Opportunities and Challenges for Multinational Enterprises and Foreign Direct Investment in the Belt and Road Initiative

Miraj Ahmed Bhuiyan
Guangdong University of Finance and Economics, China

Isidora Beraha
Institute of Economic Sciences, Serbia

IGI Global
PUBLISHER of TIMELY KNOWLEDGE

A volume in the Advances in Finance, Accounting, and Economics (AFAE) Book Series

Published in the United States of America by
IGI Global
Business Science Reference (an imprint of IGI Global)
701 E. Chocolate Avenue
Hershey PA, USA 17033
Tel: 717-533-8845
Fax: 717-533-8661
E-mail: cust@igi-global.com
Web site: http://www.igi-global.com

Library of Congress Cataloging-in-Publication Data

Names: Bhuiyan, Miraj Ahmed, 1984-, editor. | Beraha, Isidora, 1980- editor.
Title: Opportunities and challenges for multinational enterprises and foreign direct investment in the belt and road initiative Miraj Ahmed Bhuiyan, and Isadora Beraha, editors.
Description: Hershey, PA : Business Science Reference, [2022] | Includes bibliographical references and index. | Summary: "This book is driven by major developments in the world economy and fills the gap in the literature by providing new insights into some of the main opportunities and challenges faced by multinational enterprises seeking to pursue their foreign investment activities and gain access to new markets., specifically focusing on cross-border investment and how multinational enterprises are able to exploit new global business opportunities"-- Provided by publisher.
Identifiers: LCCN 2021035391 (print) | LCCN 2021035392 (ebook) | ISBN 9781799880219 (hardcover) | ISBN 9781799880226 (paperback) | ISBN 9781799880233 (ebook)
Subjects: LCSH: International business enterprises. | Investments, Foreign. | China--Foreign economic relations. | Trade routes--China--Strategic aspects | International economic integration--Strategic aspects.
Classification: LCC HD62.4 .O734 2021 (print) | LCC HD62.4 (ebook) | DDC 338.8/8--dc23
LC record available at https://lccn.loc.gov/2021035391
LC ebook record available at https://lccn.loc.gov/2021035392

This book is published in the IGI Global book series Advances in Finance, Accounting, and Economics (AFAE) (ISSN: 2327-5677; eISSN: 2327-5685)

British Cataloguing in Publication Data
A Cataloguing in Publication record for this book is available from the British Library.

Advances in Finance, Accounting, and Economics (AFAE) Book Series

Ahmed Driouchi
Al Akhawayn University, Morocco

ISSN:2327-5677
EISSN:2327-5685

Mission

In our changing economic and business environment, it is important to consider the financial changes occurring internationally as well as within individual organizations and business environments. Understanding these changes as well as the factors that influence them is crucial in preparing for our financial future and ensuring economic sustainability and growth.

The **Advances in Finance, Accounting, and Economics (AFAE)** book series aims to publish comprehensive and informative titles in all areas of economics and economic theory, finance, and accounting to assist in advancing the available knowledge and providing for further research development in these dynamic fields.

Coverage

- Labor Economics
- Economic Indices and Quantitative Economic Methods
- Economics Geography
- Microeconomics
- Finance and Accounting in SMEs
- Economic Downturn
- Interest Rates and Annuities
- Economics of Intellectual Property Rights
- Borrowing and Lending
- Investments and Derivatives

IGI Global is currently accepting manuscripts for publication within this series. To submit a proposal for a volume in this series, please contact our Acquisition Editors at Acquisitions@igi-global.com or visit: http://www.igi-global.com/publish/.

The Advances in Finance, Accounting, and Economics (AFAE) Book Series (ISSN 2327-5677) is published by IGI Global, 701 E. Chocolate Avenue, Hershey, PA 17033-1240, USA, www.igi-global.com. This series is composed of titles available for purchase individually; each title is edited to be contextually exclusive from any other title within the series. For pricing and ordering information please visit http://www.igi-global.com/book-series/advances-finance-accounting-economics/73685. Postmaster: Send all address changes to above address.

Titles in this Series

For a list of additional titles in this series, please visit: http://www.igi-global.com/book-series/advances-finance-accounting-economics/73685

Advanced Machine Learning Algorithms for Complex Financial Applications
Mohammad Irfan (CMR Institute of Technology, India) Mohamed Elhoseny (American University in the Emirates, UAE) Salina Kassim (International Islamic University of Malaysia, Malaysia) and Noura Metawa (University of Sharjah, UAE)
Engineering Science Reference • © 2022 • 335pp • H/C (ISBN: 9781668444832) • US $270.00

Finance for Sustainability in a Turbulent Economy
Abdul Rafay (University of Management & Technology, Pakistan.)
Business Science Reference • © 2022 • 315pp • H/C (ISBN: 9781668455807) • US $250.00

AI-Enabled Agile Internet of Things for Sustainable FinTech Ecosystems
Sandeep Kautish (Lord Buddha Education Foundation, Nepal) and Guneet Kaur (Independent Researcher, UK)
Engineering Science Reference • © 2022 • 300pp • H/C (ISBN: 9781668441763) • US $270.00

Applications, Challenges, and Opportunities of Blockchain Technology in Banking and Insurance
S. L. Gupta (Birla Institute of Technology, Noida, India) Pooja Kansra (Mittal School of Business, Lovely Professional University, India) and Gagan Kukreja (College of Business Administration, University of Bahrain, Bahrain)
Business Science Reference • © 2022 • 303pp • H/C (ISBN: 9781668441336) • US $250.00

Institutions, Resilience, and Dynamic Capabilities of Entrepreneurial Ecosystems in Emerging Economies
Shivani Inder (Chitkara Business School, Chitkara University, India) Amandeep Singh (Chitkara Business School, Chitkara University, Punjab, India) and Sandhir Sharma (Chitkara Business School, Chitkara University, India)
Business Science Reference • © 2022 • 303pp • H/C (ISBN: 9781668447451) • US $240.00

COVID-19's Impact on the Cryptocurrency Market and the Digital Economy
Nadia Mansour (University of Sousse, Tunisia & University of Salamanca, Spain) and Salha Ben Salem (University of Monastir, Tunisia)
Business Science Reference • © 2022 • 251pp • H/C (ISBN: 9781799891178) • US $215.00

Modern Regulations and Practices for Social and Environmental Accounting
Teresa Eugénio (Centre of Applied Research in Management and Economics (CARME), School of Technology and Management, Polytechnic Institute of Leiria, Portugal) Graça Azevedo (University of Aveiro, Portugal) and Ana Fialho (CEFAGE, University of Évora, Portugal)
Business Science Reference • © 2022 • 345pp • H/C (ISBN: 9781799894100) • US $240.00

IGI Global
PUBLISHER of TIMELY KNOWLEDGE

701 East Chocolate Avenue, Hershey, PA 17033, USA
Tel: 717-533-8845 x100 • Fax: 717-533-8661
E-Mail: cust@igi-global.com • www.igi-global.com

Table of Contents

Section 3

Detailed Table of Contents

Motivated by the Chinese government's foreign direct investment (FDI) promotion policies, this paper is attempting to examine the implications of these policies to the Belt and Road (B&R) regions under the unique institutional settings. By applying the software tool CiteSpace, which is developed for visual analyze of science mapping (Chen, 2017), this paper aims to investigate the dynamics of Chinese cross-border investment activities in B&R countries, taking the China-Pakistan Economic Corridor as an example, and discuss the question whether & how these policies and activities could drive more Chinese multinational enterprises (MNEs) to exploit these emerging business opportunities in B&R regions, as well as investigate what is the trend of Chinese FDI in B&R.

The chapter consists of highlighting how CPEC initiated and linked China to the Arabian Sea by the shortest route through Pakistan. The chapter then elaborates Chinese and Pakistani relations in detail started from the birth of the PRC to the current joint venture of CPEC. This part of the work also covers Beijing's short- and long-term interests for they invest billions of dollars in the war torn state of Pakistan. Firstly, it defines CPEC in the contour of BRI that covers the regions of Asia, Africa, and Europe including more than 64 countries of these regions with investment of trillions of dollars to maintain the Chinese economic growth that has lasted for three decades. Secondly, with special reference to CPEC, PRC expects the shortest route to connect Kashghar with the Indian Ocean and permanently put an end to the Malacca dilemma. Thirdly, the study identifies Pakistan as a strong counter actor to India. Finally, it explains their political, diplomatic, economic, and strategic interests associated to the flagship project.

This chapter analyzes the role played by Chinese investment within the Belt and Road Initiative (BRI) in promoting outward FDI from Morocco to African countries. The authors used panel data of 29 African countries from 2004 to 2021 and robust weighted least squares (RWLS) with m-estimation and Welsch function. The empirical results confirmed that inflows of Chinese FDI attract Moroccan FDI outflows in African countries because of the signal effect that these countries are "good locations" for investment. Secondly, the authors found that joining the BRI affects Moroccan FDI positively in African countries due to the commitment of these countries to improve their institutional quality related to the protection of property rights and enforcement of contracts. Finally, the findings suggest that Chinese FDI inflows and the BRI moderate positively the effect of infrastructure (transport, ITC, etc.) on the attraction of Moroccan FDI in African countries.

This research analyses the results of the Belt and Road Initiative in 17 Central, Eastern, and Southeastern European countries that signed the China-Central and Eastern European Countries Initiative. The subject of the research is the extent to which the initiative would provide benefits for the growth and development of these countries. Special attention will be paid to the link between infrastructure development and FDI, and whether environmental standards are taken into account in the projects belonging to the domain of the Initiative. The authors analyse which areas of economy belong to Chinese investments in the selected countries, and whether the countries have taken into account strategically important investments for the society and the country's economy. One of the goals of the research will be whether in the previous period the countries regularly settled their debts to China and how the COVID-19 crisis has had an impact on debt repayment.

The aim of this chapter is to examine the impact of investment in research and development on economic growth, as well as the nature of the impact of trade openness and foreign direct investment on extended Balkan Silk Road economies. The authors used the general econometric specification of the regression panel model and for the period from 2002 to 2018. The results showed that expenditures on research and development and trade openness have a significant positive effect on the gross domestic product of the countries with lower GDP per capita, while foreign direct investment in these countries has a neutral and nonsignificant impact on gross domestic product. For the countries with higher GDP per capita, expenditures on research and development have a marginally negative effect on the gross domestic product. Trade openness is significantly positive, while foreign direct investments have a significant but neutral effect on the gross domestic product. The main limitations of the research are the use of data on total R&D investment and foreign trade relations instead of sectoral.

Foreign direct investment (FDI) is a very important element of economic integration because it creates an opportunity for accelerated development, technological innovation, and corporate restructuring. Western Balkan countries mainly focused their activities on attracting investments from EU countries. However, as investments from these countries have been reduced recently, the countries of the Western Balkans have opened their markets to incoming Chinese investments. Serbia is currently the first country in the Western Balkans. Based on the inflow of Chinese investments, and in the coming period, we can expect a trend of intensive growth of Chinese investments related to the "Belt and Road" Initiative, which will lead to additional development of the Serbian economy. The main subject of this research focuses on the distribution of Chinese investments on a global scale, as well as the importance of the "Belt and Road" Initiative for both multinational companies and recipient countries of Western Balkans, with special reference to Serbia.

The subject of the research is Chinese investments in the modernization and reconstruction of railway infrastructure in Serbia, with a focus on the construction of the Belgrade-Budapest high-speed rail line up to 200 km/h, on the sections Belgrade-Stara Pazova and Novi Sad-Subotica-Kelebija. The research aims to analyze the impact of Chinese investment projects on the railway infrastructure in Serbia and examine the effects of projects' implementation at different levels, including the challenges they face. The analysis covers the traffic, technical-technological and financial aspects of the project. The importance of building a high-speed railway through Serbia, but also of the shortest railway connection from Western and Central Europe in the countries of Southern Europe and the Middle and the Far East, is considered, especially in the context of the cooperation within the BRI. The research results are the presentation of the effects railway infrastructure projects have on the development of Serbian economy, as well as the challenges that arise during the implementation process.

The focus of this chapter is the analysis of economic relations between Montenegro and China and the implications that the intensified economic cooperation may have on the political, regional, and global levels. Special attention is paid to the construction of the priority section of the Bar-Boljare highway and the financial arrangement concluded on those grounds between Montenegro and the Chinese Exim

Preface

INTRODUCTION

In a comprehensive and multidisciplinary manner, the book *Opportunities and Challenges for Multinational Enterprises and Foreign Direct Investment in the Belt and Road Initiative* brings together the findings of research on the role of multinational companies on foreign direct investment flows and their effects on international trade and economic growth in selected countries. The findings from authors worldwide contribute significantly to answering many of the issues that surround the project as the world's largest global infrastructure development strategy, with implications for politics, economics, and society.

China initiated a global development strategy named Belt and Road Initiative (BRI) in 2013. Multiple infrastructure projects to connect Eurasian markets with China by train and sea are part of the plan, which would connect at least 71 nations and involve investments worth more than USD 1 trillion by 2027 (Li, Liu & Qian, Li, Liu, et al., 2019; Macaes, 2018). Participation in the Initiative by host nations has demonstrable economic benefits. Many BRI nations, especially the tiny, landlocked, and unstable ones, have significant infrastructure shortfalls, resulting in inadequate integration into regional and global markets (Ruta et al., 2019).

The BRI establishes significant connectivity networks, including a complex network of aviation e-services and trade network systems. It has promoted economic and financial development in regions covered by the BRI in infrastructure construction and interconnection and attracted significant foreign direct investment flows. At the bottom of the escalation of the China-US trade dispute is a more fundamental shift where China has become the US's strategic competitor, and political-economic tensions have continued to climb.

The book *Opportunities and Challenges for Multinational Enterprises and Foreign Direct Investment in the Belt and Road Initiative* analyzes the opportunities and challenges of multinational enterprises (MNEs) and cross-border foreign investment transactions. BRI will assist the Chinese economy by utilizing the benefits of liberalized trade in products, services, capital, and public procurement. Simultaneously, it will bring about significant changes in international business, such as by encouraging business-to-business (B2B) and peer-to-peer (P2P) collaboration (Visvizi et al.,2019). It will also impact outbound foreign direct investment trends (OFDI). In the BRI, geography plays a role, as does geopolitics. Given the far-reaching consequences that BRI is anticipated to have in business, economics, society, and politics, it is critical to define and simplify the debate to identify the essential processes and causal links. From these various perspectives, it is necessary to examine the FDI status of the multinational companies (MNCs) in BRI regions.

The following chapters and valuable references adopt an economic and international business perspective to address these issues and present novel and state-of-the-art research insights into the role of MNEs and their influence on the Silk Road Economic Belt. This book covers economic determinants, foreign direct investment promotion policies, and the trade gravity model. These premier reference sources are excellent resources for business leaders and CEOs, policymakers, geopolitical experts, politicians, government officials, sociologists, libraries, students, higher education educators, researchers, and academicians interested in the BRI and its implications for economic development.
This book included the following topics:

- Determinant Factors on Foreign Direct Investments
- Determinants between China and "One Belt- One Road" Countries
- China Pakistan Economic Corridor
- Belt and Road Initiative Investments in African Countries
- Impact of the Belt and Road initiative on Europe
- BRI investment impact on Balkan Silk Road Countries
- Foreign Direct Investment during COVID-19 Lockdown

ORGANIZATION OF THE BOOK

The book is organized into 12 chapters. A brief description of each of the chapters follows:

Chapter 1: The Influence of Determinant Factors on Foreign Direct Investments – The Influence of Determinant Factors on Foreign Direct Investments

The first chapter aims to analyze and interpret the determinants of foreign direct investment by analyzing the actual member countries of the European Union over the period 2005-to 2019. The chapter will consist of three parts:1. The role and importance of FDI & theories related to FDI. 2. The evolution of FDI in the member countries of the EU. 3. The Determinants of FDI & Case study on the influence of determinant factors on foreign direct investment. Given that FDI is significant in economic growth and represents an essential feature of the economy, this chapter analyzes the factors that could influence the FDI. The selected elements are Trade Freedom Index, Economic Freedom, Trade Balance, Exports and Imports, Governmental Debt, Fiscal Freedom Index, Financial Freedom Index, Inflation, Unemployment rate, and Labor Freedom Index. The analysis was performed on the European Union member countries, and the sample period is 2005-2019.

Chapter 2: An Empirical Study of Trade Status and Determinants Between China and "One Belt-One Road" Countries – Based on Trade gravity Model

"One Road-One Belt" (Belt and Road Initiative, BRI), reminiscent of the Silk Road, is a massive infrastructure and trade project initiated by China. The initiative would stretch from East Asia to Europe, somehow recognized by the international community. Despite criticism of this project, it is considered an effective tool for promoting regional and bilateral trade deals. This chapter has pointed out the problems that hindered the bilateral trade among countries along the route. Based on Trade gravity Model, the bilateral trade model between China and the countries along the "Belt and Road" was empirically tested in this chapter, followed by some suggestions.

Chapter 3: Chinese Foreign Direct Investment in the Belt and Road Initiative

The Chinese government has made the Belt and Road Initiative (BRI) a national paramount strategy, and it shows up the commitment of the Chinese government to a more open economy. It is a significant attempt made by China to explore new forms of international economic cooperation with new partners, thus sustaining its economic growth. This chapter investigates the dynamics of foreign direct investment in the BRI regions. The roles of Chinese Investment in BRI will be critically examined, and how this role will strengthen the region's green economy is discussed here. This chapter, in turn, provides recommendations about BRI development.

Chapter 4: China Pakistan Economic Corridor – A Challenging Initiative

This chapter highlights how CPEC initiated and linked China to the Arabian Sea by the shortest route through Pakistan. In addition, it elaborates on China and Pakistan relations in detail, starting from the PRC's birth to the current joint venture of CPEC. This part of the work also covers Beijing's short and long-term interests that they invest billions of dollars in the War-torn state of Pakistan. Firstly, it defines CPEC in the contour of BRI that covers the regions of Asia, Africa, and Europe, including more than sixty-four countries of these regions with an investment of trillions of dollars to maintain the Chinese economic growth that lasted for three decades. Secondly, with special reference to CPEC, PRC expects the shortest route to connect Kashghar with the Indian Ocean and permanently end the Malacca Dilemma. Thirdly, this chapter also examines its time-tested ally, Pakistan as a strong counter actor to India. Finally, it explains the flagship project's political, diplomatic, economic, and strategic interests.

Chapter 5: Do Belt and Road Initiative and Chinese Investments Promote Moroccan FDI in African Countries? An Empirical Investigation Using Panel Data

This chapter analyzes the role played by Chinese investment within the Belt and Road Initiative (BRI) in promoting outward FDI from Morocco to African countries. The authors used panel data of 29 African countries from 2004 to 2021 and Robust Weighted Least Squares (RWLS) with M-estimation and Welsch function. The empirical results confirmed that inflows of Chinese FDI attract Moroccan FDI outflows in African countries because of the signal effect that these countries are "good locations" for investment. Secondly, the authors found that joining the BRI affects Moroccan FDI positively in African countries due to the commitment of these countries to improve their institutional quality related to the protection of property rights and enforcement of contracts. Finally, the findings suggest that Chinese FDI inflows and the BRI moderate the effect of infrastructure (Transport, ITC, etc.) on the attraction of Moroccan FDI in African countries positively.

Chapter 6: Impact of the Belt and Road Initiative on the countries of Central, Eastern, and Southeastern Europe

This chapter analyses the Belt and Road Initiative results in 17 Central, Eastern, and Southeastern European countries that signed the China-Central and Eastern European Countries Initiative. Special attention was paid in the chapter to checking the link between FDI and environmental standards in the projects belonging to the initiative. It also analyzed which areas of the economy belong to Chinese investments in the selected countries and whether the countries have taken into account strategically important investments for the society and its economy. One of the goals of this chapter is whether the countries regularly settled their debts to China in the previous period and how the COVID-19 crisis has impacted debt repayment.

Chapter 7: The Impact of Investment on the Economic Activity of the Balkan Silk Road Countries

This chapter examines the impact of investment in research and development on economic growth and the effects of trade openness and foreign direct investment on extended Balkan Silk Road economies. The authors used the general econometric specification of the regression panel model for the period from 2002 to 2018. The results showed that expenditures on research and development and trade openness have a significant positive effect on the gross domestic product of the countries with lower GDP per capita. In contrast, foreign direct investment in these countries has a neutral and nonsignificant impact on gross domestic product. For the countries with higher GDP per capita, expenditures on research and development have a marginally negative effect on the gross domestic product. Trade openness is significantly positive, while foreign direct investments have a significant but neutral impact on the gross domestic product. The main limitations of the research are the use of data on total R&D investment and foreign trade relations instead of sectoral.

Chapter 8: "Belt and Road" Initiative as a Development Chance for the Western Balkan Countries – The Case of Serbia

Foreign direct investment (FDI) is an essential element of economic integration because it creates an opportunity for accelerated development, technological innovation, and corporate restructuring. Western Balkan countries mainly focused their activities on attracting investments from EU countries. However, as investments from these countries have been reduced recently, the countries of the Western Balkans have opened their markets to incoming Chinese investments. Serbia is currently the first country in the Western Balkans, based on the inflow of Chinese investments, and in the coming period, we can expect a trend of intensive growth of Chinese investments related to the "Belt and Road" Initiative, which will lead to additional development of the Serbian economy. The main subject of this chapter focuses on the distribution of Chinese investments on a global scale and the importance of the "Belt and Road" Initiative for both multinational companies and recipient countries of the Western Balkans, with particular reference to Serbia.

Chapter 9: The Role and Significance of Chinese Investments in the Modernization of Railway Infrastructure in Serbia

Chapter nine discusses Chinese investments in the modernization and reconstruction of railway infrastructure in Serbia, focusing on constructing the Belgrade - Budapest high-speed rail line up to 200 km/h on the sections Belgrade - Stara Pazova and Novi Sad - Subotica - Kelebija. This chapter aims to analyze the impact of Chinese investment projects on the railway infrastructure in Serbia and examine the effects of projects' implementation at different levels, including the challenges they face. The analysis covers the traffic, technical-technological and financial aspects of the project. The importance of building a high-speed railway through Serbia and the shortest railway connection from Western and Central Europe to the countries of Southern Europe and the Middle and the Far East is considered, especially in the context of the cooperation within the BRI. The research results show the effects railway infrastructure projects have on the development of the Serbian economy and the challenges that arise during the implementation process.

Chapter 10: Montenegro and BRI Initiative – Between Economic Performances and Global Political Challenges

The focus of this chapter is the analysis of economic relations between Montenegro and China and the implications that the intensified economic cooperation may have on the political, regional, and global levels. Special attention is paid in this chapter to the construction of the priority section of the Bar-Boljare highway, and the financial arrangement concluded on those grounds between Montenegro and the Chinese Exim Bank. China's presence in the Western Balkans has gained importance recently through the Belt and Road Initiative project. Therefore, this chapter seeks to answer how Montenegro can use all the benefits of this initiative to strengthen its national economy and increase its citizens' living standards. That can be crucial as Montenegro faces economic consequences of the COVID-19 pandemic, and FDI inflows are a precondition to reducing the infrastructure gap within the convergence criteria in the EU accession process.

Chapter 11: China's Trade and Investment in the Western Balkans Under the Belt and Road Initiative – Focus on North Macedonia

As an integral part of the China Belt and Road Initiative (BRI) and the 17+1 cooperation platform are the fundamental framework for China's foreign policy towards most parts of the world, including the Western Balkan (WB). Through its global initiative and cooperation platform, China creates opportunities for facilitating trade and increasing export, financial integration, and more significant Chinese investment, major infrastructure projects, and their funding. This chapter analyzes the actual situation regarding these aspects in the WB countries, primarily focusing on North Macedonia. The analysis indicates that there has been some progress in cooperation. But the WB countries (excluding Serbia) have failed to maximize their interests either in bilateral collaboration or in the framework of the BRI initiative. Conclusively, despite all the great expectations, the trade exchange, Chinese investments, and the realized infrastructure projects do not reach a significant level.

Chapter 12: Foreign Direct Investment During the COVID-19 Lockdown

Foreign Direct Investment has been proved essential in stimulating economic growth in developing countries. Foreign Direct Investment has several benefits: transferring technology and knowledge, improving management capacity, increasing employment, improving competitiveness, and achieving a favorable balance of payments. Because of these advantages, countries are keen to attract more FDI. In this sense, this chapter analyzes to what extent lockdown during COVID 19 era may have affected FDI inñows. In addition, it explored the new role of Foreign Investment Promotion agencies in updating FDI policies and implementing new ones- Digital policies- to boost FDI entry.

CONCLUSION

The Belt and Road Initiative provides prospects for cooperation and development for all countries. Today, it is the largest platform for foreign direct investment, creating political, economic, and social development potentials. MNCs are eager to cooperate with Chinese companies to expand further in the Belt and Road markets, bringing their technology and global reach to the table. MNCs participate in the BRI by forming partnerships with Chinese businesses. As a result of this collaboration, MNCs and Chinese companies will be able to fully exploit their respective advantages, resulting in a superior outcome. Research on potential opportunities and challenges faced by MNCs, the status of their investments and effects on international trade and economic growth in host countries is becoming increasingly valuable for forming future investment promotion policies, given the increasing importance of the role they play in the development of the global trade network.

This book adds to our understanding of the nature of BRI and its ties to the foreign direct investment of multinational companies. Because many of the countries along the BRI are developing, the book focuses on the potential for international companies to contribute to their infrastructure development, trade expansion, and economic growth through foreign direct investment. A unique and comprehensive approach and valuable guidelines for further research and policymaking in investment promotion and economic development are provided by a multidisciplinary perspective on this current topic and insight into the findings of research in different countries.

Miraj Ahmed Bhuiyan
Guangdong University of Finance and Economics, China

Isidora Beraha
Institute of Economic Sciences, Serbia

REFERENCES

Li, J., Liu, B., & Qian, G. (2019). The Belt and Road Initiative, cultural friction and ethnicity: Their effects on the export performance of SMEs in China. *Journal of World Business*, *54*(4), 350–359. doi:10.1016/j.jwb.2019.04.004

Macaes, B. (2018). *Belt and road: A Chinese world order*. C Hurst US & Co.

Ruta, M., Dappe, M. H., Lall, S., Zhang, C., Constantinescu, C., Lebrand, M., Mulabdic, A., & Churchill, E. (2019). *Belt and Road Economics: Opportunities and risks of transport corridors*. World Bank Publications.

Visvizi, A., Lytras, M. D., & Jin, P. (2019). Belt and Road Initiative (BRI): New forms of international and cross-industry collaboration for sustainable growth and development. *Sustainability*, *12*(1), 193. doi:10.3390u12010193

Acknowledgment

We would like to thank IGI global Publishing for giving us this opportunity to handle this project. We thank Katie McLoughlin (Assistant Development Editor-Book, Development, IGI Global) for her continuous support. We also thank the whole IGI Global Publishing team members involved in the entire process.

We want to acknowledge the help of all the authors who have contributed and shared their knowledge with us. In addition, our gratitude and warm regards go to all of the reviewers that took part in the review process. Without their support, this book would not have become a reality.

We wish to acknowledge the valuable contributions of the reviewers regarding the improvement of quality, coherence, and content presentation of chapters. The authors also served as referees; we highly appreciate their double task.

Section 1

Chapter 1
The Influence of Determinant Factors on Foreign Direct Investments

Iulia Cristina Iuga
https://orcid.org/0000-0002-2831-3055
1 Decembrie 1918 University, Romania

ABSTRACT

The chapter aims both to analyze and interpret the determinants of foreign direct investment by conducting an analysis on the actual member countries of the European Union over the period 2005-2019. The chapter consists of three parts: 1) the role and importance of FDI and theories related to FDI, 2) the evolution of FDI in the member countries of the EU, and 3) the determinants of FDI: a case study on the influence of determinant factors on foreign direct investment. Given that FDI is significant in terms of economic growth and represents an important feature of the economy, the author has decided to analyze the factors that could influence FDI. The selected factors are trade freedom index, economic freedom, trade balance, exports and imports, governmental debt, fiscal freedom index, financial freedom index, inflation, unemployment rate, and labor freedom index. The analysis will be performed on the member countries of the European Union and the sample period is 2005-2019.

INTRODUCTION

The financial markets have evolved into a more integrated framework, globally, because of increasing liberalization of exchange controls and market access. This integration, enhanced by increased competition among market players, has led to the introduction of new financial instruments with wide market access and lower transaction costs, therefore attracting investors of numerous nationalities and countries (economies).

Foreign Direct Investment (FDI) is a key element in this rapidly evolving international economic integration, also referred to as globalization. FDI provides a means for creating stable linkages that serve as bridges across economies. In addition, under the appropriate circumstances, FDI may represent the

DOI: 10.4018/978-1-7998-8021-9.ch001

impetus for the host economy to extensively promote its products to international markets. Therefore, besides the positive effects on the development of international trade, FDI is an important source of capital for several economies. The FDI contains many management dimensions, such as bonds, portfolio investment in foreign stocks (Xinxin et al., 2021).

Today, the world is struggling through major challenges and a new reality, which we must face; to this end, the present study could provide a distinct standpoint by means which to consider from a different perspective the dependence of macroeconomic indicators against FDI and the facets that could add a beneficial impact on both the economic and social life. Firstly, foreign direct investments have a vast history, being regarded as essential to economic development. Secondly, they represent a distinctive method for connection to the economic system, including periods during which the economy comes up against difficulties.

The paper aims both to analyze and interpret the determinants of foreign direct investment, by conducting an analysis on the actual member countries of the European Union over the period 2005-2019.

As regards the objectives of this paper, they are: to acquire more in-depth theoretical concepts related to FDI; to establish the determinants of FDI; to conduct the proper analysis of the determinants; to determine the impact produced; to carry out the linear regression model in order to determine the relevance of the analysis and the determinants; to determine the most pertinent determinants and their correlation with FDI.

The topicality of the subject is denoted by the fact that FDI was and remains to be an important aspect of both social and economic life. The concept of FDI has gradually replaced the traditional forms of capital investment, and today, the concept refers to the contribution brought about by the association of foreign part with a state would bring to the economy. In addition, FDI has adapted at the same time both to detrimental contexts and to financing needs. Furthermore, FDI plays the role of accelerators for other traditional manufacturing indicators, i.e., both for human and natural resources, including science, technology, or even knowledge itself. FDI has a huge potential given that it can channel and enhance the local environment, at the level of all economies, regardless of whether they are less developed economies, in transition, or even developed economies.

This study intends to answer the question, "*What are the determinants that attract FDI to european countries?*"

The paper will consist of three parts:

1. *The role and importance of FDI. Theories related to FDI.* In this part, the theoretical aspects of paramount importance will be provided through scholarly literature, complemented by the role and importance of FDI in the world economy.
2. *The evolution of FDI in the member countries of the EU.* This part will cover the evolution of FDI in each EU member state.
3. *The Determinants of FDI. Case study on the influence of determinant factors on foreign direct investment.* Given that FDI is significant in terms of economic growth and represents an important feature of the economy, the authors have decided to analyze, through this paper, the factors that could influence FDI. The selected factors are Trade Freedom Index, Economic Freedom, Trade Balance, Exports and Imports, Governmental Debt, Fiscal Freedom Index, Financial Freedom Index, Inflation, Unemployment rate, and Labor Freedom Index. The analysis will be performed on the member countries of the European Union and the sample period is 2005-2019.

For the purpose of conducting the proposed analysis was used the Eviews Program, the data were obtained from the www.globaleconomy.com website, the World Bank database, and where it was imposed due to the limitations encountered (data confidentiality and lack of access to some reference sources) the data were obtained from the economic reports of the countries. Data retrieval was performed for 14 indicators (dependent variable FDI and 13 independent variables: Trade Freedom Index, Economic Freedom, Trade Balance, Exports and Imports, Governmental Debt, Fiscal Freedom Index, Financial Freedom Index, Inflation, Unemployment rate, and Labor Freedom Index) in all 27 Member states of the EU over the period 2005-2019, therefore were obtained models with 405 observations. A collective analysis of the determinants of FDI has been performed and further a detailed analysis of the impact generated by each group on FDI has been carried out.

Regression analysis helps us to understand how the dependent variable evolves when one of the independent variables varies, as a result allowing the mathematical determination of the variables that have a greater impact on the dependent variable. The model is estimated with the help of the Ordinary Least Square (OLS) method by using panel data.

LITERATURE REVIEW

FDI is an important source of economic growth, even during the most delicate moments, such as those times when economic growth is under pressure. This is due to the fact that FDI "is complementary to public sources of funding and provide the capital required for developing an economy, besides creating new employment opportunities in the company which they invest, they further encourage the development of other companies upstream and downstream; they are not only a flow of capital, but also of technology, knowledge and organizational practices, which stimulate and generate economic growth. Foreign investors impose their working methodology on the company they develop and bring new technologies to, which increase both employees' efficiency and the company's competitiveness. These beneficial outcomes are spreading throughout the chain of enterprises involved in the production of a certain product or service, whereas enterprises that adapt to survive on the market are characterized by long-term stability. What defines FDI is precisely the sustainable interest of the investors in the company in which they invest. On that account, an investor who lied down the foundation of a new company will not easily relinquish their investments even during turbulent economic times. (Horobeț and Popovici, 2017)

The role of investments in an economy is a major one. They belong to the category of factors of paramount importance that significantly contribute to economic growth. Numerous studies argue and demonstrate that they generate positive effects on the entire socio-economic sphere.(Chowdhury & Mavrotas, 2006; Hansen & Rand, 2006; Blonigen, 2005; Crescenzi et al., 2021; Munir & Ameer, 2020).

The FDI concept has replaced gradually the traditional forms of capital investment. Today, the notion of foreign investment commonly refers to the contribution brought about by the alliance of a foreign party, commonly a transnational company, with a state that will bring to the economy of that particular state. (Rusu, 2000)

In the broadest sense, adopted by the international community, as well as for the purpose of this study, the concept of foreign investment contract refers to the legal relations between a state and a foreign company, intending to carry out an investment project. As a rule, these contracts are concluded between a country with a developing or transition economy and a foreign investor, are of a long-term nature and commonly their object is the exploitation of natural resources, furthermore, referred in the legal literature to as transnational investment contracts or economic development contracts (Pogany, 1992).

The Organization for Economic Co-operation and Development (OECD) designed a document that defines FDI, entitled *The Benchmark Definition of Foreign Direct Investment (OECD, 2008).* Through the instrumentality of the document are addressed such issues as the recognition of statistical reporting deficiencies, the potential of considering the expansion of multinational enterprises' business at a global scale, and the improvement of their funding. In addition, the document also provides a set of standards recommended to public authorities aimed at a more appropriate and statistically accurate measurement of FDI.

Another influential aspect is that the International Monetary Fund (IMF) has adopted the recommendations designed by OECD, covered in the document entitled *Balance of Payments and International Investment Position Manual* (IMF, 2009) and currently, official FDI statistics comply with the OECD framework.

In addition, after an extensive research in the specialized literature (Nepal et al., 2021; Raza et al., 2019; Sokhanvar, 2019; Bermejo et al., 2018), we can assert that FDI represents both financial and resources flows, which cross both the legal and economic states' borders. They are the long-term relationship between a resident and non-resident entity and commonly involve a considerable managerial influence from the investor's side.

Alshamsi et al. (2015) examined the impact of inflation rate and GDP per capita on inward foreign direct investment inflows in United Emirates over the time of 1980 to 2013. They found that GDP per capita had a positive and statistically significant impact on FDI inflows, while inflation rate did not have the expected sign and it was not statistically significant

Using multiple regression, Kaur and Sharma (2013) explored the determinants influencing FDI in India. According to their findings, the key determinants of FDI inflows are trade openness, inflation, and currency reserves. Inflation and the exchange rate both have a negative impact on FDI and GDP.

Demirhan and Masca (2008) used panel data analysis to evaluate the drivers of foreign direct investment (FDI) inflows in 38 developing countries from 2000 to 2004. The inflation rate and the tax rate have a negative and statistically significant link with FDI net inflows.

Singhania and Gupta (2011) employed a dummy variable to account for changes in FDI policy, as well as to trace the influence of macroeconomic variables such as GDP, inflation rate, international trade, money supply growth, and patents on FDI inflows in India. According to the study, only GDP, inflation rate, and scientific research had an influence on FDI inflows.

A relation of FDI can coexist between several inter-related enterprises, i.e., the relation may be extended to subsidiaries, affiliated subsidiaries, and associated enterprises. Subsequently the establishment of FDI, all financial flows (future) of the inter-related bodies, "are recorded as direct investment transactions/ positions. (Voiculescu, 2015)

In the matter of Romania, FDI is defined by the National Bank of Romania, the National Office of the Trade Register, and the legislation in force. According to the National Bank of Romania, FDI represents the long-term relationship investment between a resident entity and a non-resident entity; it commonly involves a considerable managerial influence exerted by the investor on the enterprise he had invested in (BNR, 2014).

Reenu and Sharma (2015) used yearly data from 1991 to 2010 to perform a study on the drivers of FDI inflows in the post-liberalization period in India, applying an ordinary least square (OLS) regression analysis. According to their findings, market size, trade openness, interest rate, and inflation are the most important predictors of FDI inflows.

Sayari, Sari, and Hammoudeh (2018) explore the impact of FDI and the value-added components of GDP on EF in 30 European nations throughout Western Europe, Central and Eastern Europe, and the Middle East. The findings indicate a long-run positive relationship between EF and FDI in Western, Central, and Eastern European nations.

Mehmet Nasih Tag, Suleyman Degirmen (2022) using the GMM-system estimation approach and a large sample of panel data covering 19 years of observations from 127 countries, find evidence suggesting that foreign direct investment is increasing in countries with institutions that ensure the rule of law, expanding trade freedoms and reducing regulatory barriers to investment and doing business.

After examining 38 African nations, Kandiero and Chitiga (2014) discovered a negative link between FDI inflows and real exchange rate appreciation.

Dkhili and Dhiab (2018) present the importance of EF to attract the FDI inflow and thusly achieving economic growth.

Imtiaz and Bashir (2017) use panel regression to study macroeconomic factors to determine the determinants of attracting FDI inflows in South Asian nations Pakistan, Nepal, India, Sri Lanka, and Bangladesh from 1995 to 2014. They demonstrated that trade freedom, infrastructure quality, market size, human capital, and economic freedom all have a positive and statistically significant impact on FDI.

THE ROLE AND IMPORTANCE OF FDI. THEORIES RELATED TO FDI.

The Potential Role of FDI

FDI's role is paramount due to several reasons. They are more than capital flows, representing also flows of technology, managerial practices, organizational practices, knowledge, creators of new employment opportunities, provides the capital required for the economies' development, and implicitly generates economic growth. Also, they are characterized by long-term stability and the source which economic growth can rely on even during delicate periods when economic growth is under pressure.

The positive macroeconomic implications primarily relate to such issues as the stimulation of domestic investments, support of both economic development and growth of capital investments, assistance to privatization and reorganization, generation of beneficial effects on the trade balance, and contribution to the increase of state budget revenues and further implications.

Regarding the stimulation of domestic investments, we can argue that domestic enterprises that could gain access to the foreign investors' distribution channels ultimately would develop an interest in increasing the manufacturing capacity and improving the quality of goods produced and sold. In addition, they can convert to suppliers for foreign investors.

The support of economic growth can be achieved through the generation of a new manufacturing capacity, creation of additional employment opportunities, and other analogs aspects, as well by the emergence of a new type of consumer and taxpayer.

The support of capital investments' growth is attributable primarily to the access of foreign investors to external sources of capital. Since they represent a direct source of foreign capital, FDI can cover the deficit that occurred as a result of potential shortages of financial resources on the local markets.

This engenders positive outcomes on the balance of external payments. In such a manner, positive effects are triggered on the trade balance on the condition that production is intended with priority for exports, through the direct investors, or if it is the case, imports are substituted by production intended for the domestic market.

In addition, as far as goes the positive effects caused by FDI on the trade balance, these emerge when the domestic production substitutes the imports and when the foreign investors directly and with priority intends production for exports.

As regards the increase of state budget revenues, FDI assists this aspect through the new taxpayers who start being part of the host country's economy.

It is also important to consider that the impact of FDI on the host country's economy varies from one country to another, as they can also bring about adverse effects. Considering this, studies reveal that the lack or deficiencies in employment, competition, or bankruptcy policies play a crucial role, hence the authorities in most Central and Eastern countries have appealed to obtain further commitments from foreign investors on both the future of their investment and the number of employees. (Hunya, 2000). Although the practice proved that not all commitments made have been honored, there are situations when foreign investors have not complied with contracts they entered with national/ regional authorities, which led to negative social and economic effects.

Consequently, we conclude that integrity, healthy and well-established principles are vital in any field of activity, particularly when the economy and social environment are at stake.
The effects of investments can be classified into five key categories:

1. Economic effect. In an economic system, the investment activity plays a triple role:
    a. in the first place, economic agents, triggers of investment actions, who implement various investment projects, enhance their supply of goods and/or services by increasing their productive capacity and achieving additional revenues (stimulating the increase of efficiency in all areas).
    b. secondly, any investment project will cause additional needs or demands in related sectors, upstream (suppliers of raw materials, materials, and utilities, etc.) or downstream (distributors or consumers of goods and services provided). A chain increase in revenues will implicitly occur for all involved economic agents, conducive to the movement of capital. Investments are carried out in a cascading manner, involving new and new added value at all levels and for all contributors to economic life.
    c. investments ensure the improvement of the competitive position in relation to other economic agents.
2. Social effect. From a social perspective, investments play a requisite role in employment, in improving the quality of life, in raising the living standards, health protection, environmental protection, and in increasing the quality of the workforce.
3. International effect through increasing the level of a country's participation in the international economic circuit.
4. Technological effect through the acceleration of promoting technological progress and the development of research.
5. Marketing and image effect through increasing company's image and increasing consumer confidence in the company's products. It will inherently lead to increased sales and eventually to increased market share.

A particular importance is attached to FDI since they are an important external financing source of capital formation and, they facilitate the transfer of resources, human capital, and technological progress across countries. In this light, they are a vital means through which the transition economies can promote both economic growth and the development of the entire socio-economic environment.

Theories of FDI

Although foreign direct investment cannot be regarded as a recent economic phenomenon, as they are also associated with the Industrial Revolution, they have been ignored by economic theory until the late 1950s. The volume of foreign direct investment has considerably increased globally at an accelerated rate, "from \$ 13.3 billion in 1970 to \$ 51.1 in 1980, \$ 208 billion ten years later and \$ 1414 billion in 2020 (Jones, 1996). In this sense, the literature has initiated the persistent and sustained development of this aspect of the economy.

With respect to the classical theories on international trade and the report of the specialized literature, we can argue that they have been developed, relating more to FDI and the international movement of factors of productions. In this regard, the development of international trade has been attached to the factor endowment theory (Helpman 1984) and the specific factor models (Markusen and Venables 1998). Given that these theories delineate the idea of imperfect competition and product differentiation, they also apply to FDI.

In the same manner, **classical location theory** (Weber 1909) may be attributed to FDI given that the optimal location for a company is to establish the production process in the area that accounts for the lowest cost. As maintained by Hanink (1997), and according to classical location theory, FDI indicates potential, when the low-cost factor of production is located in another country.

The international investment development model carried out by Dunning (1993) is incorporated into the theories related to FDI, it establishes bridges between the outflows and inputs of investments relating to the stage of development of a certain country's economy. Conform to this model, the economy grows as the flow of outputs exceeds that of inputs. The positive and negative flow is strongly influenced by both the politico-economic system and the level of the global economic integration of that country's economy.

Given the model developed by Dunning, the evolution of FDI in Romania indicates that until the years 1998-1999, Romania has attracted modest flows of foreign investments, compared to its economic potential, approximately \$ 1 billion, whereas Romania's investments abroad were insignificant (\$11 million in 2020). This aspect as was about to change over the period 2004-2008, Romania scored a remarkable evolution attracting annual direct investment flows of over €5 billion (in 2006 and 2006 even over € 9 billion), whereas Romanian investment abroad remained extremely low (Voiculescu, 2015). Although, starting with the year 2009, given the global financial crisis and its inherently effects, the FDI attracted in Romania have considerably decreased.

The study conducted by Hymer (1976) predicts that the increasing risk and the added costs involved in managing a business from distance, the affiliated companies (transnational companies) must earn higher profits than those made in the country of origin. In such a manner, the competitive advantage of a transnational company is transferred abroad, a position that is incredibly difficult to be obtained by domestic companies. Although the economics of industrial organization reinforces that the specific advantages of a company and its adopted strategies may lead to the preservation and increase of market share, those industries employ a certain proportion of factors of production which are most appropriate to the country that provides that combination. However, the economics of industrial organization focuses primarily on strategic aspects and company-specific advantages and less on country-level factors (Voiculescu, 2015). Other theories assist the ideas found in Hymers's study, namely the transition cost theory, the product life cycle theory, and the eclectic theory.

The transition cost theory developed by Williamson (1975) has its origins in Coase's theory (1937), it indicates the importance of trade for enterprises, which is a beneficial element as through it they can avoid the costs related to the non-recognition of markets. As such, FDI constitutes more than a plain form of capital induction, by expanding on a large scale, internationally, the management of control over affiliated structures abroad.

Vernon (1966), since the mid-60s developed the product lifecycle theory, improving it afterward. The theory explains the geographical process of locating production units. Comprises four stages of development. In the first stage of the life cycle, new products are introduced by the company that holds the technological supremacy in a location where it can gain advantages from the agglomeration of economies. The foreign demand for that product is met through export. In the second stage, the company begins to establish production units abroad as it identifies the opportunity of cost reduction through foreign direct investments or if its position on the market starts to be threatened. As a rule, the first production unit abroad is planned to be established in a country with a high level of income. In the third stage, the newly established production unit sells the products on the host country's markets and exports them to the home country market. The production unit in the country of origin produces and sells the products for exports to third countries. In the fourth stage, the production unit in the host country expands its exports to third countries. When the technological advance is lost and the product peaks the maturity stage, the production units would be relocated to a location with low production costs, from where the products will be exported to the country of origin as well. (Voiculescu, 2015).

Dunning (1993) has attempted to combine various theories on foreign direct investment, as a result, has emerged the **eclectic theory,** which is based on the idea that foreign companies do not hold information as useful as possessed by domestic companies. As such, FDI will be channeled towards the implementation of production units. This is feasible only if they have certain advantages (for instance, ownership, locational, internalization advantages).

In addition, in the scholarly literature, we find microeconomic theories related to FDI.

The theory of the internationalization of the firm developed by Luostarinen (1979) explains the internationalization process of the firm through the following fourth stages: beginning, development, growth, and maturity. FDI can also be regarded from the point of view of being the result of a company's growth. Therefore, the theory of internationalization formulated by Luostarinen is similar to the theory developed by Hakanson (1979) that explains the way a company is developing, raising from a single production unit to a transnational company.

In the scholarly literature, we also find ***the classical theories of industrial location,*** which is explained the regional distribution of FDI. Into account are taken the wages, infrastructure, and transport costs, whereas recent theories have strengthened the supply-demand role (Krugman, 1991). In addition, FDI can be regarded as a catalyst for local development in the same manner that transnational companies participate and contribute to enhancing the economic growth in host countries (Hayter, 1997). Therefore, governments call for their involvement and interference in the decision-making process regarding the location of the production units of transnational companies.

Hence, both the role of domestic advantages and the role of the host government which aims to balance the differences between the real local attractiveness of the country and the conditions that a location must meet for the multinational company to be considered attractive are considered important (Voiculescu, 2015).

THE EVOLUTION OF FDI IN THE EU MEMBER COUNTRIES

According to Figure 1, we can mention that most member countries of the European Union have experienced decreases in FDI given the world economic crisis that originated in December 2007 in the USA. A series of causes have contributed to the emergence of the crisis, yet the main cause is associated with the collapse of the USA real estate market in December 2007. It has worsened in 2008 and this is also denoted in the present analysis. Also, Figure 1 shows that the impact of the crisis has been immediate, with a dramatic decrease over the years 2008-2011 in most Member Countries of the European Union: Austria, Belgium, Bulgaria, Czechia, Croatia, Denmark, Estonia, France, Germany, Greece, Italy, Latvia, Lithuania, Luxembourg, Malta, the Netherlands, Portugal, Romania, Slovenia, and Spain, whereas the effect of the crisis was delayed with a dramatic decrease later, over the period 2013-2015 in Cyprus, Ukraine and Slovakia and even around 2006, as is the case for Finland, Sweden, and Ireland.

Figure 1. FDI in EU member states
Source: Author's processing

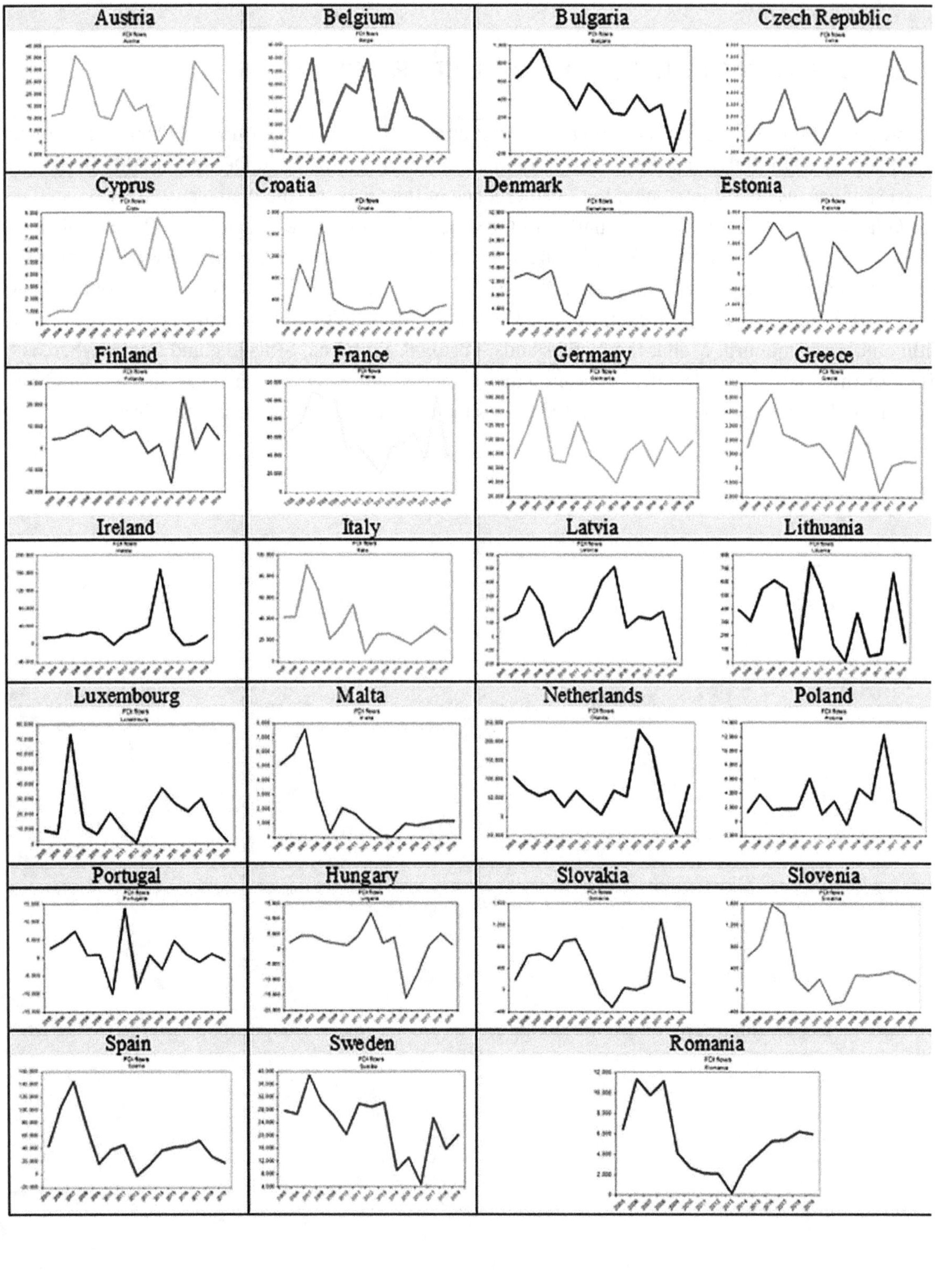

In addition, identical trends are noticed in the case of certain countries from geographical areas. The crisis first was felt in the developed countries of Western Europe, its onset taking place with a delay of 6-8 months, following after in Eastern Europe. Poland, however, is the only country from Eastern Europe that has not experienced the effects of the crisis, moreover, recording economic growth even during the recession in the rest of Europe. Given the "low private debt, exchange rate flexibility and the robust domestic demand" Poland could avoid the economic downturn.

THE DETERMINANTS OF FDI: CASE STUDY ON THE INFLUENCE OF DETERMINANT FACTORS ON FOREIGN DIRECT INVESTMENT

Data and Methodology

Since FDI is of paramount importance in terms of economic growth and inherently represents an important aspect of the economy, we will analyze the factors that could influence FDI. The selected factors are Trade Freedom Index, Economic Freedom, Trade Balance, Exports and Imports, Governmental Debt, Fiscal Freedom Index, Business Freedom Index, Investment Freedom Index, Financial Freedom Index, Inflation, Unemployment rate, and Labor Freedom Index.

The countries of the study comprise the actual member countries of the European Union; Austria, Belgium, Bulgaria, Czechia, Cyprus, Croatia, Denmark, Estonia, Finland, France, Germany, Greece, Ireland, Italy, Latvia, Lithonia, Luxembourg, Malta, the Netherlands, Poland, Portugal, Romania, Slovakia, Slovenia, Spain, Sweden and Hungary and the period analysis is 2005-2019.

The data were obtained from the Global Economy's website, the World Bank's database, and where it was imposed due to the limitations encountered (data confidentiality and lack of access to some reference sources) the data were obtained from the economic reports of the countries. Data retrieval was performed for 14 indicators (1 dependent variable FDI and 13 independent variables: Trade Freedom Index, Economic Freedom, Trade Balance, Exports and Imports, Governmental Debt, Fiscal Freedom Index, Business Freedom Index, Investment Freedom Index, Financial Freedom Index, Inflation, Unemployment rate, and Labor Freedom Index) in all 27 Member states of the EU over the period 2005-2019, therefore were obtained models with 405 observations.

Dependent Variable: FDI

Foreign direct investment (FDI) is determined based on the methodology provided by the Balance of Payments Manual and The International Investment Position Manual published by the International Monetary Fund, 6th edition (BPM6). The inflow of FDI in direct investment enterprises is the sum of the flow of equity (equity investments and reinvested earnings) which is the direct investors' share of earnings in the reference period, and the value of net debts that the direct investment enterprise has accumulated in relation with the foreign direct investor/ sister companies in the same period, thus:

$Fi = AC +/- Pr + D - Ca$

Where:

Fi = Foreign direct investment Inflow
AC = Contributed Capital
Pr = Reinvested profit or loss
D = debt flow in relation to the foreign direct investor
Ca = the flow of claims on the foreign direct investor.

Model

Regression analysis helps us to understand how the dependent variable evolves when one of the independent variables varies, as a result allowing the mathematical determination of the variables that have a greater impact on the dependent variable. The model is estimated with the help of the Ordinary Least Square (OLS) method by using panel data.

The Ordinary Least Squares Method is the most common method of approximating a dependency y=y(x), through an analytical function. Through this method can be obtained efficient results with respect to the linear regression equation.

The empirical function is posed as follows (equation 1):

$$FDI = f(TF, EF, TB, Exp, Imp, GD, FFI, BFI, IFI, FinFI, Infl, UR, LFI) \quad (1)$$

Where:

FDI = foreign direct investments;
EF = economic freedom;
TF = trade freedom;
TB=trade balance;
Exp = exports;
Imp = imports;
GD =government debt;
FFI = fiscal freedom index;
BFI = business freedom index;
IFI = investment freedom index;
FinFI = financial freedom index;
Infl = inflation;
UR = unemployment rate;
LFI=labor freedom index.

Analysing Table 1. with the estimation of the parameters of the linear regression model, we can see a probability of less than 1% for Exp, Imp, FFI, IFI.

Table 1. Parameters of the model (dependent variable: FDI) (EU-27)

Variable	Coefficient
C	35255.84
TF	615.3073**
EF	-909.5066**
TB	321.6909**
Exp	119.0091***
Imp	202.1279***
GD	-97.23415
FFI	-342.8776***
BFI	36.87714
IFI	-4.658883***
FinFI	-284.1757*
Infl	-252.7045
UR	-600.7253**
LFI	3.058198
R-squared 0.547382 Adjusted R-squared 0.532295 Prob(F-statistic) 0.000000 (405 observations)	

significance levels: *p < .05; **p < .01; ***p < .001.
Source: author's processing

However, the Ordinary Least Squares Method or "Panel Least Squares" are not always considered efficiently ("is not efficient as a general rule" - Wooldridge, 2009) in the scholarly literature, thus we will deepen the proposed analysis by performing Fixed Effects Method or "Fixed effects" followed by the Random Effects Method or " Random Effects" (Table 2.), and for assessing which one of the models (Fixed Effects or Random Effects) is suitable to be accepted we will use the Hausman Test.

Table 2. Fixed effects vs. random effects. comparisons. (EU-27)

Variable	Coefficient	
	Fixed Effects	Random Effects
C	55538.11	43622.73
TF	319.8498	-427.8664
EF	-524.1746	571.7015
TB	449.5665	344.5495
Exp	188.9670	-136.1895
Imp	182.4708	217.5388
GD	-142.6903	-150.5314
FFI	-272.1567	-418.4290
BFI	118.7257	94.83987
IFI	-132.2613	-44.88774
FinFI	-191.5211	-302.2302
Infl	-206.3927	-84.76413
UR	-279.4688	459.4846
LFI	285.0518	69.87992
	R-squared 0.631306 Adjusted R-squared 0.591803	R-squared 0.320978 Adjusted R-squared 0.298344

significance levels: *p < .05 **p < .01 ***p < .001.
Source: author's processing

To determine which of these two models (Fixed effects or Random effects) is more suitable to be accepted, we will perform the Hausman test. Therefore, we formulate the following two hypotheses:

Null hypothesis - H0: Random-effects model (Random effects) is suitable.
The alternative hypothesis - H1: Fixed effects model (Fixed effects) is suitable.

Following the Hausman test (Table 3.), we can notice that after we compared the Fixed Effects Method and the Random Effects Method, we obtained a value lower than the significance level (5%) for p-value. On that account, we reject the null hypothesis and accept the alternative hypothesis, namely the Fixed Effects Method. Therefore, we will focus on the linear regression model with fixed effects.

Table 3. Hausman test (EU-27)

Test Summary		Chi-Sq. Statistic	Prob.
Cross-section random		34.791211	0.0000
Cross-section random effects tests comparisons:			
Variable	Fixed	Random	Prob.
TF	319.8498	-427.8664	0.0032
EF	-524.1746	571.7015	0.0056
TB	449.5665	344.5495	0.0000
Exp	188.9670	-136.1895	0.0000
Imp	182.4708	217.5388	0.0000
GD	-142.6903	-150.5314	0.0112
FFI	-272.1567	-418.4290	0.0025
BFI	118.7257	94.83987	0.0001
IFI	-132.2613	-44.88774	0.0056
FinFI	-191.5211	-302.2302	0.0000
Infl	-206.3927	-84.76413	0.0000
UR	-279.4688	459.4846	0.0000
LFI	285.0518	69.87992	0.0000

Source: authors' processing

Furthermore, through the Fixed Effects method (Table 2) we will analyze the systemic importance indicators obtained:

The indicator *Coefficient* designates the estimations of the independent variables in addition to the constant-coefficient C. The coefficient of the independent variables indicates the extent to which the dependent variable varies, in our case, FDI. The positive or negative sign of the coefficient indicates the direction of the relation between the variables. Therefore, the Trade Freedom Index has a positive coefficient of 319.8498, Economic Freedom has a negative coefficient of -524.1746, Trade Balance has a positive coefficient of 449.5665, Exports account for a positive coefficient of 188.9670, Imports have a positive coefficient of 182, 4708, Government debt has a negative coefficient -142.6903, Fiscal Freedom Index has a negative coefficient -272.1567, Business Freedom Index have a positive coefficient of 118.7257, Investment Freedom Index have a negative coefficient -132.2613, Financial Freedom Index has a negative coefficient -191.5211, Inflation also has a negative coefficient of -206.3927, the Unemployment Rate's coefficient is -279.4688, and the Freedom of Labor Index has a positive coefficient 285.0518.

Therefore, the independent variables whose coefficient is positive are Trade Freedom Index, Trade Balance, Exports, Imports, Business Freedom Trade, Labor Freedom Index, and the independent variables whose coefficient is negative are: Economic Freedom, Government Debt, Fiscal Freedom Index, Investment Freedom Index, Financial Freedom Index, Inflation and Unemployment rate.

R-squared indicates the proportion of the variance with the help of cumulated independent variables. This is one of the indicators that reveal whether the regression model is well selected. It also indicates what percentage of the total variance for a dependent variable is caused by the independent variables. Hence, we can notice that the value of the adjusted coefficient of multiple determination coefficient

(R-squared = 0,631306) reveals that 63.13%o of FDI is influenced by independent variables. R-squared values range from 0 and 1, the closer its value is to 1, the better the regression is specified.

Another important aspect to be taken into account is that each time a new independent variable is introduced in the regression that is somewhat correlated with the dependent variable, the R-squared increases, but in the same manner, a degree of freedom is lost. As a result, we will also take into consideration *Adjusted r-squared* which in the scholarly literature is considered an improved measure of R-squared. Adjusted r-squared takes into consideration the number of independent variables. This aspect explains why when we introduce a new independent variable R-squared can increase and Adjusted R-squared can decrease, in this manner, penalizing the introduction of independent variables which do not have a major influence on the dependent variable. In the case of the present model, the Adjusted R-squared is 0,591803, the variation of the independent variables is 59,18%, and the difference is 40,82% being considered the influence of other independent external variables on FDI. Since the indicators R-squared and Adjusted R-squared have values close to 1, we can assume that the linear regression model is well-chosen.

In this light, we can formulate the linear regression equation. Through it, we can determine the impact of the independent variables on FDI.

Linear regression equation (equation 2):

$$Y = \beta_1 X_1 + \beta_2 X_2 + \ldots + \beta_\rho X_\rho , \quad (2)$$

where:

Y is the dependent variable

β_1, β_2, β_ρ are the coefficients

X_1, X_2, X_ρ, are the independent variables

Replacing, the following equations results (equation 3):

FDI = 55538,11 + 319,8498 TF (Trade Freedom Index) - 524,1746 EF (Economic Freedom) + 449,5665 TB (Trade Balance) +188,9670 Exp (Exports) + 182,4708 Imp (Imports) – 142,0903 GD (Government Debt) – 272,1567 FFI (Fiscal Freedom Index) + 118,7257 BFI (Business Freedom Index) – 132,2613 IFI (Investment Freedom Index) -191,5211 FinFI (Financial Freedom Index) – 206,3927 Infl (Inflation) – 279,4688 UR (Unemployment rate) + 285,0218 LFI (Labor freedom index). (3)

Through this equation (equation 3), we can argue that in the case of independent variables with a negative coefficient, when they increase the dependent variable will decrease, and in the case of variables with a positive coefficient, the dependent variable will also increase. Therefore, when Economic Freedom will increase by one unit, FDI will decrease by €524.1746 million, at the increase of the index Government debt with one unit FDI will decrease by €142.0903 million, at the increase of the Fiscal Freedom Index by one unit FDI will decrease by €272.1677 million, at the increase of Investment Freedom Index with one unit FDI will decrease by €132.2613 million, at the increase of the Financial Freedom Index with one unit the FDI will decrease by €191.5211 million, at the increase of the Inflation with one unit the FDI will decrease by €206.3927 million, and in case of increasing the Unemployment Rate by one unit, the FDI will decrease by €279.4688 million.

In the case of variables with a positive coefficient, when they increase by one unit, FDI will also increase. Thus, at the increase by one unit of Trade Freedom Index, FDI will increase by $€319,8498 million, in the case of Trade Balance, FDI will increase by €449,5665 million, at the increase of Exports, FDI will increase by €188,9670 million, in the case of Imports, FDI will increase by €182,4708 million, at the increase of Business Freedom Index, FDI will increase by €118, 7257 million, and in the case of Labor Freedom Index, FDI will increase by €285,0218 million.

RESULTS AND DISCUSSION

Taking into account that has been selected thirteen independent variables, they will be grouped into three large groups (Table 4.) aiming at performing a more accurate analysis of their influence on the dependent variable, namely FDI.

Table 4. The grouping of independent variables

No	Group Name	Indicators
1	International Trade	Trade freedom index
2		Economic freedom, the overall index
3		Trade balance
4		Exports
5		Imports
6	Business	Government debt
7		Fiscal freedom index
8		Business freedom index
9		Investment freedom index
10		Financial freedom index
11	Macroeconomy	Inflation
12		Unemployment rate
13		Labor freedom index

Sursa: Author-created table

The Influence of International Trade Group on FDI

As we can notice from Table 5., the R-squared value is 0,620903, which reflects the fact that 62,09% of the total variance in FDI is due to the independent variables selected in this group. In the model obtained from International Trade Group, Adjusted R-squared illustrates more accurately the variance of the independent variables, it has a value of 59, 93%, and the difference of 41,07% is accounted for the influence of other external factors (unanalyzed factors in this case study) on the dependent variable.

Following the analysis of these systemic importance indicators for the obtained model, we can outline that the linear regression equation formulated through the Fixed Effects Method relating to the International Trade Group, is successful, focusing on the significant indicators: R-squared has a value of 62,09%, Adjusted R-squared has a value of 58,93% and Fisher's Exact Probability Test has the value 0, whereas Durbin -Watson stat has 1,670232.

Table 5. Estimation of parameters for the linear fixed effects regression model.

Variable	Coefficient
C	45997.81
TF	15.12790**
EF	-342.2200**
TB	310.4497**
Exp	231.7319***
Imp	227.6110***
R-squared 0.620903 Adjusted R-squared 0.589396 Prob(F-statistic) 0.000000 Durbin Watson stat 1,670232 (405 observations)	

significance levels: *p < .05; **p < .01; ***p < .001.
Source: Author's processing

The Influence of Business Group on FDI

In the case of the model obtained for the Business Group (Table 6.), R-squared has a value of 0,618661, which conveys the idea that 61,86% of FDI total variance is caused by the selected independent variables from this group. Adjusted R-squared shows a value of 58,695 and the difference of 41,31% represents the influence of other external factors on the dependent variable. Fisher's Probability Test has the value of 0, whereas the Durbin-Watson stat's value is 1,634546. Therefore, following the analysis of these systemic importance factors related to the model obtained, we can epitomize that the linear regression equation performed through the Fixed Effects Method in the case of Business Group, is accepted.

Table 6. Estimation of parameters for the linear fixed effects regression model.

Variable	Coefficient
C	67295.07
GD	-176.7671
FFI	-295.7411***
BFI	182.1038
IFI	-131.7531***
FinFI	-342.0111*
R-squared 0.618661 Adjusted R-squared 0.586968 Prob(F-statistic) 0.000000 Durbin Watson stat 1.634546 (405 observations)	

significance levels: *p < .05; **p < .01; ***p < .001.
Source: author's processing

The Influence of Macroeconomic Group on FDI

In the matter of the model obtained for Macroeconomic Indicators Group (Table 7.), R-squared has a value of 0,609011, which denotes that 60,90% of FDI total variance is attributable to the independent variables included in this group. Fisher's Probability Test has a value of 0, whereas the Durbin-Watson stat has 1,604089. As R-squared reveals, combined, these three variables (Inflation, UR, LFI) have an influence of 60,90%. In addition, Adjusted R-squared, which distinguishes a more precise dimension of the variance of the independent variable shows a value of 57,86%, and the difference of 42,12% represents the influence of other external factors on the dependent variable.

Table 7. Estimation of parameters for the linear fixed effects regression model.

Variable	Coefficient
C	10246.70
Infl	-14.35475
UR	-499.2693**
LFI	194.5271
R-squared 0.609011 Adjusted R-squared 0.578694 Prob(F-statistic) 0.000000 Durbin Watson stat 1.604089 (405 observations)	

significance levels: *p < .05; **p < .01; ***p < .001.
Source: author's processing

Therefore, as a result of the in-depth analysis, performed individually on each group, we can conclude that all three models obtained are accepted, thus the independent variables of all three groups are statistically significant, cumulatively influencing FDI. In addition, we can notice that, from these three groups, the ***International Trade Group*** is the most relevant in terms of systemic importance, revealing that 62,09% (R--squared) of the total variance of the dependent variable is attributable to the independent variables of this group. ***Business Group*** designates an influence of 61,86% on FDI, whereas ***Macroeconomics Group*** indicates a value of 60,90%

CONCLUSION

Flows of Foreign Direct Investments have revealed specular developments in the last decade, having a considerable impact on most aspects of the economic activity. It explains their inclusion as a particular form of the factors of production, regarded as "classical", the capital.

In the same manner, FDI act as a catalyst on other classical factors of production, more precisely, on natural and human resources. Moreover, they also prove to affect the newly added factors of production by the economic theory, namely, science, knowledge, and technology. Also, they engender other complementary effects regarding the domestic capital, in all economies, regardless of whether they are economies in transition, developed, or developing.

A particular importance is given to Foreign Direct Investment since they are an important source of external financing in capital formation and facilitates the transfer of resources, human capital, and technological progress across countries. In such a manner, they constitute a vital means through which the economies of transition can promote economic growth and the development of the entire socio-economic environment. FDI remains, indeed, one of the key factors of economic growth. Empirical theories and studies argue that the wider FDI is approached (comprising natural, human, and technological resources), the higher sustainable economic growth the countries that invest will achieve, thus ensuring a healthy environment for future generations.

The Eviews program was used for performing the analysis of the indicators and for determining their influence on FDI. The models obtained allow to formulate own conclusion concerning the interdependence of factors of the economic system and to obtain significant observations for the comparison of this model across the member countries of the European Union. The Linear Regression Model was studied with several factors presented in this paper, removing those that were not relevant to our case study. The selection of the determinant factors was performed after going through several specialized studies and articles that approached, to some extent, the matter of this paper.

It has been noted that the **participation analysis** of a national economy to the global economy can be achieved through economic indicators. This subject is extensive, and the methods of analysis are numerous. Since FDI is an aspect of great importance, we decided to examine a series of determinants that may significantly influence FDI, using the Eviews Programme. The selected determinants (Trade Freedom Index, Economic Freedom, Trade Balance, Exports and Imports, Governmental Debt, Fiscal Freedom Index, Business Freedom Index, Investment Freedom Index, Financial Freedom Index, Inflation, Unemployment rate, and Labor Freedom Index) have been grouped into three categories (International Trade Group, Business Group, Macroeconomic Group). A collective analysis of the determinants on FDI has been performed, further has been strengthening through the in-depth analysis of the impact produced by each group on FDI.

On this basis, we conclude that all three models obtained are accepted, thus the independent variables of all three groups are statistically significant, cumulatively influencing FDI. In addition, we can notice that, from these three groups, the ***International Trade Group*** is the most relevant in terms of systemic importance, revealing that 62,09% (R--squared) of the total variance of the dependent variable is attributable to the independent variables of this group. ***Business Group*** designates an influence of 61,86% on FDI, whereas ***Macroeconomics Group*** indicates a value of 60,90%

In the period after the onset of the global economic crisis (2008-2016), FDI record predominant upward trends in the case of CEE countries (Central and Eastern European), which denotes that the taxes imposed on foreign investors an appropriate character, and the exports can be considered the main cause of attracting FDI to these countries.

Numerous studies argue and demonstrate that FDI produces positive effects on the entire socio-economic sphere. First, economic agents, triggers of investment actions, who implement various investment projects, enhance their supply of goods and/or services by increasing their productive capacity and achieving further revenues (stimulating the increase of efficiency in all areas). Secondly, any investment project will cause additional needs or demands in related sectors, upstream (suppliers of raw materials, materials, and utilities, etc.) or downstream (distributors or consumers of goods and services provided. A chain increase in revenues will implicitly occur for all involved economic agents, conducive to the movement of capital. Investments are performed in a cascading manner, involving new and new added value at all levels and for all contributors to economic life.

From an economic perspective, investments ensure the improvement of the competitive position in relation to other economic agents. If we consider through the lens of the social effect, investments play a requisite role in employment, in improving the quality of life, in raising the living standards, health protection, environment protection, and in increasing the quality of the workforce. Internationally, FDI outlines the increase of the level of a country's participation in the international economic circuit. From the technological effect perspective, FDI encourages the acceleration of promoting the technological progress and the development of research and from the perspective of the marketing and image effect, they increase both company's image and consumer confidence in the company's products. It will inherently lead to increased sales and eventually to increased market share.

Moreover, the author considers that is imperative to reassess the entire socio-economic perspective since we are currently facing a new challenge of adaptation and rehabilitation, which is not occurring accidentally in the lives of the whole world. The author considers that ethics is vital in each branch of the economy and not only. Through education population could, indeed, evolve for the better, thus laying the foundation of a healthy framework in terms of non-formal education. If the population had deep roots in principles, the things would truly gain honor and integrity.

On the other side, through economic „education" could be obtained further, appropriate, real and complete professional training. In this manner, each individual would make a major contribution to the growth and development of the entire economy, starting to be noticed in the little things and after in greater things. Both the human and the material factor contributes to the attraction of FDI in a country, but let us imagine what impact would have on the entire global economy, especially during delicate periods such as the one we are facing at the moment, in addition, it would have as support the culture and more particularly the bases of moral values. In this manner, greater transparency, progress in preventing and combating the fiscal evasions, and, at the same time, encouraging a fair and ethical approach to the whole economic and social life would be achieved, with positive effects for both the present and future generations.

As the study case designates that there is a variation of other independent factors external to the present paper, the scholarly literature itself reveals the complexity of the economic growth, this phenomenon is influenced by a multitude of factors, whose analysis and quantification of influence on economic growth requires long and detailed studies. The author considers that this paper lays the foundation for potential future research directions related to the issue approached. In this chapter, the author has managed to cover only a small part of everything that represents FDI and its determinants.

This research received no specific grant from any funding agency in the public, commercial, or not-for-profit sectors.

REFERENCES

Alshamsi, K. H., Hussin, M. R. B., & Muhammad, A. (2015). The impact of inflation and GDP per capita on foreign direct investment: The case of United Arab Emirates. *Investment Management and Financial Innovations*, *12*, 132–141.

Bermejo, C. J., & Richard, A. (2018). Does Foreign Direct Investment Generate Economic Growth? A New Empirical Approach Applied to Spain. *Economic Geography*, *94*(4), 425–456. doi:10.1080/00130095.2017.1393312

Blonigen, B. A. (2005). A Review of the Empirical Literature on FDI Determinants. *Atlantic Economic Journal*, *33*(4), 383–403. doi:10.100711293-005-2868-9

BNR. (2014). *Investițiile Străine Directe în România, în anul 2013*. Institutul Național de Statistică, București. www.bnr.ro

Chowdhury, A., & Mavrotas, G. (2006). FDI and Growth: What Causes What? *World Economy*, *29*(1), 2006. doi:10.1111/j.1467-9701.2006.00755.x

Coase, R. (1937). The nature of the firm. *Economica*, *4*, 386-405. http://walterewilliams.com/courses/articles/CoaseEconomica.pdf

Crescenzi, R., Di Cataldo, M., & Giua, M. (2021). FDI inflows in Europe: Does investment promotion work? *Journal of International Economics*, *132*, 103497. Advance online publication. doi:10.1016/j.jinteco.2021.103497

Demirhan, E., & Masca, M. (2008). Determinants of Foreign Direct Investment Flows to De-veloping Countries: A Cross-Sectional Analysis. *Prague Economic Papers*, *17*(4), 356–369. doi:10.18267/j.pep.337

Dkhili, H., & Dhiab, L. (2018). The Relationship between Economic Freedom and FDI versus Economic Growth: Evidence from the GCC Countries. *Journal of Risk and Financial Management*, *11*(4), 81. doi:10.3390/jrfm11040081

Dunning, J. H. (1993). *Multinational enterprises and the global economy*. Addison-Wesley Publishing Company.

Gabor, H. (2000). Home Country Patterns of Foreign Direct Investment in Central and East European Countries. *Russian and East European Finance and Trade*, *36*(2), 87–104. doi:10.2307/27749524

Håkanson, L. (1979). *Towards a theory of location and corporate growth*. Willey.

Hanink, D. M. (1997). Principles and applications of economic geography. In Economy, Policy, Environment. John Wiley and Sons, Inc.

Hansen, H., & Rand, J. (2006). On the Causal Links Between FDI and Growth in Developing Countries. *World Economy*, *29*(1), 21–41. doi:10.1111/j.1467-9701.2006.00756.x

Hayter, R. (1997). Dynamics of Industrial Location: The Factory, the Firm and the Production System. John Wiley & Sons Ltd.

Helpman, E. (1984). A simple theory of international trade within multinational corporations. *Journal of Political Economy, Vol*, *92*(3), 451–471. doi:10.1086/261236

Horobeţ, A., & Popovici, O. (2017). Investiţiile Străine Directe: Evoluţia şi importanţa lor în România. *Studiu realizat în parteneriat de Academia de Studii Economice Bucureşti şi Consiliul Investitotilor Străini*, 2. https://www.researchgate.net/profile/Alexandra_Horobet/publication/321016706_INVESTITIILE_STRAINE_DIRECTE_EVOLUTIA_SI_IMPORTANTA_LOR_IN_ROMANIA/links/5a0806a1a6fdcc65eab3c7e7/INVESTITIILE-STRAINE-DIRECTE-EVOLUTIA-SI-IMPORTANTA-LOR-IN-ROMANIA.pdf

Hymer, S. H. (1976). *The International Operations of National Firms: a Study of Direct Foreign Investment.* MIT Press.

IMF. (2009). *Balance of Payments and International Investment Position Manual* (6th ed.). https://www.imf.org/external/pubs/ft/bop/2007/pdf/bpm6.pdf

Imtiaz, S., & Bashir, M. F. (2017). Economic freedom and foreign direct investment in South Asian countries, Theoretical and Applied Economics. *Asociatia Generala a Economistilor din Romania, 24*(2), 277–290. Available at: https://econpapers.repec.org/article/agrjournl/v_3axxiv_3ay_3a2017_3ai_3a2(611)_3ap_3a277-290.htm

Jones, G. (1996). *The evolution of international business: an introduction.* Routledge. https://onlinelibrary.wiley.com/doi/epdf/10.1111/aehr.372br1

Kandiero, T., & Chitiga, M. (2014). Trade openness and foreign direct investment in Africa. *Suid-Afrikaanse Tydskrif vir Ekonomiese en Bestuurswetenskappe*, *9*(3), 355–357. doi:10.4102ajems.v9i3.1093

Kaur, M., & Sharma, R. (2013). Determinants of foreign direct investment in India: An empirical analysis. *Decision (Washington, D.C.)*, *40*(1/2), 57–67.

Krugman, P. R. (1991). *First Nature, Second Nature, and Metropolitan Location.* NBER Working Papers 3740, National Bureau of Economic Research.

Luostarinen, R. (1979). Internationalization of the firm. Academiae Oeconomicae Helsingiesnsis, Series A: 30 Helsinki School of Economics.

Markusen, J. R., & Venables, A. J. (1998). Multinational firms and the new trade theory. *Journal of International Economics*, *26*(2), 183–204. doi:10.1016/S0022-1996(97)00052-4

Munir, K., & Ameer, A. (2020). Nonlinear effect of FDI, economic growth, and industrialization on environmental quality: Evidence from Pakistan. *Management of Environmental Quality, 31*(1), 223–234. doi:10.1108/MEQ-10-2018-0186

Nepal, R., Nirash, P., Bhawna, T., & Harvie, C. (2021). Energy security, economic growth and environmental sustainability in India: Does FDI and trade openness play a role? *Journal of Environmental Management, 281*, 111886. Advance online publication. doi:10.1016/j.jenvman.2020.111886 PMID:33421939

OECD. (2008). *Benchmark Definition of Foreign Direct Investment: Fourth Edition*. https://www.oecd.org/daf/inv/investmentstatisticsandanalysis/40193734.pdf

Pogany, S. I. (1992). Economic Development Agreements. *ICSID Review. Foreign Investment Law Journal, 7*(1), 1–20. doi:10.1093/icsidreview/7.1.1

Raza, S. A., Shah, N., & Arif, I. (2019). Relationship Between FDI and Economic Growth in the Presence of Good Governance System: Evidence from OECD Countries. *Global Business Review*. Advance online publication. doi:10.1177/0972150919833484

Reenu, J., & Sharma, A. K. (2015). Trends and determinants of foreign direct investment in India: A study of the post-liberalization period. *South Asian Journal of Management, 22*(3), 96–98.

Rusu, M. (2000). *Investițiile străine directe*. Paideia Publishing House.

Sayari, N., Sari, R., & Hammoudeh, S. (2018). The impact of value added components of GDP and FDI on economic freedom in Europe. *Economic Systems. Elsevier, 42*(2), 282–294. doi:10.1016/j.ecosys.2017.03.003

Singhania, M., & Gupta, A. (2011). Determinants of foreign direct investment in India. *Journal of International Trade Law & Policy, 10*(1), 64–82. doi:10.1108/14770021111116142

Sokhanvar, A. (2019). Does foreign direct investment accelerate tourism and economic growth within Europe? *Tourism Management Perspectives, 29*, 86–96. doi:10.1016/j.tmp.2018.10.005

Tag & Degirmen. (2022). Economic freedom and foreign direct investment: Are they related? *Economic Analysis and Policy, 73*, 737-752. doi:10.1016/j.eap.2021.12.020

Vernon, R. (1966). International investment and international trade in the product cycle. *The Quarterly Journal of Economics, 80*(2), 190. doi:10.2307/1880689

Voiculescu, D. (2015). *Investițiile Străine Directe- Vector al dezvoltării economice*. Niculescu Publishing House.

Wang, X., Xu, Z., Qin, Y., & Skare, M. (2021). *Foreign direct investment and economic growth: a dynamic study of measurement approaches and results*. Economic Research-Ekonomska Istraživanja., doi:10.1080/1331677X.2021.1952090

Williamson, O. E. (1975). *Markets, and hierarchies: analysis and antitrust implications: a study in the economics of internal organization*. Free Press.

Wooldridge, J. M. (2009). *Econometrics: Panel Data Methods*. https://www.cemmap.ac.uk/uploads/cemmap/programmes/Background%20reading%20May%202016.pdf

KEY TERMS AND DEFINITIONS

FDI Determinant Factors: Factors that influence the evolution of FDI.

Foreign Direct Investments: A foreign direct investment (FDI) is a long-term investment relationship between a resident entity (local company) and a non-resident entity.

International Trade: International trade represents the exchange of goods and services across international borders or territories.

Macroeconomy Factors: A macroeconomic factor is an influential fiscal, natural, or geopolitical event that broadly affects a regional or national economy. Macroeconomic factors tend to have a large impact on economies.

Regression Analysis: Helps us to understand how the dependent variable evolves when one of the independent variables varies, as a result allowing the mathematical determination of the variables that have a greater impact on the dependent variable.

Chapter 2
An Empirical Study of Trade Status and Determinants Between China and "One Belt–One Road" Countries:
Based on the Trade Gravity Model

Miraj Ahmed Bhuiyan
https://orcid.org/0000-0001-9321-972X
Guangdong University of Finance and Economics, China

Zhang Qian Nan
Guangdong University of Finance and Economics, China

Xiao Na He
Guangdong University of Finance and Economics, China

ABSTRACT

"One Road-One Belt" (Belt and Road Initiative, BRI), reminiscent of the Silk Road, is a massive infrastructure and trade project initiated by China that would stretch from East Asia to Europe and be recognized by the international community. Despite of criticism of this project, it is considered as an effective tool for promoting regional and bilateral trade deals. In this chapter, the authors have pointed out the problems that hindered the bilateral trade among countries along the route. Based on trade gravity model, bilateral trade model between China and the countries along the "Belt and Road" was empirically tested followed by some suggestions.

DOI: 10.4018/978-1-7998-8021-9.ch002

INTRODUCTION

Research Background and Significance

Today's world is experiencing unprecedented changes. On the one hand, some developing countries represented by China have achieved remarkable development, promoting globalization and continuous reform of the current economic governance system. On the other hand, some powerful countries like the United States tried to deviate from the trend of economic globalization and advocated trade protectionism, which may hinder or even destroy the stability of the current international order. "One Belt- One Road" initiative, in September 2013, conveyed the strong desire and determination of China to build a better world with all other countries. "One Belt- One Road" is recognized by the international community. Over the years, the initiative has been implemented in action. More and more countries are willing to actively implement the "one belt and one road" initiative in all aspects of cooperation.

"One belt- One road" is an effective way to promote bilateral trade. This initiative has achieved good results in various fields over the past six years. In terms of trade connectivity, first, the level of trade and investment facilitation has been further improved. China has set up 12 pilot free trade zones open to the world, and the average tariff has been dramatically reduced. Second, trade between China and other countries along the border has increased in size. China has established bilateral e-cooperation mechanisms with many countries along the belt and road. "One Belt- One Road" initiative will improve the economic and trade contacts between participating countries by 4.1%, so "The belt and road" cooperation is a booster for expanding bilateral trade flows and achieving trade linkage. It is also a powerful platform for countries to deepen exchanges and cooperation and participate in and actively promote economic globalization.

China's "One Belt- One Road" initiative is closely related to trading. Studying the trade status and its influencing factors between China and the participating countries is significant. Since the trade situation of China along the belt and road has been analyzed, the factors affecting bilateral trade can be broadened. China's "One Belt- One Road" trade scale, trade liberalization, better implementation of China's opening-up strategy, and China's opening-up policy will also be of some reference value.

Main Contents and Research Methods

Main Contents

The main content of this paper is divided into four parts:

The first part describes the development status of China and the countries along with the "Belt and Road", the growth of trade, and the main problems in the countries along the "Belt and Road" from 2008 to 2018, including Central Asia, South Asia, Central, and Eastern Europe, West Asia and ASEAN countries. Understanding the development status of economic and trade cooperation between China and countries along the "Belt and Road" and the impact of the "Belt and Road" initiative on bilateral trade cooperation is also explained.

A bilateral trade model between China and countries along the "Belt and Road" is constructed in the second part. The bilateral trade model's independent and dependent variables were set based on the trade gravity model. The independent variables were the bilateral trade volume. The dependent variables included three essential variables and three dummy variables.

The bilateral trade model between China and the countries along the "Belt and Road" was tested empirically in the Third part. The overall empirical analysis of the bilateral trade model and the robustness test by region were performed using Eviews9.0, and the regression results were specifically explained as well.

The fourth part puts forward some suggestions to promote the expansion of the trade scale. Based on the conclusions drawn from the regression results of the bilateral trade model, combined with the trade development situation of the countries along the "Belt and Road," relevant suggestions are made to promote China and the countries along the "Belt and Road." We put forward four targeted suggestions to promote trade between China and the "one belt and one road" countries.

Research Methods

This paper mainly adopts four research methods. The details are as follows:

The first is the method of combining normative research and empirical research. The article collects and organizes many domestic and foreign documents related to the influencing trade factors of countries along the "Belt and Road." Through the comprehensive classification and comparison of the similarities and differences between the literature, we can understand the current research situation of the topic selection and lay the foundation for further determining its research contents. Based on the analysis of previous studies, this paper puts forward two hypotheses and constructs a trade gravity model to empirically analyze the correctness of the assumptions to increase the persuasiveness of the topic selection.

The second is a combination of qualitative analysis and quantitative analysis. The article qualitatively analyzes the trade development of the countries along the "Belt and Road" and quantitatively explain the development trend of the trade volume of the relevant countries through relevant data. The measurement part adopts the trade gravity model and performs regression analysis on the constructed model based on random effects. The results of the empirical study are explained in detail to deepen the empirical conclusions of the article further.

Literature Review

Foreign Research on Factors Affecting Trade in "One Belt- One Road"

As the "Belt and Road" has become an international public product benefiting hundreds of millions of people worldwide, all countries are generally concerned about the stimulating effect of the implementation of the "Belt and Road" initiative on their economies, so there are not a few foreign studies on the economic and trade issues of the "Belt and Road." Fardella and Prodi (2017) analyzed the impact of the "Belt and Road" initiative on bilateral trade in Europe and found that the development of new railway connections will benefit most of the Nordic and Central European countries. Irshad (2018) estimated the bilateral trade potential between Pakistan and China. Research shows that the bilateral trade volume between the two countries is positively affected by GDP, religion, WTO, the opening of trade between the two countries, and the shared border while being negatively affected by geographic distance and inflation. Shakur (2018) investigated the trade costs associated with China-EU agricultural trade from 2001 to 2015, and the results showed that the implementation of the "Belt and Road" initiative would reduce high trade costs, thereby significantly increasing China-EU bilateral agricultural trade. The research of Siobhan and Nadia (2019) found that the construction and improvement of transportation facilities under the "Belt and Road" initiative will significantly reduce trade costs, thereby helping economies along the "Belt and Road" increase trade volume. Ramasamy and Yeung (2019) compared the impact of the two "Belt and Road" initiatives (improving infrastructure and improving border management) on the trade of countries that signed the project, especially the countries along the six economic corridors. Improvements in leadership have the most significant impact on the exports of transit countries.

In the academic research on trade influencing factors, empirical analysis mainly uses the measurement method of the trade gravity model. Papalia and Bertarelli (2015) used the gravity model of structural heterogeneity to study the heterogeneous effect of trade flows in trade integration regions (such as APEC and E.U.) Kazar (2018) found bilateral trade increases with the similarity of domestic market size and country size. Hussain, Wasim & Nadeem (2019) use factor analysis and gravity model to estimate the impact of complex infrastructure such as transportation and telecommunications on bilateral export trade. In addition, there are also a few kinds of literature using the general equilibrium model to study the influence factors of trade. Alen (2019) "One Belt- One Road" and the other two countries, using the general equilibrium model, analyze the impact of infrastructure construction and Optimization on trade in the context of "one belt and one road".

Domestic Research on Factors Affecting Trade in "One Belt - One Road"

The "Belt and Road" initiative has received close attention from the international community as soon as it was put forward, and related issues have also become a hot topic in China's domestic academic areas. Tan and Zhou (2015) use the trade inefficiency model to study the impact of the four major factors of free trade agreements, trade facilitation, maritime infrastructure, and the openness of the financial industry on the trade of the southern countries of the "Belt and Road". Li (2016) analyzed the commodity trade structure between China and countries along the route and focused on the positive effect of establishing free trade zones on the growth of the trade scale . Liu, Li, and Chen (2016) analyzed the effect of cultural similarity and integration between China and countries along the "Belt and Road" on bilateral trade. Zhang (2017) concluded from the empirical analysis of the gravity model of export and import trade that economic scale, geographical distance, and language similarity are the three main factors that determine the volume of import and export trade. In addition, signing FTAs and improving government supervision efficiency and quality can also Strengthen bilateral trade ties. In the empirical analysis, Yang and Zhang (2018) take economic scale and geographical distance as explanatory variables and focus on the positive impact of diplomatic relations on trade relations, and this factor also has a lag effect. Fang and Ma (2018) analyzed the factors affecting the cultural trade of countries along the "Belt and Road." Besides the influence of core variables (economic scale, geographical distance, and common border), the study also showed that improving tariff levels and extending customs clearance would impede cultural trade between the two sides. Deng (2019) empirically found that economic scale and population size, financial system distance, common language, and free trade agreements can also increase bilateral cultural trade. The empirical analysis of the influencing factors of the "Belt and Road" trade mainly includes measurement methods such as the trade gravity model, structural vector autoregressive model, and trade inefficiency model. Zuo (2016) empirically analyzed the influencing trade factors of 11 countries along the route based on the trade gravity model and found differences in the trade potential of each region. Zhang and Zhang (2017) identified in the analysis framework of the APR model that economic scale, cultural similarity, and WTO accession have a significant positive effect on the trade efficiency of the "Belt and Road" countries. Cao and Lin (2017) found that the volatility of the RMB exchange rate is directly proportional to the bilateral trade volume by constructing an SVAR model. Hou (2018) uses a complex network model and a trade gravity model to analyze the trade patterns of countries along the route and the influencing factors of trade flows. Zhang and Yu (2018) combined the idea of the adjacency effect and used the export trade model to study the impact of transportation infrastructure on the bilateral trade of countries along with the "Belt and Road". Wan (2019) studied the influence of economic volume, trade dependence, WTO accession, and APEC on the bilateral trade flow between China and countries along the "Belt and Road" based on the expanded trade gravity model. Li and Du (2019) use the stochastic frontier gravity model to study the influencing factors of trade flows and use the trade inefficiency model to study the trade potential of 33 countries along the route. Empirical evidence shows that an open financial environment promotes export trade.

Summary

In the process of sorting out the relevant literature at home and abroad, we can find that the existing literature has comprehensively considered the influencing factors of bilateral trade cooperation between China and countries along the belt and road, which has laid the foundation for theoretical demonstration and innovation in the economy, trade, investment, and other aspects. However, the sample countries selected in the current research are relatively limited, mainly concentrated in certain countries or a few regions. The identical factor has different degrees of influence on different areas of the countries along the "Belt and Road." There are few papers on this in-depth study. Based on the analysis and reference of previous studies, the article puts forward two hypotheses: First, economies of scale, quality of port infrastructure, signing of free trade agreements, and accession to APEC will have a positive effect on bilateral trade, while geographic distance will have a negative impact. On bilateral trade, geographical distance will have a negative impact. Second, the degree of influence of the same factor on countries in different regions along the route is heterogeneous. To this end, the article will collect and sort out the import and export trade volume data between China and 45 countries along the "Belt and Road" during the 11 years from 2008 to 2018. First, establish a trade gravity model and perform regression analysis on the entire model based on random effects. The countries are divided into five groups according to their geographical locations, and the regional robustness tests are conducted to empirically study the main factors affecting the growth of bilateral trade between China and the countries along the "Belt and Road", and analyze the differential impact of these factors on different regions. Further, put forward robust measures to promote the growth of bilateral trade between China and countries along the "Belt and Road" and promote the sustainable development of the "Belt and Road" initiative.

CURRENT STATUS OF TRADE DEVELOPMENT BETWEEN CHINA AND COUNTRIES ALONG THE "BELT AND ROAD"

The "Belt and Road" initiative has stimulated the economic development of countries along the route from all aspects, greatly improved the quality of life of local people, and enabled more citizens to enjoy various benefits. This part mainly focuses on the perspective of trade connectivity, analyzes the trade growth of countries along the "Belt and Road" from 2008 to 2018, and understands the impact of the "Belt and Road" initiative on bilateral trade cooperation between China and countries along the route. To cover as many cooperation areas as possible, the article uses 45 countries in the five regions along the route as sample countries, including 5 Central Asia, 6 South Asia, 14 Central and Eastern Europe, 10 ASEAN, and 10 West Asia.

Current Situation of Trade Development Between China and Five Central Asian Countries

China has a long history of exchanges with Central Asia. As early as the Han Dynasty, China began a journey of foreign exchanges with Central Asia. Today, the "Belt and Road" initiative has helped the two sides continue to expand their cooperation in all aspects. Regarding economic and trade cooperation, the opening of the China-Kazakhstan agricultural green channel has facilitated agrarian products' "going out" strategy in the rich Xinjiang region. The smooth operation of international freight trains has promoted Ningxia's opening up toward the west. In terms of economic volume, the gross domestic product of the five Central Asian countries showed a fluctuating growth trend from 2008 to 2018, and the scale of trade continued to expand. Kazakhstan's GDP ranks first among the five countries. Uzbekistan and Turkmenistan have seen their GDP rise during the last 11 years. As Uzbekistan is rich in cherries and mung beans, its exports of fruits and vegetables to China have also increased. In 2018, China became Uzbekistan's fifth-largest fruit and vegetable export market.

Figure 1. Bilateral trade volume between China and five Central Asian countries from 2008 to 2018 unit: U.S. $100 million
Source: World Bank Database

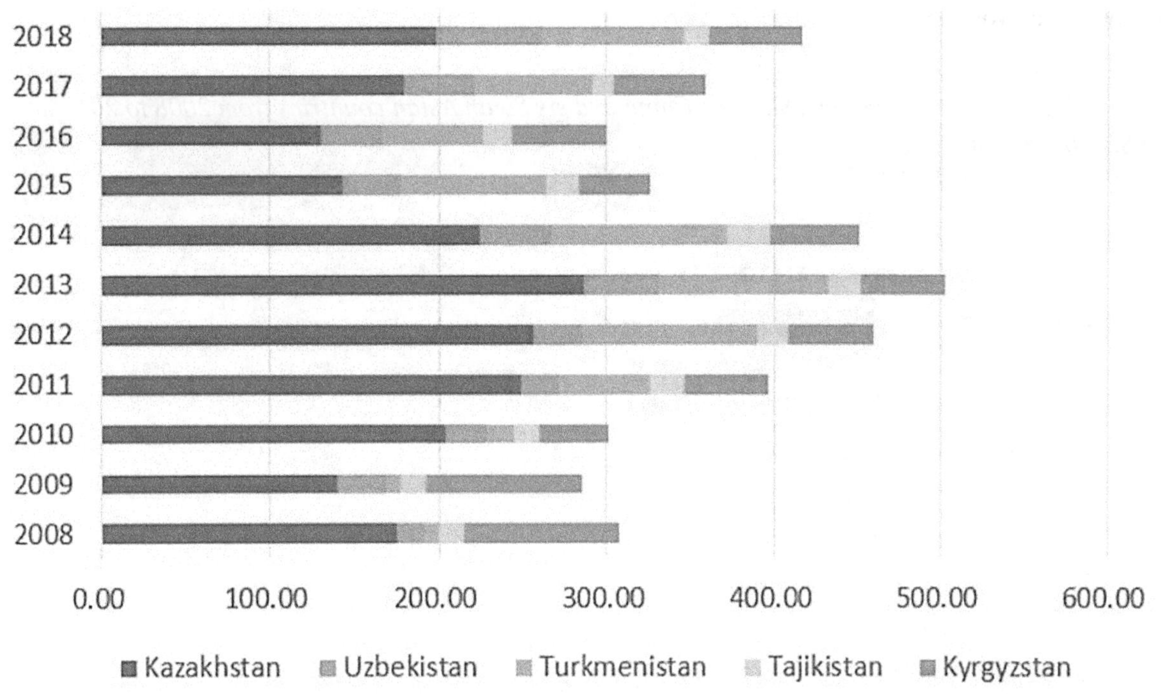

From the perspective of bilateral trade volume, the growth of bilateral trade between China and the five Central Asian countries has different characteristics. First of all, China and Kazakhstan have maintained close cooperation for a long time, but the bilateral trade volume has dropped significantly since 2013. The main reason may be that Kazakhstan mainly exports mineral products to China, and the commodity structure is relatively single. In addition, the decline of international raw material prices is another major adverse factor. Secondly, among the five Central Asian countries, the bilateral trade between Turkmenistan and China is not large, but it is the country with the fastest growth rate of bilateral trade. As can be seen from Figure 1, compared with 2008, the bilateral trade volume between China and Turkmenistan increased more than ten times in 2018, which is mainly due to Turkmenistan's rich natural resources, especially the rapid growth of natural gas exports. After long-term close cooperation and development, the scale of bilateral trade between China and Turkey has dramatically increased in the past 20 years.

Trade Development Between China and South Asia

China and South Asia are geographically adjacent, with similar cultures and customs, and have a solid foundation for cooperation. There are three economic corridors in South Asia, and the vital position of the China-Pakistan Economic Corridor is self-evident. On the one hand, many basic engineering projects in the "Belt and Road" plan have been implemented, such as Hambantota Port in Sri Lanka, Payara Coal-fired Power Station in Bangladesh, China-Malaysia Friendship Bridge in the Maldives, and Shangma Xiangdi in Nepal, A hydropower station. On the other hand, China and South Asian countries have increasingly deepened their economic and trade cooperation to promote convenient infrastructure. The trade scale between China and the six countries in South Asia is expanding year by year in terms of total trade volume.

Figure 2. Bilateral trade volume between China and six South Asian countries from 2008 to 2018 unit: U.S. $100 million
Source: World Bank Database

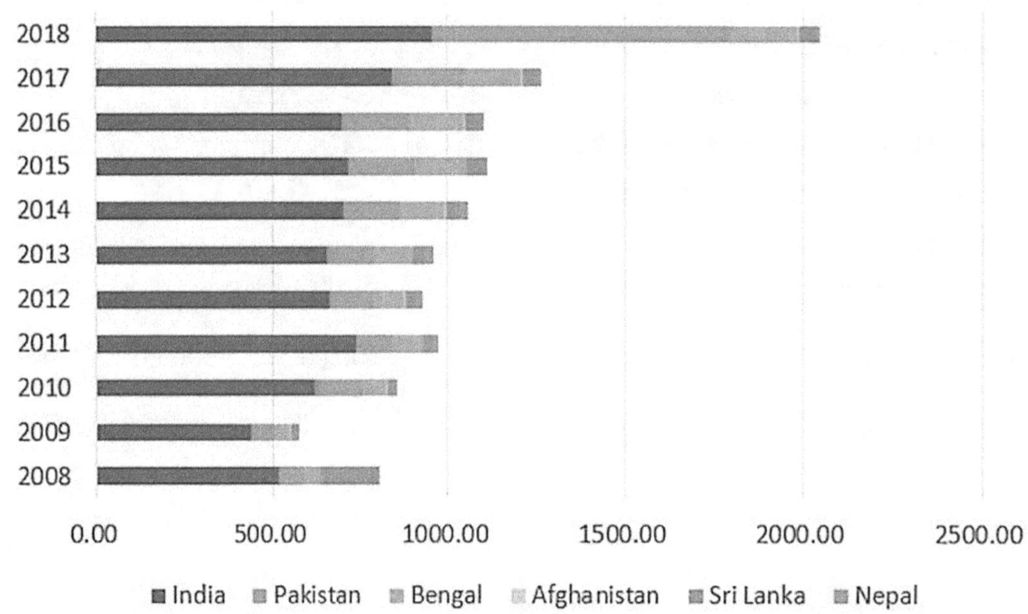

As shown in Figure 2, the trade scale of India, Pakistan, and Bangladesh occupies a dominant position among the six countries in South Asia. The bilateral transaction volume between China and the remaining five countries, including Afghanistan and Sri Lanka, is relatively small. However, as the One Belt-One Road initiative progresses, China and the six South Asian countries will develop more extensive economic and trade cooperation. First, among the six South Asian countries, the bilateral trade volume between China and India has increased yearly. As of 2018, the bilateral import and export trade volume between China and India has risen to US$95.731 billion, far exceeding the rest of the countries. The remarkable development of China-India cooperation has benefited from many factors, including the profound cultural foundation, the convenience of geographical location, and the similarity of population characteristics. In addition, China's strong infrastructure construction capabilities also cater to India's urgent needs, and India's developed software and Internet service industries also complement China's advantages. Secondly, since the beginning of 2017, the bilateral trade volume between China and Pakistan has increased significantly. This is mainly due to the leading role of the China-Pakistan Economic Corridor. Many projects under its framework have effectively solved the two significant problems of power shortage and backward transportation infrastructure faced by Pakistan and created many benefits for Pakistan every year. Thirdly, the bilateral trade volume between China and Bangladesh has been increasing yearly, especially in terms of contracting projects, and China-Bangladesh economic and trade cooperation has entered a new stage.

Current Situation of Trade Development Between China and Central and Eastern European Countries

Since 2012, China has maintained close cooperative relations with Central and Eastern European countries. Now the "16+1" cooperation mechanism has lasted for seven years. In April 2019, Greece's accession officially expanded the "16+1" model into the "17+1" cooperation framework. This means that the "one belt" initiative has been recognized more and more in central and Eastern Europe, and the cooperation between China and the east and central European countries has excellent potential for development.

Figure 3. Bilateral trade volume between China and 14 central and Eastern European countries from 2008 to 2018 unit: U.S. $100 million
Source: World Bank Database

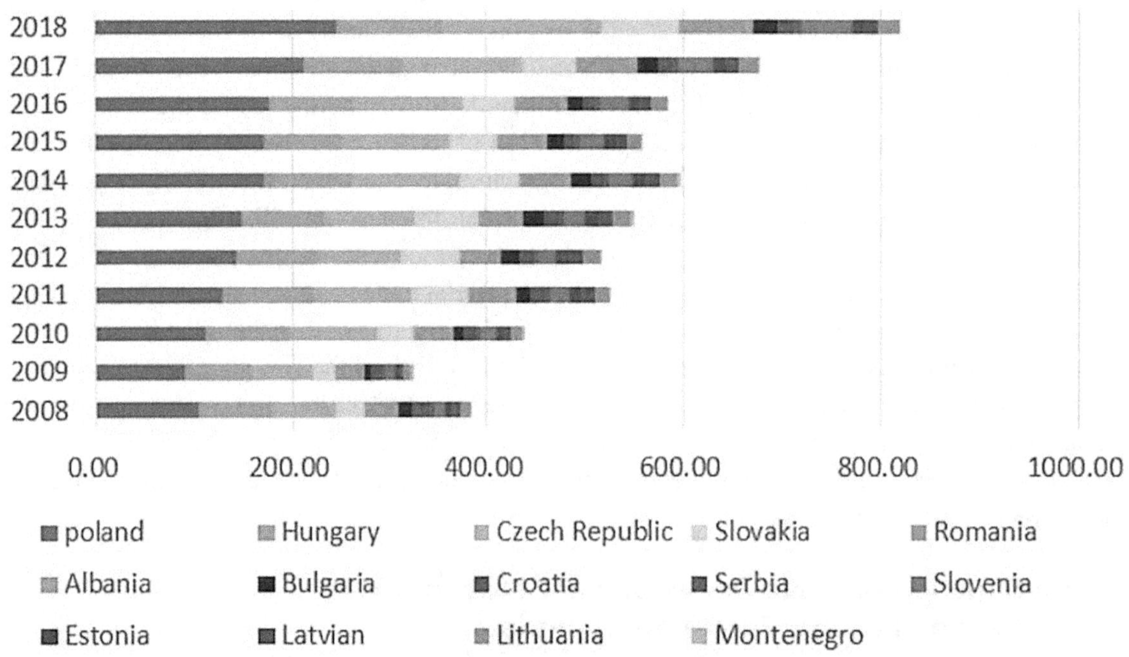

As shown in Figure 3, the total trade volume of Poland, the Czech Republic, and Hungary accounts for 63% of the total trade volume between China and Central & Eastern. Poland is known as the jewel of the "Belt and Road" among them. Compared with other Central and Eastern European countries, Poland occupies a significant advantage in geographical location, population, land area, and economic aggregate. Coupled with its stable financial situation and mature business environment, these factors will undoubtedly boost the long-term development of pragmatic cooperation. In addition, the total volume of bilateral trade between China and other central and Eastern European countries is not large, but it also shows a trend of gradual growth. In particular, Slovenia has a very significant growth rate, and there are broad prospects for economic and trade cooperation with China.

The Current Situation of Trade Development Between China and ASEAN Countries

Over the past six years, the "Belt and Road" initiative has won great praise from local leaders in the ASEAN region, and the cooperation and development between ASEAN countries and China in all aspects is a good development trend. The Belt and Road Initiative has achieved many fruitful results in Southeast Asia. Construction of the China-Laos railway has begun, the China-India-Yawan high-speed railway has been fully completed, and the China-Vietnam Yongxin project will soon be put into operation. Over the years, China has continued to maintain its position as the largest trading partner of ASEAN.

Figure 4. Bilateral trade volume between China and ten ASEAN countries from 2008 to 2018 unit: U.S. $100 million
Source: World Bank Database

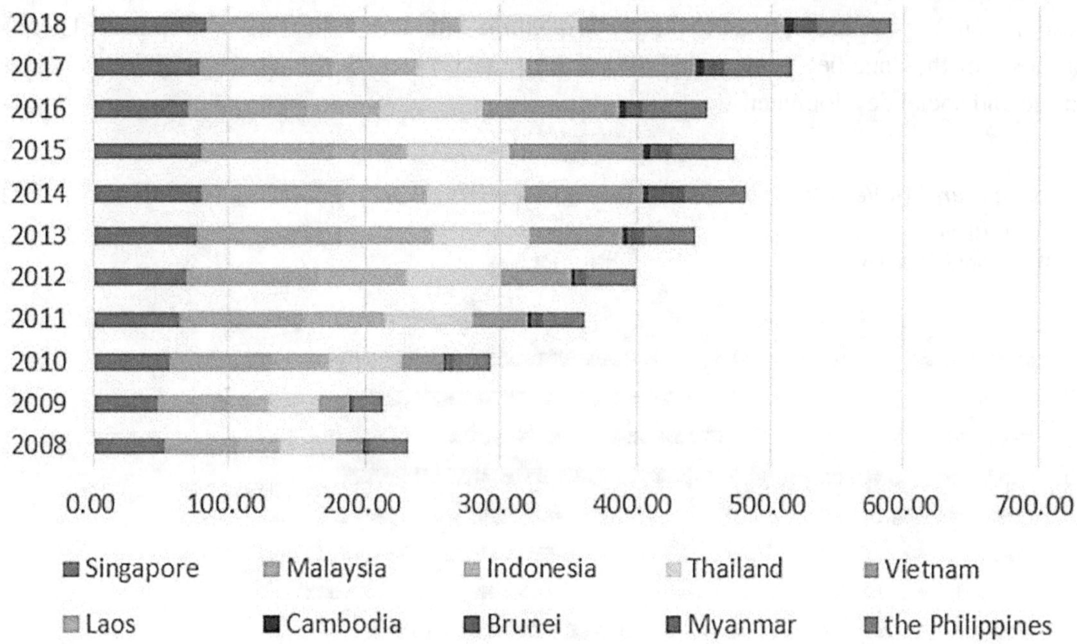

As shown in Figure 4, the bilateral trade volume between Singapore, Malaysia, Indonesia, Thailand, Vietnam, and the Philippines is developing rapidly, while the remaining four countries have seen relatively small increases. First of all, the rapid development of Vietnam is the most eye-catching. The trade structure between China and Vietnam is becoming more and more reasonable. The areas of bilateral trade cooperation are no longer limited to low-tech industries such as agricultural and sideline products but are more capital-intensive and technology-intensive. It can be seen that the degree of economic and trade cooperation between the two countries is constantly deepening. Secondly, the development of the Philippines is also very gratifying. The bilateral trade volume between China and the Philippines has grown from 72 million U.S. dollars in 1975 to 5.131 billion U.S. dollars in 2017, making significant progress. With the continuous deepening of China-ASEAN Free Trade Area cooperation and the gradual implementation of the "ASEAN Interconnection Master Plan 2025", China-Philippines cooperation has enormous room for development. With the joint efforts of China and ASEAN countries, the two sides will continue to deepen bilateral trade cooperation on the convenient platform provided by the "Belt and Road" initiative.

Current Situation of Trade Development Between China and Countries in West Asia

West Asia is well-known as the "world oil treasure house." Its exports to China have always been dominated by energy and resources such as oil, natural gas, and mineral resources. However, the level of the manufacturing industry in West Asia is low, and public infrastructure such as transportation, water & electricity is very backward. Local residents often face problems such as insufficient power supply and inconvenient transportation. Today, China's "One Belt, One Road" initiative has brought good news to improve the quality of public infrastructure in West Asia. At the same time, the rich oil and other energy and resources in West Asia also cater to the needs of China's modern industrial development. Therefore, the proposal of the "one belt - one road" initiative is consistent with the interests of the two sides in economic and social development.

Figure 5. Bilateral trade volume between China and ten West Asian countries from 2008 to 2018 unit: U.S. $100 million
Source: World Bank Database

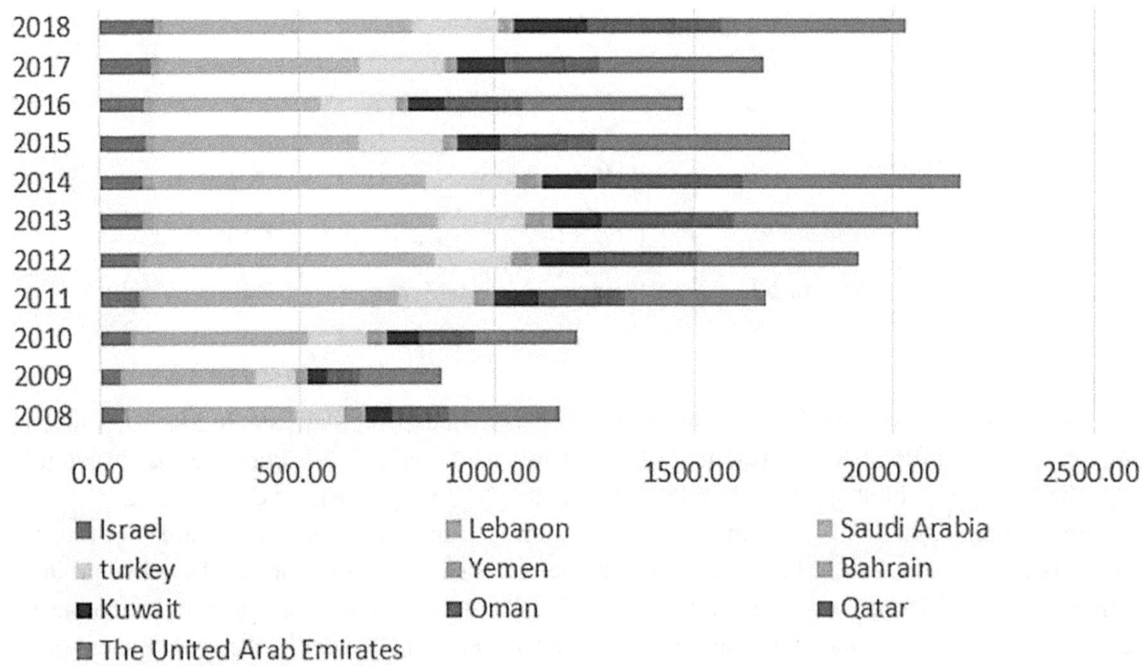

It can be seen from Figure 5 that the overall bilateral trade volume between China and ten countries in West Asia shows a fluctuating growth trend. My country and Saudi Arabia have conducted frequent trade exchanges in recent years. As the mutual complementarity of energy and industrial cooperation between the two sides has gradually strengthened, the projects planned by the "Belt and Road" Initiative have been implemented to a greater extent in West Asia. There are still many influencing factors that are not conducive to economic and trade cooperation between the two sides. The most prominent problem is the political instability in West Asia and the turbulent situation in these countries, which brings significant challenges to bilateral cooperation. In addition, issues such as religious conflicts, ethnic discrimination, and cultural estrangement also bring a crisis of trust to each other. Some differences will inevitably occur in cooperation, which hinders further exchanges and cooperation between the two sides. Despite the difficulties, under the "Belt and Road" initiative, China and countries in West Asia have worked hard to reach a consensus on cooperation and enhance mutual understanding's cultures, thus laying a foundation for the continued positive development of bilateral economic and trade cooperation.

BILATERAL TRADE MODEL SET AND DATA SELECTION

According to the previous literature review, it is very suitable to use the trade gravity model to measure the influencing factors of bilateral trade volume. Therefore, this section will set the independent and dependent variables of the empirical analysis based on the trade gravity model. The dependent variable is the bilateral trade volume, and the independent variables include three essential and three dummy variables. The article adopts a logarithmic form for each variable in the model to stabilize the data. The explanation of variables and the explanation of expected symbols are conducive to making full preparations for the next step of empirical analysis.

The Setting of Bilateral Trade Model and Selection of Explanatory Variables

The trade gravity model is widely used in academic research on trade flows. The traditional trade gravity model holds that the farther the distance between the two countries is, the smaller the trade gravity is, the less the possibility of cooperation between the two sides; and the larger the economic volume of the two countries, the greater the gravity of trade, the more likely the two countries will have trade cooperation. Therefore, early economists set the basic form of the trade gravity model as follows:

$$X_{ij} = b_0 + b_1 Y_i + b_2 Y_j + b_3 D_{ij} \tag{1}$$

In this model, X represents the scale of trade between the two countries, Y represents the GDP of the economy, and D represents the geographic distance between the two countries. Since then, dummy variables such as common language and common boundary were introduced into the model by scholars in the 1980s and 1990s. In addition, Lucian (2001), Wang (2007), and other Chinese and foreign scholars also use the gravity model to analyze the system quality index variables, such as estimating the trade flow between members of the preferential trade agreement. The expanded trade gravity model can more comprehensively measure the impact of qualitative and quantitative factors such as politics, economy, and institutions on the scale of bilateral trade between the two countries. Therefore, this article draws on this idea and uses the bilateral trade volume between China and the countries along the "Belt and Road". TRA is the explained variable. The gross domestic product (GDPi and GDPj, respectively) of China and the countries along with the "Belt and Road", the geographic distance between the two countries DIS and the quality of port infrastructure WEF are used as the explanatory variables, and three dummy variables are added, including common border (BOR), free trade agreement (FTA) and Shanghai Economic Cooperation Organization (APEC)

$$\begin{aligned} \ln TRA_{ij} &= a_0 + a_1 \ln GDP_{it} + a_2 \ln GDP_{jt} + a_3 DIS_{ij} + a_4 \ln WEF_{jt} \\ &+ a_5 \ln BOR_j + a_6 \ln FTA_j + a_7 \ln APEC_j + \mu \end{aligned} \tag{2}$$

Where j represents different countries, T represents different periods, and a_0 is a constant term, a_1, a_2, a_3, a_4, a_5, a_6 and a_7 is the coefficient of the parameter to be estimated, μ refers to the random error term of the model.

Data Source and Variable Description of Bilateral Trade Model

The article collects "One Belt- One Road", 45 countries' data in 2008-to 2018, and establishes the trade gravity model. This model takes China's "One Belt- One Road" and the other side of the "I" country as the dependent variable. The data are from the world bank database, and the sum of imports and exports between China and the sample countries is compiled and summed up by adding J to the TRA. Based on the above-mentioned extended trade gravity model, this model selects seven independent variables, namely GDPi、GDPj、DISij、WEF、BOR、FTA, and APEC. The meanings of the explanatory variables and the relevant data sources are shown in Table 1.

Table 1. Meanings of explanatory variables and data sources

Explanatory Variables	Meaning	Expected Symbol	Data Sources
GDP_i	China's economic volume, unit: 100 million U.S. dollars	+	World Bank Database https://data.worldbank.org.cn/
GDP_j	The economic volume of countries along the "Belt and Road", unit: US$100 million	+	World Bank Database https://data.worldbank.org.cn/
DIS_{ij}	Geographical distance between China and the capitals of countries along the route, in kilometers	−	CEPII database http://www.cepii.fr/CEPII/en/bdd_modele/bdd.asp
WEF	The quality of port infrastructure is divided into 1~7 grades	+	World Bank Database https://data.worldbank.org.cn/
BOR	Do China and the "Belt and Road" countries have a common border	+	CEPII database http://www.cepii.fr/CEPII/en/bdd_modele/bdd.asp
FTA	Does China sign free trade agreements with trading countries	+	China Free Trade Zone Service Network http://fta.mofcom.gov.cn/
APEC	Are the countries along the "Belt and Road" a member of APEC	+	APEC official website https://www.apec.org/

GDPi and GDPj respectively represent the economic volume of China and country j along the "Belt and Road". Measured by GDP, the size of a country's economic volume is closely related to its import and export capabilities. In the bilateral trade model, the GDP levels of the two countries can reflect the country's supply capacity and potential demand for related trade products, and its expected impact on the bilateral trade volume is positive.

DISij represents the geographical distance between China and the country of study. Most previous studies believe that the farther the geographical distance is, the higher the trade and information costs will be. With the development of trade cost theory, scholars further proposed that geographic distance will reduce the breadth and depth of trade and even affect the trade price of products, thereby reducing the trade volume between the two countries. Therefore, in the bilateral trade model, the expected sign of the explanatory variable DISij is negative.

WEF stands for the quality of port infrastructure. This indicator can measure the construction of a country's marine transportation infrastructure. It can indicate the port and logistics performance of the country and indirectly reflect the level of a country's trade facilitation. Therefore, the higher the quality of port infrastructure construction, the better the customs clearance procedures and improved trade facilitation, thereby promoting trade between the two sides. The expected sign is positive. The World Bank database divides the index into 1~7 levels. The closer to 1, the poorer the quality of port infrastructure, and the closer to 7, the more efficient and better the quality of port infrastructure.

BOR represents whether China and the "Belt and Road" countries have a common border. Generally speaking, there will be a certain degree of similarity in cultural customs between countries that share a common border, with a higher degree of cultural integration and a closer geographical distance, reducing trade costs and providing more opportunities for trade cooperation. Therefore, the expected sign of this variable is positive. At the same time, this variable is a dummy variable. If China and the research target country share a common border, i.e., border, the value is 1; otherwise, the value is 0.

FTA and APEC represent whether China has signed free trade agreements with trading countries and whether it is a member of APEC. Free trade agreements are agreements signed between two or more countries aimed at promoting the circulation of production factors such as commodities, services, human resources, and capital, eliminating trade barriers, and promoting economic development. Signing a free trade agreement can bring preferential tariff policies to the signatories. At the same time, it can simplify customs procedures, optimize customs clearance procedures, and improve customs clearance efficiency. These factors are conducive to reducing customs clearance costs and trade costs, promoting trade facilitation, and increasing bilateral trade. APEC is also an institutional arrangement to promote world economic growth and promote the multilateral free trade system through investment facilitation and trade facilitation. Therefore, the expected signs of FTA and APEC in the model are both positive, and these two variables are also dummy variables. If China has signed a free trade agreement with a trading country or the trading country is an APEC member, the value is 1; otherwise, the value is 0.

THE EMPIRICAL PROCESS OF THE BILATERAL TRADE MODEL BETWEEN CHINA AND COUNTRIES ALONG THE "BELT AND ROAD"

This part uses Eviews9.0 to conduct an empirical analysis of the bilateral trade model. Before the overall regression, the article first conducts unit root and cointegration tests on the relevant panel data of 45 countries along the "Belt and Road" to avoid non-stationary and pseudo-regression data. After passing Hausman's test, the article uses random effects to perform regression analysis on the overall bilateral trade model. To further illustrate the degree of influence of various factors on trading countries in different regions, the article will divide the 45 countries along the route into five groups Central Asia, South Asia, Central, and Eastern Europe, ASEAN, and West Asia for robustness testing.

The Empirical Process of the Overall Bilateral Trade Model

As the article selected relevant data from 2008 to 2018, involving three dimensions of time, country, and variables, it is suitable to use a static panel model for analysis. Pseudo-regression is prone to appear in the panel model, so the article chooses four methods of unit root test to measure the stability of the data to avoid this problem. It can be seen from Table 2 that the original sequence of "LNWEF" is stationary data, while the original series of "LNTRA?", "LNGDPi?" and "LNGDPj?" are non-stationary data, indicating a unit root, and it is necessary to make a difference for the relevant variables and continue to test them.

Table 2. Unit root test of each explanatory variable

	ADF-Fisher Test	LLC Test	IPS Test	PP-Fisher Test
LNTRA	191.907 (0.00)	-19.09 (0.00)	-4.46 (0.00)	91.444 (0.4377)
$LNGDP_i$	163.938 (0.00)	-20.10 (0.00)	-3.01 (0.00)	9.680 (1.00)
$LNGDP_j$	140.698 (0.0005)	-7.56 (0.00)	-1.96 (0.026)	116.539 (0.0314)
LNWEF	165.131 (0.00)	-19.35 (0.00)	-4.24 (0.00)	218.508 (0.00)

Note: the data in brackets are the concomitant probability of the statistics, and the data above the brackets are t statistics.

The first-order difference series of "LNTRA?" is stationary, while the first-order difference series of "LNGDPi?" and "LNGDPj?" are still non-stationary data. Therefore, these two variables need to be further tested for the second-order difference series. The results in Table 3 show that the quadratic difference sequence of "LNGDPi?" and "LNGDPj?" is stable.

Table 3. Unit root test for non-stationary explanatory variables

	ADF-Fisher Test	LLC Test	IPS Test	PP-Fisher Test
$\Delta LNTRA$	191.907 (0.00)	-19.09 (0.00)	-4.46 (0.00)	-4.021 (0.00)
$\Delta LNGDP_i$	163.938 (0.00)	-20.10 (0.00)	-3.01 (0.00)	68.312 (0.957)
$\Delta\Delta LNGDP_i$	163.938 (0.00)	-20.10 (0.00)	-3.01 (0.00)	183.234 (0.00)
$\Delta LNGDP_j$	162.667 (0.00)	-7.56 (0.00)	-2.541 (0.055)	259.867 (0.00)
$\Delta\Delta LNGDP_j$	162.667 (0.00)	-7.56 (0.00)	-4.360 (0.00)	259.867 (0.00)

Note: Δ is the first-order difference sequence, and △ is the second-order difference sequence. The data in brackets is the concomitant probability of the statistic, and the data above the bracket is the t statistic.

From the above analysis, we can see that there is a unit root for the "LNTRA?" sequence and two-unit roots for the "LNGDPi?" and "LNGDPj?" sequences; that is, the variable data of the bilateral trade model is not stationary. According to the above analysis, regression analysis cannot be carried out directly at this time. For this non-stationary panel variable, the authors chose the ADF cointegration test. The results are shown in Table 4. Whether it is the ADF cointegration test within or between dimensions, the corresponding p values are all rejected at the 1% significance level of the null hypothesis, which indicates that there is a cointegration relationship between the panel data of the bilateral trade model at this time. The phenomenon of pseudo regression can be avoided when performing regression analysis.

Table 4. ADF cointegration test

Explained Variable	Explanatory Variable		t Statistics	Probability Value p
LNTRA	$LNGDP_i$、$LNGDP_j$、LNWEF	In-group statistics	-4.222998	0.0000
		In-group statistics	-6.419179	0.0000

The article uses the statistical test method of the Hausman test to determine the appropriate measurement method for the bilateral trade model. According to the principle of the test, if the p-value of the test result is far more than 0.05, the null hypothesis is accepted and chooses a random effect; otherwise, the fixed effect is selected. The test results are shown in Table 5. The p-value of the Hausman test result is 0.1221, indicating that the bilateral trade model uses random effects to measure the effect better.

Table 5. Hausman test

Testing Method	Chi-Sq.Statistic	Chi-Sq.d.f.	Prob
Random cross section	7.273261	4	0.1221

After dealing with the non-stationarity of the panel data and determining the random effects of the model, this paper uses Eviews 9.0 to conduct a multiple regression analysis on the bilateral trade model and obtains the degree of influence of each variable on the bilateral trade volume from 2008 to 2018. This paper adopts the method of gradually introducing regression variables to strengthen the explanation of GDP, geographical distance, port infrastructure quality, and other influencing factors. The empirical results are shown in Table 6 model (1) ~ (5).

We can see from Table 6 that the modified R2 of the model (5) is 0.58, the F statistic is 97.24, and the p-value is 0.00. It can be seen that the overall goodness of fit of the bilateral trade model is relatively good, and it is significant at the level of 1%. The significance level of LNGDPi and LNGDPj in each model exceeds 1%. The regression coefficients of LNGDPi and LNGDPj were 0.571, 0.567, 0.561, 0.542, 0.542 and 0.724, 0.707, 0.718, 0.766, 0.764, respectively. For every 1% increase in GDPi, the bilateral trade volume will increase by approximately 0.54%, and for every 1% increase in GDPj, the bilateral trade volume will increase by approximately 0.76%. Therefore, the economic scale of China and the countries along the "Belt and Road" can significantly promote bilateral trade. The growth of GDP and the driving force of the GDP of trading countries is greater. The sign of the LNDIS regression coefficient is sometimes positive and sometimes negative. However, from the perspective of the model (5), the regression coefficient is -1.115, and the p-value is 0.06, indicating that for every 1% increase in geographic distance, the bilateral trade volume decreases by approximately 1.115%, and Significant at the 10% level, which is consistent with the expectations. The regression coefficients of LNWEF are all positive. For every 1% increase in the port infrastructure quality index, the bilateral trade volume will increase by approximately 0.33%, which is significant at the 5% level.

The three dummy variables BOR, FTA, and APEC, can all positively affect the increase of bilateral trade volume, and FTA has a higher degree of influence. From the perspective of the model (5), for every 1% increase in BOR, the bilateral trade volume will increase by approximately 0.23%; for every 1% increase in FTA, the bilateral trade volume will increase by approximately 1.67%, which is significant at the level of 1%; for every 1% increase in APEC, The bilateral trade volume increased by approximately 0.04%.

Table 6. Regression results of bilateral trade model

	(1)	(2)	(3)	(4)	(5)
$LNGDP_i$	0.570869*** (12.95008)	0.566665*** (12.86719)	0.561290*** (12.73171)	0.541612*** (12.50870)	0.542468*** (12.46479)
$LNGDP_j$	0.723938*** (0.060473)	0.706809*** (11.51611)	0.718168*** (11.70002)	0.766241*** (13.46972)	0.763891*** (13.15731)
LNDIS	0.088173 (0.216167)	0.007831 (0.019096)	0.555110 (1.065979)	-1.126008** (-1.972980)	-1.114786* (-1.884687)
LNWEF		0.246261 (1.489121)	0.275402* (1.657242)	0.326361** (2.004394)	0.326372** (2.000689)
BOR			0.736166* (1.668727)	0.219180 (0.574093)	0.231719 (0.554164)
FTA				1.641467*** (4.475906)	1.665468*** (3.478030)
APEC					0.044916 (0.082993)
C	-8.607024** (-2.448278)	-8.079963** (-2.294449)	-12.97248*** (-2.853963)	1.745031 (0.348955)	1.651219 (0.318757)
修正的R^2	0.555450	0.556544	0.558287	0.578381	0.576933
F统计量	206.7452	155.9942	125.8748	113.9455	97.23748
P值	0.000000	0.000000	0.000000	0.000000	0.000000

Note: the data in brackets are regression coefficients, and the data in brackets are t statistics. "*", "* *", "* *", "* *" were significant at 10%, 5% and 1% levels, respectively.

The Robustness Test of the Regional, Bilateral Trade Model

There are many countries along the "Belt and Road." To further illustrate the impact of the economic scale, geographical distance, and other factors on China's bilateral trade volume with various regions, the article will study the group of countries and conduct robustness tests on panel data in Central Asia, South Asia, Central & Eastern Europe, ASEAN, and West Asia. The regression results are shown in Table 7.

Table 7. Robust regression analysis of bilateral trade model

	Central Asia	South Asia	Central and Eastern Europe	ASEAN	West Asia
$LNGDP_i$	0.063991 (0.284467)	0.214647 (1.407646)	0.682336* (14.77180)	0.845174* (10.11135)	0.248225* (3.776103)
$LNGDP_j$	0.941409* (3.549798)	0.903117* (14.31794)	0.915398* (25.45924)	0.660635* (8.432675)	1.056731* (9.861981)
LNDIS	-2.633330 (-0.658406)	-1.858127* (-3.193092)	0.225623 (0.847972)	-1.357584*** (-1.744177)	-1.648303 (-0.799799)
LNWEF	0.167756 (0.331002)	1.627423* (3.718248)	0.759197* (5.782335)	0.903672** (2.478173)	1.258311* (3.928803)
C	19.62017 (0.591457)	8.439539*** (1.724144)	-13.65348* (-5.714424)	-1.568486 (-0.248570)	6.519313 (0.358005)
ADjustedR^2	0.298518	0.860002	0.870770	0.754835	0. 682457
F statistics	6.744970	100.8227	258.7343	84.89976	59.56509
P Value	0.000202	0.000000	0.000000	0.000000	0.000000

Note: the data in brackets are regression coefficients, and the data in brackets are t statistics. "*", "* *", "* *", "* *" were significant at 1%, 5% and 10% levels, respectively.

It can be seen from table 7 that except for Central Asia, the goodness of fit of bilateral trade models in other regions is relatively high, especially in South Asia and Central and Eastern Europe, with the revised R2 values of 0.860 and 0.871, respectively. The significance level of the P-value in each region is more than 1%. In Central Asia and West Asia, the gap between China's GDP and the GDP of trading countries on the bilateral trade volume is very obvious. The regression coefficients of LNGDPi and LNGDPj in Central Asia are 0.064 and 0.941, respectively, while those in West Asia are 0.248 and 1.058, respectively. In the ASEAN region, China's GDP has a greater impact on the bilateral trade volume than the GDP of trading countries, with the regression coefficients of 0.845 and 0.661, respectively. Except for central and Eastern Europe, LNDIS has a negative impact on bilateral trade volume. The degree of hindrance of geographical distance to bilateral trade volume from small to large is as follows: ASEAN (- 1.358) < West Asia (- 1.648) < South Asia (- 1.858) < Central Asia (- 2.633). The quality of port infrastructure in each region positively affects bilateral trade volume. For every 1% increase in LNWEF in South Asia, bilateral trade volume will increase by about 1.63%, which is significant at 1%. For every 1% increase in LNWEF in Western Asia, LNTRA increases by 1.26%, which is also significant at 1%. The regression coefficients of LNWEF in CEE and ASEAN are 0.759 and 0.904, which are significant at 1% and 5%, respectively.

Regression Results of Bilateral Trade Model

Both the overall regression results and the regional regression tests show that the bilateral trade model constructed in the article has a good fit, which can better reflect the economic scale, geographical distance, port infrastructure quality, and three control variables (common border, FTA and APEC) impact on bilateral trade between China and countries along the "Belt and Road". The specific analysis is as follows:

First, the scale of the economy has a positive effect on the growth of bilateral trade between China and countries along the "Belt and Road". The article uses China's GDP and the GDP of trading countries to comprehensively measure the impact of economic scale on bilateral trade and more accurately shows that the strength of a country's economic strength will have a significant stimulating effect on the country's trade. The regression results show that the economic scale of the trading countries in Central Asia, South Asia, Central, and Eastern Europe, and West Asia has a more obvious positive effect on the growth of bilateral trade. The main reason may be that these countries are importing countries for China's exports. The huge demand capacity shows that the "Belt and Road" initiative meets the economic development needs of all countries and has a broad space for development.

Second, geographic distance has a negative effect on the growth of bilateral trade volume between China and the countries along the "Belt and Road." Generally speaking, the farther the distance between the two countries is, the higher the various trade costs of trade exchanges between the two sides will be, and the less conducive to the development of bilateral trade. However, from the regression results of the article, the negative impact of geographic distance on trade is not absolute. The signs of geographic distance in models (1) ~ (3) are opposite expectations. The article believes that there are two main reasons: with the advent of the Internet information age, people can freely conduct large-scale cross-border e-commerce transactions online, and the hindrance of geographical distance to bilateral trade is getting smaller and smaller or even negligible. Second, with implementing the "Belt and Road" project, China and its partner countries have become increasingly close in terms of facility connectivity. Not only have they signed a series of transport agreements involving sea, land, and air transport, but also successfully built railways and highways extending in all directions, making transportation more convenient and efficient, thereby reducing the adverse impact of geographic distance on bilateral trade.

Third, the quality of port infrastructure positively affects the growth of bilateral trade between China and countries along the "Belt and Road". Shipping has always been an important means of transportation of goods in the development of foreign trade by countries worldwide. With the rapid development of land transportation, air transportation, and even multimodal transportation, the role of sea transportation in connecting countries' trade is becoming more and more critical. The quality of port infrastructure is an important indicator that determines shipping efficiency. The regression results show that in Southeast Asia and West Asia, where shipping is developed, high-standard port infrastructure quality can bring good development benefits to the opening of regional trade.

Fourth, having common borders, signing FTAs , and joining APEC positively affect the growth of bilateral trade between China and countries along the "Belt and Road." First of all, the countries with a common border have more in common in the cultural backgrounds, language, customs, etc. It is easier to reach consensus in business exchanges, which creates an excellent cultural environment for the smooth development of bilateral trade. Secondly, signing an FTA can bring more preferential tariff policies to trading countries, eliminate the hindrance of tariff and non-tariff barriers as much as possible, and create a stable trading environment for the growth of bilateral trade. Finally, joining APEC shows that member states share common economic development objectives and social development aspirations and create a harmonious institutional environment for the promotion of bilateral trade.

PROPOSALS TO PROMOTE THE STRENGTHENING OF BILATERAL TRADE BETWEEN CHINA AND COUNTRIES ALONG THE "BELT AND ROAD"

Through regression analysis, it can be seen that the article summarizes the conclusions from two dimensions: First, from the overall regression model, the economic scales of China and trading countries are conducive to the expansion of bilateral trade, and the positive effect of trading countries' GDP is stronger.

Geographical distance will hinder the growth of bilateral trade volume. The higher the quality of port infrastructure, the better the bilateral economic and trade cooperation. Signing FTA and joining APEC is also beneficial to in-depth cooperation between the two parties. Second, from the group regression model, the regression coefficient sign of each variable is still consistent with the hypothesis. Except for the Central Asia region, the goodness of fit of the models in the other areas is also relatively high and passed the robustness test. Based on the above mentioned conclusions, the article puts forward four targeted suggestions to promote the strengthening of bilateral trade between China and the countries along the "Belt and Road".

Deepen Economic and Trade Cooperation and Promote Economic Development

Since the launch of the "Belt and Road" initiative, China has always followed the principle of extensive consultation, joint contribution, and shared benefits, guided by the spirit of the Silk Road, and has carried out cooperation in various fields with countries along the "Belt and Road". Economic and trade cooperation between China and relevant countries continues to improve. The empirical analysis of the article shows that both the expansion of China's economic scale and the economic growth of trading countries will significantly promote the increase in bilateral trade. Therefore, China should continue to increase bilateral trade with countries along with the "Belt and Road", especially Kazakhstan, Turkmenistan, and Uzbekistan in Central Asia. China and these countries have broad prospects for trade cooperation and huge opportunities for trade development. In addition, Saudi Arabia and the UAE in West Asia have abundant natural resources and have huge development potential with China in energy trade. Based on fully understanding the trade structure of partner countries, China can promote innovation in trade methods by establishing bilateral e-commerce cooperation mechanisms and launching new cross-border e-commerce models. While increasing the total trade volume, it should also focus on optimizing the trade structure, promoting the export of high-tech products, and continuously promoting trade benefits.

Speed Up the Signing of FTA and Promote the Construction of Free Trade Zones

The construction of a free trade zone is an important economic development strategy proposed by China. The resolution of Sino-US trade frictions is still in a complex negotiation stage. It is even more urgent to promote the implementation of the free trade zone strategy to eliminate trade barriers with signatories. Promoting trade liberalization between countries has become an urgent task at present. The signing of free trade agreements between China and various regions is in full swing, and a series of good results have been achieved. The China-Sri Lanka Free Trade Area negotiations, have attracted much attention. As the "Pearl of the Indian Ocean", Sri Lanka occupies a very important geographical location advantage on the Maritime Silk Road. The signing of a free trade agreement meets economic development needs between the two countries, but the current trade deficit between Sri Lanka and China is severe. Besides, Sri Lanka itself is in the quagmire of foreign debt, which hinders the two parties from accelerating the pace of signing the FTA. Because of the significant stimulus effect of signing FTA on bilateral trade volume, China should strive to seek the common will of all countries to cooperate, more proactively promote negotiations with countries along the route, and accelerate the establishment of higher-quality and higher-level free trade areas, and trade partners.

Strengthen Modern Logistics Cooperation and Reduce the Hindrance of Geographical Distance

The empirical analysis of the article shows that geographic distance will have a negative impact on bilateral trade. In order to promote the implementation of facility connectivity in the "five links", reduce the barriers of geographic distance, and strengthen the modern logistics cooperation between China and the countries along the "Belt and Road" is necessary. With the rapid development of emerging information technologies such as the sharing economy and artificial intelligence, a number of new platform-based logistics companies have sprung up, and the logistics development mode is in the stage of transformation and upgrading. The continuous advancement of the "Belt and Road" initiative puts forward higher requirements for logistics cooperation between China and the regions along the route. However, the current level of logistics cooperation between China and its trading partners is still low, especially in Central and Eastern European countries such as Montenegro, Lithuania, Bosnia, and Herzegovina Slovenia. Various problems are emerging one after another, such as poor quality of infrastructure, the Logistics information level is low, international logistics channels are not well connected, etc. Opportunities and challenges coexist in the logistics cooperation with countries along the "Belt and Road." In terms of specific measures, attention should be paid to integrating the relevant resources of China's logistics supporting facilities, speeding up the construction of supporting facilities, and striving to form a modern logistics network system with all-round sea, land, air, and rail interoperability.

Improve the Construction of Port Infrastructure and Optimize the Trading Environment

The quality of port infrastructure is a crucial factor in determining the level of logistics performance and an important indicator to measure the level of trade facilitation. It is also of great significance for promoting the interconnection of infrastructure and trade between China and countries along the "Belt and Road" initiative route. In recent years, China has paid more and more attention to participating in port construction and operation projects in countries along the "Belt and Road", especially in the vicinity of the Indian Ocean. Few port-building projects are there; For example, the establishment of Huangjing Port in Malaysia has improved Malaysia's port construction capabilities and served the busy Malacca Strait routes more efficiently and conveniently, becoming a key link in boosting the development of the Maritime Silk Road. At present, China's port construction level is becoming more and more competitive in the international arena. However, it cannot be ignored that the construction of China's port infrastructure still faces problems such as low quality, long customs clearance cycles, and low customs clearance convenience. To this end, China should continue to improve port infrastructure construction, shorten the customs clearance cycle, and improve port convenience. At the same time, countries should continue to explore the construction plan of a free trade port, use the port as a bridge to promote the construction of a large maritime logistics channel, pay more attention to the security, intelligence of the port, and build a comprehensive, professional and three-dimensional infrastructure. At the age of the Tech era, thus creating more convenient customs clearance conditions for China's economic and trade cooperation with countries along the route is necessary.

REFERENCES

Cao, W., & Lin, S. (n.d.). Changes in the RMB exchange rate, the effects of neighboring countries' exchange rates and bilateral trade: An empirical study based on the SVAR model between China and the five Southeast Asian countries. *International Trade Issues*, (11), 152-163.

Deng, Z. (2019). *Research on Influencing Factors of Cultural Trade between China and Countries Along the Belt and Road under the Background of "One Belt One Road"*. Hunan Normal University.

Fang, Y., & Ma, R. (2018). Cultural trade potential and influencing factors between China and the countries along with the "Belt and Road": an empirical study based on the stochastic frontier gravity model. *World Economic Research*, (1).

Fardella, E., & Prodi, G. (2017). The Belt and Road Initiative Impact on Europe: An Italian Perspective. *China & World Economy*, *25*(5), 125–138. doi:10.1111/cwe.12217

François, de S., Alen, M., & Michele, R. (2019). Common transport infrastructure: A quantitative model and estimates from the Belt and Road Initiative. *Journal of Development Economics*, 143.

Hou, W. (2018). *Analysis of the trade pattern and influencing factors between China and the countries along the "Belt and Road"*. China University of Geosciences.

Hussain, Z., Hanif, N., Wasim, A. S., & Nadeem, M. (2019). Empirical analysis of multiple infrastructural covariates: An application of gravity model on Asian economies. *Asian Economic and Financial Review*, *9*(3), 299–317. doi:10.18488/journal.aefr.2019.93.299.317

Irshad, M. S., & Hamza, A. (2018). An empirical analysis of Pakistan's bilateral trade and trade potential with China: A gravity model approach. *Cogent Economics & Finance, 6*(1).

Kazar, G., Kazar, A., & Sert, T. S. (2018). Bilateral Trade in European Sports Industry: Linder versus Hecksher-Ohlin-Samuelson. *International Journal of Economics and Financial Issues*, *8*(1), 48.

Li, X. (2016). *Research on the Influencing Factors and Potentials of Bilateral Trade between China and Countries along with the "Belt and Road"*. Liaoning University.

Li, X., Du, T., & Wang, S. (2019). Research on the Influencing Factors and Potentials of Trade between China and Countries along the "One Belt and One Road". *International Economic Cooperation*, (3), 17–29.

Liu, H., Li, W., & Chen, H. (2014). How does cultural fusion affect China's bilateral trade with countries along the "Belt and Road": An empirical test based on micro-trade data from 1995 to 2013. *International Trade Issues, 398*(2), 5-15.

Papalia, R. B., & Bertarelli, S. (2015). Trade costs in bilateral trade flows: Heterogeneity and zeroes in structural gravity models. *World Economy*, *38*(11), 1744–1762. doi:10.1111/twec.12259

Ramasamy, B., & Yeung, M. (2019). C H. China's one belt one road initiative: The impact of trade facilitation versus physical infrastructure on exports. *World Economy*, *42*(6), 1673–1694. doi:10.1111/twec.12808

Shakur, S. (2018). Impact of trade cost on China-EU agri-food trade. *Journal of Chinese Economic and Business Studies*, *16*(3), 259–274. doi:10.1080/14765284.2018.1482089

Siobhan, M., Nadia, R., & Michele, R. (2019). How much will the Belt and Road Initiative reduce trade costs? *International Economics,159.*

Tan, X., & Zhou, M. (2015). The 21st Century "Maritime Silk Road" Trade Potential and Its Influencing Factors-An Empirical Study Based on Stochastic Frontier Gravity Model. *International Trade Issues*, (2), 3–12.

Wan, Y. (2019). An Empirical Study on the Influencing Factors of Bilateral Trade between China and Countries Along the "One Belt and One Road". *Exploration of Economic Issues*, (11), 134–141.

Yang, Q., & Zhang, C. (2018). Influencing factors of trade flow between China and the countries along the "Belt and Road". *International Economic Cooperation*, (5).

Zhang, H. (n.d.). Research on the trade potential between China and the areas along the "Belt and Road". *International Trade Issues*, (7), 87–97.

Zhang, J., & Zhang, P. (n.d.). Research on the trade efficiency and influencing factors between China and the "Belt and Road" countries. *International Economics and Trade Research*, (8), 5-24.

Zhang, Y., & Yu, J. (2018). Transportation infrastructure, proximity effects, and bilateral trade: An empirical study based on trade data between China and the "Belt and Road" countries. *Contemporary Finance*, (3), 98–109.

Zuo, X. (2016). Analysis of the trade influence factors and trade potential between China and neighboring countries under the strategic background of the Silk Road Economic Belt-Based on the Research of the Extended Gravity Model. *Financial Development Review*, (7), 130–145.

Chapter 3
Chinese Foreign Direct Investment in the Belt and Road Initiative

Poshan Yu
https://orcid.org/0000-0003-1069-3675
Soochow University, China & Australian Studies Centre, Shanghai University, China

Zhu Meng
Independent Researcher, China

Emanuela Hanes
Independent Researcher, Austria

Nyaribo Wycliffe Misuko
https://orcid.org/0000-0002-7890-2931
School of Graduate Studies, KCA University, Kenya

ABSTRACT

Motivated by the Chinese government's foreign direct investment (FDI) promotion policies, this paper is attempting to examine the implications of these policies to the Belt and Road (B&R) regions under the unique institutional settings. By applying the software tool CiteSpace, which is developed for visual analyze of science mapping (Chen, 2017), this paper aims to investigate the dynamics of Chinese cross-border investment activities in B&R countries, taking the China-Pakistan Economic Corridor as an example, and discuss the question whether & how these policies and activities could drive more Chinese multinational enterprises (MNEs) to exploit these emerging business opportunities in B&R regions, as well as investigate what is the trend of Chinese FDI in B&R.

DOI: 10.4018/978-1-7998-8021-9.ch003

INTRODUCTION

The Chinese government has made the Belt and Road (B&R) a paramount national strategy and it demonstrates the commitment of the Chinese government to a more open economy (Du & Zhang, 2018). It is a significant attempt made by China to explore new forms of international economic cooperation with new partners, thus sustaining its economic growth (Ge et al., 2020). Through the B&R, the synergy of foreign direct investment (FDI) between regions is greater, and the comprehensive effect is conducive to promoting green finance (Huang, 2016).

In terms of the possibility of creating a new economic pillar and contributing new policy thinking for economic development, the B&R does provide many important opportunities, although it also contains significant uncertainties and risks (Huang, 2016). By applying CiteSpace, a dynamic analysis software (Du, 2021), we can find the research hotspots and frontiers in B&R, which have attracted researchers' attention and analysis. Regional cooperations, such as the China-Pakistan Economic Corridor (CPEC), promote B&R's development. In the FDI in B&R, Chinese multinational enterprises are widely regarded as a means of expanding reach in influence especially in the countries involved in B&R (Du & Zhang, 2018; Chen et al., 2021).

Motivated by the Chinese government's FDI promotion policies, this paper is attempting to examine the implications of these policies to the B&R regions under the unique institutional settings. By applying CiteSpace, which is developed for visual analyze of science mapping (Chen, 2017), this paper aims to investigate the dynamics of Chinese cross-border investment activities in B&R countries, taking the China-Pakistan Economic Corridor as an example, and whether & how these policies and activities would drive more Chinese MNEs to exploit these emerging business opportunities in B&R regions, and investigate what is the trend of Chinese FDI in B&R.

BACKGROUND

The Silk Road is an ancient land commercial trade route that started in ancient China and connected Asia, Africa and Europe. Its original function was to transport silk, porcelain and other commodities produced in ancient China. Later, it became the main route for exchanges between the East and the West in economic, political, cultural, and other aspects.

In terms of transportation modes, the Silk Road is mainly divided into the land Silk Road and the Maritime Silk Road.

The land Silk Road dates back to the Western Han Dynasty (202 BC - 8 AD). It was established by Emperor Wu, who sent Zhang Qian as an envoy to the Western Regions, starting from the capital Chang'an (now Xi'an) and ending in Rome. This road is considered to be the intersection of ancient Eastern and Western civilizations linking the Eurasian continent, and silk was the most representative cargo.

The Maritime Silk Road refers to the maritime channel for economic and cultural exchanges between ancient China and the rest of the world. It was first opened in the Qin (221 BC to 207 BC) and Han dynasties (202 BC to 220 AD). Starting from Guangzhou, Quanzhou, Ningbo, Yangzhou and other coastal cities, from the South China Sea to the Arabian Sea, and even as far as the "Maritime Silk Road" of maritime trade on the east coast of Africa (Hook, 2022).

Over time, the Silk Road has become a collective name for all political, economic and cultural exchanges between ancient China and the West.

B&R or Belt and Road is the abbreviation of "Silk Road Economic Belt" and "21st Century Maritime Silk Road" (Saud et al., 2019), and it's also considered as China's "Going global strategy" (Rauf et al., 2020). It covers more than 60 countries, 47.6% of the global population, 27.8% of total world trade and nearly 30% of the world's GDP (Huang, 2016; Chin & He, 2016; World Bank, 2018; Belt and Road Initiative Big Data Report, 2018).

In September and October 2013, during Chinese President Xi Jinping's visits to Central Asia and Southeast Asian countries, he proposed major initiatives to jointly build the "Silk Road Economic Belt" and the "21st Century Maritime Silk Road", which have received high attention from the international community. These include 1) the Silk Road Economic Belt, whose strategy covers the economic integration of Southeast Asia, the economic integration of Northeast Asia, and ultimately leads to Europe, forming a general trend of economic integration in Eurasia (Du & Zhang, 2018). 2) The 21st Century Maritime Silk Road Economic Belt, and its strategy is to form a closed loop of sea and land between the three continents of Europe, Asia and Africa and the Silk Road Economic Belt (Ge et al., 2020).

B&R improves infrastructure and strengthens trade and investment links, seeking to deepen connectivity and cooperation on a transcontinental scale (Bastos, 2020), which is expected to reduce trade costs between China and the other B&R countries significantly (Soyres at al., 2019). It's also a great vision for China to integrate with Asia, Europe and Africa (Du & Zhang, 2018).

Since the 21st century, China's economy has maintained a steady and long-term growth trend, and it has played an increasingly irreplaceable role in global trade. Bastos (2020) also mentioned that internal supply shocks following extensive policy reforms and falling global trade barriers contributed to the growth in China's trade. At the Boao Forum for Asia in April 2021, B&R has become a heated discussion topic among participants. At the meeting, Xi Jinping delivered a keynote speech on "Together in the Same Boat to Overcome the Difficulties, Share the Destiny and Create the Future", and proposed that we should build B&R with high quality. In the same year, the theme of the 18th China - The Association of Southeast Asian Nations (ASEAN) Expo has also been determined as "high-quality joint construction of the Belt and Road, and joint promotion of sustainable development cooperation". "High-quality development" has become the theme of B&R. Chen (2016) commented that foreign investment has become a powerful driving force for China and the other B&R countries, leading to mutual benefit and common development. In the future development trend, China is moving towards the goal of becoming an investment powerhouse (Du & Zhang, 2018), and how to promote FDI has become a main concern.

The world today is undergoing complex and profound changes. The deep-seated impact of the international financial crisis continues to manifest. The world economy is slowly recovering and developing differently. The international investment and trade pattern as well as multilateral investment and trade rules are undergoing profound adjustments (Ge et al., 2020). The development problems faced by all countries are still severe. Facing the trend of economic globalization and global multi-polarization, we need a freer global trading system and a more open world economy (Chen et al., 2021; Du & Zhang, 2018).

However, the international community's views on B&R are quite mixed. The comparison with America's Marshall Plan, the view of it being a mechanism for international economic cooperation instead of international aid, and the thought that it was the evidence of Chinese ambition to replace American-led international economic architecture with a so-called "China model" is put forward to show doubts (Huang, 2020).

MAIN FOCUS OF THE CHAPTER

Literature Focus Analysis and the China-Pakistan Economic Corridor

In order to better understand the development process and research situation in and related to China, we use the literature visualization analysis software CiteSpace to draw a knowledge map of FDI policies included in the China Academic Journals Publishing Library (CNKI) database and Web of Science (WoS).

CiteSpace is a dynamic analysis software developed by Prof. Chaomei Chen of Drexel University. As a document visualization analysis software, it mainly analyzes target documents through co-citation analysis theory and pathfinding network algorithms, and at the same time draws a series of visualization maps to analyze the potential dynamics of the discipline, track the research hotspots, and explore the frontiers of discipline development (Du, 2021).

The software version we selected for this analysis is CiteSpace5.8.R2 (64-bit), and the data source is CNKI and WoS. By searching for the subject terms "FDI" and "policies" in the advanced search mode, and selecting the combination, after excluding interviews, reviews, news items, event notices and other non-academic articles, as well as some research that with low topic relevance, 1166 (WoS) and 3150 (CNKI) valid documents were finally obtained.

As a refinement of the research focus of the article, keywords can reflect the core content of the article to a certain extent. After extracting high-frequency keywords for a certain period of time, we can obtain research hotspots in this period (Du, 2021).

Set the node type to "Keyword" in CiteSpace, and the time slice is one year to construct a co-occurrence map of keywords in the financial development of the double cycle. By reading the keyword map (figure 1 & 2) and reading related literature, it is found that, in the subject terms of "FDI policies", the researchers' focus is mainly on "economic "growth", "multinational", "policies", "CO_2 emission", "energy consumption" and "trade growth" to investigate what effects these policies have on economy development (Bastos, 2020; Bird et al., 2020; Chen et al., 2019; Chen & Tang, 2014; Du & Zhang, 2018; Han et al., 2021; Yu et al., 2020), and how they influence CO2 emission and energy consumption (Cai et al., 2016; Huntington, 2015; Liu et al., 2020; Mirza et al., 2019; Rauf et al., 2020; Wang et al. 2019). The development of multinationals is strongly influenced by these policies and how they respond matters a lot (Amighini, 2013; Chen et al., 2021; Chen et al., 2018; GoldBees, 2017; Julan & Wang, 2013; Nugent & Lu, 2021; Yu et al., 2019; Zhang et al., 2021).

Figure 1. WoS keywords map

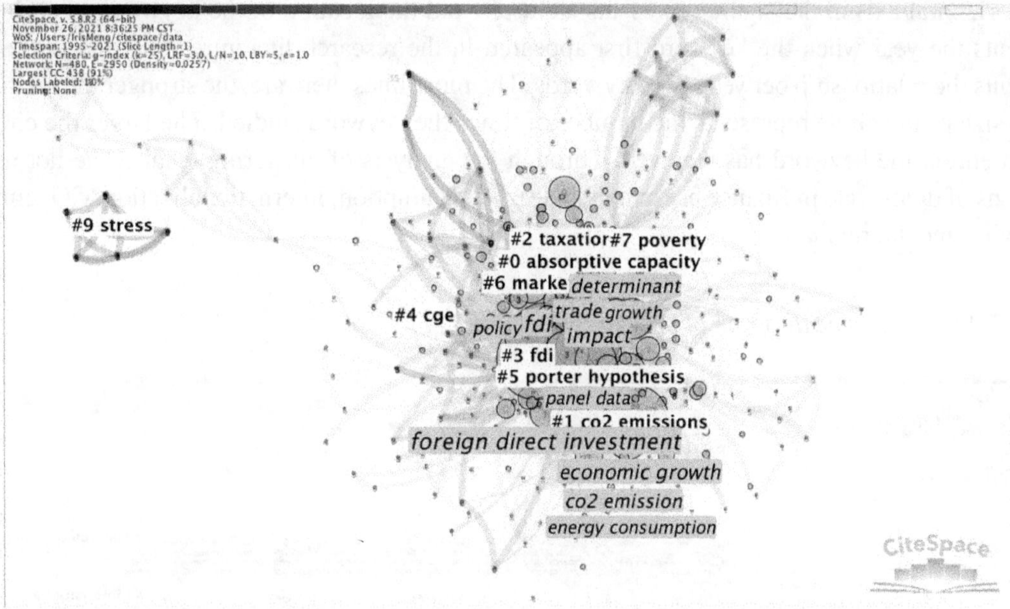

Figure 2. CNKI keywords map

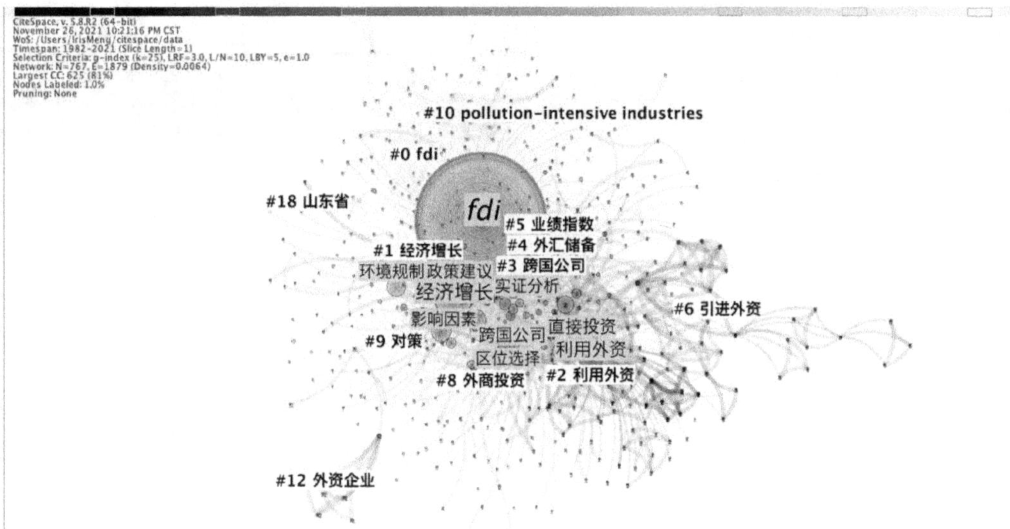

In order to have an increasingly clear understanding of the branch composition of the research field in China, the keywords are clustered through a co-occurrence network, and the clustering method is selected as K cluster (cluster by keyword), and a sequence diagram of keyword clustering is generated. Each horizontal axis in the figure represents a cluster, and the location of the keyword on each cluster represents the year when the keyword first appeared in the research literature. The line in the figure represents the relationship between two keywords. The more lines there are, the stronger the relationship is. The size of the circle represents the number of times the keyword studied. The larger the circle, the more attention the keyword has received. Through the analysis of clustering results, the hot research directions of dual-cycle in finance are mainly: energy consumption, internationalization, CO_2 emissions and environmental regulation.

Figure 3. WoS sequence diagram of keywords clustering (1)

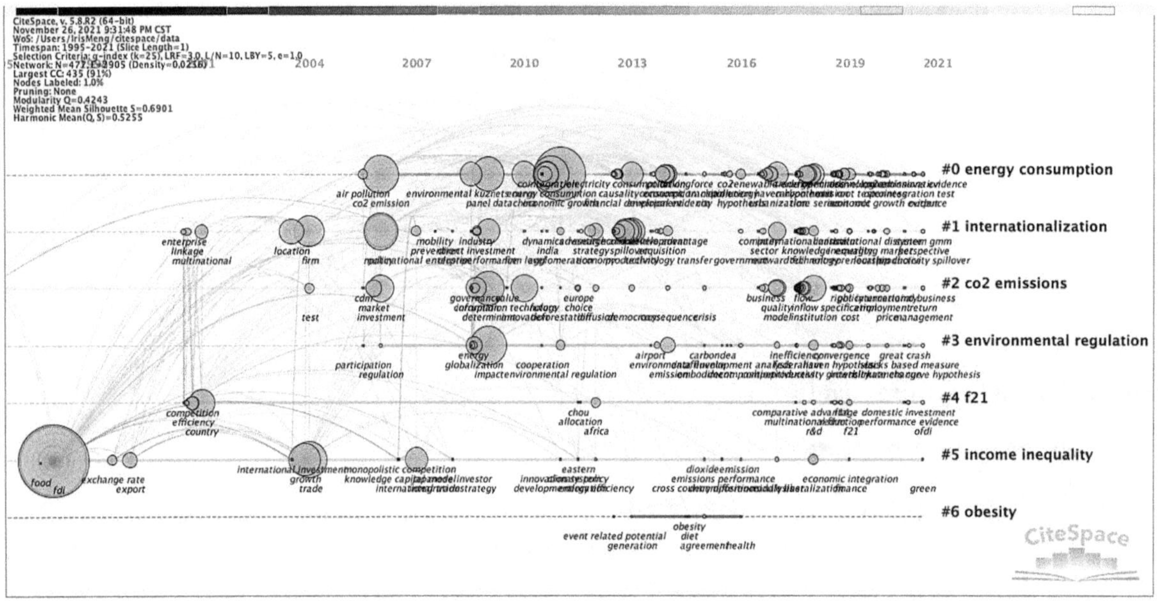

Figure 4. CNKI sequence diagram of keywords clustering (1)

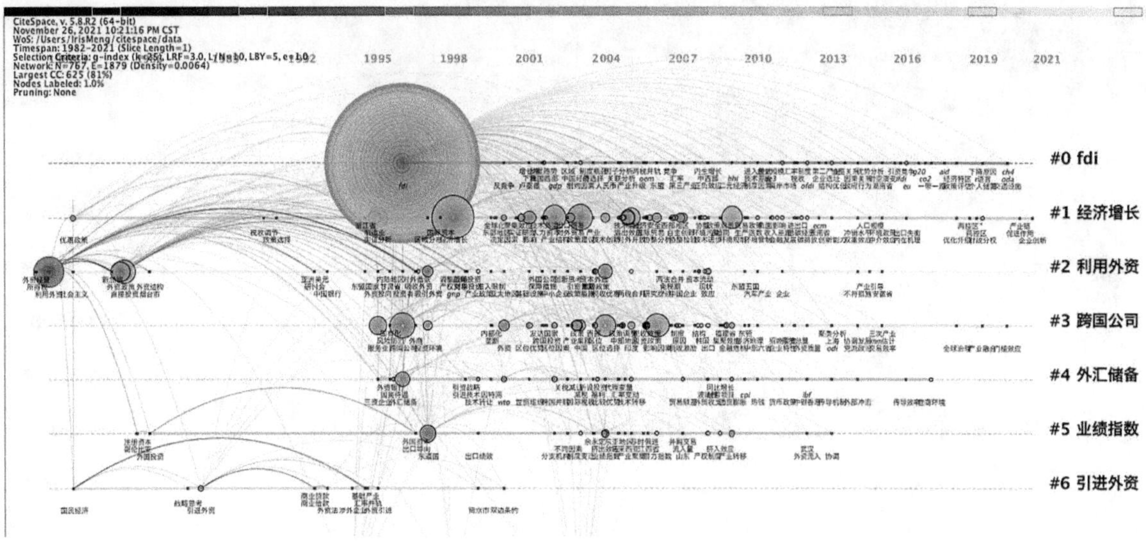

The focuses of studies home and abroad are different. In papers downloaded from WoS, more attention is paid to sustainability sectors. Choosing the key word "FDI", most link lines are distributed in cluster "energy consumption", "CO2 emissions" and "environmental regulation", indicating that from 2000s, researchers abroad studying FDI focus more on sustainability development. While in CNKI database, research focuses mainly on economy with link lines distributed in the clusters "economic growth", "foreign capital utilizing" and "multinational".

Figure 5. WoS sequence diagram of keywords clustering (2)

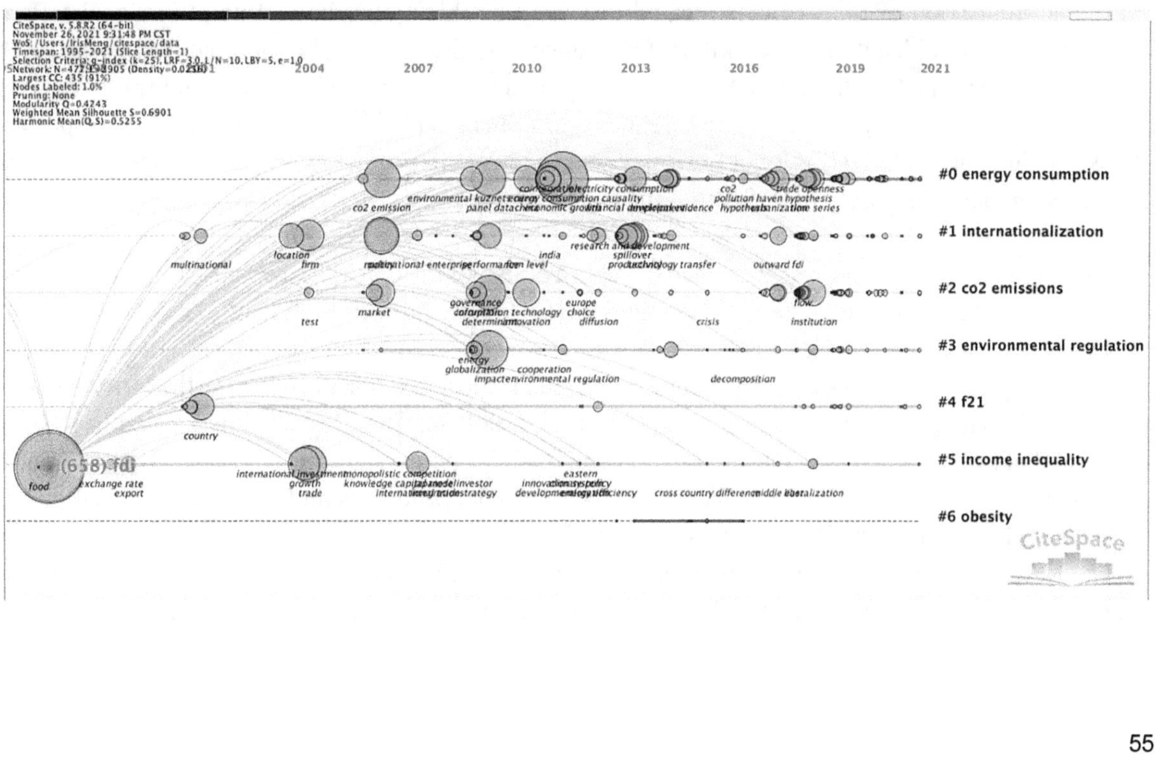

Figure 6. CNKI sequence diagram of keywords clustering (2)

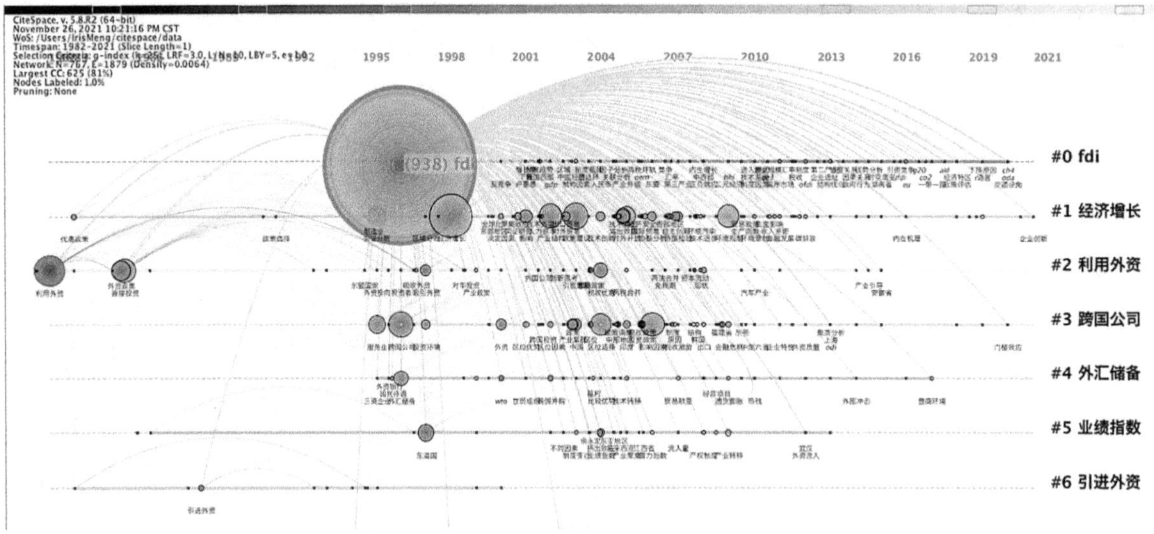

It can be seen from the analysis that researchers have paid great attention to energy and economic development. Here we have to mention a very important part of B&R - the China-Pakistan Economic Corridor (CPEC).

As a landmark project for the joint construction of B&R, construction of the CPEC started in 2013 (Rehman & Ali, 2021). In 2015, it was clarified that the CPEC was a core B&R interest area with focus on the Gwadar Port, energy, transportation infrastructure and industrial cooperation (Mirza et al., 2019; Mukhtar et al., 2022). Over the past eight years, the construction of the CPEC has made significant progress, which has provided assistance for the sustainable development of Pakistan's economy and brought tangible benefits to the Pakistani people.

The starting point of the CPEC is located in Kashgar, China, and the end point is Gwadar Port, Pakistan, with a total length of 3,000 kilometers, connecting the Silk Road Economic Belt in the north and the 21st Century Maritime Silk Road in the south. The "four-in-one" channel and trade corridor covered by roads, railways, oil and gas pipelines and optical cables is known as the flagship project of B&R (Mukhtar et al., 2022). It not only plays a strong role in promoting the development of China and Pakistan, but also closely links South Asia, Central Asia, North Africa, and Gulf countries through economic and energy cooperation.

Looking back on the achievements since the construction of the corridor, the CPEC project has been progressing smoothly in the past eight years, and the first phase has achieved fruitful results.

There are many iconic projects going on along the way.

For example, the Sugijinari Hydropower Project (SK Project for short) is one of the priority projects of the CPEC. The project investment is 1.962 billion US dollars. The SK project is located in Khyber Province, Pakistan, about 256 kilometers from Islamabad. The power station plans to install four impulse generator sets with a total installed capacity of about 873,500 kilowatts and an average annual power generation of 3.081 billion kilowatt hours (Lin, 2021).

The Karot Hydropower Station is built on the Jhelum River (Jhelum), a tributary of the Indus River in northern Pakistan, with a total installed capacity of 720,000 kilowatts and a total investment of more than 1.7 billion US dollars. It is also the first hydropower investment project written into the joint statement of the Chinese and Pakistani governments. After completion, it will provide Pakistan with more than 3.2 billion kWh of clean energy every year, and it is expected to reduce carbon dioxide emissions by 3.5 million tons per year (Lin, 2021). While promoting Pakistan's energy construction and economic and social development, it will optimize the energy structure and contribute to the global "carbon neutrality".

The energy shortage problem in Pakistan has been greatly alleviated, the construction of transportation infrastructure has been improved, and the corridor project has created a large number of employment opportunities and jobs for the Pakistani people during the construction process (Rehman & Ali, 2021). These achievements have laid a solid foundation for the next stage of the development of the CPEC (Mirza et al., 2019). With the deepening of the CPEC, Pakistan will usher in more investment opportunities, and more factories will be stationed in the special economic zone, which will help continue to enhance the development of Pakistan's industry, agriculture, scientific and technological information and other fields, and benefit more Pakistani people.

Chinese Outward FDI - Related Policies

The authors believe that the development of foreign investment cooperation can facilitate a country's participation in economic globalization. Judging from the development experience of foreign investment in other countries in the world, governments of various countries have adopted various measures to promote their own foreign investment cooperation and cultivate multinational enterprises, including formulating national-level foreign investment cooperation strategies and laws, and implementing financial assistance, as well as management services, assistance and participation in international competition and management of transnational operations.

At the 18th National Congress of the Communist Party of China in 2012, the Party Central Committee with President Xi Jinping at the core put forward a major theoretical policy to make the market play a decisive role in resource allocation and improve the effectiveness of the government (Central Committee of the Communist Party of China, 2013).

Since 1978, when China adopted its opening up and reforming policy, the Chinese government has actively been attracting FDI. Since then, as is shown in Table 2 Chinese FDI related policies, China's foreign direct investment policy had undergone a huge change from restriction to encouragement. During the first three decades, dramatic expansion of exports to and FDI from the developed economies contributed to China's rapid economic growth (Huang, 2016). Kang, Peng, Zhu and Pan (2018) found that the B&R diminished the resource-seeking motivation and improves the market-seeking motivation of China's outward FDI (OFDI).

After this phase, China's FDI policy entered a phase of FDI restriction prior to 2000. Following the wave of globalization, China joined the World Trade Organization in 2001. In the same year, the Fifth Plenary Session of the 15th Central Committee of the Communist Party of China passed the "Proposal of the Central Committee of the Communist Party of China on Formulating the Tenth Five-Year Plan for National Economic and Social Development". The state began to propose and implement the "Going Out" strategy, gradually abolishing FDI approval restrictions, and actively encouraging FDI (Li, 2016; Han et al., 2021).

From the overall strategic point of view, Chinese FDI has undergone a process of gradual developing from strict restriction to encouragement and support. With the continuous relaxation and optimization of foreign investment policies, China's "Going Out" will enter a period of rapid development. In recent years, the Chinese government has issued a series of documents to encourage Chinese companies to conduct overseas investment and transnational operations in accordance with international rules, while at the same time continuously regulating the overseas investment behavior of Chinese companies to promote the green and sustainable development of China's overseas investment. In B&R, China plans to cooperate with countries along the route in five areas: policy coordination, facilities connectivity, unimpeded trade, financial integration and people-to-people bonds (Flint & Zhu, 2018; Yu et al., 2020; Fu et al., 2020). The 2014 APEC meeting was held in China, and China's leadership proposed to build a mutually beneficial and win-win "community of interests" and a "community of destiny" for common prosperity and development between the Asia-Pacific countries, actively responding to changes in the global situation, and coordinating the overall domestic and international situations; in the same year, China initiated the establishment of the Asian Infrastructure Investment Bank and the Silk Road Fund for infrastructure construction, resource development, production capacity cooperation and financial co-operation in B&R countries to provide investment and financing support. At the same time, the Chinese government has provided diversified support services and supporting measures to enable enterprises to "go global" more successfully. In terms of financial support, the government has gradually expanded the scale of special funds to support foreign investment and cooperation, encouraging banking institutions and insurance institutions to innovate products and optimize services, in order to provide services for Chinese companies' overseas investment. Under the B&R, the promotional effect of institutional quality on facilitation of FDI can be enhanced significantly (Chen et al., 2019).

The Dynamics of Chinese FDI in B&R Regions

China has increasingly drawn global attention due to its provision of FDI (Cheng & Ma, 2010). And Chinese OFDI to B&R countries has increased by over 20% according to Du and Zhang (2018), Yu, Qian and Liu (2019), Chen and Len (2020).

Figure 7. Chinese FDI in B&R Countries
Source: CSMAR Unit:10 thousand dollars

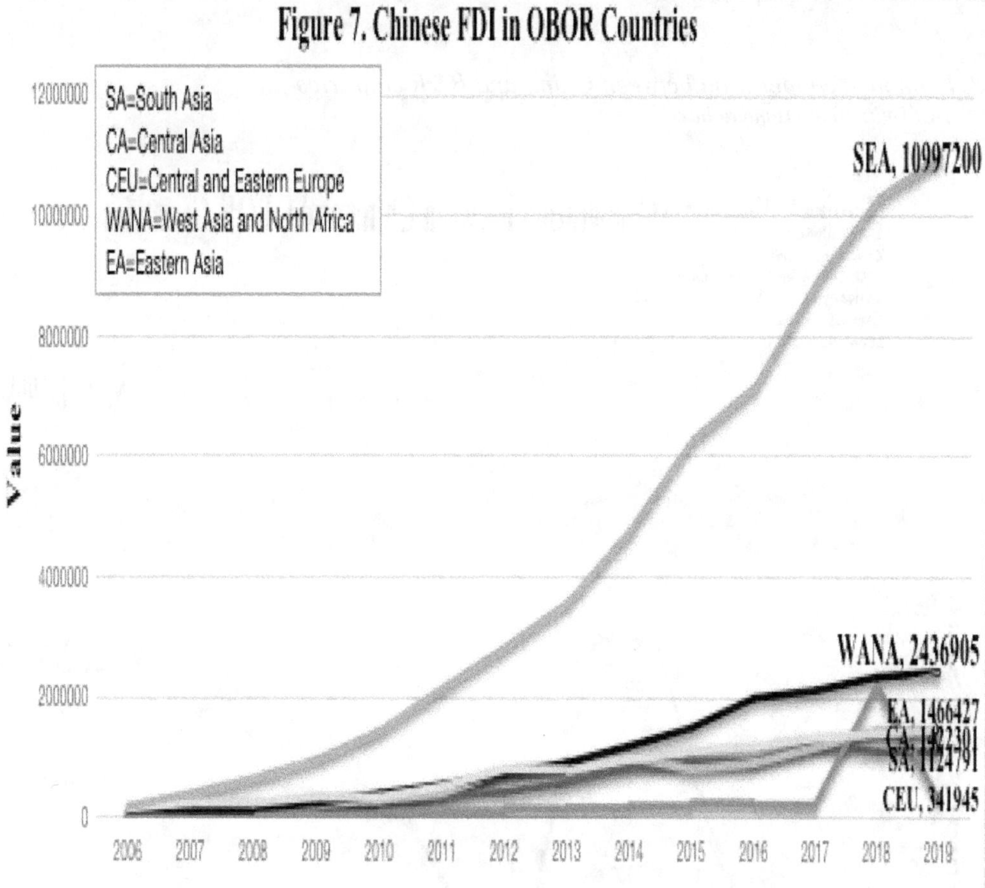

We divide the B&R into six sections: South Asia (SA), Central Asia (CA), Central and Eastern Europe (CEU), West Asia and North Africa (WANA), East Asia (EA), and Southeast Asia (SEA). In Figure 7, we constructed a line chart of China's OFDI in B&R countries. It can be seen that China's total outward direct investment has shown an upward trend. The total amount of investment has been rising. Especially the amount of investment in Southeast Asia has risen rapidly, and its total amount exceeds the sum of the total of the other five regions. According to Figure 7, before the B&R, China's total investment in Southeast Asia was about 35 billion dollars, and the total investment in other sectors was less than 10 billion dollars. The total amount of the FDI is now about 150 billion dollars, and the investment in the other five sectors is about 20 billion dollars.

Southeast Asia has received far more investment than other regions, mainly because China and Southeast Asia are connected by land and sea, and there are large numbers of Chinese and overseas Chinese in the region. China and Southeast Asian countries (except Singapore) form a vertical division of labor. The other side's minerals and agricultural products are the bulk materials that China needs to import, and its industrial products are what the other side needs. At the same time, ASEAN is the focus and priority direction of China's B&R construction, and the core of B&R is to solve the problem of connectivity. China is bringing more and more major engineering projects to Southeast Asian countries through practical actions, providing these countries with opportunities to connect with the frontiers of world infrastructure development.

Figure 8. Economic cooperation between China and B&R countries
Source: CSMAR Unit: 10 thousand dollars

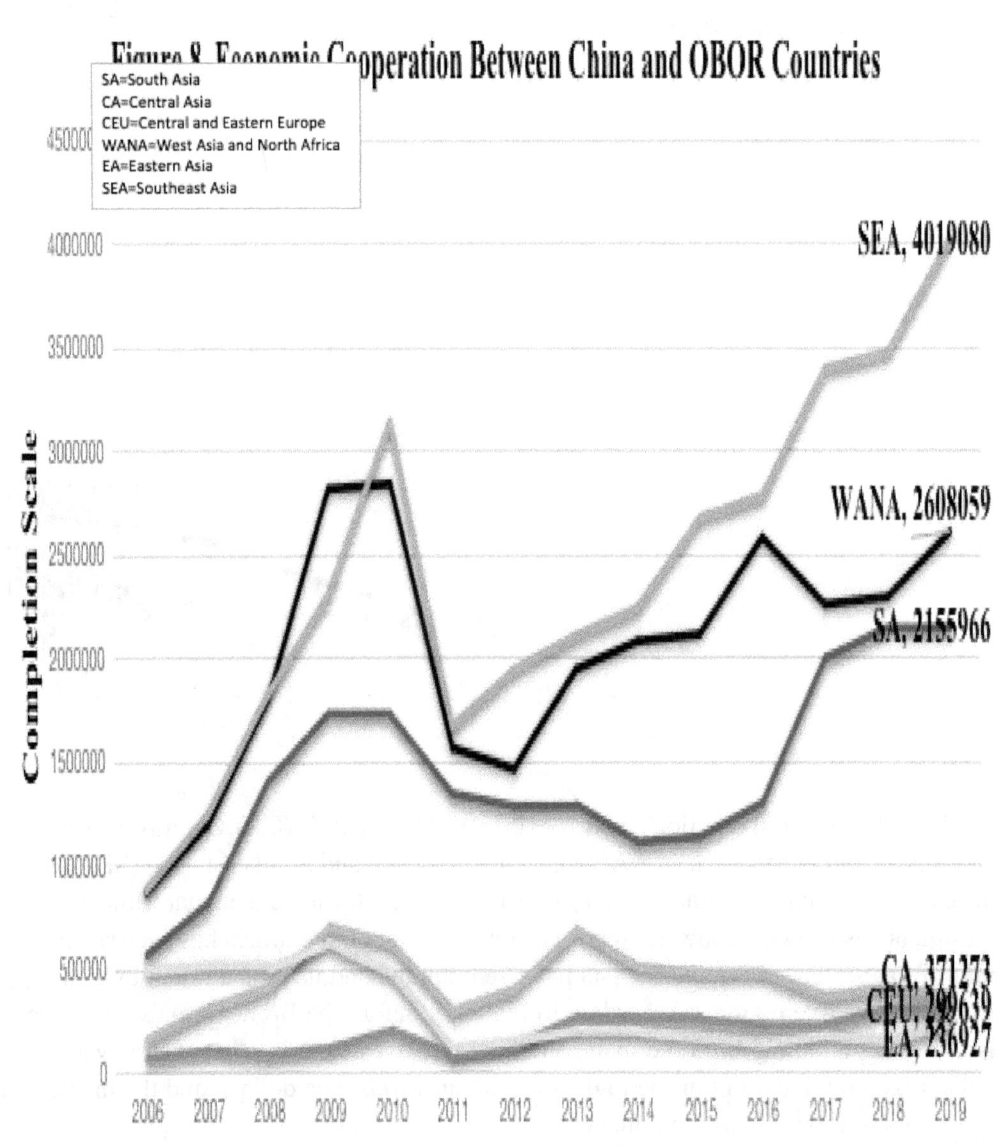

From the perspective of the completion scale of economic cooperation between China and B&R countries, despite some fluctuations in 2010, the total amount of economic cooperation in these sectors has generally increased from 2006, from less than 10 billion dollars to the current level. Economic cooperation here is measured in the whole value of consultation services, labor service cooperation and contact work, between China and B&R countries.

By 2019, there were already three regional sectors - Southeast Asia, West Asia and North Africa, and South Asia - that have completed more than 20 billion dollars of investment, and the transaction volume with Southeast Asia even reached 40 billion dollars. The level of economic cooperation is increasing continuously between China and B&R countries thanks to the before-mentioned increased investments and deep cooperation in infrastructure constructions (Fu et al., 2020; Han et al., 2021; Rehman & Ali, 2021). Southeast Asia is still the region with the fastest growth in trade volume and the largest total trade volume. The demand for infrastructure investment and construction in Southeast Asian countries continues to be strong. Countries in the region invest in energy, transportation, public utilities, construction, and other fields. The market space is huge. In addition, the development of cross-border e-commerce platforms is also indispensable. For example, Shopee, one of the largest cross-border e-commerce companies in Southeast Asia, has vigorously promoted trade by expanding overseas warehouses, building its own logistics system, and supporting railway transportation construction.

Table 1. Correlation and covariance

Regions	Correlation	Covariance
South Africa	0.5772959	> 0
Central Asia	0.085942148	> 0
Central and Eastern Europe	0.526368349	> 0
West Asia and North Africa	0.481831339	> 0
Eastern Asia	-0.773088847	< 0
Southeast Asia	0.840366366	> 0

For Table 1, we use correlation coefficients to measure the strength of the relationships between Chinese FDI and economic cooperation with China in these six regions in order to answer the question whether more Chinese FDI can bring about more economic cooperation. The answers are quite different in different regions. The results show that in Southeast Asia, the economic effect of Chinese FDI is quite obvious, the value of correlation being over 0.8. In regions such as West Asia and North Africa, Central and Eastern Europe, and South Africa, the values are around 0.5, which are still positive, reflecting that more Chinese FDI can lead to more economic cooperation but not that much. However, in Eastern Asia, things are quite different. The increase in investment from China results in much less economic cooperation. This would be mainly due to the emergence of the North Korean nuclear issue and the potential geopolitical uncertainties of China, Japan and South Korea in regional economic interests, which have slowed down the speed of regional cooperation.

Figure 9. China's economic cooperation with countries in B&R
Source: CSMAR

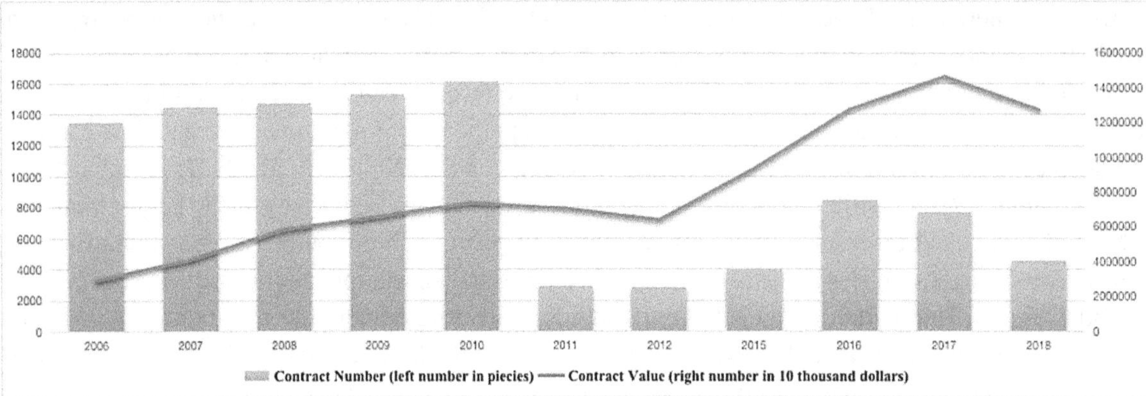

Judging from the amount of China's economic cooperation contracts with countries in B&R (figure 9), the number of contracts has shrunk rapidly since 2011, and was less than a quarter of 2010. However, in terms of contract value, 2011 was only a small drop from 2010. In part, since 2012, while the number of China's economic cooperation contracts with B&R countries has been slowly increasing, the contract value has also increased rapidly. The value of coefficient of correlation is -0.46. In 2017, the number of China's economic cooperation contracts with B&R countries has reached almost three times the amount of 2012, which can imply that although the number of contracts decreased so rapidly, the value of each contract can be much greater than before due to the increasing total value of all the contracts.

Besides, one third of China's export revenue was made up of exports to B&R economies. Bastos (2020) pointed out that although they have been more of export markets than sources of import for China, the share of imports from B&R economies has an upward trend, rising to almost 30% in 2015, which was 5% higher than that in 1995. Meanwhile, China is an important trade partner, especially as an import source, for many B&R economies. The exports of B&R economies were also boosted, but it was attenuated by increased competition in export markets.

Overall, the implementation of the B&R has gained remarkable achievements. As of May 2020, the Chinese government has signed 200 cooperation documents with 138 countries and 30 international organizations to jointly build the B&R. The total trade in goods with the above-mentioned countries has reached 1.9 trillion dollars, accounting for 41.5% of China's total trade in goods. From 2013 to 2019, Chinese companies' non-financial direct investment in countries along the B&R totaled more than 100 billion U.S. dollars, with an average annual growth rate of 4.4%; from 2013 to 2019, countries along the B&R directly invested in China more than 50 billion U.S. dollars and more than 22,000 enterprises have been established. The dynamic of Chinese FDI in B&R regions still has a huge potential to exploit.

The Investment Roles Generated by the Chinese Government and MNEs in B&R Regions

Since 2013, China has mobilized a huge number of national resources to support B&R at an unusual rate. According to estimates by the Development Research Center of the State Council, from 2016 to 2020, the total infrastructure investment demand of countries involved in B&R was estimated at at least

10.6 trillion dollars. Chen et al. (2021) found that the overall efficiency of resource allocation within Chinese enterprises can be significantly improved by China's OFDI.

Figure 10. Chinese overseas investing entities in 2019, by legal status
Source: 2019 Statistical Bulletin of China's Outward Foreign Direct Investment

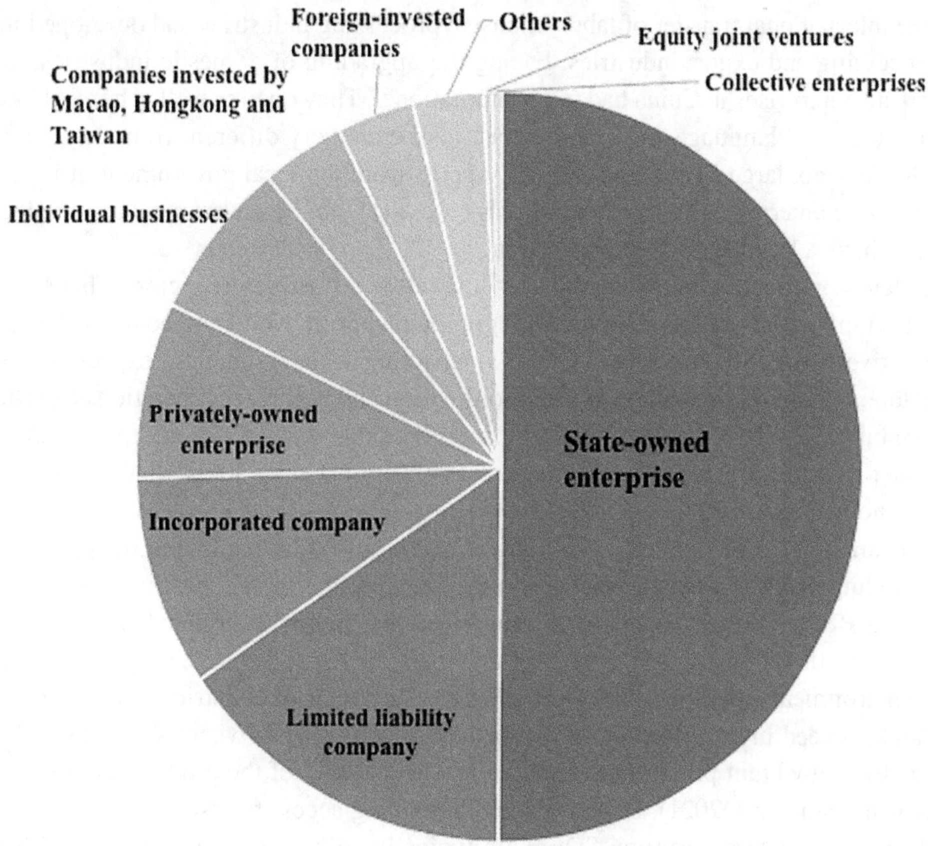

Figure 10 presents that State-owned enterprises (SOEs) account for half of China's overseas investing entities. Facing the business opportunities and risk exposure of B&R, SOEs with economic strength and ability have better opportunities to participate in international projects in B&R regions. It is worth noting that the B&R infrastructure investment itself has the characteristics of low yield and high risk in terms of its investment areas and targets, which means that neither foreign funds nor private sector funds are very willing to invest in infrastructure construction. Therefore, the Chinese government has to rely mainly on policy funds for financing. For instance, the Chinese government's investment through the China Development Bank, the Asian Infrastructure Investment Bank and the Silk Road Fund have become the main source of the B&R.

In 2016, at the sub-forum of "International Capacity Cooperation: Consolidating New Impetus for Global Economic Growth", Senior Vice President and Chief Economist of the World Bank from 2008 to 2012, Professor Justin Yifu Lin, said that in the past, China's foreign investment and cooperation were dominated by large SOEs. At the same time, he pointed out that the main reasons were: (1) As a resource-scarce country, China has a great demand for resources and focuses on resource development abroad; (2) China's capacity in engineering construction, especially railway construction, is the strongest in the world, and the developing countries we work with are basically weak in infrastructure. These two types of cooperation have high capital requirements and large scale of construction, and only large SOEs are capable of participating.

During the period of reform and opening up, Chinese enterprises seized the window of opportunity period for the international transfer of labor-intensive processing industries and developed many labor-intensive processing and export industries. Facing the upgrading of domestic industries, many labor-intensive private enterprises in China had to go international. They operate well at home. However, after going abroad, the local language, laws, and infrastructure are very different from those in China, and given that they are not large SOEs who can get support from the local government, it is actually very difficult for private enterprises to go global. In this case, the Chinese government and the local governments actually have a lot of room for cooperation.

In B&R, state-controlled acquirers played a leading role in infrastructure sectors. That's why the B&R is considered an infrastructure-led economic integration blueprint. Non-state-controlled acquirers were particularly active in non-infrastructures sectors, which might be the result of the expected improvements in infrastructure, expected government policy coordination and political cooperation etc. (Du & Zhang, 2018). Amighini et al. (2013) argued that SOEs and privately-owned firms are motivated by different things. Private firms are attracted by profits and are risk-averters, while SOEs usually follow the strategy needs of their home country (Shi et al., 2021).

China is characterized as state capitalism under an authoritarian regime. SOEs play a pivotal role in the commanding heights of the national economy, and they are the reliable forces to achieve government goals. But B&R is still more market-oriented and less political- oriented (Han et al., 2021). Lu (2018) pointed out that it has been imperative for Chinese SOEs to improve corporate society responsibility and environmental performance. They should both meet host countries' rising expectations and standards, and succeed in an increasingly competitive global market where sustainable development matter. In contrast, a vibrant private sector makes up the majority of the production of national output and employment (Shi et al., 2021). Disadvantaged in gaining access to resources such as capital, land etc., non-state-owned enterprises (non-SOEs) are typically willing to cooperate well with and please the local or national bureaucrats (Du & Wang, 2013; Kung & Ma, 2016). They tend to follow the call of the government in fulfilling various national or local goals. Thus, examining how Chinese enterprises respond to this national economic strategy can help shed light on the mechanisms of implementation of the national strategy and the functioning of a state capitalism model (Du & Zhang, 2018).

Discussion About Green Economy in B&R Regions From Chinese FDI Perspective

Based on the triple difference estimation, Nugent and Lu (2021) find that in the sectors with overcapacity problems, China's OFDI to B&R countries increased by 79%, and in the sectors with pollution problems, China's OFDI to B&R countries increased by 113%. They put forward the speculation that the prioritization of China's B&R-oriented FDI sectors has been primarily induced by China's concern for these two issues within the country.

Figure 11. Level of importance of green investment for promotion of China's B&R 2020
Source: 2019 Statistical Bulletin of China's Outward Foreign Direct Investment

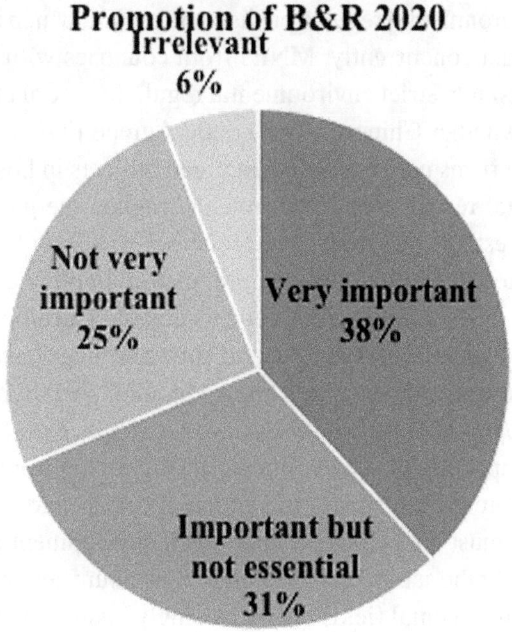

It is found that Chinese overseas acquisitions of targets in the B&R countries increased considerably in the years following the B&R, and attention has been paid to the field of green investment (Zhang et al., 2021). In Figure 11, we show that nearly 70% enterprises view the green investment for promotion of China's B&R as first priority, 38% enterprises consider green investment for promotion of China's B&R very important and 31% think it important but not that essential. Since the B&R was put forward, the concept of green development has permeated it. The topic of green has attracted worldwide attention. Policymakers all over the world strive to produce sustainable solutions against environmental degradation and uncontrolled climate change (Huntington, 2015). Chinese companies that hope to "go global" actively practice the concept of green development and participate in the construction of the green B&R. As Chen et al. (2019) mentioned, institutional quality can positively affect the degree of FDI facilitation. So, more and more investment institutions who are gradually increasing the ecological value of green investment reached a consensus and began to explore how to coordinate the "win-win goal" of capital pursuit of profit and environmental sustainability. From a global perspective, the "greening" of the economy has become a new engine of economic growth, and the development of green finance and green investment has become a trend (Jin et al., 2022). China is currently in a critical period of economic restructuring and the transformation of development patterns. The demand for green finance to support the domestic green industry and sustainable economic and social development, as well as the greening of foreign investment, is constantly increasing. Zhang et al., (2021) also mentioned that green economic growth can be promoted by public green finance and the spending on human resources and research and development (R&D) of green technologies. Therefore, the development of green B&R projects via forming sustainable regional cooperation, such as developing green infrastructure, promoting green energy and providing green finance, is a future trend.

China's foreign investment needs to be green. Chen et al. (2019) argued that the effect of institutional quality, which can promote FDI facilitation, is influenced by factors such as laws and regulations. From the angle of inbound FDI, environmental regulation discourage FDI, which means tougher environmental regulation brings less FDI, and concurrently, MNEs from countries with better environmental protections are insensitive to increasingly strict environmental regulations (Cai et al., 2016). At the same time, Liu et al. (2020) found that whether Chinese firms conduct green FDI is influenced by host countries' energy environment. Chinese firms prefer to invest in green projects in host countries which have better political environments, natural resource endowments and higher energy efficiencies. The same logic can apply to OFDI. If China establishes strict environmental laws, regulations and legislation, China's MNEs can be insensitive to toughing environmental regulation in other countries, and will have wider range of choice to gain FDI. The "2030 Agenda for Sustainable Development" and the "Paris Agreement" indicate that policies related to environment and climate change have shifted from a narrow focus on the environment to the new world order, and the economic, social and cultural fields have begun to shift to low-carbon development. The United Nations Conference on Sustainable Development has had a direct and important impact on the development of China's environmental law and has promoted the development of China's foreign investment in a green direction. Moreover, in addition to economic interests, the B&R countries must cooperate towards green development and mitigate global warming together (Zhang et al., 2021). At the same time, challenges that countries around the world are concerned about in the political and environmental fields are increasingly visible, such as environmental pollution, desert greening, population expansion, species extinction, scarcity of natural resources, global warming and sustainable development, and so on. Environmental protection has gradually become one of the inevitable factors that influence social, political and economic decision-making. The importance of environmental issues has risen to an extremely high degree in international public opinion. The more international consumers want greener products and are willing to spend money to use new technologies that help reduce greenhouse gas emissions. Zhang et al. (2021) also pointed out that the government's spending on R&D is considered a significant driver, although it might bring about a less polluting economic growth. And most economic experts support the notion that technology is the preferable option to facilitate green economic growth. This requires governments' or enterprises' responsibility to take action on environmental issues, and greening needs to be included in the scope of investment.

Chinese MNEs Opportunities and Challenges in BRI Regions

Chen et al. (2016) have pointed out that Chinese enterprises actively responded to China's "Going Global" policies. Since Chinese enterprises typically have high confidence in the success of B&R, they may be encouraged by the bright prospects of B&R and respond actively to increase OFDI ahead of their counterparts from other countries (Du & Zhang, 2018). However, it can't be ignored that China faces growing external risks in overseas investment projects (Dang & Zhao, 2020).

Chinese MNEs are facing development opportunities in terms of innovation and development, economic integration, changes in global value chains in industrial transformation and upgrading, and compliance operations, but they are also facing multiple challenges. Under the fierce international competition, the impacts were stronger on industries that produce goods that are nearer final use (Bastos, 2020). The B&R aims to promote highly efficient resource allocation, deep regional integration, and also to improve the distribution of global value chains. Improved regulatory quality, political stability, government effectiveness and rule of law can significantly promote countries' global value chain participation (Ge et al., 2020).

In terms of regional economic integration, China hopes to improve connectivity with the rest of Asia via the B&R (Bird et al., 2020). Although East Asian countries have reached some relatively broad basic principles in the process of East Asian integration, they lack political consensus on major issues such as goals and paths, and lack the means to promote the East Asian Economic Community. For Central Asia, the work of Bird, Lebrand and Venables (2020) found that the B&R enabled cities in Central Asia, some of which may experience rapid population growth and increases in income, to develop manufacturing centers. Facing the global supply chain's development in a shorter, faster and smarter direction, multinational companies no longer plan and acquire supply chains mainly on the basis of cost, and the layout and reshaping of the global value chain will be affected. Besides, Chinese corporate compliance and integrity management risks also exist. A study which contained 1814 B&R-related projects found that nearly 15% projects had problems in fields such as debt, labor, environmental standards, national security and corruption (Horsley, 2016; ICG, 2018). Many Chinese companies are not familiar with the relevant laws and regulations of the country where the project is located, which can easily lead to legal disputes and affect corporate competitiveness.

Meanwhile, cultural differences, such as differences in language, religious belief, legal origin, between countries are the primary causes of cultural risk for FDI (Dang & Zhao, 2020), which still deserves more attention. Rapaille (2001) also underlined that among the various external risks that get involved in enterprises' overseas investment projects, cultural risk is one of the most important risk exposures.

CONCLUSION

China's FDI in the B&R countries has an important influence, especially in terms of infrastructure construction, which brings infinite convenience to the host country, and CPEC can be a good example. However, because China's FDI is mainly in the development of energy and infrastructure construction, the scale of the project is large and requires a lot of funds, so the FDI is mainly dominated by Chinese state-owned enterprises, but this has brought criticism from international public opinion. The infrastructures project promotion is full of difficulties and often further complicated by the weak institutional and legal regimes in the developing world (Carrai, 2020). The fact is that China is very strong in political power, and infrastructure construction can further strengthen regional connectivity. In terms of future planning, China is working hard to build a green B&R and actively face the current national development and sustainable development of the world as the "greening" of the economy has become a new engine of economic growth. The key point is to achieve the carbon peak in 2030 and carbon saturation in 2060, which is inseparable from the efforts to build a green B&R.

ACKNOWLEDGMENT

The authors extend sincere gratitude to:

- Our colleagues from Soochow University, the Australian Studies Centre of Shanghai University, KCA university and Krirk University as well as the independent research colleagues who provided insight and expertise that greatly assisted the research, although they may not agree with all of the interpretations/conclusions of this chapter.
- China Knowledge for supporting our research.

• The Editors and the International Editorial Advisory Board (IEAB) of this book who initially desk reviewed, arranged a rigorous double/triple blind review process and conducted a thorough, minute and critical final review before accepting the chapter for publication.

• All anonymous reviewers who provided very constructive feedbacks for thorough revision, improvement and fine tuning of the chapter.

REFERENCES

Amighini, A. A., Rabellotti, R., & Sanfilippo, M. (2013). Do Chinese state-owned and private enterprises differ in their internationalization strategies? *China Economic Review*, *27*, 312–325. doi:10.1016/j.chieco.2013.02.003

Bastos, P. (2020). Exposure of belt and road economies to China trade shocks. *Journal of Development Economics*, *145*, 145. doi:10.1016/j.jdeveco.2020.102474

Big B. R. I. Data Report. (2018). *Big Data Report on Trade Cooperation under the Belt and Road Initiative 2018*. https://www.yidaiyilu.gov.cn/wcm.files/upload/CMSydylgw/201805/201805080457024.pdf

Bird, J., Lebrand, M., & Venables, A. J. (2020). The Belt and Road Initiative: Reshaping economic geography in Central Asia? *Journal of Development Economics*, *144*, 144. doi:10.1016/j.jdeveco.2020.102441

Cai, X., Lu, Y., Wu, M., & Yu, L. (2016). Does environmental regulation drive away inbound foreign direct investment? Evidence from a quasi-natural experiment in China. *Journal of Development Economics*, *123*, 73–85. doi:10.1016/j.jdeveco.2016.08.003

Carrai, M. A. (2021). Adaptive governance along Chinese-financed BRI railroad megaprojects in East Africa. *World Development*, *141*, 141. doi:10.1016/j.worlddev.2020.105388

Central Committee of the Communist Party of China. (2013). *Decision of the Central Committee of the Communist Party of China on Several Major Issues Concerning Comprehensively Deepening the Reform*. People's Publishing House.

Chen, C. (2017). Science mapping: A systematic review of the literature. *Journal of Data and Information Science*, *2*(2), 1–40. doi:10.1515/jdis-2017-0006

Chen, C., Ibekwe-Sanjuan, F., & Hou, J. (2010). The structure and dynamics of cocitation clusters: A multiple-perspective cocitation analysis. *Journal of the American Society for Information Science and Technology*, *61*(7), 1386–1409. doi:10.1002/asi.21309

Chen, F., Jiang, G., & Wang, W. (2019). Institutional quality and its impact on the facilitation of foreign direct investment: Empirical evidence from the Belt and Road countries. *Journal of Chinese Economic and Foreign Trade Studies*, *12*(3), 167–188. doi:10.1108/JCEFTS-07-2019-0041

Chen, H. (2016). China's 'One Belt, One Road' initiative and its implication for Sino-African investment relations. *Transnational Corporations Review*, *8*(3), 178–182. doi:10.1080/19186444.2016.1233722

Chen, L., Guo, S., Liu, J., & Gerschewski, S. (2021). Outward FDI and efficiency in within-firm resource allocation-Evidence from firm-level data of China. *Economics*, 74.

Chen, M. X., & Lin, C. (2020). Geographic connectivity and cross-border investment: The belts, roads and skies. *Journal of Development, 146*, 12–13. doi:10.1016/j.jdeveco.2020.102469

Chen, W., Dollar, D., & Tang, H. (2018). Why is China investing in Africa? Evidence from the firm level. *The World Bank Economic Review, 32*(3), 610–632.

Chen, W., & Tang, H. (2014). Export Promotion of OFDI from Emerging Markets – Transaction-Level Evidence from China. *Academy of Management Journal.*

Cheung, Y., & Qian, X. (2009). Empirics of China's outward direct investment. *Pacific Economic Review, 44*(3), 213–341.

Chin, H., & He, W. (2016). *The Belt and Road Initiative: 65 Countries and Beyond.* https://www.fbicgroup.com/sites/default/files/B%26R_Initiative_65_Countries_and_Beyond.pdf

Dang, L., & Zhao, J. (2020). Cultural risk and management strategy for Chinese enterprises' overseas investment. *China Economic Review, 61*, 61. doi:10.1016/j.chieco.2020.101433

Du, J. (2021). A Review Of Twenty Years Of Research On Chinese Discourse Identity Construction Based On CiteSpace. *Advanced Management Science, 10*(1), 12–18.

Du, J., & Wang, Y. (2013). Reforming SOEs under China's state capitalism. *Unfinished Reforms in the Chinese Economy*, 1-38.

Du, J., & Zhang, Y. (2018). Does one belt one road initiative promote Chinese overseas direct investment? *China Economic Review, 47*, 189–205. doi:10.1016/j.chieco.2017.05.010

Flint, C., & Zhu, C. (2018). The geopolitics of connectivity, cooperation, and hegemonic competition: The Belt and Road Initiative. *Geoforum, 99*, 95–101. doi:10.1016/j.geoforum.2018.12.008

Freymann, E. (2021, March 25). The U.S. can't keep waiting for China's Belt and Road Initiative to fail. *Fortune*. https://fortune.com/2021/03/24/china-belt-road-initiative-soft-power/

Fu, Y., Wu, D., Wang, Y., & Wang, H. (2020). Facility location and capacity planning considering policy preference and uncertain demand under the One Belt One Road initiative. *Transportation Research Part A, Policy and Practice, 138*, 172–186. doi:10.1016/j.tra.2020.05.012

Ge, Y., Dollar, D., & Yu, X. (2020). Institutions and participation in global value chains: Evidence from belt and road initiative. *China Economic Review, 61*, 61. doi:10.1016/j.chieco.2020.101447

GoldenBees. (2017). *The 2017 GoldenBees Chinese Companies' Corporate Social Responsibility Report*. http://images.mofcom.gov.cn/csr/201712/20171219174229375.pdf

Han, Y., Wang, H., & Wei, D. (2021). *The Belt and Road Initiative, sister-city partnership and Chinese outward FDI.* Economic Research-Ekonomska Istrazivanja. doi:10.1080/1331677X.2021.1997618

Hook, G. D. (2022). China's Silk Road. Encyclopedia of Violence, Peace, & Conflict, 1, 562-570.

Horsley, J. P. (2016). *China Promotes Open Government as it Seeks to Reinvent Its Government Model.* https://law.yale.edu/sites/default/files/china-law-documents/2016_horsley_china_promotes_open_government.pdf

Huang, Y. (2016). Understanding China's Belt & Road Initiative: Motivation, framework and assessment. *China Economic Review*, *40*, 314–321. doi:10.1016/j.chieco.2016.07.007

Huntington, H. G. (2015). Crude oil trade and current account deficits. *Energy Economies*, *50*, 70–79. doi:10.1016/j.eneco.2015.03.030

International Crisis Group. (2018). *China-Pakistan Economic Corridor: Opportunities and Risks*. www.crisisgroup.org/asia/south-asia/pakistan/297-china-pakistan-economic-corridor-opportunities-and- risks.

Jacques, M. (2021). *G7 no longer able to order world around: Martin Jacques*. https://www.globaltimes.cn/page/202106/1225664.shtml

Jin, Y., Tang, Y. M., Chau, K. Y., & Abbas, M. (2022). How government expenditure Mitigates emissions: A step towards sustainable green economy in belt and road initiative project. *Journal of Environmental Management*, *303*, 113967. doi:10.1016/j.jenvman.2021.113967 PMID:34810022

Kang, L., Peng, F., Zhu, F., & Pan, A. (2018). Harmony in Diversity: Can the One Belt One Road Initiative Promote China's Outward Foreign Direct Investment? *Sustainability*, *10*(9), 3264. doi:10.3390u10093264

Li, F. (2016). A study on China's foreign direct investment policy. *Globalization*, 10.

Lin, H. (2021). *The Map and Project Overview of China-Pakistan Economic Corridor*. Wechat. https://mp.weixin.qq.com/s/LkjYS34hjGDFkgeYt0Zqmw

Lin, Y. (2016). *International production capacity cooperation: Gathering new impetus for global economic growth*. https://business.sohu.com/20160324/n441896100.shtml

Liu, H., Wang, Y., Jiang, J., & Wu, P. (2020). How green is the "Belt and Road Initiative"? Evidence from Chinese OFDI in the energy sector. *Energy Policy*, *145*, 145. doi:10.1016/j.enpol.2020.111709

Lu, M. (2018). *Corporate Social Responsibility and Environmental Responsibility. Another Road to China's Sustainable Development*. Brill Nijhoff.

Mirza, F. M., Fatima, N., & Ullah, K. (2019). Impact of China-Pakistan economic corridor on Pakistan's future energy consumption and energy saving potential: Evidence from sectoral time series analysis. *Energy Strategy Reviews*, *25*, 34–46. doi:10.1016/j.esr.2019.04.015

Mukhtar, A., Zhu, Y., Lee, Y., Bambacas, M., & Cavusgil, S. T. (2022). Challenges confronting the'One Belt One Road' initiative: Social networks and cross-cultural adjustment in CPEC projects. *International Business Review*, *31*(1), 101902. doi:10.1016/j.ibusrev.2021.101902

Nugent, J. B., & Lu, J. (2021). China's outward foreign direct investment in the belt and road initiative: What are the motives for Chinese firms to invest? *China Economic Review*, *68*, 68. doi:10.1016/j.chieco.2021.101628

Peel, M., & Fleming, S. (2021, May 2). West and allies relaunch push for own version of China's Belt and Road. *Financial Times*.

Rapaille, G. C. (2001). *7 secrets of marketing in a multicultural world*. Executive Excellence Pub.

Rauf, A., Liu, X., Amin, W., Rehman, O. U., Li, J., Ahmad, F., & Bekun, F. V. (2020). Does sustainable growth, energy consumption and environment challenges matter for Belt and Road Initiative feat? A novel empirical investigation. *Journal of Cleaner Production*, *262*, 262. doi:10.1016/j.jclepro.2020.121344

Rehman, O. U., & Ali, Y. (2021). Optimality study of China's crude oil imports through China Pakistan economic corridor using fuzzy TOPSIS and Cost-Benefit analysis. *Transportation Research Part E, Logistics and Transportation Review*, *148*, 148. doi:10.1016/j.tre.2021.102246

Saud, S., Chen, S., & Haseen, A. (2020). The role of financial development and globalization in the environment: Accounting ecological footprint indicators for selected one-belt-one-road initiative countries. *Journal of Cleaner Production*, *250*, 250. doi:10.1016/j.jclepro.2019.119518

Shao, X. (2020). Chinese OFDI responses to the B&R initiative: Evidence from a quasi-natural experiment. *China Economic Review*, *61*, 61. doi:10.1016/j.chieco.2020.101435

Shi, J., Hu, X., Li, Y., & Feng, T. (2021). Does The Belt And Road Initiative Reshape China's Outward Foreign Direct Investment In ASEAN? Shifting Motives Of State-Owned And Private-Owned Enterprises. *The Singapore Economic Review*, *66*(01), 161–183. doi:10.1142/S0217590819500772

Silverstein, K. (2019, December 5). *As China's 'Belt And Road' Initiative Replaces U.S. On Global Stage, The Implications for Energy And Trade*. https://www.forbes.com/sites/kensilverstein/2019/12/05/as-the-us-becomes-isolationist-china-is-becoming-globalist-the-implications-for-energy-and-trade/?sh=2eb6804719f4

Soyres, F., Mulabdic, A., Murray, S., Rocha, N., & Ruta, M. (2019). How much will the Belt and Road Initiative reduce trade costs? *Inter Economics*, *159*, 151–164. doi:10.1016/j.inteco.2019.07.003

Tang, R. W. (2019). FDI expansion speed of state-owned enterprises and the moderating role of market capitalism: Evidence from China. *International Business Review*, *28*(6), 101596. doi:10.1016/j.ibusrev.2019.101596

Wang, S., Zhao, D., & Chen, H. (2019). Government corruption, resource misallocation, and ecological efficiency. *Energy Economics*, 85.

World Bank. (2018). *Belt and Road Initiative*. https://www.worldbank.org/en/topic/regional-integration/brief/belt-and-road-initiative

Yu, P., Chen, Z., & Hu, Y. (2020). The Impact of Belt and Road Initiative on Regional Financial Integration – Empirical Evidence from Bond and Money Markets in Belt and Road Countries. *Chinese Economy*, *54*(4), 286–308. doi:10.1080/10971475.2020.1857061

Yu, S., Qian, X., & Liu, T. (2019). Belt and road initiative and Chinese Firms' outward foreign direct investment. *Emerging Markets Review*, *41*, 41. doi:10.1016/j.ememar.2019.100629

Zhang, D., Mohsin, M., Rasheed, A. K., Chang, Y., & Taghizadeh-Hesary, F. (2021). Public spending and green economic growth in BRI region: Mediating role of green finance. *Energy Policy*, *153*, 153. doi:10.1016/j.enpol.2021.112256

ADDITIONAL READING

Chen, S., Hou, J., & Xiao, D. (2018). "One belt, one road" initiative to stimulate trade in China: A counter-factual analysis. *Sustainability*, *10*(9), 3242–3242. doi:10.3390u10093242

Cheng, L. K. (2016). Three questions on China's "belt and road initiative". *China Economic Review*, *40*, 309–313. doi:10.1016/j.chieco.2016.07.008

Cheung, Y., Wong, M. D., Chinn, M., & Fujii, E. (2006). The Chinese economies in global context: The integration process and its determinants. *Journal of the Japanese and International Economies*, *20*(1), 128–153. doi:10.1016/j.jjie.2004.12.001

Johnston, L., Morgan, S., & Wang, Y. (2015). The gravity of China's African export promise. *World Economy*, *38*(6), 913–934. doi:10.1111/twec.12229

Lin, X., Xiao, Y., Liang, Y., & Zhang, X. (2017). A research on the belt and road initiatives and strategies of RMB internationalization. *Business and Management Research*, *6*(1), 13–27. doi:10.5430/bmr.v6n1p13

Liu, H., Tang, Y., Chen, X., & Poznanska, J. (2017). The determinants of Chinese outward FDI in countries along "One Belt One Road.". *Emerging Markets Finance & Trade*, *53*(6), 1374–1387. doi:10.1080/1540496X.2017.1295843

Mao, H., Liu, G., Zhang, C., & Atif, R. M. (2019). Does belt and road initiative hurt node countries? A study from export perspective. *Emerging Markets Finance & Trade*, *55*(7), 1472–1485. doi:10.1080/1540496X.2018.1553711

APPENDIX 1

Table 2. Chinese FDI Related Policies

File Name	Release Time	Distribution Department	The Main Idea
Measures for the Administration of Foreign Exchange for Foreign Investment abroad	1989	State Administration of Foreign Exchange	The foreign exchange administration department is responsible for examining foreign exchange risks and foreign exchange sources of foreign exchange funds for overseas investment, and requires enterprises to submit certificates of foreign exchange sources of funds
Opinions on Strengthening the Management of Overseas Investment Projects	1991	National Planning Commission	Limit outbound investment
Provisions on the preparation and approval of project proposals and feasibility studies for overseas investment projects	1991	National Planning Commission	Chinese enterprises, companies or other economic organizations are allowed to invest, buy stocks and other means to Hong Kong and Macao and the Soviet Union, Eastern Europe, etc., to organize or participate in the organization of non-trade projects, and not to allow Chinese enterprises to carry out overseas investment in other countries and regions
Interim Pr ovisions on the Establishment of Offshore Trading Companies and Trade Representative Offices	1997	Ministry of Foreign Trade and Economic Cooperation	Chinese enterprises can set up trading companies in overseas regions other than Hong Kong, Macao and Taiwan
Opinions on Encouraging Enterprises to Carry Out Overseas Tape Processing and Assembly Business	1999	State Economic and Trade Commission, Ministry of Finance, Ministry of Foreign Trade and Economic Cooperation	To support Chinese enterprises to "go out" by means of overseas processing trade
Notice on issues related to the pilot work of overseas investment approval	2003	Ministry of Commerce	Carry out a pilot reform of overseas investment approval authority and simplify the approval procedures below, and take the lead in piloting in 12 cities, including Beijing, with local approval authority increased from $1 million to $3 million
Provisions on the Approval of Overseas Investment Start-up Enterprises	2004	Ministry of Commerce	Support and encourage all kinds of ownership enterprises with comparative advantages to invest negatively in overseas investment to start enterprises
Decision of the State Council on the Reform of the Investment System	2004	State council	The management of overseas investment changes from the approval system to the approval system, and it is clear that the National Development and Reform Commission is responsible for approving overseas investment projects, and the Ministry of Commerce is responsible for approving overseas start-up enterprises
Interim Measures for the Approval of Overseas Investment Projects	2004	National Development and Reform Commission	Further decentralized overseas examination and approval authority, China's investment in resources development projects of more than 200 million U.S. dollars and other large-scale foreign exchange projects of more than 50 million U.S. dollars, by the Lone Aojia Development and Reform Commission after examination and approval to the State Council for approval
Notice on Credit Support for Key Projects of Foreign Investment Encouraged by the State	2004	National Development and Reform Commission, Export-Import Bank of China, etc.	Every year, "special loans for overseas investment" are arranged, and eligible enterprises can enjoy preferential interest rates on export credit
Notice on Issues Related to the Pilot Reform of Foreign Exchange Management for Expanding Foreign Investment abroad	2005	State Administration of Foreign Exchange	Extend the pilot reform of foreign exchange management for overseas investment to the whole country, increase the local foreign exchange approval authority from US$3 million to US$10 million, and increase the foreign exchange purchase quota for overseas investment from US$3.3 billion to US$5 billion.
Notice on adjusting the way domestic banks provide financing external guarantee management for foreign investment enterprises	2005	State Administration of Foreign Exchange	Abolish the system of approval and approval of foreign guarantees from foreign investment enterprise financing banks

Continued on following page

Table 2. Continued

File Name	Release Time	Distribution Department	The Main Idea
Notice on the Trial of Special Preferential Measures for Export Credit Insurance to Support Individual Private and Other Non-Public Enterprises to Explore the International Market	2005	Ministry of Commerce, China Export Credit Insurance Company	Promote non-public enterprises to actively explore the international market
Overseas Investment Industry Guidance Policy	2006	National Development and Reform Commission	It clearly stipulates the incentive and prohibited projects for overseas investment, and gives greater policy support to the incentive projects, mainly in the areas of financial support, tax incentives, foreign exchange support, customs facilitation and information provision
Several Opinions on Encouraging and Guiding Foreign Investment Cooperation of Non-Public Enterprises	2007	Ministry of Finance, People's Bank of China, All-China Federation of Industry and Commerce and Ministry of Commerce	For eligible non-public enterprises, they may apply for financial support from the international market development funds of small and medium-sized enterprises, the interest-bearing funds of overseas processing trade loans, the special funds for the risk of foreign contracting project guarantees, the financial discount funds for loans for foreign contracting projects, the funds for joint ventures and cooperation projects for foreign countries and the special funds for foreign economic and technical cooperation.
International Financial Markets Report 2007	2008	People's Bank of China	China's overseas investment foreign exchange source of funds review and approval of the transfer of funds will be cancelled, actively support enterprises to "go out"
Regulations of the People's Republic of China on the Administration of Foreign Exchange	2008	State council	Convert the foreign exchange management system from compulsory settlement of foreign exchange to voluntary settlement of foreign exchange
Measures for the Administration of Overseas Investment	2009	Ministry of Commerce	Continue to promote and improve the facilitation of foreign investment, and delegate the approval authority for overseas investments of less than US$100 million, which shall be approved by the provincial Ministry of Commerce departments
Directory of Government-approved Investment Projects	2013	State council	The approval authority for overseas investments of less than $1 billion will no longer be required to be submitted to the NDRC departments at all levels for approval, as long as they do not involve sensitive areas and regions, whether state-owned or private enterprises, and only need to submit forms for the record
Measures for the Administration of approval and filing of overseas investment projects	2014	National Development and Reform Commission	The State shall, in accordance with different circumstances, implement the approval and filing management of overseas investment projects
Newly revised Measures for the Administration of Overseas Investment	2014	Ministry of Commerce	Increase the decentralization of government, eliminate the requirement for approval of overseas investments of a specific amount or more, and set up special purpose companies abroad, and establish a management model of "filing as the main and approval as a supplement"
Regulations on the Central Operation and Management of Foreign Exchange Funds of Multinational Corporations (Trial)	2014	State Administration of Foreign Exchange	Allow domestic and multinational companies with foreign exchange receipts and expenditures of more than $100 million in the previous year to transfer funds more freely
Notice on Further Improvement and Adjustment of Foreign Exchange Management Policies for Capital Projects	2014	State Administration of Foreign Exchange	Further relaxing the management of the upfront expenses of foreign direct investment of domestic institutions, i.e. if the cumulative amount of the upfront expenses of foreign direct investment does not exceed US$3 million and does not exceed 15% of the total investment of the Chinese side, the domestic institution may register the upfront expenses with the local foreign exchange bureau on the basis of its business license and the code certificate of the organization. If the amount exceeds US$3 million, or exceeds 15% of the total investment of the Chinese side, the domestic institution shall also provide the relevant authenticity supporting materials to the local foreign exchange bureau and register the upfront expenses

Continued on following page

Table 2. Continued

File Name	Release Time	Distribution Department	The Main Idea
Decision on amendments to the relevant provisions of the <Measures for the approval and filing of overseas investment projects> and <Measures for the approval and filing of foreign investment projects>	2014	National Development and Reform Commission	The requirement for approval by the National Development and Reform Commission for overseas investment projects with a Chinese investment of US$1 billion or more has been eliminated. The approval of out-of-degree investment projects is further decentralized
Regulations on the Administration of Cross-Border Guaranteed Foreign Exchange	2014	State Administration of Foreign Exchange	By eliminating or narrowing the scope of registration of cross-border guarantees, clarifying the scope of foreign exchange management and regulatory responsibilities of cross-border guarantees, and further realizing the harmonization of cross-border guaranteed foreign exchange management policies and the basic convertibility of cross-border guarantees
Measures for the Administration of approval and filing of overseas investment projects	2014	National Development and Reform Commission	Greatly increase the approval authority of overseas investment projects, narrow the scope of approval of the general overseas investment projects are subject to the filing system
Measures for the Administration of Overseas Investment	2014	Ministry of Commerce	Minimize the scope of project approval and shorten the operating time of outbound investment projects
Several Opinions of the State Council of the CPC Central Committee on Building a New System of Open Economy	2015	State council	Establish and implement the national strategy of "Going Out in the new period, establish the status of enterprises and individuals as the main body of foreign investment, and strive to improve the quality and efficiency of foreign investment
Notice on further simplifying and improving foreign exchange management policies for direct investment	2015	State Administration of Foreign Exchange	Further deepen the reform of foreign exchange management of capital projects, promote and facilitate the operation of cross-border investment funds by enterprises, standardize direct investment in foreign exchange management business, and improve management efficiency
Vision and Action to Promote the Construction of the Silk Road Economic Belt and the 21st Century Maritime Silk Road	2015	National Development and Reform Commission, Ministry of Foreign Affairs, Ministry of Commerce	Act on the signing of the cooperation framework, the construction of project cooperation, the improvement of policy measures and the play of a platform role
Government Work Report	2018	State council	Guide the healthy development of foreign investment, promote international cooperation in production capacity, and move high-speed rail, nuclear power and other equipment to the world
Reform and opening-up program for further deepening China's (Guangdong, Tianjin, Fujian) Free Trade Pilot Zone	2018	State council	According to their own characteristics, the three provinces and cities have formulated their own characteristics, each with a focus on the pilot tasks
Government Work Report	2019	State council	The government has launched a series of major initiatives to jointly build a "Belt and Road" leading effect to continue to release, cooperation mechanisms with countries along the route continue to improve, economic and trade cooperation and people-to-people exchanges accelerated. We should promote all-round opening up to the outside world and cultivate new advantages in international economic cooperation and competition. Promote the co-construction of B&R. Adhere to the common construction and sharing, abide by market principles and international rules, play the role of the main body of enterprises, promote infrastructure connectivity, strengthen international capacity cooperation, and expand third-party market cooperation. The second B&R International Cooperation Summit Forum is to be held. Promote the healthy and orderly development of foreign investment cooperation

Continued on following page

Table 2. Continued

File Name	Release Time	Distribution Department	The Main Idea
Guidance on Accelerating the Transformation and Upgrading of Agricultural Mechanization and Agricultural Machinery and Equipment Industry	2019	State council	In accelerating the development of high-quality agricultural machinery and equipment industry, it is required to optimize the layout of agricultural machinery and equipment industrial structure. Support enterprises to strengthen research and development and production of agricultural machinery and equipment, optimize the allocation of resources, and actively cultivate internationally competitive agricultural machinery and equipment production enterprise groups. Promote advanced agricultural machinery technology and products "Going Out", encourage advantageous enterprises to participate in foreign aid and international cooperation projects, enhance international business capacity, service B&R .

Sources:(Li,2016;http://www.chinagoabroad.com/zh/article/19157;https://www.sohu.com/a/432467841_99908530,)

APPENDIX 2

Table 3. Green-B&R policies

File Name	Release Time	Distribution Department	The Main Content
Environment Protection for Overseas Investment and Cooperation	2013	Ministry of Commerce, Ministry of Environmental Protection (MEP) (now Ministry of Ecology and Environment MEE)	The guidance document adopts a host-country approach, recommends enterprises to conduce environmental impact assessment and appraisal with respect to host country regulation, comply with the host country emission standards, protect and compensate for ecosystem and biodiversity in local context, and encourages enterprises to release environmental performance information
Vision and Actions on Jointly Building Silk Road Economic Belt and 21st Century Maritime Silk Road	2015	National Development and Reform commission (NDRC), Ministry of Foreign Affairs, Ministry of Commerce	Document laying out the foundations and strategy of B&R
Guidance on Establishing the Green Financial System	2016	• People's Bank of China (PBOC) • Ministry of Finance (MOF) • Development and Reform Commission (NDRC) • Ministry of Environmental Protection (MEE) • China Banking Regulatory Commission (CBRC/CBIRC) • Securities Regulatory Commission (CSRC/CSIRC)) • China Insurance Regulatory Commission	The guidance is the foundation of the green financial system of China. Although it has only indirect bearing for China's overseas finance, it is nevertheless the yardstick for China's green financial development
Guidelines on Further Guiding and Regulating Overseas Investments	2017	National Development and Reform commission (NDRC), Ministry of Commerce, People's Bank of China (PBOC), Ministry of Foreign Affairs (MOFA)	Guidelines laying out regulations for overseas investments, including green, open, harmounious, shared, win-win and opening-up guiding principles
Guidance on Promoting Green Belt and Road	2017	Ministry of Ecology and Environment of People's Republic of China	A summary of high-level opinions on greening the Belt and Road Initiative, including ecological civilization philosophy, environmental governance and high-level ambitions
The Belt and Road Ecological and Environmental Cooperation Plan	2017	Ministry of Environmental Protection (MEP) (now Ministry of Ecology and Environment)	High-level ambitious plan to make B&R ecologically sustainable, while abiding to local laws
The Belt and Road Ecological and Environmental Cooperation Plan	2017	Ministry of Environmental Protection (MEP)	The document lays out cooperation on eco-environmental protection in the B&R. It elaborates on several priority areas, including "Study on Green Investment and Financing"
Guiding Principles on Financing the Belt and Road	2017	Ministry of Finance of People's Republic of China	The principles were signed by finance ministers from 27 finance ministers (including China, Hungary, Cambodia, UK, Switzerland). They focus on cooperation, innovation and the important role in infrastructure

Continued on following page

Table 3. Continued

File Name	Release Time	Distribution Department	The Main Content
Joint Communique of Leaders' Roundtable of Belt and Road Forum for International Cooperation	2017	B&R Forum	The document lays out ideals and cooperation modes for the B&R. It was signed by 31 heads of state, the Secretary-General of the UN, the President of the World Bank Group and the Managing Director of the IMF
Vision and Actions on Energy Cooperation in Jointly Building Silk Road Economic Belt and 21st-Century Maritime Silk Road	2017	National Development and Reform commission (NDRC), National Energy Administration (NEA)	White paper laying out energy cooperation in the B&R
China's Arctic Policy - Artic Silk Road White Paper	2018	State Council Information Office of the People's Republic of China	The guidance document to develop the Artic
Approval Procedures for Large-scale Export Credit and Export Credit Insurance Projects	2018	• Ministry of Commerce of People's Republic of China; Ministry of Finance of People's Republic of China; •People's Bank of China; • China Banking Regulatory Commission	Approval Procedures for Large-scale Export Credit and Export Credit Insurance Projects to manage project risks
Belt and Road Green Investment Principles (GIP)	2018	Green Finance Leadership Program	Non-binding principles for public and commercial banks to invest in green investments. The document was signed by 30 banks during the 2nd B&R Forum in April 2019
Green Industry Guidance Catalog (2019 Edition)	2019	• National Development and Reform Commission (NDRC) • Ministry of Industry and Information Technology (MIIT) • Ministry of Natural Resources (MNR) • Ministry of Ecology and Environment (MEE) • Ministry of Housing and Urban-Rural Development (MHURD) • People's Bank of China (PBOC) • National Energy Board	The China green industry guidance serves to guide e.g., public investments into "green" industries. While not directly relevant to the B&R, it is a yardstick for China's green financial industry
The Belt and Road Initiative Progress, Contributions and Prospects	2019	Office of the Leading Group for Promoting the Belt and Road Initiative	A list of achievements regarding • Policy coordination, • Infrastructure connectivity, • Unimpeded trade • Financial integration • Closer people-to-people ties • Industrial cooperation and ambitious prospects, such as • Peace • Prosperity • Opening up • Green development • Innovation • Connected civilizations • Clean government

Continued on following page

Table 3. Continued

File Name	Release Time	Distribution Department	The Main Content
Debt Sustainability Framework for Participating Countries of the Belt and Road Initiative	2019	Ministry of Finance of People's Republic of China	The debt sustainability framework (BRI-DSF) is applicable to the debt sustainability analysis of B&R low-income countries. It is a non-mandatory policy framework to conduct debt sustainability analysis and manage debt risks to support lending decisions
President Xi Jinping's Belt and Road Forum Keynote speech	2019	B&R Forum	Speech laying out Chinese President Xi's vision for the next phase of the Belt and Road Initiative
Joint Communique of the Leaders' Roundtable of the 2nd Belt and Road Forum for International Cooperation	2019	B&R Forum	The final communique of the Belt and Road Forum 2019 with signatures from 38 heads of government, one vice president, the UN Secretary General and IMF's Managing Director. It lays out ambitions of the Belt and Road Initiative
List of Deliverables of the Second Belt and Road Forum for International Cooperation	2019	n/a	The document lays out 283 results in six categories: • Initiatives proposed or launched by China • Bilateral and multilateral documents signed during or immediately before the second BRF • Multilateral cooperation mechanisms under the BRF framework • Investment projects and project lists • Financing projects • Projects by local authorities and enterprises
Belt and Road Cooperation: For a Better World	2019	B&R Forum Advisory Council	The report takes stock and gives recommendations how to improve the B&R cooperation
Guiding Opinions on Promoting Investment and Financing to Address Climate Change	2020	Ministry of Ecology and Environment (MEE), National Development and Reform Commission (NDRC), People's Bank of China (PBoC), China Banking and Insurance Regulatory Commission (CBIRC), and China Securities Regulatory Commission (CSRC)	The guidance spells out climate finance ambitions at home and in the B&R, including a possibility to move away from the host-country principle

Source: https://green-bri.org/bri-policies/

Section 2

Chapter 4
China-Pakistan Economic Corridor:
A Challenging Initiative

Ijaz Khalid
Abdul Wali Khan University, Pakistan

ABSTRACT

The chapter consists of highlighting how CPEC initiated and linked China to the Arabian Sea by the shortest route through Pakistan. The chapter then elaborates Chinese and Pakistani relations in detail started from the birth of the PRC to the current joint venture of CPEC. This part of the work also covers Beijing's short- and long-term interests for they invest billions of dollars in the war torn state of Pakistan. Firstly, it defines CPEC in the contour of BRI that covers the regions of Asia, Africa, and Europe including more than 64 countries of these regions with investment of trillions of dollars to maintain the Chinese economic growth that has lasted for three decades. Secondly, with special reference to CPEC, PRC expects the shortest route to connect Kashghar with the Indian Ocean and permanently put an end to the Malacca dilemma. Thirdly, the study identifies Pakistan as a strong counter actor to India. Finally, it explains their political, diplomatic, economic, and strategic interests associated to the flagship project.

INTRODUCTION

China Pakistan Economic Corridor (CPEC), from its commencement is a hotly debated phenomenon among the scholars, think tank organizations and policy institutions across the World. It's a joint venture of both the iron brothers of China and Pakistan that connect Kashghar to Gwadar deep sea port that ultimately links western China through the Indian Ocean to Middle East, Europe and Africa (Rakisits, 2015). This project will ensure billions of dollars investment from China to Pakistan that will developed its underdeveloped regions of Khyber Pakhtunkhwa, Gilgit-Baltistan and Baluchistan through a network of roads, railway lines, bridges and other modern means of communications (Ahmar, 2014). It will also benefit China's most backward region of Xinjiang by giving direct access to Arabian Sea through Gawadar Sea port (Tariq Ali, 2022). The corridor will connect the two partners strategically

DOI: 10.4018/978-1-7998-8021-9.ch004

and economically through the transportations of millions of tons of goods from China to Middle East, African countries and to the big market of Europe (McCartney, 2022). This corridor not only links the time tested friends but will also connect the major regions of Asia including Central Asia, West Asia, Middle East and Eastern and Western Europe (Ahmed, 2019). For Pakistan, it would not be wrong that for the first time in the history of Pakistan it could get the fruits of its geo-strategic position and economic rebirth (Ahmar, 2015).

The 21st century dominated by the regional and World strategic environment across the World that led to the development and establishment of geo-strategic and geo-economic partnership among the allied states (Jackson, 2013). The driving force behind this partnership is state national interests and national security for that states reshaped its policies and strategies because it could no longer achieve the national interest and security alone and without partnership and alliance system but this alliance system is different from the one which has been practiced in 19th and 20th centuries, it is both economic and political partnership (Xuetong, 2006). The core of these partnerships growing cooperation among the states in the areas of industrial projects, infrastructure development, defense, commerce, and other economic areas that promotes cooperation and peace in the region and across the World (Massarrat Abid, 2015).

The role of China realized by everyone in the World that has been changed from a third World and rigid state to international norms and institutions to more vibrant and flexible actor that share responsibility of being not only an economic power but also an political stake holder in the contemporary World economic and political order (Laffan, 2018). In this regard Beijing is playing a central role not only in Asia but across the globe due to its largest status in the World in terms of population and the second largest economy in the World (Rosecrance, 2006). After achieving the economic power status, now Beijing set its stage for the World multilateral diplomatic revolution which was the missing and ignored chapter of Chinese foreign relations, But it doesn't mean that PRC will replace it economic policies for the sake of diplomatic mission rather this rapid diplomatic activities will boost-up the existence Chinese rising economic position in the World (Massarrat Abid, 2015).

The rise of China as an economic and political power has a lot of questions for the western World in general and particularly for the region alongside of China (Li, 2005). To make it clear and to show the real motives of China being a rising power, the PRC leadership introduced the "Good Neighbor Policy" in 2003 when Hu Jintao came to power as a president. According to this strategy Beijing tried to realize that China sought to promote independent and peaceful relationship rather than conflictive relations (Ikenberry, 2008). Hu also marked that the rise of China is peaceful and Beijing withhold the five principles of UN peaceful coexistence and the neighbor should not worry about the peaceful rise of China. By this way China changed the behavior of its regional states into friendly and converted the region into trade hub (Massarrat Abid, 2015).

As mentioned above that in 21st century states are seeking strategic and economic partnership for achieving it objectives. China and Pakistan are the two neighboring states and had good relations from 1950s till date (Li, 2005). Both states developed strong relations on the basis of trust and cooperation. Pakistan being a poor and third World state always rely on foreign aid and support to deter its traditional rival's India. For that purpose Pakistan adopted the alignment policy with the US and West to get economic and security assistance to counter the India aggression but it was in 1970s when Pakistan found all these security pacts not fulfilling it demands and left the alignment policy (Selman, 2009). Zulfiqar Ali Bhutto being a prime minister of Pakistan adopted the independent foreign policy along with making Pakistan a nuclear state because by conventional weapons Pakistan cannot defeat its rival India as the history is witnessed in 1971 war. Pakistan played core role in patching the Sin-US relations in 1971 when it secretly arrange Henry Kissinger meeting with Mao Zhe Dong (Schaller, 1975). The Afghan War of 1979 was once again clubbed Pakistan with the US but it could not hurt the Sino-Pak relations. Post 9/11 2011 both the states added the missing chapter of economic cooperation in their relations which ignored in history (Massarrat Abid, 2015).

The US being a hegemonic power kept close relations with Pakistan but in crises it kept the principles of neutrality between India and Pakistan. Keeping the historical diplomatic experiences with the US, Pakistan is now trying to diverting the dependence on the US and making new supporter to counter the larger traditional rival, India. For this determination, Pakistan got tremendous importance not only in the region but also across the globe to have friendship with the new super power of the 21st century, China. Recently, both the states revive the historical and traditional trade Silk Route and will connect Kashghar (China) to Gwadar (Pakistan) which is known a China Pakistan Economic Corridor (CPEC) (Massarrat Abid, 2015).

SINO-PAKISTAN RELATIONS

Diplomatic Terms

Being diversity in ideological aspects, Pakistan was one of the first Muslim countries to recognize newly established People's Republic of China in October 1949 but keeping in mind the Indian threat perception post-independence, Pakistan joined the SEATO and CENTO, which were arguably aimed at containing China, but at Bandung Conference in Indonesia, Pakistan make it clear that we have join SETO to protect our self not for containment strategy against China (Qandeel Siddique, 2014).. During this period, Indo-China friendship was also quite strong and have slogan of "Hindi-Cheeni Bhai Bhai". In 1954 China and India formally signed peaceful co-existence treaty, which were based on the five principles of UN Charter (Qandeel Siddique, 2014).

It was in 1961, when the largest communists' states were started to split and adopted hostile relations against each other while Indian enjoyed strong relations with USSR and Pakistan with US. In 1962 India-China border conflict united Islamabad and Beijing more closer apart from diplomatic relations to political ally against the common enemy. China has border clashes with most of its fourteen geographic neighbors including Japan, Vietnam, Russia, India and Korea, Pakistan remain one of the few neighbors with whom Beijing has not clashed (Amin, 2010). In 1963, the boarder issue between China-Pakistan on territory of Kashmir, Pakistan quietly handed over 5180 square kilometer of Kashmir to China and cleared the demarcations issues. The US adopted policy of encircling China and to isolate it in international community while Pakistan played crucial role in entering China to World politics and forming bridge between US and China (Amin, 2010).

Political Terms

Pakistan did a lot for the restoration of China's authorized right in UN Security Council which was given by the US to Taiwan. No one can ignore the role of Pakistan for arranging a secret visit of Hennery Kissinger sectary of state in 1971 to Beijing that led to the visit of Richard M. Nixon to China, which opened up PRC to the Western World and specially USA. This historic role that was played by Pakistan for its neighbor became the base of cooperative relations between the two states. This land mark achievement of Pakistan also remembered by the Chinese leadership that later led to terms of Iron Brothers, Friendship higher than Himalayas, Sweater than Honey and Deeper than Ocean. Pakistan involvement in war of Afghanistan in 1980's was comprehended by Beijing and support Pakistan's oriented forces against the Red Army in Afghanistan. Post-Cold war both the neighboring states were strengthened their relations when the US imposed sanctions on Pakistan and let alone to handle situations in Afghanistan. Islamabad took Beijing in confidence when it clubbed itself with the US against the War in Afghanistan post 9/11 2001. China also shows its solidarity with Pakistan when US raid on bin Laden's compound in Abbottabad in May 2011 and show its will to attack on Pakistan (Siddique, 2014).

The Importance of China to Pakistan can be experienced from first visit of PM Nawaz Sharif on July 4 2013 to China, as it was surprise for those who thought that PM will visit to Saudi Arabia due to his close personal and family relations and spent eight years in Saudi Arabia when he was disposed by General Pervez Musharraf in 1999. China has *second* largest economy, disturbing the dominance of the US. China has invested heavily in South Asia and so the US is interested in countering-Chinese influence in the region. Despite of diversity in language, culture, ideology and history, Sino-Pak relationship is growing day by day. As the Beijing invested billions of dollars in unstable Pakistan now PRC has more concerns and feeling to have a sable and peaceful Pakistan to achieve its economic objectives. The killing of Chinese people in Pakistan still did not affect this relationship because both of the states knows that there are outside forces involved in region to counter-weighting Sino-Pak partnership, for this purpose China is co-operating with Pakistan in defense and military equipment (Siddique, 2014).

Economic Terms

Historically speaking, Sino-Pak relations dominated by political issues rather than economic areas which were considered to be the missing aspect in their relations. But post-Cold War turn the Chinese policies into economic oriented and their policy towards Pakistan were also colored by economics especially post CPEC. Both enjoying trade relations volume of US$12 billion but the trade in favor of China not in Pakistan (Kumar, 2006). Before launching CPEC, Pakistan has a balance of economic relations with China as compare to the US but the joint project altered the nature and volume of relations between the two states. What is important to note here is that, Chinese made Pakistan economically dependent that can also pose threats to its own business community and its domestic economic development (Shabir, 2007).

Defense Relations

Since it its birth, Pakistan heavily dependent on Western and the US for purchasing its arms but post-Cold War Pakistan reduced its burdens on them and focused on China as the main supplier of arms to Pakistan. It was in 2013, when Pakistan emerged as the largest beneficiary of Beijing's arms and China declared as the largest supplier of military and nuclear technology (Lee, 2009) With China support, Pakistan built two power plants of Chashma 1 while another accord was signed to build Chashma 3 and 4 which has just completed in 2017. It shows the defense relations of both states and their cooperation in the area of nuclear program are strong. Despite of NSG concerns about the Chinese support of Pakistan nuclear activities, Beijing expedite its program with Pakistan and declared it as the Israel of China that has automatically answer to anyone who criticize their relations must think about the US support of Israel. (Yang, 2011).

The defense commitment can also be understand from the incident of Osama operation inside Pakistan by the US and its aftermath warning of attacking Islamabad. During this time the Chinese foreign office issued a clear warning to Washington that, any attack on Islamabad would be construed attack on Beijing. Again post Osama operation similar support from the PRC leadership was issued that caused isolated Pakistan in the World community. To the US criticism and aggression to intervene in Pakistan that ultimately breaches its sovereignty, Beijing backed Pakistan and the Chinese Premier Wen Jiabao told in this occasion. He said, *whatever changes may occur in regional or global level we will support Pakistan and both China and Pakistan will be good friends, neighbors and best partner forever.* He also issued warning that, *no country has the right to intervene in the internal affairs of Pakistan* (Shahid, 2011). It was for the first time when Beijing stood and took firm stance on Pakistan and the US received warning from a major power for the first time since 1945. On the other hand it also indicates the level of friendship between the two states. Beijing has intentions to use strategic friendship with Pakistan for countering Indian and American influence in the region.

CHINA'S INTERESTS IN CPEC

Chinese motivated by three main objectives to go for CPEC in a situation where Pakistan heavily smashed by the War on terror and burning in the issues of security and energy. Keeping in mind the development in South Asia where US strengthened its relations with India to use it as a counter to China also multiplied by the Malacca Dilemma that can slow down the Chinese three decades double digit economic growth but Chinese authorities are well aware of these developments and planned CPEC to counter all these issues with good manner (Wolf, 2021).

To strengthen Pakistan Economically; China and Pakistan enjoyed long term diplomatic, political and military relations based on trust and respect for each other sovereignty since the inception of both but the missing chapter in their relations was added post 9/11 2001 when Chinese policy maker adopted economic oriented policies and feel the need of Pakistan in its long term geo-economic strategy. The importance of Pakistan to the Chinese were severe when the US adopted strong relations with India for two reasons, one to counter China regional influence and second to use the India in the issues of South China Sea (Ali., 2022). For that purpose, it is logical that Beijing would seek to apply a dreadful counterweight to India to level the score with US in the South Asia politics. Unlike US, Chinese rightly conceived the real problems of Pakistan that hurdles its economic growth which are security and energy crises (Wolf, 2021). To put an end to the issue of energy, China plan to invest $55 billion in Pakistan and with reference to security Chinese also greatly concerns with elements of Xinjiang Uyghur Autonomous Region. Some Chinese media also pointed out finger on Pakistani individuals who trains and equipped these groups to operate in Xinjiang but during Musharraf era all these concerns were cleared by Pakistan and it was proved when Pakistan kill the leader of ETIM in a drone attack near Pak-Afghan border.

Secondly, the Chinese interests in CPEC to divert energy sea trade routes to and from the Middle East. China 75% of international trade going through the Strait of Malacca and Indian Ocean where huge U.S. naval presence could blockades the choke points of the Strait of Malacca that would leads to the conflict between the two largest economies of the World (Ali., 2022). For that purpose Gwadar operated by Chinese to directly link it western China and reduce the dependency on US influenced sea routes of Indian Ocean, Strait of Malacca, East and South China Sea to sustain and ensure free flow of imports and exports to the region of Middle East, Africa and Europe with any obstacle (Ali., 2022).

Lastly, the Chinese huge investment in a country like Pakistan could not justify only for supporting Pakistan economically and diverting its maritime sea routes through CPEC but the goals of Beijing are not regional but touching the global levels (Ullah, 2022). For that purpose, PRC plan to build rail network to connect Kashghar with Gwadar. This would help China to link economic partners of South East Asia to Europe, Middle East and African Markets by land corridors and maritime trade routes. On the basis of this rationale, Chinese operated the Gawadar port to meet its economic objectives but also it is hotly debated around the World that Chinese will use the port for the naval purposes to ensure the security of its maritime routes from the piracy incidents to achieve strategic objectives.

For understanding CPEC and Beijing's interests in the CPEC, we must understand the broader agenda and strategy of Chinese policy maker who chalk out the whole system of corridors across the Asia, Europe and Africa. The new leadership of Xi Jinping spoke about the "Silk Road Economic Belt" in 2013 when he was on official visit to Kazakhstan. In early 2015 the policy maker also came up with another vision of "21st Century Maritime Silk Road" through South East and South Asia. China marked both of these visions collectively as "One Belt, One Road" (OBOR) (Zimmerman, 2015).

International system dominated by western powers and in later century by the US along with its western allies through its much practices values of democracy and capitalism. The history of international politics is full of the emergence and decline of non-western powers but all of them failed to defeat western oriented values and compelled them to adopt the same values. Unlike other non-western powers, China emerged as an economic power within very short period of thirty years committed to capitalism economically and communism politically. The US and west tried to transformed the hostile powers in the colors of US and western political culture and China is not an exception.

Mao Foreign Policy

China emerged as a communist state in 1949 but practice capitalism when the US and western powers relaxed their relations with Beijing in late 1970s. This development on the one hand relaxed the tension between Washington and Beijing but with the rapid rise of China as an economic power and responsible actor of international politics produced tension in Sino-US relations in particularly and to the western powers in general (Godehardt, 2016). This tension of current major powers will ultimately lead to conflict of Washington and Beijing and consider China as a threat to the existence established norms of international political and economic order (Godehardt, 2016).

To counter the US policy of isolating China, Mao adopted three different and diverts strategies to achieve its foreign policy objectives. Firstly, "Leaning to One Side strategy", According to this strategy Mao make it clear to lean to one side and choose the communist bloc as an alliance. Initially Mao was not in mood to adopt this policy of aligning itself to the Moscow but it was due to the US policies that compelled Mao to clubbed China with USSR. Secondly, "The Double Anti", this strategy put China hostile to both of the super powers when Beijing found itself in clash with Soviet Union in 1969. During this time China developed close relations with the third World states of Asia, Africa and Latin America that gave an identity to Chinese people and some scholar considered China the master of third World states but Beijing negate that sort of notions for itself and did not claimed any leadership status. Lastly, "The One United Front Strategy". After Sino-Soviet split in 1969 China realized that it could no longer afford to be hostile with both the super powers and relaxed its relations with the US and Western states that ultimately led to the collapse of USSR in 1990. As a result the policies of Mao were security oriented and he was very rigid and committed to the values of communism and strongly opposed the Western oriented values of democracy and capitalism and their dominated World order and agencies.

Deng's Reforms of Modernization

When Deng Zhao Ping came to power in 1978, he put China on the opposite side and made economy as the top priority of the nation and kept politics secondary. To achieve its objectives he adopted the Openness and reforms program and introduced the Modernization of Agriculture, Industry, Defense, Science and technology that consequently explore China to the rest of the international community and brought positive results in terms of economic development. After Deng, Jiang Zemin and Hu Jintao both of them continue the policies of Deng modernization and reform program that marked China as one of the economic due to it double digit economic growth for the last thirty years. The 9/11 2001 attacks and the post 9/11 US policies faced China with both challenges and opportunities.

Xi Jinping Assertive Policies

Chinese interests in the post Hu has clearly elaborated by the new leadership of Xi Jinping when he came to power in 2012. What China needs and what would be the destination of its people were the questions that everyone in the World wants to know about the second largest economy and the most populous country in the World. In this regard the Beijing new leadership clearly talks about its vision when Xi spoke in January 16, 2013 and he said,

By the time the People's Republic celebrates its 100th anniversary, we will become a prosperous, strong, democratic, civilized, and harmonious socialist modernized country on its way to the ultimate great rejuvenation of the Chinese nation. This is the greatest dream of the Chinese nation in modern history (Lin, 2015).

Keeping in mind the XI vision, one can remind that after Deng the Chinese people got another leadership that not only pursuing the policies of openness and reforms but also chalked out the future planning for conducting the domestic and foreign policy. Xi clearly marked prosperity that simply means the Beijing's current economic policy that was continuing since Deng (Lin, 2015). The Communist Party of China pursuit long term history of planning which they outlined as an ambitious vision is called "The Chinese Dream by XI" that will be achieve in the mid of this century. This vision is the aggregate of policy aims proposed to augment prosperity, encourage social stability, guarantee a higher standard of life for citizens, and advance China's position as a World power. The PRC policy makers are hopeful about the result of this vision that it will bring happiness to the individuals. In effect, Beijing adopted the numerous domestic and foreign policy to advance this vision. Internally, since 2002, the CCP focused on the five areas included economic, political, social, cultural and environmental to be improved for the smooth running of China rapid economic growth that was designed by the Deng in 1980.externally, with its rising power as a global power status Beijing needs to address the economic security issues by adopting to formulate the new World order and seek regional cooperation to ease the tension between China and conflictive state (Lin, 2015).

To ensure quality of life in any society the economic development must be based on Balance sustainable growth otherwise it will leads to separatism, terrorism and extremism. Since 2002 China also faced this economic issue of balance growth and the gap between the eastern China and Southern and Western China that is widen with passing every single day that consequently created the issue Tibet and Sinkiang separatist elements in the shape of Eastern Turkistan Islamic Movement (ETIM) which posed severe threats to Beijing National sovereignty. So economically, PRC policy makers addressed economic issue of balance growth that heavily affect the quality of life in western and Southern regions to increase urbanization and also double the income of rural areas (Lin, 2015).

Secondly, to overcome on three deferent sovereignty issues of separatism, terrorism and extremism in diverse areas of Taiwan, Xinjiang, and Tibet are counted as the core interests of Beijing while making priorities of their national interests. Along with these land issue of sovereignty, Authorities in PRC also took hard stance to the maritime issues that challenged Beijing assertion but the presidency of Xi jin Ping said that we will not give up an inch to anyone who attempts to violate the sea law of China. Finally, Beijing committed to protect its raw materials markets that provides and maintain the economic development and marked this task as also the core interests of China that is not open for any negotiation and cannot be compromised for any dialogue (Lin, 2015).

One Belt One Road Initiative (OBOR)

There are three reasons that why China need land corridors for the smooth running and sustainable development of economic growth which is continue for the last three decades since Deng committed China to modernization and reform program. Firstly, when Ho Jin Tao talked about the Malacca dilemma in November 2003, Secondly, the US increased the deployment of naval forces and provided seven aircraft strike groups including in East and South China Sea and Pacific region, lastly, the balance growth and the gap between East and western China and its connection with Xinjiang problem.

This image explains the motives behind the Chinese planning of OBOR that pointed out in the images the increased presence of America in the regions of South China Sea, Indian Ocean and Mediterranean Sea that may block China and contain it in maritime business (Amineh, 2022).

Figure 1.

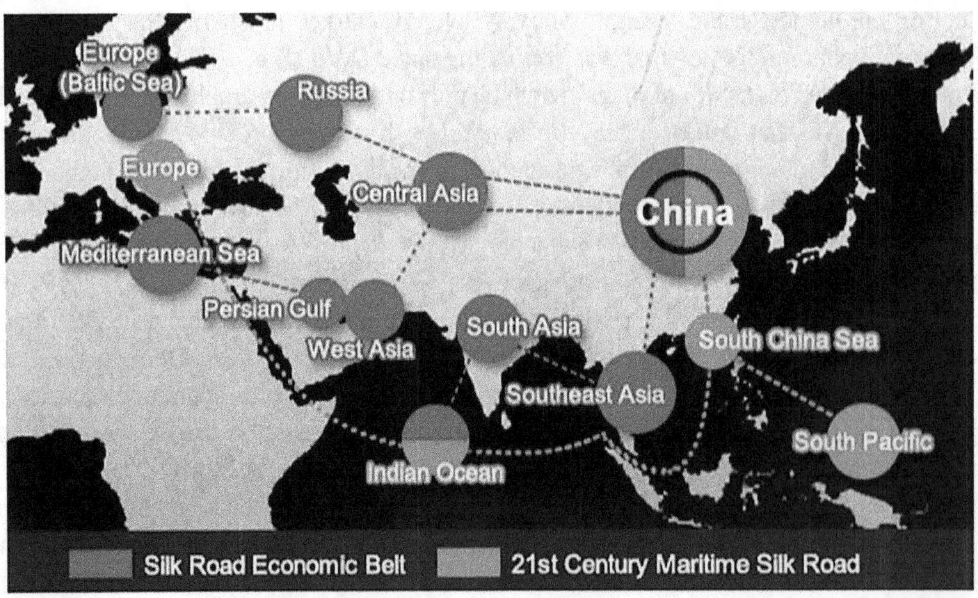

The US Increased Presence in the Region

The US administration decided to strengthen the US Naval ability by providing seven aircraft carriers strike groups (CSG) to enable Navy's combat power with other US allies that posted in five divers slots in the maritime regions. The US also conducted joint exercises with its allies including, India, Japan, South Korea, Taiwan and Arab States to show its strong presence in the areas which were that threatened by hostile nation in the World including China.

This was the spark for China to think about its sea lanes of communications (SLOC) that was heavily dependent on the sea routes and to replace it by land routes for trade and commercial links with Middle East, African nations and Europe when the US started to show its naval mighty power in the region. In 2004 Chinese economy was based on foreign trade of which 90% was passing through sea routes of Yellow Sea, East China Sea and South China Sea that were under the strong influence of US and its allies including Japan, Philippines, Indonesia and Taiwan. The major check point in all of these sea routes is the Strait of Malacca that was responsible for 82% of crude oil passed through this check point and it is controlled by the mighty Naval powers the US and its allies. Here for Beijing two options is available, one to deter the threat posed by the US and its allies by showing more naval power to the opposite powers but China at this level is incapable to deter US policies and strategies through force. The second options are to search for an alternative to replace the sea routes by land routes to avoid the clash with the US in the Pacific region and areas where China travelling it's 90% of its international trade to ensure it sustainable growth in double digit.

Trans-Pacific Partnership (TPP)

Under *"The US Back to Asia"* or *"Asia Pivot"* policy the US adopted different strategies to pursue its interests in the Pacific region. Among those strategies Trans-Pacific Partnership (TPP) is one which initiated in later Bush era but was formally started during Obama era in 2010, which initially started from four countries and consequently covered twelve countries of Asia Pacific region including USA. The specific objective of TTP is, to make their economies integrated that will ultimately leads to common business and trade interests and political align in one block excluding China. Being target of the TTP, Beijing adopted many strategies to counter the US Back to Asia policy and plan to integrate the region economically and resolve the issue political with peaceful means. The immediate response to TTP, PRC launched the Regional Comprehensive Economic Partnership (RCEP) that excluded USA. Beijing took two years to come up with rationalize and long term comprehensive policy response to not only TTP but also to counter the US presence in the regions that surrounded China. In this regard PRC announced its two side of strategy by combining Silk Road Economic Belt and Maritime Silk Road which also known OBOR. The initiative has seven land base economic corridors that cover Asia, Europe and Africa. The details of corridors are under which explain the comprehensive thinking of the Chinese elite policy makers who chalk out an economic and military strategy for the 21st century. It includes: The China-Mongolia-Russia corridor, The New Eurasian Land Bridge, from central China to Europe via Kazakhstan, Russia and Belarus, The China-Central Asia-Western Asia Corridor, The China Pakistan Economic Corridor (CPEC), The Indo-China Peninsula Corridor, The Bangladesh-China-India-Myanmar Corridor.

The image below clearly explains the seven corridor of Chinese OBOR that connect PRC with Asia, Europe and African continent.

Figure 2.

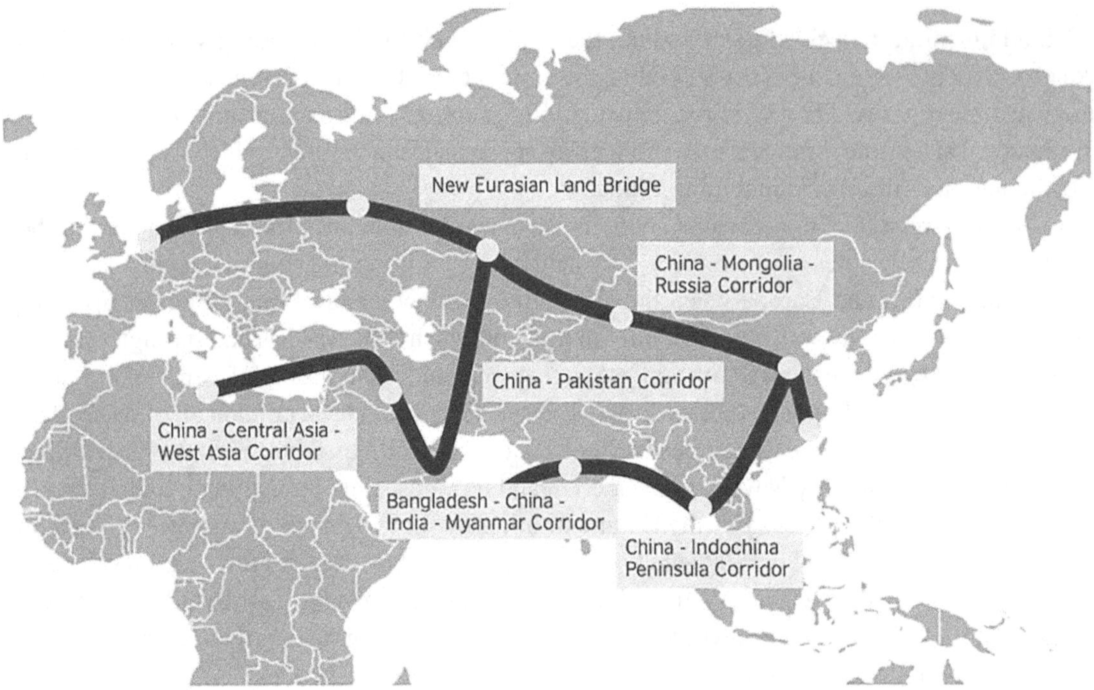

The six economic corridors designed to link China with developing countries

The OBOR is not only the new shape of another Silk Road but it also the start of Chinese academic, political, and public discourse. In a short period of time this OBOR initiative become a dominant depiction for China's foreign policy and diplomatic experiences, regional neighborhood relations and specially for the domestic economic development. The geography of OBOR is not define and its open to every nation of the World that is why most of the maps of this strategy which was published by the Chinese officials does not show the national borders but only the corridors, regions and the cities (Godehardt, 2016).

It was in 2014 when the Chinese modernized their thinking about the OBOR due to two developments. Firstly, by the local provincial support for the belt and road initiative that gave socio-economic support and strengthens in all dimensions. Secondly, the diverse composition of participants led to the creation of new ideas of potentials aspects of cooperation among the states which are the members of the corridors. It was not only the traditional infrastructure that links the nations for trade but also, cover the issues of environment, questions of urbanization, and the build-up of linkages between key cities along the Silk Road that included in the OBOR program (Godehardt, 2016).

Figure 3.
Figure: Accessed on August 20, 2017, at https://www.scmp.com/sites/default/files/2015/11/03/obor.png

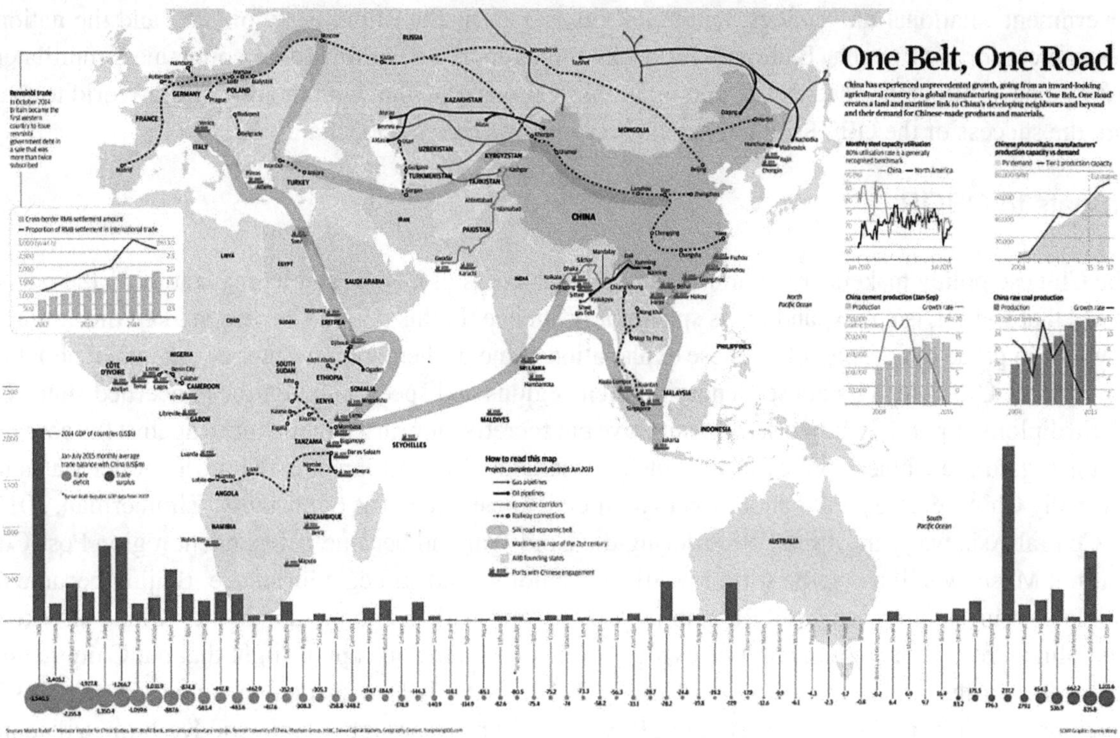

OBOR: Main Features

The Chinese OBOR initiative is not a grand strategy as a counter-model to the established norms, values; rules that shaped the current international political and economic World order but rather a proactive Chinese policy response to the rising complexity in the World that provide an alternative concept of how international politics could be planned in the future. It also represents a loose political notion in which new mechanisms of cooperation are fashioned. That's why OBOR is very different from the rule Eurocentric model of international order and institutions (Godehardt, 2016). Below are the main features of the OBOR initiative:

Firstly, it strengthen cooperation among the member states, to create a network of cooperation I many aspects at divers political level that consequently maximizing cooperation and minimizing the conflict among the member states. Keeping in mind this objective the Chinese main focus is on the economic opportunities and avoid security issues and conflicts. Secondly, it is *flexible and open;* it has no determined geography and opens to all the nations of the World to be part of the initiative that's why the Chinese official has not yet published and present any map of the corridors and that is the example of openness and inclusiveness. The beauty of this initiative covers the diverse nations and divers' interests of these nations which lead to the cooperation and common interests because it based on the win-win situation. In simple words the OBOR is one program that includes diverse actors, different interests of these nations but as a result and the successful completion and implementation of the program all the diverse interests would lead o the common interests of all the nations of OBOR. Thirdly, it is based on broad economic and political system of network that promotes connectivity among the states which include in the Silk Road for that purpose OBOR supported by all institutions within China including, Provincial and local governments, national universities, think tank organizations the ruling party of CPC and the national electronic and print media. Externally, it seeks the support of multinational companies, multilateral institutions, multilateral mechanism and bilateral relations of China with the rest of the World to make sure the success of the OBOR initiative to achieve its objectives (Godehardt, 2016).

Threats to OBOR

The Chinese policy makers are optimistic about the success of OBOR and its realization to the outside World that Beijing is not expanding its sphere of influence. In this regard Chinese marked this initiative as win-win game but despite of all these explanation some of the regional states are skeptical about the activities of OBOR and its consequences on their regions and specifically on the concerned state. The World diplomats publicly supported the initiative but secretly they raised their voiced against the corridor. In this regard the Chinese policy leaders clearly marked USA and Japan is the most spoiler states but internally Chinese have great connection to their civil society in terms of business (Zimmerman, 2015).

Central Asia was part of the USSR during the Cold War and became independent region Post-Cold War but Moscow still has some sort of political, economic and strategic influence. Beijing became the first largest investor crossing the Russian in 2009. Along with economic dominancy China also keeping political role in the region but it faces high level corruption and capital flight that put Chinese huge investment in the region on risk (Zimmerman, 2015). India is also suspicious about China's OBOR development with special reference to the CPEC that will pass through Jammu and Kashmir, a disputed area between Pakistan and India. Being part of the Chinese oriented institutions of AIIB and BRICS New Delhi refused to become part of the OBOR as they believe a national agenda of the Beijing not multilateral like other institutions. Furthermore Indian also join the US oriented projects and support policies in which they would establish North-South Economic Corridors (Zimmerman, 2015).

PAKISTAN'S INTERESTS IN CPEC

Pakistan needs economic uplift in the terms of provision of jobs, construction of roads, economic zones and so on so forth. Pakistan and people of Pakistan will get benefit from energy projects, employment, communication projects and all sort of socio-economic development that the CPEC has to offer. But we have doubts and misunderstandings on the issue which may harm our national prospects.

Economic Interests

One can remind the major decisions in Pakistan foreign policy that was started from the alignment policy in 1950s with the US and West, the 1965 war, the 1971 war and the break of Pakistan into two pieces, the Nuclearization of Pakistan, the Afghan war of 1979, post-Cold War situation in Afghanistan, post 9/11 2001 terrorists attacks and war in Afghanistan and lastly the China Pakistan Economic Corridor 2015. Among all these major decisions of Pakistan foreign policy CPEC will achieve what Pakistan is looking for to get benefits of geo-strategic position linking the on the one hand Europe, Africa, Middle East and India to the resources rich areas of the Central Asian Republics (CARs) and with Russia and

China while on other hand it also considered as a bridge for the CARs, Russia and Western China to do their business through CPEC (Ali, 2022). It is also assessed that in coming one decade the World two third trades would be goes through CPEC and Pakistan will be a hub of international trade.

To ensure Economic Rebirth of Pakistan, Pakistan from its inception in 1947 till date has relied on foreign aid and assistance for running the state machinery but no program or policy could made Pakistan economically, politically stable country of the region. Every state has some phases towards the development while chalking out the foreign policy objectives but Pakistan still in the first phase of its foreign policy objectives and considered a security oriented foreign policy and does not enter to economic or political stability stage. Those who are expert on Pakistani politics blamed diverse factors for this great negligence, some marked the inefficient political leadership, military interference in the politics, the behavior of India towards Pakistan, that led Pakistan to adopt security oriented policies (Massarrat Abid, 2015).

The only one positive signal to Pakistani society is Pak-China relations on which every Pakistani is agreed and there are no opposite opinion about that. In this regard CPEC is consider to be the game-changer, fate-changer whatever terminology one give it but for Pakistan it's a rebirth in terms of economic development because it's a win-win situation for both China and Pakistan in which both states will get benefits. Chinese investment in Pakistan will boost its GDP 274 billion $ by over 15%. Post 9/11 2001, Pakistan was known for dangerous country, failed state and the center of terrorism but now enjoyed more fiscal position than India reducing its budget deficit to 4.7% of GDP in 2014 while India 7%. Another indicator of Pakistan economic recovery is that it is cheaper and competitive in terms of as an emergent market for the foreign investors.

To *overcome the energy issue,* in modern era the industrial revolutions comes when a state has sufficient level of energy and it is considered to be life line of every state economy. Like other countries of the region with growing population and industrial modernization, Pakistan also need energy for its economic development but unfortunately due to involvement in the War on terror Pakistan faced sever energy crises? No satisfactory solution to the issue has yet been found and the citizens are facing the problem of power supply in this modern technology era. The business of people has been heavily damaged by the deliberately load shedding across the country especially in the major cities of Pakistan. In this regard CPEC is the ideal to get rid of the energy crises when it will inject 35 billion$ out of 45.6 billion$ in the energy sector while the rest are divided on the other sectors (Massarrat Abid, 2015).

Table 1. Electricity in Pakistan -2030

Investment policy area	Policy measures (examples)
Policy actions at the national level	
Investment facilitation	• Alleviation of administrative burdens and bureaucratic obstacles for firms • Use of online tools and e-platforms
Investment retention and aftercare by investment promotion agencies (IPAs)	• COVID-19-related information services • Administrative and operational support during the crisis • Move to online services
Investment incentives	• Financial or fiscal incentives to produce COVID-19-related medical equipment • Incentives for conversion of production lines • Incentives for enhancement of contracted economic activities
State participation in crisis-affected industries	• Acquisition of equity in companies, including nationalization
Local small and medium enterprises (SMEs) and supply chains	• Financial or fiscal support for domestic suppliers (such as SMEs)
National security and public health	• Application and potential reinforcement of FDI screening in pandemic-relevant industries
Other State intervention in the health industry	• Mandatory production • Export bans • Import facilitation
Intellectual property (IP)	• General authorization of non-voluntary licensing, to speed up research and development (R&D) • IP holder-specific non-voluntary licensing, to enable imports of medication
Policy actions at the international level	
International support measures for investment	• International pledges in support of cross-border investment
IIAs	• Reform of IIAs in support of public health policies and to minimize investor–State dispute risks

Source: accessed, August 20, 2017. https://defence.pk/pdf/attachments/electricity-jpg.371623/

To develop infrastructure: it is necessary for every state to improve its infrastructure if it wants to be economically develop. For the flow of people and goods the state needs build its roads, railways, Sea and Dry ports and other means of communication through which state achieve economic interests. The already poor infrastructure became worse with the starting of War on terror which lasted for 15 years and severely destroyed the infrastructure of Pakistan. Pakistan through CPEC will seek to improve its war torn infrastructure by connecting it with the regions of Asia, Europe, CARs and Middle Eastern states and will remove all the trade barriers that will lead to free trade zones and will create peaceful environment for international trade. In this regard Pakistan wants to be the center of international trade and to improve the living standard of its citizens. This joint project would be used for the creation of economic and industrial cities that would link all the four provinces of Pakistan, AJK, Fata and Gilgit-Baltistan to expand benefits of the initiative through the country (Massarrat Abid, 2015).

To eliminate Poverty: CPEC is considered to be the game changer in terms of poverty eradication from Pakistan and it is estimated that millions of people will lift from poverty and misery. Completion of infrastructure will lead to the economic development that will create economic and industrial zones and cities which consequently improve the existence industries of garments, industrial parks, textiles, construction of dams, and installation of nuclear reactors. All of these developments will generate employment and business opportunities for the people of Pakistan. Along with this Pakistan also seek to have more modern equipped hospitals, technical and vocational training institutions and the most important the supply of clean water that will provide the quality life to the people of Pakistan (Massarrat Abid, 2015).

Political Interests

The China Pakistan Economic Corridor is one of the most ambitious mega projects that Islamabad has initiated during its sixty eight years of co-existence with Beijing as closest strategic and economic partner (Masood, 2016). It has been termed as a game changer and transitional due to vast politico-economic expectations connected to CPEC. Now how much these expectations are realistic and rational to achieve its goals and how much it is just a misleading and exaggerated publicity? Is Pakistan so much serious as China in the execution of this project? (Masood, 2016).

Strategic Interests

Pakistan's army is assisting the Chinese project not only in developmental sector but is providing tight security comprised of fifteen thousand personnel under the command of major General undertaking protection of railways, roads and fiber networks (Irshad, 2015). To develop additional links for neighboring states, Pakistan's land access to Central Asia and Russia and in repose Iran's approach to China through Karakorum Highways along with India's involvement in Chabahar port in Iran for connecting it with a road network to Afghanistan, will open up opportunities for regional states in order to complement rather than to confront one another. In short this project will not only bring prosperity in the underdeveloped parts of Pakistan but a sustained development in China as well (Khan A. U., 2014). The engagement of the private sector in the project by both states would be greatly advantageous in relation to participation, dissemination of technologies and managerial skills on a broader scale also. Since last two years the project has got momentum in the fields of infrastructure and energy projects (Abid M. &., 2015).

PLAN OF CPEC

For the last six decades China and Pakistan enjoyed and achieved many landmarks in their bilateral relationships. During the first decade both states have developed strong diplomatic relations cleared all the demarcations of their international boundaries which based their relations on respect and trust. To prove its true relations based on win-win principles china launched another landmark decision to connect its western part with Pakistan's most neglected area of KP and Baluchistan. In this regard China Pakistan Economic Corridor (CPEC) is the vision of the leadership of both countries for transforming this relationship to strategic economic cooperation and contour of CPEC came to the attention in July 2013. CPEC will take the China Pakistan relationship to new heights. (Shah, 2016)

The CPEC was part of the long term and grand strategy of the Chinese One Belt One Road initiative that was chalk out by the new leadership of Xi Jin Ping when he came to power in November 2012 as a policy response to the US policy of Asia Pivot. To convert the Chinese dream into reality they started from China Pakistan Economic Corridor in 2013 with the Prime Ministerial visits of Premier Li Keqiang and Nawaz Sharif in May and July 2013. To understand the official plan of the project the China Pakistan Institute (PCI) was set up in Pakistan to analyze the real developments about the project that is headed by Senator Mushahid Husain. In order to analyze the Ministerial visits PCI conducted Round Table discussion that was chaired by the Mushahid Husain and attended by Chinese and Pakistani academicians, think tank officials and media representatives, as well as officials from the Chinese Embassy in Pakistan (Sayed, 2013). ,

Figure 4.
Figure: Accessed on August 20, 2017 copied from, http://www.be2c2.com/wp-content/uploads/2015/11/China-Pakistan-Economic-Corridor-CPEC-infographics.jpg

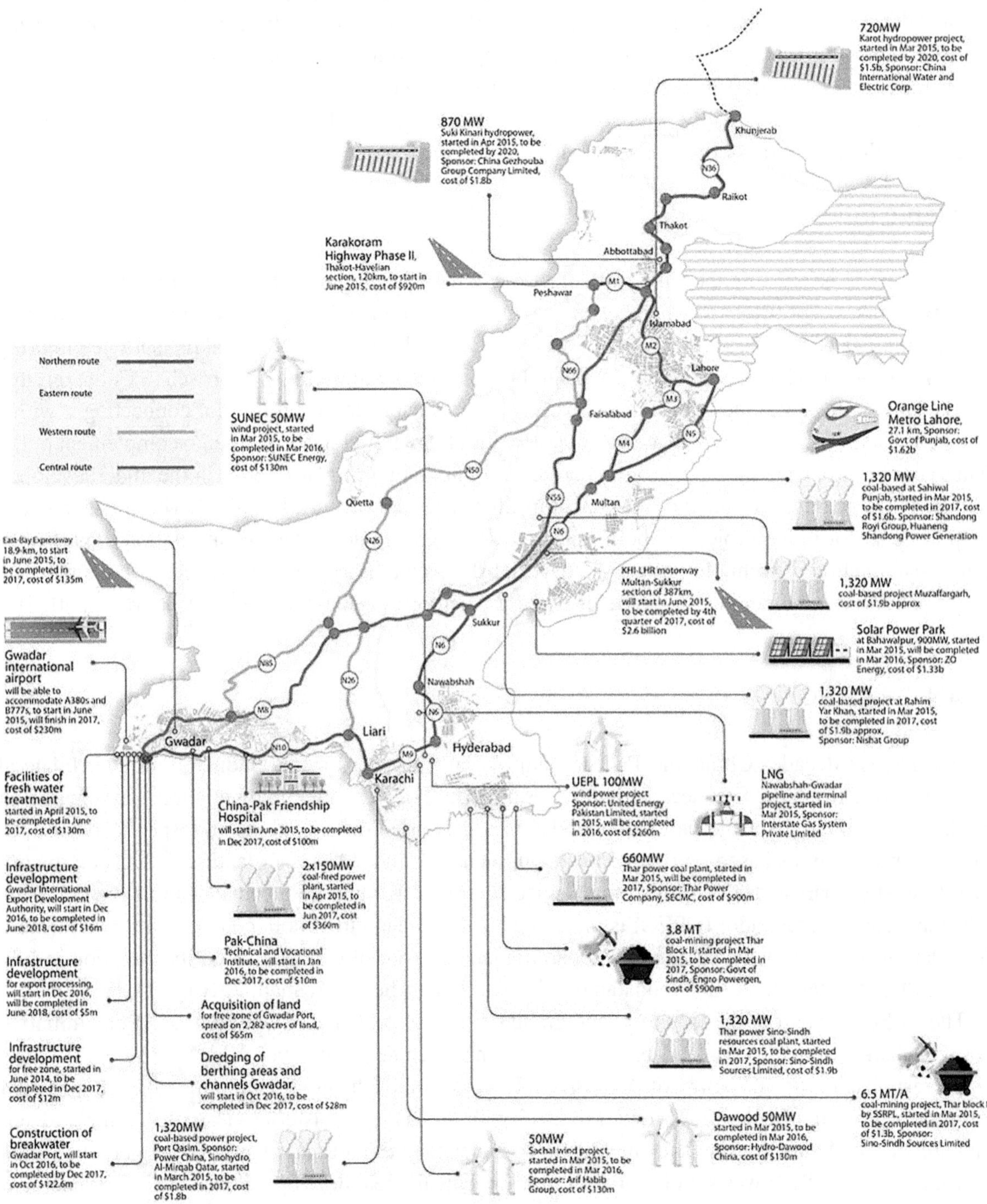

To make any project successful in Pakistan the chairman emphasized, that now Pakistan should take practical steps to improve its domestic security and make Pakistan as a viable place for foreign investors in general and especially for the Chinese who are working in Pakistan. He also declared the sensitive areas and pointed out to give priority to the Baluchistan and Gilgit-Baltistan. For that purpose he also proposed an Industrial Security Force (ISF) to guarantee maximum preventive measures. Along with these forces the chairman also indicated that in order to ensure security to foreign investors the government also reform bureaucratic procedures that prevented the implementation of major projects. He appreciated the current government of Nawaz Sharif's decision to create a monitoring cell at the Prime Minister House to oversee the outcomes of implementation of the projects with China (Sayed, 2013).

CPEC will connect China and Pakistan through huge network of roads, highways, railways and pipelines. It is estimated that the road will run 2700 kilometers from Gwadar to Kashghar. It is estimated that the total budget that was allocated for the project is $46 billion. In this project it is also decided to construct a motorway of about 1100 kilometers that connect the major cities of Pakistan of Lahore to Karachi which has already connected to Lahore-Islamabad motorway. In the corridor it is also plan to widen the Karakorum highway that directly linked to Rawalpindi and Chinese borders of western part. The news also highlighted that a network of pipelines shall also be chalk out for the transportation of liquid natural gas and oil from Iran, Middle East and African nations to China (Ziying, 2016).

Gwadar Port

In 21st century, the World Politics dominated by the Sea politics due to increase commercial and business activities that made the affairs of the more complex.In this context the major powers always kept an eye on the crucial spots of the Oceans that are strategically significant and important to control for the protection of Communications Sea Lanes. Gwadar port is one of them that is considered to be the significant deep sea port of Pakistan which located at the heart of Persian Gulf, Strait of Hormuz. Historically, it waspart of the Omani Sultanate but in 1958 purchased by Pakistan (Malik, 2012). Initially, it was under Port Singapore Authority (PSA) to construct the port but its importance increased when the port handed over to the China Overseas Port Holding Company (COPHC) in 2013.The port got tremendous attention when CPEC was launched in 2015 and the work speed upwith a rapid pace. The port also became a source of concerns for the other regional and global powers when Beijing announced a new plan to mark the port as the hub of international business and politics by launching the programs of developing of Gwadar city, Power Generation Plants and International Airport. Ultimately, the port operationalizes and has started shipment, seasonal cargo that generates business and commercial activities (Z., 2005).

CHALLENGES TO CPEC

CPEC being an important and one of the first and fast growing project of the Chinese One Belt One Road initiative has great importance for not only the partner states but also for the regions which has impacts on them. In order to implement this project the partner countr faces a lot of constrains within China, Pakistan and the regions around (Haider, 2015). In this regard, CPEC will not be implemented and would be completed without internal and external challenges due to four reasons.

Firstly, keeping in mind the historical experiences of Chinese workers found security threats in Pakistan which has great impacts on the implementation of this joint mega venture. In order to tackle this issue Pakistan must provide security to Chinese workers and technicians.

Secondly, Chinese investing huge money in Pakistan but also put on some responsibility to provide its capacity building and professional skills to meet the deadlines of construction of roads, railways and power stations on the part of Pakistan which has always seen very difficult for the state of Pakistan. Any failure in this part would be multiply the negative perception with reference to the success of CPEC as it was seen in the Pak-Iran Gas project.

Thirdly, Pakistani officials repeatedly stated that the project will sabotage by foreign forces for which covert sponsor can be used to make CPEC damage by means of terrorism. Fourthly, like other mega projects CPEC is also became the victim of corruption, nepotism and inefficiency (Massarrat Abid, 2015).

The main hub of the CPEC is Gwadar port that will provide a safe way of international trade to China Central Asia and even Russia and according to some analysts in the coming decade 2/3 of the World trade would go through CPEC. On the one side it provides great opportunities to the Partner states but on the other side it will also pose threat to these states (Abid, 2015). Secondly, Indian raised serious concerns about the CPEC going through the Pakistan Occupied Kashmir (POK) to which they considered to dispute area between India and Pakistan (Abid, 2015).

Conflict on Routes

Unfortunately Pakistan major projects were the victim of political conflicts and rivalries among the major political parties. Kala Bagh Dam is one of the great examples in this regard. The project was designed to overcome the energy shortage in the country but it became the victim of political controversies which contributed to the current energy crises. CPEC again becoming the target of political parties and their grievances against each other that led to slow down the completion of the project. The mega project of CPEC started in 2015 when Pakistan was ruling Pakistan Muslim League Nawaz (PMLN) a national party which is considered to be a Punjab oriented political party. The rest of the parties has put up their grievances about the $46 billion project that only benefit Punjab and the minority provinces were ignored in the fruits of the corridor. Pakistan People Party (PPP) and Awami National Party (ANP) and even Pakistan TehrikInsaf (PTI) have strong reservations on the handling of project. Here are approaches of different political parties about the priority of building the CPEC routes.

CONCLUSION

China Pakistan Economic Corridor being part of the China's Belt and Road initiative is a game changer, flagship project of both the neighboring states of China and Pakistan. CPEC also considered being the Zipper of Eurasian and African continent that connects most of the OBOR members in Asia, Middle East, Central Asia and the emerging economies of the African nations by a network of rail and road. It's a symbol of their long term diplomatic, political, strategic and economic relations that was based on trust and cooperation from the time of their inception in 1950s. Both the states have based their bilateral relations on common interests and mutual cooperation that led to develop a consensus on the issues related to them, to the regions that surrounded them and to the World in general. The World has associated different terms to their bilateral relations like, "the Iron Brothers, friendship Sweater than Honey Higher than Himalayas, deeper than the Ocean."

The Beijing's interests in Pakistan were increased when the American adopted a mix policy of engagement and containing China. The American presence in Afghanistan, South China Sea and the adopting of Asia pivot policy realize the Chinese leadership to counter the US policy of containing China. The sparks of their policies also emerged in the shape of Malacca Dilemma and the question of sovereignty in the Xinjiang province. For the Beijing, CPEC has political economic and strategic interest that can provide best answers to these gravest and challenged issues of economic and sovereignty. On the other hand for Pakistan, CPEC is counted as an opportunity of millennium as it was shattered by the US War on Terror. Diplomatically, it was isolated in the region, politically it has no role to play, economically it was on the verge of collapse, its infrastructure was heavily devastated but with CPEC, Pakistan got a new life and included in the World top $300 billion economies. Politically, Pakistan also got a new balancer (China) to its traditional rival India by the concept of balance of threat.

The plan of the study provides a long term comprehensive strategy to rebuild Pakistan politically, economically and strategically that enable to counter India. It also provide Pakistan a network of rail, road, energy and development while on other hand CPEC in its planning declared Gwadar port as a Hub of international business not only for China and Pakistan but also for the three regions of South, Central Asia and Middle East. For China *Gwadar* Port is the initiative of Beijing's maritime dominancy and foot print in the Indian Ocean that could easily surveillance its navigation route. There are some objections on the Beijing's presence in the deep Sea port by the Indian and American but this will not change the plan of the CPEC. Keeping in minds these factors both PRC and Pakistan are well aware of the Challenges that posed threat to the completion and operation of the CPEC. There broadly two type serious threats to CPEC. Internally, like the other mega project in Pakistan the political controversies of different political parties representing divert parts of the state have diverted opinion about the huge investment of Beijing in Pakistan. This political disagreement was also coupled by the Civil-Military relations in Pakistan, which is a permanent issue in understanding the nature of its politics. Externally, the Indian has the gravest concerns about the CPEC as it passes through the *Gilgit-Baltidtan (GB)* which is considered being part of Jammu and Kashmir. China issued many warnings to India not to hurt CPEC but they have their own calculation along with American who also believes on the containment of China and declared a *Hybrid War* on CPEC. So both internal and external challenges have a lot of concerns for both China and Pakistan to handle in the near future.

REFERENCES

Ahmad, I. (2010). The US Af-Pak strategy: Challenges and opportunities for Pakistan. *Asian Affairs: An American Review*, 37–45.

Ahmed, Z. S. (2019). Impact of the China–Pakistan Economic Corridor on nation-building in Pakistan.". *Journal of Contemporary China*, *28*(117), 400–413. doi:10.1080/10670564.2018.1542221

Ali, G. (2022). CPEC: A Gateway to Regional Connectivity. In *Crossing the Himalayas* (pp. 92–99). Springer. doi:10.1007/978-981-16-5808-2_7

Ali., Y. (2022). Risk Assessment in Supply Chain Networks of China–Pakistan Economic Corridor (CPEC). *Chinese Political Science Review*, 3-22.

Amineh, M. P. (2022). China's capitalist industrial development and the emergence of the Belt and Road Initiative. In *The China-led Belt and Road Initiative and its reflections*. Routledge. doi:10.4324/9781003256502-2

Ananthalakshmi, A. K. (2013). *India "concerned" by China role in Pakistan's Gwadar port.* South Asia News.

Andrew, K. (2016). India's Geopolitical Hate for Pakistan is Sabotaging the North-South Corridor. *Katehon*, 4.

Andrew, K. (2017). CPEC and the 21st Century Convergence of Civilizations. *Katehon*, 1-2.

Andrew, K. (2017). The Secret Behind Russia's CPEC Saga. *Regional Rapport, 4.*

Ash, R. F. (1996). The Chinese Economy Under Deng Xiaoping. Shangaye: Clarendon Press.

Baum, R. (1996). *Burying Mao: Chinese politics in the age of Deng Xiaoping*. Princeton University Press.

Bradsher, K. (2017). U.S. Firms Want In on China's Global 'One Belt, One Road' Spending. *The New York Times*.

Breslin, S. (2013). China and the global order: Signalling threat or friendship? *International Affairs*, *89*(3), 123–234. doi:10.1111/1468-2346.12036

Brewster, D. (2016). Silk Roads and Strings of Pearls: The Strategic Geography of China's New Pathways in the Indian Ocean. *Geopolitics*, 6-13.

Chung, C. P. (2006). Confronting terrorism and other evils in China: all quiet on the western front?. *Unknown*, 12-23.

Clarke, M. (2007). China's Internal Security Dilemma and the "Great Western Development": The Dynamics of Integration, Ethnic Nationalism and Terrorism in Xinjiang. *Asian Studies Review*, *31*(3), 31–45. doi:10.1080/10357820701621350

Economy, E. C. (2014). China's Imperial President: Xi Jinping Tightens His Grip. *Foreign Affairs*, 80–99.

Editorial. (2017, January 7). *Sixth JCC on CPEC.* Islamabad, Pakistan: Parliaments Times.

Fallon, T. (2015). The new silk road: Xi Jinping's grand strategy for Eurasia. *American Foreign Policy Interests*, 112-134.

Fazil, M. D. (2016). 5 Reasons Gwadar Port Trumps Chabahar. *The Diplomate*, 2.

Ferdinand, P. (2016). Westward ho—the China dream and 'one belt, one road': Chinese foreign policy under Xi Jinping. *International Affairs*, *92*(4), 62–71. doi:10.1111/1468-2346.12660

Grieger, G. (2016). One Belt, One Road (OBOR): China's regional integration initiative. European Parliamentry Research Service, 1-5.

Guihong, Z. (2003). US security policy towards South Asia after September 11 and its Implications for China: a Chinese perspective. *Strategic Analysis*, 24-34.

Hali, S. M. (2016). One Belt and One Road: Impact on China-Pakistan Economic Corridor. *Strategic Studies*, 12-18.

Hsu, S. (2017). *Trump's Support For China's One Belt, One Road Initiative Is Bad For U.S., Good For World*. Forbes.

Jeganaathan, J. (2015). OBOR'and South Asia: Can India and China Cope with the Emerging 'New Normal'in the Region? *Fudan Journal of the Humanities and Social Sciences*, 12–19.

Korybko, A. (2015). Pakistan is the "Zipper" of Pan-Euroasian Integration. Russian Institute of Strategic Studies, 1.

Korybko, A. (2017). Pakistan's Response to Hybrid War on CPEC? *Regional Rapport*, 1-3.

Lim, A. C. (2016). China's 'Belt and Road' and Southeast Asia: Challenges and Prospects. *IPP Review*, 22-27.

Lo, C. (2015). China's Silk Road strategy. *The International Economy*, 29-34.

Louis, R. (2015). The China-Pakistan Economic Corridor. Regional Dynamics and China's Geopolitical Ambitions. The National Bureau of Asian Research.

Malik, D. A. (2017). Modi's Perversion of the CPEC. Institute of Strategic Studies, 1-2.

McCartney, M. (2022). *The Dragon from the Mountains: The China-Pakistan Economic Corridor (CPEC) from Kashgar to Gwadar*. Cambridge University Press.

Pereire, K. G. (2006). Jihad in China? Rise of the East Turkestan Islamic Movement (ETIM). Institute of Defence and Strategic Studies Commentaries, 12-23.

Shiyuan, H. (2002). Ethno-Separatism and Terrorism. *Ethonational Studies*, 4-25.

Sing, G. (2016, March 9). *Chinese support to Pakistan*. New Delhi, India: Ministry of External Affairs.

Singh, P. (2015). The China Pakistan Economic Corridor and India. Institute of Defence Studies and Analyses, 3.

Tariq Ali, J. H. (2022). Bilateral Economic Impacts of China–Pakistan Economic Corridor.". *Agriculture*, 144.

Ullah, S. H. (2022). Empirical nexus between Chinese investment under China–Pakistan Economic Corridor and economic growth: An ARDL approach. *Cogent Business & Management*.

Wayne, M. I. (2007). *China's War on Terrorism: Counter-Insurgency, Politics and Internal Security*. Routledge. doi:10.4324/9780203936139

Wolf, S. O. (2021). *China-Pakistan Economic Corridor of the Belt and Road Initiative*. Springer.

Zimmerman, T. (2015). The New Silk Roads: China, the US, and the Future of Central Asia. *NYU Center on International Cooperation*, 13-15.

Chapter 5
Do the Belt and Road Initiative and Chinese Investments Promote Moroccan FDI in African Countries?
An Empirical Investigation Using Panel Data

Jihad Ait Soussane
Economics, Ibn Tofail University, Morocco

Zahra Mansouri
Economics, Ibn Tofail University, Morocco

ABSTRACT

This chapter analyzes the role played by Chinese investment within the Belt and Road Initiative (BRI) in promoting outward FDI from Morocco to African countries. The authors used panel data of 29 African countries from 2004 to 2021 and robust weighted least squares (RWLS) with m-estimation and Welsch function. The empirical results confirmed that inflows of Chinese FDI attract Moroccan FDI outflows in African countries because of the signal effect that these countries are "good locations" for investment. Secondly, the authors found that joining the BRI affects Moroccan FDI positively in African countries due to the commitment of these countries to improve their institutional quality related to the protection of property rights and enforcement of contracts. Finally, the findings suggest that Chinese FDI inflows and the BRI moderate positively the effect of infrastructure (transport, ITC, etc.) on the attraction of Moroccan FDI in African countries.

DOI: 10.4018/978-1-7998-8021-9.ch005

INTRODUCTION

The rise of competition in developed economies pushes foreign investors to think of African territories since it is becoming an area of entrepreneurial development and a strategic partner for any economy. Africa has become the new Eldorado of the global economy. According to Mckinsey Global Institute (Bughin et al.,2016), the African emergence can take place on the horizon of 2040 due to three main factors: a demographic potential through population densification of 1.1 billion people of working age, the rise in commodity prices that will increase the Gross Domestic Product up to 3 billion USD, and the emergence of a middle class of 128 million households with a regular income and a significant consumption expenditure.

On the one hand, Morocco presents itself in Africa through its multinational enterprises (MNEs). Moroccan direct investment flows in sub-Saharan Africa experienced an average annual growth rate of 4.5% between 2008 and 2016. In addition, the average annual flows of these FDI to sub-Saharan Africa is estimated at 100 million USD in 2010, representing 92% of the total flow of Moroccan direct investments abroad. In 2015, these average annual flows were estimated at 300 million USD, representing 40% of the flow of Moroccan direct investments abroad. The top receivers of Moroccan FDI flows are Cote d'Ivoire and Nigeria. Moreover, the sectoral distribution of Moroccan FDI flows is 44% in the banking sector, 21% in the holding company, 9% in real estate, and the rest in telecommunications, transport, insurance, energy, and mining (Office des Changes, 2017).

On the other hand, China is also present in Africa within the Belt and Road Initiative. Bilaterally, China has invested in 49 African countries which have already signed memoranda of understanding. Geographically, 22 countries in West Africa, 12 countries in East Africa, 9 in North Africa, and six countries in Central Africa. These memoranda of understanding formalize Chinese FDI in African countries with the recognition of local governments. It facilitates the investment process for Chinese MNEs in these countries[1].

Generally, the Belt and Road Initiative projects in Africa are emerging in sectors related to infrastructure and logistics to improve territorial competitiveness in Africa. China is investing in ports and port areas along the coastline from the Gulf of Aden to the Suez Canal to the Mediterranean Sea. In addition, China uses its connectivity projects (20% of all its projects in Africa, including rail and road lines) to link its industrial (10% of all its projects, including mineral processing) and energy projects (15% of all its projects, including oil and renewables) in the African hinterland to infrastructure projects (nearly 45 percent of all its projects, including ports) along the coastline African. It appears to have made significant progress on the Mali-Guinea cross-border railway project, the Chad-Cameroon pipeline, Sudan (Port Sudan) –Chad – Niger – Mali-Senegal (Port of Dakar) rail line, and the Central African Republic-Chad water diversion project (Transaqua Project).

The research conducted by this chapter is of great interest to public decision-makers and the private sector as joining the Belt and Road Initiative is an indicator of the territorial competitiveness of African countries. The African continent remains a black box for foreign investors because information on economic stability, macroeconomic aggregates, and any relevant information for investors are not published or reliable. To this end, foreignness liability remains a thing for any firm wishing to invest in Africa. However, the Belt and Road Initiative is a good indicator of territorial performance, and it is a sign of the territorial health of host countries insofar as the massiveness and importance of Chinese investments constitute a signal effect for other investors so that they can follow the Chinese by minimizing the risks associated with ignorance of the local business climate in Africa[2].

This chapter aims to study the effect of the Belt and Road Initiative on the location choice of Moroccan FDI in African countries. In other words, the authors will conduct an empirical investigation using the hypothesis testing method to validate the idea that Chinese infrastructure investments contribute to the African attractiveness of inward FDI in general and Moroccan FDI in particular.

Hence, this chapter analyzes the direct effect of Chinese FDI and joining the Belt and Road Initiative on Moroccan FDI in Africa. The first two hypotheses considered Chinese investments as an explanatory variable of Moroccan FDI in Africa in the context of the literature on the signal and agglomeration effects explained below. Furthermore, the chapter analyzes the indirect impact of Chinese FDI and joining the Belt and Road Initiative on Moroccan FDI in Africa. The third hypothesis considers Chinese investments as a moderating variable that indirectly impacts Moroccan FDI by improving the effectiveness of other infrastructure-related determinants of FDI like logistics performance, information & communication technologies, and energy supply.

The theoretical framework of the research topic resorts to models related to international economics and international business. The research hypothesis deals with FDI as an explanatory variable and a dependent variable simultaneously. Thus, the eclectic paradigm introduced by Dunning (1988) explains the dynamics between different country-origin of FDI. In addition, the Economic Geography model, developed initially by Krugman (1991), explains the role of the agglomeration effect on FDI attraction. The authors built the conceptual framework on three hypotheses that fill the research gap in the literature on FDI location choice, which omits the impact of investment treaties and investment from a given country on the FDI location choice of a third-party country.

From this reflection, the central research hypothesis is as follows: To what extent do Chinese investments and joining the Belt and Road Initiative play a role in the location decision of Moroccan FDI in Africa? Practically, research hypotheses are as follows: Do Chinese investments constitute a signal effect for Moroccan FDI in Africa? Does joining the Belt and Road Initiative motivate Moroccan Multinational-Enterprises to locate their investment in African countries? Do joining the BRI and Chinese investment positively moderate Moroccan FDI location decisions in African countries? The empirical analysis works on panel data of 29 African countries from 2004 to 2021 using Robust weighted least square (RWLS) with M-estimation.

The chapter is organized as follows: the first section discusses the theoretical framework on which the research hypothesis is based. The second section presents the conceptual framework by developing the hypotheses within a literature review. The third section explains the empirical strategy, and the fourth section discusses empirical results.

THEORETICAL FRAMEWORK

The central research hypothesis argues that Moroccan FDI follows Chinese FDI invested in African countries because Chinese investment is supposed to affect the African economy positively and encourages other countries like Morocco to invest within. In other words, the relationship between FDI and the economic variables of the host country is circular. Hence, the theoretical framework considers models explaining the dynamic between FDI and the host economy.

The eclectic paradigm of Dunning (1988) represents one of the foundations of the integrative approach that explains FDI movements and determines their impacts on the host economy in circular logic. In other words, a country-specific advantage may become firm-specific and vice versa. It is a double game: for example, when a country develops its specific advantages, it enhances the attraction of FDI. Additional investment emerges with new country-specific advantages, which will allow its emerging firms to improve their Ownership. Ownership denotes the firm-specific advantages which depend on the host country-specific advantages and chosen penetration mode to gain market share. Location indicates country-specific advantages influenced by the firm-specific advantages that lead them to control Research & Development and the penetration modes as if firms set up a head office in the country. Internalization denotes a process that depends on the advantages provided by the host country and firm-specific advantages.

However, internationalization theories have often focused on the FDI location determinants by excluding the spatial effect of location choice, which explains the empirical invalidity of several models in some cases. Krugman (1991) argues that spatial variables and geography play a significant role in the location choices of FDI, thus explaining their impact on host economies. This model is called Economic Geography.

The spatial organization of industrial activity is the cornerstone of the contribution of Krugman's model, where forces are acting on the balances of the location of foreign direct investment. These FDI location balances result from the spatial and temporal confrontation between two forces as follows:

- Centripetal forces: these are forces that opt for the polarization of industrial activities.
- Centrifugal forces: these are forces that opt for the dispersion of industrial activities.

Krugman proposes a structure of monopolistic competition where there are two sectors, manufactured and agricultural, and two regions. First, this model assumes the following three assumptions:

1. There is an increasing return to scale in both sectors. The manufacturing sectors produce differentiated goods and services, while the agricultural sectors produce homogeneous goods.
2. Perfect mobility of labor factors in the manufacturing sectors while labor factors in the agricultural sectors are immobile on an international scale.
3. The existence of economies of scale and decreasing transportation costs between the two regions generate the center-periphery structure with an agglomeration of industrial activities in the form of clusters. These transport costs are of the 'iceberg' type. The iceberg transportation cost model is a simple economic model based on paying the cost of transporting a good with a portion of the transported good rather than other resources.

Assuming that the labor factor is perfectly mobile between regions, the increase in the real wage pushes workers to move towards the industrial center, which will generate an accumulation of the labor factor in this industrial center, resulting in an agglomeration business in this location. Consequently, the central region is experiencing an increase in the variety of goods and services produced by this agglomeration, which partially explains the decrease in the price index of manufactured goods and, Ipso facto, an increase in the real wage. For the peripheral region, this interregional migratory movement accompanied by the agglomeration of industrial activities leads to a dispersion of agricultural activities.

Krugman explains the phenomenon of the agglomeration of industrial activities in the central region by introducing the of Vertical-Linkage effects, upstream and downstream, as follows:

- The upstream Backward-Linkage effect is when firms seek a region where there is perfect labor mobility allowing the worker to move towards this center by taking advantage of the increase in wages real.
- The downstream Forward-Linkage effect is when firms seek regions where consumers opt for the diversity of goods and services.

Roughly speaking, according to Krugman's model (1991), mobile labor represents the centripetal force in the appearance of agglomerations. Furthermore, districts and clusters are distinguished:

- In the broad sense, an industrial district is an agglomeration of firms that produce and market goods & services of the same sector.
- In the strict sense, a cluster is a concentration of firms that benefit from a network along the production chain (suppliers, customers, and competitors), competitive factors of production (skilled labor and capital), and institutional factors (government spending and good governance) (Carlos, 2005).

However, the models of Economic Geography proposed and developed by several authors (Krugman, 1991; Baldwin, 1999; Krugman & Venables, 1995) cannot explain the location equilibria of foreign direct investment in the form of an agglomeration due to the omission of other centripetal forces (technological spillovers, positive externalities, network effect, public spending) and other centrifugal forces (sclerosis of innovation, congestion phenomenon, negative externalities). These new contributions are input into what is called the New Economic Geography.

Krugman introduced the New Economic Geography to fill the gaps of the classical Economic Geography, in which it opts to explain the spatial distribution of industrial activities in the form of FDI by integrating other centripetal forces and centrifugal as omitted variables in the old model:

- The centripetal, or agglomeration, forces added by this model are any factor related to the search of multinational firms for suppliers of raw materials and intermediate goods, qualified human capital, and proximity to the market. Thus, the positive externalities result from the firms participating in this agglomeration.
- Centrifugal forces are all factors related to negative externalities that arise when centripetal forces exceed their optimal thresholds as congestion, pollution, and rivalry, which causes fierce competition between firms and the dispersion of these industrial activities.

In other words, the agglomerations of economic activities may also induce congestion and possible deagglomeration economies so that a net effect of agglomeration economies will only be present if this compensates more than these countervailing forces (costs (Saito & Wu, 2016; Jones, 2016, De Groot et al. 2016).

However, Mainguy (2004) argues that it is difficult to separate the determinants of FDI from their impact on host economies in this model because the causation between FDI and economic factors has a circular logic. For instance, economic growth in the host country causes the emergence of agglomerations in the central region in which firms begin to achieve significant economies of scale, competitiveness, and increase in Research & Development. Consequently, MNEs are attracted to the performance and establish themselves through FDI. These investments will contribute to economic growth. It's a two-way game.

However, Mainguy argues that MNE prefers the most attractive territories in terms of better infrastructure, well-trained human capital, strong demand, and a structure of foreign trade (imports and exports).

LITERATURE REVIEW AND HYPOTHESES DEVELOPMENT

Hypothesis 1: Chinese FDI in African Countries Positively Affect Moroccan FDI

The literature has recognized the importance of firm agglomeration, through which it externalizes benefits to other offshoring firms. Marshal (1920) is the pioneer in highlighting this effect. Moreover, the paradigm of the New Geographical Economy (Krugman & Venables, 1996) presents three conditions so the agglomeration can make a profit for the companies: 1/ the effects of spillover between firms. 2/ the access to production factors (labor and capital) relevant to overly specialized sectors. 3/ Vertical linkage. If all these conditions come together, agglomeration would allow firms to achieve efficiency. However, Decoster and Strange (1993) argue that despite the absence of these conditions so the agglomeration effect can be efficient, firms decide to follow other conglomerate firms because, from a rational point of view, in an uncertain business climate and a new territory to invest in, companies prefer to mitigate the risks by imitating the footsteps of other companies and following them towards the agglomerations.

Moreover, a previously existing investment constitutes a signal to other investors that it is a 'good location' to locate projects where profitability is high compared to the 'bad location', which does not have a pre-existing investment significantly. It pushes companies to understand the mechanism of choice and be encouraged to choose the 'good location' for their investment.

Empirically, the majority of studies at that time did not separate between the Marshal-like efficiency factor and the demonstration effect and measured agglomeration at the aggregate level without distinguishing between domestic and foreign firms. Head et al. (1995) were the first to disaggregate the agglomeration effect by studying Japanese sectoral FDI in the regions of the United States during the 1980s using conditional logit regression. They concluded that the number of Japanese subsidiaries established influences the location decision of Japanese FDI more than the number of domestic American firms.

Krugman (1997) joins Decoster and Strange in pointing out that as foreign firms face more uncertainties than domestic firms in the host country, they may have strong incentives to follow previous investors because of the signal they send relative to the reliability of the host country location. In other words, even if the efficiency reasons for the development of Marshall agglomerations are not many or complete, firms may choose the identical location country because of demonstration effects. Krugman (1997) and Barry and Bradley (1997) alluded to such demonstration effects when discussing the strong growth of inward FDI in Ireland over the past 15 years.

Barry and Bradley (1997) claim that surveys of executives of newly arrived firms in the computer, instrument engineering, pharmaceutical, and chemical industries indicate that their location decision is affected strongly by other key market players already located in Ireland. Krugman (1997) argues that Ireland now has the advantage as a reliable host country for new investors. For example, in the electronics industry, Ireland hosts 20 American high-tech companies in the top 25 (White, 2000). According to Krugman (1997), this demonstration effect attracts other firms setting up in Ireland close to the large companies in the sector. According to Barry et al. (2001), for several reasons, Ireland provides an insightful case for investigating the importance of efficiency agglomeration effects in attracting inward FDI: First, there is the strong presence of foreign-owned multinational firms in the Irish economy, as shown by data from the Irish Census of Industrial Production: in 1998, foreign multinationals accounted for 47% of manufacturing employment, 82% percent of net production, and 88 percent of manufacturing exports. Second, the substantial presence of foreign-invested firms in the high-tech sector allows us to analyze the relative importance of traditional agglomeration and demonstrate effects between sectors differentiated by the degree of technology. Third, the differences between US firms and the second most predominant source country (UK). The illustrative differences show that US-owned firms have much higher labor productivity than UK firms, are much more export-oriented, and are more likely to be located in high-tech sectors.

The majority of studies have concluded a positive impact of agglomeration on FDI. Coughlin et al. (1991) studied a panel of 50 American states from 1981 to 1983 using the conditional Logit estimation technique. They used the logarithm of employment as a measure of agglomeration. These authors use employment as Hilber & Voicu (2007) for the case of 31 regions of Romania from 1990 to 1997 and Blonigen et al. (2005) for 11 countries from 1985 to 1991. Wheeler & Mody (1992) studied 42 countries from 1982 to 1988 using the OLS method and the logarithm of the infrastructure/industrialization index as a proxy for agglomeration. Woodward (1992) analyzed the case of 324 regions in the American United States between 1980 and 1989 using the logarithm variable of the number of foreign affiliates. Braunerhjelm & Svensson (1996) studied 18 OECD member countries from 1978 to 1990 using the employee share as an agglomeration proxy. Barrell & Pain (1998) studied a panel of 9 European countries during the period 1967-1996 using the logarithm of the stock of FDI in the host country. Also, Hubert and Pain (2002) for 8 European countries during 1981-1996. Ford and Strange (1999) used FDI flows per capita for 7 European countries from 1980 to 1995. Urata and Kawai (2000) used the Log of FDI flows for 81 Turkish regions from 1996 to 2003.

These studies used the logarithm of the number of firms: Crozet et al. (2004) for 92 French regions from 1985 to 1995 and Disdier and Mayer (2004) for 19 European countries from 1980 to 1999. Debaere et al. (2010) for 29 Chinese regions during 1992-2004, Defever (2006) for 23 European countries during 1997-2002, Hong (2009) for 21 regions of China, and Devereux et al. (2007) for 88 regions of the United Kingdom during 1986-1992, Basile et al. (2009) for 47 European regions during the period 1991-1999. However, a few studies have found that agglomeration can determine FDI. Smith and Florida (1994) studied 3112 American regions in 1988 using the distance to assemble as a proxy. Sun et al. (2002) used the logarithm of cumulative FDI flows for 36 Chinese regions from 1986 to 1998 and found a negative impact on FDI. Békés (2006) used the logarithm of population density for 20 regions of Hungary from 1990 to 1995. Ramasamy et al. (2012) used the number of projects per output for 59 countries from 2006 to 2008.

Vide (2014) investigates FDI location decision factors of Austrian and German MNE in Brazil. The author used a multinomial nested logit model to show that FDI-specific country agglomeration (investor-nation), industry-specific sector, labor quality, and physical infrastructure were the important FDI location decision factors for German and Austrian MNE in Brazil. Young & Shi-Young (2015) studied the agglomeration effects on Korean MNEs' location decisions. They concluded positive agglomeration effects on vertical FDI and negative ones on horizontal FDI. However, they indicate that vertical FDI occurs after worldwide MNE position themselves, and, thus, vertical FDI can be operated to increase access to new markets and reduce agglomeration effects.

Agustina & Flath (2019) studied the different types of agglomeration for the location decision of greenfield FDI in the manufacturing sector in Indonesia. Using the multinomial logit model and micro-level data of principle licenses from the Indonesia Investment Coordinating Board (IICB), the authors concluded that the agglomeration shows a significant and positive but small impact compared to other factors like infrastructure and the labor market. Choi et al. (2020) examined the determinants of Chinese outward FDI, especially the preexistent FDI coming from China. Using panel data of outward Chinese FDI in 18 countries in the period 1997–2017 and the random-effects GLS model, the authors found that agglomeration of preexistent Chinese MNE has a significant effect on outward FDI from China, which means that agglomeration of Chinese firms in host countries has predictive power for Chinese MNE location choices.

Hypothesis 2: Signing on the BRI by African Countries Positively Affects Moroccan FDI

The authors present the hypothesis claiming that investment agreements between China and African countries may constitute a determinant of Moroccan FDI. Despite that literature focused on the effect of bilateral investment treaties (BIT) on bilateral FDI, the authors argue that bilateral investment treaties affect FDI inflows from a third country. The authors deduct from the literature two explanations of which establishing a BIT can promote inward FDI to developing countries from third-party countries as follows:

- The signaling effect: Signing a BIT signals to other countries that the host country is serious about improving its property rights. This improvement is relevant to other foreign investors, not only from the BIT contracting countries.
- Improved institutional quality: signing a BIT may be considered a way to improve the quality of formal institutional and good governance. In Other Words, when a developed country signs a BIT with a developing country, investors from other countries consider it an improvement of the institutional quality of the host country and increase their FDI outflows.

Signing an investment treaty signals to foreign investors that the host country is susceptible to providing a favorable business climate to MNE clear from corruption, expropriation, and other traits of low institutional quality. However, the BRI is an informal network of states agreeing under non-binding Memorandums of Understanding (MOUs). In other words, BRI is not a ratified or signed investment agreement. Some BRI participants signed a BIT with China, while others did not. It could limit the commitment effect that reduces risks and increase bilateral FDI. While the signaling effects may be relevant for any level of the international investment agreement, the commitment effect is significant only when the signing parties ratify the BIT.

Empirical studies have found a positive impact of BITs on FDI, from which this chapter suggests few. Egger & Pfaffermayer (2004) confirmed the signaling effect concluding that both signed and ratified BITs positively affect the stock of outward FDI of 19 home countries and 54 host countries from 1982 to 1997. While both investment agreement types have a positive effect, they find that ratified treaties have a superior impact than those merely signed, which indicates that investment treaties have a more significant commitment effect than the signaling effect. Elkins et al. (2006) and Neumayer & Spress (2005) find that all forms of bilateral investment agreements signal to foreign investors that the host country is prepared to undertake liberal reforms regarding its business climate and legal system.

Furthermore, few studies have analyzed the effect of the BRI on outward Chinese FDI: Hofman (2016) argues that Tajikistan may welcome Chinese MNE operating in farmland investment after signing the BRI to help develop its agriculture market. Huang et al. (2017) use a case study to highlight environmental and social challenges facing Pakistan when engaging in the BRI and receiving Chinese FDI. They also emphasize the positive attitude of Pakistan towards Chinese outward FDI after sinning on the BRI. Yu et al. (2019) studied the Chinese outward FDI. Overall, the BRI positively impacts Chinese FDI activities. However, the direction and magnitude of this impact depend on the host countries' willingness to participate in the initiative. The BRI promotes more outward FDI to developing countries that welcome China's economic engagement and alters the effect of Chinese domestic push factors on the patterns of its outward FDI. In addition, Chinese firms in construction and infrastructure, manufacturing, and trade-related sectors are more responsive to the BRI than firms in other sectors.

Hypothesis 3: Signing on the BRI and Increasing Chinese FDI Positively Moderate the Effect of Infrastructure of African Countries on Moroccan FDI

The literature has widely recognized the role of infrastructure in FDI attractiveness, as a well-developed infrastructure improves market interconnectivity and FDI attractiveness (Donaubauer et al., 2016), while poor quality of infrastructure disrupts connectivity between market players, hence hindering the entry of FDI (Pradhan et al., 2013).

In general, good quality of infrastructure leads to lower trade-related costs and improves Doing Business, which affects the attractiveness of FDI by providing a good infrastructure as a comparative advantage (Donaubauer et al., 2016).

Dumon (2014) argues that FDIs affected by the infrastructure are generally of the efficiency-seeking type because good infrastructure is a set of efficient transport systems, efficient communication systems, a reliable energy supply, and reliable water and waste management system.

However, infrastructure may not affect FDI inflows due to the hypothesis that infrastructure may be endogenous: Pradhan et al. (2013) argue that FDI brings technology to host countries which improves the quality of their infrastructure.

The empirical literature agrees that the infrastructure positively impacts the inflows of FDI by using different variables to represent the whole infrastructure. Wheeler and Mody (1992) studied American FDI in 42 developing countries between 1982 and 1984, where they found that the quality of infrastructure (energy, communication, and transport) positively impacts American FDI. They added that American MNEs are interested in the infrastructure of the developing countries but indifferent when it comes to the developed countries because they assume that they already have a good infrastructure. Therefore, an improvement in the level of their infrastructure has a negligible marginal impact on the economy.

Cheng & Kwan (2000) worked on the case of Hong Kong and Singapore and found that good infrastructure attracts FDI. Houghwout (2001) showed that public infrastructure impacts FDI indirectly through the spillover effects generated by clusters and agglomeration. Nunnenkamp & Spatz (2002) analyzed the case of Pakistan and Nepal. They concluded that the poor quality of the infrastructure hinders FDI. Asiedu (2002) worked in 34 sub-Saharan countries from 1980 to 2000 using the OLS method. She found that the development of infrastructure positively impacts FDI, of which an increase of 1 unit of infrastructure causes an increase in FDI per capita of 1.12%.

Fung et al. (2005) studied FDI in China and concluded that both types of infrastructure positively impact FDI, with a superior impact of physical infrastructure on FDI than the communicational. Castro et al. (2007) studied the role of road networks using two proxy variables, the number of paved roads per capita and the total length of roads per capita. They found that a 10% increase in the road leads to a 17-33% increase in FDI, and an increase in energy supply causes a 12-14% high in FDI. Kazembe &

Namizinga (2007) studied the case of Malawi and found that firms operated efficiently and produced goods at a lower cost due to the existence of good infrastructure. Similarly, Cordero & Paus (2008) analyzed the case of Costa Rica and concluded that they succeeded in attracting FDI thanks to flexible access to roads, good communication, and continuous access to water and electricity at reasonable costs.

Seetanah (2009) studied the impact of transport and non-transport infrastructure on service and manufacturing FDI in Mauritius over the period 1981-to 2005. He concluded that transport infrastructure positively impacts manufacturing FDI and non-transport infrastructure positively impacts service FDI. Jordaan (2004) demonstrated that the quality of the infrastructure increases the productivity of the investment that attracts FDI by taking the case of telecommunications (the number of telephone lines as a proxy). However, the author argues that the availability of the infrastructure is not sufficient because it is necessary to consider its reliability also. Straub (2011) studied the case of developing countries with poor infrastructure that significantly paralyzes the attraction of FDI. Rehman et al. (2011) studied the case of Pakistan during the period 1975-2008, where they found that infrastructure positively impacts short-term and long-term FDI. Babatunde (2011) studied a panel of sub-Saharan countries from 1980 to 2003. The author concluded that infrastructure positively impacts FDI under the premise of open trade. Voorpijl (2011) studied the case of Kenya and found that availability and access to good infrastructure networks is a determinant of FDI.

Chakrabarti et al. (2012) empirically analyzed the relationship between FDI and physical infrastructure in India over the period 2002-to 2007. They concluded a non-linear impact of infrastructure on FDIs whose FDIs are insensitive to infrastructure only to the delay of a given point. Benhame (2012) studied a panel of Asian countries between 1980 and 2009 and found that urban infrastructure positively impacts FDI. Anyadike (2012) studied the case of Nigeria between 2000-2010 and worked on many forms of infrastructures such as road networks and energy supply. He found that poor infrastructure negatively impacts FDI. Ang (2012) studied a panel of Chinese regions and found that infrastructure (physical, technological, and financial) determine FDI through its multiplier effects on openness and access to foreign markets. Moosa (2012) analyzed a panel of 18 Arab countries and found that energy availability is a relevant determinant for efficiency-seeking FDI. Dumon (2014) argues that market-seeking FDI is interested in well-maintained infrastructure because sales of goods and services in territory require a good infrastructure of roads, highways, ports, and other forms of infrastructure. It lowers transport costs, increases the return on investment, and attracts FDI.

RESEARCH DESIGN AND METHODOLOGY

Sample Description and Data Sources

The empirical study works on panel data of 29 African countries during the period 2004-2021. The sample selection is due to the significance of foreign investment of Moroccan and Chinese firms in those countries. Therefore, those absent from the data are because the investment within is too non-significant to consider. The sample countries are Algeria, Benin, Burkina Faso, Cameroon, Chad, Congo, Democratic Republic of Congo, Ivory Coast, Egypt, Ethiopia, Gabon, Ghana, Guinea, Guinea-Bissau, Equatorial Guinea, Kenya, Madagascar, Mali, Mauritius, Mauritania, Niger, Nigeria, Central-African Republic, Rwanda, Senegal, Tanzania, Togo, Tunisia, and Uganda.

The data on foreign direct investment are collected from the database of The International Trade Center[3]. Data on the countries joining the BRI are from Green Finance & Development Center database[4]. The source of data on infrastructure variables is all taken from the database of the World Bank[5].

Variables Description

According to the research topic, the authors aim to identify the role of China in the location decision of Moroccan firms in African countries. Therefore, foreign direct investment (FDI) is the practical proxy variable usually used when dealing with this research topic on internationalization and multinational enterprises. In particular, the authors use the flow of outward FDI of Moroccan investors. In addition, the authors use a binary variable to indicate joining BRI: 0 is before the BRI, and 1 is after the BRI. For the infrastructure variables, they are presented as follows:

The access to electricity rate is the percentage of the country's population with access to electricity. Air transported freight is the volume of freight, express, and diplomatic bags measured by million in metric tons times kilometers traveled carried on each flight stage. Internet users' rate is the percentage of the population using the Internet from any location in the last three months via a computer, mobile phone, or personal digital. Logistics Performance Index score indicates the perceptions of a country's logistics based on the efficiency of customs clearance processes, quality of trade and related transport infrastructure, ease of arranging shipments at competitive prices, the quality of infrastructure services, the ability to track and trace consignments, and the frequency with which shipments arrive at the consignee on time. The index ranges from 1 to 5, and the highest score represents the best performance.

The Liner Shipping Connectivity Index captures how well countries are connected to global shipping networks. It is based on five components of the maritime transport sector: the number of ships, their container-carrying capacity, maximum vessel size, number of services, and number of companies that deploy container ships in a country's ports. The scores of this index range from 0 for the worst to 100 for the best. Ores and metals exports are the percentages of ores and metals in merchandise exports.

Empirical Model

To identify the role played by China in Morocco's FDI location decision, the authors formulate the general hypothesis as a linear equation to measure the marginal effect of Chinese FDI and BRI on Moroccan outward FDI into African counties as follows:

The dependent variable is the Moroccan foreign direct investment regressed by the independent variables relative to the Chinese investment within the sample countries in Africa. Additionally, the authors use Chinese involvement as an auxiliary variable to control the effect of infrastructure development on the investment behavior of Moroccan MNE. The following equations capture the research hypotheses:

$$FDI_{it} = \alpha_i + \beta_1 FDIC_{it} + \beta_2 (FDIC.AER)_{it} + \beta_3 (FDIC.ATF)_{it} + \beta_4 (FDIC.IUR)_{it} + \beta_5 (FDIC.LPI)_{it} + \beta_6 (FDIC.LSCI)_{it} + \beta_7 (FDIC.OME)_{it} + \varepsilon_{it} \quad (1)$$

$$FDI_{it} = \alpha_i + \beta_1 BRI_{it} + \beta_2(BRI.AER)_{it} + \beta_3(BRI.ATF)_{it} + \beta_4(BRI.IUR)_{it}$$
$$+\beta_5(BRI.LPI)_{it} + \beta_6(BRI.LSCI)_{it} + \beta_7(BRI.OME)_{it} + \varepsilon_{it} \quad (2)$$

FDI_{it} denotes the flow of outward Moroccan FDI in millions of USD into African country i in year t. $FDIC_{it}$ denotes the flow of outward Chinese FDI in millions of USD into African country i in year t. AER_{it} indicates the access to electricity rate in the African country i in year t in percentage, ATF_{it} denotes the airport transported freight in African country i in year t in millions of tones. IUR_{it} denotes the internet user rate in African country i in year t in percentage. LPI_{it} denotes the logistic performance index of African country i in year t ranging in a scale from 1 to 5. $LSCI_{it}$ denotes the Linear Shipping connectivity index of African country i in year t ranging from 0 to 100. OME_{it} denotes the ores and metals export the in African country i in year t in percentage. α denotes the specific fixed effect of each country to control for the omitted factors relatively stable over time, and ε is the normally distributed error term.

Equation (1) deals with the first hypothesis claiming that higher inflows of Chinese FDI into African counties attract flows of Moroccan FDI. Equation (2) formulates the second hypothesis that joining BRI affects Moroccan FDI positively toward African countries. The third hypothesis is present in both equations as the moderation effect of Chinese investment on the infrastructure as a determinant of the outflow of Moroccan FDI into African countries.

Estimation Method

The present sample constitutes panel data where N=29 (29 African countries) and T=18 (from 2004 to 2021). Thus, the suitable estimation method is Robust weighted least square (RWLS) with M-estimation. The covariance type for the estimation is Huber Type with Welsch function for the weight. The used Scale estimate used is MAD (zero centered).

RESULTS AND DISCUSSION

Table 1. The effect of Chinese FDI inflows on Moroccan FDI in African countries

Variable	Coefficient	Std. Error	Z-statistic
FDIC	0.144337***	0.006425	22.46319
FDIC*AER	-0.000194***	2.60E-05	-7.461480
FDIC*ATF	5.35E-05***	6.71E-06	7.984565
FDIC*IUR	0.000949***	7.13E-05	13.30912
FDIC*LPI	-0.059600***	0.002669	-22.32804
FDIC*LSCI	0.000408***	5.80E-05	7.036281
FDIC*OME	-0.000360***	5.75E-05	-6.260851
Adjusted Rw^2	0.05372		
Rn^2 statistic	1144.484***		

Note: ***, **, * indicates significate level respectively at 1%, 5% and 10% respectively. Estimation method: Robust weighted least square (RWLS) with M-estimation. The covariance type for the estimation is Huber Type with Welsch function for the weight. Scale estimate used is MAD (zero centered).

Source: Authors' estimates

Table 1 represents the estimate of equation (1) with an included observation of 68 after adjustment. The model is globally significant (Rn^2 statistic is significant at 1% level) with a low level of Adjusted Rw^2 (0.053792) which makes sense because FDI is explained by multiple variables, not only by the agglomeration effect.

The empirical results show that FDIC affects FDIM positively at a significance level of 1%: an increase in Chinese FDI of 1 million USD causes an increase in Moroccan FDI of 0.144337 million USD. The results confirm Hypothesis (1) that Chinese FDI affects Moroccan FDI positively, which means that Chinese FDI plays a significant role in developing host economies and enhances their productivity by transferring technology and know-how. Knowing that Chinese FDI is a sign of a good location, the improvement of the economic climate encourages Moroccan MNE to invest more in African economies.

Additionally, the chapter concludes that infrastructure indicators like Airport transported freight (ATF), Internet user rate (IUR), and Linear Shipping Connectivity Index are moderated positively by Chinese FDI at the significance level of 1%. In other words, an increase in Chinese investment in African economies boost the effect of infrastructure indicators on Moroccan FDI location choice. Other infrastructure indicators (access to electricity rate, Logistic Performance Index, and Ores and metal exports) are negatively affected by Chinese FDI at the significance level of 1%, which means that an increase in Chinese investment in African countries hinders the effect of these infrastructure indicators on Moroccan FDI location choice.

Table 2. The effect of joining BRI on Moroccan FDI in African countries

Variable	Coefficient	Std. Error	Z-statistic
BRI	129.4721***	2.168099	59.71690
BRI*AER	-4.643109***	0.029653	-156.5833
BRI*ATF	0.014648***	0.001881	7.787208
BRI*IUR	4.172284***	0.035455	117.6788
BRI*LPI	24.55159***	0.719233	34.13580
BRI*LSCI	1.762185***	0.016936	104.0500
BRI*OME	-5.876339***	0.034110	-172.2769
Adjusted Rw^2	0.05372		
Rn^2 statistic	1144.484***		

Note: ***, **, * indicates significate level respectively at 1%, 5% and 10% respectively. Estimation method: Robust weighted least square (RWLS) with M-estimation. The covariance type for the estimation is Huber Type with Welsch function for the weight. Scale estimate used is MAD (zero centered).

Source: Authors' estimates

Table 2 represents the estimate of equation (2) with an included observation of 67 after adjustment. The model is globally significant (Rn^2 statistic is significant at 1% level) with a high level of Adjusted Rw^2 (0.868993).

The empirical results show that joining the BRI affects FDIM positively at a significance level of 1%: the mean difference between countries who joined who didn't join the BRI is 129 million USD. The results confirm Hypothesis (2) that joining the BRI by African countries affects Moroccan FDI positively, which means that signing investment treaties with China constitutes a sign to other countries like Moroccan that African countries who joined the BRI are ready to improve the quality of the institution and their business climate. Knowing that they are committed to respecting property rights and contract enforcement, improving the business climate and institutional quality encourages Moroccan MNE to invest more in African countries.

Additionally, the chapter concludes that infrastructure indicators like Airport transported freight (ATF), Internet user's rate (IUR), Logistic Performance Index, and Linear Shipping Connectivity Index are moderated positively by signing the BRI at a significance level of 1%. In other words, joining the BRI by African economies enhance the positive effect of infrastructure indicators as a determinant of Moroccan FDI location choice. Other infrastructure indicators (access to electricity rate, Ores, and metal exports) are negatively affected by joining the BRI at a significance level of 1%, which means that joining the BRI hinders the effect of these infrastructure indicators on Moroccan FDI location choice in African countries.

CONCLUSION

The chapter discusses the role of Chinese investment and the BRI in promoting Moroccan FDI into African countries. To this end, the theoretical framework on which the work is based resorts mainly to internationalization theories like the eclectic paradigm (Dunning, 1988) and Economic Geography (Krugman, 1991).

The conceptual framework consisted of formulating and developing three research hypotheses: The first one claims that Chinese FDI in African countries attracts Moroccan FDI. The second one argues that joining the BRI affects Moroccan FDI positively. The third one argues that Chinese FDI and the BRI moderate the effect of infrastructure on outward FDI in African countries.

The empirical analysis worked on panel data of 29 African countries from 2004 to 2021 using Robust Weighted Least Square (RWLS) estimation method with M-estimation and Welsch function for the weight. The empirical results confirm Hypothesis (1) that Chinese FDI causes an increase in outflow of Moroccan FDI as a sign of a 'good location' to invest. Equally, Hypothesis (2) is confirmed in the extent that joining the BRI attracts Moroccan FDI into African countries because signing an investment treaty constitutes a signal and commitment effect that the developing is willing to improve institutional quality like protecting pretty rights and enforcing contracts. Finally, the empirical tests confirm Hypothesis (3) that Chinese investments positively moderate the effect of infrastructure on Moroccan FDI.

The implication of the findings: establishing bilateral relations with China seems beneficial to the extent that investment within the Belt and Road Initiative enhances the infrastructure quality and promotes FDI attractiveness. Thus, the decision-makers should recognize the mutually beneficial cooperation with China as a global economic power that aims to develop its partner.

The future research topics will deal with the effect of BRI on the FDI attractiveness of other regions like Europe, Asia, and the Americas, to compare the results with the present study.

REFERENCES

Agustina, A., & Flath, D. (2019). Agglomeration and Location Decision of Foreign Direct Investment (FDI) in Indonesia. *Jurnal Ekonomi & Kebijakan Publik*, *10*(2), 87–98. doi:10.22212/jekp.v10i2.1477

Ang, J. B. (2012). Determinants of Foreign Direct Investment in China. *Journal of Policy Modeling*, *30*(3), 185–189.

Anyadike, N. O. (2012). Poor Infrastructure: The Hindrance to Foreign Investment and Economic Development in Nigeria. *Interdisciplinary Journal of Contemporary Research in Business*, *4*(4), 1–15.

Asiedu, E. (2002). On the Determinants of Foreign Direct Investment to Developing Countries: Is Africa Different? *World Development*, *30*(1), 107–119. doi:10.1016/S0305-750X(01)00100-0

Babatunde, A. (2011). Trade Openness, Infrastructure, FDI and Growth in Sub-Saharan African Countries. *Journal of Management Policy and Practice*, *2*(7), 27–36.

Baldwin, R. E. (1999). Agglomeration and endogenous capital. *European Economic Review*, *43*(2), 253–280. doi:10.1016/S0014-2921(98)00067-1

Barrell, R., & Pain, N. (1998). Real exchange rates, agglomerations, and irreversibilities: Macroeconomic policy and FDI in EMU. *Oxford Review of Economic Policy*, *14*(3), 152–167. doi:10.1093/oxrep/14.3.152

Barry, F., & Bradley, J. (1997). FDI and Trade: The Irish Host-Country Experience. *Economic Journal (London)*, *107*(445), 1798–1811. doi:10.1111/j.1468-0297.1997.tb00083.x

Barry, F., Gorg, H., & Strobl, E. (2011). *Foreign Direct Investment, Agglomeration and Demonstration Effects: An Empirical Investigation.* Center for Economic Policy Research, Discussion paper n° 2907.

Basile, R., Castellani, D., & Zanfei, A. (2009). National boundaries and the location of multinational firms in Europe. *Papers in Regional Science*, *88*(4), 733–748. doi:10.1111/j.1435-5957.2009.00238.x

Behname, M. (2012). Foreign Direct Investment and Urban Infrastructure: An Evidence from Southern Asia. *Advances in Management & Applied Economics*, *2*(4), 253–259.

Békés, G. (2006). *Location of manufacturing FDI in Hungary: How important are inter-company relationships?* Magyar Nemzeti Bank (Hungarian National Bank) Working Paper No. 2005/07. Budapest: Magyar Nemzeti Bank.

Braunerhjelm, P., & Svensson, R. (1996). Host country characteristics and agglomeration in foreign direct investment. *Applied Economics*, *28*(7), 833–840. doi:10.1080/000368496328272

Bughin, J., Chironga, M., Desvaux, G., Ermias, T., Jacobson, P., Kassiri, O., & Zouaoui, Y. (2016). *Lions on the Move II: Realizing the Potential of Africa's Economies*. McKinsey Global Institute.

Carlos, F. (2005). Improving The Competitiveness Of SMEs Through Enhancing Productive Capacity. In *United Nations Conference on Trade and Development, Proceedings of Four Meetings*, 182.

Castro, L., Paulo, R., & Saslavsky, D. (2007). *Infrastructure and the Location of Foreign Direct Investment: A Regional Analysis.* The 12th Annual Meeting of the Latin American and Caribbean Economic Association (LACEA).

Chakrabarti, R., Subramanian, K., Sairam, S., & Kuntluru, S. (2012). *Infrastructure and FDI: Evidence from district-level data in India*. Academic Press.

Cheng, L. K., & Kwan, Y. L. (2000). What Are the Determinants of the Location of Foreign Direct Investment? The Chinese Experience. *Journal of International Economics*, *51*(2), 79–400. doi:10.1016/S0022-1996(99)00032-X

Chidlow, A., Salciuviene, L., & Young, S. (2009). Regional determinants of inward FDI distribution in Poland. *International Business Review*, *18*(2), 119–133. doi:10.1016/j.ibusrev.2009.02.004

Choi, P. M. S., Chung, C. Y., Lee, K. Y., & Liu, C. (2020). Agglomeration Effects and Foreign Direct Investment Location Choice: Cross-country Evidence from Asia. *Journal of Korea Trade*, *24*(1), 35–58. doi:10.35611/jkt.2020.24.1.35

Cohen, S. D. (2007). *Multinational Corporations and Foreign Direct Investment*. Oxford University Press. doi:10.1093/acprof:oso/9780195179354.001.0001

Cordero, J., & Paus, E. (2008). *Foreign Investment and Economic Development in Costa Rica: The Unrealized Potential*. Discussion Paper, No. 13. Working Group on Development and Environment in the Americas. Tufts University.

Coughlin, C. C., Terza, J. V., & Arromdee, V. (1991). State characteristics and the location of foreign direct investment within the United States. *The Review of Economics and Statistics*, *73*(4), 675–683. doi:10.2307/2109406

Crozet, M., Mayer, T., & Mucchielli, J. L. (2004). How do firms agglomerate? A study of FDI in France. *Regional Science and Urban Economics*, *34*(1), 27–54. doi:10.1016/S0166-0462(03)00010-3

De Groot, H. L. F., Poot, J., & Smit, M. (2016). Which agglomeration externalities matter most and why. *Journal of Economic Surveys*, *30*(4), 756–782. doi:10.1111/joes.12112

Debaere, P., Lee, J., & Paik, M. (2010). Agglomeration, backward and forward linkages: Evidence from South Korean investment in China. *The Canadian Journal of Economics. Revue Canadienne d'Economique*, *43*(2), 520–546. doi:10.1111/j.1540-5982.2010.01582.x

DeCoster, G. P., & Strange, W. C. (1993). Spurious Agglomeration. *Journal of Urban Economics*, *33*(3), 273–304. doi:10.1006/juec.1993.1017

Defever, F. (2006). Functional fragmentation and the location of multinational firms in the enlarged Europe. *Regional Science and Urban Economics*, *36*(5), 658–677. doi:10.1016/j.regsciurbeco.2006.06.007

Devereux, M. P., Griffith, R., & Simpson, H. (2007). Firm location decisions, regional grants and agglomeration externalities. *Journal of Public Economics*, *91*(3-4), 413–435. doi:10.1016/j.jpubeco.2006.12.002

Disdier, A. C., & Mayer, T. (2004). How different is eastern Europe? Structure and determinants of location choices by French firms in eastern and western Europe. *Journal of Comparative Economics*, *32*(2), 280–296. doi:10.1016/j.jce.2004.02.004

Donauber, J., Meyer, B. E., & Nunnenkamp, P. (2016). A new global index of infrastructure: Construction, rankings and applications. *World Economy*, *39*(2), 236–259. Advance online publication. doi:10.1111/twec.12290

Dumon, M. (2014). *Top 6 Factors That Drive Investment in China*. https://www.investopedia.com/articles/economics/09/factors-drive-investment-in-china.asp

Dunning, J. H. (1988). The Eclectic Paradigm of International Production: A Restatement and Some Possible Extensions. *Journal of International Business Studies*, *19*(1), 1–31. doi:10.1057/palgrave.jibs.8490372

Egger, P., & Pfaermayer, M. (2009). The Impact of Bilateral Investment Treaties on Foreign Direct Investment. *Journal of Comparative Economics*, *32*(4), 788–804. doi:10.1016/j.jce.2004.07.001

Elkins, Z., Guzman, A. T., & Simmons, B. A. (2006). Competing for capital: The diffusion of bilateral investment treaties, 1960-2000. *International Organization*, *60*(4), 811–846. doi:10.1017/S0020818306060279

Ford, S., & Strange, R. (1999). Where do Japanese manufacturing firms invest within Europe and why? *Transnational Corporations*, *8*(1), 117–140.

Fung, C.K., Garcia-Herrero, A., Lizaka, H., & Siu, A. (2005). Hard or soft? Institutional reforms and infrastructure spending as determinants of foreign direct investment in China. *Japanese Economic Review*, *4*(56), 408-416.

Head, K., Ries, J., & Swenson, D. (1995). Agglomeration benefits and location choice: Evidence from Japanese manufacturing investments in the United States. *Journal of International Economics*, *38*(3-4), 223–247. doi:10.1016/0022-1996(94)01351-R

Hilber, C., & Voicu, I. (2010). Agglomeration economies and the location of foreign direct investment: Empirical evidence from Romania. *Regional Studies*, *44*(3), 355–371. doi:10.1080/00343400902783230

Hofman, I. (2016). Politics or profits along the "Silk Road": What drives Chinese farms in Tajikistan and helps them thrive? *Eurasian Geography and Economics, 57*(3), 457–481. doi:10.1080/15387216.2016.1238313

Hong, J. (2009). Firm heterogeneity and location choices: Evidence from foreign manufacturing investments in China. *Urban Studies (Edinburgh, Scotland), 46*(10), 2143–2157. doi:10.1177/0042098009339425

Houghwout, A. F. (2001). Infrastructure and Social Welfare in Metropolitan America. *Economic Policy Review, 7*(3), 1–16.

Huang, Y. Y., Fischer, T. B., & Xu, H. (2017). The stakeholder analysis for sea of Chinese foreign direct investment: The case of "One Belt, One Road" initiative in Pakistan. *Impact Assessment and Project Appraisal, 35*(2), 158–171. doi:10.1080/14615517.2016.1251698

Hubert, F., & Pain, N. (2002). Fiscal incentives, European integration and the location of foreign direct investment. *Manchester School, 70*(3), 336–363. doi:10.1111/1467-9957.00306

Jones, J. (2017). Agglomeration economies and the location of foreign direct investment: A meta-analysis. *Journal of Regional Science, 57*(5), 1–17. doi:10.1111/jors.12335

Jordaan, J. C. (2004). *Foreign direct investment and neighbouring influences* (Doctoral dissertation). University of Pretoria.

Kazembe, P., & Namizinga, N. (2007). *The Impact of Foreign Direct Investment on Development: Policy Challenges for Malawi*. Integrated Framework Policy Analysis Working Paper Series, No. 6. Government of Malawi Ministry of Industry, Trade and Private Sector Development Integrated Framework Policy Analysis.

Krugman, P. (1991). Increasing Returns and Economic Geographic. *Journal of Political Economy, 99*(3), 483–499. doi:10.1086/261763

Krugman, P. R., & Venables, A. J. (1996). Integration, Specialization, and Adjustment. *European Economic Review, 40*(3-5), 959–967. doi:10.1016/0014-2921(95)00104-2

Mainguy, C. (2004). L'impact des investissements directs étrangers sur les économies en développement. *Région et Développement, 20*, 65–89.

Marshall, A. (1920). *Principles of Economics* (8th ed.). Macmillan.

Moosa, I. A. (2012). *The Determinants of Foreign Direct Investment in Mena Countries: An Extreme Bounds Analysis. Research Report 0421. Department of Economics and Finance, La Trobe University*. University of Chicago Press.

Neumayer, E., & Spess, L. (2005). Do bilateral investment treaties increase foreign direct investment to developing countries? *World Development, 33*(10), 1567–1585.

Nunnenkamp, P., & Spatz, J. (2002). Determinants of FDI in developing countries: has globalization changed the rules of the game? Kiel Institute for World Economics, 1122.

Office des Changes. (2017). *Echanges Maroc-Afrique Subsaharienne*. Département des Statistiques des Echanges Extérieurs.

Pradhan, R. P., Norman, N. R., Badir, Y., & Samadhan, B. (2013). Transport infrastructure, foreign direct investment and economic growth interactions in India: The ARDL bounds testing approach. *Procedia: Social and Behavioral Sciences*, *104*, 914–921.

Ramasamy, B., Yeung, M., & Laforet, S. (2012). China's outward foreign direct investment: Location choice and firm ownership. *Journal of World Business*, *47*, 17–25.

Rehman, A., Muhammad, I., Hassan, A. M., & Muhammad, A. (2011). The Impact of Infrastructure on Foreign Direct Investment: The Case of Pakistan. *International Journal of Business and Management*, *6*(5), 268–276.

Saito, H., & Wu, J. (2016). Agglomeration, congestion, and U.S. regional disparities in employment growth. *Journal of Regional Science*, *56*(1), 53–71.

Seetanah, B. (2009). A Sector-Wise Panel Data Study on the Link between Transport Infrastructure and FDI in Mauritius. *9th Global Conference on Business & Economics*.

Smith, D. F., & Florida, R. (1994). Agglomeration and industrial location: An econometric analysis of Japanese-affiliated manufacturing establishments in automotive-related industries. *Journal of Urban Economics*, *36*, 23–41.

Straub, S. (2011). Infrastructure and development: A critical appraisal of the macro-level literature. *The Journal of Development Studies*, *47*(5), 683–708.

Sun, Q., Tong, W., & Yu, Q. (2002). Determinants of foreign direct investment across China. *Journal of International Money and Finance*, *21*, 79–113.

Urata, S., & Kawai, H. (2000). The determinants of the location of foreign direct investment by Japanese small and medium sized enterprises. *Small Business Economics*, *15*, 79–103.

Voorpijl, R. (2011). *Foreign Direct Investments in Kenya: The Gains and Losses of Foreign Involvement*. Radboud University.

Wheeler, D., & Mody, A. (1992). International investment location decisions: The case of U.S. firms. *Journal of International Economics*, *33*, 57–76.

Woodward, D. P. (1992). Locational determinants of Japanese manufacturing start-ups in the United States. *Southern Economic Journal*, *58*(3), 690–708.

Yu, S., Qian, X., & Liu, T. (2019). Belt and road initiative and Chinese firms' outward foreign direct investment. *Emerging Markets Review*, *41*(C), 100629.

KEYS TERMS AND DEFINITIONS

Agglomeration: A conglomerate of firms in one geographical that share infrastructure and benefit from synergy.

Belt and Road Initiative: An infrastructural project developed by China to connect international trade and promote the global economy.

Foreign Direct Investment: A financial instrument used by multinational enterprises to create subsidiaries abroad. Technically, FDI is any participation above 10% in a firm's share capital.

Infrastructure: A set of technical and economic equipment that supports creating added value. it could be physical (road, railroad, airports, ports), energetic (electricity and fuel cost and supply), and soft (information and communication technologies).

Institutional Quality: The absence of corruption, respecting property rights, and the rule of law.

Internationalization: The process of investing abroad while considering location factors.

Multinational Enterprise: Any firm having at least one subsidiary in a foreign territory. It could be operating in any sector (Industry, service, agriculture) and having any size (small, medium, or large).

ENDNOTES

1 https://greenfdc.org/belt-and-road-initiative-about/

2 idem

3 https://www.investmentmap.org/investment/time-series-by-industry

4 https://greenfdc.org/countries-of-the-belt-and-road-initiative-bri/

5 https://data.worldbank.org/indicator/

Chapter 6
Impact of the Belt and Road Initiative on the Countries of Central, Eastern, and Southeastern Europe

Mirela Mitrašević
Faculty of Business Economics, University of East Sarajevo, Bijeljina, Bosnia and Herzegovina

Miloš Radoslav Pjanić
Faculty of Economics, University of Novi Sad, Serbia

ABSTRACT

This research analyses the results of the Belt and Road Initiative in 17 Central, Eastern, and Southeastern European countries that signed the China-Central and Eastern European Countries Initiative. The subject of the research is the extent to which the initiative would provide benefits for the growth and development of these countries. Special attention will be paid to the link between infrastructure development and FDI, and whether environmental standards are taken into account in the projects belonging to the domain of the Initiative. The authors analyse which areas of economy belong to Chinese investments in the selected countries, and whether the countries have taken into account strategically important investments for the society and the country's economy. One of the goals of the research will be whether in the previous period the countries regularly settled their debts to China and how the COVID-19 crisis has had an impact on debt repayment.

INTRODUCTION

In this chapter, we have analysed the results of the Belt and Road Initiative (BRI) in 17 countries of Central, Eastern and Southeastern Europe, the member states of the China - Central and Eastern European Countries Initiative, which originally included 16 former communist European countries, and, afterwards, Greece joined the Initiative at the 8th summit in Dubrovnik in April 2019. (China-CEE Institute, 2019)

DOI: 10.4018/978-1-7998-8021-9.ch006

The "17+1" platform differs from other Chinese-led initiatives since it includes local cooperation between Central, Eastern and Southeastern European countries and Chinese cities and provinces, aiming to compensate for the asymmetry in market size. Additionally, the "17+1" platform implies a higher frequency of summits. The first summit was held in 2012 in Warsaw, Poland, when the document CHINA's Twelve Measures for Promoting Friendly Cooperation with Central and Eastern European Countries was adopted. Since then, member states' representatives have met annually to set new goals for future cooperation. Until 2018, the summits were held in Bucharest (2013), Belgrade (2014), Suzhou (2015), Riga (2016), and Budapest (2017). Even though in 2012 these 16 countries enthusiastically accepted this form of cooperation, until 2018 the economic results were not at a satisfactory level. The guidelines of the Sofia Summit 2018 for the first time outlined the need for more balanced trade, reciprocity in terms of market access, open tenders for infrastructure construction, and tangible economic results for the BRI countries. The need for increased transparency was expressed especially regarding the activities of the Initiative, which at that time included 16 European countries, as mostly the information within summit guidelines could be obtained. Croatia hosted the 8th summit in Dubrovnik in April 2019 when the inclusion of Greece led to the transformation into the "17+1" platform.

Our goal is to analyse, based on the available data, whether this cooperation provides certain benefits for the growth and development of the member states. The emphasis is on two areas through which the cooperation between China and Central, Eastern and Southeastern Europe countries is manifested: infrastructure projects and Foreign Direct Investment (FDI).

Since foreign direct investments are one of the most important factors for stimulating trade, employment growth, and establishing overall macroeconomic stability, in this paper we are going to deal with the Chinese motives for investing in Central and Eastern and Southeastern Europe (Wang, 2016; McCaleb & Szunomár, 2017; China-CEE Institute, 2018)

Poor infrastructure causes an increase in transaction costs and limits the access to both local and global markets and, ultimately, makes the country unattractive to FDI. Reducing transportation costs and travel time along with the improvements related to regulating the business environment can have a positive impact on trade and investment, and, consequently, on development itself.

The "17+1" platform includes the so-called "no strings attached" Chinese financing, implying preferential loans from Chinese policy banks, as well as financing from Chinese or mutual funds. A number of projects, especially in Southeast Europe, are financed through the Export-Import Bank of China, which is controlled by the State Council of the People's Republic of China. In addition to being available much faster than the loans from western financial institutions, Chinese loans are characterized by long maturities. (Grieger, 2018) Almost 79% of Chinese infrastructure construction projects in the region of Central, Eastern and Southeastern Europe are located in the countries of the Western Balkans, with as many as 75-85% of these projects being financed from Chinese loans (Matura, 2021).

Furthermore, we are going to analyse which areas of the economy belong to Chinese investments and whether the countries have taken into account strategically important investments. The subject of the last part of the research is the Regulation 2019/452, which has been in force since 11th October 2020, establishing a framework for FDI screening in the EU.

Bearing in mind that ten years have passed since the official launch of the Initiative, and that the last two years have been marked by the COVID-19 crisis, one of the goals of our research, based on the available data, is to answer the question whether strengthening the relations between China and 17 Central, Eastern and Southeastern countries through the Belt and Roads Initiative has the potential to significantly contribute to the competitiveness of these countries and what prerequisites need to be met.

LITERATURE REVIEW

Numerous factors have been identified in the literature as the Chinese motives for the BRI.

According to Wang (2016), the Initiative arose because of several reasons: the pressure of the economic slowdown in Chine, American pivot to Asia, and deteriorating of the relations with the neighbouring countries after overcoming the global financial crisis that began in 2008. McCaleb & Szunomár (2017) state that in the case of Chinese multinational companies, the motives for investing in Central and Eastern Europe are not only relatively low labour and land costs, educated workforce needed for production and the access to rich EU markets, but also institutional factors and other less measurable aspects, such as good political relations and diplomatic gestures, including the possibility of obtaining visas and permanent residence permits for Chinese citizens. Some authors such as Coenen, et al. (2020) question the impact of the infrastructure and investment development strategy that officially includes more than 130 countries and its expansion on the environment. Zhou & Esteban (2018) consider it to be an initiative that serves as a decisive strategic manoeuvre for China to ensure security and improve the power status in the international order, moving from the position of a rule maker to a rule creator. Zhao (2019) examines the design, goals and implementation of the BRI six years after its inception. He outlines that although the BRI has been originally designed to serve China's ambitious geostrategic and geoeconomic interests, many developing countries have supported the Initiative because of infrastructure development. The article "EU ambassadors band together against Silk Road" published by Handelsblatt in April 2018 on the report drawn up by EU ambassadors which strongly criticized the Chinese Belt and Road Initiative project stated that only the Hungarian ambassador refused to sign the document, as well as that the countries that relied on Chinese investments, such as Hungary and Greece, also showed in the past that they could not resist Chinese pressure (Heide, et al., 2018). Chinese influence in the Czech Republic, Hungary, Poland and Slovakia, is the subject of the analysis within the international project ChinfluenCE that reflects similar researches conducted by the research centres in EU member states that are not a part of the "17+1" format. Pelaudeix (2021) points out that Beijing's foreign policy in the EU is in fact an attempt to exploit EU vulnerabilities and, ultimately, weaken the relevance and legitimacy of EU institutions by using foreign direct investment and cyber attacks and bypassing elected EU representatives. Nevertheless, it is believed that the format can hardly be utilised as a political instrument due to the fact that 11 countries belong to the EU and that they are obliged to respect the European regulations.

CHINA'S BELT AND ROAD INITIATIVE

The Belt and Road Initiative was launched to integrate and develop the Asian, European and African continents and their neighbouring seas; primarily through infrastructure development, trade liberalization, and economic cooperation. (Arduino & Gong, 2018). The vision and activities regarding the joint construction of the Silk Road Economic Belt and the 21st Century Maritime Silk Road issued by the Chinese government in 2015 means that the Belt and Road passes through the continents of Asia, Europe and Africa, connecting East Asia and Europe (NDRC, 2015).

Figure 1. Silk ROAD ECONOMIC BELT and 21st century Maritime Silk Road
Source: World Bank (2019)

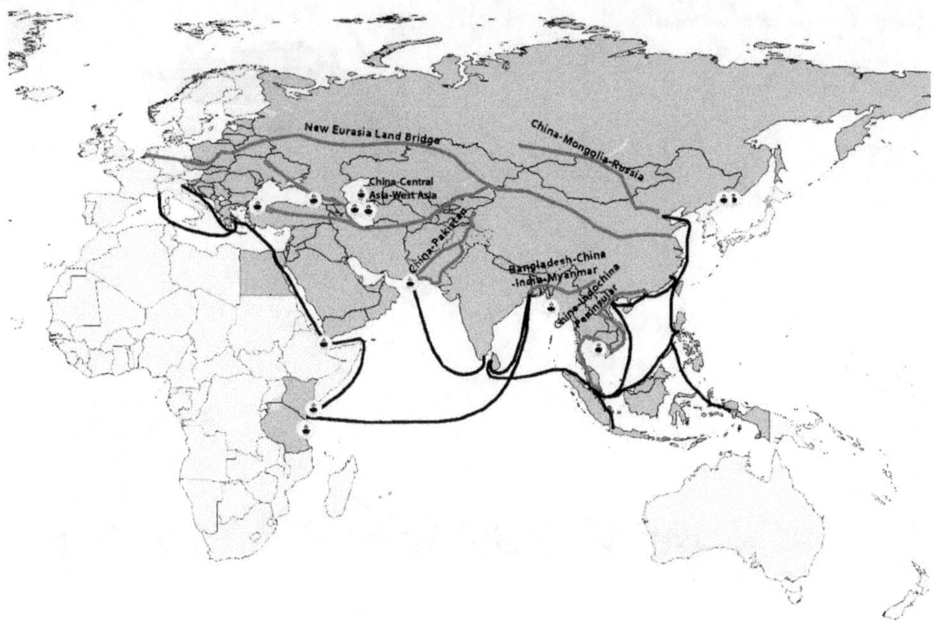

The land part of the BRI, so-called Silk Road Economic Belt, which connects China with Central and South Asia and Europe as well, was presented by President Xi Jinping in his speech in September 2013 at Nazarbayev University in Kazakhstan.

A month later, Xi Jinping, during his speech in the Indonesian Parliament, proposed "21st Century Maritime Road". The maritime road connects China with the countries of Southeast Asia, Gulf countries, East and North Africa, and Europe as well. The official draft, vision and activities regarding the joint construction of the 21st Century Land and Maritime Silk Road indicate that these projects will be developed along six economic corridors (Derudder, Liu, & Kunaka, 2018):

1. China-Mongolia-Russia Economic Corridor,
2. New Eurasian Land Bridge,
3. China-Central Asia-West Asia Economic Corridor,
4. China-Indochina Peninsula Economic Corridor,
5. China-Pakistan Economic Corridor, and
6. Bangladesh-China-India-Myanmar Economic Corridor.

The planned development covers an area of 70 percent of the world's population, 55 percent of the global GDP, and 75 percent of the energy reserves (Lechmacher Padilla-Taylor, 2015).

In the China Belt and Road Initiative (BRI) Investment Report H1 2021 it was pointed out that, in January 2021 according to the official information, 140 countries signed Memorandum of Understanding (MoU) for bilateral cooperation under the Belt and Road Initiative framework, however, for 7 countries stated in the official Chinese media, the signing of the Memorandum could not be confirmed (Wang, 2021a) (Figure 2).

Figure 2. The countries of the Belt and Road Initiative
Source: Green Finance & Development Centre, FISF Fudan University

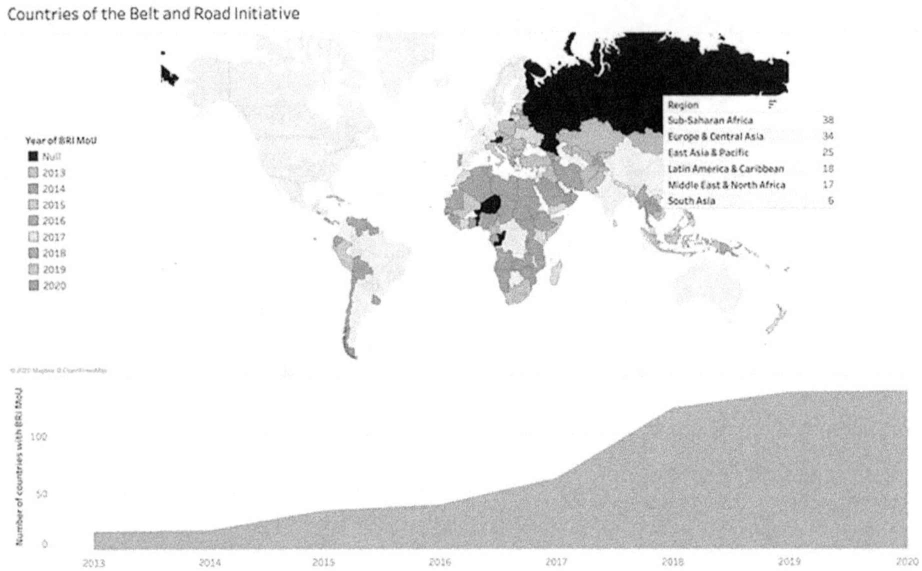

The BRI, along with infrastructure development, includes policy coordination, uninterrupted trade, financial integration, and cultural and scientific exchange (NDRC, 2015). It was pointed out that these activities indicate China's desire to play a leading role in transport infrastructure development, in all phases of infrastructure projects' life-cycle, and all modes of transport (Lisinge, 2020).

The Chinese Belt and Road Initiative covers a wide network of railways, pipelines, ports and roads including 64 countries (Hofman, 2015). Within these 64 countries there are 16 European countries with which China launched the "16+1" Initiative in 2012.

CHINA - CENTRAL AND EASTERN EUROPEAN COUNTRIES INITIATIVE

China - Central and Eastern European Countries Initiative, colloquially known as the "16+1" Initiative, was launched by the Ministry of Foreign Affairs of the People's Republic of China (PRC) in 2012. It aims to strengthen and expand the cooperation between China and 16 former communist countries in Central, Eastern and Southeastern European in trade and investment, transport connection, finance, agriculture, science and technology, healthcare system, education, and culture. Sixteen member states of the Initiative are: Albania, Bosnia and Herzegovina, Bulgaria, Croatia, the Czech Republic, Estonia, Hungary, Latvia, Lithuania, Macedonia, Montenegro, Poland, Romania, Serbia, Slovakia, and Slovenia. The thing which connects them is that they are all former communist countries. However, currently they have quite different economic development, as well as a legal status related to EU membership. The "16+1" format is a key platform for promoting the Belt and Road Initiative and these countries are included in the BRI based on their specialization as well.

The China-CEE Institute (2018) has identified various motives for Chinese companies regarding the 16+1 Initiative. In addition to 16 member states of the Initiative, Chinese public companies in the infrastructure sector can also participate in the construction of highways and ports in the Balkan countries. Moreover, thanks to the expertise in the medium and high technology sectors, Chinese public companies can participate in the nuclear or automotive industry. Thus, the project creates a basis for Chinese companies to profit from the construction of roads and high-speed railways, ports, pipelines, and electricity networks.

The thing which motivated the governments of Central, Eastern and Southeastern Europe to accept the Initiative was the 2008 financial crisis which caused insufficient funding for new EU member countries since the EU was in deep recession (Ross, 2016). Therefore, Chinese suggestions which involved financing, a rapid loan approval and implementation process seemed to be an attractive alternative (Poulain, 2011).

One of the first documents produced within the "16+1" format is the report entitled "China's Twelve Measures for Promoting Friendly Cooperation with Central and Eastern European Countries" which contains China's promise to provide a special credit line of 10 billion dollars and to focus on cooperation projects in the areas such as infrastructure, high and new technologies, and the green economy (The Ministry of Foreign Affairs of the PRC, 2012).

Unlike other initiatives organised by China, "16+1" format includes local cooperation between the countries of Central, Eastern and Southeastern Europe and Chinese cities and provinces. Moreover, it aims to compensate for the asymmetry in market size. The "16+1" format also includes holding summits. Summits are a part of the Cooperation between China and Central and Eastern European Countries, whose secretariat is located in Beijing. The first summit was held in Warsaw, Poland, in 2012 when the document China's Twelve Measures for Promoting Friendly Cooperation with Central and Eastern European Countries was adopted. Since then, the representatives of the member states met every year to set new goals for the future cooperation, and by 2018, summits were held in Bucharest (2013), Belgrade (2014), Suzhou (2015), Riga (2016), and Budapest (2017).

Even though in 2012 these 16 countries enthusiastically accepted the offered form of cooperation, by 2018 some of them expressed dissatisfaction with the economic results. The official data show that the volume of trade between China and the BRI countries increased before 2012, but after that time continued at a much slower pace. Furthermore, Chinese export to CEE countries increased more than these countries' export to China. As for imported goods in the EU in 2020, China had the largest share (22.4%), while it participated with 10.5% in exported goods which ranked it third. (Eurostat, 2021)

Figure 3. EU trade in goods with China, 2010-2020
Source: Eurostat (2021)

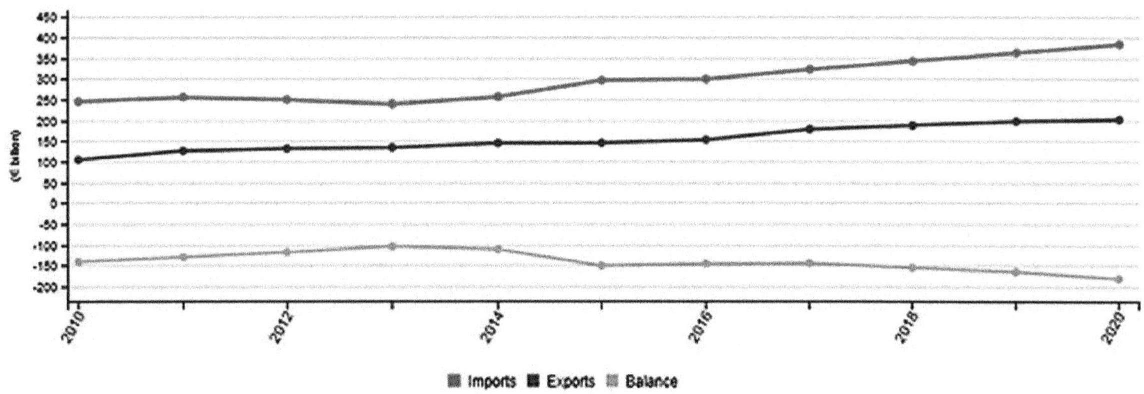

Additionally, Chinese investments did not reach the expected level in the region of Central, Eastern and Southeastern Europe, which will be further discussed in the following part of the research that will address the issue of Chinese direct investments in the member states of the “17+1” Initiative.

Such results caused disappointment and scepticism in Central, Eastern and South-Eastern European countries which had unrealistic expectations about the effects of the Initiative (European Parliament, 2019). The document posted on the website of the European Parliament (2019) states that unsatisfactory economic results for these countries may not only result from the apparent asymmetry in market size, but also due to trade and investment barriers.

The guidelines of the Sofia Summit 2018 for the first time emphasized the need for more balanced trade, reciprocity in terms of market access and open tenders for infrastructure construction, as well as tangible economic results for the BRI countries. Moreover, since the information outside the summit guidelines was extremely scarce, there were requests for greater transparency regarding the activities of the “16+1” Initiative. Pendrakowska (2018) points out that a lack of prescribed procedures, as well as ambiguities related to the BRI project, affect the perception of the results of the cooperation.

The European Parliament (2019) website outlined that all Central, Eastern and South-Eastern European countries, except for Albania and Estonia, established sectoral coordination mechanisms, but there was still no empirical evidence that the Initiative contributed to sufficient economic results to offset significant costs of holding frequent meetings, especially for small countries.

Croatia hosted the 8th summit in Dubrovnik in April 2019, when the inclusion of Greece led to the first expansion of the cooperation pattern and the transformation into the “17+1” Format (Xinhua, 2019).

Figure 4. Members of China's "17+1" format
Source: Kavalski (2020)

Chinese policy banks and state-owned commercial banks provide the largest sources of financing the BRI, while additional investments are made by Chinese companies, non-Chinese companies and banks, international organizations and partner country governments (Coenen, et al. 2020). A number of projects, especially in Southeast Europe, are financed through the Export-Import Bank of China (Exim Bank) controlled by the State Council of the People's Republic of China (Abu Dayeh & Janíčko, 2021).

Figure 5. The sources of funding to support BRI projects
Source: Authors, based on He (2019)

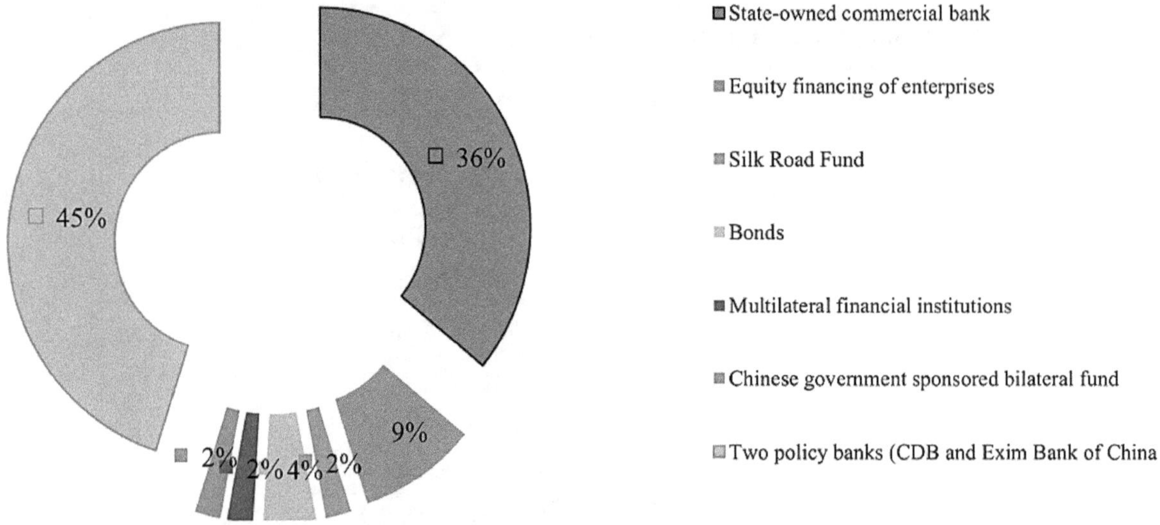

As shown in Graph 2 as much as 45% of the funds for supporting BRI projects in 2018 came from two policy banks: Exim Bank and CDB bank. State-owned commercial banks participated with 36%. Chinese loans have long maturity, their interest rates vary depending on size and maturity date, and may also be available much faster than the loans from Western financial institutions. Their distinguishing feature is that in the case of court disputes, they fall under the jurisdiction of Chinese courts, and not the courts of a host country (European Parliament, 2019).

CHINESE FOREIGN DIRECT INVESTMENT IN CENTRAL, EASTERN AND SOUTHEASTERN EUROPE

In order to list the effects of economic cooperation "17+1", it is necessary to have reliable data on the amount of Chinese investments.

However, the website of the European Court of Auditors (2020) points out that it is not always possible to categorize these projects as BRI projects, as there is not a publicly available inventory of official BRI projects. Due to the limitations of FDI statistics, the Commission (DG TRADE) has created a new non-public database, EC-JRC Foreign Ownership Database which uses enterprise-level data and excludes small businesses which are not required to disclose their balance sheets publically. The EC-JRC's foreign ownership database includes foreign ownership of more than 50% of the capital of unlisted companies and the ownership of the largest shareholders for publicly listed companies.

Matura (2021) pointed out that there is a significant limitation in researching foreign direct investment in "17+1" countries because it needs to be separated from infrastructure projects. It is also worth mentioning that when a Chinese company acquires a multinational company, its subsidiaries in the region are automatically re-categorized as a Chinese investment. The Minister of Foreign Affairs and Trade Peter Szijjártó addressed the issue in the Hungarian Parliament in June 2019, explaining that out of sixteen Chinese investments in Hungary, as many as eleven were realized through the acquisition of international companies (Szijjártó, 2019). This can be illustrated in the example of the acquisition of Lexmark International Technology by a Chinese company Apex Technology and PAG Asia Capital in 2016, the acquisition of German industrial robotics company KUKA in late 2016 by a Chinese company Midea, the acquisition of Bosch's SEG Automotive Germany GmbH in late 2017 by Zhengzhou Coal Mining Machinery Group (Prague Security Studies Institute, 2019).

Typically, BRI projects are mainly financed by Chinese state-owned enterprises, including state-owned political banks and commercial banks, and in compliance with EU rules, such subsidies, if granted by a member state, are treated as a state aid. In June 2020, White Paper on Foreign Subsidies to Protect the EU Single Market was published, which partially addressed the issue (European Commission, 2020).

According to Kratz, et al. (2021) China invests in most European Union countries, and its largest investments are concentrated in France, Italy, Germany, and United Kingdom. Based on the data in Table 1, we can calculate that 46% of China's outward FDI to the countries of Central, Eastern and Southeastern Europe in 2018 are in Poland, Hungary, and Romania, while relatively more significant investments are recorded in Serbia, Croatia, and Montenegro (Brown, 2020).

Table 1. China's outward FDI (stock) in the "17+1" countries in the period 2014-2018

Country	2014 Billion EUR	2015 Billion EUR	2016 Billion EUR	2017 Billion EUR	2018 Billion EUR
Albania	0,006	0,006	0,007	0,004	0,005
Bosnia and Herzegovina	0,005	0,007	0,009	0,003	0,003
Bulgaria	0,140	0,217	0,158	0,209	0,149
Croatia	0,010	0,011	0,011	0,032	0,060
Czech Republic	0,201	0,206	0,217	0,137	0,243
Estonia	0,003	0,004	0,004	0,003	0,050
Greece	0,100	0,111	0,046	0,152	0,212
Hungary	0,459	0,526	0,298	0,273	0,280
Latvia	0,001	0,001	0,001	0,001	0,010
Lithuania	0,011	0,012	0,014	0,014	0,011
Montenegro			0,004	0,033	0,055
North Macedonia	0,002	0,002	0,002	0,002	0,031
Poland	0,272	0,324	0,305	0,338	0,456
Romania	0,158	0,336	0,373	0,258	0,266
Serbia	0,025	0,046	0,079	0,142	0,236
Slovakia	0,106	0,118	0,079	0,070	0,086
Slovenia	0,004	0,005	0,026	0,022	0,035

Source: Authors, based on China National Statistical Bureau's (2018)

Note: US Dollar to Euro Exchange Rates: 2014: 0,826; 2015: 0,92094; 2016: 0,9504; 2017: 0,8332; 2018: 0,87097

Table 2 shows the cumulative values of China's outward FDI (stock) in "17 + 1" countries which were EU members in the period 2000-2019 and 2000-2020, based on which we can conclude that among all the analysed countries Poland had the largest transaction in 2020.

Table 2. China's outward FDI (stock) in the "17+1" countries which are EU members

Country	Cumulative Value 2000-2019 Billion EUR **	Cumulative Value 2000-2020 Billion EUR ***
Bulgaria	0,400	0,400
Croatia	0,400	0,400
Czech Republic	1,000	1,200
Greece	1,900	1,900
Hungary	2,400	2,700
Poland	1,400	2,200
Romania	1,200	1,300
Slovakia	0,100	0,200
Slovenia	0,300	0,400

Source: **Authors, based on Kratz, et al. (2020)
***Authors, based on Kratz, et al. (2021)

Taking into account the infrastructure projects and the amount of FDI, the largest Chinese presence in the analysed region in 2020 was recorded in Serbia in the amount of 9,7 billion euros, followed by Hungary – 5,4 billion euros, Romania – 2,8 billion euros, Poland – 2,7 billion euros, and Bosnia and Herzegovina – 1,9 billion euros. However, China's presence in the Western Balkans is more important in the field of infrastructure projects compared to FDI (Matura, 2021). The report of the Centre for Strategic and International Studies in Washington DC states that the EU is by far the largest donor to Serbia, and that China is in the fifth place (Conley et al. 2020:4).

The COVID-19 crisis has caused the investments in European countries of the BRI to fall by 36%, but according to Wang (2021b) these countries were the least affected by the crisis. Actually, the COVID-19 crisis has had the greatest impact on the investments in African regions which fell by over 65% between 2019 and 2020. Some authors argue that the pandemic will threaten the ability of some countries to pay off the debts to China (Mouritz, 2020; Kratz et al., 2020; Kynge & Yu, 2020; Buckley, 2020).

As shown in Graph 3, despite high expectations in the past decade, Chinese investments did not reach a significant level in the region of Central, Eastern and Southern Europe, especially in EU member states. The largest participation was recorded in Hungary and Romania, regarding the Western Balkans countries mostly in Serbia and Albania.

Figure 6. Share of Chinese investments in total foreign direct investments (2019)
Source: Authors, based on Kratz, et al. (2020)

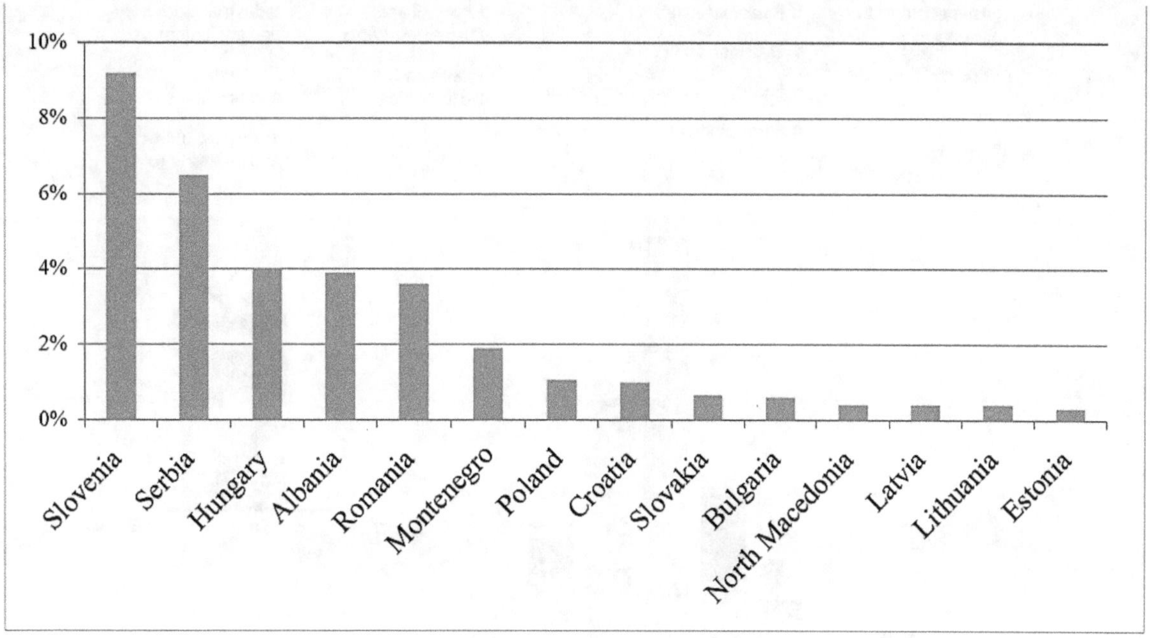

Examples of BRI-Funded Programs in the Selected Countries of Central, Eastern and South-Eastern Europe

Chinese investments in Europe are diverse. However, the transport, construction and infrastructure sectors account for the largest share (Kratz et al. 2021). The graph shows that in 2020, the top target were transport, construction, and infrastructure sectors with 25%.

Figure 7. Completed Chinese FDI in the EU-27 and UK by industry 2000-2020
Source: Kratz, et al. (2021)

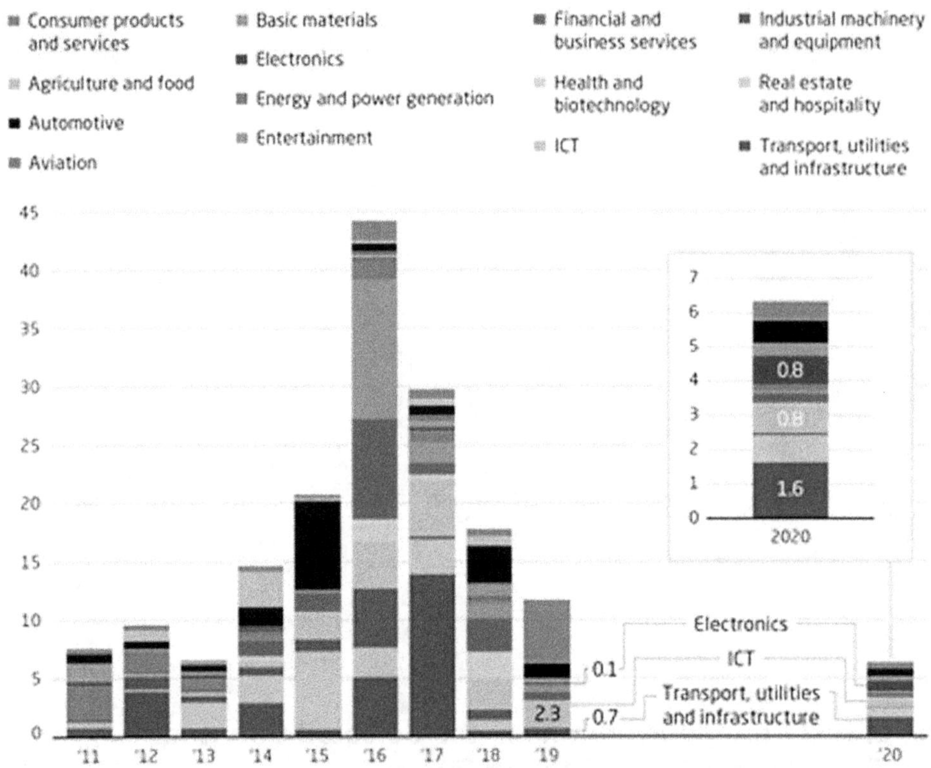

The largest transaction in 2020 was GLP's acquisition of Goodman Group's warehousing portfolio in Central and Eastern Europe (GLP is a leading global investment manager and business builder in logistics, real estate, infrastructure, finance, and related technologies), including the transactions in Poland, Slovakia, Hungary, and the Czech Republic. As much as 18% of the total investments were made in the procurement of goods and computer software, and the electronics industry ranked third in terms of investments.

Abu Dayeh & Janíčko (2021) emphasize that Central Europe attracts Chinese outward direct investments mainly in the form of M&A, while the Balkan states use it for the infrastructure they urgently need to build.

Infrastructure investments enable China to monitor and control the activities in key logistics hubs. Pelaudeix (2021) points out that key logistics hubs are of strategic importance, but in addition to economic risks, there are also some security risks depending on the proximity of military infrastructure.

One of strategically most important investments in mid-2016 was the acquisition of 51% stake in the largest port in Greece Piraeus by a Chinese shipping company COSCO, one of the world's largest shipping companies. Greece is of great importance to China. China considers the port Piraeus, the closest port in the northern Mediterranean to Suez Canal, to be the gateway for Asian goods in the Balkans and southern Europe.

In 2015, a Chinese company China Railway Group won a contract to build a high-speed railway from Budapest to Belgrade, which should further speed up the supply of Chinese goods in Europe (Goh, 2015) and it is expected to shorten the travel time between the two capital cities. The extension of the high-speed railway to Skopje and Athens should provide freight trains with another alternative for China's access to the Aegean and Mediterranean Sea (Chan, 2016). Chinese companies have expressed interest in transformation of Szombathely airport into a major European cargo base and in the infrastructure development of Debrecen airport. However, these investments were not realized, because the European Commission postponed them with the explanation that there was a problem with transparency and it questioned the relation between price and quality on the domestic field.

In Serbia, significant Chinese infrastructure projects include:

- The bridge named after a renowned Serbian scientist Mihajlo Pupin on the Danube in Belgrade. The total value of the project was 203 million USD, and 85% of the funding came from the Chinese Export-Import Bank, and the remaining 15% from the City of Belgrade. China's Road and Bridge Corporation was responsible for its construction. (Stakić &Zakić, 2016).
- The construction of the Corridor 11 sections. The highway should connect Belgrade with the port of Bar in Montenegro. The large part of the investment was financed from the loan in Export-Import Bank (Exim Bank).(Brown, 2020)

Shanghai Electric Power Construction, Pinggao Group and Sinohydro Corporation, Chinese companies in building electronic communications infrastructure, won the tenders for the construction of electrical networks in Poland in the period 2013-2015 (Prague Security Studies Institute, 2019).

Impact of Infrastructure on Foreign Direct Investment

Chen & Lin (2018) conducted one of the most comprehensive studies on the impact of various transport costs, infrastructure and institutional factors on foreign direct investment in the member states of the BRI. Their research indicates that longer delivery time presents an obstacle to foreign direct investment flow, limiting the countries' ability to trade. The results suggest that reducing the travel time by one day may increase the total inflow of foreign direct investment in the BRI countries by 7 percent. The effects of transport and infrastructure costs differ significantly in the analysed countries. The results also suggest that the positive effect of the reduced transport costs on foreign direct investment may be enhanced when accompanied by better regulated business environment. Domazet & Marjanović (2018) also emphasized the importance of creating a favorable investment environment which would encourage investors to invest their capital in a particular country. In one of the following studies, these authors analyzed the interconnectedness of multinational companies, their investments and the economy of a country and concluded that the primary task of economic policy makers is to monitor world trends, harmonize domestic regulations and create an investment climate that would benefit foreign investors (Marjanović & Domazet, 2021).

The following graph (Graph 5.) displays that the proposed transport network of the BRI could increase the total foreign direct investment flows in the economies of the Belt and Road corridors.

Figure 8. Expected increase in the total foreign direct investment flows in the economies of the Belt and Road corridors
Source: Authors, based on Chen and Lin (2018)

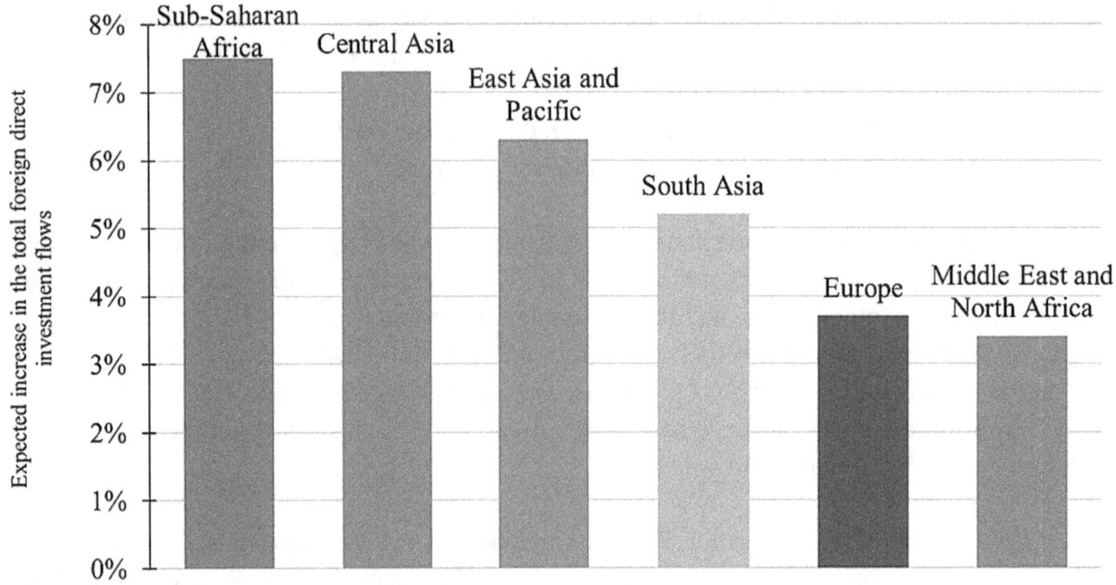

Risks Associated With the BRI

According to the Ministry of Foreign Affairs of the PRC (2016), the Chinese side encourages strong domestic companies with a good reputation to participate in the construction of the railway and port network, electricity network, and the Internet. However, in practice, in most such infrastructure projects Chinese business contractors are involved more than the local ones (Escobar, 2016). Apart from not contributing to increasing employment in the countries where the construction projects take place, the hired Chinese workers are usually subject to the Chinese labour law, and the Chinese imported materials and equipment are exempt from VAT or customs duties in the host countries (European Parliament, 2019). These risks could negatively affect the goal of ensuring reciprocity and equal conditions in the EU-China relation. Furthermore, there is a risk that environmental, social and management standards are not sufficiently respected in the implementation of these projects. (European Court of Auditors, 2020)

Some of the key criticisms of the Initiative relate to the non-compliance with environmental standards. (Buckley, 2020; Teo et al., 2019; Hughes, 2018)

The European Green Deal has been promoted as one of the main priorities for the European Commission, with the aim of having a net zero greenhouse gas emission by 2050. Even though it was announced at the Second Forum for International Cooperation, the Belt and Road 2019 that the environmental standards would be respected, energy projects in which coal is used as a raw material are still conducted. One such project financed by Chinese loans is planned in an Bosnia and Herzegovina. (Petkova, 2021)

The following table (Table 3.) shows the restrictions on foreign investment in China for which there are no such restrictions in the EU. The table shows that foreign investors have limited access to the Chinese market in several sectors. After entering the Chinese market, the foreign legal framework is defined in such a way that it puts European companies at a disadvantage compared to their Chinese counterparts.

Table 3. Sectoral restrictions of foreign investments in China

Sectors	Restrictions
Exploration & exploitation of oil and natural gas	Joint Venture only
Printing of publications	Minority only
Automobile manufacturing	Max 50%
Banks	Max 20%
Insurance companies	Max 50%
Repair, design & manufacturing of ships Aircraft design & production Production of satellite television broadcasting Nuclear power stations Construction & operation of power grids Construction & operation of network of railways Construction & operation of civil airports Telecommunication companies	Minority only

Source: Authors, based on Holslag (2019)

The 2019 Business Confidence Survey, published by the European Chamber of Commerce in China, pointed out that 20% of the respondents felt compelled to transfer technology to maintain the market access in China, stressing a lack of reciprocity in EU-China relation. (European Chamber of Commerce, 2019).

Almost 79% of the Chinese infrastructure projects in Central, Eastern and Southeastern Europe are located in the Western Balkans, with as much as 75-85% of projects financed by Chinese loans. Taking into account the GDP of these economies, the total value of the projects is significant. The volume of the loans offered by China reaches 18% of GDP in Montenegro, 12% in Serbia, 10% in Bosnia and Herzegovina, and 7% in Northern Macedonia (Matura, 2021).

In order to implement the BRI, China has approved loans without sufficiently considering the long-term sustainability of the projects and credit risks. This has contributed to excessive indebtedness in third countries such as an EU candidate Montenegro (Hurley et al., 2018). Since its main source of income, tourism, due to the COVID-19 crisis decreased, this country cannot repay its loans. The total government debt now stands at 103% of economic output, of which 18% can be attributed to the principal of the Chinese loan granted at an interest rate of 2% (CEIC Data, 2020). This risk could also be potentially materialized in the EU if this project financing form of the BRI would be implemented in the member states. Consequently, the infrastructure of the national or strategic importance could become the property of Chinese creditors in the event of loan default. The document published by the European Court of Auditors (2020) states that most of these loans are executed by the state-owned enterprises (SOE), and this way of execution implies that there is no need to take ownership of the infrastructure.

In order to limit China's influence in the EU, a framework for screening foreign direct investment has been established, which will be discussed in more detail in the following section.

FRAGMENTED SCREENING OF CHINESE INVESTMENTS

The expected increase in Chinese investments on the territory of the European Union caused concern among EU regulators. As a result, a new Regulation 2019/452 was adopted, establishing a framework for FDI screening in the EU, applicable from 11th October 2020 (Gadocha, 2020). The Regulation stipulates certain conditions for the screening mechanism, but does not impose an obligation on member states to adopt it (European Commission 2021b).

The Regulation specifies that during the foreign direct investment screening process a member state, another member state or the Commission could take into account the potential effects of FDI on infrastructure, including energy, transport, communications, data warehousing, critical technologies, artificial intelligence, space or nuclear technology, the access to sensitive information or the ability to control sensitive information. The Regulation should contribute to the transparency of Chinese foreign direct investment, including the information on investors, ownership and the sectors in which they operate, the value of the investment and its financing, as well as a completion date. Bambalas & Romeris (2019) outline that the real impact of the Regulation on Chinese FDI flows in the EU will be known only after the Regulation becomes applicable, but we should be aware of the fact that the FDI from China to the EU had begun to decline before that the Regulation was adopted due to the changes in China's domestic policy.

The European Commission and the member states are already cooperating in this regard to ensure the smooth implementation of the Regulation at both EU and national levels. In the middle of 2021, 18 member states implemented the screening mechanisms, while before the Regulation was adopted, it had existed in 11 member states. Companies planning to invest in the EU should be aware of the potential impact of the Regulation 2019/452 on their transactions.

The Regulation includes an indicative list of the factors covering the following areas: critical infrastructure, critical technologies, the supply of critical inputs, the access to sensitive information, information control, the freedom and pluralism of the media, all of which help the member states and the Commission determine whether an investment is likely to affect security or the public order.

According to the European Commission's first annual report on the experience with the Foreign Direct Investment Regulation, published on 23rd November 2021, the European Commission reviewed 265 transactions by June 2021. The largest number of investors came from the US, the UK, China, Canada and the United Arab Emirates. On the reporting date, 212 cases were closed in Phase 1, 14% requested additional information in Phase 2, and 6% were still active. Most of the investments that required additional information were related to the Manufacturing and Information and Communication Technologies sectors. The report shows that 91% of the formally reviewed files were approved, as many as 79% without any conditions, and the other 12% with certain conditions. The other investments were not realized because 2% of them were prohibited, and 7% were terminated for unknown reasons. (European Commission, 2021a) This approach should provide the control of the investments of strategic importance which, given the structure of the EU market, may have implications for several member states.

CONCLUSION

By January 2021, over 130 countries in Asia, Africa, Europe, Latin America and the Caribbean joined the Belt and Road Initiative, the concept which had been presented by President Xi Jinping during his visit to Kazakhstan in September 2013. The Initiative covers a wide network of railways, pipelines, ports and roads, as well as building infrastructure and investment, uninterrupted trade, cultural and scientific exchange. Having in mind the strategic, economic and political importance of the Initiative, it became the subject of a number of various researches published in a number of scientific and professional literature.

The focus of our research is on the countries of the China - Central and Eastern European Countries Initiative which was launched in 2012 and included 16 former communist countries until 2019 when Greece also joined at the 8th Summit in Dubrovnik (Croatia). The motivation of the countries of Central, Eastern and Southeastern Europe to access the Initiative was that the financial crisis in 2008 when the EU did not provide enough funds to the newly joined EU countries. Therefore, the alternative offered by China, enabling the process of granting the financing of the investments in the field of infrastructure, new technologies and green economy, made it attractive for Central and Eastern European countries. Furthermore, Chinese technology and equipment became more accessible to these countries, thus enabling high speed infrastructure construction.

China's motivation for the cooperation with the countries of Central, Eastern and Southeastern Europe is, above all, the ability to access various European markets. Moreover, this is an opportunity for Chinese construction companies to participate in the construction of infrastructure in the mentioned countries. In practice, Chinese contractors are more involved in infrastructure projects than the local ones. Therefore, these projects do not provide the possibility of significant job creation for the local population. It should be emphasized that from 75 to 85% of the infrastructure construction projects in the region of Central, Eastern and Southeastern Europe are financed from Chinese loans. As China has approved loans without sufficiently considering credit risks, this has contributed to the over-indebtedness of an EU candidate Montenegro. Bearing in mind that the crisis is still ongoing, the effects of the new crisis on China's Initiative in the area of the countries covered by the 17 + 1 Initiative are still uncertain and will significantly depend on crisis's duration. In addition, Chinese investments have not reached a significant level in the region of Central, Eastern and Southeastern Europe, especially not in the EU member states.

The expectations of the countries of Central, Eastern and Southeastern Europe, which enthusiastically accepted this form of cooperation, have not been fully met and some countries expressed their dissatisfaction with the economic results at the summit in Sofia 2018. This summit stressed the need to increase transparency regarding "16+1" activities with more balanced trade, the reciprocity of market access and open tenders in infrastructure construction, as well as tangible economic results for the BRI countries. Moreover, there is a risk that the environmental standards are not sufficiently respected during the implementation of these projects. Considering that it is necessary to limit Chinese influence in the region, the EU has established the Framework for foreign direct investment screening which does not impose any obligations to the member states to obey the Framework.

Since the researches indicate that reduced transport costs and travel time, along with the improvements related to the regulation of the business environment can have a positive impact on trade and investment, and thus on development as well, future research will be focused on whether the effects of the Initiatives would affect the volume of investments in the analysed countries.

REFERENCES

Abu Dayeh, B., & Janíčko, M. (2021). Determinants of Chinese Foreign Direct Investment in Central and Eastern Europe. *Central European Business Review, 10*(3), 19–36. doi:10.18267/j.cebr.254

Arduino, A., & Gong, X. (2018). *Securing the Belt and Road Initiative*. . doi:10.1007/978-981-10-7116-4

Bambalas, A., & Romeris, M. (2019). China's One Belt One Road Initiative and the Eu's Fdi Screening Regime: Scope, Eu's Attitude and Impact. *Social Transformations in Contemporary Society, 7.*

Brown, R. C. (2020). China's BRI in Central Eastern European Countries: "17+1" Connectivity, Divisiveness, or Pathway to EU-CHINA FTA? *San Diego International Law Journal, 22*(1), 1–40.

Buckley, P. J. (2020). China's Belt and Road Initiative and the COVID-19 crisis. *J Int Bus Policy, 3*(3), 311–314. doi:10.105742214-020-00063-9

CEIC Data. (2020). *Montenegro Government Debt: % of GDP*. Global Economic Data, Indicators, Charts and Forecasts. Available at: https://www.ceicdata.com/en/indicator/montenegro/government-debt–of-nominal-gdp

Chan, L. (2016). *Belt and Road Opportunities in Central and Eastern Europe*. Available at: https://perma.cc/6RX7-PUK7

Chen, M., & Lin, C. (2018*). Foreign Investment across the Belt and Road: Patterns, Determinants and Effects.* Policy Research Working Paper 8607, World Bank.

China-CEE Institute. (2018). 16+1 Cooperation and China-EU Relationship. Budapest: China-CEE Institute.

China-CEE Institute. (2019). *Greece External Relations Briefing: Dubrovnik Summit Welcomes Greece.* Available at: https://china-cee.eu/2019/05/09/greece-externalrelations-briefing-dubrovnik-summit-welcomes-greece/

China National Statistical Bureau's. (2018). *2018 Statistical Bulletin of China's Outward Foreign Direct Investment*. China Statistics Press.

Coenen, J., Bager, S., Meyfroidt, P., Newig, J., & Challies, E. (2020). Environmental Governance of China's Belt and Road Initiative. *Environmental Policy and Governance, 31*(1), 3-17. doi:10.1002/eet.1901

Conley, H. A., Hillman, J. E., McCalpin, M., & Ruy, D. (2020). *Becoming a Chinese Client State. The Case of Serbia*. Center for Strategic & International Studies. Available at https://csis-websiteprod.s3.amazonaws.com/s3fs-public/publication/200924_Chinese_Client.pdf

Derudder, B., Liu, X., & Kunaka, C. (2018). *Connectivity along Overland Corridors of the Belt and Road Initiative*. MTI Global Practice Discussion Paper; No. 6. World Bank.

Domazet, I., & Marjanović, D. (2018). Foreign Direct Investment and Economic Development: Comparative Analysis of Bulgarian, Romanian and Serbian Economies. In Western Balkans Economies in EU Integration: Past, present and future. CEMAFI International Association.

Escobar, P. (2016). Silk Roads, Night Trains, and the Third Industrial Revolution in China. *New Perspectives Quarterly*, *33*(1), 24–31. doi:10.1111/npqu.12020

European Chamber of Commerce. (2019). *Business Confidence Survey*. Available at: https://www.eurochambres.eu/

European Commission. (2020). *White paper on levelling the playing field as regards foreign subsidies*. Available at: https://ec.europa.eu/competition-policy/system/files/2021-06/foreign_subsidies_white_paper_en.pdf

European Commission. (2021a). *First Annual Report on the screening of foreign direct investments into the Union*. Available at: https://trade.ec.europa.eu/doclib/docs/2021/november/tradoc_159935.pdf

European Commission. (2021b). *List of screening mechanisms notified by Member States*. Available at: https://trade.ec.europa.eu/doclib/docs/2019/ june/tradoc_157946.pdf

European Court of Auditors (ECA). (2020). *The EU's response to China's state-driven investment strategy*. Available at: https://www.euractiv.com/wp-content/uploads/sites/2/2020/09/ECA_EU-China-review_EMBARGO-THU-10-SEP-09H00-CET.pdf

European Parliament. (2019). *China, the 16+1 format and the EU*. Available at: https://www.europarl.europa.eu/RegData/etudes/BRIE/2018/625173/EPRS_BRI (2018)625173_EN.pdf

Eurostat. (2021). *China-EU - international trade in goods statistics*. Available at: https://ec.europa.eu/eurostat/statistics-explained/index.php?title=China-EU_-_international_trade_in_goods_statistics

Gadocha, P.M. (2020). Assessing the EU Framework Regulation for the Screening of Foreign Direct Investment—What Is the Effect on Chinese Investors? *The Chinese Journal of Global Governance*.

Goh, B. (2015). China Railway Group Team Wins $1.6 Bln Hungary High-Speed Rail Contract. *Reuters*. Available at: https://greenfdc.org/countries-of-the-belt-and-road-initiative-bri

Grieger, G. (2018). *China, the 16+1 Format and the EU*. Members' Research Service PE 625.173. Available at: http://www.europarl.europa.eu/RegData/etudes/ BRIE/2018/625173/EPRS_BRI(2018)625173_EN.pdf.

He, A. (2019). *The Belt and Road Initiative: Motivations, Financing, Expansion and Challenges of Xi's Ever-expanding Strategy. CIGI Papers, No. 225*. Centre for International Governance Innovation.

Heide, D., Hoppe, T., Scheuer, S., & Stratmann, K. (2018). *EU ambassadors band together against Silk Road*. Handelsblatt.

Hofman, B. (2015). *China's One Belt One Road Initiative: What We Know Thus Far*. Available at: https://blogs.worldbank.org/eastasiapacific/china-one-belt-one-road-initiative-what-we-know-thus-far

Holslag, J. (2019). The Silk Road Trap. Polity Press.

Hughes, A. C. (2018). Understanding and Minimizing Environmental Impacts of the Belt and Road Initiative. *Conservation Biology*, *33*(4), 883–894. doi:10.1111/cobi.13317 PMID:30900273

Hurley, J., Morris, S. & Portelance, G., (2018). *Examining the Debt Implications of the Belt and Road Initiative from a Policy Perspective.* Centre for Global Development, CGD Policy Paper 121.

Kavalski, E. (2020). *Is China out the window in the CEE?* Available at: https://www.echo-wall.eu/currents-context/chinaout-window-cee

Kratz, A., Huotari, M., Hanemann, T., & Arcesati, R. (2020). *Chinese FDI in Europe: 2019 Update.* MERICS.

Kratz, A., Rosen, D. H., & Mingey, M. (2020). *Booster or Brake? COVID and the Belt and Road Initiative.* Rhodium Group. Available at: https://rhg.com/research/booster-or-brake-covid-and-the-belt-and-road-initiative

Kratz, A., Zenglein, M. J., & Sebastian, G. (2021). *Chinese FDI in Europe: 2020 Update.* Mercator Institute for China Studies. Available at: https://merics.org/en/report/chinese-fdi-europe-2020-update

Kynge, J., & Yu, S. (2020). China faces wave of calls for debt relief on "Belt and Road" projects. *Financial Times.*

Lechmacher, W., & Padilla-Taylor, V. (2015). Hurdles Ahead Along the "New Silk Road." *Financial Times Blog.* Available at: http://blogs.ft.com/beyondbrics/2015/09/17/hurdles-ahead-along-the-new-silk-road/

Lisinge, R. T. (2020). The Belt and Road Initiative and Africa's regional infrastructure development: Implications and lessons. *Transnational Corporations Review, 12*(4), 425–438. doi:10.1080/19186444.2020.1795527

List of screening mechanisms notified by Member States. (n.d.). Available at: https://trade.ec.europa.eu/doclib/docs/2019/june/tradoc_157946.pdf

Marjanović, D., & Domazet, I. (2021). Foreign Direct Investments: A Key Factor for Business Globalization. In Handbook of Research on Institutional, Economic, and Social Impacts of Globalization and Liberalization. IGI Global. doi:10.4018/978-1-7998-4459-4.ch006

Matura, T. (2021). *Chinese Investment in Central and Eastern Europe: A reality check.* CEECAS. Available at: https://bird.tools/wp-content/uploads/2021/04/72d38a_373928ea28c44c7f9c875ead7fc49c44.pdf

McCaleb, A., & Szunomár, Á. (2017). Chinese foreign direct investment in Central and Eastern Europe. In J. Drahokoupil (Ed.), *Chinese investment in Europe: Corporate strategies and labour relations* (pp. 121–140). ETUI Aisbl.

Ministry of Foreign Affairs of the PRC. (2016). Available at: https://www.fmprc.gov.cn/web/zyxw/t1413173.shtml

Mouritz, F. (2020). Implications of the COVID-19 Pandemic on China's Belt and Road Initiative. *Connections: The Quarterly Journal, 19*(2), 115-124.

NDRC. (2015). *Vision and actions on jointly building the Silk Road Economic Belt and 21st-century Maritime Silk Road.* Available at: https://en.ndrc.gov.cn/newsrelease/201503/t20150330_669367.html

Pelaudeix, C. (2021). *The rise of China and EU vulnerability.* https://halshs.archives-ouvertes.fr/halshs-03323014/document

Pendrakowska, P. (2018). Poland's perspective on the Belt and Road Initiative. *Journal of Contemporary East Asia Studies*, *7*(2), 190–206. doi:10.1080/24761028.2018.1552491

Petkova, M. (2021). The Environmental Impact of Chinese Projects in the Western Balkans. Association for International Affairs (AMO).

Poulain, L. (2011). China's New Balkan Strategy. Central Europe Watch, 1(2), 7.

Prague Security Studies Institute. (2019). *Comparative Analysis of the Approach towards China: V4+ and One Belt One Road.* Available at: https://ceias.eu/wp-content/uploads/2019/05/COMPARATIVE_ANALYSIS_full_05.pdf

Ross, J. (2016). *China Strengthening Links with Eastern Europe.* Available at: http://www.china.org.cn/opinion/2016- 05/17/content_38470993.htm

Stakić, N., & Zakić, K. (2016). Challenges of business and financial transformation of China in New Normal Economy. *The Review of International Affairs*, *67*(1161), 80–100.

Szijjártó, P. (2019). *The Speech of H.E. Péter Szijjártó in the Hungarian Parliament, Assembly day 72, Speech No. 60.* Hungarian National Assembly.

Teo, H. C., Lechner, A. M., Walton, G. W., Chan, F. K. S., Cheshmehzangi, A., Tan-Mullins, M., Chan, H. K., Sternberg, T., & Campos-Arceiz, A. (2019). Environmental Impacts of Infrastructure Development under the Belt and Road Initiative. *Environments*, *6*(6), 72. doi:10.3390/environments6060072

The Ministry of Foreign Affairs of the PRC. (2012). *China's Twelve Measures for Promoting Friendly Cooperation with Central and Eastern European Countries.* Available at: http://www.fmprc.gov.cn/mfa_eng/ topics_665678/wjbispg_665714/t928567.shtml

Wang, N. C. (2021a). *China Belt and Road Initiative (BRI) Investment Report H1 2021.* Green BRI Centre, International Institute of Green Finance (IIGF).

Wang, N. C. (2021b). *China's Investments in the Belt and Road Initiative (BRI) in 2020, Green BRI Centre, International Institute of Green Finance.* IIGF.

Wang, Y. (2016). Offensive for defensive: The Belt and Road Initiative and China's new grand strategy. *The Pacific Review*, *29*(3), 455–463. doi:10.1080/09512748.2016.1154690

World Bank. (2019). *Belt and Road Economics: Opportunities and Risks of Transport Corridors.* World Bank.

Xinhua. (2019). *Full text of the Dubrovnik Guidelines for Cooperation between China and Central and Eastern European Countries – Xinhua.* Available at: http://www.xinhuanet.com/english/2019-04/13/c_137973910.htm

Zhao, S. (2019). China's Belt-Road Initiative as the Signature of President Xi Jinping Diplomacy: Easier Said than Done. *Journal of Contemporary China*, 1–17. doi:10.1080/10670564.2019.1645483

Zhou, W., & Esteban, M. (2018). Beyond Balancing: China's Approach towards the Belt and Road Initiative. *Journal of Contemporary China*, *27*(112), 1–15. doi:10.1080/10670564.2018.1433476

Chapter 7
The Impact of Investment on the Economic Activity of the Balkan Silk Road Countries

Duško Bodroža
https://orcid.org/0000-0002-6219-1338
Institute of Economic Sciences, Serbia

Miloš Kolavčić
Faculty for Banking, Finance, and Insurance, Belgrade Banking Academy, Serbia

ABSTRACT

The aim of this chapter is to examine the impact of investment in research and development on economic growth, as well as the nature of the impact of trade openness and foreign direct investment on extended Balkan Silk Road economies. The authors used the general econometric specification of the regression panel model and for the period from 2002 to 2018. The results showed that expenditures on research and development and trade openness have a significant positive effect on the gross domestic product of the countries with lower GDP per capita, while foreign direct investment in these countries has a neutral and nonsignificant impact on gross domestic product. For the countries with higher GDP per capita, expenditures on research and development have a marginally negative effect on the gross domestic product. Trade openness is significantly positive, while foreign direct investments have a significant but neutral effect on the gross domestic product. The main limitations of the research are the use of data on total R&D investment and foreign trade relations instead of sectoral.

INTRODUCTION

In the past ten years, China has become one of the major financiers of infrastructure projects in the transport and energy sectors of the Balkan region (Holzner and Schwarzhappel, 2018). As one of the fastest-growing economies globally, China wants to become an economic superpower. In order to achieve its goal, one of the strategies for that goal is to establish the cheapest transport connection from the Far

DOI: 10.4018/978-1-7998-8021-9.ch007

East to the European market. This connection is named The Balkan Silk Road. It is the transport route and logistics corridor that China has begun to establish in the Balkan region as part of the Belt and Road Initiative (BRI) (Bastian, 2017). The route begins in the Greek port of Piraeus, passes through Skopje and Belgrade, and broadens to Hungary. Besides this route, the Belt and Road initiative includes other Balkan countries, i.e. Albania, Montenegro and Bosnia and Herzegovina. BRI envisages large investments into roads, railways, ports, bridges, thermal power plants and supporting infrastructure and operating systems. Through these projects, China aims to improve transport and energy infrastructure in the Balkan region by supporting its global trade in different manufacturing and services sectors (Siddiqui, 2019).

These investments will diversify sources of access to capital in the Balkan region and have a positive impact on the acceleration of economic activity through GDP growth (Lakshmanan, 2011, Erić et. al, 2021) and increase productivity by reducing transport costs within and across observed countries (Bastian, 2017). Taking part in the new Silk Road represents a great development opportunity for the Balkan region to be actively involved in international trade, technological and financial flows. Performing the analysis, the authors want to investigate the effects of investments on the observed countries' economic activity in the recent period. The obtained results will be used to assess the expected future effects of the BRI on the Balkan Silk Road countries.
In accordance with the objective of the research, two hypotheses will be tested:

H1: Investment in research and development has a significant positive impact on the country's gross domestic product

H2: Foreign trade relations, measured by trade openness and foreign direct investment, have a significant but indirect impact on economic growth

In the analysis, the authors used the general econometric specification of the regression panel model. The sample includes 7 countries of the Balkan Peninsula (Serbia, North Macedonia, Bosnia and Herzegovina, Croatia, Slovenia, Bulgaria, and Greece) and Hungary, which is part of the extended Balkan Silk Road. The time interval of the data is 17 years and covers the period from 2002 to 2018., a panel set of data includes 136 observations.

This chapter is organized as follows. After the introduction, Section 2 brings a theoretical basis and literature review related to the subject of research. Section 3 presents the BRI data facts, as well as investments trend and worth of construction total and by sector in observed the Balkan Silk Road countries. Afterward, in section 4 the research methodology is presented. Section 5, the results of the research were discussed. Finally, section 6 presents the chapter's conclusions.

LITERATURE REVIEW

Investments in the modern economy take over the function of a major development factor and, along with trade, become a key component of growth and development. Analysis of the effects that investments have on the economy is a very complex assignment. The rich literature on economic growth does not primarily deal with the role of investment, but certain findings and conclusions from this literature are very important when we consider investment as a driver of economic growth. For most countries, the contribution of investment to economic activity is significant. It represents a combination of positive effects, starting with the boosting of economic activity in the country, employment growth, and most importantly, the transfer and spillover of knowledge and technology (Borenzstein et al., 1998, Mehic et al., 2013, Pegkas, 2015, Dinh et al. 2019, Đukić et al., 2016).

Since the early 1990s, a number of empirical analyses have been conducted based on models of endogenous growth. An important question is how to calculate innovation at the macroeconomic level. Investments in research and development and patent statistics are often used as an indicator of innovation. The pioneering work was presented by Lichtenberg (1992), who investigated the relationship between research and development investment and productivity based on comparative data for 74 countries from 1964 to 1989. In the study, he concluded that private sector expenditures have a positive effect on growth, while public sector investments do not create a positive effect, and sometimes have a negative impact. There are numerous analyses of panel data assessing the relationship between research and development investment and economic growth, and the results obtained vary for different panels, time periods, variables, and econometric methods. De Melo (1997) claims that the impact of investments on technologically backward countries is much greater than in developed countries.

Silaghi et al. (2014) analyzed private and public sector investment in research and development in Central and Eastern European countries from 1998 to 2008. Their conclusion was that private sector investment in research and development has a statistically significant impact on the economic growth of European Union countries, while public sector investment has had a neutral impact. Pece et al. (2015) using multiple regression models confirmed the positive relationship between economic growth and number of patents, number of trademarks and R&D expenditures. Huňady and Orviska (2014) based their research on a regression analysis of panel data for 26 European countries in the period from 1999 to 2000, in which they concluded that research and development expenditures have a positive impact on economic growth with a shifted effect of two years, while the effect was negative for the current year. Based on a panel model of data for 30 developing countries in the period from 2000 to 2006, Samimi and Alerasoul (2009) concluded that due to low amounts of investment in research and development, a cause-and-effect relationship with economic development could not be established. As the literature review shows, there is still an open question about the overall impact of research and development expenditure on the economic growth of European countries.

The assessment of the impact of trade openness on economic growth is widely discussed in the scientific literature. An empirical measure of trade openness, defined as the ratio of exports plus imports to GDP - is the measure most often used in empirical studies; as Busse and Königer (2012) did and concluded from a panel model for 108 countries (of which 87 are developing countries) that trade openness has a significant positive impact on economic growth. Andersen and Babula (2009) identified channels through which international trade can impact economic growth: (1) facilitating access to foreign products and technologies, (2) facilitating the international distribution of knowledge, (3) expanding the size of the market for new products. Previous research showed that international trade has a positive impact on economic growth through facilitating capital accumulation, modernizing industry, and technological progress (Iwaisako & Futagami, 2013). Were (2015) analyzed the effect of trade openness (trade, export and import as a share of GDP) on economic growth on panel data for 85 countries with significantly different levels of development, when he concluded that there is a significant positive impact in developed and developing countries but it's effect was insignificant for the least developed countries which largely include African countries. Zaman et al. (2021) using the annual panel data of BRI countries from 2013 to 2018 showed that trade openness has a negative and insignificant impact on economic growth. Observing the CEE countries, the results usually showed the positive impact of trade openness on economic growth (Gurgul and Lach, 2014, Çetintaş, and Barişik, 2009).

The link between foreign direct investment and economic growth has attracted much attention from scientists around the world (Vo et al. 2019). Consensus on their relationship has not yet been reached, as theoretical and empirical literature offer contradictory conclusions about the impact of foreign direct investment on the gross domestic product of the host country. The researchers examined the relationship between foreign direct investment and economic growth in 4 directions, when it comes to neoclassical (exogenous) and endogenous models of economic growth: (1) determinants of economic growth, where foreign direct investment is one of the independent variables, (2) determinants foreign direct investment, where the gross domestic product is one of the independent variables, (3) the channels through which foreign direct investment affects growth, (4) the cause-and-effect relationship between the variables. Based on panel data for 90 developed and developing countries and the time span from 1980 to 2002, Johnson (2006) concluded that foreign direct investment has a significant positive effect on the economic growth of developing countries, but not developed countries. Alfaro et al. (2004) concluded that foreign direct investment is one of the key initiators of growth for the 20 members of the Organization for Economic Co-operation and Development (OECD). Jyun-Yi and Chih-Chiang (2008) did not identify a link between foreign direct investment and economic growth in a database for 62 countries between 1975 and 2000. Bodroža and Đukić (2018) using the panel data regression analysis for CEE countries in the period 1996 – 2014 found that FDI did not have a significant impact on economic growth.

As for the BRI route, it will have a positive impact on global economic development through shortening travel times and boosting trade and investment (World Bank, 2019). WB envisaged that travel times along the route countries will decline by up to 12 percent and an average of 3 percent at the rest of the world. Also, the same study estimates that trade will grow from between 2.8 and 9.7 percent for route economies and between 1.7 and 6.2 percent for the world economies. Furthermore, it is expected that foreign direct investments will increase by 7.6% in low-income countries and 3.4% -7.5% in other countries along the route.

DATA FACTS

The magnitude of The Belt and Road initiative is significant best shown by the fact that its combines more than a third of the global GDP of all involved countries, and 61 percent of the world's population (OECD, 2018). It involved 7 regions and more than 100 economies that have direct cooperation with China. In the period 2013-2021., in different projects, Chinese companies in the Belt and Road Initiative economies invested $ 60.470 million, while the worth of its construction was $ 34.010 million. Observed by region, Chinese companies invested the most in East Asia ($117,760 million), while construction worth was highest in the Sub-Saharan Africa region ($ 123,450 million).

Table 1. Investment and worth of construction in the Belt and Road Initiative, 2013-2021

Region	Investment, mill USD	%	Construction, mill USD	%
East Asia	117,760	36,7	91,250	19,3
West Asia	54,880	17,1	115,130	24,3
Europe	54,060	16,8	24,170	5,1
South America	40,850	12,7	14,470	3,1
North America	1,970	0,6	5,690	1,2
Sub-Saharan Africa	34,140	10,6	123,450	26,1
Arab Middle East and North Africa	17,600	5,5	99,720	21,0
TOTAL	**321,260**	100,0	**473,880**	100,0

Source: China Global Investment Tracker

Of all China investments, from 2013 to 2021, Balkan Silk Road countries attracted a total of USD 10,630 million in investment. China invested the most in Serbia (USD 4,440 million) and Greece (USD 3,840 million). As for the other Balkan Silk Road countries, Slovenia attracted USD 1,390 million, Bosnia and Herzegovina USD 420 million, Hungary USD 320 million and Croatia USD 220 million.

Figure 1. China's investment in Balkan silk road countries, 2013-2021
Source: Source: China Global Investment Tracker

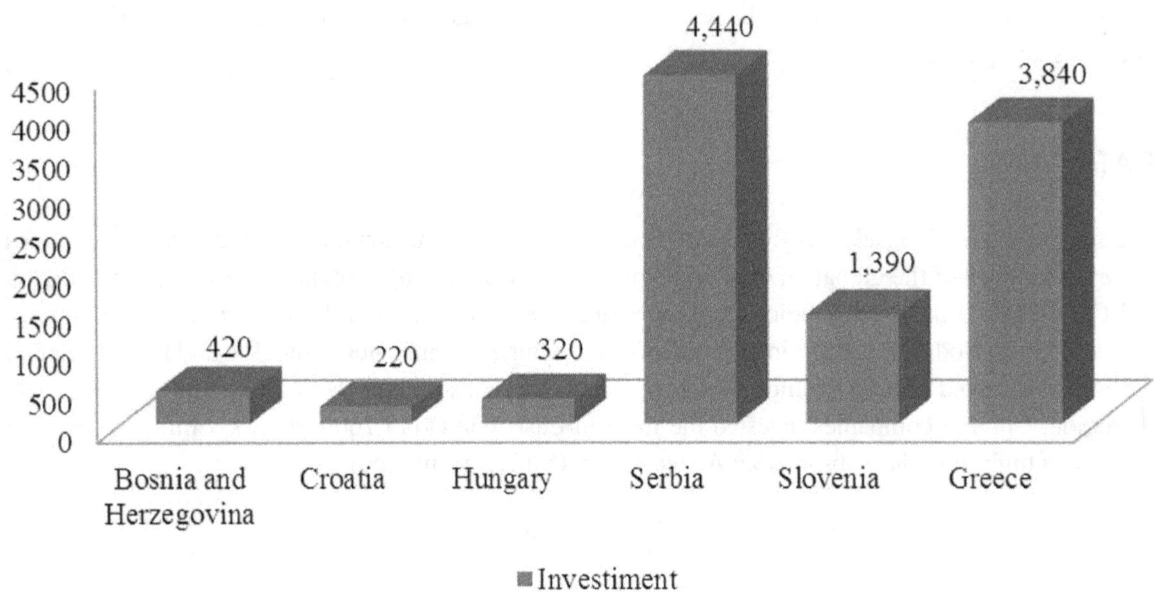

In the observed period, China invested in Balkan Silk Road countries the most in the energy sector (35.2% of total investment), transport (21.4% of total investment), and metals (20.6% of total investment). The next figure shows total investment in Balkan Silk Road countries by sector.

Figure 2. China investment in Balkan silk road countries by sector, 2013-2021
Source: Source: China Global Investment Tracker

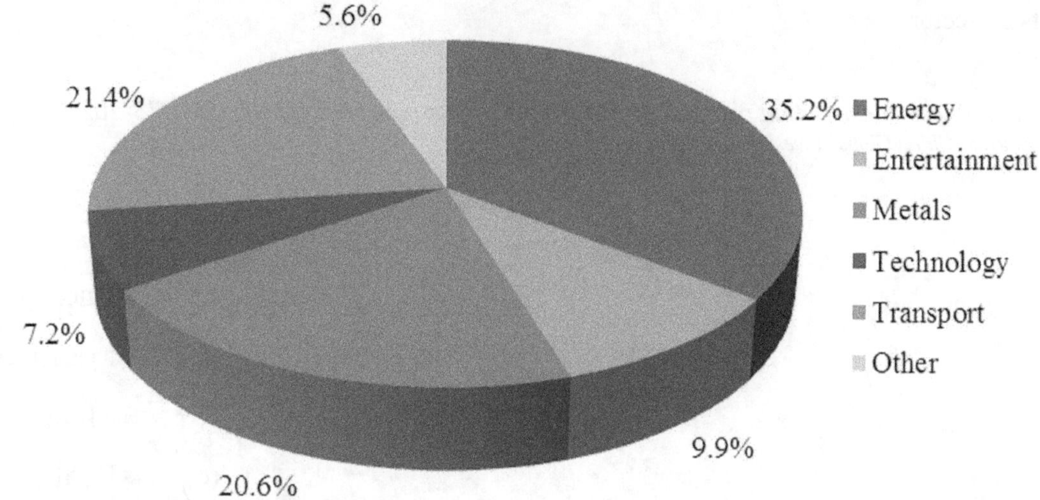

Chinese construction projects implemented between 2012 and 2021 were worth $11,150 million in credit loans from Chinese banks. These loans are guaranteed by the state. Most of China's construction projects were implemented in Serbia ($5,290 million), Hungary ($2,080 million) and Bosnia and Herzegovina ($1,080 million).

Figure 3. Chinese construction projects in Balkan Silk Road countries, 2013-2021
Source: Source: China Global Investment Tracker

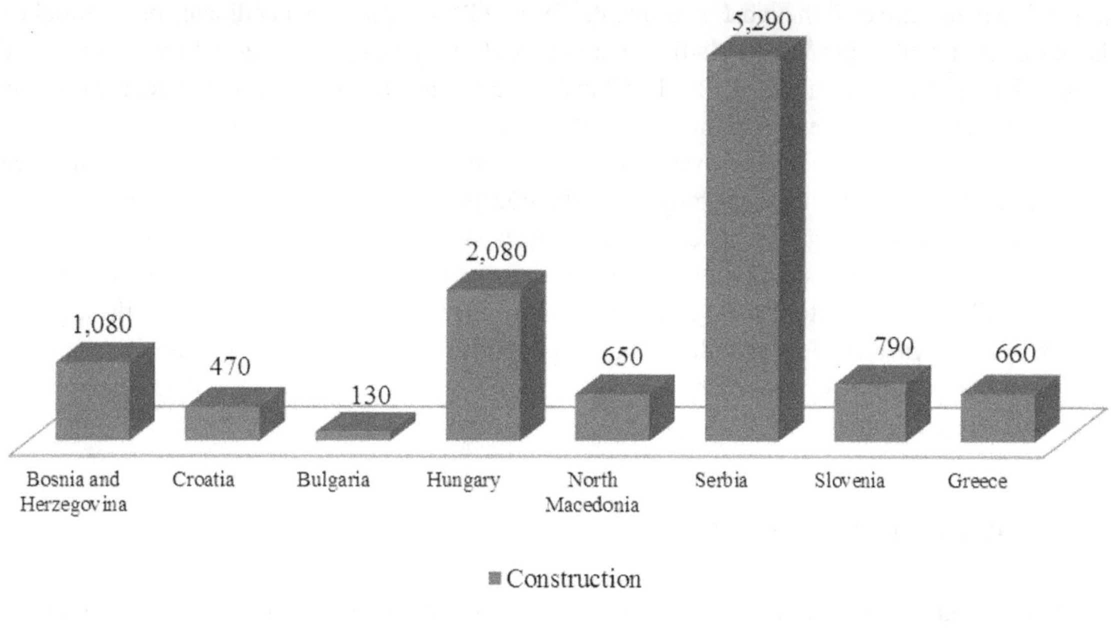

Between 2013 and 2021, China mainly assigned construction projects in the transport (66.8% of total loans) and energy (23.9% of total loans) sectors. The next figure shows the share of all construction projects by sector.

Figure 4. Chinese construction projects in Balkan Silk Road countries by sector, 2013-2021
Source: Source: China Global Investment Tracker

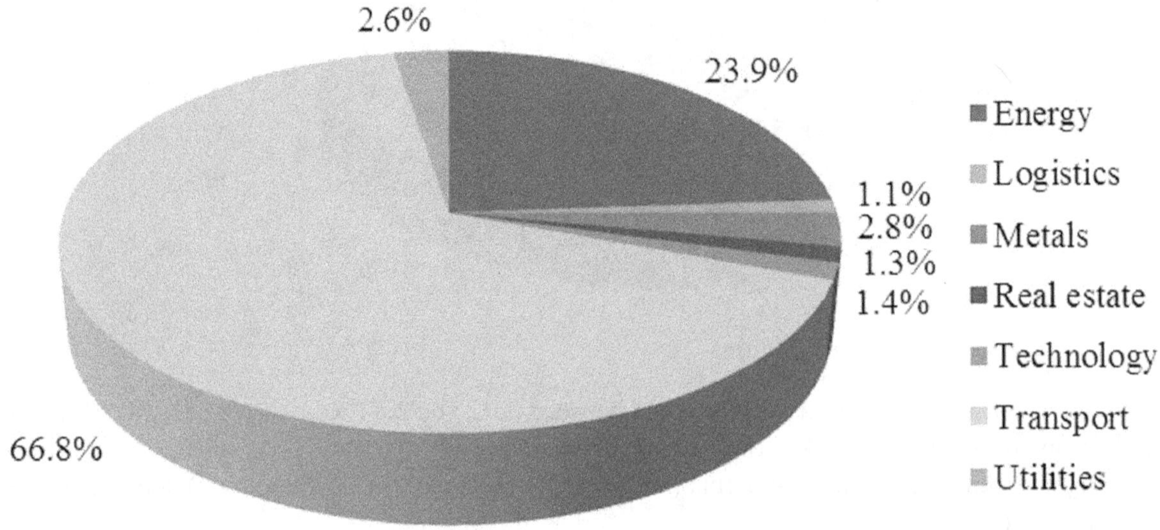

As we can see from the presented data, since 2013, China has significantly invested in Balkan Silk Road countries. Most of the investments have been observed in Serbia, while sectors energy, transport, and metals sectors attracted the most investment. Observed economies are candidates or potential candidates for EU membership but they still lag significantly in development behind the average of the European Union (Bodroža and Lazić, 2021). China's investment can significantly impact the economic performance and competitiveness of the Balkan Silk Road countries on their way to the EU.

The credit loans which were approved in order to finance construction projects in the Balkan Silk Road countries were mostly used for projects in the transport and energy sectors. Although these are projects that will, in the long term, affect the attractiveness of the region, i.e. attract FDI and accelerate economic growth, there should be caution because these projects are financed from credit loans. In addition, Chinese contractors and workers are mainly engaged in the development of these projects (Barisitz and Radzyner, 2017). The following is an analysis of the impact of investments in research and development (R&D), trade openness and foreign direct investments (FDI) on gross domestic product of Balkan Silk Road countries.

RESEARCH METHODOLOGY

The research methodology is aimed at examining the impact of investments in research and development, trade openness and foreign direct investments on the value of the gross domestic product of the country.

The general econometric specification of the regression panel model is:

$$y_{it=x_{it}'\beta+u_{it},t=1,..,T;i=1,..,N.}$$

Where y_{it} is a dependent variable, β is the m-dimensional vector of the coefficients, x_{it} is the m-dimensional vector of explanatory variables, u_{it} is an error of a stochastic nature (noise), t is an index that refers to time (years), and i is a country-specific index.

In order to increase the normality of the data, the logarithm of the dependent variable gross domestic product per capita was performed. Although the trade openness is expressed as in relation to the gross domestic product per capita variable was transformed in the logarithm of the value due to higher absolute amounts. Other independent variables are retained in their original form.

The panel model developed in this chapter has the following form:

$$\ln GDPpc_{it} = \beta_1 R\&D_{it} + \beta_2 \ln TRO_{it} + \beta_3 FDI_{it} + u_{it}$$

$\ln GDPpc_{it}$ - Gross domestic product per capita (constant 2015 US$)
$R\&D_{it}$ - Research and development expenditure (% of GDP)
$lnTRO_{it}$ - Trade (% of GDP)
FDI_{it} - Foreign direct investment, net inflows (% of GDP)

The sample includes 7 countries of the Balkan Peninsula (Serbia, North Macedonia, Bosnia and Herzegovina, Croatia, Slovenia, Bulgaria and Greece) and Hungary, which is part of the extended Balkan Silk Road. The time interval of the data is 17 years and covers the period from 2002 to 2018. In the process of data collection, the author applied the desk method and used the World Bank database, as a secondary data source. At the beginning of the data processing, a panel set of data was formed, which includes 136 observations, since the sample covered 8 countries (N), and the research period is 17 years (T). Further processing of the panel series was carried out using the statistical software 'STATA'.

The initial panel data set was further divided into two-panel clusters based on the average gross domestic product per capita in the observed period.

Table 2. Panel clusters

Country	Average GDP per Capita	Panel Cluster
Bosnia and Herzegovina	$4,118.86	Lower GDP pc
North Macedonia	$4,223.91	
Serbia	$5,091.58	
Bulgaria	$6,199.21	
Croatia	$11,703.33	Higher GDP pc
Hungary	$11,795.99	
Greece	$20,445.43	
Slovenia	$20,453.92	

Source: Author's review

"Lower GDP pc" panel cluster (LGDPpc) consists of three countries that are not members of the European Union and Bulgaria, which, although a member, had a similar level of average gross domestic product per capita in the period between 2002 and 2018.

"Higher GDP pc" panel cluster (HGDPpc) consists of four countries which are members of the European Union with significantly higher gross domestic product per capita.

The reason for creating two panel clusters is to analyze what impact each of the independent variables has on the gross domestic product of countries with different levels of development.

The panel data applied in the research has the character of balanced and macro panel data, because each time series in the model is of the same length, and the units of observation in the research are countries.

The advantage of panel analysis is that data, which are not sufficient for time series analysis or for spatial analysis, combined into panel data can give quality empirical results. Panel analysis has found application in all areas of the economy at the micro and macro level.

Before performing the analysis of the regression panel model, the time series stationarity was tested using *Levin-Lin-Chu* test (*Levin-Lin-Chu unit root test).* Stationarity of data is extremely important in research because, as Gujarati (2004) states, if regression analysis were performed on non-stationary data, false research results would be obtained.

Since the correlation matrix between the dependent and independent variables was set, an analysis of the correlation coefficients was performed, in order to determine the existence of correlation and the nature of the relationship between the variables. The correlation between the variables was determined by applying Pearson's Coefficient Correlation.

Analysis of the presence of heteroskedasticity, autocorrelation, cross-section dependence and multicollinearity, characteristic for econometric estimation of panel models, were performed, because these are problems that can lead to error in estimating regression panel model. If the values of the random error are distributed randomly and the same are distributed for all independent variables (all random errors have the same variance), the assumption of homoskedasticity is not violated. However, if we can notice some pattern in the grouping of random error values, there is probably a violation of the assumption, and we have a heteroskedasticity problem. The standard error of these estimated values will be biased and unobjective (Baltagi, 2005). Heteroskedasticity was examined using *Wald* test (Greene, 2000) (*Modified Wald test for heteroskedasticity).*

In time series in which random errors are correlated between observation periods, autocorrelation occurs. Autocorrelation often occurs in time series in which a random error, which refers to one observation, begins to become dependent on a random error, which refers to another observation. The dependence of the observation in a certain period of time on the observations in the previous time periods conditions the occurrence of serial correlation, i.e. autocorrelations. Wooldridge (2002) presented an attractive test to identify autocorrelation in panel data series, which requires relatively few assumptions and is very easy to perform. *Wooldridge* test, compared to other tests with more parameters, has less power, but, on the other hand, is more robust, i.e. stable (Drukker, 2003).

In panel data, common shocks, such as recession, or spillover effects per observation unit, are common, affecting all comparative data in the panel over a period of time. Such common shocks, in the panel model, may reflect a violation of the assumption of the absence of correlation of random errors between comparative data and (or) correlation of these shocks (contained in the random error) with regressors. Then it is about the existence of dependence between comparative data, i.e. the dependence of cross-sectional data (*Cross-sectional dependence - CSD*). The existence of dependencies between comparative data was examined using *Pesaran* test (Pesaran, 2004).

Multicollinearity occurs when there is a large dependence between two variables. Multicollinearity is considered to be a data problem, not a model or method of estimating coefficients. In order to identify the presence of multicollinearity between the independent variables used in the research, it is most often used *VIF* test (*Variance Inflation Factor test*). The VIF test shows whether one independent variable is in a strong linear relationship with other independent variables.

In addition, due to the specificity of the model, the problem of possible endogeneity, i.e. simultaneous interdependence of the dependent variable gross domestic product *(lnGDPpc)* was examined and independent variables expenditure on research and development *(R&D),* because it can be assumed that countries with a higher level of gross domestic product allocate a larger amount of funds for research and development. *Durbin-Wu-Hausman* test was performed as the endogeneity test of the variables,, which makes it possible to individually test the endogeneity of each of the variables in the equation, but also the potential endogeneity of the set of variables.

RESULTS

When performing econometric analysis on panel data, the first step in the analysis represents testing the presence of a unit root in time series. In other words, in order for the analysis to be valid, it is necessary for the series to show properties stationarity. For this reason, the analysis was started by examining stationarity time series of variables using the Levin-Lin-Chu (LLC) test.

Levin, Lin, and Chu (2002) state that the following hypotheses should be tested during testing:

H0: The panel series is not stationary (contains a unit root).

X1: The panel series is stationary (does not contain a unit root).

Table 3. Unit root test result

Variable	Panel Cluster	Level	Statistic	P - Value
lnGDPpc	LGDPpc	Original	-3.08	0.00
	HGDPpc	Original	-0.91	0.18
		first difference	-1.52	0.06
R&D	LGDPpc	Original	-0.90	0.18
	HGDPpc	Original	1.35	0.91
		first difference	-1.93	0.03
lnTRO	LGDPpc	Original	-2.09	0.02
	HGDPpc	Original	-1.89	0.03
FDI	LGDPpc	Original	-2.16	0.02
	HGDPpc	Original	-0.32	0.37
		first difference	-3.46	0.00

Source: Author's review

Based on the obtained results, it can be concluded that in LGDPpc panel cluster only the variable R&D is not stationary (0.18), while in the case of all other variables the condition of stationarity is satisfied. Given that the non-stationarity of only one independent variable was noted, with a p-value of 0.18, further analysis will be performed without transforming the initial data. In HGDPpc panel cluster, dependent variable lnGDPpc as well as two independent variables R&D and FDI showed first-order non-stationarity. For this reason, all three variables were transformed with first-order differentiation. As after the first-order differentiation variables showed stationarity, in such a transformed form it will be used in further analysis of this panel cluster.

Table 4. Correlation matrix

LGDPpc	lnGDPpc	R&D	lnTRO	FDI	HGDPpc	fd_lnGDPpc	fd_R&D	lnTRO	fd_FDI
lnGDPpc	1.00				**fd_lnGDPpc**	1.00			
R&D	0.76* (.0.00)	1.00			**fd_R&D**	-0.18 (0.15)	1.00		
lnTRO	0.67* (0.00)	0.28* (0.02)	1.00		**lnTRO**	0.28* (0.02)	0.05 (0.68)	1.00	
FDI	0.13 (0.28)	0.04 (0.74)	0.09 (0.46)	1.00	**fd_FDI**	0.06 (0.61)	-0.31* (0.01)	-0.05 (0.67)	1.00

Source: Author's review

Results of the Correlation Matrix presented in Table 4 show that for the LGDPpc panel cluster between independent variables R&D and lnTRO and dependent variable there is a strong positive and significant correlation. There is a statistically significant positive correlation between lnTRO and lnGDPpc in HGDPpc panel cluster. In both panel clusters there is no high correlation between independent variables even there is a significant correlation between lnTRO and R&D in LGDPpc and fd_FDI and fd_R&D

in HGDPpc. Thus we can assume that there will be no problem of multicollinearity in the model. As independent variable FDI showed nonlinear relation to the dependent variable, its squared value was added to the model for both panel clusters as an additional independent variable.

Table 5. VIF test

LGDPpc			HGDPpc		
Variable	**VIF**	**1/VIF**	**Variable**	**VIF**	**1/VIF**
R&D	1.11	0.90	fd_R&D	1.11	0.90
lnTRO	1.17	0.85	lnTRO	1.13	0.88
FDI	8.81	0.11	fd_FDI	1.15	0.87
FDIsq	8.98	0.11	fd_FDIsq	1.18	0.85
Mean VIF	5.02		Mean VIF	1.14	

Source: Author's review.

The VIF test showed that there is no multicollinearity between the independent variables, because the test result is close to 1 for HGDPpc panel cluster and close to 5 for LGDPpc panel cluster. If the VIF value is greater than 10, there is a strong presence of multicollinearity (Bowerman and O'Connell, 1990).

The panel model for the LGDPpc panel cluster has the following form:

$$\ln GDPpc_{it} = \beta_1 R\&D_{it} + \beta_2 \ln TRO_{it} + \beta_3 FDI_{it} + \beta_4 FDIsq + u_{it}$$

The panel model for the HGDPpc panel cluster has the following form:

$$\ln GDPpc_{it} = \beta_1 fd\_R\&D_{it} + \beta_2 \ln TRO_{it} + \beta_3 fd\_FDI_{it} + \beta_4 fd\_FDIsq + u_{it}$$

Table 6. Residual test results (random errors)

Term	Test	H0	Panel Cluster	Statistic	P - Value
Heteroskedasticity	Modified Wald test for heteroskedasticity	All random errors have the same variance	LGDPpc	chi2 (4) = 28.25	0.00
			HGDPpc	chi2 (4) = 2.84	0.58
Autocorrelation	Wooldridge test for serial correlation in panel data	There is no first-order autocorrelation	LGDPpc	F (1,3) = 292.44	0.00
			HGDPpc	F (1,3) = 12.717	0.04
Cross-sectional dependence	Pesaran's test of cross section independence	There is no cross-sectional dependence	LGDPpc	Z = 4.20	0.42
			HGDPpc	Z = 6.60	0.67

Source: Author's review

Residual tests results, which are presented in Table 6, show that we cannot reject the null hypothesis according cross-sectional dependence in both panel clusters, thus it can be concluded that there is no strong cross-sectional dependence between comparative data. In terms of autocorellation test clearly reject the null hypothesis in both panel clusters, which indicates that random errors are correlated between observation periods. Heteroskedasticity test result for LGDPpc panel cluster reject the null hypothesis, which point out that random errors are not distributed randomly, while in HGDPpc panel cluster there is no heteroskedasticity problem because p-value of test was greater than 0.05. The obtained results imply that the problems of heteroskedasticity and autocorrelation should not be neglected when evaluating the regression panel model.

Table 7. Hausman test

Panel Cluster	H0	Statistic	P - Value
LGDPpc	Random error is not correlated with any regressor	chi2 (3) = 26.76	0.00
HGDPpc		chi2 (3) = 53.79	0.00

Source: Author's review

The model Hausman test was done, in order to decide whether a model with a fixed or random effects is more appropriate. He is based on assumption that both evaluators are consistent if there is no correlation between β_1 and independent variables x_{it}. In case both evaluators are consistent, the grades will converge in large samples the true values of the parameters. As test shows that the null hypothesis should be rejected, we can conclude that the random effect evaluator is not consistent, and we should use fixed effect evaluators in both panel clusters.

Table 8. Endogenity test

Panel Cluster	Test	H0	Statistic	P - Value
LGDPpc	Durbin	The variables are exogenous	chi2 (1) = 0.76	0.38
	Wu-Hausman		F (1,58) = 0.69	0.41
HGDPpc	Durbin		chi2 (1) = 0.68	0.41
	Wu-Hausman		F (1,58) = 0.63	0.43

Source: Author's review

Both endogeneity tests, presented in Table 8, showed that the null hypothesis cannot be rejected, i.e. it can be concluded that there is no simultaneous interdependence of the independent variable R&D (investment in research and development) and dependent variables lnGDPpc (gross domestic product per capita) in both panel clusters.

Table 9. Results of the model estimation

LGDPpc			HGDPpc		
Variable	**FE**	**FGLS**	**Variable**	**FE**	**FGLS**
R&D	0.304** (0.019)	0.319*** (0.000)	fd_R&D	-0.065 (0.016)	-0.310 (0.421)
lnTRO	0.688*** (0.002)	0.462*** (0.000)	lnTRO	0.055 (0.277)	0.042** (0.012)
FDI	-0.008 (0.340)	0.003 (0.348)	fd_FDI	0.000 (0.958)	0.000 (0.871)
FDI_sq	0.000 (0.439)	-0.000 (0.400)	fd_FDI_sq	0.000 (0.006)	0.000* (0.056)
Constant	5.257*** (0.000)	6.211*** (0.000)	Constant	-0.237 (0.305)	-0.172** (0.025)
No. of Obs.	68	68	No. of Obs.	64	64

Dependent variable: lnGDPpc (gross domestic product per capita)
Levels of significance: * p<0.1, ** p<0.05, *** p<0.01
R-Squared is not possible to compute for FGLS
Source: Author's review

The model was estimated using two different estimators Fixed Effects (FE) and Feasible Generalized Least Squares (FGLS). Based on the results of the Hausman tests, Fixed Effects (FE) estimator was applied with a robust standard errors option due to the results of the residual tests which indicate the presence of autocorrelation in both panel clusters and heteroskedasticity in LGDPpc panel cluster data set.

In a situation where there are problems of heteroskedasticity, autocorrelation and dependence between comparative data, and the panel data set is of type T > N, the usual approach is to use a model of derived generalized least squares to evaluate the model (Feasible Generalized Least Squares Method - FGLS), because it is robust to the mentioned problems with residuals (Kmenta, 1986).

The results of the estimation shown in Table 9, clearly indicate that expenditures on research and development and trade openness have a significant positive effect on gross domestic product of the countries from lower gross domestic product per capita panel cluster (with a statistical significance of 1%). This result shows that assuming that other factors do not change, an increase in investment in research and development by 1% affects the growth of gross domestic product from 0.31% to 0.32%. An increase in trade openness by 1% leads to growth of gross domestic product from 0.46% to 0.69% which makes it the variable with the greatest positive impact. Foreign direct investment have a neutral and nonsignificant impact on gross domestic product in LGDPpc panel cluster. The explanatory power of the model is estimated at 78% in the case of FE which can be considered as satisfactory, while it is not possible to estimate R-Squared when FGLS is applied.

Opposite to the results for LGDPpc panel cluster expenditures on research and development have a marginally negative effect on the gross domestic product of countries with the higher gross domestic product per capita. Trade openness has a significantly positive effect and increase by 1% affects the growth of gross domestic product from 0.04% to 0.05% which is much weaker than the impact that this variable has on less developed countries. Foreign direct investments have a significant but neutral effect on the gross domestic product (with a statistical significance of 1%) which coincides with the result obtained for countries with lower levels of development when it comes to this variable.

DISCUSSION

The obtained results confirm numerous previous studies that analyzed the impact of trade openness on the economic growth of the country. Nowbutsing et al. (2012), Zeren and Ari (2013), Yebolah et al. (2012), Karras (2003), Nourzad and Powell (2003) are some of the studies that analyzed the impact of trade openness on the country's gross domestic product. These surveys included panel data from different sets of countries and different time periods, and what they all had in common was that they showed that trade openness has a positive and significant impact on the growth of the country's gross domestic product.

There is also a group of opinions that believe that trade openness affects the gross domestic product, only through the improvement of certain policies and sectors. To exploit the full potential of trade openness in developing countries, macroeconomic and private sector stability are needed, as well as the accumulation of human capital, Rodrik (1992). In order to successfully apply the technology of developed countries, the country must have a high level of "social capability", Howitt (2000). Insufficient investment in human capital and research and development negatively affects the country's "absorption capacity" to adopt new technologies.

The obtained results confirm the findings of Freimane and Bāliņa (2016), who concluded that there is a significant positive impact of investment in research and development on gross domestic product based on the analysis of panel data of the European Union countries for the period from 2001 to 2013. There are many studies that use OECD data in order to analyze the relationship between research and development expenditure and economic growth. Sylwester (2001) found a statistically meaningful relationship between R&D expenditure and economic growth. On the other side numerous authors have found a significant and positive impact of expenditures on research and development on economic growth based on panel data from different OECD countries covering various time periods Falk (2007), Saraç (2009), Freire-Seren (1999) and Gülmez and Yardımcıoglu (2012).

Göçer (2013) used 11 developing Asian country's data covering the period 1996-2012 and found a positive association between R&D expenditure and economic growth in these countries. The author calculated that an increase in R&D expenditures by 1% accelerates economic growth by 0.43%, which is quite close to the findings of this article regarding LGDPpc panel cluster.

Numerous authors have previously dealt with the impact of foreign direct investment on economic growth and so far no clear consensus has been reached, as the results have gone to different directions. Despite the fact that in most studies the results showed a positive impact of foreign direct investment on economic growth, it is possible that they will cause a negative effect through increased dependence, and suppression of domestic investments Lipsey (2002). The results of this article correspond to previous studies Azman-Saini et al. (2010), Carkovic and Levine (2002), which based on the analysis of panel data concluded that there is no strong and direct relationship between foreign direct investment and economic growth, supporting the "neutrality hypothesis".

In the previous period, China has a high involvement in Balkan Silk Road countries through investment and direct lending for construction projects. Even though the Chinese presence in the region is a great chance to attract foreign direct investments and economic development, the authors want to point out certain economic risks of Chinese involvement. First, most of the activities on those projects are done by Chinese companies and workers (Ghossein et al., 2018). Excluding national companies and domestic labor significantly reduces the potential economic benefits for Balkan Silk Road countries (Barisitz and Radzyner, 2017). Additionally, most construction projects are financed in the form of credit loans creating the risk of unsustainable debt for some economies (Hurley et al., 2018, Holzner and Schwarzhappel, 2018). Also, it can create financial dependence on China's debt overload (Bastian, 2017).

CONCLUSION

The emergence of the Belt and Road initiative as China's new development strategy and plan for global connectivity and cooperation of many countries between Asia and Europe, including almost all Balkan countries. The Balkans are the hub for Eurasian traffic and the only route through which China can enter the European market. Financing infrastructure projects and investing in the Balkan region, China wants to support the flow of Chinese goods from Asia to wealthier European economies.

In the previous period, China has invested significant funds in the Balkan Silk Road countries and approved credit loans to finance construction, mainly in the transport and energy sectors. Those activities in the Balkan region can have a significant impact on its economic development and affect the attractiveness of the region, i.e to attract FDI. Taking this fact into account, the authors investigated the impact of investment in research and development on economic growth, as well as the nature of the impact of foreign trade balance and foreign direct investment on the Balkan Silk Road countries.

The results showed that expenditures on research and development and trade openness have a significant positive effect on the gross domestic product of the countries with lower GDP per capita (Bosnia and Herzegovina, North Macedonia, Bulgaria and Serbia). Assuming that other factors do not change, an increase in investment in research and development by 1% affects the growth of gross domestic product from 0.31% to 0.32%. An increase in trade openness by 1% leads to growth of gross domestic product from 0.46% to 0.69%. Foreign direct investment had a neutral and nonsignificant impact on gross domestic product for these countries. On the other side, for the countries with higher GDP per capita (Croatia, Greece, Hungary and Slovenia) expenditures on research and development have a marginally negative effect on the gross domestic product. Trade openness has a significantly positive effect and an increase by 1% affects the growth of gross domestic product from 0.04% to 0.05%. Foreign direct investments have a significant but neutral effect on the gross domestic product which coincides with the result obtained for countries with lower levels of development when it comes to this variable.

Despite the expected multiple positive effects, the authors point to several economic risks, especially for construction projects. Most of the activity on those projects is done by Chinese companies which may reduce their economic benefits. These projects are financed in the form of credit loans from Chinese banks, leading to over-dependence on China. Additionally, it creates the risk of unsustainable debt and potential debt repayment problems. These risks become even bigger especially significant by the COVID-19 pandemic. Due to the slow economic activity, some Balkan countries may face problems in repaying loans and implementing initiated construction projects.

The main limitation of the research is the use of data on total R&D investment and foreign trade relations instead of sectoral. Additional limitations are not using the value or share of Chinese in total investments by country, which in fact should be considered as an independent variable. Due to the unavailability of consistent data by sector, the authors were forced to use aggregate data concerning each of the observed variables. The recommendation is to investigate the impact of investment in R&D and foreign trade relations on the economic growth of each sector separately, mainly the energy, metal, and transport sectors. The results can help decision-makers focus their measures on the sectors that contribute most to economic growth. Additionally, due to the lack of data for foreign direct investment and research and development expenditures, it was not possible to extend the research to all countries on the Balkan Silk Road, as well as to observe an even longer time span, which would probably give even more stable results.

FUNDING STATEMENT

This research received no specific grant from any funding agency in the public, commercial, or not-for-profit sectors.

ACKNOWLEDGMENT

This research has been funded by the Ministry of Education, Science and Technological Development of the Republic of Serbia

REFERENCES

Azman-Saini, W. N. W., Baharumshah, A. Z., & Law, S. H. (2010). Foreign direct investment, economic freedom and economic growth: International evidence. *Economic Modelling*, *27*(5), 1079–1089. doi:10.1016/j.econmod.2010.04.001

Bakari, S. (2017). *Trade and Economic Growth in Germany*. LIEI, Faculty of Economic Sciences and Management of Tunis (FSEGT). MPRA Paper No. 77404.

Bakari, S., & Sofien, T. (2019). The impact of trade openness, foreign direct investment and domestic investment on economic growth: New evidence from Asian developing countries. Economic Research Guardian. *Weissberg Publishing*, *9*(1), 46–54.

Baltagi, B. H. (2005). *Econometric analysis of panel data*. John Wiley & Sons Ltd.

Barisitz, S., & Radzyner, A. (2017). *The New Silk Road, part I: A stocktaking and economic assessment. Focus on European Economic Integration, Q3/2017, Oesterreichische Nationalbank*. Austrian Central Bank.

Bashir, M. F., Benjiang, M. A., Qin, Y., & Bashir, M. A. (2021). Evaluation of One Belt One Road publications: A bibliometric and literature review analysis. *Environmental Science and Pollution Research International*, *28*(28), 37016–37030. doi:10.100711356-021-14621-y PMID:34050514

Bastian, J. (2017). *The potential for growth through Chinese infrastructure investments in Central and South-Eastern Europe along the Balkan Silk Road*. European Bank for Reconstruction and Development.

Blavasciunaite, D., Garsviene, L., & Matuzeviciute, K. (2020). Trade balance effects on economic growth: Evidence from European Union Countries. Economies. Academic Press.

Bodroža, D., & Đukić, M. (2018). Influence of FDI Inflows on Economic Activity in CEE Countries. Western Balkans Economies in EU Integration: past, present and future. CEMAFI International Association.

Bodroža, D., & Lazić, M. (2021). Economic Impact of the COVID-19 Pandemic on Western Balkan Countries. *Economic Analysis: Applied Research in Emerging Markets, 54*(2), 30–40.

Borenzstein, E., De Gregorio, J., & Lee, J. W. (1998). How does foreign direct investment affect economic growth? *Journal of International Economics, 45*(1), 115–135. doi:10.1016/S0022-1996(97)00033-0

Bowerman, B. L., & O'Connell, R. T. (1990). *Linear statistical models: An Applied Approach*. Duxbury Press.

Buckley, P. J., Clegg, J., & Wang, C. (2002). The impact of inward FDI on the performance of Chinese manufacturing firms. *Journal of International Business Studies, 33*(4), 637–655. doi:10.1057/palgrave.jibs.8491037

BusseM.KönigerJ. (2012). Trade and Economic Growth: A Re-Examination of the Empirical Evidence. Available at SSRN: https://ssrn.com/abstract=2009939 doi:10.2139/ssrn.2009939

Carkovic, M. & Levine, R. (2002). *Does foreign direct investment accelerate economic growth?* University of Minnesota Department of Finance working Paper.

Çetintaş, H., & Barişik, S. (2009). Export, import and economic growth: The case of transition economies. *Transit. Stud. Rev., 15*(4), 636–649. doi:10.100711300-008-0043-0

Chan, M. H. T. (2018). The Belt and Road Initiative – the New Silk Road: A research agenda. *Journal of Contemporary East Asia Studies, 7*(2), 104–123. doi:10.1080/24761028.2019.1580407

Dinh, T. T.-H., Vo, D. H., The Vo, A., & Nguyen, T. C. (2019). The Vo, A., & Nguyen, TC. (2019). Foreign Direct Investment and Economic Growth in the Short Run and Long Run: Empirical Evidence from Developing Countries. *Journal of Risk and Financial Management., 12*(4), 176. doi:10.3390/jrfm12040176

Drukker, D. M. (2003). Testing for serial correlation in linear panel-data models. *The Stata Journal, 3*(2), 168–177. doi:10.1177/1536867X0300300206

Đukić, M., Jovanoski, I., Munitlak-Ivanović, O., Lazić, M., & Bodroža, D. (2016). Cost-benefit analysis of an infrastructure project and a cost-reflective tariff: A case study for investment in wastewater treatment plant in Serbia. *Renewable and Sustainable Energy Reviews, 59*, 1419–1425.

Erić, D., Đukić, M., & Bodroža, D. (2021). *Finansijska tržišta X.O. Belgrade*. Data Status, Republic of Serbia.

Falk, M. (2007). R&D spending in the high-tech sector and economic growth. *Research in Economics, 61*(3), 140–147. doi:10.1016/j.rie.2007.05.002

Freimane, R., & Bāliņa, S. (2016). Research and development expenditures and economic growth in the EU: A panel data analysis. *Economics and Business, 29*(1), 5–11. doi:10.1515/eb-2016-0016

Freire-Serén, M. J. (1999). *Aggregate R&D expenditure and endogenous economic growth* (UFAE and IAE Working Papers No. WP 43699). Barcelona, Spain: Unitat de Fonaments de l'Anàlisi Econòmica (UAB) and Institut d'Anàlisi Econòmica (CSIC).

Ghossein, T., Hoekman, B., & Shingal, A. (2018). *Public procurement in the Belt and Road Initiative*. Discussion paper no. 10, The World Bank Group.

Göçer, I. (2013). Effects of R&D expenditures on high technology exports, balance of foreign trade and economic growth. *Maliye Dergisi*, (165), 215–240.

Greene, W. (2000). *Econometric Analysis*. Prentice-Hall.

Gujarati, D. (2004). *Basic Econometrics*. United States Military Academy.

Gülmez, A., & Yardımcıog˘lu, F. (2012). The relationship between R&D expenditures and economic growth in OECD Countries: Panel cointegration and panel causality analyses (1990–2010)]. *Maliye Dergisi*, (163), 335–353.

Gurgul, H., & Lach, L. (2014). Globalization and economic growth: Evidence from two decades of transition in CEE. *Economic Modelling*, *36*, 99–107. doi:10.1016/j.econmod.2013.09.022

Holzner, M., & Schwarzhappel, M. (2018). *Infrastructure Investment in the Western Balkans: A First Analysis*. European Investment Bank and The Vienna Institute for International Economic Studies.

Howitt, P. (2000). Endogenous Growth and Gross country Income Differences. *The American Economic Review*, *90*(4), 111–130. doi:10.1257/aer.90.4.829

Huňady, J., & Orviská, M. (2014). The Impact of Research and Development Expenditures on Innovation Performance and Economic Growth of the Country – the Empirical Evidence. *CBU International Conference Proceedings 2014, 2*, 119–125.

Hurley, J., Morris, S., & Portelance, G. (2018). *Examining the Debt Implications of the Belt and Road Initiative from a Policy Perspective. CGD Policy Paper No. 121*. Center for Global Development.

Iwaisako, T., & Futagami, K. (2013). Patent protection, capital accumulation, and economic growth. *Economic Theory*, *52*(2), 631–668. doi:10.100700199-011-0658-y

Johnson, A. (2006). *The effects of FDI inflows on host country economic growth*. The Royal Institute of technology. Centre of Excellence for studies in Science and Innovation.

Jyun-Yi, W., & Chih-Chiang, H. (2008). Does foreign direct investment promote economic growth? Evidence from a threshold regression analysis. *Economic Bulletin*, *15*, 1–10.

Karras, G. (2003). Trade openness and economic growth can we estimate the precise effect? *Applied Econometrics and International Development AEEADE*, *3*(1), 7–25.

Kmenta, J. (1986). *Elements of Econometrics* (2nd ed.). Macmillan.

Lakshmanan, T.R. (2011).The broader economic consequences of transport infrastructure investments. *Journal of Transport Geography, 19*(1), 1-12. . doi:10.1016/j.jtrangeo.2010.01.001

Laura, A., Chanda, A., & Kalemli-Ozcan, S. (2004). FDI and economic growth:The role of local financial markets. *Journal of International Economics*, *64*(1), 89–112. doi:10.1016/S0022-1996(03)00081-3

Levin, A., Lin, C. F., & Chu, C. S. J. (2002). Unit root tests in panel data: Asymptotic and finite-sample properties. *Journal of Econometrics*, *108*(1), 1–24. doi:10.1016/S0304-4076(01)00098-7

Lichtenberg, F. R. (1992). *R&D investment and international productivity differences* (Working Paper No. 4161). Cambridge.

Lill, A., & Babula, R. (2009). The link between openness and long-run economic growth. *Journal of International Commerce and Economics, 2*, 31–50.

Lipsey, R. E. (2002). *Home and host country effects of FDI.* NBER Working Paper No. 9293.

Mehic, E., Silajdzic, S. & Babic-Hodovic, V. (2013). The Impact of FDI on Economic Growth: Some Evidence from Southeast Europe. *Emerging Markets Finance and Trade, 49*(1), 5-20. doi:10.2753/REE1540-496X4901S101

Nourzad, F., & Powell, J. J. (2003). Openness, growth, and development: Evidence from a panel of developing countries. *Scientific Journal of Administrative Development, 1*(1), 72–94.

Nowbutsing, A., Ramsohok, S., & Ramsohok, K. (2012). *The impact of openness on economic growth: Case of Indian Ocean rim countries.* ICTI.

OECD. (2018). The Belt and Road Initiative in the global trade, investment and finance landscape. In *OECD Business and Finance Outlook 2018*. OECD Publishing. doi:10.1787/bus_fin_out-2018-6-

Pegkas, P. (2015). The impact of FDI on economic growth in Eurozone countries. *Journal of Economic Asymmetries, 12*(2), 124–132. doi:10.1016/j.jeca.2015.05.001

Pesaran, M. H. (2004). *General diagnostic tests for cross section dependence in panels.* Cambridge Working Papers in Economics 0435, University of Cambridge.

Rodrik, D. (1992). The limits of trade policy reforms in developing countries. *The Journal of Economic Perspectives, 6*(1), 87–105. doi:10.1257/jep.6.1.87

Samimi, A. J., & Alerasoul, S. M. (2009). R&D and economic growth: New evidence from some developing countries. *Australian Journal of Basic and Applied Sciences, 3*(4), 3464–3469.

Saraç, T. B. (2009). *Aras¸tırma-Gelis¸tirme Harcamalarının Ekonomik Büyüme Üzerindeki Etkisi: Panel Veri Analizi* [The effect of research-development expenditures on economic growth: A panel data]. *EconAnadolu 2009: Anadolu International Conference in Economics*, Eskis¸ehir, Turkey.

Siddiqui, K. (2019). One Belt and One Road, China's Massive Infrastructure Project to Boost Trade and Economy: An Overview. *International Critical Thought, 9*(2), 214–235. doi:10.1080/21598282.2019.1613921

Silaghi, M., Alexa, D., Jude, C., & Litan, C. (2014). Do business and public sector research and development expenditures contribute to economic growth in Central and Eastern Europe Countries? A dynamic panel estimation. *Economic Modelling, 36*, 108–119. doi:10.1016/j.econmod.2013.08.035

Sylwester, K. (2001). R&D and economic growth. *Knowledge, Technology & Policy, 13*(4), 71–84. doi:10.1007/BF02693991

Titus, A. O. (2007). Causality between exports, imports, and economic growth: Evidence from transition economies. *Economics Letters, 94*(3), 389–395. doi:10.1016/j.econlet.2006.08.025

Vo, D.H., The Vo, A., & Zhang, Z. (2019). *Exchange Rate Volatility and Disaggregated Manufacturing Exports: Evidence from an Emerging Country*. Academic Press.

Wang, C., Lim, K. M., Zhang, X., Zhao, L., & Lee, P. T. L. (2020). Railway and road infrastructure in the Belt and Road Initiative countries: Estimating the impact of transport infrastructure on economic growth. *Transportation Research Part A, Policy and Practice*, *134*, 288–307. doi:10.1016/j.tra.2020.02.009

Were, M. (2015). Differential effects of trade on economic growth and investment: A cross-country empirical investigation. *Journal of African Trade*, *2*(1–2), 71–85. doi:10.1016/j.joat.2015.08.002

Wooldridge, J. M. (2002). *Econometric analysis of cross section and panel data*. The MIT Press Cambridge.

World bank. (2019). *Belt and road economics*. International Bank for Reconstruction and Development / The World Bank.

World Bank. (2021). *Data base*. https://data.worldbank.org/

Yeboah, O. A., Naanwaab, C. B., Saleem, S., & Akuffo, A. S. (2012). *Effects of trade openness on economic growth: The case of African countries*. Academic Press.

Zaman, M., Pinglu, C., Hussain, S. I., Ullah, A., & Qian, N. (2021). Does regional integration matter for sustainable economic growth? Fostering the role of FDI, trade openness, IT exports, and capital formation in BRI countries. *Heliyon*, *7*(12), e08559. Advance online publication. doi:10.1016/j.heliyon.2021.e08559 PMID:34917822

Zeren, F., & Ari, A. (2013). Trade openness and economic growth: A panel causality test. *International Journal of Business and Social Science*, *4*(9), 317–324.

ADDITIONAL READING

Barisitz, S., & Radzyner, A. (2017). *The New Silk Road, part I: a stocktaking and economic assessment. Focus on European Economic Integration, Q3/2017, Oesterreichische Nationalbank*. Austrian Central Bank.

Bashir, M. F., Benjiang, M. A., Qin, Y., & Bashir, M. A. (2021). Evaluation of One Belt One Road publications: A bibliometric and literature review analysis. *Environmental Science and Pollution Research International*, *28*(28), 37016–37030. doi:10.100711356-021-14621-y PMID:34050514

Chan, M. H. T. (2018). The Belt and Road Initiative – the New Silk Road: A research agenda. *Journal of Contemporary East Asia Studies*, *7*(2), 104–123. doi:10.1080/24761028.2019.1580407

Dinh, T. T.-H., Vo, D. H., The Vo, A., & Nguyen, T. C. (2019). The Vo, A., & Nguyen, TC. (2019). Foreign Direct Investment and Economic Growth in the Short Run and Long Run: Empirical Evidence from Developing Countries. *Journal of Risk and Financial Management.*, *12*(4), 176. doi:10.3390/jrfm12040176

Freimane, R., & Bāliņa, S. (2016). Research and development expenditures and economic growth in the EU: A panel data analysis. *Economics and Business*, *29*(1), 5–11. doi:10.1515/eb-2016-0016

Göçer, I. (2013). Effects of R&D expenditures on high technology exports, balance of foreign trade and economic growth. *Maliye Dergisi*, (165), 215–240.

Holzner, M., & Schwarzhappel, M. (2018). *Infrastructure Investment in the Western Balkans: A First Analysis*. European Investment Bank and The Vienna Institute for International Economic Studies.

OECD. (2018). The Belt and Road Initiative in the global trade, investment and finance landscape. In *OECD Business and Finance Outlook 2018*. OECD Publishing. doi:10.1787/bus_fin_out-2018-6-

Wang, C., Lim, K. M., Zhang, X., Zhao, L., & Lee, P. T. L. (2020). Railway and road infrastructure in the Belt and Road Initiative countries: Estimating the impact of transport infrastructure on economic growth. *Transportation Research Part A, Policy and Practice*, *134*, 288–307. doi:10.1016/j.tra.2020.02.009

KEY TERMS AND DEFINITIONS

Balkan Silk Road: The transport route and logistics corridor that China has begun to establish in the Balkan region.

Belt and Road Initiative: A development strategy focusing on networking and cooperation between the Republic of China and the rest of Eurasia.

Foreign Direct Investment: Investing in a company that is resident in another country that provides long-term connections, interest, and ownership control over that company

Gross Domestic Product: The total value of goods and services produced in the country during the year.

Panel Data: Consist of repeated observations over time on the same set of cross-sectional units.

Panel Regression: The modeling method adapted to panel data, in which one or more variables are observed across time intervals for several statistical units.

Research and Development: The process of creating new scientific and technological knowledge.

Trade Openness: The sum of a country's exports and imports as a share of that country's GDP, represents the involvement of the state in international flows of goods and capital.

APPENDIX

Figure 5. Relation between trade openness and expenditures on research and development

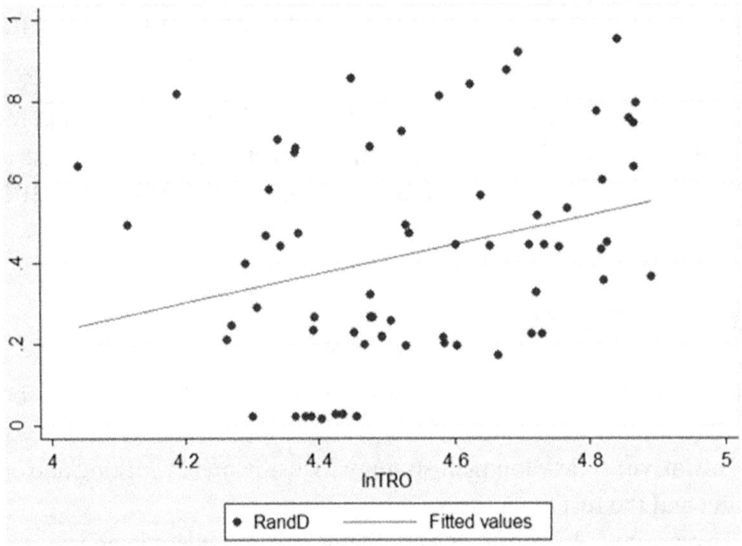

Figure 6. Relation between foreign direct investments and expenditures on research and development

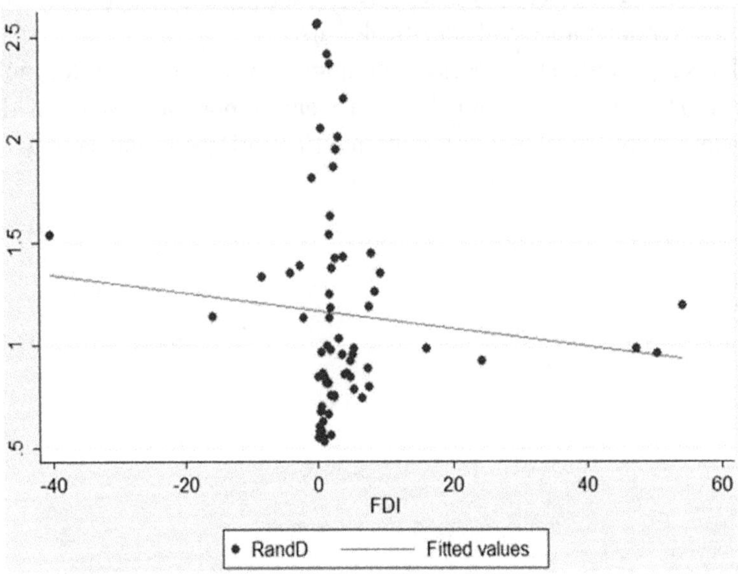

Figure 7. Relation between foreign direct investments and gross domestic product per capita

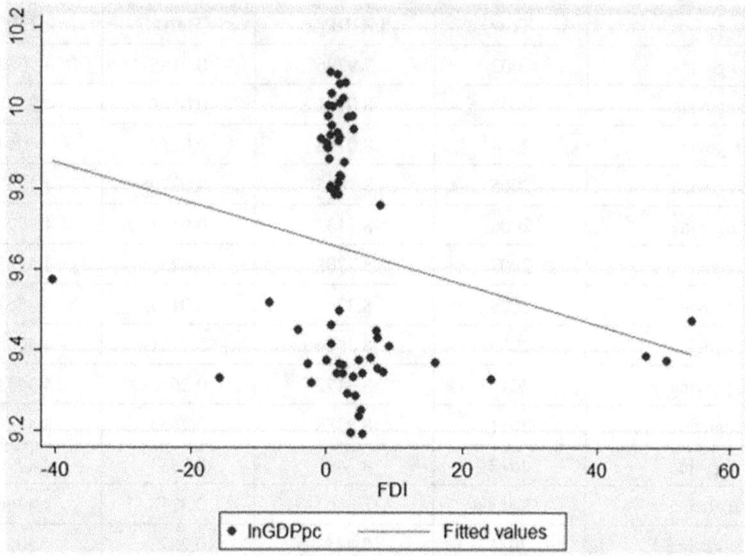

Table 10. Panel data set

Country	Year	lnGDPpc	R&D	lnTRO	FDI
Bosnia and Herzegovina	2002	7.9796	0.0185	4.3660	3.9795
Bosnia and Herzegovina	2003	8.0181	0.0185	4.3891	4.4923
Bosnia and Herzegovina	2004	8.0768	0.0152	4.4044	8.7580
Bosnia and Herzegovina	2005	8.1605	0.0270	4.4350	5.5584
Bosnia and Herzegovina	2006	8.2132	0.0197	4.3799	6.5759
Bosnia and Herzegovina	2007	8.2708	0.0252	4.4255	11.6737
Bosnia and Herzegovina	2008	8.3261	0.0184	4.4562	5.2575
Bosnia and Herzegovina	2009	8.3004	0.0211	4.3006	0.7864
Bosnia and Herzegovina	2010	8.3172	0.2653	4.3941	2.5840
Bosnia and Herzegovina	2011	8.3388	0.2653	4.4755	2.5295
Bosnia and Herzegovina	2012	8.3460	0.2653	4.4790	2.2761
Bosnia and Herzegovina	2013	8.3867	0.3213	4.4766	1.7240
Bosnia and Herzegovina	2014	8.4154	0.2573	4.5059	2.9356
Bosnia and Herzegovina	2015	8.4611	0.2186	4.4925	2.3619
Bosnia and Herzegovina	2016	8.5048	0.2159	4.4921	1.8517
Bosnia and Herzegovina	2017	8.5463	0.2005	4.5846	2.8178
Bosnia and Herzegovina	2018	8.5913	0.1949	4.6029	2.9825
Bulgaria	2002	8.3445	0.4647	4.3211	5.5153
Bulgaria	2003	8.4026	0.4722	4.3696	9.9162
Bulgaria	2004	8.4726	0.4709	4.5333	11.7462
Bulgaria	2005	8.5492	0.4427	4.6023	13.7202
Bulgaria	2006	8.6226	0.4422	4.7100	22.9044
Bulgaria	2007	8.6935	0.4303	4.8171	31.2470
Bulgaria	2008	8.7596	0.4477	4.8266	18.9142
Bulgaria	2009	8.7317	0.4936	4.5293	7.4902
Bulgaria	2010	8.7439	0.5666	4.6387	3.6362
Bulgaria	2011	8.7736	0.5324	4.7661	3.6475
Bulgaria	2012	8.7829	0.6036	4.8202	3.2930
Bulgaria	2013	8.7918	0.6368	4.8655	3.5639
Bulgaria	2014	8.8161	0.7928	4.8697	1.9158
Bulgaria	2015	8.8616	0.9520	4.8418	4.3744
Bulgaria	2016	8.9061	0.7722	4.8108	2.7587
Bulgaria	2017	8.9479	0.7431	4.8650	3.3907
Bulgaria	2018	8.9855	0.7557	4.8587	2.7272
Croatia	2002	9.1959	0.9503	4.3963	3.6225
Croatia	2003	9.2504	0.9498	4.4011	5.2777
Croatia	2004	9.2908	1.0303	4.4029	3.1321
Croatia	2005	9.3317	0.8561	4.4010	3.9640

Continued on following page

Table 10. Continued

Country	Year	lnGDPpc	R&D	lnTRO	FDI
Croatia	2006	9.3802	0.7401	4.4269	6.5799
Croatia	2007	9.4299	0.7911	4.4255	7.6736
Croatia	2008	9.4488	0.8866	4.4123	7.4199
Croatia	2009	9.3738	0.8447	4.2542	4.8659
Croatia	2010	9.3628	0.7429	4.2943	2.5569
Croatia	2011	9.3642	0.7510	4.3623	1.9772
Croatia	2012	9.3431	0.7510	4.3784	2.5617
Croatia	2013	9.3414	0.8116	4.4032	1.5917
Croatia	2014	9.3420	0.7831	4.4536	5.4586
Croatia	2015	9.3743	0.8401	4.5148	0.1042
Croatia	2016	9.4157	0.8631	4.5312	0.8003
Croatia	2017	9.4615	0.8627	4.5838	0.8482
Croatia	2018	9.4981	0.9719	4.6037	1.9483
Greece	2002	9.9037	0.5465	3.9190	0.0222
Greece	2003	9.9576	0.5465	3.8752	0.6973
Greece	2004	10.0045	0.5273	3.9100	0.8930
Greece	2005	10.0076	0.5790	3.9299	0.2779
Greece	2006	10.0595	0.5612	3.9675	1.9799
Greece	2007	10.0892	0.5766	4.0522	0.6145
Greece	2008	10.0832	0.6618	4.0831	1.6175
Greece	2009	10.0366	0.6256	3.8659	0.8383
Greece	2010	9.9790	0.5984	3.9357	0.1795
Greece	2011	9.8734	0.6720	4.0401	0.3864
Greece	2012	9.8054	0.6996	4.1281	0.6867
Greece	2013	9.7848	0.8113	4.1412	1.2332
Greece	2014	9.7984	0.8333	4.1976	1.1471
Greece	2015	9.8009	0.9612	4.1787	0.6487
Greece	2016	9.8002	0.9939	4.1592	1.3981
Greece	2017	9.8149	1.1311	4.2708	1.7252
Greece	2018	9.8324	1.1773	4.3839	1.8993
Hungary	2002	9.1927	0.9836	4.7734	5.3890
Hungary	2003	9.2356	0.9187	4.7588	4.8739
Hungary	2004	9.2850	0.8612	4.8156	4.3576
Hungary	2005	9.3285	0.9214	4.8503	24.2763
Hungary	2006	9.3696	0.9786	5.0037	16.1369
Hungary	2007	9.3736	0.9560	5.0463	50.3691
Hungary	2008	9.3858	0.9787	5.0643	47.4242
Hungary	2009	9.3180	1.1307	4.9764	-2.1295

Continued on following page

Table 10. Continued

Country	Year	lnGDPpc	R&D	lnTRO	FDI
Hungary	2010	9.3315	1.1376	5.0588	-15.7076
Hungary	2011	9.3535	1.1862	5.1142	7.5641
Hungary	2012	9.3447	1.2607	5.1095	8.3937
Hungary	2013	9.3659	1.3869	5.1016	-2.6424
Hungary	2014	9.4100	1.3491	5.1260	9.2573
Hungary	2015	9.4499	1.3465	5.1196	-4.2061
Hungary	2016	9.4740	1.1901	5.1021	54.1692
Hungary	2017	9.5189	1.3319	5.1072	-8.4766
Hungary	2018	9.5728	1.5334	5.0952	-40.2908
North Macedonia	2002	8.0699	0.2446	4.2702	2.8418
North Macedonia	2003	8.0897	0.2106	4.2637	2.4067
North Macedonia	2004	8.1336	0.2324	4.3928	5.4399
North Macedonia	2005	8.1782	0.2283	4.4525	2.3221
North Macedonia	2006	8.2269	0.1937	4.5278	6.2299
North Macedonia	2007	8.2885	0.1709	4.6643	8.7983
North Macedonia	2008	8.3409	0.2236	4.7147	6.1727
North Macedonia	2009	8.3365	0.1968	4.4679	2.7605
North Macedonia	2010	8.3687	0.2163	4.5838	3.2044
North Macedonia	2011	8.3909	0.2228	4.7291	4.8398
North Macedonia	2012	8.3855	0.3268	4.7204	3.4674
North Macedonia	2013	8.4135	0.4389	4.6526	3.7204
North Macedonia	2014	8.4483	0.5165	4.7233	0.5358
North Macedonia	2015	8.4854	0.4441	4.7336	2.9470
North Macedonia	2016	8.5128	0.4359	4.7552	5.1476
North Macedonia	2017	8.5230	0.3544	4.8214	3.3673
North Macedonia	2018	8.5509	0.3652	4.8920	5.1149
Serbia	2002	8.1998	0.6397	4.0407	2.9379
Serbia	2003	8.2449	0.4914	4.1137	6.1782
Serbia	2004	8.3337	0.2895	4.3072	3.7755
Serbia	2005	8.3905	0.3953	4.2907	5.8375
Serbia	2006	8.4442	0.4399	4.3426	17.6928
Serbia	2007	8.5107	0.5788	4.3255	10.2458
Serbia	2008	8.5700	0.6697	4.3654	7.7706
Serbia	2009	8.5463	0.8173	4.1900	6.4859
Serbia	2010	8.5576	0.7023	4.3403	4.0490
Serbia	2011	8.5856	0.6833	4.3670	10.0096
Serbia	2012	8.5837	0.8532	4.4482	2.9447
Serbia	2013	8.6170	0.6837	4.4764	4.2553

Continued on following page

Table 10. Continued

Country	Year	lnGDPpc	R&D	lnTRO	FDI
Serbia	2014	8.6057	0.7231	4.5243	4.2487
Serbia	2015	8.6286	0.8115	4.5788	5.9087
Serbia	2016	8.6666	0.8395	4.6236	5.7878
Serbia	2017	8.6927	0.8735	4.6777	6.5520
Serbia	2018	8.7422	0.9197	4.6959	8.0408
Slovenia	2002	9.7582	1.4433	4.6410	7.8749
Slovenia	2003	9.7867	1.2479	4.6282	1.8073
Slovenia	2004	9.8288	1.3703	4.7145	2.2174
Slovenia	2005	9.8643	1.4178	4.7897	2.6813
Slovenia	2006	9.9170	1.5371	4.8659	1.7528
Slovenia	2007	9.9789	1.4270	4.9209	3.9255
Slovenia	2008	10.0118	1.6267	4.9033	1.9454
Slovenia	2009	9.9243	1.8118	4.7285	-0.6889
Slovenia	2010	9.9333	2.0513	4.8481	0.6627
Slovenia	2011	9.9398	2.4130	4.9365	1.7003
Slovenia	2012	9.9109	2.5606	4.9585	0.0720
Slovenia	2013	9.8992	2.5649	4.9681	0.2149
Slovenia	2014	9.9255	2.3655	4.9805	2.0416
Slovenia	2015	9.9466	2.1957	4.9856	4.0152
Slovenia	2016	9.9773	2.0115	4.9881	3.2329
Slovenia	2017	10.0237	1.8664	5.0580	2.4680
Slovenia	2018	10.0634	1.9504	5.0826	2.8412

Chapter 8
"Belt and Road" Initiative as a Development Chance for the Western Balkan Countries:
The Case of Serbia

Darko Marjanović
Institute of Economic Sciences, Serbia

Isidora Beraha
Institute of Economic Sciences, Serbia

Ivana Domazet
https://orcid.org/0000-0002-3493-4616
Institute of Economic Sciences, Serbia

ABSTRACT

Foreign direct investment (FDI) is a very important element of economic integration because it creates an opportunity for accelerated development, technological innovation, and corporate restructuring. Western Balkan countries mainly focused their activities on attracting investments from EU countries. However, as investments from these countries have been reduced recently, the countries of the Western Balkans have opened their markets to incoming Chinese investments. Serbia is currently the first country in the Western Balkans. Based on the inflow of Chinese investments, and in the coming period, we can expect a trend of intensive growth of Chinese investments related to the "Belt and Road" Initiative, which will lead to additional development of the Serbian economy. The main subject of this research focuses on the distribution of Chinese investments on a global scale, as well as the importance of the "Belt and Road" Initiative for both multinational companies and recipient countries of Western Balkans, with special reference to Serbia.

DOI: 10.4018/978-1-7998-8021-9.ch008

INTRODUCTION

In the process of globalization, capital as the most mobile factor in creating a global economy can accelerate the economic development of the country in which it is invested, since it is placed where the conditions are most favorable. Accordingly, one of the goals of every country is to attract as much foreign direct investments (FDI) as possible, given that they are one of the factors of success of national economies in the global market (Domazet & Marjanović, 2017a; Stancheva-Gigov, 2018). The volume and intensity of FDI distribution at the global level depends, above all, on the conditions in the world economy. Considering the forms of international capital movements, FDI are the most represented in the financing of national economies of developing countries. The dynamics of the global FDI structure has changed in the last ten years, with a growing trend in developing countries. This is not surprising since foreign investors have recognized all the advantages and benefits that arise from these investments. In the process of attracting FDI, countries apply numerous measures to provide a favorable investment climate and ensure greater competitiveness in the international capital market. To achieve that, political and social stability in the country is needed, prevailing stable economic conditions, favorable foreign trade, customs, and foreign exchange treatment of joint investments, as well as the availability of reliable and trained labor force.

Depending on the target sector, FDI can have different effects on the economic development of the host countries. Additionally, FDI are important not only for strengthening the national economy, but also as a prerequisite for economic integration because they create stable and long-term relations between economies. Attracting foreign investment is a necessary factor for most countries to achieve stable growth. Accordingly, all policies affecting investments must be harmonized and synergistically linked nationally and internationally. Investment policies should be based on the country's overall development strategy, and establish open, stable, and predictable conditions for investors.

Accelerated process of globalization, liberalization of foreign investments and deregulation in many spheres of activity has enabled a growing choice of locations for Chinese companies. Because of this, the countries of the Western Balkans are trying to create an economic environment that is beneficial for Chinese investors and to enable them to perform their activities smoothly and profitably.

As the fastest growing economy, China is the world's largest manufacturing producer, characterized by large supply of cheap working force, significant investments in education, and advanced technology (Beraha & Redžepagić, 2016). One of the goals of the Chinese state is to participate more actively in the world market and to become a leader in the world economic system. In line with this, China has launched the" Belt and Road" Initiative (BRI), which is an economic framework developed with the aim of connecting and strengthening its integration, primarily with the markets of Central and Eastern Europe. This initiative should greatly contribute to the implementation of large infrastructure projects in European countries, as well as connecting the economies of the Western Balkans. The main task is aimed at increasing investments and imports, lowering tariffs, developing free trade zones, improving the business environment, as well as deepening bilateral and multilateral cooperation.

BACKGROUND

At the end of 2013, the Chinese President Xi Jinping announced that China plans to implement one of the most ambitious foreign policy and economic projects in the coming period – Belt and Road Initiative

(BRI). In the first quarter of 2015, the National Development and Reform Commission announced an action plan for BRI. The Chinese initiative promotes the development of infrastructural goods, which will significantly contribute to the economic and social development of the country. This will open the way to Western countries, primarily to Europe and its market, which is very attractive to Chinese investors. It is this novelty that represents a new direction when it comes to Chinese foreign policy, given that it is a new economic model that aims to strengthen China's position as an economic superpower (Julien & Mitsuo, 2018).

The BRI is considered one of the most ambitious projects in the China's foreign and economic policy. The main goal is to make China even stronger and more economically dominant in the world market, and the first task is to expand and build a new infrastructure network, primarily towards European countries (Cai, 2017). The new transport, energy and telecommunications infrastructure promoted by the BRI will contribute to connecting China with Europe and Asia, which will have a significant impact on the economic development of these regions (Rolland, 2017). For European countries, this is an exceptional opportunity both economically and in every other respect, given that it will significantly contribute to the development of these countries (Casarini, 2015). The inflow of investments from China is significant for all Western Balkans countries, including Serbia, because it contributes to developing these economies, economic stability, and strengthening and maturing the business environment (Marjanović et al., 2021). Given that the consequences of the global financial crisis are still being felt in European countries, the Initiative provides an opportunity to strengthen financial security by gaining access to a new source of funding (Pardo, 2018).

The BRI aims to stimulate the economic development of the regions of Asia, Europe and Africa, given that this region covers about 60% of the world's population and about 30% of world GDP. This Initiative is characterized by an active dialogue between all participants on unimpeded trade, mutual exchange, and financial support (Huang, 2016). According to Dunford & Liu (2019), The Chinese BRI is an open call to states, with the aim of increasing connectivity and encouraging international economic, political, and cultural cooperation. Therefore, the Initiative is an open and mutually beneficial model of cooperative economic, political, and cultural exchange in countries on the ancient "Silk Road" (Liu & Dunford, 2016). There is a good chance that the BRI will change the pattern of the international trade network that is currently in force, which is very likely to affect the global supply chain management (Cui & Song, 2019). According to the data obtained by Zhai (2018), the BRI will bring significant benefits to the world economy in terms of prosperity and trade growth, even if conservative assumptions about total investments within the Initiative come true.

The research results obtained by Khan & Khan (2019) indicate that there is a long-term link between FDI and financial development, and that the positive role of financial development in FDI inflows is very important for the Chinese government and policy makers. FDI have positive effects on growth only above a certain threshold of institutional quality, which clearly indicates that reforms that will precede FDI attraction policies should be implemented (Jude & Levieuge, 2017; Li & Tanna, 2019). Xiaoyang Chen & Lin (2018) analyzed the economic effects of FDI and concluded that the "New Silk Road" significantly reduces transportation costs, which, with an increase in FDI, can contribute to GDP, trade, and employment growth in countries, which are part of the Chinese BRI. Aibai et al. (2019) analyzed the impact of FDI on the financial development of host countries, where they took 50 countries that joined the BRI as a base. The results showed that FDI could significantly improve the development of the financial sector (financial market). If the country performs well in terms of economic activity, legal and political system, business environment and infrastructure, one can say with certainty that it is a potential investment destination (Groh & Wich, 2012; Milovic et al., 2020). In addition to the fact that foreign investors bring modern technology and knowledge to the host country, they increase competition in the local market, which can to some extent harm domestic companies. In addition, the obtained results imply that technological capabilities do not prevent domestic companies from the harmful effects of competition associated with incoming FDI (Jin et al., 2019).

FDIs have a significant impact on modernization, increased production, and exports, as well as employment growth. Therefore, it is very important to create an appropriate investment climate in the country. In this way, they send a clear message to investors that the country has good performance and that it can quickly and easily adjust its investment policy to the requirements of foreign investors (Marjanović & Domazet, 2021). One of the ways to attract multinational companies is to approve tax incentives, which is especially characteristic for developing countries (Azemar & Dharmapala, 2019). Tax incentives, especially those approved in the income tax system, are very important for foreign investors when making an investment decision (Marjanović, 2018). Country characteristics such as size, openness and institutional stability significantly determine the pace of FDI (Bolivar et al., 2019). The economic development of most countries directly correlates with the inflow of foreign investments (Marjanović & Domazet, 2018). They significantly affect the economic growth of the host country (Milovic & Jocovic, 2017) and the constancy of its macroeconomic performance (Bekmurodova, 2020). If the financial market is developed, bilateral FDI increases both in the host country and in the source country, which clearly indicates that the development of the financial market increases foreign investment (Donaubauer et al., 2019).

In the coming period, the BRI will increasingly show its positive value as well as its strategic importance. The results of empirical research (Ma et al., 2019) indicate that (a) China's FDI significantly promotes international trade between China and European countries and (b) the BRI influences the promotion of bilateral trade between China and European countries.

RESEARCH METHODOLOGY AND OBJECTIVES

FDI is considered one of the most important characteristics of the modern global economy. Nowadays, they are a necessity, especially in developing countries. The growing need for enterprise restructuring and modernization, along with limited domestic resources, create an environment in which the potential benefits of FDI are gaining in importance. FDI significantly contributes to strengthening the competitiveness of the domestic economy. Therefore, the development effects of these investments enable an increase in exports, transfer of modern technology, GDP growth and a reduction in the inflation rate.

FDI, their determinants and effects have been the subject of many analyzes and studies over the last twenty years. The positive effects of FDI contribute to improving the economic performance of the host country. This primarily refers to the transfer of knowledge and technology, increasing productivity, competitiveness, and exports. The rapid growth of FDI flows indicates a significant and growing role of corporations in global trade, and especially in global production.

The methodology used in this chapter includes a quantitative approach based on numerical data and their mutual comparison. The analysis used official data from the China Global Investment Tracker, which is a comprehensive public data set covering Chinese global investments. The China Global Investment Tracker is published by the American Enterprise Institute and the Heritage Foundation, and monitors China's construction activities and global investments since 2005 worth at least $100 million. The analysis covers the period from 2013 to 2020.

The chapter is segmented into three interrelated units, which represent the main objectives of this paper:

1. to determine the significance of the BRI for the construction of the Eurasian Economic Corridor,
2. to show the global investments of Chinese companies, with a special focus on Europe and the Western Balkan region,
3. to determine the inflow and importance of Chinese investments in the development of the Serbian economy.

Based on the defined methodology and set objectives, the focus of the chapter is on the BRI. Since investments are one of the basic pillars of this Initiative, it is especially important to show the direction and values of Chinese investments with special reference to their importance for the development of the Serbian economy. In addition to the fact that the strategic partnership between China and Serbia is at a very high level, the Chinese government considers Serbia as a country that can significantly contribute to the development of the BRI. The reason for such a standpoint stems from the fact that Serbia is geographically well positioned, and that it has directed its overall policy towards creating conditions that benefit Chinese investors.

MAIN FOCUS OF THE CHAPTER

Significance of the Belt and Road Initiative for the Construction of the Eurasian Economic Corridor

The official presentation of the BRI is related to 2013 and the official visit of the Chinese President to Kazakhstan and Indonesia. The Chinese state media often call this initiative the "New Silk Road". The BRI represents two initiatives in one. The Belt initiative covers overland routes for road and rail transportation, while the Road covers maritime roads and the port system involved in the initiative. Together, they provide a large network of routes connecting the participating countries. The primary focus of BRI is the construction and development of infrastructure in the countries participating in the implementation of this project.

Box 1. Map of BRI regions and projects

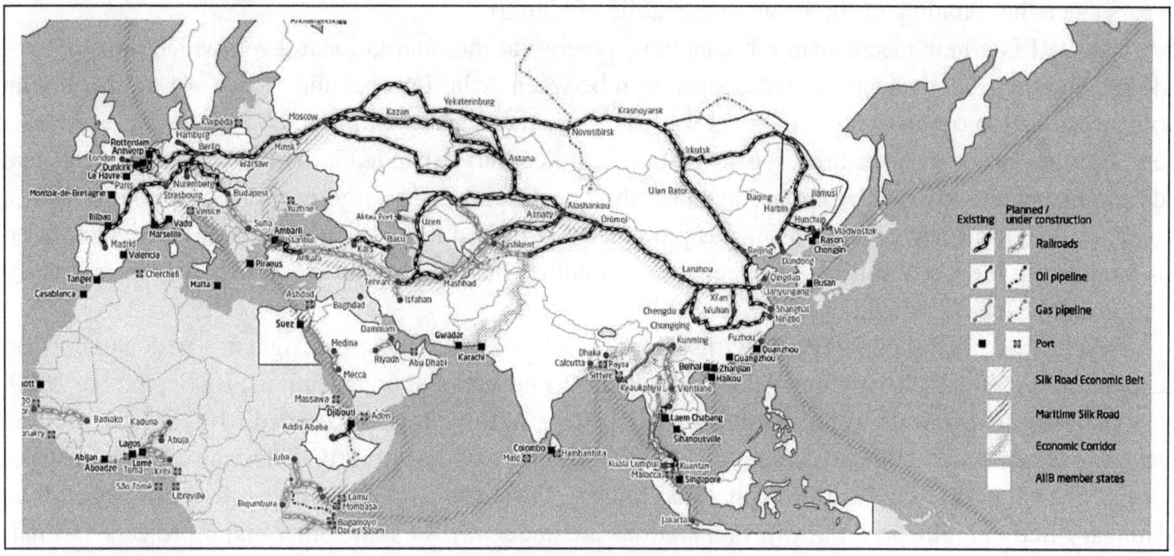

Source: MERICS (https://merics.org/en/analysis/mapping-belt-and-road-initiative-where-we-stand)

Box 1 shows the economic belt "Silk Road", which connects China, Russia and Europe. As for the Maritime Silk Road, on the one hand, it stretches from the Chinese coast to Europe, while the other direction goes from the Chinese coast through the South China Sea and the South Pacific (Lu et al., 2018). Therefore, the Chinese development strategy of the BRI is focused on cooperation and connecting countries located on the route of the six economic corridors. These corridors should connect China and (a) Mongolia and Russia, (b) Eurasian countries, (c) Central and Western Asia, (d) Pakistan, (e) other countries of the Indian subcontinent, and (f) Indochina and the South Pacific (OECD, 2018). Priority areas for cooperation are (a) policy coordination; (b) infrastructure connectivity; (c) unimpeded trade; (d) connecting financial institutions; and (e) connecting the population. The main goals of the project are to build a single market capable of comprehensive exchange of goods and cultures, as well as to improve cooperation between the countries participating in the project, with an emphasis on capital investment and development of new technologies.

The development of the Initiative, which aims to strengthen trade ties around the world and connect China with other countries, plays a central role in the plan to open up the Chinese market. Other measures include increasing investment and imports, lowering tariffs, developing free trade zones, improving the business environment, and deepening bilateral and multilateral cooperation. This project envisages investments worth about $1000 billion, while the Chinese government has provided about $200 billion and another $340 billion that Chinese contractors have managed to secure through construction contracts with countries that will be involved in the project. According to the development strategy, China plans to take on a bigger role in global events in the coming period, as well as to achieve the best possible cooperation with countries that have a developed industry, primarily steel production. Therefore, one of the tasks of this project is the development of countries in Asia and Europe that have not yet reached full economic development, as well as their economic and political integration. Through the realization of this Initiative, the Chinese government is primarily seeking to make China a global superpower, that will surpass America and Europe in economic terms. According to the initial plans presented, it is obvious that the Chinese government intends to complete the project by 2049 at the latest (one hundred years since the founding of the People's Republic of China).

The BRI is a new mechanism for achieving synergy at the international level, which aims at economic and cultural connections and cooperation between Asia, Europe, and Africa. At the beginning of the realization of this project, the goal was to restore the ancient "Silk Road", which connected Asia and Europe. However, over time, the scope of the project has expanded to include new territories and development initiatives. The project includes the construction of a large network of roads, railways, seaports, electricity networks, oil and gas pipelines and related infrastructure facilities. The fact that it is included in the Constitution of the People's Republic of China in 2017 clearly shows how seriously this project is being worked on.

Despite the impact of the coronavirus, by November 2020, China has signed 201 documents on cooperation within the BRI with 138 countries and 31 international organizations. By September 2020, China's total investments in the countries participating in this project exceeded $100 billion, and the value of construction projects is more than $720 billion. Work is currently underway on the construction of the China-Laos railway, the Sino-Thai railway, the Jakarta-Bandung high-speed railway and the Hungary-Serbia high-speed railway. Preparations are underway for some other major projects - China-Kyrgyzstan-Uzbekistan railway, eastern arm of Pan-Asian Railway Network, China-Nepal railway and reconstruction of Karachi-Peshawar railway. Maritime projects related to the ports of Gwadar (Pakistan), Hambantota (Sri Lanka), Piraeus (Greece) and Khalifa (UAE) are also being successfully developed. Among the numerous projects within the BRI, those related to the connection stand out, with special emphasis on the express railway line between China and Europe, where a significant segment is the project of modernization of the Belgrade-Budapest railway. Therefore, connecting is one of the foundations of the BRI, given that it is important not only because of the physical flows of people, goods, labor and capital, but also for the transfer of knowledge and values. The seriousness of Chinese plans speaks volumes in the presence of Chinese companies in most European countries, with the Western Balkans region being particularly interesting to Chinese investors, given that these countries are on the "New Silk Road".

The development of the BRI is of great importance for Chinese companies, which can enter new locations and invest their capital. The role of host countries is important in this process because they need to adjust their investment policies to current market conditions, which will contribute to attracting multinational companies to their territories. The growth of foreign direct investment is very important for every country as it can contribute to increasing production, developing human capital, promoting foreign trade, and increasing revenue (Domazet & Marjanović, 2018). The motives of Chinese companies to invest in a particular country are most often the demand for resources, the demand for a new market, and the demand for efficiency. When the motive is a demand for resources, Chinese investors will invest capital in countries that are part of the Initiative, which can offer resources at significantly lower costs compared to the home country (China) or another country. In addition to providing adequate resources, it will significantly strengthen its competitive position both in a given country and in its immediate environment. Another motive for Chinese companies is the expansion of the market, so it is important for the state to adjust its system, usually through various incentives, because in that way it will become an attractive investment destination for Chinese investors. The third important motive of Chinese companies is the demand for greater efficiency, given that more efficient management of branches will enable the maximum use of the advantages offered by certain location.

The BRI as the China's main infrastructure project has faced a major problem due to the coronavirus pandemic that has swept the world since March 2020. The global economic impact of the SARS-CoV-2 coronavirus along with the simultaneous collapse of economies around the world is creating startling new challenges for this Chinese project. The huge global quarantine caused by the COVID-19 virus is a powerful strike to many BRI participants. The big problem is that the leading routes for railway and maritime infrastructure of the BRI include agreements with some of the world's poorest economies and some of the biggest credit risks. With the recovery of the Chinese economy, the BRI project is making significant progress, which speaks in favor of the fact that China is the first major economy to recuperate since the beginning of the coronavirus pandemic, with growth of about 3.2 percent in the last quarter of 2020, and a tendency of continuous progress in the coming period.

The BRI is an endeavor from which much is rightly expected. Undoubtedly, apart from the desire to connect the continents, and the creation of new economic partners, China intends to set rules and principles according to which the cooperation between the partners will function in the future as well. Restoring relations with the countries on the former "Silk Road" is certainly the right path.

Value and Distribution of Chinese Investments - Global Level, Europe, Countries of the Western Balkans

The BRI should contribute to synergies between all countries involved in this project to achieve development goals. Considering global governance, BRI focuses on innovations in directions and models of cooperation to accelerate economic globalization. The BRI seeks to encourage all countries to participate in globalization and contribute to economic development. Therefore, it is necessary to find a way to accelerate globalization, which is a central part of this initiative. Therefore, it is not surprising that China has succeeded in its economic development, based, among other things, on projects that are a useful way to encourage globalization. Since it is led by developed countries, in the process of globalization, the rules of developed market economies apply (Stancheva-Gigov, 2016). In contrast to these countries, there are developing countries to which globalization provides an opportunity, but also poses certain challenges. However, due to the difficult course of globalization that has been visible in recent years, many countries are opting for bilateral negotiations, and more transparent bilateral trade, and investment agreements.

From a global perspective, in the period from 2013 to 2020, Chinese companies invested significant funds. According to the official report of China Global Investment Tracker, the distribution of investments by regions in that period was as follows (Figure 1): (1) Europe - $345,450 million, (2) USA - $145,280 million, (3) North America - $29,880 million, (4) South America - $114,320 million, (5) East Asia - $217,440 million, (6) Australia - $63,270 million, (7) West Asia - $200,530 million, (8) Arab Middle East and North Africa - $119,480 million and (9) Sub-Saharan Africa - $190,250 million. The total amount of investments at the global level in the given period was around $1,425,900 million.

Figure 1. Distribution of Chinese investments by regions: 2013-2020. (mil. $)
Source: Authors, based on China Global Investment Tracker

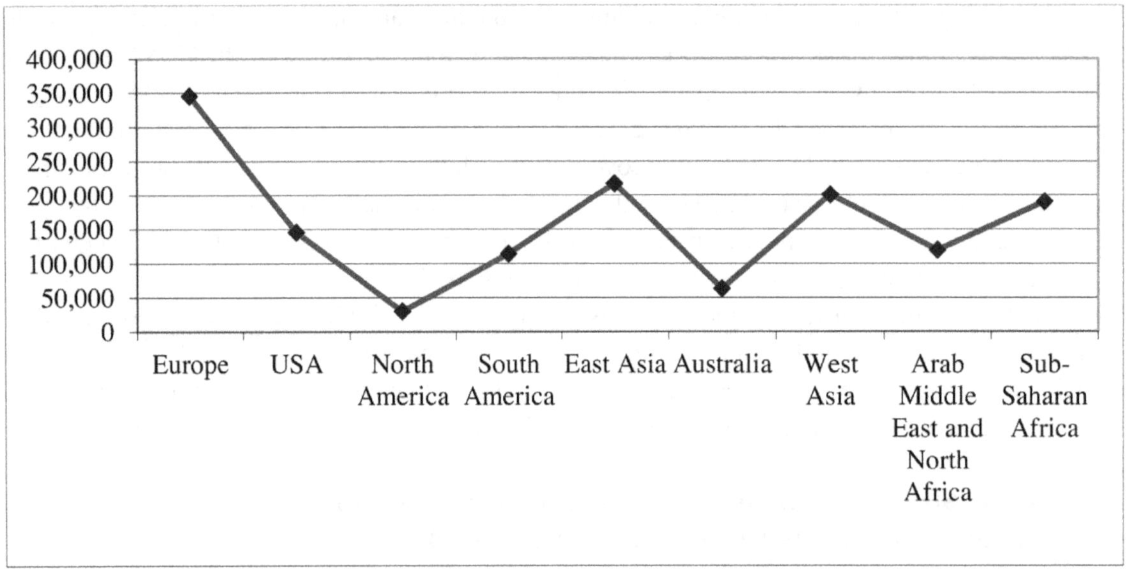

The distribution of Chinese investments by regions in the period 2013-2020, shows that Chinese companies directed their business towards all regions, with the amounts varying depending on the attractiveness of the market itself. Comparing the world's regions in terms of the inflow of Chinese investments, Figure 2 clearly shows that Chinese companies direct their investments to European countries, which should not be surprising, considering that this region is very important for the realization of the Chinese BRI project.

Figure 2. Share of Chinese investments by regions: 2013-2020 (%)
Source: Authors, based on China Global Investment Tracker

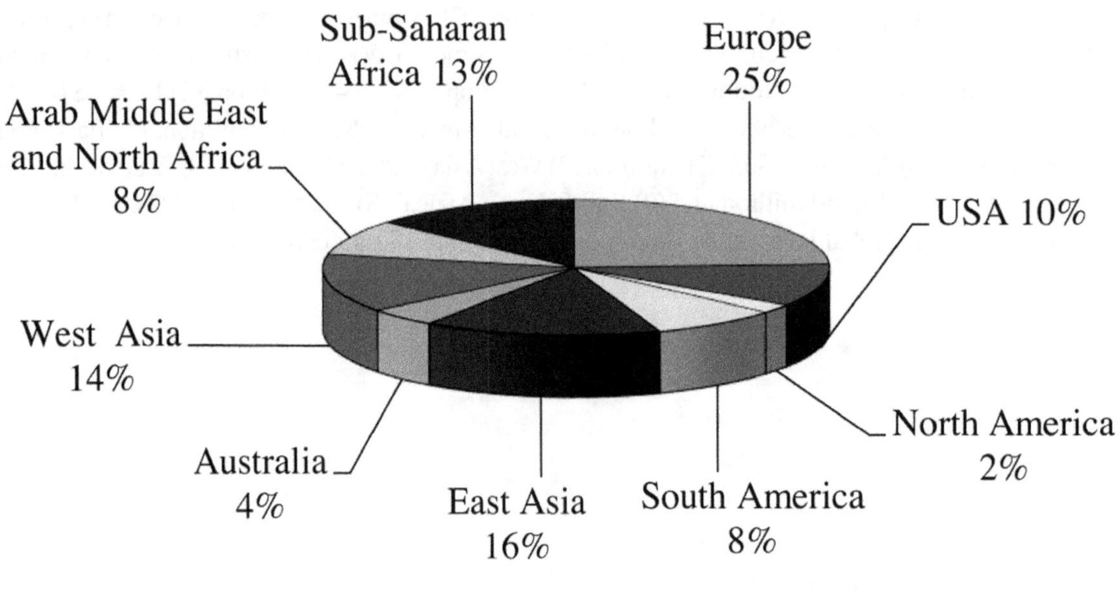

If we take a closer look at the percentage share of Chinese investments by region in the period 2013-2020, over 70% of investments are going to regions that are potentially attractive for the implementation of the BRI.

With the launch of the BRI (2013), China has become one of the most important actors in the field of international relations. The Initiative has enabled China to increase its presence in various regions of the world. If observed from a global level, Europe should certainly lead, given that the volume of China's trade with 17 Central and Eastern European countries in 2020 reached almost $103 billion, with a tendency to increase in the coming years.

Chinese investors have directed their investments in Europe to the following industries: Transport ($64,650 million), Agriculture ($54,580 million), Energy ($42,020 million), Entertainment ($36,600 million), Finance ($32,930 million), Technology ($31,340 million), Real estate ($22,030 million), Logistics ($21,190 million), Tourism ($15,300 million), Health ($6,530 million), Metals ($4,190 million), Utilities ($3,060 million), Chemicals ($360 million) and Other ($10,670 million).

Figure 3. Share of Chinese investments in Europe, by industry, 2013-2020 (percentage)
Source: Authors, based on China Global Investment Tracker

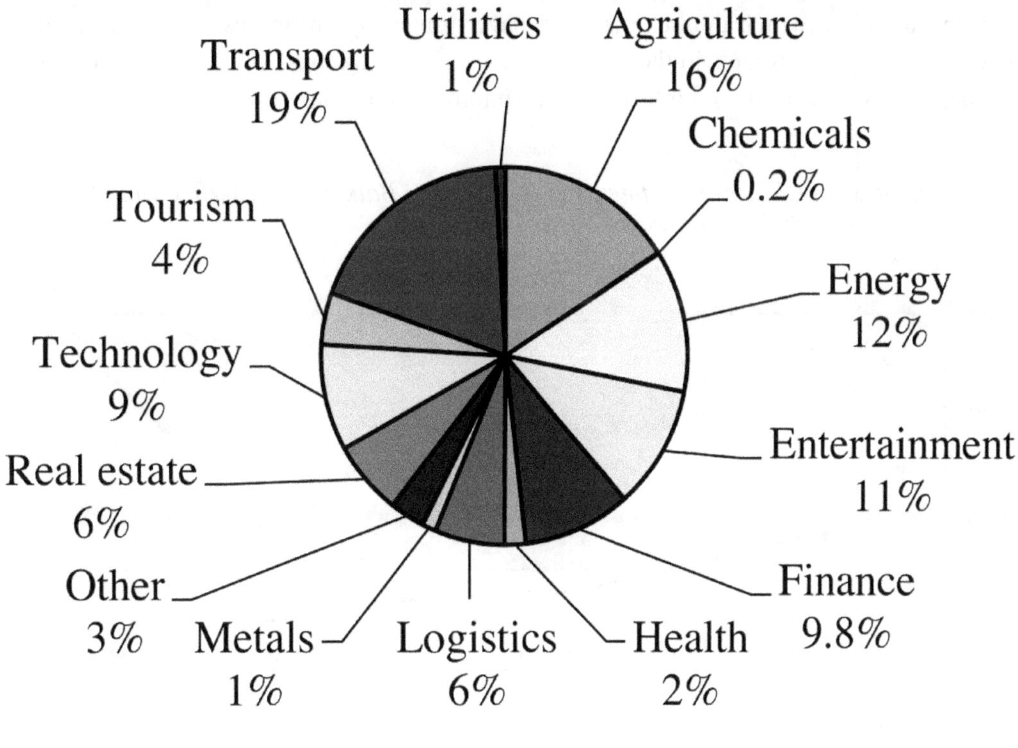

Considering that the observed period coincides with the activities related to the implementation of the project "One Belt, One Road", and as capital projects that have been completed or started are very important for this phase, almost 1/5 of all investments are directed to the transport sector (Figure 3). Creating competitive advantages in the Western Balkans will have a positive impact on foreign investors, which will contribute to the growth of FDI in some other sectors that were less attractive (Domazet & Marjanović, 2017b).

In the first nine months of 2020, total imports and exports between China and European countries involved in the BRI amounted to about $960 billion. Non-financial direct investments in countries within that initiative amounted to about 13 billion dollars, which is an increase of about 30% compared to 2019. The number of freight train departures from China to 92 European cities and 21 European countries reached over 10,000 and about 927,000 TEU (unit for measuring shipping containers) by the middle of November 2020, which is an increase of about 55% compared to the same period in 2019.

The region of the Western Balkans has a very important role in the BRI, since it has become the main center connecting Asia with the European market. Given that this project is just the beginning, there is no doubt that the route connecting Greece, Northern Macedonia and Serbia will be one of the main links between the Chinese and European markets (Zuokui, 2016). Since countries of the Western Balkans significantly lag behind the countries of the European Union, the increase in foreign investment will be important for their economic growth and development. In the absence of large investments from developed EU countries, the countries of the Western Balkans are trying to adapt their markets to the requirements of Chinese investors. The Chinese BRI can enable the realization of large infrastructure projects and connect the economies of the Western Balkans with the EU countries. In the past ten years, China has significantly increased its presence in the Western Balkans region. China finds its commitment to such activities in the fact that the countries of the Western Balkans have not yet become members of the European Union, which implies that they have limited opportunities to attract large European investments. Chinese investments in these countries are mostly focused on the infrastructure, telecommunications, energy, transport, and information technology industries.

Figure 4. Distribution of Chinese investments in the Western Balkans: 2013-2020 (mil. $)[1]
Source: Authors, based on China Global Investment Tracker

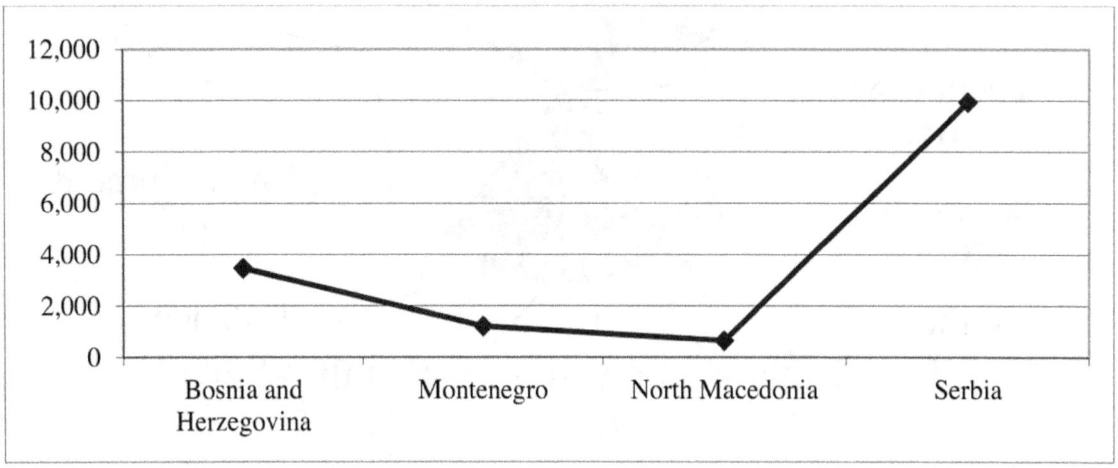

Chinese investments in the Western Balkans have been growing steadily for years. In the period 2013-2020, Chinese companies invested about $15 billion in the countries of the Western Balkans, of which the largest amount of investment (about $10 billion) was directed to Serbia (Figure 4).

Table 1. Total amount of Chinese investments in the Western Balkans over the years (mil. $)

Godina	2013	2014	2015	2016	2017	2018	2019	2020
Iznos	980	2,210	460	750	3,080	3,660	760	2,140

Source: China Global Investment Tracker

The largest inflow of Chinese investments in the countries of the Western Balkans (Table 1) was recorded in 2018 in the amount of about $3,660 million. Of the total amount of Chinese investments in 2018, the largest part was directed to Serbia in the transport sector ($2,300 million). Looking at the industries in which Chinese investments were made, in the period from 2013 to 2020, the distribution in the countries of the Western Balkans was as follows: transport ($6,970 million), energy ($3,990 million), metals ($2,180 million), utilities ($310 million), Other ($260 million), technology ($170 million) and real estate ($160 million).

The future of cooperation between China and the countries of the Western Balkans depends on the results of the process of integration into the European Union. In the years to come, it is not to be expected that any of the countries of the Western Balkans will become a member of the European Union, which gives these countries the opportunity to strengthen their cooperation with China. Although there is no doubt that China has become a relevant factor in the Western Balkans, especially in Serbia, there are several challenges for the prospective collaboration between these countries. All the countries of the Western Balkans have expressed their will to continue their path to membership in the European Union. In that sense, the future of cooperation between the Western Balkan countries and China can be found in the relations between the European Union and China. The European Union's growing concern about China's growing influence in the Western Balkans could also have negative consequences for China. However, the future of the Western Balkans' integration into the European Union is not clearly defined. Such a situation leaves room for the influence of other interested parties, which could lead to certain negative consequences for certain actors in the process. The possibility of negative consequences lies in the absence of control mechanisms, dependence on political elites and unstable state institutions in the Western Balkans. The solution could be found in the rapid accession of the Western Balkan countries to the European Union.

The Importance of Chinese Investments in the Development of the Serbian Economy

Serbia is one of the first countries to express support for the BRI and to participate in several projects under the Initiative. Having understood the initiative and recognized all the benefits of cooperation in that process, Serbia is the first country to have signed a bilateral agreement with China on cooperation in the "One Belt, One Road" project. In the previous period, Serbia tried to create a business environment through interstate relations, but also made significant progress in terms of Chinese direct investments. In the past seven years, China and Serbia have expanded cooperation in all areas, which has greatly encouraged Serbia's economic and social development. The goal is to deepen cooperation with China further, given that the two countries share the same economic vision of the 21st century - a vision of sustainable development and economic interdependence. China's strategic goal in cooperation with Serbia is aimed at developing and promoting the route of the mainland part of the Maritime Silk Road - the railway-road traffic corridor from the Port of Piraeus to Central Europe, with a strategic route through the territory of Serbia.

After Serbia and China signed a co-operation agreement on joint construction under the BRI, trade between the two countries grew by almost 56 percent. The value of projects in which Chinese companies participated reached about $5 billion.

Figure 5. Inflow of Chinese investments in Serbia, 2013-2020 (mil. $)
Source: Authors, based on China Global Investment Tracker

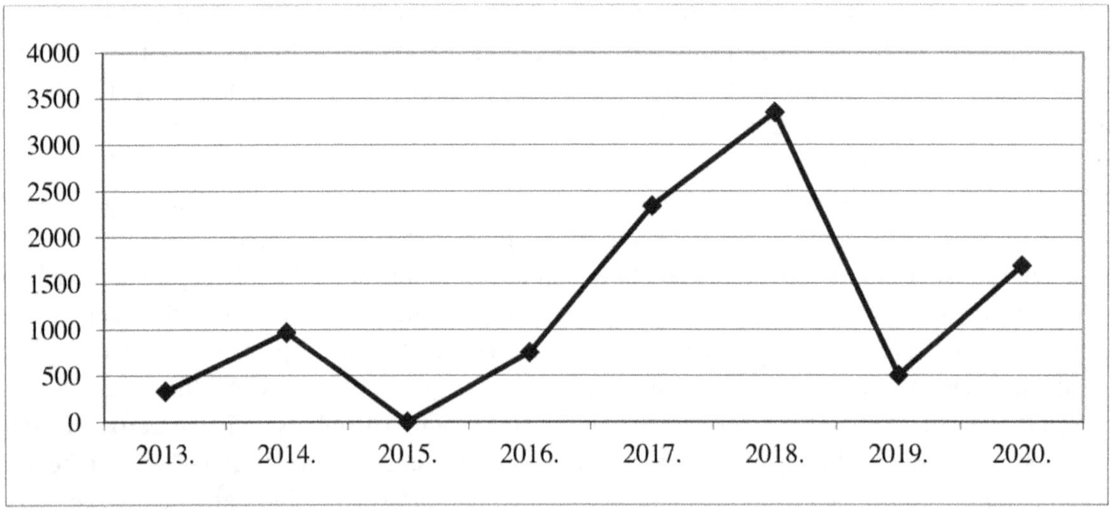

From the moment the realization of the project "One Belt, One Road" started, Chinese investments in Serbia have mostly had a growth trend (Figure 5). The largest value of Chinese investments was recorded in 2018, around $3,350 million. Chinese investments were reduced during 2019, and it was to be expected that the consequences of the COVID-19 pandemic, which affected the entire world, would cause an even more significant reduction in Chinese investments in Serbia in 2020. However, despite the negative consequences caused by the coronavirus, there was no drop in investments. On the contrary, they increased to about $1,690 million, during 2020. Graph 6 shows that Chinese companies invested the most in two sectors during 2020: transport (investors: Shandong Gaosu and China Communications Construction Company) and metals (investor: Zijin Mining).

Figure 6. Chinese investments in Serbia, by sectors, 2013-2020 (mil. $)
Source: Authors, based on China Global Investment Tracker

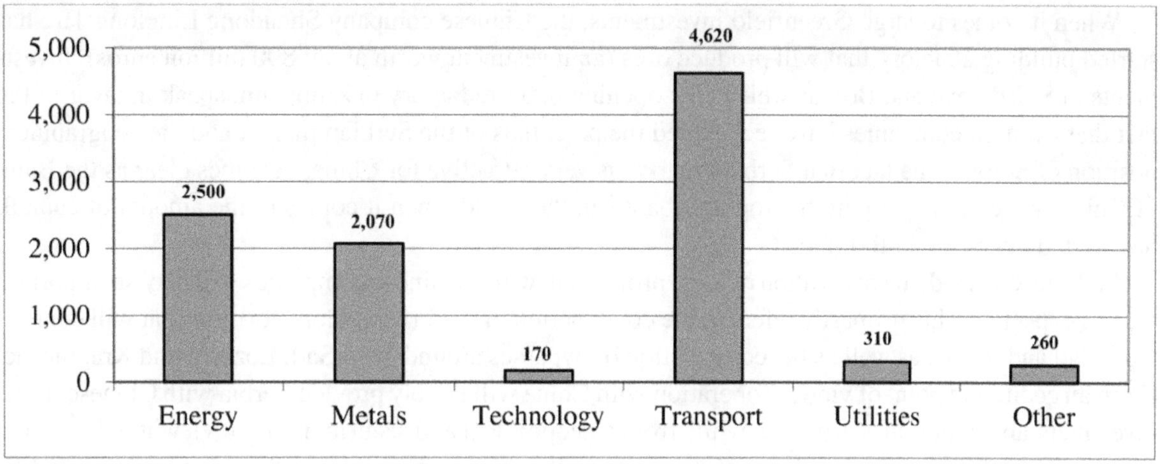

Of the total amount of investments that Chinese companies invested in Serbia in the period from 2013 to 2020, about 45% was directed to transport, about 25% to energy and about 21% to the metals industry, while significantly less was invested in other sectors. In the observed period, Chinese investors mainly invested in the transport industry, consequently in the automotive sub-industry, as well as in the reconstruction of road and traffic infrastructure. Chinese companies have so far invested about $3 billion in the reconstruction of road and traffic infrastructure. The largest funds were invested in the construction of highways, bridges, and other infrastructure facilities. Some of the most important projects are the Zemun-Borča bridge (Pupin's bridge), the section of Corridor 11 (Preljina-Požega), as well as the bypass around Belgrade. One of the most important projects within the BRI, which is now being implemented, is the reconstruction and modernization of the railway that connects Belgrade and Budapest. The reconstruction of this part of the railway infrastructure will connect the Greek port of Piraeus with Central Europe, which is very important both for the global BRI project and for Serbia, given that there will be a significant increase in revenues from the transport of goods.

The primary goal of attracting FDI in the automotive sector in developing countries is to encourage the development of the domestic automotive parts and components industry (Beraha, 2016). The interest of Chinese companies in investing in the automotive sector in Serbia has grown significantly in the past few years. As a result, the plant of the "Minth Automotive Europe" company, in which about 100 million euro was invested, was opened in Loznica. The Energy sector has also attracted significant Chinese funding, specifically the gas industry but also alternative energy sources. Chinese companies have directed significant funds to this sector, with special emphasis on the construction of an energy plant – thermal power plant Kostolac B-3.

Chinese companies have also directed investments in the metals sector, more precisely in companies engaged in the production of copper and steel. China has invested large funds in Serbian companies that significantly contribute to the development of the national economy, primarily in RTB Bor and steel plant in Smederevo. Serbia's strategic partner in the Smederevo ironworks is the Chinese company HBIS, which made an excellent move with this investment, given that the plant is in a good location on the Danube and thus represents a significant springboard for placing Chinese steel in Central and Western

Europe. In addition, an agreement was signed with the mining giant Zijin Mining on the opening of the Timok mine, where the investment will be worth about $470 million.

When it comes to large Greenfield investments, the Chinese company Shandong Linglong Tire has started building a factory that will produce tires (an investment worth about 800 million euros). Investments in Smederevo and Bor, as well as the opening of a tire factory in Zrenjanin, speak in favor of the fact that Chinese companies have recognized the potentials of the Serbian market and the geographical position of Serbia. The fact that Serbian market is very attractive for China, becomes clear as the Bank of China, which ranks among the top four banks in the world when it comes to the amount of capital, has started operating in Belgrade.

In the next period, the realization of large projects, in which Chinese companies will play an important role, is expected. This primarily refers to the construction of the Fruška-Gora corridor that will connect Novi Sad and Ruma, as well as the construction of bypasses around Novi Sad, Loznica and Kragujevac. From an economic point of view, cooperation with China will largely provide Serbia with Chinese direct investment and better infrastructure, while from a geopolitical and security point of view it will provide stronger support in international organizations as well as prosperity in the Balkan region (Jojić, 2017).

SOLUTIONS AND RECOMMENDATIONS

From a strategic perspective, the countries of the Western Balkans are a great opportunity for China. First, they are not part of the EU and therefore not subject to the strict control procedures that Chinese investment currently faces in the EU and other Western countries, while on the other hand they benefit from various trade agreements with the EU and the rest of the world. Second, they are close to the port of Piraeus in Greece, which Chinese are currently managing. In addition, given the state of their economies, labor costs are significantly lower than in the EU. One of the tasks that China has set for itself in the coming period is the growing coordination with the institutions of the European Union. Considering that EU has a great influence in the Western Balkans, it is extremely important for China to improve cooperation with the EU, because in that way it will enable faster development of the "One Belt, One Road" project. It is to be expected that such cooperation and support between China and the EU will significantly contribute to faster and more efficient construction of the China-Europe sea-land express transport, which will partly pass-through Serbia.

In the coming years, China will increasingly focus its activities on the countries of the Western Balkans, with special emphasis on investing in Serbia through current and planned projects. Therefore, it can be concluded that Serbia is a very interesting market through which China will try to consolidate and strengthen its position in the Western Balkans, which it will achieve through even more intensive investment in Serbia. To achieve its strategic economic goals, Serbia has considered China one of the most important foreign trade and financial partners in the past ten years. The volume of trade between China and Serbia has increased significantly, more than twice over the past ten years (Jovičić, Stevanović & Beraha, 2020). Due to the insufficient financial resources for the realization of the planned economic development goals, Serbia is trying to open its market for the new investments. To a large extent, China is trying to make the most of it by investing its own financial resources on favorable terms. By investing in the Serbian economy, Chinese investors can contribute to achieving a common interest, which will have a positive impact on China's "New Silk Road" development strategy (Dimitrijević, 2017).

The countries of the Western Balkans, especially Serbia, will strive to create an even stronger connection with China in the coming period. Strategic cooperation between these countries will significantly contribute to the increase of Chinese direct investments, which can lead to increasing economic growth and development of both Serbia and other countries in the Western Balkans. In that sense, the BRI can not only contribute to the progress of these countries, but also of the entire region. It is particularly important that each of these countries align its development and investment policies with the needs of Chinese companies, thus creating a more competitive environment compared to some other European regions. Accordingly, it is very important to adopt an adequate strategy that will enable countries to attract Chinese investments. The investment sectors that will be the bearers of these activities in the future should be clearly presented within that strategy. This means that countries need to represent sectors and sub-sectors with potential for progress and consequently for investment. State cooperation within the "One Belt, One Road" project is the first and foremost goal for attracting Chinese capita. Also, providing an adequate economic environment is of great importance.

Starting from the second quarter of 2020 and the worldwide COVID-19 pandemic, the movement of foreign direct investment has been significantly limited (Pjanić & Mitrašević, 2021). If the crisis continues, the consequences will be directly reflected in the inflow of foreign investments, and it is to be expected that they will decrease due to great uncertainty for capital investment, limited financing, and limited fiscal space. In a situation where there is less free capital on the market, it is very important that the countries of the Western Balkans use their chances in the most efficient and best way and attract Chinese direct investments. Therefore, it is very important that these countries pursue an active tax policy, but also strive to maintain the stability of basic macroeconomic indicators, primarily GDP. In the analysis of the Western Balkan countries, Serbia is in the most convenient position as it has adapted solidly to the new situation. This is reflected both through the completion of already launched projects and through the attraction of new investments. The partnership with the Chinese state and strategic cooperation have led to new investments that will certainly contribute to the economic growth of the country, but also ensure a faster continuation of the BRI initiative implementation.

It will be very important to bring the Serbian market even closer to Chinese investors in the coming period. To achieve that, it will be necessary to direct state activities to the planning of specific projects and creating free zones that are especially relevant for Greenfield investments. The main task should be to create favorable conditions for investors that would be a clear signal that Serbia wants to be a partner in the implementation of international projects and above all in the implementation of the global Chinese initiative. Expectations are that Serbia will continue to provide incentives because it will attract investments of Chinese companies that have not yet invested in Serbia, as well as encourage further investments of those companies that already operate in the Serbian market.

FUTURE RESEARCH DIRECTIONS

The global economic environment significantly contributes to the development of international relations, as they are extremely important for state, regional and local communities that aim to ensure diversification and strengthen their economic base. The components necessary to ensure a high level of economic growth are attracting FDI and developing export opportunities. This is one of the tasks set before economic development experts as their goal is to offer proposals on how to use the country's resources as efficiently as possible to attract FDI and improve export potentials. Accordingly, to attract as many FDI as possible, each country should take the initiative to promote exports and FDI or improve efficiency of already adopted ones.

The emphasis in this chapter is on the presentation of the importance of the BRI initiative for the construction of the Eurasian economic corridor, as well as on the presentation of the inflow of Chinese investments at the global level with special reference to Serbia. Future research can be extended to Central and Eastern European countries as China plans to implement the "One Belt, One Road" project in these countries as well. Accordingly, it would be especially important that the analysis focuses on the competitiveness of these countries because this is one of the basic preconditions for new Chinese investments. The research would use data from some of the world's databases (World Bank, UNCTAD, and IMF) and selected official data (FDI inflow, GDP, exports, imports, employment, etc.). Additionally, a detailed analysis of sectors/industries in Central and Eastern European countries would be particularly important to determine the value of Chinese investment since the beginning of "One Belt, One Road" project. Based on this analysis, sectors that are attractive for Chinese investments would be mapped and the economic development of these countries would be anticipated. Certainly, presenting measures used by Central and Eastern European countries to secure new investments would be important. On the other hand, such an analysis would indicate the limitations and possible ways to overcome them in order for these countries to attract more Chinese investments in the coming period.

The results obtained in such a research would provide guidance for all Central and Eastern European countries in terms of the direction of their economic and investment policy. In this way, the preconditions for new investment would be met because Chinese investors would perceive these countries as attractive destinations. This is especially relevant for China as this region is of strategic importance for the implementation of the BRI.

CONCLUSION

Countries that, through their overall policies, provide an environment with stable conditions for free and profitable business will certainly attract FDI faster and easier compared to those countries where the investment environment is not sufficiently favorable. To attract as much foreign capital as possible, the countries of the Western Balkans have liberalized the regulations that determine the framework for foreign investments. In the last ten to fifteen years, we are witnessing the success of these countries as with high FDI inflows they have achieved high export rates and attracted a significant number of large projects of multinational companies.

In the past ten years, Chinese companies have mainly invested in developing countries, among which the region of the Western Balkans stands out. Investors from China have recognized all the advantages offered by the countries of the Western Balkans (favorable geographical position, cheap labor, availability of raw materials, market size, etc.), which has contributed to their growing interest for investment.

Southeast Europe is strategically very important for China, and the Western Balkans countries will be the main hub for the new "Silk Road", as one of three important corridors. Owning to incentive measures within the implementation of the FDI attraction policy, and partly due to other factors i.e.., economic growth, increasing macroeconomic stability, geopolitical factors, cheap labor, etc., Serbia has become an attractive destination for Chinese investors. Investments in infrastructure have been the main driver of GDP growth in Serbia in recent years, which has resulted in a growing interest in cooperation in this area with the EU and international development institutions, as well as with China. Thanks to the demanding economic reforms it has implemented in the previous period, Serbia has positioned itself as one of the most important investment destinations in Central and Eastern Europe.

Also, many prominent Chinese investors have been attracted by Serbia's various potentials. Serbia and China have nurtured very good relations for years, which is confirmed by cooperation at all levels. Accordingly, it is not surprising that China is currently Serbia's most reliable political and economic partner. On the other hand, Serbia has become a key strategic partner of China in the region of Central and Eastern Europe, especially after the launch of the 16 + 1 multilateral cooperation mechanism, within the BRI. China is increasing its presence as an investor in the Serbian market mainly through the purchase of state-owned companies or through Greenfield investments. The share of Chinese investments in total FDI in the country during 2019 exceeded 20%, with a clearly visible upward trend in the past few years. Chinese investors have not only shown a strong sense of responsibility, but some of them have already successfully completed projects in Serbia. The Serbian government, in turn, received preferential loans and technology, which led to significant growth in its energy sector. Both countries expected to benefit from "One Belt, One Road" initiative through promoting industry, including infrastructure construction, energy, agriculture, information technology, tourism, and manufacturing.

In the coming period, attention should be focused on creating competitive advantages based on which Chinese investors will map Serbia in their investment plans as a country that provides favorable conditions for investment and business development.

ACKNOWLEDGMENT

This chapter is financed by the Ministry of Education, Science and Technological Development of the Republic of Serbia.

REFERENCES

Aibai, A., Huang, X., Luo, Y., & Peng, Y. (2019). Foreign Direct Investment, Institutional Quality, and Financial Development along the Belt and Road: An Empirical Investigation. *Emerging Markets Finance & Trade*, *55*(14), 3275–3294. doi:10.1080/1540496X.2018.1559139

Azémar, C., & Dharmapala, D. (2019). Tax sparing agreements, territorial tax reforms, and foreign direct investment. *Journal of Public Economics*, *169*, 89–108. doi:10.1016/j.jpubeco.2018.10.013

Bekmurodova, G. (2020). Theoretical Features of FDI (Foreign Direct Investment) and its Influence to Economic Growth. *International Journal of Management Science and Business Administration*, *6*(2), 33–39. doi:10.18775/ijmsba.1849-5664-5419.2014.62.1004

Beraha, I. (2016). Revitalizacija srpske automobilske industrije - da li je uloga Fijata ključna? *Zbornik Matice srpske za društvene nauke*, *67*(159/16), 767-783.

Beraha, I., & Redžepagić, S. (2016). Trade and Cooperation Between the Emerging Economies: What is the BRICS Position? In Europe and Asia - Economic Integration Prospects. CEMAFI International.

Bolivar, L. M., Casanueva, C., & Castro, I. (2019). Global Foreign Direct Investment: A network perspective. *International Business Review, 28*(4), 696–712. doi:10.1016/j.ibusrev.2019.01.007

Cai, P. (2017). *Understanding China's Belt and Road Initiative*. Lowy Institute for International Policy.

Casarini, N. (2015). Is Europe to Benefit from China's Belt and Road Initiative? *IAI Working Papers, 15*.

Chen, X. M., & Lin, C. (2018). *Foreign Investment across the Belt and Road Patterns, Determinants and Effects*. World bank group. Policy Research Working Paper 8607.

Cui, L., & Song, M. (2019). Economic evaluation of the Belt and Road Initiative from an unimpeded trade perspective. *International Journal of Logistics Research and Applications, 22*(1), 25–46. doi:10.1080/13675567.2018.1492532

Dimitrijević, D. (2017). *Capacities for Development Serbia's Cooperation with China*. China-CEE Institute. Working paper, No. 4.

Domazet, I., & Marjanović, D. (2017). Foreign Direct Investment in the Function of Economic Development-Example of Selected Countries in the Western Balkans. *International Letters of Social and Humanistic Sciences, 79*, 1-15.

Domazet, I., & Marjanović, D. (2017). Tax incentives as a factor of economic growth. In The state and the market in economic development. Brisbane, Australia: The International Institute for Development Studies.

Domazet, I., & Marjanović, D. (2018). FDI as a Factor of Improving the Competitiveness of Developing Countries: FDI and Competitiveness. In Foreign Direct Investments (FDIs) and Opportunities for Developing Economies in the World Market. Hershey, PA: Business Science Reference.

Donaubauer, J., Neumayer, E., & Nunnenkamp, P. (2019). Financial market development in host and source countries and their effects on bilateral foreign direct investment. *World Economy, 43*(3), 534–556. doi:10.1111/twec.12884

Dunford, M., & Liu, W. (2019). Chinese perspectives on the Belt and Road Initiative. *Cambridge Journal of Regions, Economy and Society, 12*(1), 145–167. doi:10.1093/cjres/rsy032

Groh, A. P., & Wich, M. (2012). Emerging economies' attraction of foreign direct investment. *Emerging Markets Review, 13*(2), 210–229. doi:10.1016/j.ememar.2012.03.005

Huang, Y. (2016). Understanding China's Belt & Road Initiative: Motivation, framework and assessment. *China Economic Review, 40*, 314–321. doi:10.1016/j.chieco.2016.07.007

Jin, B., Garcia, F., & Salomon, R. (2019). Inward foreign direct investment and local firm innovation: The moderating role of technological capabilities. *Journal of International Business Studies, 50*(5), 847–855. doi:10.105741267-018-0177-1

Jojić, S. (2017). *How Serbia perceives "The Belt and the Road" Initiative and 16+1 Cooperation*. China-CEE Institute. Working paper, No. 9.

Jovičić, E., Stevanović, S., & Beraha, I. (2020). Serbia-China Bilateral Trade Relations: Major Challenges and Opportunities. *Economic Analysis, 53*(2), 133–144.

Jude, C., & Levieuge, G. (2017). Growth Effect of Foreign Direct Investment in Developing Economies: The Role of Institutional Quality. *World Economy*, *40*(4), 715–742. doi:10.1111/twec.12402

Julien, C., & Mitsuo, M. (2018). China's 'Belt and Road' Initiative — Mapping the World's Normative and Strategic Implications. *Journal of World Trade*, *1*, 163–185.

Khan, H., & Khan, U. (2019). Financial development and FDI inflows in China. Kiel Institute for the World Economy. Economics Discussion Papers No. 2019-54.

Li, C., & Tanna, S. (2019). The impact of foreign direct investment on productivity: New evidence for developing countries. *Economic Modelling*, *80*, 453–466. doi:10.1016/j.econmod.2018.11.028

Liu, W., & Dunford, M. (2016). Inclusive globalization: Unpacking China's Belt and Road Initiative. *Area Development and Policy*, *1*(3), 323–340. doi:10.1080/23792949.2016.1232598

Lu, H., Rohr, C., Hafner, M., & Knack, A. (2018). *China Belt and Road Initiative: Measuring the impact of improving transport connectivity on international study.Santa Monica, Calif., and Cambridge*. RAND Corporation. doi:10.1007/978-981-13-0101-8

Ma, D., Lei, C., Ullah, F., Ullah, R., & Baloch, Q. B. (2019). China's One Belt and One Road Initiative and Outward Chinese Foreign Direct Investment in Europe. *Sustainability*, *11*(24), 7055. doi:10.3390u11247055

Marjanović, D. (2018). Competitiveness of the Serbian Economy through the Prism of Tax Incentives for Foreign Investors. *Economic Analysis*, *51*(3-4), 95–104. doi:10.28934/ea.18.51.34.pp95-104

Marjanović, D., & Domazet, I. (2018). *Unapređenje makro konkurentnosti – fiskalni aspekti [Improving macro competitiveness - fiscal aspects]*. Institute of Economic Sciences.

Marjanović, D., & Domazet, I. (2021). Foreign Direct Investments: A Key Factor for Business Globalization. In Institutional, Economic, and Social Impacts of Globalization and Liberalization. Hershey, PA: Business Science Reference. doi:10.4018/978-1-7998-4459-4.ch006

Marjanović, D., Jovičić, E., & Stojanović, D. (2021). The Global Distribution of Chinese Investments: Importance for the Economy of Serbia. *Ekonomika (Nis)*, *67*(1), 43–55. doi:10.5937/ekonomika2101043M

Milovic, N., & Jocovic, M. (2017). Impact of foreign direct investment on competitiveness of montenegrin economy. *Transformations in Business & Economics*, *16*(1), 223-23.

Milovic, N., Jocovic, M., & Martinovic, N. (2020). Analysis of the Impact of Macroeconomic Stability on the Level of Global Competitiveness of Western Balkan Countries. *Journal of Central Banking Theory and Practice*, *2*, 23–37.

OECD. (2018). *China's Belt and Road Initiative in the Global Trade, Investment and Finance Landscape*. OECD Publishing.

Pardo, R. P. (2018). Europe's financial security and Chinese economic statecraft: The case of the Belt and Road Initiative. *Asia Europe Journal*, *16*(3), 237–250. doi:10.100710308-018-0511-z

Pjanić, M., & Mitrašević, M. (2021). Foreign Direct Investments in Serbia. *Culture of Polis-Journal for Nurturing of Democratic Political Culture*, *18*(44), 253-265.

Rolland, N. (2017). *China's Eurasian Century? Political and Strategic Implications of the Belt and Road Initiative*. National Bureau of Asian Research.

Stancheva-Gigov, I. (2016). Foreign direct investment and economic growth: Empirical analysis. *Economic Development, 18*(1-2), 337–350.

Stancheva-Gigov, I. (2018). Transnational companies and their technological power - investments in technology development and technology transfer. *Economic Development, 20*(3), 55–68.

Zhai, F. (2018). China's belt and road initiative: A preliminary quantitative assessment. *Journal of Asian Economics, 55*, 84–92. doi:10.1016/j.asieco.2017.12.006

Zuokui, L. (2016). *Europe and the "Belt and Road" Initiative: Responses and Risks*. China Social Sciences Press.

ADDITIONAL READING

Bandiera, L., & Tsiropoulos, V. (2020). A Framework to Assess Debt Sustainability under the Belt and ROad Initiative. *Journal of Development Economics, 146*, 146. doi:10.1016/j.jdeveco.2020.102495

Clarke, M. (2018). The Belt and Road Initiative: Exploring Beijing's Motivations and Challenges for its New Silk Road. *Strategic Analysis, 48*(2), 84–102. doi:10.1080/09700161.2018.1439326

Lai, K. P. Y., Lin, S., & Sidaway, J. D. (2020). FInancing the Belt and Road Initiative (BRI): Research agendas beyond the "dept-trap" discourse. *Eurasian Geography and Economics, 61*(2), 109–124. doi: 10.1080/15387216.2020.1726787

Liu, W., Zhang, Y., & Xiong, W. (2020). Finacing the Belt and Road Initiative. *Eurasian Geography and Economics, 61*(2), 137–145. doi:10.1080/15387216.2020.1716822

Mitrovic, D. (2018). China's Belt and Road Initiative: Connecting and Transforming Initiative. *The Belt & Road Initiative in the Global Arena*, 17-34.

Mobley, T. (2019). The Belt and Road Initiative: Insights from China's Backyard. *Strategic Studies Quarterly, 13*(3), 52–72.

Oliveira, G., Murton, G., Rippa, A., Harlan, T., & Yang, Y. (2020). China's Belt and Road Initiative: Views from the ground. *Political Geography, 82*, 82. doi:10.1016/j.polgeo.2020.102225 PMID:32836922

Soyres, F., Mulabdic, A., Murray, S., Rocha, N., & Ruta, M. (2019). How much will the Belt and Road Initiative reduce trade costs? *Inter Economics, 159*, 151–164. doi:10.1016/j.inteco.2019.07.003

Wang, H. (2019). China's Approach to the Belt and Road Initiative: Scope, Character and Sustainability. *Journal of International Economic Law, 22*(1), 29–55. doi:10.1093/jiel/jgy048

Wen, X., Ma, H. L., Choi, T. M., & Sheu, J. B. (2019). Impacts of the Belt and Road Initiative on the China-Europe trading route selections. *Transportation Research Part E, Logistics and Transportation Review, 122*, 581–604. doi:10.1016/j.tre.2019.01.006

Yang, G., Huang, X., Huang, J., & Chen, H. (2020). Assessment of the effects of infrastructure investment under the belt and road initiative. *China Economic Review*, *60*, 60. doi:10.1016/j.chieco.2020.101418

KEY TERMS AND DEFINITIONS

Belt and Road Initiative (BRI): Is a strategy initiated by the People's Republic of China that seeks to connect Asia with Africa and Europe via land and maritime networks with the aim of improving regional integration, increasing trade and stimulating economic growth. It is a global infrastructure development strategy adopted by the Chinese government in 2013 to invest in nearly 70 countries and international organizations.

Competitiveness: The ability of a country to produce goods and services that pass the test of the international market in free and equal market conditions, while retaining and increasing the real income of the population in the long run.

Countries of the Western Balkans: Balkan countries (Serbia, Bosnia and Herzegovina, Northern Macedonia, Albania, and Montenegro) that are not the members of the EU.

Economic Development: The process of continuous economic growth in a dynamic environment.

Eurasian Economic Space: The Customs Union of Belarus, Kazakhstan and Russia was found on January 1, 2010, and was later renamed the Eurasian Customs Union. The four freedoms of movement, modeled on the European Union (goods, capital, services, and people), were fully implemented on 25th of January 2012, with the establishment of the Eurasian Economic Area.

Foreign Direct Investment (FDI): Is a category of cross-border investment in which an investor resident in one economy establishes a lasting interest in and a significant degree of influence over an enterprise resident in another economy. FDI is an important channel for the transfer of technology between countries, promotes international trade through access to foreign markets, and can be an important vehicle for economic development.

Multinational Company (MNC): Is a corporate organization that owns or controls production of goods or services in at least one country other than its home country.

ENDNOTE

1 Data for Albania are not available in official China Global Investment Tracker reports.

Chapter 9
The Role and Significance of Chinese Investments in the Modernization of Railway Infrastructure in Serbia

Danijela Stojanović
https://orcid.org/0000-0002-9728-8586
Institute of Economic Sciences, Serbia

Elena Jovičić
Institute of Economic Sciences, Serbia

Nenad Stanisavljević
https://orcid.org/0000-0003-1723-7103
Infrastructure of Serbian Railways, Serbia

ABSTRACT

The subject of the research is Chinese investments in the modernization and reconstruction of railway infrastructure in Serbia, with a focus on the construction of the Belgrade-Budapest high-speed rail line up to 200 km/h, on the sections Belgrade-Stara Pazova and Novi Sad-Subotica-Kelebija. The research aims to analyze the impact of Chinese investment projects on the railway infrastructure in Serbia and examine the effects of projects' implementation at different levels, including the challenges they face. The analysis covers the traffic, technical-technological and financial aspects of the project. The importance of building a high-speed railway through Serbia, but also of the shortest railway connection from Western and Central Europe in the countries of Southern Europe and the Middle and the Far East, is considered, especially in the context of the cooperation within the BRI. The research results are the presentation of the effects railway infrastructure projects have on the development of Serbian economy, as well as the challenges that arise during the implementation process.

DOI: 10.4018/978-1-7998-8021-9.ch009

INTRODUCTION

In the last few years, the share of Chinese loans in infrastructure projects financing in Serbia has increased, and Chinese companies are currently carrying out works on large transport projects. According to the latest data of the Public Debt Administration, Serbia signed eleven contracts with the Export-Import Bank of China (herein Exim Bank) for the financing of infrastructure and energy projects worth about 3.2 billion euros in the period from 2010 to 2021.

The growing economic presence of China in Serbia was primarily a result of the signing of the Agreement on Economic and Technical Cooperation in the Field of Infrastructure in August 2009 between the Governments of Serbia and China, which is considered the essential Agreement laid the foundation for the establishment and encouragement of cooperation between both countries. Furthermore, bilateral cooperation was deepened by the launching multilateral framework "16+1" and the Belt and Road initiative (BRI) in 2012, 2013, respectively.

Besides the growing investment activities, deepening cooperation has also fostered bilateral trade relations. China became the third-largest trade partner of Serbia in 2020, while the total trade volume has more than doubled in the past decade (Beraha & Jovičić, 2021). In terms of exports, there was a more substantial increase – Serbia's exports increased almost 45 times compared to 2010 (Jovičić et al., 2020).

On the other hand, China has become the world's leading creditor in the last two decades, with loans worth over 700 billion U.S. dollars. China's trade with 17 Central and Eastern European countries (CEEC) reached a remarkable $ 103.15 billion in 2020 (Ministry of Commerce of the People's Republic of China, 2020).

The Western Balkans, as the gateway to Southeast Europe, has a key role to play in connecting the Silk Road and opening the way for Chinese exports to Europe and beyond.

BACKGROUND

Belt and Road Initiative

The President of the People's Republic of China Xi Jinping announced "One Belt, One Road" in 2013, while the action plan for the "Belt and Road" initiative was announced by the National Development and Reform Commission on March 28, 2015. In this way, China potentially took over the most important international project of the twenty-first century (Cai, 2017; Zhang et al., 2018).

Under the auspices of the BRI, China invests in transport and energy infrastructure, vital to the country's economic and social development, such as railways, airports, ports, roads, telecommunications, and electricity networks across the Eurasian, Asian and African continents, across the land belt. The Silk Road "and the Maritime Silk Road of the Twenty-first Century." (Li et al., 2018; Coenen et al., 2020).

The BRI aims to foster China's ongoing development and thus also seeks to foster the development opportunities of a new era for other developing countries. Chinese outbound investment exceeded inbound investment for the first time in 2015 (Johnston, 2019).

In the article (Wen et al., 2019) the importance of considering the reliability of the infrastructure for the choice of trading routes is emphasized. Analyzes of the presented study could produce insightful implications for proper logistics planning in developing other agreements on economic cooperation and trade worldwide.

“Belt and Road” is an ambitious foreign policy initiative of China, which will significantly influence the future of global trade, especially in Asia, Africa, and Europe. This initiative includes the massive development of trade routes between and within these regions, referring to the historic “Silk Road,” but on a much broader scale. According to the Chinese government, at least 64 countries are expected to participate in this initiative, including approximately two-thirds of the world’s population and one-third of the global economy.

The Silk Road includes the expansion of large-scale land transport infrastructure (Silk Road economic belt component), together with the development of new ports in the Pacific and Indian Ocean (21st Century Silk Road Component) (Ascensão et al., 2018).

Given that the Belt and Road Initiative is very important and that Chinese investment projects are receiving a lot of attention in the Western Balkans, which aspire to be part of the Belt and Road Initiative (BRI), a large number of authors indicate growing interest in researching this topic.

Considering the relations between China and the Western Balkans from 1949 to 2013, when the implementation of BRI began, the author Arezina (2021) concludes that their mutual cooperation has significantly improved after the Great Recession and the Eurozone crisis, that most factors have a positive impact cooperation between the Western Balkans and China. She states that several dozen joint projects have been completed so far, many of which are of strategic importance for the countries of the Western Balkans. The authors (Markovic Khaze & Wang, 2021) state in their report that China’s only strategic partner in the region is Serbia, thanks to intensive engagement during these years.

Authors Zakić & Radišić (2019) state that before BRI, the value of Chinese investment projects in the Balkan countries was 11.77 billion US dollars, and after BRI 19.34 billion US dollars. This confirms that there is a positive correlation between the levels of investment projects in the Balkans and BRI. The largest Chinese investment projects in the Western Balkans are in the infrastructure, especially in the transport infrastructure, and are financed mainly by loans, and subsequently by foreign direct investments (Jaćimović et al., 2021).

Chinese Investments in Serbian Transport Infrastructure

Transport infrastructure across the Western Balkans has become one of the most attractive sectors for Chinese companies and banks in the last decade. According to Rogelja (2020), there was a total of €8.7bn worth of road construction deals at various stages of approval, with about half of this amount already completed, under construction or in advanced stages of planning in 2019. Being the key partner of China in the region of Western Balkans, Serbia received the highest amount of Chinese investments directed to transport infrastructure (Marjanović et al., 2021).

Regarding the Chinese investments in the transport infrastructure of Serbia, three main projects can be singled out (Zakić & Radišić, 2019). The first project is the building of the Zemun-Borča bridge (also known as Mihajlo Pupin Bridge) across the river Danube, the first Chinese large-scale infrastructural project completed in Southeast Europe. The agreement between the Republic of Serbia and the People’s Republic of China was concluded in 2010, and the bridge was opened in December 2014 during the China-CEEC summit 16+1 in Belgrade. The project was realized by the China Road and Bridge Company (CRBC) and financed by the Exim Bank. The project’s total cost, including all connecting roads building, amounted to 260 million USD. The Exim Bank provided a loan of 217 million U.S. dollars (85% of the total amount), while the Republic of Serbia financed the rest (15%).

The second project is related to constructing several sections of the Belgrade-South Adriatic E-763 road (so-called Corridor 11). The section Belgrade (Surčin)-Obrenovac long 17.6 km was completed by the CCCC in 2019 through the loan granted by Exim Bank (198 million dollars). The Sections Obrenovac-Ub and Lajkovac-Ljig (total length of both sections completed in 2019 is 50.2 km. Shandong Hi-speed Group Co Ltd was engaged as the main contractor, and Exim Bank provided a loan (301 million U.S. dollars). The section Preljina – Pozega construction began in May 2019 and the completion is expected in the second half of 2022. The length of the section is 30.9 kilometers, while the value of the works is 501 million U.S. dollars (the Exim Bank loan provides 445 million U.S.dollars).

The third project announced as the "16+1" initiative's flagship project and the BRI's most important European project relates to building the high-speed railway between Belgrade and Budapest. Two Chinese companies, „China Railway International Company" and China Communications Construction Company Ltd (CCCC), are in charge of that project, while Exim Bank assists in financing. The project's total cost is around €3.8 billion, where €2 billion is estimated for the 160-km Hungarian section and €1.8 billion for 183km on the Serbian side. The project can be considered one of the most important transport infrastructure projects in the framework of the cooperation between Serbia and China, while it is also much more financially demanding than the above-mentioned transport projects (see Figure 1). The total amount of loans provided to all five projects is nearly 3 billion U.S. dollars, with the largest amount (61%) given to the Belgrade-Budapest railway line construction project.

Figure 1. Share of the individual projects in the total Chinese loans provided to the transport infrastructure projects
Source: authors compilation

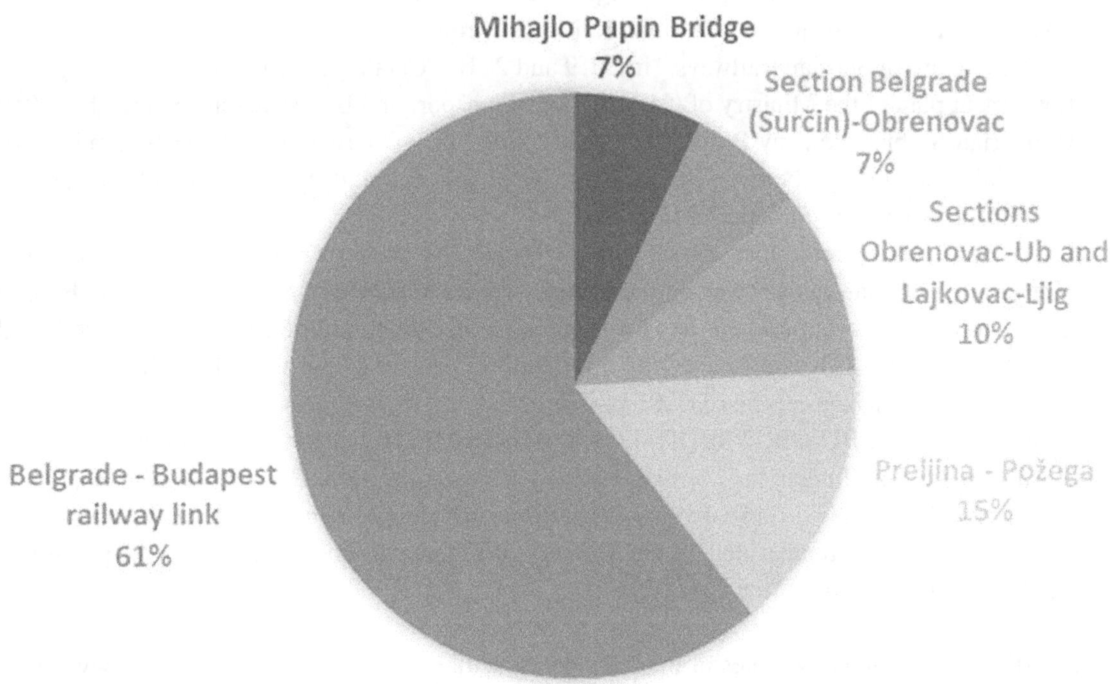

The project Belgrade-Budapest railway construction is of strategic importance especially to the Chinese side, since it creates a connection between the Greek port of Piraeus and Western Europe and enables faster transport of Chinese goods (Szunomár, 2019; Matura, 2020; Tomaszewska & Dahl, 2020). Furthermore, it allows China to create a sound foundation for its political and economic presence in the region of Central and Eastern Europe (Rencz, 2019; Kaczmarski & Jakóbowski, 2015).

When it comes to Serbia, apart from the development of infrastructure, the high-quality railway connection to Central and Western Europe will also contribute to the increase of the Serbian economy competitiveness that was on an insufficient level for many years (Baranenko & Stevanović, 2013). The positive effects could be especially expected in terms of exports, which is one of the key factors for the stimulation of economic development (Baranenko & Đukić, 2012). The transit railway traffic through Serbia will be increased, bringing larger foreign exchange revenues to the economy and the Serbian railway. In addition, by shortening the travel of passenger trains, the quality of life and standard of living in this part of the country rises.

RESEARCH METHODOLOGY AND OBJECTIVES

The methodology in this chapter implies a quantitative approach, based on the collection of numerical data and their presentation. The analysis used official and internal data from "Infrastructure of Serbian Railways." which are in the following documents:

- Business program of the Joint Stock Company for Public Railway Infrastructure Management "Infrastructure of Serbian Railways." Belgrade 2017 - 2022
- ID card of the "Infrastructure of Serbian Railways" project
- "Infrastructure of Serbian Railways." in 2019 and 2018 - Catalog of projects
- Investment plan of the Ministry of Construction, Transport and Infrastructure (September 2019)
- Hungarian-Serbian Railway Project: Reconstruction and modernization of the Belgrade - Novi Sad - Subotica railway - border with Hungary (Kelebija) - Belgrade Center – Stara Pazova railway section and Novi Sad - Subotica section
- Preferential buyer credit loan agreement on project od modernization and reconstruction of Hungarian – Serbian railway line on the territory of the Republic of Serbia, for section Belgrade Center – Stara Pazova, between the Government of the Republic of Serbia – represented by the ministry of finance as borrower and the Export-Import bank of China as lender („Službeni glasnik RS" – International agreements 11/2017 – 78)
- PREFERENTIAL BUYER CREDIT LOAN AGREEMENT On Project of Modernization and Reconstruction of Hungarian - Serbian Railway Connection in the Territory of the Republic of Serbia, for Section Novi Sad-Subotica-State Border (Kelebija) between the Government of the Republic of Serbia - represented by the Ministry of Finance as borrower and The Export-Import Bank of China as lender (May 21, 2019)

The official institutional websites of the National Assembly of the Republic of Serbia (www.parlament.rs), the Public Debt Administration (www.javnidug.gov.rs), the Ministry of Construction, Transport and Infrastructure (www.mgsi.gov.rs) and "Infrastructure of Serbian Railways" (www.infrazs.rs) were used as sources of information.

The paper is divided into eight interrelated units, which represent the main directions of research and goals, namely: Belt and Road Initiative, Chinese Investments in Transport Infrastructure in Serbia, Belgrade-Budapest High Speed Railway, Belgrade Center-Stara Pazova, Belgrade-Novi Sad and Novi Sad - Subotica - Kelebija, Effects of building a high-speed railway for Serbia and China, the first direct railway cargo line from China to Serbia, the first Chinese railway project in Serbia.

Given the deepening cooperation between China and Serbia and the growing investment in transport infrastructure, the main objectives of this paper:

1. to determine the inflow and importance of Chinese investments in the development of railway infrastructure in Serbia;
2. to analyze the impact of the Chinese investment projects on the development of Serbian railway infrastructure, providing an overview of the most important cases' essential features;
3. to analyze the positive effects of these projects, and the challenges arising during the projects' execution;
4. to analyze the realization and international significance and role of the construction of the Belgrade-Budapest high-speed railway, as one of the most important investments and infrastructure projects in Serbia and the region;
5. to determine opportunities for further Chinese investments in the development of railway infrastructure in Serbia.

THE MAIN FOCUS OF THE CHAPTER

In the field of infrastructure projects implemented on the basis of an interstate agreement between Serbia and China, and financed by loans from the Chinese "Exim Bank", the construction of a high-speed railway up to 200 kilometers per hour between Belgrade and Budapest stands out as a larger and more significant investment and infrastructure project in this part of Europe.

High-Speed Railway Belgrade – Budapest

The Belgrade-Budapest high-speed railway is part of the global project "One Belt - One Road" of infrastructural connection between Europe and Asia, initiated by China.

In November 2013, at the second summit of China and the heads of state of Central and Eastern Europe, held in Romania, the prime ministers of China, Hungary and Serbia announced cooperation in the construction of a high-speed railway between Serbia and Hungary. Reconstruction, modernization and construction of a modern railway Belgrade - Novi Sad - Subotica - state border with Hungary (Kelebija) - Budapest, includes the reconstruction of the existing single-track railway and construction of another track, to form a modern high-performance double-track railway for mixed (passenger and freight) traffic and speed up to 200 km/h.

The project of building a high-speed railway Belgrade - Novi Sad - Subotica - Kelebija implies the application of European interoperability standards. The construction of the high-speed railway through Serbia includes works on three sections long 183kilometers: Belgrade - Stara Pazova, Stara Pazova - Novi Sad and Novi Sad - Subotica - state border (Kelebija).

The investor of the project is the Joint Stock Company for Public Railway Infrastructure Management "Infrastructure of Serbian Railways".

Today, China is implementing two projects in Serbia to modernize the railway infrastructure, within the construction of a high-speed railway up to 200 km/h between Belgrade and Budapest. The first section is Belgrade Center - Stara Pazova, and the second is Novi Sad - Subotica.

Works on the sections Belgrade Center - Stara Pazova and Novi Sad - Subotica are performed by a consortium of Chinese companies China Railway International Company and China Communications Construction Company.

The total value of these two sections of the high-speed railway through Serbia is about 1.5 billion dollars, or 1,512,972,540 dollars. Of that amount, 85 percent of the funds are provided from preferential loans from the Chinese Exim Bank, with a total value of about 1 billion 285.9 million dollars, while Serbia provides the remaining 15 percent of the required funds from the state budget, or about 227 million dollars.

The project is financed in this way thanks to the Interstate Agreement between Serbia and China. The construction of the Belgrade-Budapest high-speed railway is the first cross-border project within the cooperation between China and Central and Eastern Europe countries, which is being implemented jointly by Serbia, Hungary, and China. When the high-speed railway from Belgrade to Budapest is completed in 2025, it is planned to travel by train on this international route in less than three hours.

The section of the high-speed railway from Stara Pazova to Novi Sad is being built by the Russian state railway company RZD International. Russia is the initiator of the great Eurasian Partnership, one of the goals of which is to strengthen the partnership between Russia and China, but also to deepen the economic ties between Europe and Asia. "The possibility of connecting that partnership with the Belt and Road Initiative for International Cooperation is one of the key factors in the implementation of this agenda." Coordination of development strategies of Russia and China in the field of global, regional and bilateral relations lays the foundation for successful cooperation of a number of countries, regions and organizations" (Y. Li, 2018).

Serbia is connected to Hungary, which is a member of the European Union, by high-speed railway, and the construction of the high-speed railway on the Belgrade-Stara Pazova section, built by Chinese Railways, is supervised by German Railways, so Serbia has managed to unite the world's most modern and largest, and to gather Russia, China and the European Union on the project of building a high-speed railway, thus connecting Europe and Asia. Therefore, this project is specific and, in addition to transport advantages, has a deeper state, political, economic and social significance for Serbia and the Western Balkans.

It is planned that the new high-speed line Belgrade - Subotica will be electrified and equipped with modern signal-safety and telecommunication devices, as well as the European train traffic control system ETCS - level 2, which is the highest level of high-speed train traffic regulation. In order to create conditions for the functioning of the European train traffic control system ETCS - level 2 for speeds up to 200 km/h, as well as secure platforms for voice communication and data transmission between railway staff, the introduction of GSM - R system is planned along the entire line. The GSM - R optical cable system will be used as a physical transmission medium, which is interoperable, in order to be integrated into the European railway traffic management system.

Along the entire line, it is planned to equip it with devices that will enable the realization of signalized train runs on all tracks in both directions.

The project envisages that all crossings with the road will be leveled, which means that there will be no road crossings on the entire fast line Belgrade - Novi Sad - Subotica - Kelebija (state border with Hungary). It is also planned that more than 120 new facilities (bridges, galleries, underpasses, overpasses, underpasses and culverts) will be built along the high-speed railway from Belgrade to Subotica, existing and new railway stations will be reconstructed.

Modern equipment for informing and directing the movement of passengers, as well as video surveillance, is designed to be installed in the railway stations along the entire high-speed line. Before the construction of the 183-kilometer-long high-speed railway between Belgrade and Subotica began, 35 kilometers of the railway was two-track (Belgrade - Stara Pazova), while the rest of the international highway was single-track. On average, about 115 passenger and 85 freight trains ran daily along the Belgrade-Subotica line before the start of works, and the travel time of international passenger trains was 4 hours and 37 minutes, which means that their average speed was around 40 km/h.

Due to the construction of a high-speed railway on the section Stara Pazova - Novi Sad, as of 1 February 2019, passenger railway traffic on this section of the international highway Belgrade - Subotica has been completely suspended.

Section Belgrade Center - Stara Pazova

The modernization of the Belgrade Center - Stara Pazova railway, 34 and a half kilometers long, is the first section of the project for the construction of a high-speed railway up to 200 kilometers per hour, between Belgrade and Subotica.

The two existing tracks between Belgrade and Stara Pazova are planned to be reconstructed, and two new tracks between Batajnica and Stara Pazova to be built.

Figure 2. Speed of trains on the section Belgrade - Stara Pazova
Source: authors' compilation

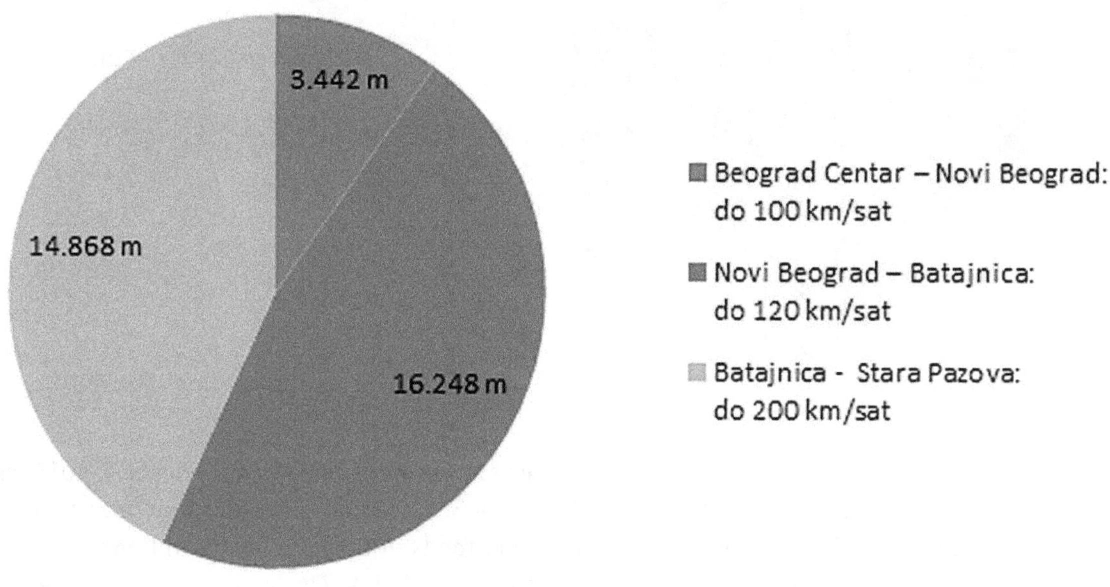

The project envisages complete reconstruction and modernization of construction and electrical infrastructure with raising the speed of trains on the following sections:

- Belgrade Center - New Belgrade: up to 100 km / h (section length 3,442 meters)
- New Belgrade - Batajnica: up to 120 km / h (section length 16,248 meters)
- Batajnica - Stara Pazova: up to 200 km / h (section length 14,868 meters)

Having in mind that a two-track high-speed railway is being built on the section Belgrade Center - Stara Pazova, that means that the consortium of Chinese railways will build a total of 29,736 meters of tracks for speeds up to 200 kilometers per hour on this part of high-speed railways through Serbia.

Significant facilities on this section of the high-speed railway are: three overpasses (Zemun Polje, Nova Pazova, Stara Pazova), one underpass (Kamendin), leveling of the railway - gallery in Batajnica, and it is planned to build a large number of underpasses in Tošin bunar stations. Altina, Zemunsko Polje, Kamendin, Batajnica and Nova Pazova. Reconstruction of railway stations (New Belgrade, Zemun, Zemunsko Polje, Batajnica, Stara Pazova and Nova Pazova) as well as building, of new station buildings (Zemun and Batajnica) is planned. The Tošin bunar stop will be relocated, and new Altina and Kamendin stops will be built.

The project for the future appearance of the stations was done by the Traffic Institute CIP, in cooperation with the Chinese company China Railway Design Corporation.

Figure 3. Contract value per section
Source: authors' compilation

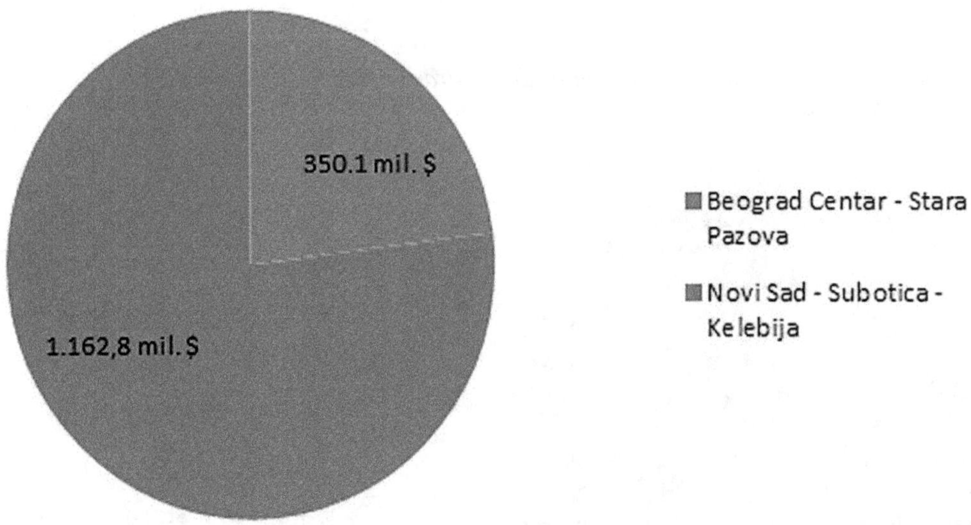

The commercial contract for the construction of this section was signed on November 5, 2016, and the value of the contract is around 350.1 million dollars, or 350,162,540. precisely. The largest amount 297.6 million dollars (85%) was provided from the credit funds of the Chinese Exim Bank, while the remaining 15% was provided from the budget of the Republic of Serbia. The last date of loan availability is November 24, 2022.

The works on this section began on June 5, 2018, and the deadline for the execution of works was three years, and by Annex 3 of the Commercial Agreement it was extended for another three months, i.e. until September 30, 2021. In accordance with Annex 6 of the contract, the deadline for the completion of works on the main tracks was December 31, 2021, and the agreed deadline for variations and other works was extended until March 1, 2022.

A special Annex 3, signed with Chinese companies on January 22, 2021, additionally contracted works on signaling, security and telecommunication facilities for speeds of up to 200 kilometers per hour, worth 58.9 million dollars. The deadline for the completion of these works was December 31, 2021.

The section of the high-speed railway Belgrade Center - Stara Pazova will be the first public transport railway on European soil built by Chinese companies and will be a confirmation of their technical-technological, organizational, personnel and financial ability to build a modern railway in Europe, respecting European standards. interoperability, with the application of the traffic safety system ETCS - level 2.

Organization of Work and Supervision Over Project Implementation

Until the middle of 2020, the supervision over the execution of works on the construction of the high-speed railway was performed by the employees of the "Infrastructure of Serbian Railways".

In the second half of 2020, the company DB (Deutsche Bahn) will supervise the realization of the project, which represents additional quality control of the work performed on this section. After the engagement of the German Railways for the supervision over the realization of the project, the protocols for monitoring the execution of certain phases of works were defined, which contributed to the intensification of the construction of the high-speed railway Belgrade - Stara Pazova. In addition, the Ministry of Construction, Transport and Infrastructure and "Infrastructure of Serbian Railways" had the obligation to agree with the engagement of each supplier of parts and equipment or contractors, who are engaged as subcontractors of Chinese Railways in the implementation of this project.

All that contributed to the intensification of works on the construction of the Belgrade-Stara Pazova high-speed railway in the second half of 2020, after the physical realization on this section amounted to only about 25 percent in June 2020, two years after the start of work.

Dynamic Testing of the Belgrade-Novi Sad High-Speed Railway

On the section Belgrade Center - Stara Pazova, where the works are performed by the Chinese consortium "China Railway International" and "China Communications Construction Company" at the end of 2021, static tests on track geometry and contact network were performed, as well as static tests of signaling and security and telecommunication systems. Dynamic testing of the Belgrade-Novi Sad high-speed line began on 17 January 2022, after the measuring cars of the German railway company "Deutsche Ban Sistemtehnik" and two locomotives for speeds up to 230 km / h arrived from Germany.

Dynamic testing includes testing the geometry of newly built high-speed tracks, contact network parameters, installed high-speed equipment, compatibility of equipment and systems and other performed construction works. During the dynamic tests, on 21 January 2022, a speed of 201.5 km / h was reached on the high-speed railway, which is a record speed of trains on Serbian railways. Prior to that, a new Dispatch Command Center for high-speed train traffic was put into operation at the Belgrade Center station.

The Construction of the First Serbian High-Speed Railway Has Been Completed and Put Into Operation

The first Serbian high-speed railway line Belgrade - Novi Sad, with trains running at a speed of 200 kilometers per hour, was put into operation on March 19, 2022. The high-speed train with the promotional name "Soko" made a journey on this section in 33 minutes.

A day later, on March 20, 2022, regular passenger railway traffic was established on this section, with a total of sixteen departures from both Belgrade and Novi Sad, and from April 4, that number was increased to the total of 20 departures from both Belgrade and Novi Sad, or 40 daily in total. Of that number, 9 departures, or a total of 18 departures, are InterCity trains that travel between Belgrade and Novi Sad for 36 minutes and stop at only one train station.

The railway traffic on the high-speed line Belgrade - Novi Sad for the first twenty days was conducted completely according to the timetable, and the promotional price of ticket on this route was a little less than two and a half euros.

Section Novi Sad - Subotica – Kelebija

On 22 November 2021, at the Novi Sad Ranžirna railway station, works began on the 108,1 km long Novi Sad - Kelebija section, as part of the construction of the Belgrade - Budapest high-speed railway. The planned completion of the works is November 2024.

The total value of high-speed railway construction on this section is 1,162,810,000 dollars, of which 988.3 million dollars from the preferential loan of the Chinese Exim Bank, i.e. 85 percent of the project value, while the remaining 15 percent is provided from the budget funds by the state of Serbia. The contract for the realization of this project was signed on July 7, 2018.

The project for the construction of a high-speed railway between Novi Sad and Subotica includes the route of a two-track railway and a station with facilities on the railway, reconstruction and modernization of the Novi Sad, Vrbas and Subotica railway junctions, leveling infrastructure that enables safe traffic at projected speeds and the introduction of a European railway traffic management system.

As part of the construction of a high-speed railway between Novi Sad and Subotica, it is planned to build a total of 56 facilities - underpasses, overpasses and similar facilities, including a 1.6-kilometer viaduct in Vrbas.

The project envisages the reconstruction of nine railway stations (Novi Sad, Sajlovo, Kisac, Stepanovicevo, Zmajevo, Backa Topola, Zednik, Naumovicevo, Subotica), as well as three new stations with station capacities (Rumenka, Vrbas and Lovcenac). It is also planned that the works in the first phase will take place in those places that do not require the suspension of railway traffic. The railway traffic between Novi Sad and Subotica, ie Kelebija, is planned to be suspended in the spring of 2022 due to the execution of works.

During the execution of works, the project envisages that trains run in alternative regional directions: Novi Sad - Bogojevo - Sombor - Subotica and Novi Sad - Zrenjanin - Senta - Subotica. The Novi Sad - Subotica railway modernization project involves the application of European interoperability standards.

Even before the official start of works on the high-speed railway Novi Sad - Subotica - Kelebija, a consortium of Chinese companies (China Railway International Company and China Communications Construction Company), began implementing two projects in the City of Novi Sad, which include the construction of the third section of the high-speed railway, but due to their traffic and functional importance of railway traffic on the high-speed line Belgrade - Novi Sad. It is about the construction of the railway underpass in Kisacka Street, in Novi Sad and the reconstruction of the Novi Sad railway station, and the completion of these works was coordinated with the launch of the Belgrade-Novi Sad high-speed railway.

The new underpass in Kisacka Street is located on the Belgrade-Novi Sad high-speed railway and is about one kilometer away from the Novi Sad railway station in the direction of Belgrade. It is planned that the dynamics of the completion of works on this facility will be harmonized with the completion of works and the launch of the newly built high-speed railway Belgrade - Novi Sad.

Considering that the previously existing railway underpass in Kisacka Street in Novi Sad did not meet the standards for train traffic for speeds up to 200 km/h, it was necessary to demolish it and build a new underpass on that location.

Work on the new underpass began on 3 October 2021. The new three-track underpass near the railway station in Novi Sad is planned to be about 41 meters long, about four and a half meters high and a total of 48 piles about 20 meters deep.

Activities on the reconstruction of the Novi Sad station began at the end of September 2021. The first phase of works at the Novi Sad railway station includes works on the first three station tracks, as well as on the tenth and eleventh tracks, then the construction of a new platform and canopy, as well as partial rehabilitation and adaptation of the Novi Sad station. At the Novi Sad station, works on the rehabilitation of floors, walls and roof are planned, as well as the energy rehabilitation of the building. Also, the replacement of the facade and carpentry is planned, as well as the arrangement and extension of the existing and construction of a new station underpass. In accordance with the new technological needs for the high-speed railway, the station also plans to adapt the premises where the new signal and telecommunication equipment will be located. The works of the first phase of the reconstruction of the Novi Sad railway station are taking place in the conditions of uninterrupted functioning of the railway traffic along the fourth station track.

Effects of High-Speed Railway Construction for Serbia and China

The construction of a high-speed railway brings mutual benefits to both Serbia and China.

Serbia and Serbian Railways

The effects that the Serbian railways and the state of Serbia achieve by building a high-speed railway can be divided into direct and indirect.

1. Direct effects
    a. Shortest and fastest connection
        i. High-speed railway Belgrade - Subotica - Budapest becomes the shortest and fastest connection of the port of Piraeus in southern Europe with Central and Central Europe;
    b. Increase in transport revenues

Thanks to the construction of the high-speed railway, international flows of passengers and goods in the region and this part of Europe will be directed to the Belgrade-Budapest railway corridor, which will bring opportunities to increase transport revenues for Serbian railways;

c. Increase in other income

By increasing the number of passenger and freight trains on the high-speed line, and thus the number of passengers and the amount of goods that will be transported, conditions are created for more successful business and higher revenues for a whole range of activities based on transport.

Thus, a larger number of high-speed passengers will contribute, for example, to increasing revenues in tourism, catering, event industry and other industries, while the improvement of rail freight transport will affect the work of, for example, freight forwarding companies, other modes of transport and trade.

d. Improving standards and quality of life

By reducing the travel of passenger trains on the high-speed railway from Belgrade to Novi Sad by half an hour, to Subotica by an hour and a half, and to the Hungarian capital by three hours, the quality of life and standard of living in this part of the country rises.

e. Further improvement of overall bilateral relations between Serbia and China.

2. Indirect effects
    a. Engagement of the Serbian companies as Chinese railways' subcontractors

Dozens of Serbian companies have been engaged as subcontractors of the Chinese consortium in projects for the construction of high-speed railways, as contractors or manufacturers of devices, parts and equipment. These companies have gained experience, but also significant references for potential engagement in third markets.

b. Increase in the competitiveness of Serbian products

The shortened time of transport of Serbian goods by fast railway to Budapest and further to the countries of the European Union will make the offer of Serbian products competitive on foreign markets.

c. Better conditions for investors

Modern and fast railway infrastructure is certainly one of the conditions that foreign investors demand from the state of Serbia, before investing money in our country. Therefore, the high-speed railway can be one of the significant advantages when attracting foreign investments to Serbia.

China and Chinese Railways

The People's Republic of China and the Chinese Railways, which are building two sections of high-speed railway through Serbia, are realizing the following benefits on this project:

1. Strategic implementation of the "Belt and Road" initiative.
   a. The "Belt and Road" initiative is being implemented in Serbia by building a high-speed railway, which means that China is realizing its foreign policy, economic and infrastructural initiative;
2. Placement of financial resources
   a. Realization of the project from the funds of the Chinese Exim Bank;
3. Employment of Chinese companies
   a. Chinese companies have been engaged in the project of building a high-speed railway China Railway International Company and China Communications Construction Company

the project of reconstruction and construction of railway stations on the route of the high-speed railway was done by China Railway Design Corporation (in cooperation with the Traffic Institute CIP), as well as some other Chinese companies;

4. Better standards

In the project of building a high-speed railway in Serbia, the Chinese railways can confirm the international standards of parts, devices and equipment that will be used on high-speed railway sections, designed with the application of rules of European interoperability standards and traffic safety systems ETCS - level 2.

The First Direct Railway Cargo Line From China to Serbia

The construction of a high-speed railway through Serbia was also an opportunity for China to demonstrate its important railway role in the European transport system. On 24 October 2019, the freight train of the Chinese Railways "China Railway Express", almost 600 meters long, with 28 containers, arrived in Belgrade from the Chinese city of Jinan, with over 500 tons of equipment for the construction of a high-speed railway through Serbia. It was about equipment and materials that met all European standards and had all the international certificates for the construction of high-speed railways.

The first direct train from China to Serbia traveled ten and a half thousand kilometers in thirty days, through Mongolia, Russia, Belarus, Poland and Hungary, to reach Serbia. In that way, the establishment of the first railway cargo line between China and Serbia was marked, which opened a new opportunity for the economies of the two countries to develop their trade relations based on railway transport.

In addition, the China Railways Express freight train sent a message to the international public that rail transport is one of the central modes of transport of the Chinese global economic initiative "Belt and Road", and that the high-speed railway from Belgrade to Budapest, whose modernization is current, an integral part of this project. In the context of the given facts, I can see the importance of the modernization of the Belgrade-Budapest railway in the economic and transport sense for China and Serbia.

In 2016, the Chinese company "Kosko" (Chinese Ocean Transport Company) became the majority owner of the largest Greek port of Piraeus. Today, the port of Piraeus ranks fourth in Europe in terms of workload, behind Rotterdam, Antwerp and Hamburg and the main port of the Mediterranean. Thanks to its geostrategic position, practically behind the Suez Canal and at the very cape of European soil, as well as the investments of the Chinese company Kosko, the port is developing rapidly. That is why the

Chinese call Piraeus "the head of the Chinese dragon in Europe", and the port itself represents the end of the Silk Road.

It takes a cargo ship 40 days to transport goods from China to Europe, by train half as long. And if there are a lot less goods on the train, the connection is important if you need to translate something that is too heavy for the plane relatively quickly (Mišev et al., 2018).

Central and Eastern Europe are an important link in the "New Silk Road" that connects China with Europe. Serbia is located at the crossroads of the main traffic corridors, ie the shortest railway connections from Western and Central Europe to the countries of southern Europe and the Middle and Far East. The "Silk Road" passes through Serbia with one of its branches.

Goods packed in containers can find their way to European markets from Chinese-owned ports on Railway Corridor 10 through Serbia, and Belgrade is becoming the main railway crossroads, where goods will be divided in the direction of Budapest and Zagreb. In this way, the Belgrade-Budapest high-speed line becomes the shortest and fastest transport connection between the port of Piraeus and Central and Central Europe.

Reconstruction of the Railway Topčider - Rakovica - Resnik: The First Chinese Railway Project in Serbia

The construction of a high-speed railway is not the first project of Chinese companies when it comes to the reconstruction and modernization of the railway infrastructure in Serbia.

The first job of a Chinese company on the reconstruction of the railway infrastructure in Serbia during 2018 was the modernization of the seven and a half kilometer long railway Topčider - Rakovica - Resnik, on the territory of the City of Belgrade. The contractor was the Chinese company "China civil engineering construction corporation", and the project worth about 24.5 million euros was financed from a loan from the European Bank for Reconstruction and Development.

The project was specific in many ways. At an international tender, the Chinese company met the strict international financial and banking criteria and won the job of reconstructing the railway infrastructure in one European country, with funding from the European Bank for Reconstruction and Development.

The works on the reconstruction of the railway began on March 30, 2017, and included the reconstruction and replacement of the construction and electrical infrastructure on the given section, in the conditions of complete suspension of traffic. This project was marked by a great delay in its realization. The complete project and all works covered by the contract were completed only in mid-January 2019. or nine months longer than planned.

SOLUTIONS AND RECOMMENDATIONS

The Belgrade-Budapest high-speed railway project has been facing several challenges since its inception.

The first challenge was the construction of a high-speed railway through Hungary, as the European Union challenged the implementation of the project in connection with a potential breach of regulation in the procurement process. Today, the high-speed railway is also being built on the territory of Hungary, and it is planned to be completed in 2025.

The countries of Western Europe criticize such cooperation of Serbia with China, objecting to its realization only on the basis of interstate agreements, without transparency and tenders, although at the same time they also cooperate to a large extent with China.

Sanja Arezina (Arežina, 2018), author of the book "China in Europe", says that it is a policy of double standards, because "on the one hand, Europe cooperates with China, and on the other hand, Europe objects to small countries like Serbia for having cooperation with China."

Another challenge was the skepticism of many experts in Serbia and abroad, especially in the European Union, when it comes to the cost-effectiveness of such a project. However, in the territory of the European Union, as well as at the level of the International Railway Union, there are only a few lines whose construction is measured by the criteria of direct profitability and economic justification.

According to the data of the Public Debt Administration from November 2021, the debts to the Chinese Exim Bank amount to 1,752,779,000 dollars, which is only slightly less than 6% in relation to the total public debt of the Republic of Serbia, which on November 30, 2021. is $ 32,227,958,000. In that way, the Chinese debt for the projects of modernization of the railway and transport infrastructure in Serbia does not significantly affect the indebtedness of the state.

One of the challenges that Serbian railways will face in the coming period with the construction of high-speed railways are new, modern and up-to-date high-speed rail technologies. Already now, the Chinese Railways in Belgrade and Novi Sad have installed two simulators for high-speed train traffic in real time and weather conditions.

In order to adapt to modern trends, in the coming period, "Infrastructure of Serbian Railways" will be forced to create smart learning environments that are already used by educational institutions, in order to train employees to work with modern and contemporary technologies. (Stojanović, et al. 2020; Petrović et al., 2021). The application of IoT technologies in the education of railway employees is becoming inevitable in the application of high technologies high-speed train traffic (Zhong, et al. 2021).

An integral part of smart environments is mobile education, which was created thanks to the rapid development and application of mobile and wireless technologies. The increasing application of mobile technologies and the Internet has influenced the transformation of many industries. And as the use of mobile phones has changed many industries, such as banking, high-speed train traffic in Serbia, but also their further commercial exploitation will take place in interaction with smart environments using advanced web, mobile, Internet of Things (IoT) technologies and augmented reality (Tomić & Stojanović, 2018; Rafay, et al., 2021). In this way, the need for additional education, and caution will be emphasized among railway employees, but also awareness raising with the aim of traffic safety as well as the ability to quickly detect and eliminate faults in conditions of increasing train speed (Righetti et al., 2020).

In September 2021, the Ministry of Construction, Transport and Infrastructure and the Ministry of Education, Science and Technological Development of the Republic of Serbia signed a Memorandum of Cooperation on the development of a training center in railway and air transport. It is planned to invest five million euros for the purchase of state-of-the-art equipment for practical training of future train drivers in railway education centers, which would include modern stationary simulators of the entire train control cabin. Thus, the state creates conditions for the training of railway staff in a smart environment in accordance with the needs of high-speed train traffic in Serbia.

Implementation of Customer Relationship Management (CRM) and smart technologies, as has been done in some other areas (e.g. librarianship), (Stokić et al., 2019) and in the field of high-speed train traffic in Serbia, through customer satisfaction with the quality of services could contribute to the development of improved relations with stakeholders and further improve the quality of railway services. Authors in the paper (Samarina & Bondarchuk, 2021) indicate that the use of digital economy technologies improves measures to optimize the process of modernization of the Trans-Siberian Railway.

Railway infrastructure modernization projects in Serbia have a great place and role when it comes to media activities "Infrastructure of Serbian Railways" (Stojanović & Stanisavljević, 2011). That is how it is in 2020 on the company's website www.infrazs.rs and a total of 151 pieces of information were published on the social networks "Serbian Railway Infrastructure", of which as many as 92 (61%) referred to the projects of modernization and reconstruction of railway infrastructure in Serbia. This is important when it comes to informing the public about the implementation and importance of modernization and reconstruction of railway infrastructure in Serbia, because public opinion that is truthfully and objectively informed can accept and support projects, which is a prerequisite for their successful implementation (Stojanović et al., 2021).

Another challenge for the railway sector in Serbia and the implementation of the high-speed railway project was the current Covid 19 virus pandemic. Numerous scientific papers suggest that institutions and sectors that are more flexible in the process of providing different ways of doing business and efficient information systems are better equipped to respond to the crisis (Stojanović, 2020; Ting et al., 2020; Alawad & Kaewunruen, 2021).

The construction of the Belgrade - Budapest high - speed railway, based on the application of modern systems, IoT devices and advanced technologies, creates conditions for the railway traffic in Serbia to successfully respond to all potential future similar challenges such as the Covid 19 pandemic.

A large number of authors deal with the impact of the Covid 19 virus on the implementation of the BRI project.

Some aurors state that all existing systems will suffer from post-crisis hysteresis, and the effects of the virus will remain long after the immediate crisis is over. They state that all institutions and institutional characteristics depend on the history and status of their systems. BRI is no exception, and the initiative will be deeply affected by the destruction of the virus and its consequences. But they also point out that adaptation is still possible (Buckley, 2020). However, the results of research in the paper Beraha and Jovičić (2021) showed that the crisis, for instance, did not have much of an impact on trade between the Western Balkans and China. The consortium of Chinese railways in Serbia also actively and at full capacity worked on the realization of the project for the construction of a high-speed railway, and during the state of emergency in Serbia due to the Covid 19 virus pandemic in the first half of 2020.

On 26 May 2020, a train with medical equipment arrived at the Novi Beograd railway station from the People's Republic of China, which Serbia procured from China to fight the corona virus. A freight train with 300 tons of medical equipment on the new "Silk Road" symbolically set off on 9 May, Victory Day, from Wuhan, a Chinese city from which the fight against the corona virus began. The direct freight train "Chinese Railways" with protective equipment consisting of 42 wagons covered a distance of a total of 10,631 kilometers between China and Serbia in seventeen days, via Kazakhstan, Russia, Belarus, Poland, the Czech Republic and Hungary. The journey of the train with medical equipment from China to Serbia has shown multiple connections between the two countries, and confirmed the importance of the "Belt and Road" initiative, in which Serbia is an active participant.

Showing its social responsibility, the company "China Railway International Corporation" donated 200,000 protective masks and six sets of thermal imaging cameras during the state of emergency in Serbia due to Covid 19. In the first four months of 2020, Chinese railways transported 8,000 tons of materials and equipment to fight the Covid 19 pandemic along the "Belt and Road" route, thus creating an international railway health corridor between China and Europe.

In that period, railway transport also confirmed its comparative transport advantages in relation to other types of transport, and emphasized its important role in the state, economic and social connection between Serbia and China, but also practically proved the economic and transport need for high-speed rail construction. international railway transfer station Belgrade - Budapest.

FUTURE RESEARCH DIRECTIONS

One of the tasks in future research may be to analyze the traffic, economic and social effects of the operation of the high-speed railway between Belgrade and Novi Sad, both in relation to other modes of transport and in relation to Serbian railways in the previous level. Also, based on the analysis and research of the effects of Chinese investments in railway infrastructure and construction of high-speed railways in Serbia, it will be possible to analyze the situation in this area and in other Western Balkan countries, with the aim of considering future development directions in this area.

In the coming period, researchers can pay special attention to the education of railway executive staff, as well as the application of IoT technologies in education for work in smart environments, and the application of high technologies for high-speed train traffic, whether students within the education system, or about railway workers who are already employed in railway sector companies. Also, a possible topic of future analyzes is the research of railway education in the conditions of necessary high expertise and increased responsibility for safety and functioning of traffic in the conditions of high-speed trains.

In addition, it would be important to analyze the impact of the corona virus pandemic on the realization of Chinese investments in railway infrastructure in Serbia, given its duration of two years now.

The following research would focus on possible implications for investment activities and other forms of cooperation between China and the Western Balkans, i.e. China and Serbia, given the change of the strategic focus from an export-oriented economy to the "Dual circulation" concept. This concept appears as the main component of the new 14th Five-Year Plan, implying a greater focus on the development of domestic production, distribution, and consumption and reducing dependence on the global market.

The results of such research on Chinese investments in Serbian infrastructure, including railway infrastructure, open up new topics and the possibility of looking at this area from a number of social angles with an aim to gain new experiences and define future directions of bilateral relations between Serbia and China at all levels.

CONCLUSION

The Belgrade-Budapest high-speed railway is part of the global project "One Belt - One Road" of infrastructural connection between Europe and Asia, initiated by China. Being constructed, the railway for speeds up to 200 km/h will represent the shortest and fastest connection of the port of Piraeus in the south of Europe with Central and Central Europe. Works on the sections Belgrade Center - Stara Pazova and Novi Sad - Subotica are performed by a consortium of Chinese companies "China Railway International Company" and "China Communications Construction Company".

The realization of this project will contribute to the improvement of political, economic and social bilateral relations between Serbia and China. Thanks to the high-speed railway construction, international flows of passengers, and especially goods, in the region and this part of Europe will be directed to the Belgrade-Budapest railway corridor, which will increase transport revenues to Serbian railways. A whole range of transport-related companies will also benefit from that project. Shortening the travel of passenger trains raises the quality of life and standard of living of the population in this part of the country. Several dozen Serbian companies have been engaged as subcontractors of the Chinese consortium on high-speed railway construction projects, which has enabled them to optimize their production and business capacities usage, as well as experience and significant references for potential engagement in third markets gaining.

Modern and fast railway infrastructure is one of the important conditions for attracting foreign investors in Serbia. Furthermore, the shortened time of transporting Serbian goods by fast railway to Budapest and further to European Union countries will make the offer of these products more competitive on foreign markets.

The project is supervised by experts from the German Railways ("Deutsch Bahn"), while "Deutsch Bahn Systemtechnik" is in charge of dynamic testing of the high-speed line Belgrade - Novi Sad. It is planned that high-speed trains up to 200 km/h will run regularly on the Belgrade-Novi Sad high-speed line in March 2022. The end of 2024 is the contractual deadline for the Belgrade-Subotica railway to be fully completed, and it is expected that in 2025 the high-speed railway will reach Budapest.

ACKNOWLEDGMENT

This chapter is financed by the Ministry of Education, Science and Technological Development of the Republic of Serbia. This chapter is also based upon work from COST Action CA18215, supported by COST (European Cooperation in Science and Technology).

REFERENCES

Alawad, H., & Kaewunruen, S. (2021). 5G Intelligence Underpinning Railway Safety in the COVID-19 Era. *Frontiers in Built Environment*, *7*, 7. doi:10.3389/fbuil.2021.639753

Arežina, S. (2018). *China in Europe*. Institute of European Studies.

Arezina, S. (2021). The Sino-Western Balkans Relations Within "Belt and Road" Initiative Amidst the World'S Grappling With the Rise of China. *Teme-Časopis Za Društvene Nauke*, *45*(1), 145–164. doi:10.22190/TEME200131009A

Ascensão, F., Fahrig, L., Clevenger, A. P., Corlett, R. T., Jaeger, J. A., Laurance, W. F., & Pereira, H. M. (2018). Environmental challenges for the Belt and Road Initiative. *Nature Sustainability*, *1*(5), 206–209. doi:10.103841893-018-0059-3

Baranenko, E., & Đukić, M. (2012). Ways for enhancement of export activities. In Managing structural changes: Trends and requirements (pp. 520–536). Academic Press.

Baranenko, E., & Stevanović, S. (2013). Strategies for enhancing competitiveness of the economy as a way to ensure faster recovery from the crisis: The experience of the EU and Serbia. *Post Crisis Recovery*, 420–433.

Beraha, I., & Jovičić, E. (2021). Uticaj pandemije COVID-19 na spoljnotrgovinsku razmenu između Kine i zemalja Zapadnog Balkana. *Makroekonomska Stabilnost i Unapređenje Konkurentnosti Zemalja Zapadnog Balkana*, 107–123.

Buckley, P. J. (2020). China's Belt and Road Initiative and the COVID-19 crisis. *Journal of International Business Policy*, *3*(3), 311–314. doi:10.105742214-020-00063-9

Cai, P. (2017). Understanding China's Belt and Road Initiative. Lowry Institute for International Policy.

Coenen, J., & Bager, S., Meyfroidt, P., Newig, J., & Challies, E. (2020). Environmental Governance of China's Belt and Road Initiative. *Wiley Online Library*, *31*(1), 3–17.

Jaćimović, D., Milović, N., Miščević, T., & Radenović, M. (2021). Does China Challenge Integration Perspective of the Western Balkan Countries? *12th SCF International Conference on "Contemporary Issues in Social Sciences,"* 164–173.

Johnston, L. A. (2019). The Belt and Road Initiative: What is in it for China? *Asia & the Pacific Policy Studies*, *6*(1), 40–58. doi:10.1002/app5.265

Jovičić, E., Stevanović, S., & Beraha, I. (2020). Serbia - China Bilateral Trade Relations : Major Challenges and Opportunities. *Economic Analysis*, *53*(2), 133–144. doi:10.28934/ea.20.53.2.pp133-144

Kaczmarski, M., & Jakóbowski, J. (2015). China on Central-Eastern Europe: "16+1" as seen from Beijing. *OSW Commentary, 166*.

Li, K. X., Jin, M., Qi, G., Shi, W., & Ng, A. K. Y. (2018). Logistics as a driving force for development under the Belt and Road Initiative–the Chinese model for developing countries. *Transport Reviews*, *38*(4), 457–478. doi:10.1080/01441647.2017.1365276

Li, Y. (2018). The greater Eurasian partnership and the Belt and Road Initiative: Can the two be linked? *Journal of Eurasian Studies*, *9*(2), 94–99. doi:10.1016/j.euras.2018.07.004

Marjanović, D., Jovičić, E., & Stojanović, D. (2021). The global distribution of Chinese investments: Importance for the economy of Serbia. *Ekonomika (Nis)*, *67*(1), 43–55. doi:10.5937/ekonomika2101043M

Markovic Khaze, N., & Wang, X. (2021). Is China's rising influence in the Western Balkans a threat to European integration? *Journal of Contemporary European Studies*, *29*(2), 234–250. doi:10.1080/14782804.2020.1823340

Matura, T. (2020). Sino–Hungarian Relations in the 21st Century. In China and Central Europe: Success or Failure? (pp. 117–136). Academic Press.

Mišev, G., Stanojević, P., & Jeftić, Z. (2018). Neki aspekti bezbednosti srpske infrastrukture na "Novom putu svile". In Novi put svile: Evropska perspektiva Bezbednosni izazovi/rizici unutar Inicijative 16+1 (pp. 193–207). Univerzitet u Beogradu – Fakultet bezbednosti.

Petrović, L., Stojanović, D., Mitrović, S., Barać, D., & Bogdanović, Z. (2022). Designing an extended smart classroom: An approach to game-based learning for IoT. *Computer Applications in Engineering Education*, *30*(1), 117–132.

Rafay, A., Mahdaliza Idrus, S., Mohamad Yusof, K., & Hasunah Mohammad, S. (2021). A survey on advanced transmission technologies for high bandwidth and good signal quality for high-speed railways. *Indonesian Journal of Electrical Engineering and Computer Science*, *23*(1), 293–301. doi:10.11591/ijeecs.v23.i1.pp293-301

Rencz, F. (2019). *The BRI in Europe and the Budapest-Belgrade railway link*. Briefing Paper.

Righetti, F., Vallati, C., Anastasi, G., Masetti, G., & di Giandomenico, F. (2020). Failure management strategies for IoT-based railways systems. *IEEE International Conference on Smart Computing (SMARTCOMP)*. 10.1109/SMARTCOMP50058.2020.00082

Samarina, M., & Bondarchuk, E. (2021). Ways to optimize process of modernization of trans-Siberian railway using digital economy technologies. *SHS Web of Conferences, 112*. 10.1051hsconf/202111200033

Stojanović, D. (2020). Analiza realizacije učenja na daljinu u Srbiji za vreme pandemije virusa COVID 19. In Black swan in the world economy 2020 (pp. 121–140). Institut ekonomskih nauka.

Stojanović, D., Bogdanović, Z., Petrović, L., Mitrović, S., & Labus, A. (2020). Empowering learning process in secondary education using pervasive technologies. *Interactive Learning Environments*, 1–14. Advance online publication. doi:10.1080/10494820.2020.1806886

Stojanović, D., & Stanisavljević, N. (2011). Internet u funkciji unapređenja odnosa sa javnošću "Železnica Srbije.". *XI Međunarodna Konferencija E-Trgovina, 2011*, 116–121.

Stojanović, D., Stanisavljević, N., & Jovičić, E. (2021). Digital marketing techniques for promotion of "Infrastructure of Serbian Railways." *E-Business Technologies*, 44–46.

Stokić, A., Stojanović, D., Bogdanović, Z., Despotović-Zrakić, M., & Radenković, B. (2019). Enhancing the customer relationship management in public libraries: Findings from three developing countries. *Library Hi Tech*, *37*(2), 251–272. doi:10.1108/LHT-07-2017-0138

Szunomár, Á. (2019). China' s investments and infrastructural expansion in Central and Eastern Europe. In S. Jian & H. Guenter (Eds.), *Opportunities and challenges: sustainability of China-EU relations in a changing world* (pp. 84–103). China Social Sciences Press.

Ting, D. S. W., Carin, L., Dzau, V., & Wong, T. Y. (2020, March 27). Digital technology and COVID-19. *Nature Medicine*, *26*(4), 459–461. doi:10.103841591-020-0824-5 PMID:32284618

Tomaszewska, P., & Dahl, M. (2020). Implementation of the Belt and Road Initiative in Selected Balkan States. *Understanding Asia: Political, Economic and Socio-Cultural Dimensions*, 69–85. Retrieved from http://kongresazja.pl/images/pdf/understanding_asia.pdf#page=69

Tomić, V., & Stojanović, D. (2018). Trends and innovations in mobile banking. In Digital transformation (pp. 290–310). Academic Press.

Wen, X., Ma, H. L., Choi, T. M., & Sheu, J. B. (2019). Impacts of the Belt and Road Initiative on the China-Europe trading route selections. *Transportation Research Part E: Logistics and Transportation Review, 122*(September), 581–604.

Zakić, K., & Radišić, B. (2019). China's Belt and Road Investment Projects in the Balkan Countries: Six Years After. *The Review of International Affairs*, *70*(1175), 48–68.

Zhang, W., Alon, I., & Lattemann, C. (2019). China's belt and road initiative: Changing the rules of globalization. *Journal of International Business Studies*, 358.

Zhong, G., Xiong, K., Zhong, Z., & Ai, B. (2021). Internet of things for high-speed railways. *Intelligent and Converged Networks*, *2*(2), 115–132. doi:10.23919/ICN.2021.0005

ADDITIONAL READING

Barisitz, S., & Radzyner, A. (2017). The new silk road, part II: Implications for Europe. *Focus on European Economic Integration Q*, *4*, 70–81.

Csapó, D. G. (2021). Funding of Transport Infrastructure in Serbia: China in Focus. *China Report (New Delhi, India)*, *57*(2), 210–228. doi:10.1177/00094455211004257

Gelpern, A., Horn, S., Morris, S., Parks, B., & Trebesch, C. (2021). *How China lends: a rare look into 100 debt contracts with foreign governments,* CEPR Discussion Paper No. DP16331

Pavlićević, D. (2014). China's railway diplomacy in the Balkans. *China Brief*, *14*(20), 8.

Soyres, F., Mulabdic, A., Murray, S., Rocha, N., & Ruta, M. (2019). How much will the Belt and Road Initiative reduce trade costs? *Inter Economics*, *159*, 151–164. doi:10.1016/j.inteco.2019.07.003

Vangeli, A. (2017). China's engagement with the sixteen countries of central, East and Southeast Europe under the belt and road initiative. *China & World Economy*, *25*(5), 101–124. doi:10.1111/cwe.12216

Vučić, M. (2020). European Union integration and the belt and road initiative: A curious case of Serbia. *Medjunarodni problemi, 72*(2), 337-355.

KEY TERMS AND DEFINITIONS

Belt and Road Initiative (BRI): Is an international initiative of the People's Republic of China aimed at improving existing and creating new trade routes, transport, and economic corridors connecting more than 70 countries of Central Asia, Europe and Africa, which will promote the development of trade relations between them and China.

ETCS (The European Train Control System): A single European standard for the control of signaling and protection of railway traffic.

European Standards of Interoperability: Technical and operational standards that satisfy the requirements and ensure the interoperability of the railway system of the EU.

Infrastructure Investments: Expenditures on new transport construction projects as well as modernization of the existing transport network.

Investments: Assets or items acquired to generate an income or profit.

Transport Infrastructure: Are facilities, structures and systems provided for transporting people and goods. The development of transport infrastructure enhances economic growth, while the quality of transport infrastructure is essential when it comes to performance in the transport sector.

Western Balkan Countries: Countries of the Western Balkans region (Serbia, Bosnia and Herzegovina, Montenegro, Northern Macedonia and Albania).

Chapter 10
Montenegro and BRI Initiative:
Between Economic Performance and Global Political Challenges

Nikola Martinović
Faculty of Economics, University of Montenegro, Montenegro

Nikola Milović
Faculty of Economics, University of Montenegro, Montenegro

ABSTRACT

The focus of this chapter is the analysis of economic relations between Montenegro and China and the implications that the intensified economic cooperation may have on the political, regional, and global levels. Special attention is paid to the construction of the priority section of the Bar-Boljare highway and the financial arrangement concluded on those grounds between Montenegro and the Chinese Exim Bank. China's presence in the Western Balkans has gained importance recently through the Belt and Road Initiative project. Therefore, this chapter seeks to answer how Montenegro can use all the benefits of this initiative to strengthen its national economy and increase its citizens' living standards. That can be crucial as Montenegro is facing economic consequences of the COVID-19 pandemic, and FDI inflows are a precondition to reduce the infrastructure gap within the convergence criteria in the EU accession process.

INTRODUCTION

Over the past thirty years, the world has seen a rapid change in the functioning of countries, regional, continental, and world organizations at the macroeconomic level, and companies and their stakeholders at the micro-level. The process of digitalization has caused a significant acceleration of globalization, allowing a more free movement of people, goods, capital, and services (Burlacu, 2018; Autio et al., 2021). As national borders are becoming less important, foreign direct investments become critical determinant of economic growth, especially for developing countries. This process is vital in the field of

DOI: 10.4018/978-1-7998-8021-9.ch010

movement of capital and for faster and better dissemination of knowledge, technology, and best practices across the globe.

Developing countries, many of which are yet to face the challenges of the transition process, often lack money for capital projects. That is an important drawback since investments in capital projects, such as the construction of adequate infrastructure and creating a favorable environment for business development, are crucial for economic growth in the long run (Domazet & Marjanović, 2018), Under such circumstances, developing countries have a critical task to create an environment and regulatory framework that will attract investments by multinational companies so their citizens can benefit from them. Some international institutions, such as the World Bank, monitor the success of countries in creating a stimulating investment climate through the annual Doing Business Index (Rogge & Archer, 2021).

The Chinese Belt and Road Initiative is in the focus of relations between China and the Western Balkans. Through this initiative, China plans to invest a large amount of money in the Western Balkans by the end of 2027. China wants to strengthen its foreign policy by increasing its presence in foreign markets. Given that the entire region, including Montenegro as its integral part, faces a severe infrastructure gap, some thought that activities and interests of China and the European Union through this project could be complementary and contribute to economic convergence. That is important because all Western Balkan countries have set membership in the European Union as their key foreign policy priority, at least declaratively, as it may be concluded from messages from the national authorities.

This chapter's main subject is the scope and importance of Chinese investments in the Western Balkans, with a focus on Montenegro. The sectoral structure of investments will be discussed in more detail, along with the analysis of the investment climate and business barriers for foreign investors that often stem from political factors.

BACKGROUND

Stimulating economic development in Asia, Europe, and Africa, which make up 64% of the world's population and almost a third of the world's GDP, is one of the main goals of the Belt & Road initiative that the People's Republic of China has been implementing since 2015 (Huang, 2016). Naturally, there is a growing interest in the background of such an ambitious economic plan, especially in the context of strong polarization and growing geopolitical tensions and pretensions in the modern economic "war" that is being fought continuously. Despite the exceptional GDP growth rates for 25 years before the launch of this initiative, which according to the World Bank, amounted to almost 10%, there was a noticeable slowdown, too (Brandt et al., 2020). High economic growth rates have not solved all the economic challenges the country was facing, so poverty reduction in China and the focus on better management of financial assets became medium-term priorities of monetary authorities (Johnston, 2019). For these purposes, the country needs new sources and drivers of economic growth and development to enable further prosperity of its economy (Li & Lin, 2017). One of the BRI initiative goals was for Chinese companies to achieve better results in foreign markets through the growth of investment activities. Available data indicate that Chinese companies are well on their way to attaining these interests (Zakić & Radišić, 2019).

On the other hand, considering China's economic strength and global significance only from the aspect of the transformation of its economy would be wrong without considering the repercussions these developments have or may have on the geopolitical level. Against this background, Cheng (2016) suggests viewing this initiative within the framework of three dominant narratives that refer to the fundamental goals of the initiative, countries that are defined as strategic investment targets, and priorities that economic performance will have over political factors when deciding on the investment. In this sense, many authors suggest that economic indicators behind this initiative are inseparable from geopolitical goals in the international struggle for supremacy, primarily with the United States (Blanchard & Flint, 2017; Flint & Zhu, 2019).

In this global game, the EU's position is very interesting as the EU may lose its influence, especially in the Western Balkans and Montenegro, as an integral part of the Western Balkans. That is why the authorities in Brussels (Pavlićević 2019; Jaćimović & Milović, 2022) are trying to maintain their status as the regional countries' main strategic foreign policy partner in the last few years by being more active and investing more in the region to remedy the aftermath of the COVID-19 pandemic.

The main task of authorities in all transition economies is to create a stimulating investment climate that will enable significant amounts of foreign direct investments. Higher FDI inflows are a prerequisite for faster inclusion of a country in international trade and cross-national capital flows (Liang et al, 2021), and a precondition to strengthen the competitiveness of any national economy (Marjanović & Domazet, 2021). Creating such an investment climate should be a priority for Montenegro and other Balkan countries to build a healthy and long-term sustainable market-oriented and functional economy. On the other hand, the empirical results of a study conducted in 2017 for a group of Western Balkan countries indicate that the inflow of foreign direct investment does not affect to a significant extent the economic development (Domazet & Marjanović, 2017).

Montenegro is one of the youngest countries in the world that regained its independence in a referendum held on 21 May 2006. In the first years after independence, Montenegro was a fairly attractive destination for foreign investors, and in 2009 it had a record 911 million euro worth of foreign investments. Despite the decline during the Global Economic Crisis, Montenegro remained the European leader among developing countries regarding FDI's share in GDP structure. In 2000-2020, FDI averaged to 12.5% of GDP, and Montenegro went the farthest on the path to EU membership among all other countries. Since 2017, Montenegro has been a member of NATO and fully confirmed its foreign policy orientation. The FDI inflow in Montenegro is correlated positively with the reduction of unemployment rates, the growth of GDP, and a better living standard for citizens (Mirković, 2019).

Considering the market size, political tensions and turmoil, underdeveloped institutions, and the rule of law, Montenegro and the WB are not attractive areas for investments at first glance. However, its geographical position makes it a hub, a transport corridor to Central and Western Europe (Tonchev, 2017). In light of this, the cost of financing or the so-called cheap money policy in place requires special attention. Chinese banks offer money at better terms than their European counterparts. Moreover, China is willing to finance projects that lack a clear commercial perspective (Feigenbaum, 2017) or oppose the principles of green economic development at first glance. Therefore, the European side fears that the money from Chinese investors will be used for projects that deviate from European standards. Historically speaking, the Western Balkans are a "seismic" political arena susceptible to different influences. Does that mean that geopolitical factors are significantly ahead of economic criteria, as the example of Western Balkan countries suggest? Why would anyone decide to finance investment projects that supposedly lack economic logic and basis? Is the much-debated debt-trap diplomacy (Brautigam, 2020) one of the "secret" goals behind this initiative? Are Montenegro and other regional countries' independent economic policies at risk from the so-called "vassal" relationship with China?

Bilateral relations between China and Montenegro are at the desired level. There is no doubt that China will be an essential partner of Montenegro in economic terms as it was in the past. Therefore, any answer to the above questions would be arbitrary unless confirmed by adequate data and empirical analysis, as in the rest of the chapter.

RESEARCH METHODOLOGY AND OBJECTIVES

Limited access to finance is a fundamental challenge faced by transition economies. International organizations such as the European Bank for Reconstruction and Development, the World Bank, and the International Monetary Fund are potential funding sources available to developing countries. Furthermore, access to external funding sources should be sought through various regional or international initiatives, such as the Belt & Road Initiative, which will be discussed in more detail in this chapter.

The methodology used in this study implies an abductive approach. The quantitative approach is reflected in the analysis of data obtained from secondary sources, databases of international institutions such as the World Bank, International Monetary Fund, European Commission, the Central Bank of Montenegro, and the Statistical Office, that are presented as descriptive statistics. The qualitative approach refers to the theoretical analysis of collected data to understand the importance of FDI inflows, especially in infrastructure projects for the growth and development of the Montenegrin economy.

The paper is divided into two thematic units, each one analyzing the importance of relations between Montenegro and China:

- Economic and political analysis of the loan from the Chinese EXIM Bank for the construction of priority sections of the Bar-Boljare highway;
- Importance of Chinese investments for the development of Montenegrin economy and the analysis of opportunities and challenges that stand in the way of intensifying economic cooperation.

As a small and highly dependent import economy, Montenegro bases its growth and development on FDI inflow as a driver of economic growth and development. At the end of the first decade of the 21st century, the global financial crisis emerged and was followed soon by the debt crisis in Eurozone (Frieden, 2017). It had a negative impact on foreign direct investment inflows in all developing countries, including Montenegro. This is especially important in the light of the above-mentioned infrastructure gap and the requirement of Montenegro for a constant inflow of capital that would enable long-term growth and development of the economy on sound basis.

That is one of the reasons why the BRI initiative and the greater presence of Chinese companies in Montenegro can be a chance for development in challenging times that are aggravated by the health crisis and its strong adverse effects on Montenegro's macroeconomic performance. However, considering the global political trends and the struggle for supremacy between China and some Western countries, the question is what kind of economic implications could that have for Montenegro and future investments from China.

MAIN FOCUS OF THE CHAPTER

Economic and Political Analysis of the Loan From the Chinese EXIM Bank for the Construction of Priority Sections of the Bar-Boljare Highway

Economic relations between Montenegro and China mostly boil down to infrastructure, especially the construction of the priority section of the Bar-Boljare highway. The project's cost-effectiveness is the subject of an ongoing national debate and how Montenegro will finance the remaining two sections of the highway, given the recent growing trend of public debt. That becomes even more important if we keep in mind that European partners (European Bank for Reconstruction and Development and European Investment Bank) were not interested in this project after conducting two feasibility studies. That is why this matter is of particular importance from the geopolitical aspect. But, first things first.

Montenegro is the only country in Europe without a single meter of a highway. Considering that tourism is strategically crucial for its economic development, Montenegro needs an adequate transport network to improve its competitiveness as a tourist destination. After the restoration of independence in 2006, the dominant narrative in the country was the need to construct a highway. Although there were formal beginnings at the regional summit in 2009, Montenegro had to wait until the middle of the next decade to begin implementing its capital infrastructure project. The great economic crisis from the end of the first decade of the XXI century, and the recommendations of the World Bank about inherent risks of such an infrastructure project in times of economic uncertainty, resulted in its later start.

In October 2014, the Governor of the Central Bank of Montenegro and the Chinese EXIM Bank signed the agreement on financing the construction of the priority section of the Bar Boljare highway, on the Smokovac-Uvac-Matesevo stretch. The costs of the project and construction of the priority section of the highway amounted to 809.6 million euros, whereby the EXIM Bank provided 85% of the funds, and Montenegro the remaining 15%. This dollar loan repayment period is 20 years with a 6-year grace period and a 2% interest rate. [1]

On the tender for the highway construction in 2013, the best bidders were China Communications Construction Company (CCCC) and its subsidiary company China Road and Bridge Corporation (CRBC). That was important from the standpoint of China too. It contributed to the Chinese economy and complemented with the BRI initiative, which was launched soon after and set the growth of Chinese investment activities in other markets.

The arrangement opened several dominant questions, from the economic, political and geopolitical aspects, and a debate about some clauses in it. Given that the above European partners did not find interest in becoming a part of the project following their studies and analyses, one might wonder why Chinese investors agreed to enter into such an arrangement and under such circumstances? According to their reports, Montenegro struggled with debts from state guarantees worth 200 million euro originating from a decade before, as supported by data of the Ministry of Finance and Social Welfare. Furthermore, Montenegro's public debt was expected to be against the convergence criteria set by the Maastricht Treaty (as later happened), which could jeopardize the debt repayment. Macroeconomic stability directly affects the competitiveness of the national economy (Milovic et al., 2021), so problems in public finances make the country a less attractive investment destination. What is more, Montenegro was not on the list of countries that should be a part of the BRI initiative at the time.

From a geopolitical perspective, Montenegro clearly defined its strategic path. In that sense, investments and closer cooperation with the People's Republic of China have a limited impact on Montenegrin foreign policy. That can be supported from experience with the Russian Federation. In the first years after the restoration of independence, i.e., during the investment boom, Russia was a dominant foreign investor in Montenegro. In that way, one may conclude that Russia might strongly influence Montenegrin foreign policy, but that is far from the truth. Not only Montenegro became a member of NATO, but it also supported and harmonized its policies with EU policies and imposed sanctions against Russia and some Russian citizens.

Accordingly, China's influence on Montenegro could be viewed as the influence of any major investor on the developing country (Grgic, 2017). That implies greater flexibility in terms of deadlines for completion and technical aspects of the project. As Montenegro is not an EU member state yet, that fact gives room for maneuver for foreign investors because some investment activities would not be possible in EU member states, especially in terms of compliance with the European Green Deal, as some authors suggest (Okano-Heijmans & Lanting, 2015). Western countries fear not only from the direct influence on foreign policy but also from the expansion of Chinese governing methods and systems that contradict Western practices. The flexibility given to the Chinese investor has been imposed as the main source of potential problems and threats to Montenegro's sovereignty.

To be exact, under the agreement on the design and construction of the priority section of the highway, signed between the Government of Montenegro and CRBC, the court in China is competent for disputes. Furthermore, if Montenegro defaults on the repayment plan, China might become the owner of the priority section of the highway. From the geopolitical standpoint, that means that China would build up its influence in Montenegro through the cheap money policy, favorable lending, and rigorous criteria and methods to protect its interests in case of default.

In addition, the question is whether Montenegro was deliberately dragged into the credit trap by China. The fact that the loan was taken in dollars and that Montenegro was not protected from currency risk could ultimately make the highway costs more expensive were often mentioned as an additional threat. In this context, we must not forget that the arrangement involved only a single 40-kilometer long section, so how would the remaining two sections be financed?

To begin the story of debt slavery, we must analyze the structure of Montenegro's public debt and the share of the loan from the Chinese EXIM Bank. An overview of 5 largest creditors, their share in the state debt at the end of the first quarter of 2021 is presented in the table below.

Table 1. Debt balance/5 largest creditors

Creditor	Balance as of 31 December 2020	Balance as of 31 March 2021	Share %
International Bank for Reconstruction and Development	181.53	186.09	5.20%
Chinese Exim Bank	640,542	681,283	19.08%
EUROBOND	1,977.45	1,750.00	49.00%
Syndicated loan - PBG	250.00	250.00	7,00%
Syndicated loan - PBG 2	250.00	250.00	7,00%
…			-
Total internal debt	**495,56**	**454,76**	11.1%
TOTAL STATE DEBT	**4,330.83**	**4,097.44**	-
Deposits	872,43	527,26	-
TOTAL STATE DEBT (including deposits)	**3,458.40**	**3,570.18**	-

Source: Ministry of Finance and Social Welfare - processed by the authors

As the available data suggest, the share of debt to EXIM Bank in total debts of Montenegro amounts to slightly over 19%. That means that Montenegro is not in debt "slavery" from this credit arrangement. Montenegro is an economy with structural problems such as illiquidity of the real sector, very negative foreign trade balance, inefficient public administration and so on. A large portion of Montenegro's debt is the result of the problems from the transition period, and usually originates from borrowings for current consumption (Martinovic & Milovic, 2021). Moreover, public debt per se is not a problem, but rather its structure and how the obtained funds are used. Namely, borrowing for capital projects such as the highways has its economic logic because it will positively affect the national economy's performance in the long run.

In this sense, it is crucial to conclude that the construction of the priority section of the highway is not the leading cause of the debt crisis in Montenegro. On the contrary, cooperation with Chinese partners enabled Montenegro to start implementing that ambitious project when European partners were reluctant to support that vitally important infrastructure project for Montenegro's future development.

Although the data presented here support the above conclusion, the dominant narrative on the socio-political stage of the country suggested that this loan is the main cause of economic problems in Montenegro. The situation became even more complex with the emergence of the COVID-19 pandemic, which further exposed all the above-mentioned structural problems of the Montenegrin economy and was used as a good argument in the regional political debate on growing Chinese influence. The media further promoted this (Deron et al., 2021) and disseminated incomplete and unconfirmed information on the true nature of economic and political relations between Montenegro and China. Due to enlargement fatigue, Brussels shed less light on Montenegro and other Western Balkan countries, which China and Russia used to strengthen their influence in the region (Khaze, 2018; Economides, 2020).

As a result of the growing debate and controversies that accompanied the construction of the highway, European partners started showing interest in the arrangement in 2021. They demonstrated readiness to help Montenegro finance its debt to China against the backdrop of fears of growing Chinese influence and the vassal relationship that might be established on the Beijing-Podgorica route. That became even more interesting after the 2020 parliamentary elections in Montenegro that changed the governing structure. The parties that make up the present majority in the Parliament were fierce in attacking economic decisions made by their predecessors, often focusing on the project of highway and the credit arrangement with Chinese partners.

In that regard, the Government of Montenegro and four banks (Merril Lynch, Goldman International, Deutsche Bank and Societe Generale) entered into a hedging arrangement in mid-2021 to protect Montenegro from currency risk.[4] That move resulted in the reduction of interest rate by 2% on the Chinese dollar-loan, converting the remaining debt into euros with a corresponding interest rate of 0.8%. In that way, Montenegro lost 109 million euros due to the unfavorable changes of the euro-dollar exchange rate in the past, as perceived by the state. Some calculations support this transaction, indicating that there will be savings from the repayment of annuities in the future and that the country additionally "protected" itself from Chinese influence.

While it is still not possible to fully identify all the economic implications of that arrangement, from a political point of view, a new space has emerged for discourse about the struggle for influence and supremacy in the Western Balkans. Thus, US officials supported and approved that decision emphasizing that it reduced the likelihood of Chinese impact on creating political opportunities in Montenegro. In addition, all regional countries are alarmed to pay special attention to their future arrangements with the People's Republic of China, stressing that China tends to use debt-trap diplomacy or dollar diplomacy (Waisová, 2020) to pursue its interests and political concessions on various grounds. The People's Republic of China condemned such an attitude of the USA and raised the question of where the USA was when Montenegro needed help in developing its capital infrastructure project. lThey dismissed the accusation calling them political manipulations to disrupt friendly relations between China and Montenegro. [5]

The above contradicting views support that Montenegro, although a tiny market, is the stage for constant struggles for geopolitical influences. Limited economic power and market potential are less important than geographical and historical significance, making Montenegro an important geopolitical target. Although socio-economic interests are key priorities of Montenegro's cooperation with the countries mentioned above, the thesis on the inextricable link between economic and political interests cannot be ignored.

It is important to point out that Chinese investments, the arrangement with EXIM Bank and the appointment of Chinese companies in the tender for the construction of the priority section of the highway, were the only logical choice in the circumstances Montenegro found itself in - without the support from European partners and with an evident need to start the implementation of the capital project. The above factors indicate that the People's Republic of China has a limited influence on Montenegro's foreign policy, and there are no fears of deepening cooperation in the field of infrastructure projects in the future.

IMPORTANCE OF CHINESE INVESTMENTS FOR THE DEVELOPMENT OF MONTENEGRIN ECONOMY AND THE ANALYSIS OF OPPORTUNITIES AND CHALLENGES THAT STAND IN THE WAY OF INTENSIFYING ECONOMIC COOPERATION

Since the restoration of independence, foreign direct investments have been among the top sources of economic growth and development of the Montenegrin economy. The Government of Montenegro adopted Strategies for Attracting FDI on several occasions, which speak in favor of the importance of foreign capital inflows as a determinant of economic development. To this end, Montenegro has signed

22 agreements on economic cooperation with partner countries, 23 agreements on mutual promotion and protection of investors, and double taxation agreements with 44 countries. The government signed the agreement on economic cooperation and double taxation with the People's Republic of China too. From the standpoint of foreign trade, China is one of the largest foreign trade partners of Montenegro in the import of goods and services. According to the Statistical Office of Montenegro, imports from China amount to between 200 and 250 million euros annually. Montenegro dominantly imports electrical devices and appliances, white goods, and computer equipment.

Membership in NATO, the status of candidate country for EU membership, membership in the World Trade Organization (WTO), World Bank (WB) and International Monetary Fund (IMF), and the use of the euro as a currency for payments, are key advantages of Montenegro in attracting FDI.

The table below shows an overview of 10 countries with the highest investments in Montenegro during the three years.

Table 2. Inflow of FDI in Montenegro - by countries (2019-2021)

Top 10 Countries / FDI Volume in 2019	Volume of FDI (000 EUR)	Top 10 Countries / FDI Volume in 2020	Volume of FDI (000 EUR)	Top 10 Countries / FDI Volume in 2021 (Jan-Aug)	Volume of FDI (000 EUR)
Russian Federation	69,972.17	Russian Federation	98,964.52	Russian Federation	82,579.28
Hungary	54,425.56	China	71,234.14	Malta	70,345.55
United Arab Emirates	48,547.04	Switzerland	63,221.43	Serbia	53,335.99
Switzerland	43,703.99	Italy	45,311.06	Italy	41,299.02
Serbia	39,234.79	USA	29,495.41	Switzerland	40,541.13
Germany	37,096.57	United Arab Emirates	28,011.02	USA	22,049.08
Virgin Islands (GBR)	35,487.65	Serbia	27,876.36	Germany	18,777.62
Turkey	34,460.46	Germany	26,914.36	United Arab Emirates	18,216.21
Bosnia and Herzegovina	33,516.53	The Netherlands	18,890.02	Azerbaijan	17,423.46
The Netherlands	33,414.62	Turkey	18,614.72	Turkey	15,666.06

Source: Central Bank of Montenegro – processed by authors

As the available data suggest, Chinese investments were on the list of top 10 countries with the largest share of investments only in 2020. According to the Central Bank of Montenegro, almost all these investments are recorded as intercompany debt. The Bulletin of the Central Bank of Montenegro lists Chinese investment in Montenegrin companies and the purchase of real estate to belong to intercompany debt. There are no details about these Chinese investments as the data are confidential. However, in 2020, the Government of Montenegro and the Chinese-Montenegrin consortium DEC International-Bemax-BB Solar-Peromonte signed the 54 million worth agreement on the reconstruction of TPP Pljevlja[6], as another major investment activity in addition to the construction of the highway. Is that an indication of an increase in Chinese investments in Montenegro, or just an isolated case?

The following graph is an overview of Chinese investments over the six years. Evidently, Chinese investments were at a fairly low level, except in 2020.

Figure 1. China investments in Montenegro 2015-2021 (000 EUR)
Source: Central Bank of Montenegro – processed by authors

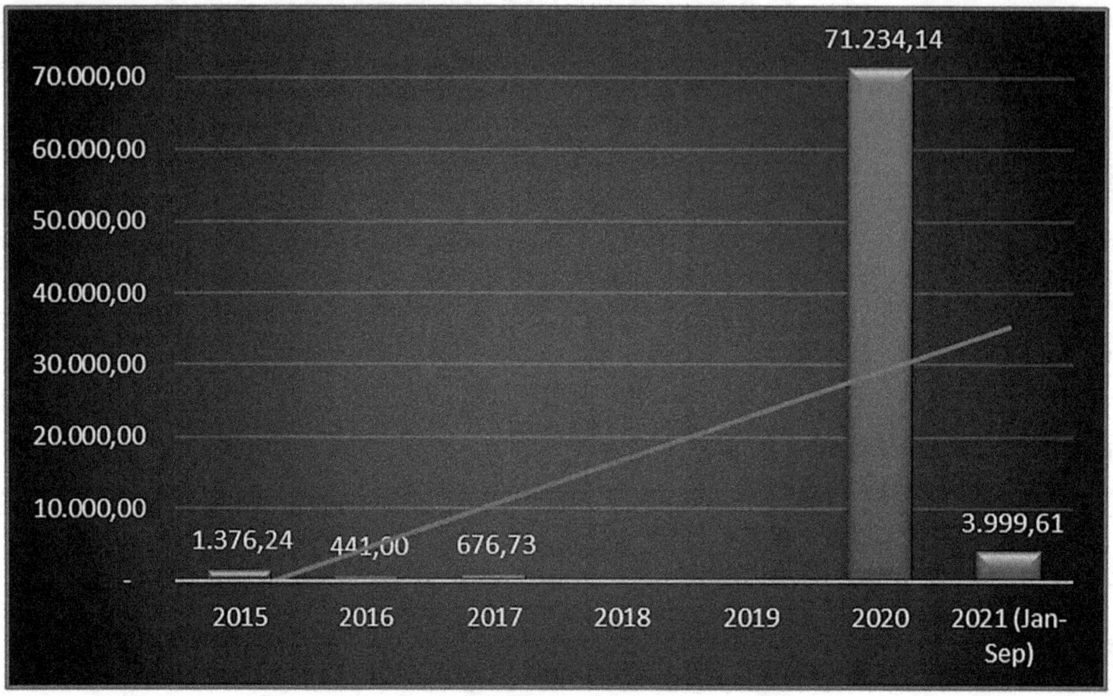

There are two conclusions. First, the scope of Chinese investments in Montenegro could not intensify Chinese influence on Montenegrin foreign policy. Even if the investments were at a much higher level, the marginal impact of such inflow on the foreign policy is evident above in the example of Russia. In conclusion, there is much room for improving economic cooperation between the two countries. Montenegro desperately needs additional funds for further economic development. That has been evident during the pandemic and the health crisis. The health crisis was an additional burden if we keep in mind that the health system of Montenegro is highly centralized, with the lack of adequate support in providing health services at the municipal level (Radević & Haček, 2019).

According to the World Bank, Montenegro is the most affected European economy, with a 15.2% drop in economic activity in 2020. Therefore, an important question is how successful Montenegro is in creating a stimulating business environment that will attract FDI, especially from Chinese multinational companies, as they are interested in having a stronger presence at foreign markets under the BRI initiative.

According to the latest Doing Business Index from the World Bank, Montenegro ranked among top 50 countries in the ease of doing business. A positive information for potential investors from China is that they have the same treatment as Montenegrin national companies. That includes investments in all industries, free movement of assets and goods, financial assets, profits, and dividends. The tax system of Montenegro is competitive and caps the general income tax rate at 9%. Establishing companies is quite simple, registration with the Commercial Court is fast and efficient, and the banking system is highly liquid. At the end of 2021, the Government of Montenegro adopted a decision to extend the economic citizenship program until the end of the current year. It is a development program that attracts FDI by financing priority programs that Montenegro has identified as key for sustainable development. In return, private investors acquire Montenegrin citizenship and all its benefits.

Furthermore, Montenegro has a valid regulation on business zones. It implies tax reliefs for users of business zones for social benefits, contributions for pension, disability, health and unemployment insurance for a period not exceeding 5 years. The Law on Business Zones stipulates that the beneficiaries may be granted additional benefits, such as reduced land rent, or reduced real estate taxes to stimulate production. In addition to state business zones, there is an ongoing call for the business zone projects implemented by the Capital Podgorica with the aim teo strengthen the Montenegrin economy's competitiveness and create a better business environment for foreign investors what is the main goal according to the Report published by Chamber Economy of Montenegro and Ministry of foreign affairs (2021). Research conducted in neighboring countries such as Serbia also speaks in favor of the great importance of tax incentives for choosing a country as an investment destination (Domazet et al., 2018).

However, these advantages are only one side of the coin, as foreign investors face many challenges that may be significant constraints. Inefficient public administration, corruption, the rule of law, and the acting status in most state institutions, slow bureaucracy – to name just some obstacles for FDI. In addition, tiny market, a large volume of the informal economy, structural unemployment and lack of skilled labor, underdeveloped road infrastructure and energy network, which are important determinants for running a company, can be considered as deterrents from the standpoint of Chinese multinational companies and their investments.

Furthermore, political challenges may be an obstacle to further improving cooperation between China and Montenegro. The Covid-19 pandemic has made the economic situation even more complex, including the global political and economic struggle for supremacy. Some authors suggest that China has been using the so-called vaccine diplomacy (Lee, 2021; Su et al., 2021) not just to improve its image in the world by helping underdeveloped countries but rather as a part of its global geopolitical strategic game. On the other hand, the USA and many other developed western countries do not accept Chinese vaccines, which can also be linked to the economic struggle for supremacy, in terms of the supply and setting conditions to use the ''preferred'' vaccine. Under such circumstances, all foreign investments, especially in the Western Balkans, are under public scrutiny in analyzing the political repercussions of such activities on a larger scale.

These are some of the reasons that may destimulate the investments of Chinese multinational companies in Montenegro in the years to come. With the current complex political situation in the country, political instability per se is a significant destimulating factor for economic activities. Solving these problems is imperative for top state officials in Montenegro to enjoy the benefits of the BRI initiative. Infrastructure and energy projects are priority areas that require investment projects by Montenegro, which complement the plans and goals of the BRI Initiative.

SOLUTIONS AND RECOMMENDATIONS

For the past twenty years, Montenegro has been the country with the largest share of FDI in the created GDP value annually. A tiny Western Balkans country with scarce opportunities to create new value and accumulate significant capital had to rely on foreign capital to ensure economic development. Considering the global character of the BRI initiative, Montenegro must strive further to strengthen regional cooperation with other Western Balkan countries to promote itself as a favorable destination for business development. In that way, the whole region becomes a more desirable destination for doing business, and improved cooperation enables free movement of goods, people, capital, and services.

Against this background, the country should consider intensifying the cooperation within the Open Balkans initiative (Serbia, Northern Macedonia, and Albania). Due attention should be paid to this initiative. It must not be a replacement for Montenegro's membership in the European Union (which has no alternative), but rather a possibility for cooperation that further reduces business barriers. Additional investments in road infrastructure by creating a regional network of highways and expressways and integration of the energy market could build on the opportunities of the Port of Bar in Montenegro, i.e. a crucial resource for maritime transport, as vital steps towards further progress. That is important, bearing in mind that China has made significant investments in the Balkans through the BRI initiative and plans to make additional investments in the years to come. Serbia is a regional leader in attracting investments from China, which is an important signal for the importance of the highway and construction activities on the remaining sections that will connect Bar and Belgrade.

Montenegro needs to establish political stability through further progress in meeting European standards, stemming from negotiating chapters with the EU, and further strengthen its rule of law. MPs in the Parliament must make additional efforts to establish political stability and build independent and professional institutions, as the current state of affairs with acting capacity negatively impacts macroeconomic performance. Historically speaking, Montenegro has always been a stage for the struggle of the supremacy of various influences, so a firm heterogeneity in the programs of political parties in the Parliament does not come as a surprise. However, that should not be a problem for Montenegro's economic interests. Reform of the public administration and the state of public finances are no less important. Ongoing weaker macroeconomic indicators, especially in the growth of public debt, show econometrical characteristics of trends of stationary time series and danger in terms of further decline in credit rating. That is a problem from the standpoint of future borrowing, which would generally be more expensive in each subsequent iteration because Montenegro will lose the status of a credible debtor. It is no less important to note that the credit rating is often the first signal to foreign investors about the national economy.

From the geopolitical standpoint, Montenegro does not have the luxury to be hurt in strategic games and struggles for global supremacy and adjust itself by classifying partner countries or potential investors as desirable or less desirable. On the other hand, geopolitical struggles can often have harmful effects on any country. In that sense, Montenegro would benefit significantly from the detente at the international level. In the Western Balkans, the interests of China and Montenegro should complement each other, so new investment projects on both sides should reduce the infrastructure gap and have a positive effect on Montenegro's subsequent accession to the European Union and convergence criteria. Some European authorities fear that Beijing is financing projects without a commercial perspective that provide a backdrop for corruptive practices. To that end, joint cooperation and implementation of projects by partners of the EU and China may be one of the models to overcome that challenge. That would open up the door for Montenegro to exploit all benefits of the BRI initiative while complying with European standards.

FUTURE DIRECTIONS FOR STUDIES

The level of foreign direct investment, construction of the priority section of the Bar-Boljare highway, opportunities available to Montenegro within the BRI initiative, and the (geo)political framework in which the economic reality takes place are the basic ideas discussed in this chapter. All of them grew in importance with the current health and financial crisis outbreak, which dramatically changed how the modern economy functions. The economists, decision-makers, and the scientific community found themselves before the question of how to ensure sustainable growth and economic development in challenging times. This question is challenging in developing and transition countries that transfer their self-governing system to a market economy system.

With geopolitical aspects in mind, this chapter pays due attention to the construction of the priority section of the Montenegrin highway. This study's disadvantage is that the situation in Montenegro was not compared to credit arrangements that Chinese lenders have had with other countries. A comparative analysis would show whether Montenegro negotiated better or worse conditions than other countries and the economic and political repercussions of such arrangements on those countries' economic and foreign policies. Another important segment of the study would be the scope of economic development of those countries at the time of borrowing for capital projects, their public finances, and strategic foreign policy, so future studies should focus in that direction.

When it comes to Montenegro, future studies should analyze the sectoral structure of the Montenegrin economy and perform segmentation in terms of industries with the greatest potential for foreign investment. In that way, Chinese investors would better understand potential market niches where they should look for their chances. Another option would be to conduct an exploratory study through in-depth interviews with local and national economic authorities and vital economic entities. That would help identify all critical development needs of the country, its regions, and municipalities. Montenegro is known for evident inequality in the development of its parts, so the priorities of cities often differ and collide with each other. Therefore, a special focus on the micro aspect of the study and presentation of adequate data would create a clearer picture of potential investors, both in terms of opportunities and challenges for doing business.

CONCLUSION

Countries implement economic measures at the macro and micro levels to increase the living standard of their citizens. A higher standard of living means quantitative financial performance such as average wages and purchasing power levels and includes qualitative aspects, such as the quality of the health and education system, road infrastructure, and transport connectivity. To improve living standards for their citizens, countries usually need significant investments, which the developing countries often lack and can not make investments in fixed capital formation. That is why the inflow of FDI is vital for analyzing any national economy and achieving its goals.

FDI inflows are subject to many factors, which may be opportunities for development or limiting factors on the road to a healthy and sustainable functioning economy. The chapter focuses on the political aspects and challenges faced by a small, highly dependent import economy in attracting FDI. We paid particular attention to the construction of the highway and the chances for further economic development that Montenegro can use from the BRI initiative. Despite many challenges, different interpretations, and presented data, it is evident that Montenegro has not become part of the Chinese debt trap. The money borrowed from the Chinese EXIM Bank is not at the root of Montenegro's financial challenges but rather structural problems that are inherent to the country's economy. Moreover, that investment had a marginal impact on Montenegro's foreign policy. In the meantime, Montenegro became a member of NATO and made progress to EU membership.

FDI inflows are crucial for the development of the Montenegrin economy, especially in the post-pandemic period when the accompanying effects of the health crisis will require remedy. The BRI initiative is emerging as one of Montenegro's opportunities to use to its advantage by creating a stimulating business environment and favorable investment climate. To minimize political challenges, joint implementation of investment projects by Chinese and European partners would contribute to the relaxation of relations and make positive economic performance. Given the evident growth of Chinese investments in the Western Balkans, keeping regional economic cooperation would strengthen competitiveness and the spillover of positive economic effects at the regional level.

REFERENCES

Autio, E., Mudambi, R., & Yoo, Y. (2021). Digitalization and globalization in a turbulent world: Centrifugal and centripetal forces. *Global Strategy Journal, 11*(1), 3–16. doi:10.1002/gsj.1396

Blanchard, J. M. F., & Flint, C. (2017). The geopolitics of China's maritime silk road initiative. *Geopolitics, 22*(2), 223–245. doi:10.1080/14650045.2017.1291503

Brandt, L., Litwack, J., Mileva, E., Wang, L., Zhang, Y., & Zhao, L. (2020). *China's Productivity Slowdown and Future Growth Potential.* World Bank Group. doi:10.1596/1813-9450-9298

Brautigam, D. (2020). A critical look at Chinese 'debt-trap diplomacy': The rise of a meme. *Area Development and Policy, 5*(1), 1–14. doi:10.1080/23792949.2019.1689828

Burlacu, S., Gutu, C., & Matei, F. O. (2018). Globalization–pros and cons. *Calitatea, 19*(S1), 122–125.

Cheng, L. K. (2016). Three questions on China's "belt and road initiative". *China Economic Review, 40*, 309–313. doi:10.1016/j.chieco.2016.07.008

Deron, L., Pairault, T., & Pasquali, P. (2021). *Montenegro, China, and the Media: A Highway to Disinformation?* (No. 07/2021). Briefing Paper.

Domazet, I., & Marjanović, D. (2018). *Foreign direct investment and economic development: Comparative analysis of Bulgarian, Romanian and Serbian economies.* Academic Press.

Domazet, I., Marjanović, D., & Stošić, I. (2018). Attractiveness of the domicile economy through tax incentives. *Ekonomika preduzeća, 66*(7-8), 434-445.

Domazet, I., & Marjanovic, D. M. (2017). Foreign Direct Investment in the Function of Economic Development-Example of Selected Countries in the Western Balkans. *International Letters of Social and Humanistic Sciences, 79.*

Economides, S. (2020, March). From fatigue to resistance: EU enlargement and the Western Balkans. *The Dahrendorf Forum.*

Feigenbaum, E. A. (2017). China and the world: Dealing with a reluctant power. *Foreign Affairs, 96*, 33.

Flint, C., & Zhu, C. (2019). The geopolitics of connectivity, cooperation, and hegemonic competition: The Belt and Road Initiative. *Geoforum, 99*, 95–101. doi:10.1016/j.geoforum.2018.12.008

Frieden, J., & Walter, S. (2017). Understanding the political economy of the Eurozone crisis. *Annual Review of Political Science, 20*(1), 371–390. doi:10.1146/annurev-polisci-051215-023101

Grgić, M. (2019). Chinese infrastructural investments in the Balkans: Political implications of the highway project in Montenegro. *Territory, Politics, Governance, 7*(1), 42–60. doi:10.1080/21622671.2017.1359106

Huang, Y. (2016). Understanding China's Belt & Road initiative: Motivation, framework and assessment. *China Economic Review, 40*, 314–321. doi:10.1016/j.chieco.2016.07.007

Jaćimović, D., & Milović, N. (2022). Montenegro: Enlargement Solidarity, Hoping for the Best.... In *European Solidarity in Action and the Future of Europe* (pp. 143–145). Springer. doi:10.1007/978-3-030-86537-5_34

Johnston, L. A. (2019). The Belt and Road Initiative: What is in it for China? *Asia & the Pacific Policy Studies, 6*(1), 40–58. doi:10.1002/app5.265

Khaze, N. M. (2018). European Union's enlargement fatigue: Russia's and China's rise in Southeast Europe? *Australian and New Zealand Journal of European Studies, 10*(1).

Lee, S. T. (2021). Vaccine diplomacy: Nation branding and China's COVID-19 soft power play. *Place Branding and Public Diplomacy*, 1–15. doi:10.105741254-021-00224-4

Li, K., & Lin, B. (2017). Economic growth model, structural transformation, and green productivity in China. *Applied Energy, 187*, 489–500. doi:10.1016/j.apenergy.2016.11.075

Liang, C., Shah, S. A., & Bifei, T. (2021). The Role of FDI Inflow in Economic Growth: Evidence from Developing Countries. *Journal of Advanced Research in Economics and Administrative Sciences, 2*(1), 68–80. doi:10.47631/jareas.v2i1.212

Marjanović, D., & Domazet, I. S. (2021). Foreign Direct Investments: A Key Factor for Business Globalization. In Handbook of Research on Institutional, Economic, and Social Impacts of Globalization and Liberalization (pp. 96-116). IGI Global. doi:10.4018/978-1-7998-4459-4.ch006

Martinović, N., & Milović, N. (2021). Dužnička kriza ekonomije Crne Gore – uzroci i posljedice. In Makroekonomska stabilnost i unapređenje konkurentnosti zemalja Zapadnog Balkana. Institut ekonomskih nauka.

Milović, N., Jocović, M., & Martinović, N. (2021). Analysis of the Impact of Macroeconomic Stability on the Level of Global Competitiveness of Western Balkan Countries. *Journal of Central Banking Theory and Practice, 2*(2), 23–37. doi:10.2478/jcbtp-2021-0012

Ministry of Foreign Affairs & Chamber Economy of Montenegro. (2021). *Montenegro investment and business opportunities*. Author.

Mirković, M. (2019). Montenegro economy briefing: Overview of Foreign Direct Investment Trends in Montenegro. China–CEE Institute, 20(2), 1-4.

Okano-Heijmans, M., & Lanting, D. (2015). *Europe's Response to China's Activism: Balancing Hope and Fear in the New Age of Global Economic Governance*. Clingandael Institute.

Pavlićević, D. (2019). Structural power and the China-EU-Western Balkans triangular relations. *Asia Europe Journal*, *17*(4), 453–468. doi:10.100710308-019-00566-y

Radević, I., & Haček, M. (2019). Decentralisation processes in Montenegrin public administration: Challenges of health system. *Lex Localis*, *17*(3), 471–492. doi:10.4335/17.3.471-493(2019)

Rogge, N., & Archer, G. (2021). Measuring and analyzing country change in establishing ease of doing business using a revised version of World Bank's ease of doing business index. *European Journal of Operational Research*, *290*(1), 373–385. doi:10.1016/j.ejor.2020.07.065

Su, Z., McDonnell, D., Li, X., Bennett, B., Šegalo, S., Abbas, J., Cheshmehzangi, A., & Xiang, Y. T. (2021). COVID-19 Vaccine Donations—Vaccine Empathy or Vaccine Diplomacy? A Narrative Literature Review. *Vaccines*, *9*(9), 1024. doi:10.3390/vaccines9091024 PMID:34579261

Tonchev, P. (2017). *China's road: Into the western Balkans*. European Union Institute for Security Studies (EUISS).

Waisová, Š. (2020). China's strategy vis-à-vis Taiwan's diplomatic friends: Is Beijing using dollar diplomacy? *Journal of Comparative Politics*, *13*(1).

Zakić, K., & Radišić, B. (2019). China's Belt and Road Investment Projects in the Balkan Countries: Six Years After. *The Review of International Affairs*, *70*, 48–68.

ADDITIONAL READING

Beeson, M., & Watson, N. (2019). Is international leadership changing hands or disappearing? China and the USA in comparative perspective. *Asian Perspective*, *43*(2), 387–415. doi:10.1353/apr.2019.0015

Bieber, F., & Tzifakis, N. (2019). *The Western Balkans as a Geopolitical Chessboard? Myths, Realities and Policy Options.* Myths, Realities and Policy Options. BiEPAG Policy Brief.

Bonomi, M., & Uvalic, M. (2019). The economic development of the Western Balkans: The importance of non-EU actors. In *The Western Balkans in the World* (pp. 36–58). Routledge. doi:10.4324/9780429243349-3

Cai, K. G. (2018). The one belt one road and the Asian infrastructure investment bank: Beijing's new strategy of geoeconomics and geopolitics. *Journal of Contemporary China*, *27*(114), 831–847. doi:10.1080/10670564.2018.1488101

Makocki, M., & Nechev, Z. (2017). Balkan corruption: the China connection. *Issue Alert, 22*.

Markovic Khaze, N., & Wang, X. (2021). Is China's rising influence in the Western Balkans a threat to European integration? *Journal of Contemporary European Studies*, *29*(2), 234–250. doi:10.1080/14782804.2020.1823340

Turcsányi, R. Q. (2020). China and the frustrated region: Central and Eastern Europe's repeating troubles with great powers. *China Report (New Delhi, India)*, *56*(1), 60–77. doi:10.1177/0009445519895626

Witt, M. A. (2019). China's challenge: Geopolitics, de-globalization, and the future of Chinese business. *Management and Organization Review*, *15*(4), 687–704. doi:10.1017/mor.2019.49

Zhang, W. (2018). *China's Belt and Road InitiativeChanging the Rules of Globalization*. Palgrave Macmillan. doi:10.1007/978-3-319-75435-2

KEY TERMS AND DEFINITIONS

Belt and Road Initiative (BRI): Also known as the New Silk Road, is a plan by the government of the People's Republic of China to build infrastructure for transportation, from China to other countries in Asia, Europe, and Africa.

Debt Trap: Is a situation where the debtor will not be able to repay the debt incurred. Debt trap situation may arise due to the higher interest rates or change in terms and conditions of debt incurred

Economic Development: Is the creation of wealth from which community benefits are realized. It is more than a jobs program, it's an investment in growing your economy and enhancing the prosperity and quality of life for all residents.

Foreign Direct Investment (FDI): Is a category of cross-border investment in which an investor resident in one economy establishes a lasting interest in and a significant degree of influence over an enterprise resident in another economy.

Geopolitics: A study of the influence of such factors as geography, economics, and demography on the politics and especially the foreign policy of a state.

National Competitiveness: Is a relative concept. It is an approximation of a country's ability to grow and to compete with other countries for human capital, investments, and other resources.

National Economy: The economy of a nation as a whole that is an economic unit and is usually held to have a unique existence greater than the sum of the individual units within it.

Western Balkans (WB): Are a group of countries that are targeted by the European Union enlargement policy. This group is originally constituted by Albania, Croatia, North Macedonia, Montenegro, Bosnia and Herzegovina, Serbia, and Kosovo.

ENDNOTES

1 See more: *Law on the Bar-Boljare Highway. Official Gazette of Montenegro no. 52/2014.*

2 As per exchange rate on 31 December 2020

3 As per exchange rate on 31 March 2021

4 See more: Ministry of Finance and Social Welfare of Montenegro

5 See more: http://me.chineseembassy.org/mon/sghd_1/202107/t20210709_9032474.htm

6 See more: https://balkangreenenergynews.com/chinese-montenegrin-consortium-wins-bid-for-eco-reconstruction-of-tpp-pljevlja/

Chapter 11
China's Trade and Investment in the Western Balkans Under the Belt and Road Initiative:
Focus on North Macedonia

Iskra Stancheva Gigov
Ss. Cyril and Methodius University in Skopje, Macedonia & Institute of Economics, Macedonia

Klimentina Poposka
Ss. Cyril and Methodius University in Skopje, Macedonia & Institute of Economics, Macedonia

ABSTRACT

The China Belt and Road Initiative (BRI) and the 17+1 cooperation platform, as an integral part of it, is the key framework for China's foreign policy towards most parts of the world, including the Western Balkans (WB). Through its global initiative and cooperation platform, China creates a range of opportunities for facilitating trade and increasing export, financial integration and greater Chinese investment, major infrastructure projects, as well as their funding. This chapter analyzes the real situation regarding these aspects in the WB countries, especially focused on North Macedonia. The analysis indicates that there has been some progress in co-operation, but the WB countries (excluding Serbia) have failed to maximize their interests either in bilateral co-operation or in the framework of the BRI initiative and the 17+1 platform. Conclusively, despite all the great expectations, the trade exchange, Chinese investments, and the realized infrastructure projects do not reach a significant level.

INTRODUCTION

China's progress and extremely rapid economic growth have globally obtained the country, an advantage, both in trade and investment. In the recent years, with its globalized approach, China aims to promote its economic model and experience as an example of supporting the development of other countries in progress, not only in Third World countries, but also in the European Union (EU), including the WB

DOI: 10.4018/978-1-7998-8021-9.ch011

region. The 17+1 cooperation platform and the global BRI initiative, launched in 2012 and 2013 are respectively the most visible examples of China's attempts to cooperate with non-neighboring countries, which has so far been left out of its foreign policy priorities. Such is the case with the five WB countries (Albania, Bosnia and Herzegovina, Montenegro, North Macedonia and Serbia). Despite the minor viable market, opportunities that were offered to Chinese investors since 2012 have been included in the "16 +1" platform[1] which existed at that time, both with Central and Eastern Europe (CEE). Later on, this regional platform became an integral part of the BRI and WB and were increasingly targeted for BRI-related projects as a result of their key strategic and geographical position for the Balkan Silk Road through infrastructure networks and logistic corridors between the Port of Piraeus (China's flagship project in the region) and the markets in Western Europe. China's geo-economic and political interests aim to use the region as a gateway and transit trading platform to Western Europe where real Chinese interests are positioned (Zeneli, 2020).

Thereby, the BRI initiative is one of the most ambitious economic and infrastructural endeavors in history that can implicit changes in the balance of power globally and has also a great potential to shift the epicenter of the world politics from West to East. Actually, the initiative leaded that China will take over the dominance of world trade through land and maritime transport networks with the Balkans, considered a strategically important region due to its proximity to the EU. However, China's influence on the WB can be seen not only by the tendency to build the express maritime and land route connecting China with Europe, but also by the indecisive policy pursued by the EU, especially in the WB region. On top of all this, regular annual summits are being held and close relations with the countries on the institutional level are maintained by the means of 17+1 cooperation mechanism which as well enables additional influence within the region.

The global initiative BRI creates opportunities for economic cooperation with the WB countries and offers numerous benefits primarily in the areas such as: trade, investment, infrastructure, etc. The 17+1 platform is also very useful for the WB countries, because it enables constant and regular communication and cooperation with China which at the same time increases the chance for attracting investments, increasing exports and financing infrastructure projects. Regarding the above-mentioned info, this chapter addresses the analysis of economic cooperation, an area in which China has the utmost importance for the WB region, with a special emphasis on foreign trade, investments and various infrastructure projects. Hence, the chapter should demonstrate to what extent and in which sectors the foreign trade is mainly realized, as well as the Chinese investments between the WB countries and China, with a special focus on North Macedonia. One of the main objectives of the BRI initiative is to facilitate the flow of goods, services, capital, people and information. Particular measures need to be taken by both sides to create an appropriate regulatory framework and remove existing barriers to trade and invest. Consequently, this research also analyzes the possible challenges and obstacles faced by the Macedonian economy and other economies of the WB countries in the implementation of import-export activities and attracting foreign investments from China. So, it is expected that certain solutions are envisaged at improving the overall economic cooperation between China and the WB, as well as North Macedonia, and some recommendations are being given to overcome the obstacles and challenges.

In order to realize the aforementioned research goal, this chapter mainly uses the following methods: analysis, synthesis, comparative method, etc. In general, the findings in this chapter are obtained through desk research, using a quantitative approach based on numerical data and their correlation. The analysis covers the period from 2013 to 2020. The official figures are provided by the following public Data Sets: UN Comtrade, China Global Investment Tracker, Chinese Investment in Central and Eastern Europe

Data Set, NBStat (Statistical Web Portal of the National Bank of the Republic of North Macedonia) and AidData's Global Chinese Development Finance Dataset.

BACKGROUND

As stated, the BRI initiative aims to connect Asia with Europe and Africa through major infrastructure projects, financial integration, trade facilitation, as well as cooperation in other areas. This initiative envisages China and all participating countries to benefit from the cooperation. However, the outcome and impact of this cooperation, as well as the resulting policies are subjects to agree upon by the WB countries. Anyway, China's goals and activities for these countries remain relatively unclear, both for the local policymakers and for the Western partners: the EU and the US. Thereby, some researchers, supporters of traditional concepts, explain the Chinese presence in the WB through the principles of Chinese foreign policy, such as "mutual benefit" and "a situation in which everyone benefits" (Zhou, 2004). Other researchers see this through the prism of recently developed concepts according to which in these countries harmonious and peaceful development is achieved in a "community of shared destiny" (State Council, 2011). Other researchers perceive China as a "real predator" in the region (Mirel, 2019) or as a threat to EU unity (Turcsanyi, 2014). Some authors point out that the WB governments, disappointed by the lack of progress with the EU accession, have welcomed China's greater economic engagement (Vetrovcova, 2018). According to some experts, another important aspect is that despite of certain benefits which come from China's economic engagement, all the countries, including China itself, the EU and the WB countries, may oppose the EU reform agenda because of the Chinese state-led engagement model (Mardell, 2020).

As pointed out, BRI is a significant potential for economic cooperation in the fields of trade, investment, tourism and infrastructure and the 17+1 platform is also expected to help participants attract Chinese investment, as well as to increase exports to China and gain much needed funding for infrastructure projects. However, since the establishment of the BRI initiative and the cooperation platform 17+1, until today, the question which has been constantly raised is: "How much the WB region manages to use the potential opportunities that they offer?" Academic experts are lately paying more attention to China's engagement and contribution to the WB. A serie of studies indicate that almost all WB countries, except Serbia, neither use the available opportunities and maximize their interests and bilateral cooperation among themselves, nor within the FP and 17+1 platform. (Krstinovska, 2020a). Another study points to the fact that when assessing China's engagement, most countries in the region feel a wider gap between expectations and fulfillment, as China appears to be mainly focused on Serbia (Mardell, 2020; Domazet & Marjanović, 2018). So far, North Macedonia, despite the will and interest of national institutions and companies, fails to significantly use the available opportunities and has few particular results that can be distinguished (Krstinovska, 2020b). In addition, the previous research has shown that China's interaction with the WB is mainly reflected in the infrastructure financing (Zweers et al., 2020) and that China's presence in the Western Balkans focuses more on construction, than on actual FDI projects (Tamás, 2021). It is considered that a large part of Chinese investments in the Western Balkans are actually loans, but not real investments. Hence, it is not surprising that in the meantime, many researchers and experts point out that the actual number and value of Chinese investment projects in the region are much lower than many would expect them to be. (Tamás, 2021; Domazet & Marjanović, 2017)

But, there are authors who point out that although the EU is the most important trade partner of the Western Balkan countries, cooperation with China in the previous decade has been growing in terms of both investment and trade (Jacimovic et al., 2018). At the same time, the findings claim that due to weak capacities and asymmetry in economic power, Serbia lacks the possibility of significant influence on the development of trade with China and that China's influence in Serbia is mostly manifested through investment, not trade (Jovičić et al.; Marjanović & Domazet, 2021). Such or similar tendencies are characteristic of all Western Balkan countries, because according to their size, economic strength and impact on international trade, they are inferior to China. (Beraha & Jovičić, 2021).

The findings so far and the opposing views and considerations confirm the justification of conducting this research which analyzes how much the WB region manages to really use the potential opportunities offered by China and whether it is making progress in economic cooperation with China, focusing on trade and attracted FDI, as well as implemented infrastructure projects.

MAIN FOCUS OF THE CHAPTER

Western Balkans and North Macedonia in the Belt and Road Initiative and the 17+1 Cooperation Platform

Traditionally, the WB countries have established good relations with China primarily as a result of historical ties and socialist past, as well as the need to cooperate with China as a growing power in the 21st century. Their mutual cooperation is basically of economic nature. On one hand, China's growing focus on WB countries comes from the need to support Chinese banks and companies to invest, export and do more business abroad, gain access to new technologies, gain new experiences in operations and become globally more competitive, while on the other hand, there is the need for WB countries to cooperate with China comes from the interest in increasing exports to the Chinese market and Chinese foreign direct investment, attracting tourists and financing infrastructure projects. Besides the bilateral cooperation, the five countries of the Western Balkans through membership in the cooperation platform 17+1 have the opportunity for multilateral cooperation. Not to forget that these five countries also support the BRI initiative and have signed a Memorandum of Understanding with China. The launch of 17+1 cooperation in 2012 and the BRI initiative from a year later, marked a turning point in China-WB relations, which was noticed primarily by the emergence of Balkan countries as potential partners in specific projects and beneficiaries of infrastructural development funds. The cooperation is based on mutual interest and raises the hopes that they will increase the benefits in order to attract Chinese investments, increase exports to China and provide the necessary finances through cheap loans to build much-needed infrastructure projects.

The five WB countries have been participating in the 17+1 Cooperation Forum from the very beginning. This cooperation platform is beneficial for the WB countries, as it establishes a permanent and regular forum for communication with China. Prior to this, countries, except Serbia, have rarely had such an opportunity. In addition, the adaptable institutional structure of the 17+1 platform and the way it develops left much room for WB countries to introduce content according to their priorities. So far, the level of involvement and ambition in 17+1 in each of these countries varies over the years.

The BRI initiative is often associated with major infrastructure projects, funded by a Chinese state-owned bank and built by a Chinese state-owned enterprise. Knowing that most projects are implemented in developing countries with limited access to finance and a relatively volatile political and macroeconomic situation, the question is whether those countries can find another source of funding. This is the case with North Macedonia and Montenegro, which using all other opportunities to finance certain infrastructural projects (highways, etc) turn to China. (Krstinovska, 2020a)

From present perspective, not each of these countries actively participates in multilateral cooperation forums and relevant high-level events led by China, nor do they have any tangible benefits from them. It is also impossible to single out any major successful project, nor to determine significant benefits. Hence, the realization of the potential success of the initiative and the fulfillment of the long-term interests of the WB countries is a subject to discuss. This is also supported by the fact that the WB countries, while not receiving actual benefits, are either forced to spend budget funds for cooperation in order to succeed. In addition, CEE participants, including the WB countries, consider only their own interests and do not see themselves as part of the wider CEE region, which certainly rises a question about the multilateral nature of the initiative. Different subregions do not seek common solutions to common problems, but act as competitors with each other. At the same time, another obstacle is the limited understanding of China in terms of its goals, opportunities and policies by North Macedonia, as well as other WB countries, except Serbia. This prevents policy makers from making informed decisions, being proactive in cooperating and maximizing national interests. (Krstinovska, 2020a)

Considering the Republic of North Macedonia in terms of reaping the benefits of the BRI, there is so far no significant achievement, especially in recent years when it is absent from most of the events in the initiative. The initial years of the 17+1 cooperation led to a big project – the construction of two highway sections, Miladinovci-Stip and Kichevo-Ohrid, but the recent events lack initiatives that proactively include the country.

Economic Cooperation between the Western Balkans and China - Trade and Investment

The WB countries, as part of the BRI and the 17+1 platform, find the main reason for cooperation with China in the economic domain - primarily in the potential increasement in exports and attracting Chinese foreign direct investment, as well as financing infrastructure projects. These aspects are the subject of analysis in the following part of this chapter.

Foreign Trade Exchange Between China and the WB Region

The pace in bilateral trade relations has accelerated in the past, for almost a decade, as all five countries have started exporting and importing more Chinese goods. In the period 2013-2020, the trade between the Western Balkans and China has been constantly growing, especially in the last four years, when there was also a constant slight increase in the share of this exchange within the total trade of these countries. This is especially dominant in the last two years, i.e. 2019 and 2020 when that share is 5.7 and 6.9, respectively (Figure 1). The trade between the Western Balkans and China in 2020 reached a value of 6,058.8 million dollars (Figure 1), which is 15.5% higher than the previous year due to China's success in the fight against the COVID- 19 virus and the ability to restore full production and take advantage of increased demand. However, it must be emphasized that China's share of trade with the Western Balkans is still relatively low.

Figure 1. Trade exchange of WB with China (volume and share), 2013-2020
Source: Authors' calculations based on UN Comtrade, 2021

Almost half of the total WB trade with China is in Serbia ($ 3,667 million) which happens to be China's strategic partner in the region. Thereby, its registered growth of the overall trade has started to increase from 2017 (Figure 2), but until then the situation was relatively steady and unchangeable.

Figure 2. Total trade of WB with China, by counties
Source: Authors' calculations based on UN Comtrade, 2021

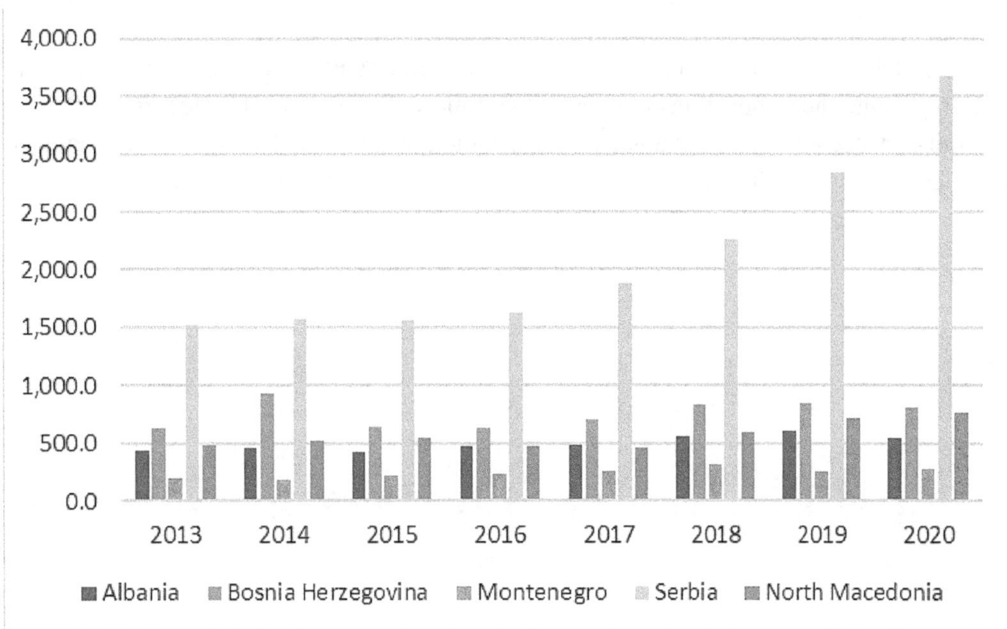

Viewed separately, the import and export aspect, it can be concluded that Serbia contributed to trade with China mainly through import activities in the analyzed period (Figure 3). The last two years are a bit of exception (2019 and 2020), because a significant increase on the export side and takes over the primacy of the largest exporter in China compared to other countries in the region has been registered (Figure 4). Until then, regarding export, the main exporters of WB in China were Albania and North Macedonia.

Figure 3. Imports of WB countries from China
Source: Authors' calculations based on UN Comtrade, 2021

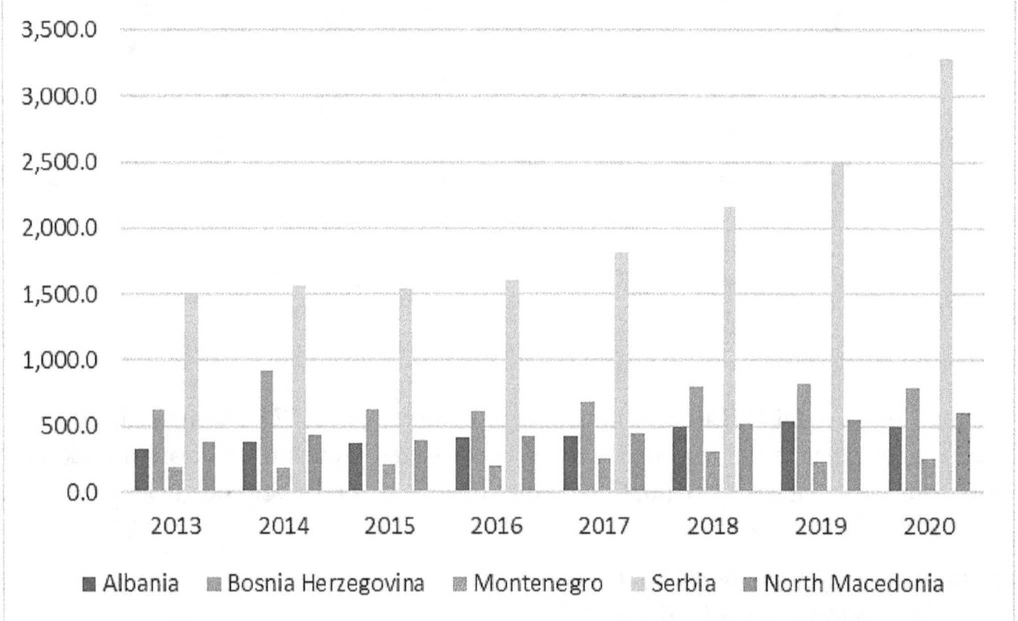

Bosnia and Herzegovina and Montenegro registered significantly low values throughout the period (Figure 4). Regarding the import aspect, after Serbia, follows Bosnia and Herzegovina with an unstable dynamic, unlike Macedonia and Albania, which throughout the period have recorded some stability. Montenegro is a country with constantly low values in the import category. (Figure 3)

Figure 4. Exports of WB countries to China
Source: Authors' calculations based on UN Comtrade, 2021

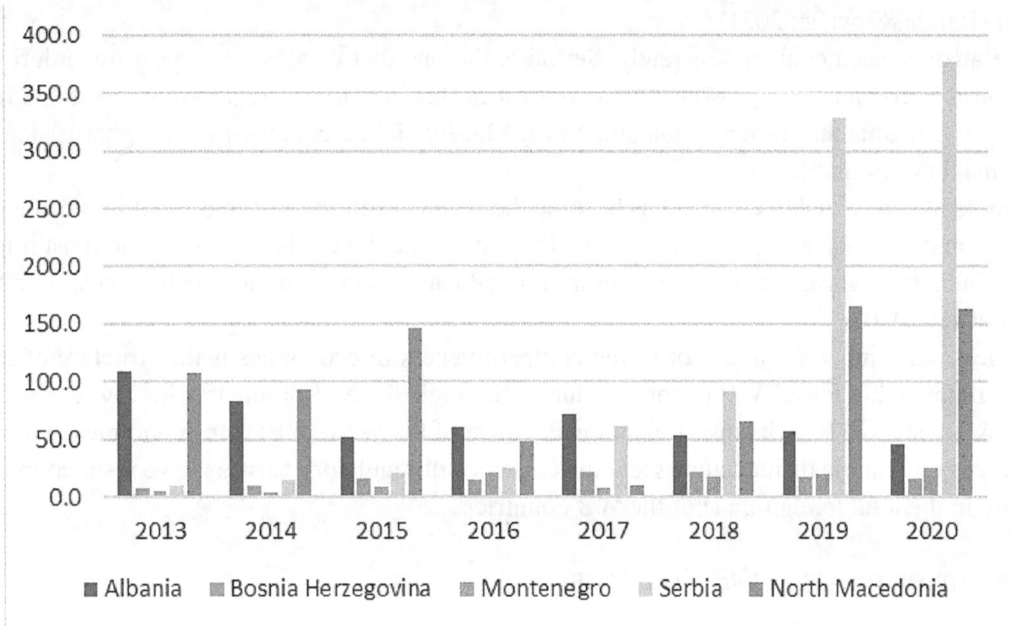

The trade exchange is strongly in favor of China, gaining a positive balance with the region, i.e. the countries of the Western Balkans are the ones that register a continuous deficit, which deepens during the entire analyzed period. The trade deficit has almost doubled for all WB countries, especially in Serbia, Albania and North Macedonia (Figure 5).

Figure 5. China trade balance by WB countries
Source: Authors' calculations based on UN Comtrade, 2021

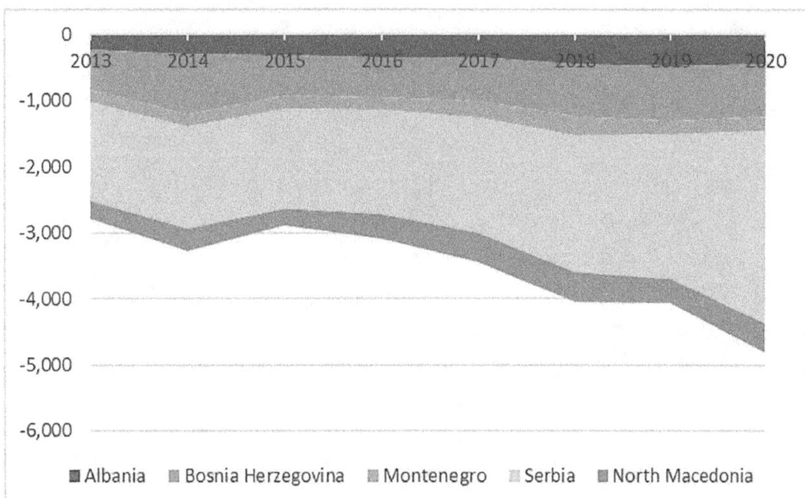

The high value of the trade deficit with China is not specific only to the Western Balkans region, but also to the most of the world economies, as China is the largest producer and the world's largest exporter (Beraha&Jovičić, 2021).

If we analyze each country separately, Serbia is the one that creates the largest trade deficit with China and it is continuously growing. As a contrast of this, other countries have more stable trend in this category. Bosnia and Herzegovina and North Macedonia are countries with higher trade deficits with China, besides Serbia.

It should also be noted that China has become the second or third most important importing partner in the region during the analyzed period. Conclusively, while the EU is still by far the most important partner, China has managed to replace other traditional partners in the region such as Russia or Turkey. (Zweers et al., 2020).

A much more important indicator of the competitiveness of economies is the structure of exports, which is unfavorable for all WB countries, due to the high share of products with lower value added (Beraha & Jovičić, 2021). The insufficient involvement of the Western Balkan economies in the global value chains of Chinese manufacturers and the existence of regulatory barriers have resulted in China's low share in the total foreign trade of the WB countries.

Chinese Investments in WB Countries

The results of the analysis for Chinese investment are similar to those for trade. Chinese investment in the Western Balkans has grown over the years, but despite all the high expectations over the past decade, Chinese investment has not reached a significant level. In the period 2013-2021, Chinese companies invested a total of about 14,000 million dollars in the Western Balkan countries (Figure 6).

Figure 6. Total investments of China in the Western Balkans, 2013-2021
Source: Authors' calculations based on China Global Investment Tracker

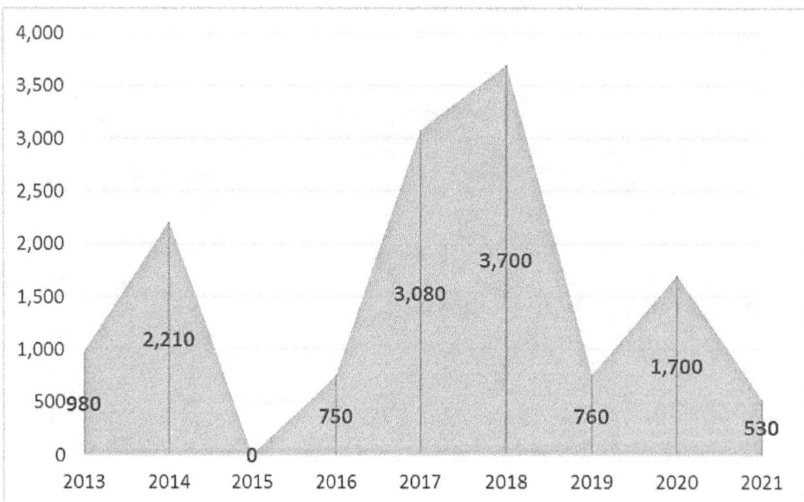

Most of these investments (around 10,000 million dollars) are directed to Serbia (Figure 7). Over the past decade, more precisely in the period after it became a member of the 17+1 cooperation platform in 2012, it has become a center for Chinese loans and investments in the region. It is a key country in terms of Chinese state investment in the Balkans not only because of the important geographical location, but also because of the ability to establish dialogue and cooperation with China. Chinese investments in Serbia are mainly present in the energy, transport and metals sectors.

Figure 7. Distribution of Chinese investments in the Western Balkans, by countries, 2013-2021
Source: Authors' calculations based on China Global Investment Tracker

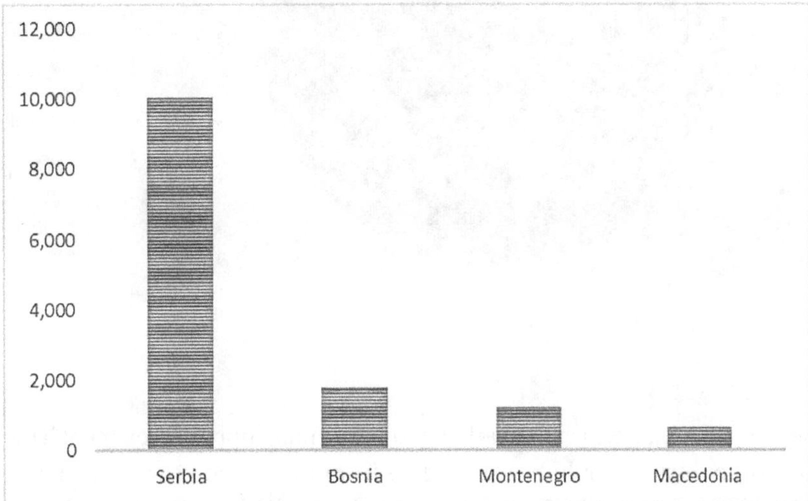

Compared to Serbia, the Chinese influence in Bosnia and Herzegovina is relatively small and Chinese investments are present on a much smaller scale. In this country the investments are mainly made in the field of infrastructure and energetics.

In Montenegro, as well, the Chinese companies are usually interested in investing in energetics and infrastructure, but the biggest project is the highway, which is not really an investment but a huge loan. It is almost the largest loan Montenegro has ever taken and the largest project Montenegro has ever implemented. The country borrowed 809 million euros from China's Exim Bank to finance the highway, which has significantly increased its public debt (Tamás, et. al, 2021).

Figure 8. Distribution of Chinese investments in the Western Balkans, by sectors, 2013-2021
Source: Authors' calculations based on China Global Investment Tracker

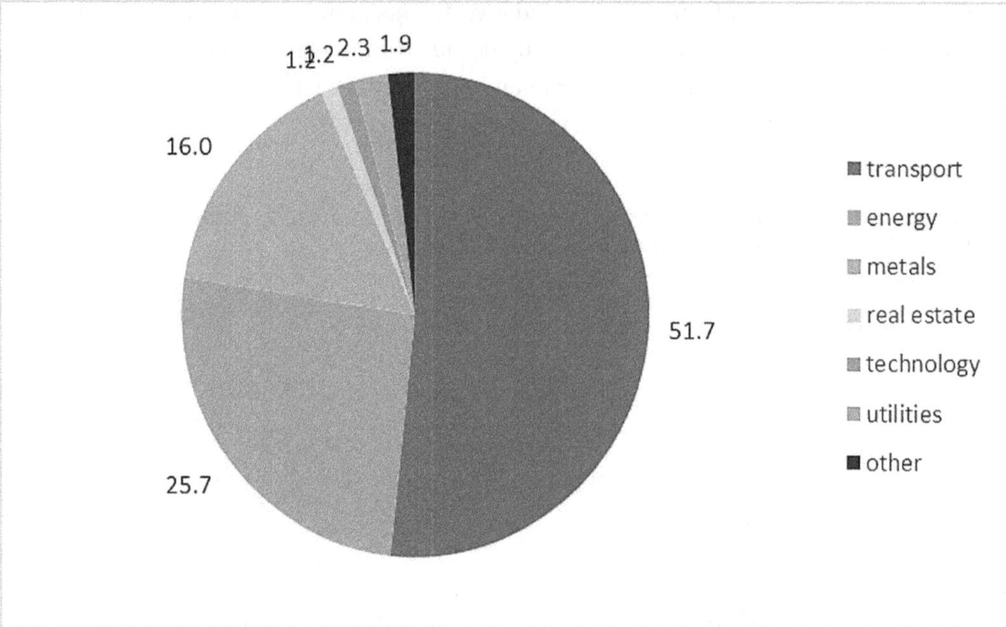

When it comes to Albania, data is not available in the China Global Investment Tracker database, so comments about this country are only based on data from the Chinese investments in the Central and Eastern Europe Data Set. Albania is the only country in the Western Balkans that has not registered any Chinese investments in the last five years, i.e. from 2016 onwards. It also remains the only Western Balkan country where Chinese companies have not won any tender for public works in infrastructure. The highest level of investment in this country was reached in September 2016, when the Chinese company Geo Jade Petroleum Corporation paid 300 million Euros for the concession for oil extraction at the Patos-Marinza Oil field, the largest oil production field in the country.

The investments from China in North Macedonia will be analyzed in more details in the next part of this chapter.

So, the conclusion is that no country in the WB region, except Serbia, has received the much-coveted Chinese investment and China is not the largest investor in any of the countries in the region.

Looking at the industries in which Chinese investments are put during the period from 2013 to 2021, the dominant share is played by the sectors: transport-with nearly 52%; energetics-with about 26% and metals- nearly 16%. The other sectors have a minimal contribution (Figure 8).

Another observation is important to have in mind and make a distinction while considering FDI from China to the Western Balkans. That is the one according to which the Research Report by the Central and Eastern European Center for Asian Studies, it is concluded that often the figures presented by governments tend to include investment plans that have been previously proposed, but have never been implemented by the Chinese side. Others include the cost of infrastructure projects built by Chinese contractors, although the costs are borne by the national government itself. Therefore, according to this research, it is emphasized that infrastructure projects financed by Chinese loans do not fit into the category of foreign direct investment of China, but are investments made by the host country and only financed by a loan that accidentally comes from China. (Tamás, et. al, 2021) Therefore, below is another analysis according to the database which for the first time collects and processes data on Chinese capital in the CEE region.

Figure 9. Infrastructure projects, FDI stocks and the estimated value of actual inflow of Chinese capital to WB countries in EUR millions
Source: Authors' calculations based on Chinese Investment in Central and Eastern Europe Data Set

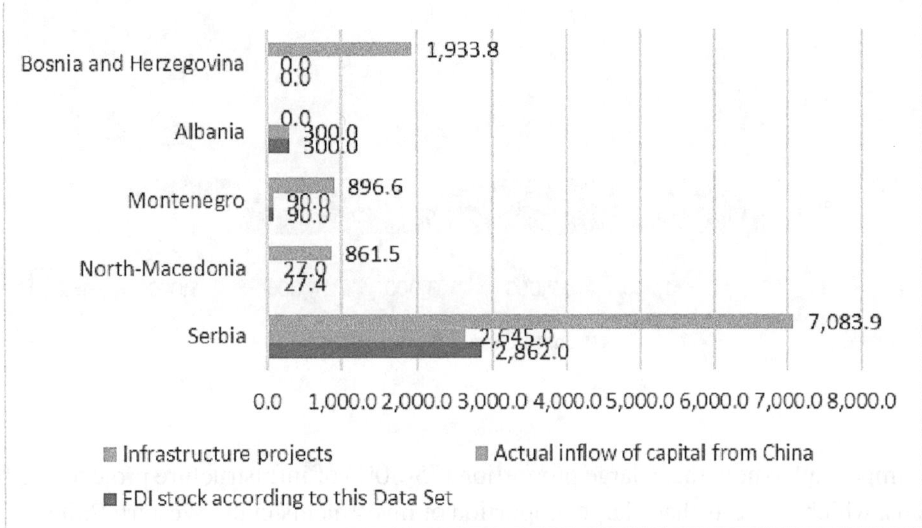

From the data provided in Figure 9, it can be concluded that there are significant differences between the value of infrastructure projects related to China, FDI inventories and the estimated value of the real inflow of Chinese capital in CEE countries. The Figure indicates that in the Western Balkans there is a dominant presence of large construction projects, and FDI figures show a much more limited presence of China in the region.

Furthermore, an important distinction needs to be made between investments that fit into the official FDI category and the actual inflow of Chinese capital into the relevant countries.[2] The Figure shows that the difference between these categories occurs only in Serbia. This means that when real financial inflows are taken into consideration instead of FDI figures (Figure 9), China's relevance is further reduced in most WB countries.

The previous is also confirmed by the data presented below from the China Global Investment Tracker database (Figure 10). This shows that when infrastructure projects and FDI figures are taken into consideration, the value of infrastructure projects greatly distorts the overall picture, as China's presence in the WB focuses mostly on construction rather than actual FDI projects. The only exception is Serbia, where China has managed to gain an important position not only in terms of infrastructure, but also in terms of classic investments such as the M&A and Greenfield projects.

Figure 10. Inflow of China's capital to Western Balkans in the form of investments and infrastructure projects, 2013-2021
Source: Authors' calculations based on China Global Investment Tracker

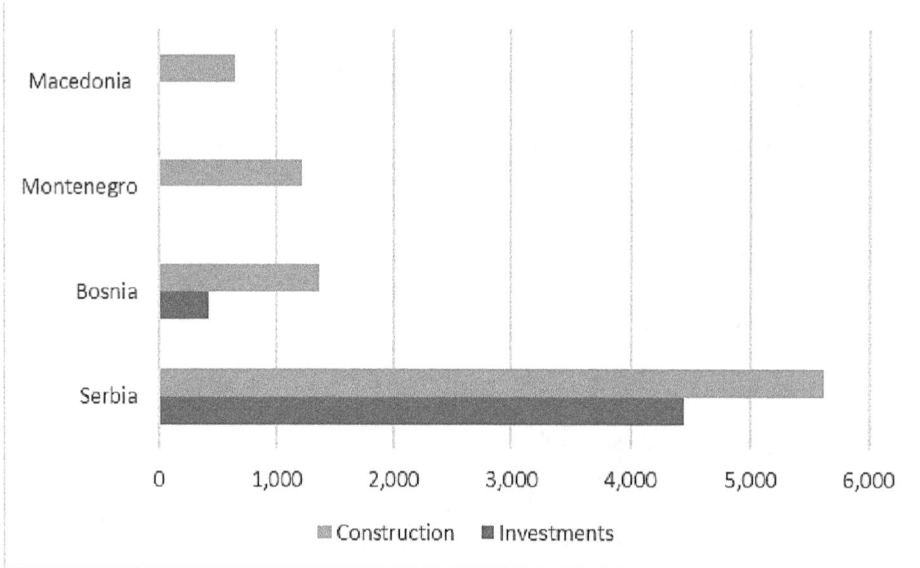

It is also important to note that a large proportion (75-80%) of infrastructure projects are financed by Chinese loans, which suggests that a large proportion of investments in the Western Balkans are actually loans, not investments. This significantly increases the public debt of the countries in the region. The level of loans offered by China can reach 18% of GDP in Montenegro, 12% in Serbia, 10% in Bosnia and Herzegovina and 7% in Northern Macedonia (Tamás, et. al, 2021). Thereby, China holds 22% of Montenegro's total public debt, 14% of North Macedonia's total public debt, 13% of BiH's public debt and 7.9% of Serbia's public debt (Sevba, 2020).

China's Presence in North Macedonia Expressed Through Trade and Investment

Despite the fact that North Macedonia is a small country, with a population of only about two million people, it still remains in the focus of China's interest. The main reason for that is its location on the route of the BRI initiative and possible future membership in the EU, as well as its membership in the WTO, NATO, UN and other organizations. As mentioned before, the 17+1 cooperation platform is the basis on which more opportunities for cooperation with China and the initiation of new investment activities have been opened. In addition, this platform is working on increasing trade, investment and improving infrastructure connectivity, which should enhance cooperation between the two sides. These several key aspects of cooperation between the Macedonian and Chinese economies are the subject of analysis in the following section.

Trade Exchange of the North Macedonia-China Route

The trade exchange between Macedonia and China has a continuity of growth, especially in the last four years of the analyzed period. Its volume in 2020 reached a level of 763.2 million dollars (Figure 11). It is expected that next year all activities on the Macedonia-China route will further contribute to increase this volume.

In 2020, exports were 163.7 million dollars, while imports reached 599.6 million dollars. Unlike imports, exports do not increase at a steady pace and there are significant differences from year to year. In 2020, both imports and exports increased equally by 1.5 times compared to their values in 2013. Thereby, achieving more imports and less exports, Macedonia realizes a negative trade balance which records continuous growth in the analyzed period. (Figure 11)

Figure 11. Trade exchange of North Macedonia with China
Source: Authors' calculations based on UN Comtrade, 2021

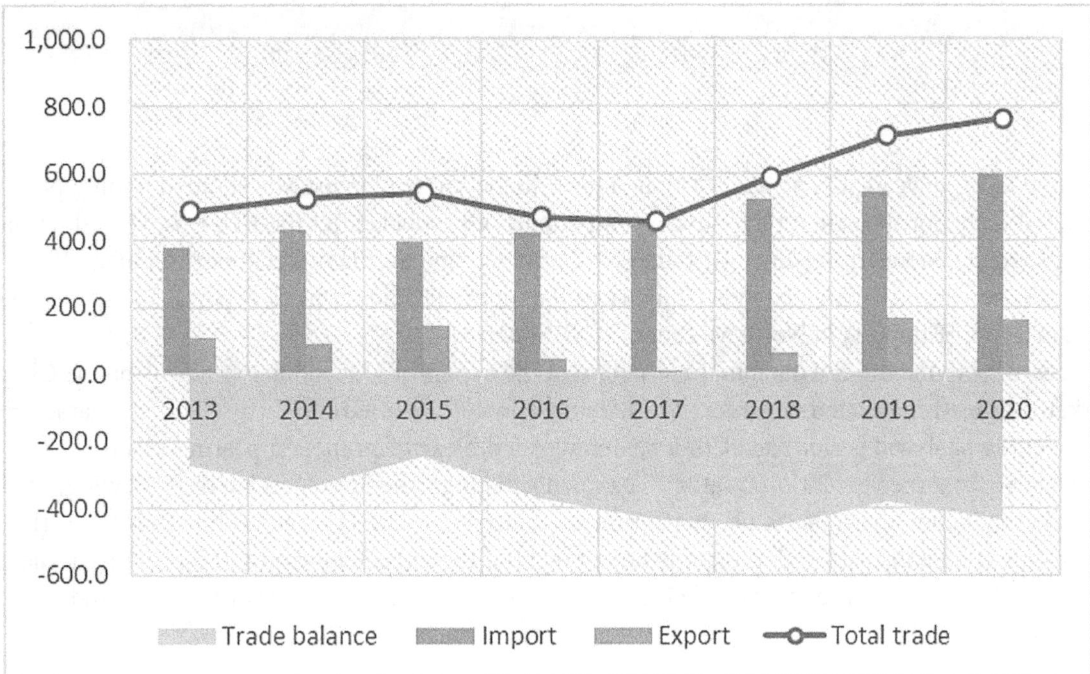

A slight increase was also registered in the share of Chinese trade in the total trade of North Macedonia, especially last year (2020, 5.0%), when the level of 2015 was reached again (Figure 12). However, it must be emphasized that this share is still relatively low.

Figure 12. Share of trade with China in the total trade exchange of North Macedonia
Source: Authors' calculations based on UN Comtrade, 2021

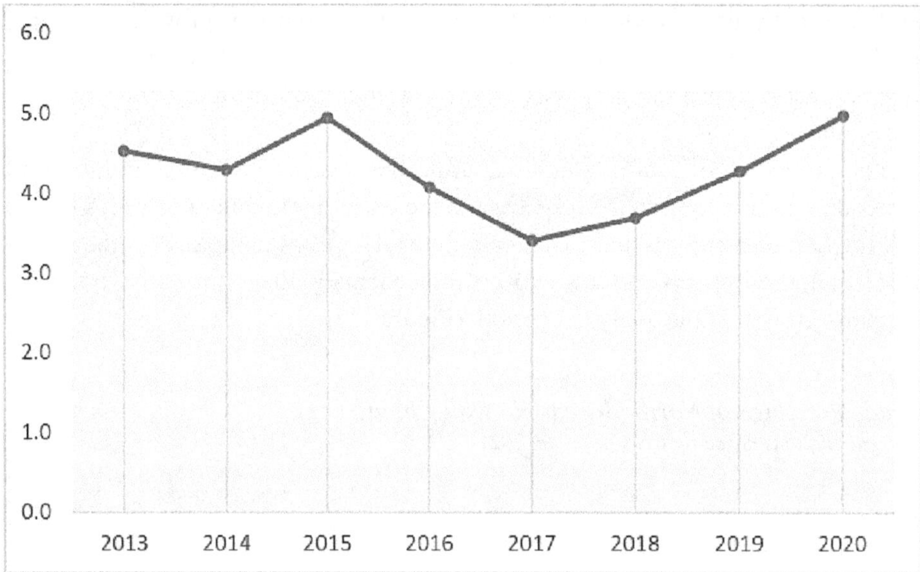

In the last five years, China has positioned itself in the top ten largest Macedonian trading partners. In 2020 it is the forth destination for export and import of products after the EU, Kosovo and Serbia in export segment and after the Great Britain, EU (Germany) and Serbia in the import segment. If the EU countries are viewed separately, then China is on the ninth place in terms of exports, and on the fourth place in terms of imports in North Macedonia (NBStat).

According to the official data, in the structure of the export of Macedonian products on the Chinese market, the most represented sectors are Manufactured goods classified chiefly by material (characteristic for the entire analyzed period) and Crude materials, inedible, except fuel (appearing as a new category of exchange from the year 2017 onwards). The mainly distinguished products are the following: marble, travertine and other limestone, wine, metal products, electrical conductors and automobile parts. (Figure 13) It should be emphasized that there is huge potential for improving exports, especially in the sectors of food and agriculture, metal and chemical industry, as well as in terms of finished products with higher added value.

Figure 13. Export structure of Macedonian products in China according to SMTC, 2013-2020 (percentage share)
Source: Authors' calculations based on National Bank of the Republic of North Macedonia (NBRNM)

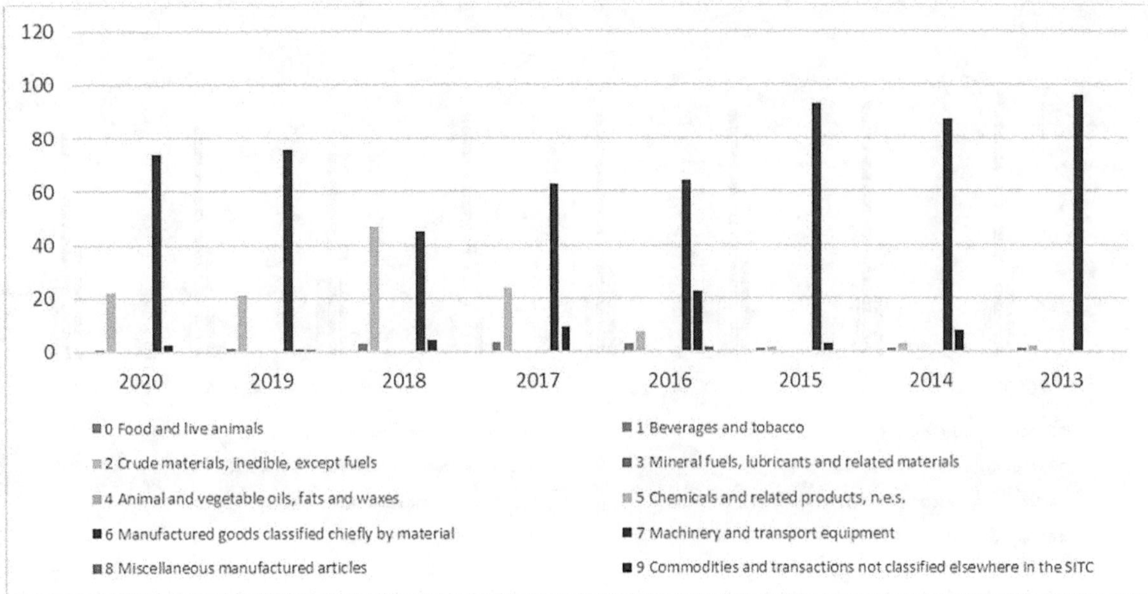

In terms of Macedonian import from China, the sectors of Machinery and transport equipment, Manufactured goods classified chiefly by material and Miscellaneous manufactured articles have the largest share. The most characteristic of these are the following products: machinery, consumer goods, textiles, iron and steel products. These production sectors are constantly present as dominant throughout the analyzed period. (Figure 14)

Figure 14. Import structure of Macedonian products from China according to SMTC, 2013-2020 (percentage share)
Source: Authors' calculations based on NBRNM

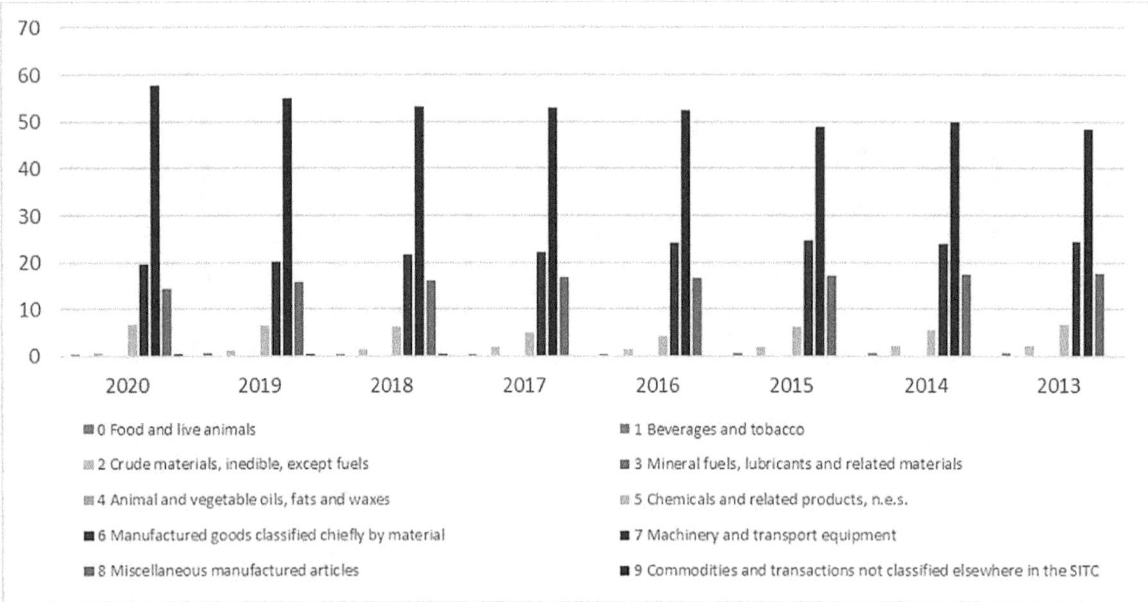

According to the mentioned above, it can be concluded that no significant progress has been made in China's exchange with North Macedonia. In order to correct this situation, the obstacles that need to be overcome and the opportunities that need to be taken to improve the trade exchange should be taken into consideration in future (some of them are listed in the Solutions and Recommendations section).

Investments in North Macedonia from China - Stoks, Flows and Structure

In the last two decades, North Macedonia has made several attempts to attract Chinese investments in the country, but the success was partial. However, the same as in other Western Balkan countries, the interest for investment by Chinese companies in North Macedonia in recent years is growing. As already known, before 2015 they were almost non-existent, but since then there have been occasional small investments, such as smaller greenfield projects and purchase of foreign companies that have shares in the ownership of Macedonian companies.

According to data from the Chinese Investment in Central and Eastern Europe Data Set, these are: the initial Chinese-Turkish investment of Weibo Group in 2015 of 3.4 million euros, out of the total announced 316 million euros of investment that was not realized; the expansion of Joyson Safety Systems - initial brownfield investment in TIDZ, Kichevo in 2015 by the American company Key Safety Systems which was purchased by Ningbo Joyson Electronic Corp, Zhejiang in 2016 and later decided to expand into a greenfield investment in 2017; the acquisition of 51% of Duferco International Trading Holding (LU), the company that owns 81.78% of Makstil Ironworks, by Hebei Group Company Ltd for iron and steel in 2015. Regarding what was previously mentioned, when it comes to greenfield investments, it appears that there are almost no such Chinese investments in the country.

Figure 15. Stoks and flows of FDI from China to North Macedonia
Source: Authors' calculations based on NBRNM

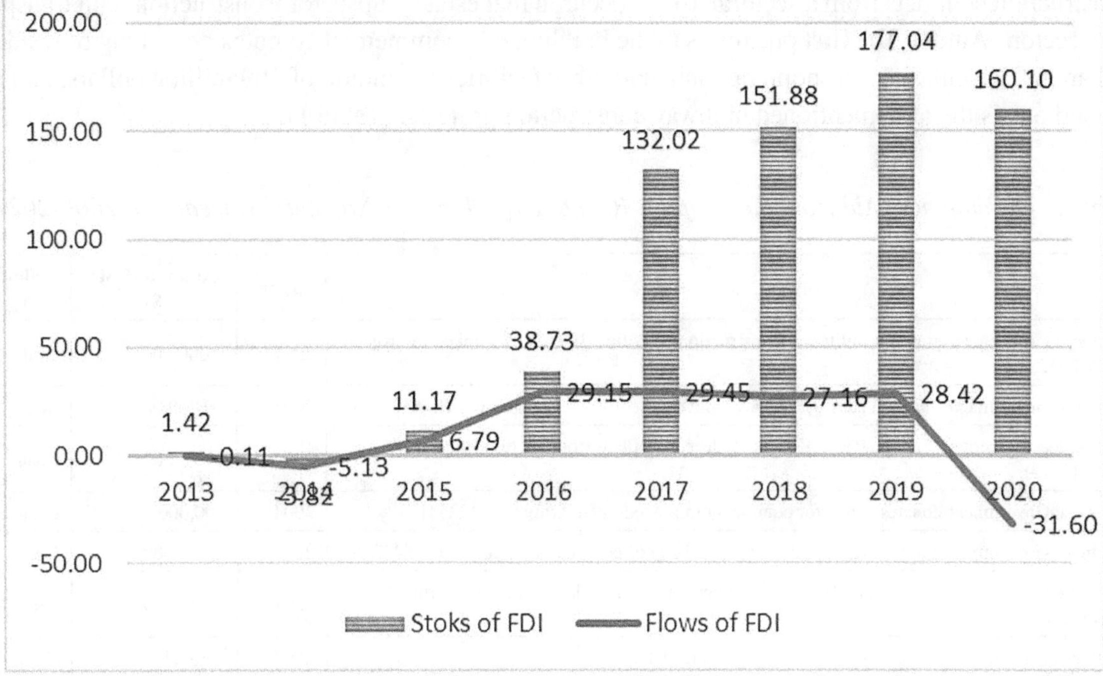

The figures show a steady increase in Chinese investment in the country, especially in the last four years. If in 2013, the cumulative amount of Chinese foreign direct investment was about 1.5 million US dollars, in 2019 they reached 177 million US dollars, and in 2020 their amount, the last available data by NBRNM, it is 160 million US dollars (Figure 15). This represents 2.2% of the total direct investments in the country. It is very likely that such flows are related to Sinohydro - Chinese construction company, that invested in highways Miladinovci - Shtip and Kichevo - Ohrid. These are the two major infrastructure projects initiated at the beginning of the 17+1 cooperation. The section Miladinovci - Shtip was completed in 2019, while the section Kichevo - Ohrid is supposed to be finished in the forthcoming period. Five years overdue due to serious technical issues. The funds for them were provided by the Chinese Export-Import Bank through a $ 10 billion credit line for infrastructure for CEE countries. But already, in recent years, in the recent events related to the 17+1 platform, no new initiatives involving the country have been noticed. Experts say there is very little real interest from China in infrastructure projects in North Macedonia.

Table 1. Chinese investments in the country, by sectors in the field of construction (in million dollars)

	Sector	Subsector	2013	2014	2016	2017	2018	2019	2020	2021
Construction contracts	Real estate	Construction						160		
	Transport	Autos	370	120						

Source: Authors' calculations based on China Global Investment Tracker

According to the data presented earlier in Figure 9 and Figure 10, it is visible that there are mainly Chinese investments in infrastructure/construction, primarily in road construction in the country. Thereby, construction contracts from a sectoral aspect occur in real estate (subsector Construction) and transport (sub sector - Autos). The first one refers to the building of a commercial complex consisting of residential and office buildings, a shopping mall, and other facilities in amount of 160 million dollars, and the second one is the aforementioned highway construction projects. (Table 1)

Table 2. Development Aid from the People's Republic of China for Northern Macedonia (2000-2021)

Project	Year	Amount (USD $)	Flow Type
Chinese Government grant for military reconstruction activities (ID#42239, Linked to Project ID#42242)	2001	1,000,000	Grant
Chinese Government financial package for post-conflict reconstruction activities (ID#42442)	2001	20,000,000	Loan
Credit loan agreement for the 80MW Kozjak Hydropower Plant Construction Project (ID#42247)	2002	89,964,628	Loan
Chinese Government donates computer equipment to Macedonian Army (ID#42254)	2004	500,000	Grant
Chinese Government grant — via ETCA — for provision of computers to schools (ID#42259)	2006	2,500,000	Grant
Chinese Government grant - via ETCA - for projects that will be determined in the future. (ID#42267)	2007	3,144,159	Grant
Chinese Government grant for unspecified projects (ID#42269)	2007	1,337,400	Grant
Chinese Government grant — via ETCA — for unspecified projects (ID#42277)	2008	1,572,080	Grant
Grant for the purposes of developing Macedonian Human Resources (ID#42274)	2008	157,208	Grant
Chinese Government grant for Goce Delcev Primary School Renovation Project (ID#42283)	2010	786,040	Grant
Chinese Embassy donates computers to Macedonia's Ministry of Defense	2011	300,000	Grant
Chinese Government grant — via ETCA — for unspecified projects (ID#42293)	2011	3,100,000	Grant
Chinese Government grant for provision of 23 school buses (ID#42300)	2011	1,320,000	Grant in kind
Hanban funds establishment of Confucius Institute at SS. Cyril and Methodius University (ID#42999)	2013	n/a	Grant
Chinese Government grant for Rajko Zinzifov Primary School Construction Project (ID#42922-Linked to Project ID#42923)	2014	5,030,655	Grant
Chinese Government commits grant funding - via ETCA — for construction of educational facilities - two new kindergartens in the municipalities of Cair and Kisela Voda (ID#42914 - Linked to ID#42923)	2015	5,030,655	Grant
Chinese Government grant for E-Education Project (ID#66762)	2016	7,000,000	Grant
Chinese Government grant — via ETCA — for renovation of schools (ID#85196)	2017	3,144,159	Grant

Source: AidData. 2021. AidData's Global Chinese Development Finance Dataset, Version 2.0. Retrieved from https://www.aiddata.org/data/aiddatas-global-chinese-development-finance-dataset-version-2-0

Conditions with Chinese investments as such are explained by several reasons: insufficient interest from the Chinese side, mismatch of Macedonian supply and Chinese demand, difference in business culture and insufficient mutual knowledge, lack of institutional capacity, and interest in cooperation with China. Considering that at the moment, China has the most infrastructural activities and projects, Macedonia should be promoted in the future as a destination for direct investments.

The country, as well, realizes much more donations and cooperation agreements with China (medical, military and cultural) than real projects and investments. (Table 2) China has a huge interest in such projects, which are not going to be called investments, and which are of vital importance for North Macedonia as a country, because they are basically public contracts for which the state either borrows or announces procurement with budget funds. This is matching with China's global strategy.

SOLUTIONS AND RECOMMENDATIONS

After perceiving the current situation in the Macedonian-Chinese cooperation, both in trade and investment, it can be emphasized that there is a huge potential for its improvement and maximization of benefits. Namely, high quality agricultural products, industrial products and services are the three key sectors in which China wants to import foreign products in future. These are all areas where Macedonia has great potential for future cooperation with China, along with infrastructure and tourism (Krstinovska, 2020b). The potential opportunities for future cooperation in these segments will be considered in the forthcoming text.

In the area of infrastructure, there are still a number of open issues and needs to be met, especially in the railway traffic along Corridor 10. As an example, the railway route throughout the country is old and needs to be reconstructed and a number of issues need to be addressed to maximize its use. Even if modernization is achieved, sustainable solutions for the operation of the railway system will have to be implemented in the future. Given the level of debt in the country, it will be necessary to find appropriate creative sources for its financing (in addition to traditional lending).

Despite the increasement in the number of Chinese tourists in the country in recent years (Krstinovska, 2020b), there is still a great field for improvement. This could be achieved through the development of content and measures that will make the country more attractive to Chinese tourists, especially by developing and promoting alternative types of tourism.

As shown in Figure 14, exports of agricultural and food products as well as tobacco account increased for less than 4% of exports to China. These data also indicates that so far wine is the only food product that has managed to enter the Chinese market. Regarding to what has already been mentioned and on the other hand knowing that food imports are becoming an increasingly popular activity in China, all this points to the significant market opportunity that opens up for the country to export these products to China. To take advantage of this opportunity, special care should be focused on being sure that the food is healthy and organic, as well as to offer products with a controlled label of origin. Moreover, Macedonian products need to be branded and properly advertised and at the same time liked by Chinese consumers, so they will be attractive to them. In the country, the Rural Development Program (2021-2027) envisages measures to support these activities which consist of co-financing the costs incurred for such and similar activities (National Strategy for Agriculture and Rural Development for the period 2021-2027, 2021).

Some analysis show that according to the increased production capacity and increased exports in recent years, the most prominent industrial sectors in North Macedonia that have an export potential to China are the Mechanical and Electrical industry, as well as the Metal industry, followed by the Chemical industry (Krstinovska, 2020b). In accordance with the above, it can be emphasized that the data from Figure 13 showes that metal products are already one of the most exported from North Macedonia to China. This indicates that in the future there is space for deepening export activities related to these products, i.e. there is still great potential that can be used. Furthermore, the data showed that the export of chemical products to China is currently small and insignificant, so these products, in some way, can also be considered as potential export products in the future.

Regarding the services, it can be said that they are a marginal part of the Macedonian export to China. This segment leaves space for deepening cooperation between the two countries because:

- on one hand, China, with its increasing development, is shifting to the production of more complex products with higher added value and is becoming an outsourced country, and
- on the other hand, North Macedonia has become an attractive destination for outsourcing, especially in ICT services due to cheaper and skilled labor.

North Macedonia, in general, and in order to facilitate the previous, in the near future should develop an appropriate policy for China that will define its priorities in terms of bilateral cooperation, BRI and 17+1. At the same time, in order to use the above-mentioned opportunities easier and more effectively, has to remove the obstacles, especially in the areas with great potential for cooperation, and to overcome the biggest challenges. These are: access to information, lack of institutional support, production volume and branding of products, language and cultural barriers, mistrust and risk of fraud. Elements that need to be worked upon in the future in order not to complicate more the cooperation are: trade and investment barriers, such as tariffs, bureaucracy, non-transparency and complex regulation, as well as different product standards.

Regarding the recommendations that would apply to the entire WB region and in order to make more successful use of the opportunities offered by China the following should be taken in consideration:

- encouraging the inclusion of the Western Balkan countries in the global value chains of Chinese manufacturers, increasing the added value in exports and removing regulatory barriers as well as trade barriers in the form of various standards and bureaucratic procedures.
- given that the WB countries are small and relatively unknown to the average Chinese, with regional cooperation between them and the formulation of a joint regional offer in the field of tourism and investment, WB would become more attractive to Chinese tourists and investors, reduce asymmetry in relation to China, and reduce the incentive for competition that often occurs in these countries.
- In addition to the above, the WB region together with the other regions (Visegrad or the Baltic) that are part of the 17+1 cooperation platform should start considering not only their interests, but also see themselves as part of the wider CEE region, as well as to act together seeking common solutions to common problems.
- knowing that almost all WB countries, except Serbia, have very limited understanding of China in terms of its goals, opportunities, policies and public policies and they need to take certain steps to overcome this. They should also invest in gaining expertise and creating a strategy that will enable policy makers to make informed decisions, be proactive in cooperation and maximize national interests.
- The region's integration into the EU would mean more stability and prosperity, which is essential for Chinese investors and providing export markets. Given that China's interests in the region are predominantly economic in nature, China sees the WB as a region with relatively untapped

economic potential that would further increase if countries became EU members. In this context, each of the countries must work as intensively and dedicatedly as possible to provide membership in the Union.

Fulfillment of at least some of the proposed measures and activities is expected to significantly improve the economic cooperation of the WB countries.

FUTURE RESEARCH DIRECTIONS

According to previous findings, some of the following researches could be extended to the other Central and Eastern European countries as part of the BRI initiative and the 17+1 cooperation platform. The comparative aspect with a larger group of countries would have a greater contribution in finding conceptual solutions for advancing the cooperation with China. It could be aimed at identifying the measures used by Central and Eastern European countries to secure new investments, the directions they take to see what the constraints are and how to overcome them. All these in order for these countries to be able to attract even more Chinese investments in the cforthoming period. It will also help determine the direction for conducting the economic and investment policy of these countries.

Moreover, analysis so far has shown that with the launch of this initiative, China has begun investing heavily in infrastructure projects in the Balkans to use the region to bring its goods into Europe, with most real FDI evading. The next process initiated by China in the region, which makes countries more dependent, is the borrowing of those countries. These loans are offered by the China Development Bank and the Export-Import Bank of China for infrastructure investments and have significantly increased the public debt of countries in the region. Hence, the following research could be aimed at assessing how much China really has a real contribution to the region, excluding Serbia. Specifically, to assess, as realistically as possible, the contribution of China using appropriate econometric models. Not only to evaluate and analyze the obvious figures, but also to put them in correlation with the real contribution and growth of the economies in order to see the justification of the future cooperation of these countries with China or it will show that all this is more in China's favor.

Given the importance of the EU for the WB countries, as well as China in achieving its goal, it would be good to assess whether the activities and implementation of projects arising from the BRI initiative in these countries violate EU rules, and if is so to analyze common possible solutions. The research can be expanded to assess in which segments and how the EU and China could start a discussion on cooperation in the WB and thus contribute to faster development of the region. In doing so, their approaches can be complementary in several areas.

CONCLUSION

The inclusion of the Western Balkan countries in the BRI initiative and the 17+1 cooperation platform has resulted in improved economic cooperation with China. However, the analysis shows that although trade and investment have grown over the years, they have not reached a significant level and still have relatively modest values. An exception to this is Serbia as China's strategic partner in the region.

Thereby, trade is strongly in favor of China, i.e. the countries of the Western Balkans register a continuous deficit in trade with China. The structure of exports is unfavorable for all WB countries, given the high share of products with lower value added. Moreover, the insufficient involvement of the Western Balkan economies in the global value chains of Chinese manufacturers, the existence of regulatory barriers as well as various standards and bureaucratic procedures have resulted in China's low share in total WB foreign trade.

Structurally, Chinese investments are present in the energy, transportation and metals sectors. At the same time, the WB region has become a major destination for Chinese infrastructure investments, but not for real FDI projects. These infrastructure projects are mostly financed by loans, which shows that a large part of investments in the Western Balkans are actually loans and not investments that increase the debt of economies.

Such situations are explained by several reasons: insufficient interest of the Chinese side, mismatch of the country's supply and Chinese demand, difference in business culture and insufficient mutual knowledge and lack of institutional capacity, as well as interest in cooperation with China.

Despite the increased potential for cooperation with China since the beginning of the PIP initiative and the 17+1 cooperation platform, the WB countries, including North Macedonia, have so far failed to maximize the benefits. Relationships for enhanced cooperation are in place, but additional steps need to be taken to maximize benefits. In order to use the opportunities for future cooperation with China more easily and effectively. It is also necessary to remove the obstacles, especially in the areas with great potential for cooperation, and to overcome the biggest challenges. All these obstacles and challenges are detailed in the chapter above.

REFERENCES

AidData. (2021). *AidData's Global Chinese Development Finance Dataset, Version 2.0*. Retrieved from https://www.aiddata.org/data/aiddatas-global-chinese-development-finance-dataset-version-2-0

Beraha, I., & Jovičić, E. (2021). *Uticaj pandemije Covid-19 na spoljnotrgovinsku razmenu između Kine i zemalja ZapadnogBbalkana [Impact of the Covid-19 pandemic on foreign trade between China and the Western Balkans] In Makroekonomska stabilnost i unapređenje konkurentnosti zemalja Zapadnog Balkana [Macroeconomic stability and improving the competitiveness of the Western Balkans]*. Institute of Economic Sciences China Global Investment Tracker. https://www.aei.org/china-global-investment-tracker/

Domazet, I., & Marjanovic, D. (2017). *Foreign Direct Investment in the Function of Economic Development - Example of Selected Countries in the Western Balkans. In International Letters of Social and Humanistic Sciences* (Vol. 79). SciPress Ltd.

Domazet, I., & Marjanović, D. (2018) Foreign Direct Investment and Economic Development: Comparative Analysis of Bulgarian, Romanian and Serbian Economies. In Western Balkans Economies in EU Integration: past, present and future. CEMAFI International Association.

Jacimovic, D., Dragutinović Mitrović, R., Bjelić, P., Tianping, K., & Rajkovic, M. (2018). The role of Chinese investments in the bilateral exports of new E.U. member states and Western Balkan countries, *Economic Research - Ekonomska Istrazivanja, 31*(1), 1185–1197. doi:10.1080/1331677X.2018.1456357

Jovičić, E., Stevanović, S., & Beraha, I. (2020). Serbia-China Bilateral Trade Relations: Major Challenges and Opportunities. *Economic Analysis*, *53*(2), 133–144.

Krstinovska, A. (2020a). The place of North Macedonia in China's strategy for the Western Balkans. Konrad-Adenauer-Stiftung, Office in Skopje.

Krstinovska, A. (2020b). The business dimension of the Belt and Road Initiative: case study on Macedonian companies. ESTIMA.

Mardell, J. (2020). *China's Economic Footprint in the Western Balkans*. Bertelsmann Stiftung. https://www.bertelsmann-stiftung.de/en/our-projects/germany-and-asia/news/asia-policy-brief-chinas-economic-footprint-in-the-western-balkans

Marjanović, D., & Domazet, I. (2021). Foreign Direct Investments: A Key Factor for Business Globalization. In Handbook of Research on Institutional, Economic, and Social Impacts of Globalization and Liberalization. IGI Global

Mirel, P. (2019). *European Union- Western Balkans: for a revised membership negotiation framework*. https://www.recom.link/ european-union-western-balkans-for-a-revisedmembership-negotiation-framework

National Strategy for Agriculture and Rural Development for the period 2021-2027. (2021). Ministry of Agriculture, Forestry and Rural Development.

NBStat, National Bank of the Republic of North Macedonia. (n.d.). http://makstat.stat.gov.mk/PXWeb/pxweb/mk/MakStat/MakStat__NadvoresnaTrgovija__DetalniPod__DetKumSMTK/150_SMTK_ZEMJI_ml.px/table/tableViewLayout2/?rxid=9f41cd3f-fff2-4841-a0f7-1e2345cf5ed5

Sevba, A. (2020). *With weak pandemic management West opens door to China's influence in Balkans*. https://www.aa.com.tr/

Tamás, M. (2021). *Chinese Investment in Central and Eastern Europe - A reality check*. Central and Eastern European Center for Asian Studies.

Tamás, M., Ágnes, S., Andrijauskas, K., Bērziņa-Cerenkova, U. A., Brînză, A., Filipova, R., Karásková, I., Karindi L., Krstinovska, A., Liperi, O., McCaleb, A., Pejič, N., Raditya-Ležaić, A., Turcsányi, R. & Vladisavljev, S. (2021). *Chinese Investment in Central and Eastern Europe Data Set*. Central and Eastern European Center for Asian Studies.

Turcsanyi, R. (2014). *Central and Eastern Europe's courtship with China: Trojan horse within the EU?* European Institute for Asian Studies. https://www.eias.org/wp-content/uploads/2016/02/EUAsia-at-a-glance-Richard-Turcsanyi-China-CEE.pdf

UN Comtrade. (2002). https://comtrade.un.org/Data/

Vetrovcova, M. (2018). Towards an "Expectations Fulfilment Gap" in 16+1 Relations? China, the EU and the Central and Eastern European Countries. In 16+1 Cooperation and China–EU Relationship. Budapest: China-CEE Institute.

White Paper China's Peaceful Development. (2011). *Information Office of the State Council*. http://www.gov.cn/english/official/2011-09/06/content_1941354.htm

Zeneli, V. (2020). *The Western Balkans: Low Hanging Fruit for China?* https://thediplomat.com/2020/02/the-western-balkans-low-hanging-fruit-for-china/

Zhou, Y. (2004). *China's Diplomacy*. China Intercontinental Press.

Zweers, W., Shopov, V., Van der Putten, F., Petkova M., & Lemstra M., (2020). *China and the EU in the Western Balkans, A zero-sum game?* Clingendael Report.

ADDITIONAL READING

Blazheska, A. (2019). *BRI – potential for economic cooperation between China and the Western Balkans: the case of the Republic of Macedonia*. http://www.crpm.org.mk/wp-content/uploads/2019/01/China-BRI-Macedonia-FINAL-1.docx

Holzner, M., & Schwarzhappel, M. (2018). *Infrastructure Investment in the Western Balkans: A First Analysis*. European Investment Bank.

Krstinovska, A. (2020). *From Rule-Taker to Rule-Shaper? China's Changing Global Role and its Implications for the Western Balkans*. Konrad-Adenauer-Stiftung Office in North Macedonia & ESTIMA.

Nechev, Z., & Nikolovski, I. (2020). Hustled Into a Dead End: The Delusional Belief In Chinese Corrosive Capital for the Construction of North Macedonia's Highways. Center for International Private Enterprise & Institute for Democracy "Societas Civilis" – Skopje.

Tonchev, P. (2017). *China's Road: into the Western Balkans*. European Union Institute for Security Studies (EUISS).

KEY TERMS AND DEFINITIONS

Belt and Road Initiative (BRI): Is one of the most ambitious global initiative created by the People's Republic of China in 2013. It has intention to connect Asia with Africa and Europe trough the land and maritime networks and open up significant potential for economic cooperation with many countries in many areas. the Belt and Road Initiative aims to carry out major infrastructure projects, financial integration, trade facilitation, as well as to achieve cooperation in other areas.

Cooperation Platform 17+1: Is cooperation mechanism with the countries of Central and Eastern Europe (CEE) that China has been leading since 2012. It holds regular annual summits, which establishes and maintains close relations at the institutional level. This platform for cooperation includes the 11 CEE member states (Bulgaria, Croatia, Estonia, Hungary, Latvia, Lithuania, Poland, Romania, Slovakia, Slovenia, and the Czech Republic) and 5 countries from the Western Balkans (Albania, Bosnia and Herzegovina, Montenegro, North Macedonia and Serbia). In 2019, Greece also joined this platform.

FDI Stocks and Flows: FDI Stocks are the total accumulated level of direct investment at the end of a given period (usually quarter or year). FDI flows are transactions recorded during the reference period (usually year or quarter). They are a measure of transactions that change FDI stock over a specific period of time. FDI flows can be negative in certain cases.

Foreign Direct Investment (FDI): Is the acquisition of a significant share in a foreign business or its full purchase in order to expand operations in a new region. FDI alows lasting interest in or effective control over an enterprise operating outside of the economy of the investor. Greenfield and brownfield investments are two different types of foreign direct investment.

Infrastructure Projects: Infrastructure project means the design, construction and development of a new facility or the renovation, modernization, or expansion of existing facilities; as well as development and maintenance of services and systems. Financing for them can be provided by private companies, public companies or combined through a public-private partnership.

International Trade: Is the exchange of goods and services between countries, allowing them to expand their products to other markets and access goods and services that are not available in their domestic markets.

Investment: Is the investing of money or capital in order to gain profitable returns, as interest, income, etc.

Western Balkan Countries: Are located in the western part of the Balkan Peninsula and not yet EU member states. These include Serbia, Bosnia and Herzegovina, Northern Macedonia, Albania, and Montenegro.

ENDNOTES

1 Currently 17+1 with the addition of Greece in 2019.

2 According to international statistic standards all Chinese owned companies are considered Chinese direct investment, not regarding the method or type of acquisition. That is, whenever a company from China acquires a multinational company (MNC), the subsidiaries of that MNC in the CEE region are henceforth automatically recategorized as Chinese investment, although the purchase price was transferred to a third country. Based on this logic, it makes sense to exclude all international M&A transactions from the list of China's investments in the region and to deduct the value of such transactions from the value of FDI figures to get a more realistic view of the level of Chinese economic activity in the CEE countries (Tamás, et. al, 2021).

Section 3

Chapter 12
Foreign Direct Investment During the COVID-19 Lockdown

Karima Toumi Sayari
https://orcid.org/0000-0001-7564-022X
Al-Zahra College for Women, Oman

ABSTRACT

Foreign direct investment has been proven to be an essential element in stimulating economic growth in developing countries. Foreign direct investment has several benefits: the transfer of technology and knowledge, improving management capacity, increasing employment, improving competitiveness, and achieving a favorable balance of payments. Because of these advantages, countries are keen to attract more FDI. In this sense, the authors assess the extent to which the lockdown during the COVID-19 era may have affected FDI inflows. In addition, they explore the new role played by foreign investment promotion agencies in terms of updating FDI policies and implementing new ones—digital policies—to boost FDI entry.

INTRODUCTION

Foreign Direct Investment (FDI) has long been regarded as a powerful engine of growth, trade, and economic expansion. FDI flows are among the main driving forces of globalization (Hobbs et al., 2021). They are central to the restructuring of the global economy. The growth of multinational enterprise (MNE) activity in foreign direct investment has outperformed more than any other type of international capital flow (UNCTAD, 2020).

Given the critical role of multinational corporations, developing countries increasingly consider FDI as a basis for economic development, modernization, income growth, and job creation. In addition to the firmly economic advantages, FDI may assist in improving environmental and social circumstances in the host country by, for example, transferring technology and leading to additional socially responsible business strategies. International trade flows, spillovers, and other externalities concerning FDI entries (Nguyen et al., 2019).

DOI: 10.4018/978-1-7998-8021-9.ch012

Furthermore, FDI promotes growth through increasing total factor productivity and, more broadly, the receiving economy's resource usage efficiency. Regarding this multitude of advantages, all countries, mainly developing ones, are facing increasing competition to attract FDI flows. This competition has intensified in an uncertain international environment. The relative importance of FDI mobilization factors has changed. Today's determining factors for attracting IDE are different from what they were in the past. As a result, foreign investors are more interested in differences in institutional structures between countries. In addition to economic factors, foreign investors are increasingly focused on the quality of institutions and public policies in their host countries. Transparent policies and organizations that effectively implement these policies are critical factors attracting IDE.

Several factors have encouraged the development of FDI and some of which are related to the institutional framework of the country:

- An economic and political environment is more favorable.
- Some countries, mainly developing ones, were also trying to attract foreign capital by offering favorable tax conditions.
- The reduction of barriers to trade and investment has favored FDI, especially those assigned to the strategies called "horizontal," in which companies want to produce in the foreign market.
- Technical innovations are an essential factor for FDI development in recent decades. More complex production processes can take the form of vertical integration in the industry field, through investments in various stages of the production process and the establishment of an internationally integrated production chain. In the case of a company with research and development capabilities and a portfolio of trademarks, economies of scale will be achieved by a leading position on the international market and the geographical dispersion of patent exploitation and trademarks;

Recently, the COVID 19 crisis has intensified, more than any other time, the need for new and adapted policies to the needs of foreign investors. With their investment promotion Agencies, the government has to alleviate the impact of this crisis. Implementing new facilities and regulations and mainly digitalizing policies during the crisis makes communication easy, reassuring investors and updating them with any news during and after the COVID.

The chapter starts with a review of FDI determinants by concentrating on the role of the institutional framework and investment climate because these determinants—in the opposite of traditional or economic ones- are under the control of government and policymakers who are responsible for adapting their regulations and FDI policies according to new circumstances. Indeed, by nature, institutions are flexible and are in continuous change, and can be adapted to new conditions. Then a description of the FDI trend during the last three-decade from 1990 to 2020 will be in section two. The objective is to see the relationship between FDI flows (increase /decrease) in parallel with the evolution of the international institutional framework. By focusing on the influence of the COVID 19 crisis as the most severe economic recession in the decade 2010-2020. This descriptive analysis will be followed by investment policy responses to the COVID-19 crisis. What is the government and Investment Promotion Agencies' role in facing this crisis and how do they manage to keep attracting foreign investors during and after this crisis. The last part of the chapter will deal with the digitalization of FDI policies as a need to alleviate the impact of the crisis and keep contacting and providing. The challenges experienced by IPAs throughout the world, the actions they have taken to respond to the epidemic, and the experiences of some countries will be discussed in this part.

METHODOLOGY

To analyze the FDI during the lockdown, the chapter utilizes a descriptive method through tables and figures taken from World Investment Report in different years accompanied with a literature review. Based on previews studies, a literature review has been made by focusing on institutional framework. In fact, Since the late 1990s, the literature on economic development has emphasized institutional quality as the primary factor explaining the difference between countries in terms of attractiveness to FDI. Table 1 summarizes factors affecting opportunities and incentives to invest for companies in terms of cost, risk and obstacle to competition.

Figure 1 shows the global trend from the 2015 to 2022 forecast and figure 2 shows FDI inflows by region to analyze the FDI trend. Since the COVID 19 crisis, recent data has evidenced the direct impact of COVID 19 on FDI as illustrated by figure 3: effect of the Pandemic on FDI. The impact manifests in a slowdown of ongoing projects due to site closures; cross borders mergers and acquisitions, and a drop in new investment decisions. Figures 4 and 5 also support the impact by comparing the evolution of total COVID-19 cases number of cases (figure 4) and the global FDI flow. The increase in cases during 2020-2021 was accompanied by a drop in FDI flows (figure 5). Despite the fact that the majority of countries and regions were impacted, Africa was the most affected one. Table 2 summarizes the pandemic impact on countries by selected economic groupings. The effect of COVID-19 on international private investment in SDGs was also showed in figure 6. It lists the investment policy instruments for responding to the Pandemic. The table exhibits the policy action in different investment policy areas and the appropriate policy measures taken. Adopting digital policies is among the urgent and effective measures to combat the Pandemic. Figures 7 and 8 display the digital FDI Initiative by balancing and connecting digital investment supply and demand and also the importance of developing a digital FDI framework.

This change towards digitalization cannot be performed only with the role of IPAs. World Association of Investment Promotion Agencies surveyed to get the initial action taken (IPAs) towards the COVID-19 Pandemic. The survey results showed that 87% of IPAs are assisting their clients throughout the Pandemic. Figure 9 summarizes the support offered by IPAs to their clients during the COVID-19.

Sabir et al. (2019) also investigated the impact of institutional quality on FDI (FDI) in both developing and developed countries. The empirical results confirm that institutional quality positively impacts FDI in all groups of countries.

LITERATURE REVIEW

Determinants of FDI

The determinants of FDI have changed over time (Bénassy-Quéré *et al.*, 2007). While economic determinants (market size, natural resources, labor cost, and good physical infrastructure) have affected FDI in many economies for long periods, FDI is progressively looking for a localization endowed with good institutional infrastructure, with a stable environment and appropriate policies (Asongu et al., 2018). The key fact is that, as we will see later, foreign investors are more interested in the stability, quality of institutions, and essentially in the capability to adapt to any new circumstances. This has implications on how policies can set an attractive investment climate.

Dunning was the pioneer of the FDI determinants theory known as the Paradigm OLI. This theory outlines three motives for a company to invest overseas. The theory combines three types of advantages: ownership-specific (O), location-specific (L), and internalization (I) specific advantages. The ownership-specific (O), location-specific (L), and internalization (OLI) Paradigm is an attempt to create an overall framework to explain why MNEs choose FDI rather than assist overseas markets via alternative models such as licensing and exporting.

Ownership advantage makes an exploitative advantage to be used in international markets. This advantage enables the firm to meet global competition and benefit from available opportunities using their existing competitive advantages to found affiliates abroad.

Location advantages address the question 'where to invest"? These advantages are specific to the host country. The FDI destination market must offer factors (land, capital, know-how, cost/ quality of labor, economies of scale) and institutional infrastructure that are advantageous for the firm to locate its investment there. **Internalization advantage** addresses the question "How to go abroad?" transaction costs of an entry mode like licensing, exports-- higher than managing the activity within the MNC's boundaries. It must be more profitable to use these advantages combined with factors located abroad; otherwise, foreign markets would be entirely served by exports (Dunning, 1992).

FDI growth has been accompanied by broad empirical research to establish an empirical link between the entry of FDI and a set of explanatory variables. For the last few decades, the relationship between institutions and FDI entry has concerned responsiveness from researchers and policymakers. The majority of these studies share the same objective, which is to see the importance of institutions for the entry of FDI in developing countries. Different parametric methods have been used: cross-section regressions, panel estimation methods, time series econometric analysis, etc. They searched to explain the entry of FDI by different factors. These reflect the economic, political, social, and institutional characteristics of a country. The dependent variable (IDE) is not always the same. Some studies use FDI flows. Others use the stock instead. Some studies use FDI in absolute terms; others use FDI as a percentage of GDP (Beugelsdijk, 2010). These differences between studies, coupled with samples from different countries and periods, largely influence the results obtained.

Globerman & Shapiro (2002) found that governance infrastructure has a significant and positive impact on FDI, an essential determinant for FDI. Bénassy-Quéré et al. (2007) achieved that variables such as corruption, political instability and weak institutions negatively affect the FDI entry. They conclude that Institutional reforms are significant because they help reduce corruption while also providing more transparency and security to investors.

Naudé (2004) revealed that flows of FDI to Africa are less affected by variables related to the economic policy since the economic variables do not have a great effect on FDI except for the export variable. However, the variables related to institutional quality better explain FDI to Africa.

The quality of institutions is important for FDI entry, mainly for developing countries, for multiple reasons. First, poor legal protection of assets rises the expropriation of a firm's assets and discourages investment. Poor quality of institutions necessary for well-functioning markets (and/or corruption) increases the cost of doing business and, as a consequence, diminishes FDI flows. And finally, to the extent that poor institutions lead to poor infrastructure (physical and institutional), probable success decreases, as does FDI into a market.

According to a World Bank examination of the relationship between public institution adequacy and FDI, the result showed that a one-point improvement in institutional adequacy is related to a 23 percent rise in the number of FDI projects (Heilbron & Whyte, 2019).

Sayari (2019) found that FDI entry depends on the quality of institutions. The study developed an institutional index measuring institutions' quality using the DEA method based on governance indicators. Good quality of institutions enhances the attractiveness of countries to investment flows. Galenkova et al. (2018) confirmed the positive impact of institutional factors on the inflow of foreign direct investment in developing countries.

Table 1. Public policies, behavior, and investment decisions - some examples

	Factors Affecting Opportunities and Incentives to Invest for Companies	
	Strong State Influence	**Weak State Influence**
Costs	• Corruption • Taxation • Red tape and bureaucracy. • Financing and infrastructure costs • Labor market regulations	• Price of factors of production on the market • Gap between production factor market and production market. • Economies of scale and potential of certain technologies.
Risks	• Predictability and credibility of public policies. Macroeconomic stability. • Property rights. • Contract execution. • Expropriation	• Responses from competition and consumers. • External shocks • Natural disasters • Supplier reliability
Obstacles to competition	• Regulatory barriers to entry and exit. • Competition law and policies •Well-functioning financial markets. • Infrastructure.	• Market size and differences between factor markets production and production market. • Economies of scale and potential of certain activities

Table 1 recapitulates factors for evaluating opportunities and incentives to invest for companies. Many factors determine the costs, risks, and barriers to competition at a given location. On the other hand, it is challenging to influence factors such as geography. Public authorities can exert more decisive influence over many different aspects of the investment climate, such as the protection of the rights of ownership, Regulation, or taxation, and the quality of infrastructure and the functioning of capital and labor markets.

Companies evaluate the interaction of government policies as part of a broader reflection aiming to act on costs, risks, and barriers to competition associated with certain opportunities. There is an interaction between the public policies implemented in these areas. Thus, the protection of property rights can facilitate access to finance. In addition, the content and impact of related formal policies depend on more general governance characteristics, including corruption and credibility. Tale 1 shows how these three factors can change the attitude of companies towards investment and what their variability is across the world.

Costs

The costs of producing and distributing products affect the range of opportunities expected to be profitable. The number of costs supported by companies is part of the ordinary commercial activity, while others derive directly or indirectly from policies and behavior of public authorities. Tax levies are the most direct apparent costs. However, in many titles, the government plays an essential role in the provision of public goods, supporting infrastructure building, and alleviating other market failures. The way he does, it can strongly influence business costs. Thus, the expenses linked to delinquency, corruption, regulations, infrastructure failures, and difficulty enforcing contracts can represent more than 25% of revenue and triple the standard tax burden. The magnitude and composition of these costs are variables among countries.

Risks

Investment decisions are geared towards the future: it is about allocating resources today, hoping that they will bear fruit tomorrow. Many risks entailed by investment activities investment are part of regular business activity, including consumer reactions and competition. It is, therefore, up to companies to assume them. The government nevertheless plays an essential role in helping companies manage risks related to protecting property rights. But, in some cases, it can, on the contrary, increase the risks and uncertainty with which economic actors are confronted.

Unclear public policy and macroeconomic instability are consistently top factors that make companies reluctant to invest. The unpredictability in the interpretation of Regulation is also of great concern. And almost 95% of companies see a discrepancy between policy formalities and their implementation. It is difficult to assess the impact of risks because not all companies have the same reaction. Some are looking for better returns, others are shortening their planning horizons, yet others are giving up altogether investing. To compensate for the additional risks they take, those operating in certain risky countries require a higher return than the one they would ask for in countries where the risk is lower.

Barriers to Competition

Companies would, eventually, prefer less competition. However, such obstacles to competition that will be beneficial to one will eliminate opportunities and increase the cost to others and consumers. Moreover, competitive pressures are pushing firms to innovate, increase productivity and provide customers and staff with the benefits of these productivity gains. The number of parameters, in particular the economies of scale and the size of the market, can influence the degree of competition in a business segment. The state can also act on competitive pressures by regulating entering and exiting the market and taking action against companies that violate the competition rules. The latter is difficult to measure globally,

Managing the conflict between providing a favorable investment environment for corporations and attaining other social goals is a significant problem for governments. Improving the investment climate does not imply eliminating all costs, risks, and impediments. Taxation and Regulation provide a favorable investment climate while safeguarding larger societal interests.

Global FDI Flows in the Last Three Decades

To better realize the impact of the crisis on the flows of investment, figures will be very helpful. In this section, a review of FDI trends will be performed by focusing on the COVID crisis period. Also, a brief history trend of global flows is done to compare the relevant picks over the three decades.

The 1990s were a period of rapid globalization and outsourcing by MNCs, with FDI in developing nations with cheap labor costs (such as China) playing a pivotal role. The industrialized economies dominated global FDI flows, whereas FDI from developing countries had a minor role in outflows but a much larger part in inflows due to outsourcing.

In 2000 FDI flows reached a peak. From 2003, as their enterprises found chances on global markets through pushing their internationalization process, emerging countries, particularly China, began to play a more important role as outward investors. They recovered in the years after that, reaching new highs in 2007, just before the Global Financial Crisis.

After the Global Financial crisis in 2008/2009 and the Euro crisis closely following in 2010, developed countries' FDI outflows and inflows experienced more ups and downs than in the two decades before. Since 2010, flows to emerging economies have been moderately constant, hovering around $675 billion on average, in a far tighter range than developed nations. The gap between inflows to developing and to developed countries decreased. In 2014 and 2018, developing economies even received more FDI than developed countries did for the first time.

Following important reductions in 2017 and 2018, international FDI flows augmented somewhat in 2019. This year, global FDI flows mounted slightly by 3%, reaching $1.54 trillion. Foreign direct investment (FDI) inflow into developed economies increased by 5% to $800 billion. It was concentrated in Europe (up 18% to $429), although primarily due to increases in a few economies, such as Ireland and Switzerland, following sharply negative inflows in 2018. On the other hand, FDI into several of the region's biggest economies has decreased. The largest receiving economy, the United States, had a 3% drop in FDI to $246 billion. In 2019, the value of net cross-border mergers and acquisitions and announced Greenfield projects fell. The overall value of Greenfield projects decreased by 14% to $846 billion. The main cause was a reduction in average project size, as investment activity defined by the number of projects declined by just 1%.

As a result of the Pandemic's impact, new projects will find it difficult to secure international funding. To prioritize the crisis response, many previously announced projects have been delayed or stopped, and others have been scrapped. The decline in new project announcements was one of the early signals of the impending crisis. That impact was clear globally in April 2020, with a decline of extra than 50% from March and more than 40% from the monthly average in 2019, owing primarily to decreases in developing economies.

The COVID-19 crisis has caused severe economic disruptions, which results in a significant drop in FDI. Global FDI flows are expected to drop by 40% in 2020, compared to $1.54 trillion in 2019. Since 2005, FDI would go below $1 trillion for the first time. In 2021, FDI is expected to drop by another 5–10% before beginning to rebound in 2022. A comeback is possible in 2022, with FDI reverting to the pre-COVID underlying trend, but only at the top bound of forecasts (UNCTAD, 2020). The following figure shows the global tern from the 2015 to 2022 forecast.

Figure 1. Global FDI inflows, 2015-2019 and 2020-2022 forecast (trillions of dollars)
Source: UNCTAD, World Investment Report (2020)

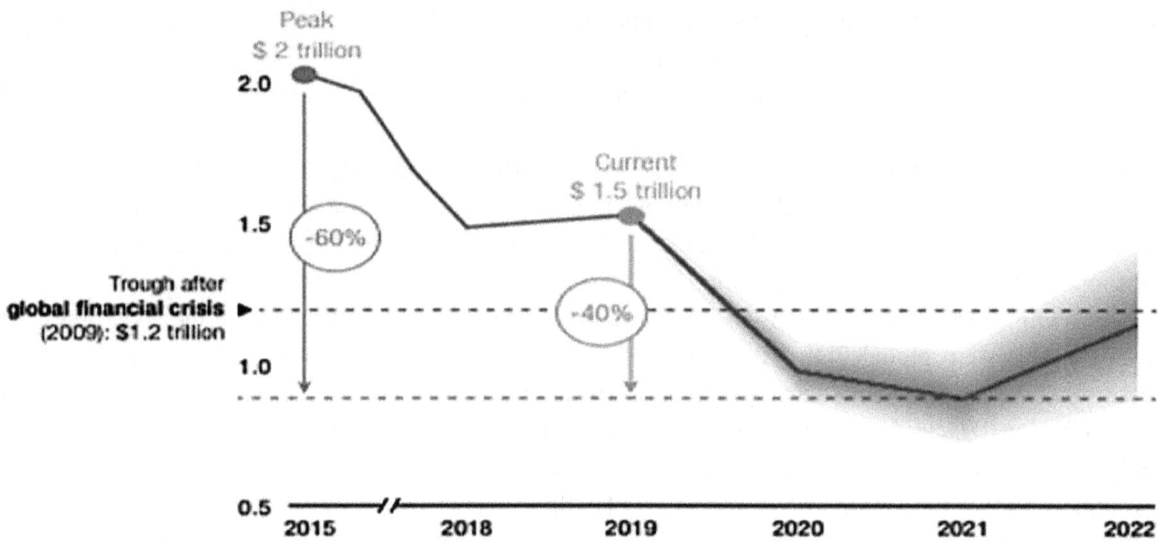

According to the report (UNCTAD, 2020). The fall in FDI was focused in industrialized countries, where flows fell by 69 percent to an estimated $229 billion. FDI flows to emerging nations declined by 12% to $616 billion, but they still represent 72 percent of global FDI, the greatest percentage. Developing economies get a record amount of FDI as well.

The drop was unevenly distributed throughout developing areas, with -37 percent in Latin America and the Caribbean, -18 percent in Africa, and -4 percent in developing Asia. Foreign direct investment (FDI) into transition economies fell by 77 percent to $13 billion.

Figure 2. FDI inflows by region, 2019 and 2020 (billions of US dollars)
Source: UNCIAD, 2020 (Preliminary estimates)

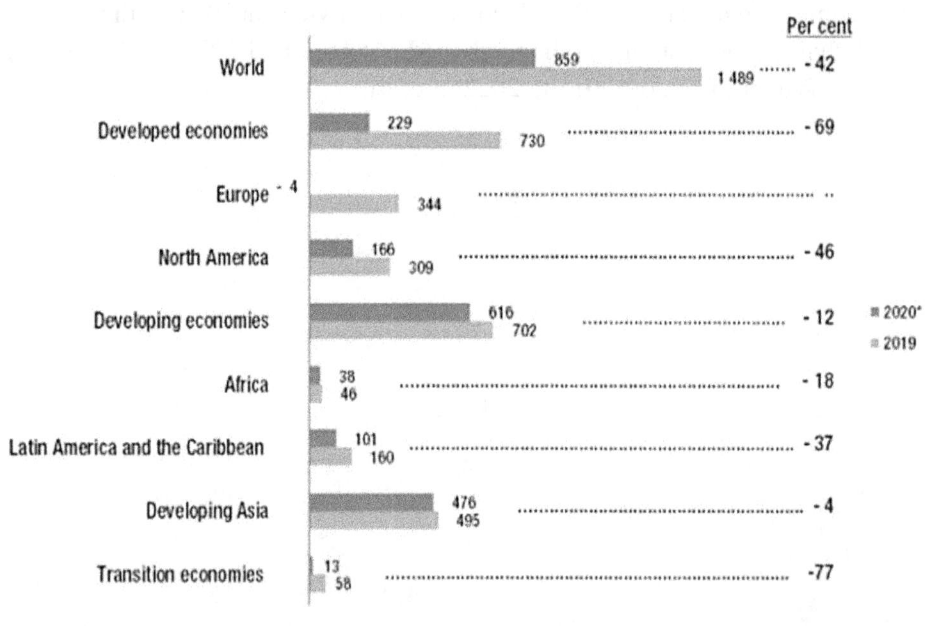

Recent data evidenced the immediate impact of COVID 19 on FDI and might have medium and long-term complications. A range of consequences on FDI is being generated by the unexpected and simultaneous relationship of supply- and demand-side shocks and policy responses to the global crisis (figure 3).

The impact of the crisis is immediate and might continue in the future. Businesses, industrial plants, and construction sites have been shut down to stop the virus from spreading. Investment projects are experiencing immediate delays in execution. Some investments continue, but other expenses are blocked totally.

Greenfield project declarations are also deferred. Similarly, numerous mergers and acquisitions (M&As) have been put on hold for the time being. M&As, like greenfield initiatives, are often long-term investments in foreign markets. Nonetheless, accomplishments of formerly announced M&A agreements have been delayed, potentially leading to cancellations. Short-term effects include reduced reinvestment margins and increased investment limitations.

Over the medium term, macroeconomic predictions for 2020 were reduced down to negative territory already in the early stages of the epidemic. If economic activity starts with policy stimulus, current predictions are for a moderate and unpredictable rebound of GDP in 2021. A significant drop in demand will significantly detrimentally impact on foreign output.

Uncertainty about the economy's future will affect fresh investment ambitions. As a result of financial difficulty and liquidity concerns, many firms are obliged to transfer whatever cash available for investment to working capital during this crisis. Over the long term, the Pandemic will force MNEs to investigate possibilities for improving supply chain resilience. It may result in a policy push for more national or regional self-sufficiency in producing critical goods.

Figure 3. Effect of the pandemic on FDI: transmission mechanisms
Source: UNCTAD, World Investment Report (2020)

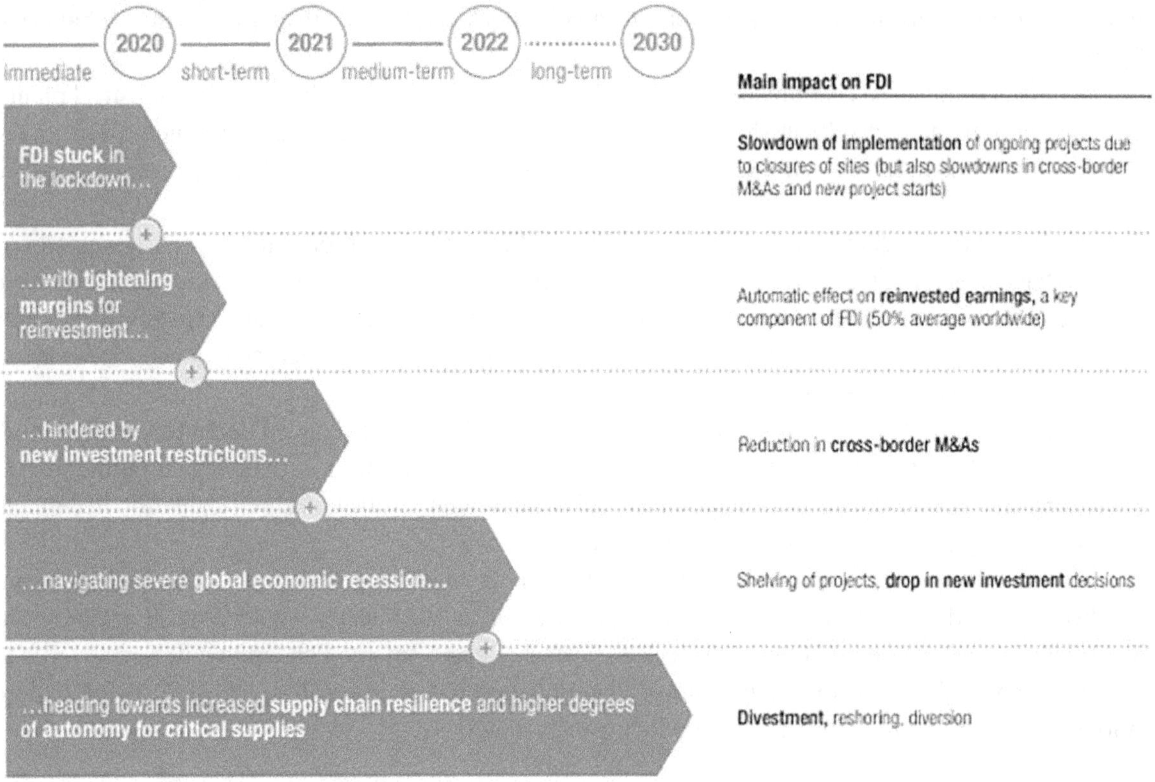

Primary indicators support the relationship between earnings impact and FDI. The industries with the most downward revisions have the most reductions in new investment projects. In the early months of 2020, industries accounting for 90% of projects in 2019 saw a more than 20% drop in the number of newly announced Greenfield projects (UNCTAD, 2020).

COVID-19's economic repercussions are a challenging responsibility. It is not known how fast economic activity will return and the extent of the harm caused by the drop in global demand and supply; policy response can be the most essential to alleviate these repercussions.

The Effect of COVID-19 on Foreign Direct Investment

Recently, few studies link FDI, COVD-19, and the BRI though researchers started to focus on establishing a relationship between FDI and COVID-19. One of the latest studies by Nawo & Njangang (2021) dealt with the effects of the COVID-19 outbreak on FDI for nations classified to have Sovereign Wealth Funds (SWFs) in 79 developed and developing countries, where China ranks the 2nd and findings revealed that the COVID-19 has a significant effect in countries with SWF. In other words, China with SWF is not significantly affected by COVID-19. However, the general outcome showed that the COVID-19 outbreak in terms of the number of death and total cases negatively correlates the FDI, which means that as the COVID-19 cases and deaths increase, the FDI of these countries decreases. However, this result does not directly tackle the BRI context.

Moreover, FDI is habitually susceptible to economic and other types of shocks. Previous research has found that financial crises negatively impact FDI entry (Dornean & Oanea, 2015). The required adoption of contagion prevention measures such as lockdowns and social distancing is one of the most distinguishing features of the COVID-19 crisis. These measures raise the costs of pre-investment research and FDI operations. Furthermore, the COVID-19 Pandemic has highlighted the vulnerability of global trade and value chains to external shocks. When a country in the global value chain experiences a large COVID-19 outbreak, which causes factory shutdowns, the entire global supply chain can be disrupted.

Since the Pandemic crisis, some studies have been done to assess the impact of lockdown on the flow of investment (Camino & Armijos, 2020). They concluded that lockdown rules harm FDI iñows. They also recommend that public policymakers focus their efforts on adequately managing the Pandemic. In their descriptive and analytical study, Manoj et al. (2020) found that the COVID -19 impacts FDI in Nepal. They also highlighted that the Pandemic is not the only obstacle to investment commitment. Other barriers are also responsible, like poor infrastructure and weak governance. This result confirms other studies on the role of institutional factors reviewed previously.

Hayakawa et al. (2022) investigated the effect of COVID 19 on the FDI flow and examined how this effect varies among two different entry modes of FDI: greenfield FDI and cross-border mergers and acquisitions (M&A). The novelty of the mentioned study is to examine the impact of COVID-19 damage on bilateral FDI flows in three dimensions.

The first dimension is the cost of COVID-19 to the host country instead of the home country.

The severity of both host and home country's damage discourages the FDI flows. The second dimension is the distinction between manufacturing and services. Many countries imposed several limitations on business procedures to encompass the spread of COVID-19. The third dimension is cross-border mergers and acquisitions against greenfield FDI. While the first type purchases the assets of a foreign company, the second requires the investor to start a new business from scratch. As a result, COVID-19 may have a more significant impact on greenfield FDI than on cross-border M&A. On the other hand, severe damage in the host country may reduce the value of acquired firms; a phenomenon is known as "fire-sale FDI." letting investors earn local companies at a lower price (Stoddard & Noy 2015). As a result, COVID-19 damage may affect the two FDI entry modes.

Hayakawa et al. (2022) examined how COVID-19 damage affected FDI flows between countries. They investigated how COVID-19 damage in origin and host countries, as measured by confirmed cases, deaths, and the harshness of social distancing policies such as government lockdown or mobility restrictions, affected the flow of FDI in 2020 and the first half of 2021.

In the case of the manufacturing sector, they achieved an immediate negative impact of the host country's COVID-19 damage on greenfield FDI and cross-border M&A. In the service sector, the host country's COVID-19 injury had a negative effect only on greenfield FDI. The following figures illustrate the evolution of the total number of cases and the global FDI flows over the Pandemic.

Figure 4. Total Covid-19 cases
Source: Worldometer- www.worldometers.info

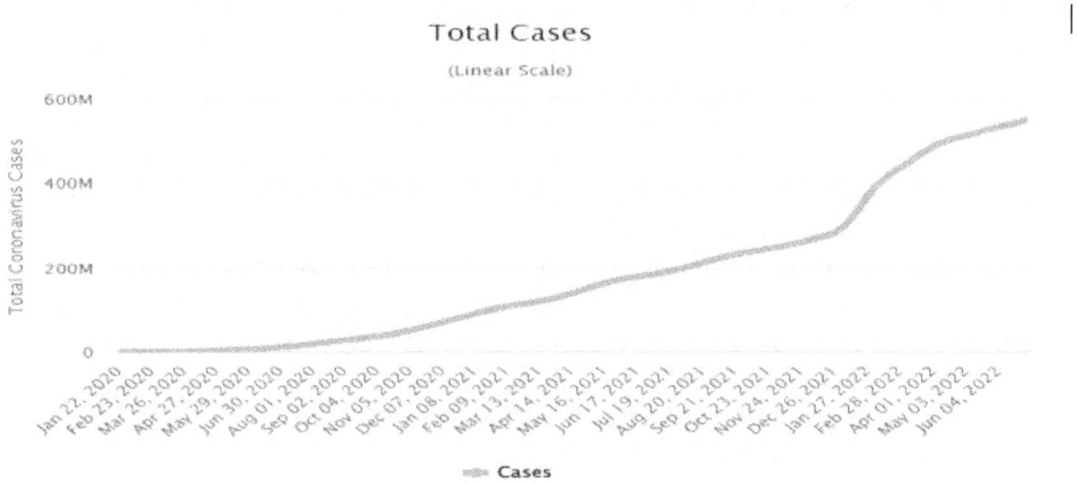

Figure 5. Global FDI flows, Q1 2013 Q2 2021 (USD billion)
Source: UNCTAD, 2021

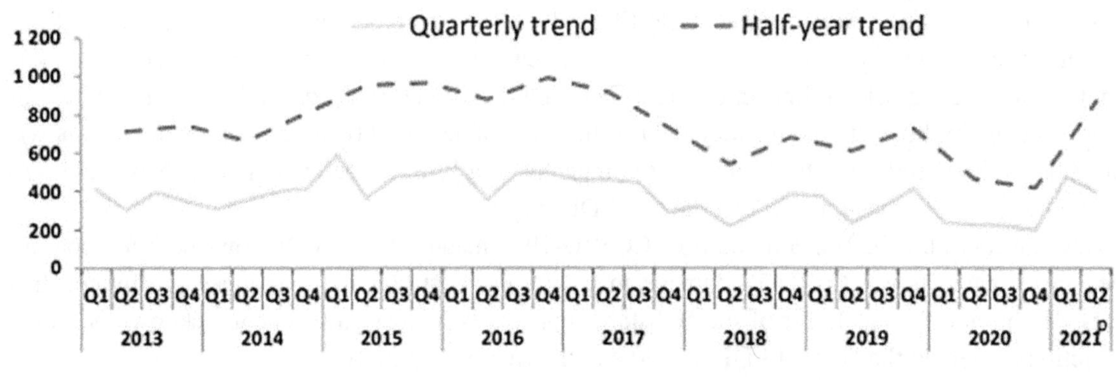

The trends in FDI in 2020 varied significantly by region. The Pandemic's impact on investment in global value chains and resource-intensive activities was disproportionately felt in developing and transition economies. Disparities in fiscal space for implementing economic support measures also influenced regional differences.

Meanwhile, in the Commonwealth countries have seen a decline of FDI inflows from 2015-to 2022 wherein a significant drop was found in 2020 (UNCTAD, 2020). The aggregate value of FDI in 2019 accounted for US$358.6 billion and has dropped to approximately US$178 billion in 2020 or a 50% decline amid the COVID-19 Pandemic. However, the decrease in 2021 and 2022 has become manageable at 18% and 7%, respectively.

Africa's FDI inflows to developing economies fell from 6.3% to 5.9% (UNCTAD, 2021). The Pandemic generated a chute of health and economic challenges in Africa that will significantly impact FDI inflows throughout 2020. Although most countries and regions were affected, FDI was essentially impacted in economies reliant on natural resources, as mentioned in the following table.

Table 2. Africa: pandemic impact on countries, by selected economic groupings

Country economic grouping	Share of inflows (Per cent) 2019	2020	Pandemic impact (Per cent change)
Oil exporters (10)	21	21	-15
Other resource-intensive economies (17)	50	44	-34
Non-resource-based economies (27)	29	35	-10

Source: NCTAD. (2020)

COVID-19 has also resulted in a drop in investment flows to developing-country sectors relevant to the Sustainable Development Goals (SDGs).

Figure 6. The impact of COVID-19 on international private investment in SDGs
Source: UNCTAD, 2021

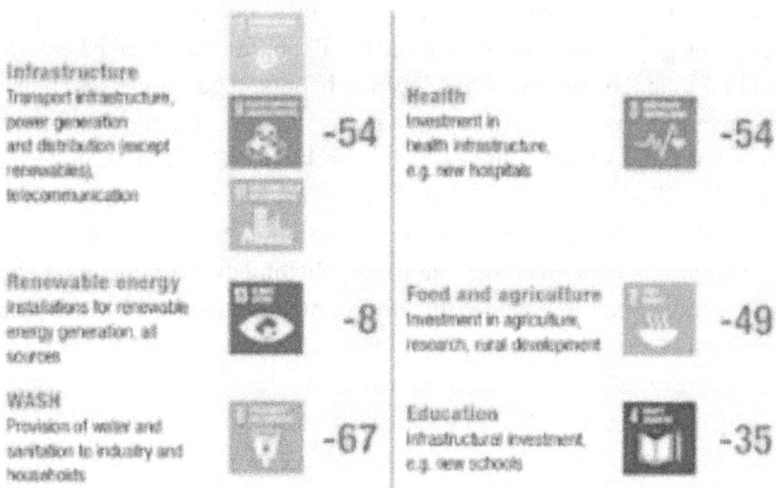

The Policy Response to Coronavirus: Flexibility of Institutions

Investment programs can help mitigate the catastrophic economic and social costs of the COVID-19 epidemic. Several nations worldwide have taken steps to encourage investment or protect important local businesses in the face of a crisis.

The liberalization of investment coupled with the mounting consideration paid by countries to FDI has corresponded with a greater focus on FDI protection and elevation. Countries are now actively attempting to appeal FDI and have established Investment Promotion Agencies (IPAs) to do so, intending to convert FDI screening into actual FDI promotion. The number of IPAs worldwide has increased substantially since the 1980s, particularly in the 1990s (UNCTAD, 2006).

IPAs are at the forefront of investment attraction and supply chain management and need to be ready to respond quickly to these challenges. These agencies contribute to a large extent to the adaptation of policies and their institutions.

COVID 19 pandemic is a recent crisis that stimulated the need for a quick adaption of existing policies. FDI literature has highlighted the role of the institutional environment and the role of investment policies in the attraction of FDI. Especially under international uncertainty.

North (1990) highlights the importance of institutions in boosting investment and economic development. According to previous research studies on the major drivers of FDI in developing countries, institutional quality, is the most essential component in encouraging economic growth. Literature on the impact of institutional quality has defined diverse conducts in which institutions affect FDI, growth, and economic development.

The most significant fundamentals of institutional structures are those that guarantee the capacity to adjust to different circumstances and adjust to new environments when required. On the other hand, the items that result in the holding and conservation of any specific policies are less important. Adaptive capacity, based in part on the population's education and its adaptation policy, maybe more significant for economic growth and FDI than the continuation of certain beliefs, regulations, and behaviors. This was significant for European expansion where there was a geographic movement to different environments with new climates, new natural resources, and even new problems. Confrontation with a new environment that offers rich opportunities, but in unfamiliar contexts, leads to some adaptations and adjustments and innovations in institutions that are in the interests of economic improvement.

The flexibility of institutions explains their role in establishing and supporting a continuous development process that is always open to change, for the following reasons: The last decades have been marked by a shift from a focus on the role of barely defined economic factors to an emphasis on the effect and implication of institutional structures on economic development. The arguments generally used, and which have always been at the heart of the analysis of the differences in economic performance between countries, are centered on conditions such as available natural resources, large market as well as other circumstances which encourage and accelerate economic performance. These arguments have been replaced by others related rather to the difference between countries in terms of the political and institutional framework and how they affect the growth process. To design a growth process, it is interesting to refer to institutional changes. Institutions are of great importance, but how they intervene in the development process is deeply influenced by the political and economic environment. If any aspect of institutions is important for growth, it is because they change all the time with changing circumstances.

Institutional flexibility facilitates efficiency and adaptability in policy management. It increases the capacity of governments to provide incentives. These can take various forms (formal investment incentives, informal privileges, and protections). Some host countries choose to improve their attractiveness through certain specific policies. Indeed, competition between countries in attracting FDI based on these policies has become a global phenomenon. There are three types of investment incentives: fiscal, financial, and regulatory incentives. Tax incentives are manifested through the reduction of various taxes. The most important financial incentives are cash grants and subsidized loans. Regulatory incentives include a set of policies, such as subsidized services or infrastructure and regulatory relief. It is reasonable that countries with more institutional flexibility will provide incentives to MNCs.

The crisis has led to new policies to facilitate, retain, and promote investment in many countries. Numerous countries have engaged in some measure to facilitate the entry of FDI by alleviating the administrative burden for firms and reducing bureaucratic obstacles to speed up production or delivery of goods during the Pandemic. The following table summarizes some investment policy instruments and the measures taken to meet the COVID crisis.

Table 3. Investment policy instruments for responding to the pandemic

Investment policy area	Policy measures (examples)
Policy actions at the national level	
Investment facilitation	• Alleviation of administrative burdens and bureaucratic obstacles for firms • Use of online tools and e-platforms
Investment retention and aftercare by investment promotion agencies (IPAs)	• COVID-19-related information services • Administrative and operational support during the crisis • Move to online services
Investment incentives	• Financial or fiscal incentives to produce COVID-19-related medical equipment • Incentives for conversion of production lines • Incentives for enhancement of contracted economic activities
State participation in crisis-affected industries	• Acquisition of equity in companies, including nationalization
Local small and medium enterprises (SMEs) and supply chains	• Financial or fiscal support for domestic suppliers (such as SMEs)
National security and public health	• Application and potential reinforcement of FDI screening in pandemic-relevant industries
Other State intervention in the health industry	• Mandatory production • Export bans • Import facilitation
Intellectual property (IP)	• General authorization of non-voluntary licensing, to speed up research and development (R&D) • IP holder-specific non-voluntary licensing, to enable imports of medication
Policy actions at the international level	
International support measures for investment	• International pledges in support of cross-border investment
IIAs	• Reform of IIAs in support of public health policies and to minimize investor–State dispute risks

Source: UNCTAD, (2020)

During the epidemic, IPAs and government ministries in charge of investment throughout the world will have a major role to react quickly and adjust their services to investor needs:

IPAs are well-positioned to benefit from synergies with other policy areas, although they may go through organizational changes. Many IPAs stress the significance of effective government coordination in providing investors with a thorough and effective response. They also recognize the benefit and necessity of cross-fertilization with other policy areas, especially in IPAs that include diverse mandates, because investment is horizontal by nature. Organizational changes are inevitable in the future as governments and IPAs reassess their approaches to investment promotion and policy. The OECD is ready to help IPAs find best practices in this area and to assist whole-of-government business climate improvements.

Table 2 lists some policy measures taken in a different area as a response to the COVID crisis. These policies are broadly divided into two main categories: at the national level and the international level. ***Nationwide,*** several states (for example, China, Myanmar, Serbia, and Thailand) have made initiatives to lessen the administrative load on businesses and decrease bureaucratic barriers to speed up production and distribution of commodities during the epidemic. Furthermore, the Pandemic has resulted in the shutdown or suspension of ordinary government services, and increased the use of online technologies and e-platforms that allow for the continuance of critical services.

Another area of investment policy is connected to the IPAs' retention of investment and intensification of aftercare. National investment promotion agencies (IPAs) have had a diverse reaction to the crisis. The majority (64 percent on 3 April 2020) reacted quickly and shifted their investor services online, with 19 percent growing their function as an online facilitator (digital policies will be discussed in the following section).

In an attempt to mitigate the pandemic negative effects, many types of incentives have been implemented to enhance production in the health sector. One category of incentives is to increase investment in those industries that are crucial to cover the virus extent (medical and pharmaceutical research). Other incentive programs involve efforts to encourage firms to develop or move production lines to medical and personal protective equipment. The third set of incentives is intended to boost contractual economic activity. They comprise, for instance, training and capacity-building subsidy programs. Several governments have stated their willingness to interfere more aggressively in the market to keep important enterprises viable: partial and full nationalization. Most State aid packages connected to the Pandemic include financial and tax assistance for SMEs. Packages often comprise guaranteed payment recovery, indirect financing to suppliers through their purchasers, tax credits and other fiscal advantages to enterprises, co-funding of development programs, and direct finance. Significant changes have occurred in practically all areas.

Internationally, several notable changes impacted the worldwide investment policy environment in 2019 and 2020, and they continue to affect the foreign investment system. The Pandemic and its mitigation strategies are also possible to cause governments to reconsider the role of International Investment Agreements (IIAs) in national development. Indeed, IIAs can come into play about government policy responses to the economic impact of the epidemic, as these actions influence the operations of foreign investors.

IIAs provide comprehensive legal safeguards that may not be accessible under the host country's local law, and they can complement the investor's rights under any contracts controlling the transaction. In general, IIAs provide that international investors have the same rights as domestic rivals and other international investors. IIAs establish explicit limitations on investment expropriation and allow foreign investors to seek compensation, and incorporate further wide assurances of investor protection in line with international law. What is new during the COVID crisis?

In 2019, nations signed at least 22 IIAs. Brazil and the United Arab Emirates were the most active economies, each with three new IIAs. This increased the size of the IIA universe to 3,284 dimensions (2,895 BITs and 389 TIPs). Furthermore, at least 12 IIAs come into force in 2019, increasing the total number of IIAs to at least 2,654 by the year's conclusion.

IPAs play an effective role in targeting FDI and can develop over time to include image building, affect investment policy, or ease inward investment barriers.

Toward a Digital Investment Policy to Better Attract Such Investment

Like any other sector, (education, health, economy,etc.), digitalization became a must during the COVID 19 pandemic. This crisis has changed the way we live in many aspects. Therefore, MNCs assessment of the investment climate has been changed with more accelerating trends towards digitalization. Similarly, the host countries have to adopt digital policies to meet the pandemic crisis.

To attract FDI in the digital economy, necessitates diverse strategies and regulations because digital companies have business models that vary from traditional ones. Digital firms depend on data and technology, often involve platform economies, and leverage non-traditional assets.

Furthermore, the epidemic and subsequent shutdown have pushed the usage of online technologies and e-platforms which allow important services to continue. International organizations, such as UNCTAD's e-Registrations platform, assist in the implementation of these solutions. (UNCTAD, 2020)

Governments that seek to recover after the pandemic crisis should encourage digital competitiveness through FDI in the digital economy, "Digital FDI." Beyond the traditional policies, the digital revolution has the potential to change traditional ways of attracting FDI. Host governments can refer to several digital policies and measures to remove any obstacles and to make the supply and value chains easier.

The need to adopt digital policies becomes more significant in the future economic depression where there will be a shortage in the sources for investment and consequently many countries will fiercely compete to attract investment in digital. The attainment in attracting foreign investment in digital infrastructure will benefit local businesses.

On the supply side, the project tries to find laws, rules, and procedures that governments may put in place to create a digitally friendly and appealing investment climate. On the demand side, the project seeks to identify businesses' digital investment requirements and objectives, as well as how they may be handled. In other words, the project seeks to understand the "demand" for digital investment opportunities. Supply and demand may therefore be well-adjusted and aligned through host nation programs that identify and solve nation-specific digital investment issues and goals.

Figure 7. Digital FDI Initiative- Balancing and connecting digital investment supply and demand
Source: Digital FDI: Policies, regulations, and measures to attract FDI in the digital economy, P6

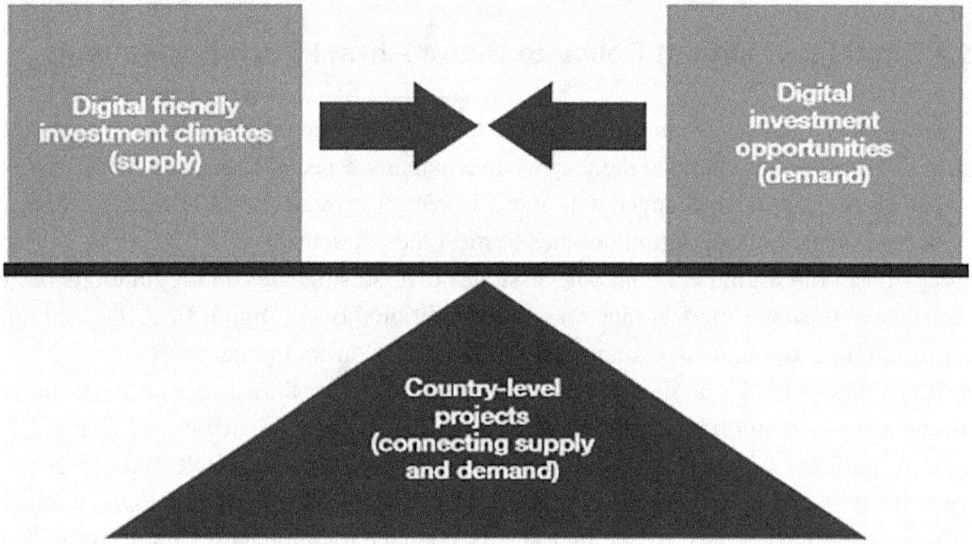

So, it is recommended for government to promote digital-friendly investment climate as a need and urgent requirement during the lockdown. As there are fewer resources for investment and hence greater competition to attract scarce capital. It will also be critical for countries to boost their digital capabilities and competitiveness following COVID-19, both to aid rapid recovery and to foster long-term pliability.

Digital FDI may be used as an additional driver of long-term growth in both the host and home countries. World Investment Report (2017) has developed a digital investment framework based on three pillars: (1) new digital activities; (2) digital adoption by traditionally non-digital firms; and (3) digital infrastructure.

Figure 8. Digital FDI framework
Source: Digital FDI: Policies, regulations, and measures to attract FDI in the digital economy, P8

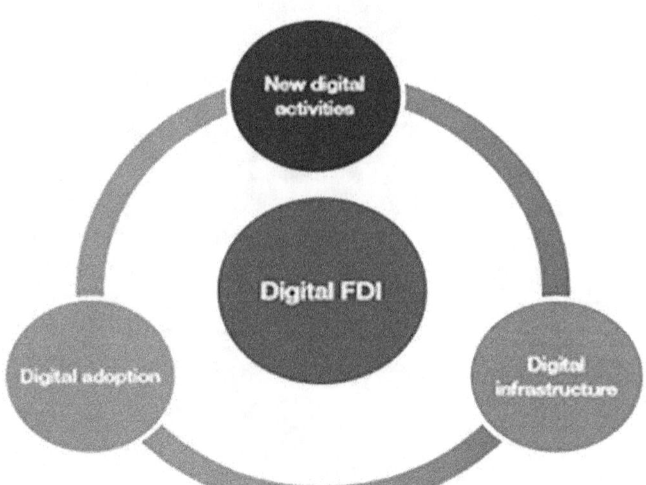

Regarding the first pillar, it empowers investment in new digital activities. The digital economy has produced a host of new business models. From social media and digital platforms to cloud computing and statistics centers, such enterprises would not exist if it weren't for the internet. Governments can hold and actively encourage such new business models to attract investment. Apropos second pillar, it empowers digital adoption by conventionally non-digital firms. Beyond new business models, the digital economy has the potential to change traditional comportments of directing corporate. Local enterprises can adopt various digital services to reduce obstacles affected by physical barriers, simplify supply and value chains and provide speedy delivery of goods and services. Certain policies, regulations, and measures can enable the adoption of new digital approaches; for instance, through telemedicine, mobile banking, and online sales.

The third pillar comprises elements that enable investment in digital infrastructure, both physical and institutional measurement. Strong and consistent physical infrastructure is crucial for the expansion and progress of the digital economy. Attracting investment in digital infrastructure requires a conducive regulatory framework; for instance, policies and regulations that encourage investment in payment processors. Success in attracting foreign investment in digital infrastructure will also depend on the nature of the existing infrastructure.

So what are the policies, regulations, and measures that need to be considered in each of the three pillars, and which matters for foreign investors?

Recently, World Economic Forum (2020) executed a global survey directed by an advisory committee of experts to see what are the concerns of investors regarding the most important policies, and measures they require, when they decided to invest in a market. A sample of 310 firms surveyed. The major number of firms being surveyed in the United States because the most digital MNEs have their parent in the US.

In terms of the large image, the top most three factors that investors care about when making decisions to invest in the digital economy are (1) the level of digital skills in the economy; (2) regulatory stability and expectedness; and (3) the regulatory framework. This confirms and supports the finding of previous studies (literature review section) which highlighted the role of the regulatory framework and quality of institutions and their flexibility in creating a well safe and predictable environment for investors to localize their production. So, the government in collaboration with IPAs has the power to shape and control the Regulation and policies of the investment climate.

The survey reveals also that investors worry about data security and protection of intellectual property rights and data privacy regulations. So, the government should implement a legal system to ensure all these properties and security. Which refers again to the importance of institutional infrastructure in assuring a good investment climate.

Implications of the COVID-19 Pandemic on China's Belt and Road Initiative

The Belt and Road Initiative began in China, but it now belongs to the entire world. It encompasses various countries and regions, various stages of development, various historical traditions, various cultures and beliefs, and several customs and regimes. It is primarily focused on Asia, Europe, and Africa, but it is open to all partners.

The COVID-19 Pandemic has largely stopped infrastructure and construction projects, some of which are part of Road Initiative (BRI). Supply chain disruptions around the world and lockdowns and travel restrictions on foreign workers, particularly Chinese workers who are frequently employed on BRI projects, are some of the main reasons for project suspensions and slowdowns. Many BRI projects are in developing countries, where controlling the Pandemic driving recovery may be more difficult than in more developed countries.

The COVID-19 Pandemic has clearly slowed BRI implementation, which is unpredictable with China's short- and long-term assumptions for international security. The Pandemic may not have occurred at the worst possible time for the implementation of China's plans to build a New Silk Road, but it appears to be a significant impediment to the overall project's success within a reasonable time frame (Górnikiewicz & Zelkowski, 2020). The COVID-19 pandemic will, undoubtedly, be an obstruction for the BRI, but the upcoming months will determine whether this is a fatal blow or whether it can evolve into a long-term promoter for the BRI along the lines of "what doesn't kill you only makes you stronger" (Mouritz, 2022).

Going Digital: Countries' Experiences

In an environment of uncertainty and possibly protectionist inclinations, investment climate improvements, backed by IPA policy advocacy, will become increasingly vital. IPAs have a critical role in policy advocacy which they believe will grow in importance over time. If FDI falls, investors will place a greater emphasis on stable business environments. IPAs are set to secure transparent and structured markets because they work at the business and public service confluence.

The reaction by COVID-19 substantially speeded up the prior trend in IPAs. First, many physical services may require a digital provision. This will require access to various Information Communication Technology (ICT) tools, from video conferencing and virtual site visitors and communication tools. With direct visits canceled by traditional means that make it more difficult or expensive to generate leads, digital media will enable IPAs to carry on serving and identify impending customers.

The COVID-19 Pandemic has greatly enhanced previous trends toward the digitalization of IPAs. Though IPAs have started the transformation earlier, the current situation caused by COVID 19 has accelerated this change towards digitalization. Therefore, the traditional services such as visits which used to be accomplished tangibly, require now to be digitalized to continue serving and identifying future customers.

World Association of Investment Promotion Agencies (WAIPA) surveyed to get the initial action taken (IPAs) towards the COVID-19 Pandemic. IPAs can lessen the impact of COVID-19 on the local economies by giving support to current enterprises, thanks to their extensive understanding of local markets and relationships with their governments. The survey results showed that 87 percent of IPAs are assisting their clients throughout the Pandemic. The figure below shows support offered by IPAs to their clients during the COVID-19 outbreak.

Figure 9. Support offered by IPAs to their clients during the COVID-19 outbreak, n=53
Source: Impact of COVID 19 from the perspective of IPAS, 2020

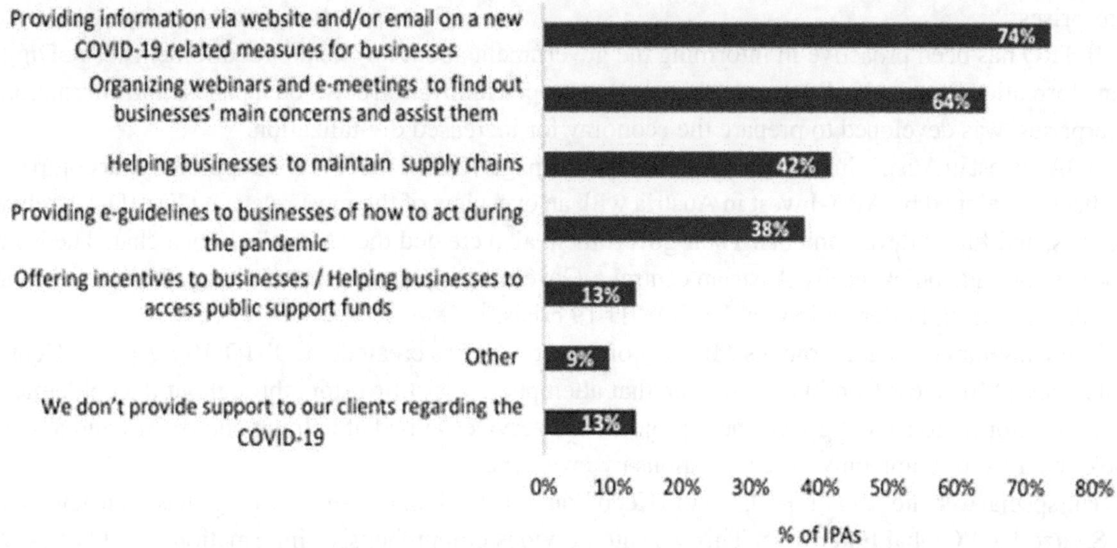

Some organizations, such as ABA-Invest in Austria, Invest in India, Switzerland Global & Enterprise, and others, set COVID-19 information platforms on their websites. In addition, 64 percent of IPAs hosted webinars and e-meetings to support their clients and learn_about their major needs and issues, while 42 percent of IPAs assist firms with supply chain management. 38% of IPAs provide e-guidelines on how to respond to a pandemic, and 11% directly offer incentives to the most impacted clients or assist them in obtaining governmental assistance funding.

Because of their ability to adapt to new situations, IPAs are essential players in governments' solutions to the COVID-19 dilemma. IPAs are frequently adaptable and quick to adjust to changing conditions since they work directly with the business sector and on various policy issues.

In their medium to long-term, IPAs are more likely to emphasize investor retention and expansion. Coordination with local and regional partners is essential in this context.

During the COVID-19 crisis, Brazil's trade and investment promotion agency established a comprehensive platform with tools to assist exporters and investors. It designed an online market intelligence platform that gives economic and trade updates by sector, for example, and held a webinar to introduce users to it. A support guide for suppliers and checklists for exporters are among the other essential resources.

Germany Trade and Invest have created a dedicated pandemic website to assure the investment community that the IPA is still working on their interests. The website provides frequent updates on corporate financing, supply networks, and economic changes. A succession of webinars has been presented on subjects such as the most recent regulatory changes linked to pandemics and the unique fast-track program for medical professionals.

In India, a comprehensive platform dedicated to pandemic-related news and resources for the investment community. It keeps track of pandemic-related developments, provides the most up-to-date information on various central and state government initiatives.

The Japan External Trade Organization (JETRO) in Japan has concentrated on delivering up-to-date information on Japan's policy measures and market environment. To better understand the requirements of investors, the agency launched an "Invest in Japan" hotline and conducted an emergency survey, the results of which were published online, better to measure the impact of the epidemic on foreign-affiliated enterprises.

JETRO has been proactive in informing the government about its clients' requirements. The Digital Transformation Partnership Program, which supports open innovation between Japanese and international enterprises, was developed to prepare the economy for increased digitalization.

ABA-Invest in Austria information portal. The web page "COMPANY-19- Support for your company" has been developed by ABA-Invest in Austria with an overview of the most relevant COVID-19, related changes, and future developments. Their government also created the "Mona" Corona chat. The Mona task is to provide quick, easily Austrian central e-Government portal companies, e.g. Business Service Portal, the essential information on the COVID-19 crisis.

The Kingdom of Saudi Arabia's Ministry of Investment has created a COVID-19 Response Centre. It also has a "Business Continuity" section that attempts to assist investors throughout the epidemic. It contains information about government projects and services aimed at helping enterprises and a handbook and a list of commonly asked questions by investors.

The special website "COVID-19: How to Keep Your International Business Going" has been developed by Switzerland Global Enterprise. This website provides comprehensive information on COVID-19's impact on the supply chain, goods movements, digital trade, an overview of the most frequent market questions, and market news.

Promoting FDI Entree During and After- Coronavirus-Disease Era

To attract, maintain, and facilitate investment in the phase of the Pandemic, bold, multidimensional, and new methods will be required. It also necessitates that governments around the region reform and strengthen their investment conditions. During and after the crisis, investment promotion frameworks and policies must develop to match each country's needs and situation. Therefore, governments concentrate on institution reorganization.

All governments must make FDI markets and sectors a greater priority to correspond with their long-term development goals. Furthermore, the reforms and policies put in place today must be designed to be sustained after the pandemic period.

The COVID-19 epidemic has hastened worldwide digital transformation by dramatically changing the link between businesses and consumers through digital technology in just a short period. As the need for online operations and services has risen, the government has adopted steps to limit COVID-19, forcing businesses to digitalize and expand their online activities.

Firms that were more digitally active were the most effective in adjusting to this new environment, while the other companies focused on modifying their business strategies.

Governments started to develop their digital competitiveness in a robust digital infrastructure and a digitally skilled and active workforce.

A fit-for-purpose regulatory framework, a national digital economy plan, and a consistent digital investment policy must all be in place to support these elements. For example, the latter would focus on attracting and supporting foreign direct investment into digital infrastructure, digital enterprises, and broader digital adoption across the economy.

Governments and administrative bodies, such as investment promotion authorities and agencies, must also use digital technology to reduce administrative costs and bureaucratic restrictions that impede product delivery and foreign investment. This means offering more efficient digital services, especially in investment facilitation through one-stop online shops that function throughout the investment cycle.

Lockdown measures have encouraged investment promotion authorities and agencies to provide remote investor services via telephone and video conferences and strengthen their online presence by centralized, easily accessible investor information, particularly on policy, financial, and regulatory changes related to COVID-19.

When attracting new FDI may be complex, retaining existing FDI is critical, and investment promotion authorities and agencies must expand their online investment services for existing investors.

While some investment promotion authorities and agencies in the region have established good practices in this area, such as those in Malaysia, the Republic of Korea, Singapore, and Thailand, many other developing countries have resisted providing these services due to a lack of access to cloud-based or virtual files and investor information.

If such services are not given, developing nation investment promotion authorities and agencies will continue to have a threatening time maintaining existing investors and recruiting new ones during the crisis.

CONCLUSION

The COVID-19 Pandemic's economic crisis is predicted to produce a significant change in developing and emerging countries. Furthermore, governments must emerge better prepared to deal with the climatic and environmental crises. The emphasis should not be solely on short-term solutions implemented during the crisis to accomplish so. The Pandemic's great impact on society and economies worldwide gives the investment community a significant opportunity to assess the efficacy of previous efforts and adapt them to the new international uncertain environment. Some of the Pandemic's consequences may linger longer than a conventional recession, necessitating continued and long-term intervention.

How investment can contribute to greater resilience, what institutions and policies are needed to address pressing problems of inequality, poverty, and the climate crisis, and how all economies can benefit to the fullest extent possible from international investment opportunities are all important considerations.

The OECD's FDI Qualities program (OECD 2020), which will propose a new policy toolset for maximizing FDI's sustainable development benefits, especially in the health sector, will substantially contribute to this reconsideration. As part of encouraging market-based economies that create a more resilient, inclusive, and climate-friendly society, the OECD will provide a forum for policymakers to draw lessons from the current crisis to help refine domestic policies and potentially complement existing investment policy instruments.

The path to recovery from the COVID-19 epidemic will be long and winding, requiring a large infusion of resources. Because public funding will be scarce, FDI will be a valuable resource. Developing economies are highly dependent on FDI inflows and foreign capital accumulation. Without improving their policies and regulations, it will be tough to attract FDI. The adoption of digital policies becomes an urgent need to facilitate communication with investors.

REFERENCES

Asongu, S., Akpan, U. S., & Isihak, S. R. (2018). Determinants of foreign direct investment in fast-growing economies: Evidence from the BRICS and MINT countries. *Financ Innov*, *4*(1), 26. doi:10.118640854-018-0114-0

Bénassy-Quéré, A., Coupet, M., & Mayer, T. (2007). Institutional determinants of foreign direct investment. *World Economy*, *30*(5), 764–782. doi:10.1111/j.1467-9701.2007.01022.x

Beugelsdijk, S., Hennart, J.-F., Slangen, A., & Smeets, R. (2010). Why and how FDI stocks are a biased measure of MNE affiliate activity. *Journal of International Business Studies*, *41*(9), 1444–1459. doi:10.1057/jibs.2010.29

Blonigen, B. A. (2005). *A Review of the Empirical Literature on FDI Determinants*. NBER Working Paper 11299. https://www.nber.org/papers/w11299

Camino-Mogro, S., & Armijos, M. (2020). *The effects of COVID-19 lockdown on Foreign Direct Investment: evidence from Ecuadorian firms*. MPRA Paper No. 104821. https://mpra.ub.uni-muenchen.de/104821/

Dimitrova, A., Rogmans, T., & Triki, D. (2020). Country-specific determinants of FDI inflows to the MENA region: A systematic review and future research directions. *Multinational Business Review*, *28*(1), 1–38. doi:10.1108/MBR-01-2019-0003

Dornean, A., & Oanea, D.-C. (2015). Impact of the Economic Crisis on FDI in Central and Eastern Europe. *Review of Economic and Business Studies*, *8*(2), 53–68. doi:10.1515/rebs-2016-0003

Dunning, J. H. (1988). The Eclectic Paradigm of International Production: A Restatement and Some Possible Extensions. *Journal of International Business Studies*, *19*(1), 1–31. doi:10.1057/palgrave.jibs.8490372

Dunning, J. H. (1992). Explaining international production. *Journal of International Development*, *4*(6), 655–655.

Dunning, J. H. (1993). *Multinational Enterprises and the Global Economy*. Addison-Wesley Publishers Company Inc.

Galenkova, A. D., Drapkin, I. M., & Mariev, O. (2018). The impact of institutional efficiency on the foreign direct investment inflows in developing countries. *CBU International Conference Proceedings, 6*(0), 141-145. 10.12955/cbup.v6.1146

Globerman, S., & Shapiro, D. (2002). Global foreign direct investment flows The role of governance infrastructure. *World Development*, *30*(11), 1899–1919. doi:10.1016/S0305-750X(02)00110-9

Górnikiewicz, M., & Zelkowski, J. (2020). Belt and Road Initiative in the Age of COVID-19 Pandemic: Implications for the Development of the Strategic Project of the People's Republic of China. *European Research Studies Journal*, *23*(3), 302–310. doi:10.35808/ersj/1884

Hayakawa, K., Lee, H. H., & Park, C. Y. (2022). The Effect of COVID-19 on Foreign Direct Investment. *Asian Development Bank Economics Working Paper Series*, (653). https://papers.ssrn.com/sol3/papers.cfm?abstract_id=4060417

Heilbron, A., & Whyte, R. (2019). *Institutions for Investment: Establishing a High-Performing Institutional Framework for Foreign Direct Investment. Finance, Competitiveness, and Innovation in Focus.* World Bank.

Hobbs, S., & Paparas, D., & AboElsoud, M.E. (2021). Does Foreign Direct Investment and Trade Promote Economic Growth? Evidence from Albania. *Economies*, *9*(1), 1–19. doi:10.3390/economies9010001

Manoj, K., Rudra, P., & Dinesh, M. (2020). *Impact of COVID -19 pandemic on foreign direct investment in Nepal from south Asian perspectives.* https://www.scribd.com/doc/215509137/Asian-in-the-Global-Economic

Melendez-Ortiz, R. (2016). *What's ahead for the WTO: Looking around the corner and beyond.* International Centre for Trade and Sustainable Development (ICTSD). https://voxeu.org/users/ricardomel-ndez-ortiz

Mihaela, P., Waqar, A., & Helian, X. (2018). The impact of institutional quality on foreign direct investment inflows: Evidence for developed and developing countries. *Economic Research-Ekonomska Istraživanja*, *31*(1), 626–644. doi:10.1080/1331677X.2018.1438906

Morisset, J. (2003). *Does a country need a Promotion Agency to attract Foreign Direct Investment? A small analytical model applied to 58 counties.* https://openknowledge.worldbank.org/handle/10986/18230

Mouritz, F. (2022). *Implications of the COVID-19 Pandemic on China's Belt and Road Initiative.* The Quarterly Journal. doi:10.11610/Connections.19.2.09

Naudé, W. (2004). The effects of policy, institutions, and geography on economic growth in Africa: An econometric study based on cross-section and Panel Data. *Journal of International Development*, *16*(6), 821–849. doi:10.1002/jid.1129

Nguyen, H. V., Phan, T. T., & Lobo, A. (2019). Debunking the Myth of Foreign Direct Investment toward Long-Term Sustainability of a Developing Country: A Transaction Cost Analysis Approach. *Sustainability*, *11*(4569), 1–26. doi:10.3390u11174569

North, D. C. (1990). *Institutions, institutional change, and economic performance.* Cambridge University Press. doi:10.1017/CBO9780511808678

OECD. (2019). *FDI Qualities Indicators: Measuring the sustainable development impacts of investment.* https://www.oecd.org/

Sabir, S., Rafique, A., & Abbas, K. (2019). Institutions and FDI: Evidence from developed and developing countries. *Financial Innovation*, *5*(8), 1–20. doi:10.118640854-019-0123-7

Sayari, K. (2019). Institutional efficiency and attraction of FDI to developing countries. *International Journal of Economic Development*, *11*(7), 54–60.

Stephenson, M. (2020). *Digital FDI: Policies, Regulations and Measures to Attract FDI in the Digital Economy.* World Economic Forum White Paper, September 2020. https://www3.weforum.org/docs/WEF_Digital_FDI_2020.pdf

Stoddard, O., & Noy, I. (2015). Fire-sale FDI? The Impact of Financial Crises on Foreign Direct Investment. *Review of Development Economics, 19*(2), 387–399. doi:10.1111/rode.12149

Trąpczyński, P. (2013). Determinants of Foreign Direct Investment Performance – a Critical Literature Review. *Oeconomia Copernicana, 4*(2), 117–132. doi:10.12775/OeC.2013.016

UNCTAD. (2010). *World Investment Report 2020: International Production Beyond the Pandemic.* https://unctad.org/system/files/official-document/wir2020_en.pdf

UNCTAD. (2014). *World Investment Report, Investing in the SDGs (Sustainable Development Goals) – A Plan of Action.* United Nations.

UNCTAD. (2014). *World Investment Report, investment and the digital economy.* https://unctad.org/system/files/official-document/wir2014_en.pdf

UNCTAD. (2020). *Investment Policy Responses to the COVID-19 Pandemic.* Investment Policy Monitor Special Issue No. 4 (May 2020). UNCTAD.

United Nations, Economic and Social Commission for Asia and the Pacific Committee on Trade and Investment. (2021). *Promoting inward and outward foreign direct investment in the post-coronavirus-disease era.* Seventh session Bangkok, 27–29 January 2021 Item 3 of the provisional agenda, ESCAP/CTI/2021/2. https://www.unescap.org/sites/default/d8files/eventdocuments/CTI7_2_item%203%20FDI%20reissued.pdf

KEY TERMS AND DEFINITIONS

COVID-19: Is a global pandemic or disease that started in 2019 spreading throughout the world.

Foreign Direct Investment (FDI): Is defined as an investment involving a long-term relationship and reflecting a lasting interest and control by a resident entity in one economy in an enterprise resident in an economy other than that of the foreign direct investor.

Institutional Determinants: This category of FDI determinants refers to institutional infrastructure: laws, policies, regulations, governance, and quality of institutions.

Integrated Development Environment (IDE): Is a software application that provides comprehensive facilities to computer programmers for software development.

Investment Promotion Agencies (IPAs): Are national or subnational institutions mandated to attract and grow investment—usually foreign direct investment.

Multinational Corporation: Is a business that operates in many different countries at the same time. In other words, it's a company that has business activities in more than one country.

Sovereign Wealth Funds (SWFs): Is composed of 79 developed and developing countries that are not heavily affected by their FDI during the COVID-19 pandemic crisis.

United Nations Conference on Trade and Development (UNCTAD): Is an intergovernmental organization intended to promote the interests of developing states in world trade.

Compilation of References

Abu Dayeh, B., & Janíčko, M. (2021). Determinants of Chinese Foreign Direct Investment in Central and Eastern Europe. *Central European Business Review*, *10*(3), 19–36. doi:10.18267/j.cebr.254

Agustina, A., & Flath, D. (2019). Agglomeration and Location Decision of Foreign Direct Investment (FDI) in Indonesia. *Jurnal Ekonomi & Kebijakan Publik*, *10*(2), 87–98. doi:10.22212/jekp.v10i2.1477

Ahmad, I. (2010). The US Af-Pak strategy: Challenges and opportunities for Pakistan. *Asian Affairs: An American Review*, 37–45.

Ahmed, Z. S. (2019). Impact of the China–Pakistan Economic Corridor on nation-building in Pakistan.". *Journal of Contemporary China*, *28*(117), 400–413. doi:10.1080/10670564.2018.1542221

Aibai, A., Huang, X., Luo, Y., & Peng, Y. (2019). Foreign Direct Investment, Institutional Quality, and Financial Development along the Belt and Road: An Empirical Investigation. *Emerging Markets Finance & Trade*, *55*(14), 3275–3294. doi:10.1080/1540496X.2018.1559139

AidData. (2021). *AidData's Global Chinese Development Finance Dataset, Version 2.0.* Retrieved from https://www.aiddata.org/data/aiddatas-global-chinese-development-finance-dataset-version-2-0

Alawad, H., & Kaewunruen, S. (2021). 5G Intelligence Underpinning Railway Safety in the COVID-19 Era. *Frontiers in Built Environment*, *7*, 7. doi:10.3389/fbuil.2021.639753

Ali., Y. (2022). Risk Assessment in Supply Chain Networks of China–Pakistan Economic Corridor (CPEC). *Chinese Political Science Review*, 3-22.

Ali, G. (2022). CPEC: A Gateway to Regional Connectivity. In *Crossing the Himalayas* (pp. 92–99). Springer. doi:10.1007/978-981-16-5808-2_7

Alshamsi, K. H., Hussin, M. R. B., & Muhammad, A. (2015). The impact of inflation and GDP per capita on foreign direct investment: The case of United Arab Emirates. *Investment Management and Financial Innovations*, *12*, 132–141.

Amighini, A. A., Rabellotti, R., & Sanfilippo, M. (2013). Do Chinese state-owned and private enterprises differ in their internationalization strategies? *China Economic Review*, *27*, 312–325. doi:10.1016/j.chieco.2013.02.003

Amineh, M. P. (2022). China's capitalist industrial development and the emergence of the Belt and Road Initiative. In *The China-led Belt and Road Initiative and its reflections*. Routledge. doi:10.4324/9781003256502-2

Ananthalakshmi, A. K. (2013). *India "concerned" by China role in Pakistan's Gwadar port.* South Asia News.

Andrew, K. (2016). India's Geopolitical Hate for Pakistan is Sabotaging the North-South Corridor. *Katehon*, 4.

Andrew, K. (2017). CPEC and the 21st Century Convergence of Civilizations. *Katehon*, 1-2.

Andrew, K. (2017). The Secret Behind Russia's CPEC Saga. *Regional Rapport, 4*.

Ang, J. B. (2012). Determinants of Foreign Direct Investment in China. *Journal of Policy Modeling*, *30*(3), 185–189.

Anyadike, N. O. (2012). Poor Infrastructure: The Hindrance to Foreign Investment and Economic Development in Nigeria. *Interdisciplinary Journal of Contemporary Research in Business*, *4*(4), 1–15.

Arduino, A., & Gong, X. (2018). *Securing the Belt and Road Initiative*. . doi:10.1007/978-981-10-7116-4

Arežina, S. (2018). *China in Europe*. Institute of European Studies.

Arezina, S. (2021). The Sino-Western Balkans Relations Within "Belt and Road" Initiative Amidst the World'S Grappling With the Rise of China. *Teme-Časopis Za Društvene Nauke*, *45*(1), 145–164. doi:10.22190/TEME200131009A

Ascensão, F., Fahrig, L., Clevenger, A. P., Corlett, R. T., Jaeger, J. A., Laurance, W. F., & Pereira, H. M. (2018). Environmental challenges for the Belt and Road Initiative. *Nature Sustainability*, *1*(5), 206–209. doi:10.103841893-018-0059-3

Ash, R. F. (1996). The Chinese Economy Under Deng Xiaoping. Shangaye: Clarendon Press.

Asiedu, E. (2002). On the Determinants of Foreign Direct Investment to Developing Countries: Is Africa Different? *World Development*, *30*(1), 107–119. doi:10.1016/S0305-750X(01)00100-0

Asongu, S., Akpan, U. S., & Isihak, S. R. (2018). Determinants of foreign direct investment in fast-growing economies: Evidence from the BRICS and MINT countries. *Financ Innov*, *4*(1), 26. doi:10.118640854-018-0114-0

Autio, E., Mudambi, R., & Yoo, Y. (2021). Digitalization and globalization in a turbulent world: Centrifugal and centripetal forces. *Global Strategy Journal*, *11*(1), 3–16. doi:10.1002/gsj.1396

Azémar, C., & Dharmapala, D. (2019). Tax sparing agreements, territorial tax reforms, and foreign direct investment. *Journal of Public Economics*, *169*, 89–108. doi:10.1016/j.jpubeco.2018.10.013

Azman-Saini, W. N. W., Baharumshah, A. Z., & Law, S. H. (2010). Foreign direct investment, economic freedom and economic growth: International evidence. *Economic Modelling*, *27*(5), 1079–1089. doi:10.1016/j.econmod.2010.04.001

Babatunde, A. (2011). Trade Openness, Infrastructure, FDI and Growth in Sub-Saharan African Countries. *Journal of Management Policy and Practice*, *2*(7), 27–36.

Bakari, S. (2017). *Trade and Economic Growth in Germany*. LIEI, Faculty of Economic Sciences and Management of Tunis (FSEGT). MPRA Paper No. 77404.

Bakari, S., & Sofien, T. (2019). The impact of trade openness, foreign direct investment and domestic investment on economic growth: New evidence from Asian developing countries. Economic Research Guardian. *Weissberg Publishing*, *9*(1), 46–54.

Baldwin, R. E. (1999). Agglomeration and endogenous capital. *European Economic Review*, *43*(2), 253–280. doi:10.1016/S0014-2921(98)00067-1

Baltagi, B. H. (2005). *Econometric analysis of panel data*. John Wiley & Sons Ltd.

Bambalas, A., & Romeris, M. (2019). China's One Belt One Road Initiative and the Eu's Fdi Screening Regime: Scope, Eu's Attitude and Impact. *Social Transformations in Contemporary Society*, *7*.

Baranenko, E., & Đukić, M. (2012). Ways for enhancement of export activities. In Managing structural changes: Trends and requirements (pp. 520–536). Academic Press.

Baranenko, E., & Stevanović, S. (2013). Strategies for enhancing competitiveness of the economy as a way to ensure faster recovery from the crisis: The experience of the EU and Serbia. *Post Crisis Recovery*, 420–433.

Barisitz, S., & Radzyner, A. (2017). *The New Silk Road, part I: A stocktaking and economic assessment. Focus on European Economic Integration, Q3/2017, Oesterreichische Nationalbank*. Austrian Central Bank.

Barrell, R., & Pain, N. (1998). Real exchange rates, agglomerations, and irreversibilities: Macroeconomic policy and FDI in EMU. *Oxford Review of Economic Policy*, *14*(3), 152–167. doi:10.1093/oxrep/14.3.152

Barry, F., Gorg, H., & Strobl, E. (2011). *Foreign Direct Investment, Agglomeration and Demonstration Effects: An Empirical Investigation.* Center for Economic Policy Research, Discussion paper n° 2907.

Barry, F., & Bradley, J. (1997). FDI and Trade: The Irish Host-Country Experience. *Economic Journal (London)*, *107*(445), 1798–1811. doi:10.1111/j.1468-0297.1997.tb00083.x

Bashir, M. F., Benjiang, M. A., Qin, Y., & Bashir, M. A. (2021). Evaluation of One Belt One Road publications: A bibliometric and literature review analysis. *Environmental Science and Pollution Research International*, *28*(28), 37016–37030. doi:10.100711356-021-14621-y PMID:34050514

Basile, R., Castellani, D., & Zanfei, A. (2009). National boundaries and the location of multinational firms in Europe. *Papers in Regional Science*, *88*(4), 733–748. doi:10.1111/j.1435-5957.2009.00238.x

Bastian, J. (2017). *The potential for growth through Chinese infrastructure investments in Central and South-Eastern Europe along the Balkan Silk Road.* European Bank for Reconstruction and Development.

Bastos, P. (2020). Exposure of belt and road economies to China trade shocks. *Journal of Development Economics*, *145*, 145. doi:10.1016/j.jdeveco.2020.102474

Baum, R. (1996). *Burying Mao: Chinese politics in the age of Deng Xiaoping*. Princeton University Press.

Behname, M. (2012). Foreign Direct Investment and Urban Infrastructure: An Evidence from Southern Asia. *Advances in Management & Applied Economics*, *2*(4), 253–259.

Békés, G. (2006). *Location of manufacturing FDI in Hungary: How important are inter-company relationships?* Magyar Nemzeti Bank (Hungarian National Bank) Working Paper No. 2005/07. Budapest: Magyar Nemzeti Bank.

Bekmurodova, G. (2020). Theoretical Features of FDI (Foreign Direct Investment) and its Influence to Economic Growth. *International Journal of Management Science and Business Administration*, *6*(2), 33–39. doi:10.18775/ijmsba.1849-5664-5419.2014.62.1004

Bénassy-Quéré, A., Coupet, M., & Mayer, T. (2007). Institutional determinants of foreign direct investment. *World Economy*, *30*(5), 764–782. doi:10.1111/j.1467-9701.2007.01022.x

Beraha, I. (2016). Revitalizacija srpske automobilske industrije - da li je uloga Fijata ključna? *Zbornik Matice srpske za društvene nauke*, *67*(159/16), 767-783.

Beraha, I., & Jovičić, E. (2021). Uticaj pandemije COVID-19 na spoljnotrgovinsku razmenu između Kine i zemalja Zapadnog Balkana. *Makroekonomska Stabilnost i Unapređenje Konkurentnosti Zemalja Zapadnog Balkana*, 107–123.

Beraha, I., & Redžepagić, S. (2016). Trade and Cooperation Between the Emerging Economies: What is the BRICS Position? In Europe and Asia - Economic Integration Prospects. CEMAFI International.

Beraha, I., & Jovičić, E. (2021). *Uticaj pandemije Covid-19 na spoljnotrgovinsku razmenu između Kine i zemalja ZapadnogBbalkana [Impact of the Covid-19 pandemic on foreign trade between China and the Western Balkans] In Makroekonomska stabilnost i unapređenje konkurentnosti zemalja Zapadnog Balkana [Macroeconomic stability and improving the competitiveness of the Western Balkans]*. Institute of Economic Sciences China Global Investment Tracker. https://www.aei.org/china-global-investment-tracker/

Bermejo, C. J., & Richard, A. (2018). Does Foreign Direct Investment Generate Economic Growth? A New Empirical Approach Applied to Spain. *Economic Geography*, *94*(4), 425–456. doi:10.1080/00130095.2017.1393312

Beugelsdijk, S., Hennart, J.-F., Slangen, A., & Smeets, R. (2010). Why and how FDI stocks are a biased measure of MNE affiliate activity. *Journal of International Business Studies*, *41*(9), 1444–1459. doi:10.1057/jibs.2010.29

Big B. R. I. Data Report. (2018). *Big Data Report on Trade Cooperation under the Belt and Road Initiative 2018*. https://www.yidaiyilu.gov.cn/wcm.files/upload/CMSydylgw/201805/201805080457024.pdf

Bird, J., Lebrand, M., & Venables, A. J. (2020). The Belt and Road Initiative: Reshaping economic geography in Central Asia? *Journal of Development Economics*, *144*, 144. doi:10.1016/j.jdeveco.2020.102441

Blanchard, J. M. F., & Flint, C. (2017). The geopolitics of China's maritime silk road initiative. *Geopolitics*, *22*(2), 223–245. doi:10.1080/14650045.2017.1291503

Blavasciunaite, D., Garsviene, L., & Matuzeviciute, K. (2020). Trade balance effects on economic growth: Evidence from European Union Countries. Economies. Academic Press.

Blonigen, B. A. (2005). *A Review of the Empirical Literature on FDI Determinants*. NBER Working Paper 11299. https://www.nber.org/papers/w11299

Blonigen, B. A. (2005). A Review of the Empirical Literature on FDI Determinants. *Atlantic Economic Journal*, *33*(4), 383–403. doi:10.100711293-005-2868-9

BNR. (2014). *Investițiile Străine Directe în România, în anul 2013*. Institutul Național de Statistică, București. www.bnr.ro

Bodroža, D., & Đukić, M. (2018). Influence of FDI Inflows on Economic Activity in CEE Countries. Western Balkans Economies in EU Integration: past, present and future. CEMAFI International Association.

Bodroža, D., & Lazić, M. (2021). Economic Impact of the COVID-19 Pandemic on Western Balkan Countries. *Economic Analysis: Applied Research in Emerging Markets*, *54*(2), 30–40.

Bolivar, L. M., Casanueva, C., & Castro, I. (2019). Global Foreign Direct Investment: A network perspective. *International Business Review*, *28*(4), 696–712. doi:10.1016/j.ibusrev.2019.01.007

Borenzstein, E., De Gregorio, J., & Lee, J. W. (1998). How does foreign direct investment affect economic growth? *Journal of International Economics*, *45*(1), 115–135. doi:10.1016/S0022-1996(97)00033-0

Bowerman, B. L., & O'Connell, R. T. (1990). *Linear statistical models: An Applied Approach*. Duxbury Press.

Bradsher, K. (2017). U.S. Firms Want In on China's Global 'One Belt, One Road' Spending. *The New York Times*.

Brandt, L., Litwack, J., Mileva, E., Wang, L., Zhang, Y., & Zhao, L. (2020). *China's Productivity Slowdown and Future Growth Potential*. World Bank Group. doi:10.1596/1813-9450-9298

Braunerhjelm, P., & Svensson, R. (1996). Host country characteristics and agglomeration in foreign direct investment. *Applied Economics*, *28*(7), 833–840. doi:10.1080/000368496328272

Brautigam, D. (2020). A critical look at Chinese 'debt-trap diplomacy': The rise of a meme. *Area Development and Policy*, *5*(1), 1–14. doi:10.1080/23792949.2019.1689828

Breslin, S. (2013). China and the global order: Signalling threat or friendship? *International Affairs*, *89*(3), 123–234. doi:10.1111/1468-2346.12036

Brewster, D. (2016). Silk Roads and Strings of Pearls: The Strategic Geography of China's New Pathways in the Indian Ocean. *Geopolitics*, 6-13.

Brown, R. C. (2020). China's BRI in Central Eastern European Countries: "17+1" Connectivity, Divisiveness, or Pathway to EU-CHINA FTA? *San Diego International Law Journal*, *22*(1), 1–40.

Buckley, P. J. (2020). China's Belt and Road Initiative and the COVID-19 crisis. *J Int Bus Policy*, *3*(3), 311–314. doi:10.105742214-020-00063-9

Buckley, P. J., Clegg, J., & Wang, C. (2002). The impact of inward FDI on the performance of Chinese manufacturing firms. *Journal of International Business Studies*, *33*(4), 637–655. doi:10.1057/palgrave.jibs.8491037

Bughin, J., Chironga, M., Desvaux, G., Ermias, T., Jacobson, P., Kassiri, O., & Zouaoui, Y. (2016). *Lions on the Move II: Realizing the Potential of Africa's Economies*. McKinsey Global Institute.

Burlacu, S., Gutu, C., & Matei, F. O. (2018). Globalization–pros and cons. *Calitatea*, *19*(S1), 122–125.

BusseM.KönigerJ. (2012). Trade and Economic Growth: A Re-Examination of the Empirical Evidence. Available at SSRN: https://ssrn.com/abstract=2009939 doi:10.2139/ssrn.2009939

Cai, P. (2017). Understanding China's Belt and Road Initiative. Lowry Institute for International Policy.

Cai, P. (2017). *Understanding China's Belt and Road Initiative*. Lowy Institute for International Policy.

Cai, X., Lu, Y., Wu, M., & Yu, L. (2016). Does environmental regulation drive away inbound foreign direct investment? Evidence from a quasi-natural experiment in China. *Journal of Development Economics*, *123*, 73–85. doi:10.1016/j.jdeveco.2016.08.003

Camino-Mogro, S., & Armijos, M. (2020). *The effects of COVID-19 lockdown on Foreign Direct Investment: evidence from Ecuadorian firms*. MPRA Paper No. 104821. https://mpra.ub.uni-muenchen.de/104821/

Cao, W., & Lin, S. (n.d.). Changes in the RMB exchange rate, the effects of neighboring countries' exchange rates and bilateral trade: An empirical study based on the SVAR model between China and the five Southeast Asian countries. *International Trade Issues*, (11), 152-163.

Carkovic, M. & Levine, R. (2002). *Does foreign direct investment accelerate economic growth?* University of Minnesota Department of Finance working Paper.

Carlos, F. (2005). Improving The Competitiveness Of SMEs Through Enhancing Productive Capacity. In *United Nations Conference on Trade and Development, Proceedings of Four Meetings*, 182.

Carrai, M. A. (2021). Adaptive governance along Chinese-financed BRI railroad megaprojects in East Africa. *World Development*, *141*, 141. doi:10.1016/j.worlddev.2020.105388

Casarini, N. (2015). Is Europe to Benefit from China's Belt and Road Initiative? *IAI Working Papers, 15*.

Castro, L., Paulo, R., & Saslavsky, D. (2007). *Infrastructure and the Location of Foreign Direct Investment: A Regional Analysis.* The 12th Annual Meeting of the Latin American and Caribbean Economic Association (LACEA).

CEIC Data. (2020). *Montenegro Government Debt: % of GDP*. Global Economic Data, Indicators, Charts and Forecasts. Available at: https://www.ceicdata.com/en/indicator/montenegro/government-debt–of-nominal-gdp

Central Committee of the Communist Party of China. (2013). *Decision of the Central Committee of the Communist Party of China on Several Major Issues Concerning Comprehensively Deepening the Reform*. People's Publishing House.

Çetintaş, H., & Barişik, S. (2009). Export, import and economic growth: The case of transition economies. *Transit. Stud. Rev., 15*(4), 636–649. doi:10.100711300-008-0043-0

Chakrabarti, R., Subramanian, K., Sairam, S., & Kuntluru, S. (2012). *Infrastructure and FDI: Evidence from district-level data in India*. Academic Press.

Chan, L. (2016). *Belt and Road Opportunities in Central and Eastern Europe*. Available at: https://perma.cc/6RX7-PUK7

Chan, M. H. T. (2018). The Belt and Road Initiative – the New Silk Road: A research agenda. *Journal of Contemporary East Asia Studies, 7*(2), 104–123. doi:10.1080/24761028.2019.1580407

Chen, L., Guo, S., Liu, J., & Gerschewski, S. (2021). Outward FDI and efficiency in within-firm resource allocation-Evidence from firm-level data of China. *Economics*, 74.

Chen, M., & Lin, C. (2018*). Foreign Investment across the Belt and Road: Patterns, Determinants and Effects.* Policy Research Working Paper 8607, World Bank.

Chen, X. M., & Lin, C. (2018). *Foreign Investment across the Belt and Road Patterns, Determinants and Effects*. World bank group. Policy Research Working Paper 8607.

Chen, C. (2017). Science mapping: A systematic review of the literature. *Journal of Data and Information Science, 2*(2), 1–40. doi:10.1515/jdis-2017-0006

Chen, C., Ibekwe-Sanjuan, F., & Hou, J. (2010). The structure and dynamics of cocitation clusters: A multiple-perspective cocitation analysis. *Journal of the American Society for Information Science and Technology, 61*(7), 1386–1409. doi:10.1002/asi.21309

Chen, F., Jiang, G., & Wang, W. (2019). Institutional quality and its impact on the facilitation of foreign direct investment: Empirical evidence from the Belt and Road countries. *Journal of Chinese Economic and Foreign Trade Studies, 12*(3), 167–188. doi:10.1108/JCEFTS-07-2019-0041

Cheng, L. K. (2016). Three questions on China's "belt and road initiative". *China Economic Review, 40*, 309–313. doi:10.1016/j.chieco.2016.07.008

Cheng, L. K., & Kwan, Y. L. (2000). What Are the Determinants of the Location of Foreign Direct Investment? The Chinese Experience. *Journal of International Economics, 51*(2), 79–400. doi:10.1016/S0022-1996(99)00032-X

Chen, H. (2016). China's 'One Belt, One Road' initiative and its implication for Sino-African investment relations. *Transnational Corporations Review, 8*(3), 178–182. doi:10.1080/19186444.2016.1233722

Chen, M. X., & Lin, C. (2020). Geographic connectivity and cross-border investment: The belts, roads and skies. *Journal of Development, 146*, 12–13. doi:10.1016/j.jdeveco.2020.102469

Chen, W., Dollar, D., & Tang, H. (2018). Why is China investing in Africa? Evidence from the firm level. *The World Bank Economic Review, 32*(3), 610–632.

Chen, W., & Tang, H. (2014). Export Promotion of OFDI from Emerging Markets – Transaction-Level Evidence from China. *Academy of Management Journal*.

Cheung, Y., & Qian, X. (2009). Empirics of China's outward direct investment. *Pacific Economic Review*, *44*(3), 213–341.

Chidlow, A., Salciuviene, L., & Young, S. (2009). Regional determinants of inward FDI distribution in Poland. *International Business Review*, *18*(2), 119–133. doi:10.1016/j.ibusrev.2009.02.004

Chin, H., & He, W. (2016). *The Belt and Road Initiative: 65 Countries and Beyond.* https://www.fbicgroup.com/sites/default/files/B%26R_Initiative_65_Countries_and_Beyond.pdf

China National Statistical Bureau's. (2018). *2018 Statistical Bulletin of China's Outward Foreign Direct Investment.* China Statistics Press.

China-CEE Institute. (2018). 16+1 Cooperation and China-EU Relationship. Budapest: China-CEE Institute.

China-CEE Institute. (2019). *Greece External Relations Briefing: Dubrovnik Summit Welcomes Greece.* Available at: https://china-cee.eu/2019/05/09/greece-externalrelations-briefing-dubrovnik-summit-welcomes-greece/

Choi, P. M. S., Chung, C. Y., Lee, K. Y., & Liu, C. (2020). Agglomeration Effects and Foreign Direct Investment Location Choice: Cross-country Evidence from Asia. *Journal of Korea Trade*, *24*(1), 35–58. doi:10.35611/jkt.2020.24.1.35

Chowdhury, A., & Mavrotas, G. (2006). FDI and Growth: What Causes What? *World Economy*, *29*(1), 2006. doi:10.1111/j.1467-9701.2006.00755.x

Chung, C. P. (2006). Confronting terrorism and other evils in China: all quiet on the western front?. *Unknown*, 12-23.

Clarke, M. (2007). China's Internal Security Dilemma and the "Great Western Development": The Dynamics of Integration, Ethnic Nationalism and Terrorism in Xinjiang. *Asian Studies Review*, *31*(3), 31–45. doi:10.1080/10357820701621350

Coase, R. (1937). The nature of the firm. *Economica, 4*, 386-405. http://walterewilliams.com/courses/articles/CoaseEconomica.pdf

Coenen, J., Bager, S., Meyfroidt, P., Newig, J., & Challies, E. (2020). Environmental Governance of China's Belt and Road Initiative. *Environmental Policy and Governance*, *31*(1), 3-17. doi:10.1002/eet.1901

Coenen, J., & Bager, S., Meyfroidt, P., Newig, J., & Challies, E. (2020). Environmental Governance of China's Belt and Road Initiative. *Wiley Online Library*, *31*(1), 3–17.

Cohen, S. D. (2007). *Multinational Corporations and Foreign Direct Investment.* Oxford University Press. doi:10.1093/acprof:oso/9780195179354.001.0001

Conley, H. A., Hillman, J. E., McCalpin, M., & Ruy, D. (2020). *Becoming a Chinese Client State. The Case of Serbia.* Center for Strategic & International Studies. Available at https://csis-websiteprod.s3.amazonaws.com/s3fs-public/publication/200924_Chinese_Client.pdf

Cordero, J., & Paus, E. (2008). *Foreign Investment and Economic Development in Costa Rica: The Unrealized Potential.* Discussion Paper, No. 13. Working Group on Development and Environment in the Americas. Tufts University.

Coughlin, C. C., Terza, J. V., & Arromdee, V. (1991). State characteristics and the location of foreign direct investment within the United States. *The Review of Economics and Statistics*, *73*(4), 675–683. doi:10.2307/2109406

Crescenzi, R., Di Cataldo, M., & Giua, M. (2021). FDI inflows in Europe: Does investment promotion work? *Journal of International Economics*, *132*, 103497. Advance online publication. doi:10.1016/j.jinteco.2021.103497

Crozet, M., Mayer, T., & Mucchielli, J. L. (2004). How do firms agglomerate? A study of FDI in France. *Regional Science and Urban Economics*, *34*(1), 27–54. doi:10.1016/S0166-0462(03)00010-3

Cui, L., & Song, M. (2019). Economic evaluation of the Belt and Road Initiative from an unimpeded trade perspective. *International Journal of Logistics Research and Applications*, *22*(1), 25–46. doi:10.1080/13675567.2018.1492532

Dang, L., & Zhao, J. (2020). Cultural risk and management strategy for Chinese enterprises' overseas investment. *China Economic Review*, *61*, 61. doi:10.1016/j.chieco.2020.101433

De Groot, H. L. F., Poot, J., & Smit, M. (2016). Which agglomeration externalities matter most and why. *Journal of Economic Surveys*, *30*(4), 756–782. doi:10.1111/joes.12112

Debaere, P., Lee, J., & Paik, M. (2010). Agglomeration, backward and forward linkages: Evidence from South Korean investment in China. *The Canadian Journal of Economics. Revue Canadienne d'Economique*, *43*(2), 520–546. doi:10.1111/j.1540-5982.2010.01582.x

DeCoster, G. P., & Strange, W. C. (1993). Spurious Agglomeration. *Journal of Urban Economics*, *33*(3), 273–304. doi:10.1006/juec.1993.1017

Defever, F. (2006). Functional fragmentation and the location of multinational firms in the enlarged Europe. *Regional Science and Urban Economics*, *36*(5), 658–677. doi:10.1016/j.regsciurbeco.2006.06.007

Demirhan, E., & Masca, M. (2008). Determinants of Foreign Direct Investment Flows to De-veloping Countries: A Cross-Sectional Analysis. *Prague Economic Papers*, *17*(4), 356–369. doi:10.18267/j.pep.337

Deng, Z. (2019). *Research on Influencing Factors of Cultural Trade between China and Countries Along the Belt and Road under the Background of "One Belt One Road"*. Hunan Normal University.

Deron, L., Pairault, T., & Pasquali, P. (2021). *Montenegro, China, and the Media: A Highway to Disinformation?* (No. 07/2021). Briefing Paper.

Derudder, B., Liu, X., & Kunaka, C. (2018). *Connectivity along Overland Corridors of the Belt and Road Initiative*. MTI Global Practice Discussion Paper; No. 6. World Bank.

Devereux, M. P., Griffith, R., & Simpson, H. (2007). Firm location decisions, regional grants and agglomeration externalities. *Journal of Public Economics*, *91*(3-4), 413–435. doi:10.1016/j.jpubeco.2006.12.002

Dimitrijević, D. (2017). *Capacities for Development Serbia's Cooperation with China*. China-CEE Institute. Working paper, No. 4.

Dimitrova, A., Rogmans, T., & Triki, D. (2020). Country-specific determinants of FDI inflows to the MENA region: A systematic review and future research directions. *Multinational Business Review*, *28*(1), 1–38. doi:10.1108/MBR-01-2019-0003

Dinh, T. T.-H., Vo, D. H., The Vo, A., & Nguyen, T. C. (2019). The Vo, A., & Nguyen, TC. (2019). Foreign Direct Investment and Economic Growth in the Short Run and Long Run: Empirical Evidence from Developing Countries. *Journal of Risk and Financial Management.*, *12*(4), 176. doi:10.3390/jrfm12040176

Disdier, A. C., & Mayer, T. (2004). How different is eastern Europe? Structure and determinants of location choices by French firms in eastern and western Europe. *Journal of Comparative Economics*, *32*(2), 280–296. doi:10.1016/j.jce.2004.02.004

Dkhili, H., & Dhiab, L. (2018). The Relationship between Economic Freedom and FDI versus Economic Growth: Evidence from the GCC Countries. *Journal of Risk and Financial Management*, *11*(4), 81. doi:10.3390/jrfm11040081

Domazet, I., & Marjanović, D. (2017). Foreign Direct Investment in the Function of Economic Development-Example of Selected Countries in the Western Balkans. *International Letters of Social and Humanistic Sciences*, *79*, 1-15.

Domazet, I., & Marjanović, D. (2017). Tax incentives as a factor of economic growth. In The state and the market in economic development. Brisbane, Australia: The International Institute for Development Studies.

Domazet, I., & Marjanović, D. (2018) Foreign Direct Investment and Economic Development: Comparative Analysis of Bulgarian, Romanian and Serbian Economies. In Western Balkans Economies in EU Integration: past, present and future. CEMAFI International Association.

Domazet, I., & Marjanović, D. (2018). FDI as a Factor of Improving the Competitiveness of Developing Countries: FDI and Competitiveness. In Foreign Direct Investments (FDIs) and Opportunities for Developing Economies in the World Market. Hershey, PA: Business Science Reference.

Domazet, I., & Marjanović, D. (2018). *Foreign direct investment and economic development: Comparative analysis of Bulgarian, Romanian and Serbian economies*. Academic Press.

Domazet, I., & Marjanović, D. (2018). Foreign Direct Investment and Economic Development: Comparative Analysis of Bulgarian, Romanian and Serbian Economies. In Western Balkans Economies in EU Integration: Past, present and future. CEMAFI International Association.

Domazet, I., & Marjanovic, D. M. (2017). Foreign Direct Investment in the Function of Economic Development-Example of Selected Countries in the Western Balkans. *International Letters of Social and Humanistic Sciences, 79.*

Domazet, I., Marjanović, D., & Stošić, I. (2018). Attractiveness of the domicile economy through tax incentives. *Ekonomika preduzeća, 66*(7-8), 434-445.

Domazet, I., & Marjanovic, D. (2017). *Foreign Direct Investment in the Function of Economic Development - Example of Selected Countries in the Western Balkans. In International Letters of Social and Humanistic Sciences* (Vol. 79). SciPress Ltd.

Donaubauer, J., Neumayer, E., & Nunnenkamp, P. (2019). Financial market development in host and source countries and their effects on bilateral foreign direct investment. *World Economy*, *43*(3), 534–556. doi:10.1111/twec.12884

Donauber, J., Meyer, B. E., & Nunnenkamp, P. (2016). A new global index of infrastructure: Construction, rankings and applications. *World Economy*, *39*(2), 236–259. Advance online publication. doi:10.1111/twec.12290

Dornean, A., & Oanea, D.-C. (2015). Impact of the Economic Crisis on FDI in Central and Eastern Europe. *Review of Economic and Business Studies*, *8*(2), 53–68. doi:10.1515/rebs-2016-0003

Drukker, D. M. (2003). Testing for serial correlation in linear panel-data models. *The Stata Journal*, *3*(2), 168–177. doi:10.1177/1536867X0300300206

Du, J., & Wang, Y. (2013). Reforming SOEs under China's state capitalism. *Unfinished Reforms in the Chinese Economy*, 1-38.

Du, J. (2021). A Review Of Twenty Years Of Research On Chinese Discourse Identity Construction Based On CiteSpace. *Advanced Management Science*, *10*(1), 12–18.

Du, J., & Zhang, Y. (2018). Does one belt one road initiative promote Chinese overseas direct investment? *China Economic Review*, *47*, 189–205. doi:10.1016/j.chieco.2017.05.010

Đukić, M., Jovanoski, I., Munitlak-Ivanović, O., Lazić, M., & Bodroža, D. (2016). Cost-benefit analysis of an infrastructure project and a cost-reflective tariff: A case study for investment in wastewater treatment plant in Serbia. *Renewable and Sustainable Energy Reviews, 59*, 1419–1425.

Dumon, M. (2014). *Top 6 Factors That Drive Investment in China*. https://www.investopedia.com/articles/economics/09/factors-drive-investment-in-china.asp

Dunford, M., & Liu, W. (2019). Chinese perspectives on the Belt and Road Initiative. *Cambridge Journal of Regions, Economy and Society*, *12*(1), 145–167. doi:10.1093/cjres/rsy032

Dunning, J. H. (1988). The Eclectic Paradigm of International Production: A Restatement and Some Possible Extensions. *Journal of International Business Studies*, *19*(1), 1–31. doi:10.1057/palgrave.jibs.8490372

Dunning, J. H. (1992). Explaining international production. *Journal of International Development*, *4*(6), 655–655.

Dunning, J. H. (1993). *Multinational Enterprises and the Global Economy*. Addison-Wesley Publishers Company Inc.

Dunning, J. H. (1993). *Multinational enterprises and the global economy*. Addison-Wesley Publishing Company.

Economides, S. (2020, March). From fatigue to resistance: EU enlargement and the Western Balkans. *The Dahrendorf Forum*.

Economy, E. C. (2014). China's Imperial President: Xi Jinping Tightens His Grip. *Foreign Affairs*, 80–99.

Editorial. (2017, January 7). *Sixth JCC on CPEC*. Islamabad, Pakistan: Parliaments Times.

Egger, P., & Pfaermayer, M. (2009). The Impact of Bilateral Investment Treaties on Foreign Direct Investment. *Journal of Comparative Economics*, *32*(4), 788–804. doi:10.1016/j.jce.2004.07.001

Elkins, Z., Guzman, A. T., & Simmons, B. A. (2006). Competing for capital: The diffusion of bilateral investment treaties, 1960-2000. *International Organization*, *60*(4), 811–846. doi:10.1017/S0020818306060279

Erić, D., Đukić, M., & Bodroža, D. (2021). *Finansijska tržišta X.O. Belgrade*. Data Status, Republic of Serbia.

Escobar, P. (2016). Silk Roads, Night Trains, and the Third Industrial Revolution in China. *New Perspectives Quarterly*, *33*(1), 24–31. doi:10.1111/npqu.12020

European Chamber of Commerce. (2019). *Business Confidence Survey*. Available at: https://www.eurochambres.eu/

European Commission. (2020). *White paper on levelling the playing field as regards foreign subsidies*. Available at: https://ec.europa.eu/competition-policy/system/files/2021-06/foreign_subsidies_white_paper_en.pdf

European Commission. (2021a). *First Annual Report on the screening of foreign direct investments into the Union*. Available at: https://trade.ec.europa.eu/doclib/docs/2021/november/tradoc_159935.pdf

European Commission. (2021b). *List of screening mechanisms notified by Member States*. Available at: https://trade.ec.europa.eu/doclib/docs/2019/ june/tradoc_157946.pdf

European Court of Auditors (ECA). (2020). *The EU's response to China's state-driven investment strategy*. Available at: https://www.euractiv.com/wp-content/uploads/sites/2/2020/09/ECA_EU-China-review_EMBARGO-THU-10-SEP-09H00-CET.pdf

European Parliament. (2019). *China, the 16+1 format and the EU*. Available at: https://www.europarl.europa.eu/RegData/etudes/BRIE/2018/625173/EPRS_BRI (2018)625173_EN.pdf

Eurostat. (2021). *China-EU - international trade in goods statistics*. Available at: https://ec.europa.eu/eurostat/statistics-explained/index.php?title=China-EU_-_international_trade_in_goods_statistics

Falk, M. (2007). R&D spending in the high-tech sector and economic growth. *Research in Economics*, *61*(3), 140–147. doi:10.1016/j.rie.2007.05.002

Fallon, T. (2015). The new silk road: Xi Jinping's grand strategy for Eurasia. *American Foreign Policy Interests*, 112-134.

Fang, Y., & Ma, R. (2018). Cultural trade potential and influencing factors between China and the countries along with the "Belt and Road": an empirical study based on the stochastic frontier gravity model. *World Economic Research*, (1).

Fardella, E., & Prodi, G. (2017). The Belt and Road Initiative Impact on Europe: An Italian Perspective. *China & World Economy*, *25*(5), 125–138. doi:10.1111/cwe.12217

Fazil, M. D. (2016). 5 Reasons Gwadar Port Trumps Chabahar. *The Diplomate*, 2.

Feigenbaum, E. A. (2017). China and the world: Dealing with a reluctant power. *Foreign Affairs*, *96*, 33.

Ferdinand, P. (2016). Westward ho—the China dream and 'one belt, one road': Chinese foreign policy under Xi Jinping. *International Affairs*, *92*(4), 62–71. doi:10.1111/1468-2346.12660

Flint, C., & Zhu, C. (2018). The geopolitics of connectivity, cooperation, and hegemonic competition: The Belt and Road Initiative. *Geoforum*, *99*, 95–101. doi:10.1016/j.geoforum.2018.12.008

Ford, S., & Strange, R. (1999). Where do Japanese manufacturing firms invest within Europe and why? *Transnational Corporations*, *8*(1), 117–140.

François, de S., Alen, M., & Michele, R. (2019). Common transport infrastructure: A quantitative model and estimates from the Belt and Road Initiative. *Journal of Development Economics*, 143.

Freimane, R., & Bāliņa, S. (2016). Research and development expenditures and economic growth in the EU: A panel data analysis. *Economics and Business*, *29*(1), 5–11. doi:10.1515/eb-2016-0016

Freire-Serén, M. J. (1999). *Aggregate R&D expenditure and endogenous economic growth* (UFAE and IAE Working Papers No. WP 43699). Barcelona, Spain: Unitat de Fonaments de l'Anàlisi Econòmica (UAB) and Institut d'Anàlisi Econòmica (CSIC).

Freymann, E. (2021, March 25). The U.S. can't keep waiting for China's Belt and Road Initiative to fail. *Fortune*. https://fortune.com/2021/03/24/china-belt-road-initiative-soft-power/

Frieden, J., & Walter, S. (2017). Understanding the political economy of the Eurozone crisis. *Annual Review of Political Science*, *20*(1), 371–390. doi:10.1146/annurev-polisci-051215-023101

Fung, C.K., Garcia-Herrero, A., Lizaka, H., & Siu, A. (2005). Hard or soft? Institutional reforms and infrastructure spending as determinants of foreign direct investment in China. *Japanese Economic Review*, *4*(56), 408-416.

Fu, Y., Wu, D., Wang, Y., & Wang, H. (2020). Facility location and capacity planning considering policy preference and uncertain demand under the One Belt One Road initiative. *Transportation Research Part A, Policy and Practice*, *138*, 172–186. doi:10.1016/j.tra.2020.05.012

Gabor, H. (2000). Home Country Patterns of Foreign Direct Investment in Central and East European Countries. *Russian and East European Finance and Trade*, *36*(2), 87–104. doi:10.2307/27749524

Gadocha, P.M. (2020). Assessing the EU Framework Regulation for the Screening of Foreign Direct Investment—What Is the Effect on Chinese Investors? *The Chinese Journal of Global Governance*.

Galenkova, A. D., Drapkin, I. M., & Mariev, O. (2018). The impact of institutional efficiency on the foreign direct investment inflows in developing countries. *CBU International Conference Proceedings*, *6*(0), 141-145. 10.12955/cbup.v6.1146

Ge, Y., Dollar, D., & Yu, X. (2020). Institutions and participation in global value chains: Evidence from belt and road initiative. *China Economic Review*, *61*, 61. doi:10.1016/j.chieco.2020.101447

Ghossein, T., Hoekman, B., & Shingal, A. (2018). *Public procurement in the Belt and Road Initiative*. Discussion paper no. 10, The World Bank Group.

Globerman, S., & Shapiro, D. (2002). Global foreign direct investment flows The role of governance infrastructure. *World Development*, *30*(11), 1899–1919. doi:10.1016/S0305-750X(02)00110-9

Göçer, I. (2013). Effects of R&D expenditures on high technology exports, balance of foreign trade and economic growth. *Maliye Dergisi*, (165), 215–240.

Goh, B. (2015). China Railway Group Team Wins $1.6 Bln Hungary High-Speed Rail Contract. *Reuters*. Available at: https://greenfdc.org/countries-of-the-belt-and-road-initiative-bri

GoldenBees. (2017). *The 2017 GoldenBees Chinese Companies' Corporate Social Responsibility Report*. http://images.mofcom.gov.cn/csr/201712/20171219174229375.pdf

Górnikiewicz, M., & Zelkowski, J. (2020). Belt and Road Initiative in the Age of COVID-19 Pandemic: Implications for the Development of the Strategic Project of the People's Republic of China. *European Research Studies Journal*, *23*(3), 302–310. doi:10.35808/ersj/1884

Greene, W. (2000). *Econometric Analysis*. Prentice-Hall.

Grgić, M. (2019). Chinese infrastructural investments in the Balkans: Political implications of the highway project in Montenegro. *Territory, Politics, Governance*, *7*(1), 42–60. doi:10.1080/21622671.2017.1359106

Grieger, G. (2016). One Belt, One Road (OBOR): China's regional integration initiative. European Parliamentry Research Service, 1-5.

Grieger, G. (2018). *China, the 16+1 Format and the EU*. Members' Research Service PE 625.173. Available at: http://www.europarl.europa.eu/RegData/etudes/ BRIE/2018/625173/EPRS_BRI(2018)625173_EN.pdf.

Groh, A. P., & Wich, M. (2012). Emerging economies' attraction of foreign direct investment. *Emerging Markets Review*, *13*(2), 210–229. doi:10.1016/j.ememar.2012.03.005

Guihong, Z. (2003). US security policy towards South Asia after September 11 and its Implications for China: a Chinese perspective. *Strategic Analysis*, 24-34.

Gujarati, D. (2004). *Basic Econometrics*. United States Military Academy.

Gülmez, A., & Yardımcıog˘lu, F. (2012). The relationship between R&D expenditures and economic growth in OECD Countries: Panel cointegration and panel causality analyses (1990–2010)]. *Maliye Dergisi*, (163), 335–353.

Gurgul, H., & Lach, L. (2014). Globalization and economic growth: Evidence from two decades of transition in CEE. *Economic Modelling*, *36*, 99–107. doi:10.1016/j.econmod.2013.09.022

Håkanson, L. (1979). *Towards a theory of location and corporate growth*. Willey.

Hali, S. M. (2016). One Belt and One Road: Impact on China-Pakistan Economic Corridor. *Strategic Studies*, 12-18.

Hanink, D. M. (1997). Principles and applications of economic geography. In Economy, Policy, Environment. John Wiley and Sons, Inc.

Hansen, H., & Rand, J. (2006). On the Causal Links Between FDI and Growth in Developing Countries. *World Economy*, *29*(1), 21–41. doi:10.1111/j.1467-9701.2006.00756.x

Han, Y., Wang, H., & Wei, D. (2021). *The Belt and Road Initiative, sister-city partnership and Chinese outward FDI*. Economic Research-Ekonomska Istrazivanja. doi:10.1080/1331677X.2021.1997618

Hayakawa, K., Lee, H. H., & Park, C. Y. (2022). The Effect of COVID-19 on Foreign Direct Investment. *Asian Development Bank Economics Working Paper Series*, (653). https://papers.ssrn.com/sol3/papers.cfm?abstract_id=4060417

Hayter, R. (1997). Dynamics of Industrial Location: The Factory, the Firm and the Production System. John Wiley & Sons Ltd.

He, A. (2019). *The Belt and Road Initiative: Motivations, Financing, Expansion and Challenges of Xi's Ever-expanding Strategy. CIGI Papers, No. 225.* Centre for International Governance Innovation.

Head, K., Ries, J., & Swenson, D. (1995). Agglomeration benefits and location choice: Evidence from Japanese manufacturing investments in the United States. *Journal of International Economics*, *38*(3-4), 223–247. doi:10.1016/0022-1996(94)01351-R

Heide, D., Hoppe, T., Scheuer, S., & Stratmann, K. (2018). *EU ambassadors band together against Silk Road.* Handelsblatt.

Heilbron, A., & Whyte, R. (2019). *Institutions for Investment: Establishing a High-Performing Institutional Framework for Foreign Direct Investment. Finance, Competitiveness, and Innovation in Focus.* World Bank.

Helpman, E. (1984). A simple theory of international trade within multinational corporations. *Journal of Political Economy, Vol*, *92*(3), 451–471. doi:10.1086/261236

Hilber, C., & Voicu, I. (2010). Agglomeration economies and the location of foreign direct investment: Empirical evidence from Romania. *Regional Studies*, *44*(3), 355–371. doi:10.1080/00343400902783230

Hobbs, S., & Paparas, D., & AboElsoud, M.E. (2021). Does Foreign Direct Investment and Trade Promote Economic Growth? Evidence from Albania. *Economies*, *9*(1), 1–19. doi:10.3390/economies9010001

Hofman, B. (2015). *China's One Belt One Road Initiative: What We Know Thus Far.* Available at: https://blogs.worldbank.org/eastasiapacific/china-one-belt-one-road-initiative-what-we-know-thus-far

Hofman, I. (2016). Politics or profits along the "Silk Road": What drives Chinese farms in Tajikistan and helps them thrive? *Eurasian Geography and Economics*, *57*(3), 457–481. doi:10.1080/15387216.2016.1238313

Holslag, J. (2019). The Silk Road Trap. Polity Press.

Holzner, M., & Schwarzhappel, M. (2018). *Infrastructure Investment in the Western Balkans: A First Analysis.* European Investment Bank and The Vienna Institute for International Economic Studies.

Hong, J. (2009). Firm heterogeneity and location choices: Evidence from foreign manufacturing investments in China. *Urban Studies (Edinburgh, Scotland)*, *46*(10), 2143–2157. doi:10.1177/0042098009339425

Hook, G. D. (2022). China's Silk Road. Encyclopedia of Violence, Peace, & Conflict, 1, 562-570.

Horobeţ, A., & Popovici, O. (2017). Investiţiile Străine Directe: Evoluţia şi importanţa lor în România. *Studiu realizat în parteneriat de Academia de Studii Economice Bucureşti şi Consiliul Investitotilor Străini*, 2. https://www.researchgate.net/profile/Alexandra_Horobet/publication/321016706_INVESTITIILE_STRAINE_DIRECTE_EVOLUTIA_SI_IMPORTANTA_LOR_IN_ROMANIA/links/5a0806a1a6fdcc65eab3c7e7/INVESTITIILE-STRAINE-DIRECTE-EVOLUTIA-SI-IMPORTANTA-LOR-IN-ROMANIA.pdf

Horsley, J. P. (2016). *China Promotes Open Government as it Seeks to Reinvent Its Government Model.* https://law.yale.edu/sites/default/files/china-law-documents/2016_horsley_china_promotes_open_government.pdf

Houghwout, A. F. (2001). Infrastructure and Social Welfare in Metropolitan America. *Economic Policy Review*, *7*(3), 1–16.

Hou, W. (2018). *Analysis of the trade pattern and influencing factors between China and the countries along the "Belt and Road"*. China University of Geosciences.

Howitt, P. (2000). Endogenous Growth and Gross country Income Differences. *The American Economic Review*, *90*(4), 111–130. doi:10.1257/aer.90.4.829

Hsu, S. (2017). *Trump's Support For China's One Belt, One Road Initiative Is Bad For U.S., Good For World.* Forbes.

Huang, Y. (2016). Understanding China's Belt & Road Initiative: Motivation, framework and assessment. *China Economic Review*, *40*, 314–321. doi:10.1016/j.chieco.2016.07.007

Huang, Y. Y., Fischer, T. B., & Xu, H. (2017). The stakeholder analysis for sea of Chinese foreign direct investment: The case of "One Belt, One Road" initiative in Pakistan. *Impact Assessment and Project Appraisal*, *35*(2), 158–171. doi:10.1080/14615517.2016.1251698

Hubert, F., & Pain, N. (2002). Fiscal incentives, European integration and the location of foreign direct investment. *Manchester School*, *70*(3), 336–363. doi:10.1111/1467-9957.00306

Hughes, A. C. (2018). Understanding and Minimizing Environmental Impacts of the Belt and Road Initiative. *Conservation Biology*, *33*(4), 883–894. doi:10.1111/cobi.13317 PMID:30900273

Huňady, J., & Orviská, M. (2014). The Impact of Research and Development Expenditures on Innovation Performance and Economic Growth of the Country – the Empirical Evidence. *CBU International Conference Proceedings 2014, 2*, 119–125.

Huntington, H. G. (2015). Crude oil trade and current account deficits. *Energy Economies*, *50*, 70–79. doi:10.1016/j.eneco.2015.03.030

Hurley, J., Morris, S. & Portelance, G., (2018). *Examining the Debt Implications of the Belt and Road Initiative from a Policy Perspective.* Centre for Global Development, CGD Policy Paper 121.

Hurley, J., Morris, S., & Portelance, G. (2018). *Examining the Debt Implications of the Belt and Road Initiative from a Policy Perspective. CGD Policy Paper No. 121.* Center for Global Development.

Hussain, Z., Hanif, N., Wasim, A. S., & Nadeem, M. (2019). Empirical analysis of multiple infrastructural covariates: An application of gravity model on Asian economies. *Asian Economic and Financial Review*, *9*(3), 299–317. doi:10.18488/journal.aefr.2019.93.299.317

Hymer, S. H. (1976). *The International Operations of National Firms: a Study of Direct Foreign Investment.* MIT Press.

IMF. (2009). *Balance of Payments and International Investment Position Manual* (6th ed.). https://www.imf.org/external/pubs/ft/bop/2007/pdf/bpm6.pdf

Imtiaz, S., & Bashir, M. F. (2017). Economic freedom and foreign direct investment in South Asian countries, Theoretical and Applied Economics. *Asociatia Generala a Economistilor din Romania, 24*(2), 277–290. Available at: https://econpapers.repec.org/article/agrjournl/v_3axxiv_3ay_3a2017_3ai_3a2(611)_3ap_3a277-290.htm

International Crisis Group. (2018). *China-Pakistan Economic Corridor: Opportunities and Risks.* www.crisisgroup.org/asia/south-asia/pakistan/297-china-pakistan-economic-corridor-opportunities-and- risks.

Irshad, M. S., & Hamza, A. (2018). An empirical analysis of Pakistan's bilateral trade and trade potential with China: A gravity model approach. *Cogent Economics & Finance, 6*(1).

Iwaisako, T., & Futagami, K. (2013). Patent protection, capital accumulation, and economic growth. *Economic Theory*, *52*(2), 631–668. doi:10.100700199-011-0658-y

Jacimovic, D., Dragutinović Mitrović, R., Bjelić, P., Tianping, K., & Rajkovic, M. (2018). The role of Chinese investments in the bilateral exports of new E.U. member states and Western Balkan countries, *Economic Research - Ekonomska Istrazivanja*, *31*(1), 1185–1197. doi:10.1080/1331677X.2018.1456357

Jaćimović, D., & Milović, N. (2022). Montenegro: Enlargement Solidarity, Hoping for the Best…. In *European Solidarity in Action and the Future of Europe* (pp. 143–145). Springer. doi:10.1007/978-3-030-86537-5_34

Jaćimović, D., Milović, N., Miščević, T., & Radenović, M. (2021). Does China Challenge Integration Perspective of the Western Balkan Countries? *12th SCF International Conference on "Contemporary Issues in Social Sciences,"* 164–173.

Jacques, M. (2021). *G7 no longer able to order world around: Martin Jacques*. https://www.globaltimes.cn/page/202106/1225664.shtml

Jeganaathan, J. (2015). OBOR'and South Asia: Can India and China Cope with the Emerging 'New Normal'in the Region? *Fudan Journal of the Humanities and Social Sciences*, 12–19.

Jin, B., Garcia, F., & Salomon, R. (2019). Inward foreign direct investment and local firm innovation: The moderating role of technological capabilities. *Journal of International Business Studies*, *50*(5), 847–855. doi:10.105741267-018-0177-1

Jin, Y., Tang, Y. M., Chau, K. Y., & Abbas, M. (2022). How government expenditure Mitigates emissions: A step towards sustainable green economy in belt and road initiative project. *Journal of Environmental Management*, *303*, 113967. doi:10.1016/j.jenvman.2021.113967 PMID:34810022

Johnson, A. (2006). *The effects of FDI inflows on host country economic growth*. The Royal Institute of technology. Centre of Excellence for studies in Science and Innovation.

Johnston, L. A. (2019). The Belt and Road Initiative: What is in it for China? *Asia & the Pacific Policy Studies*, *6*(1), 40–58. doi:10.1002/app5.265

Jojić, S. (2017). *How Serbia perceives "The Belt and the Road" Initiative and 16+1 Cooperation*. China-CEE Institute. Working paper, No. 9.

Jones, G. (1996). *The evolution of international business: an introduction*. Routledge. https://onlinelibrary.wiley.com/doi/epdf/10.1111/aehr.372br1

Jones, J. (2017). Agglomeration economies and the location of foreign direct investment: A meta-analysis. *Journal of Regional Science*, *57*(5), 1–17. doi:10.1111/jors.12335

Jordaan, J. C. (2004). *Foreign direct investment and neighbouring influences* (Doctoral dissertation). University of Pretoria.

Jovičić, E., Stevanović, S., & Beraha, I. (2020). Serbia - China Bilateral Trade Relations : Major Challenges and Opportunities. *Economic Analysis*, *53*(2), 133–144. doi:10.28934/ea.20.53.2.pp133-144

Jovičić, E., Stevanović, S., & Beraha, I. (2020). Serbia-China Bilateral Trade Relations: Major Challenges and Opportunities. *Economic Analysis*, *53*(2), 133–144.

Jude, C., & Levieuge, G. (2017). Growth Effect of Foreign Direct Investment in Developing Economies: The Role of Institutional Quality. *World Economy*, *40*(4), 715–742. doi:10.1111/twec.12402

Julien, C., & Mitsuo, M. (2018). China's 'Belt and Road' Initiative — Mapping the World's Normative and Strategic Implications. *Journal of World Trade*, *1*, 163–185.

Jyun-Yi, W., & Chih-Chiang, H. (2008). Does foreign direct investment promote economic growth? Evidence from a threshold regression analysis. *Economic Bulletin*, *15*, 1–10.

Kaczmarski, M., & Jakóbowski, J. (2015). China on Central-Eastern Europe: "16+1" as seen from Beijing. *OSW Commentary, 166.*

Kandiero, T., & Chitiga, M. (2014). Trade openness and foreign direct investment in Africa. *Suid-Afrikaanse Tydskrif vir Ekonomiese en Bestuurswetenskappe, 9*(3), 355–357. doi:10.4102ajems.v9i3.1093

Kang, L., Peng, F., Zhu, F., & Pan, A. (2018). Harmony in Diversity: Can the One Belt One Road Initiative Promote China's Outward Foreign Direct Investment? *Sustainability, 10*(9), 3264. doi:10.3390u10093264

Karras, G. (2003). Trade openness and economic growth can we estimate the precise effect? *Applied Econometrics and International Development AEEADE, 3*(1), 7–25.

Kaur, M., & Sharma, R. (2013). Determinants of foreign direct investment in India: An empirical analysis. *Decision (Washington, D.C.), 40*(1/2), 57–67.

Kavalski, E. (2020). *Is China out the window in the CEE?* Available at: https://www.echo-wall.eu/currents-context/chinaout-window-cee

Kazar, G., Kazar, A., & Sert, T. S. (2018). Bilateral Trade in European Sports Industry: Linder versus Hecksher-Ohlin-Samuelson. *International Journal of Economics and Financial Issues, 8*(1), 48.

Kazembe, P., & Namizinga, N. (2007). *The Impact of Foreign Direct Investment on Development: Policy Challenges for Malawi.* Integrated Framework Policy Analysis Working Paper Series, No. 6. Government of Malawi Ministry of Industry, Trade and Private Sector Development Integrated Framework Policy Analysis.

Khan, H., & Khan, U. (2019). Financial development and FDI inflows in China. Kiel Institute for the World Economy. Economics Discussion Papers No. 2019-54.

Khaze, N. M. (2018). European Union's enlargement fatigue: Russia's and China's rise in Southeast Europe? *Australian and New Zealand Journal of European Studies, 10*(1).

Kmenta, J. (1986). *Elements of Econometrics* (2nd ed.). Macmillan.

Korybko, A. (2015). Pakistan is the "Zipper" of Pan-Euroasian Integration. Russian Institute of Strategic Studies, 1.

Korybko, A. (2017). Pakistan's Response to Hybrid War on CPEC? *Regional Rapport*, 1-3.

Kratz, A., Rosen, D. H., & Mingey, M. (2020). *Booster or Brake? COVID and the Belt and Road Initiative.* Rhodium Group. Available at: https://rhg.com/research/booster-or-brake-covid-and-the-belt-and-road-initiative

Kratz, A., Zenglein, M. J., & Sebastian, G. (2021). *Chinese FDI in Europe: 2020 Update*. Mercator Institute for China Studies. Available at: https://merics.org/en/report/chinese-fdi-europe-2020-update

Kratz, A., Huotari, M., Hanemann, T., & Arcesati, R. (2020). *Chinese FDI in Europe: 2019 Update.* MERICS.

Krstinovska, A. (2020a). The place of North Macedonia in China's strategy for the Western Balkans. Konrad-Adenauer-Stiftung, Office in Skopje.

Krstinovska, A. (2020b). The business dimension of the Belt and Road Initiative: case study on Macedonian companies. ESTIMA.

Krugman, P. R. (1991). *First Nature, Second Nature, and Metropolitan Location.* NBER Working Papers 3740, National Bureau of Economic Research.

Krugman, P. (1991). Increasing Returns and Economic Geographic. *Journal of Political Economy, 99*(3), 483–499. doi:10.1086/261763

Krugman, P. R., & Venables, A. J. (1996). Integration, Specialization, and Adjustment. *European Economic Review*, *40*(3-5), 959–967. doi:10.1016/0014-2921(95)00104-2

Kynge, J., & Yu, S. (2020). China faces wave of calls for debt relief on "Belt and Road" projects. *Financial Times*.

Lakshmanan, T.R. (2011).The broader economic consequences of transport infrastructure investments. *Journal of Transport Geography, 19*(1), 1-12. . doi:10.1016/j.jtrangeo.2010.01.001

Laura, A., Chanda, A., & Kalemli-Ozcan, S. (2004). FDI and economic growth:The role of local financial markets. *Journal of International Economics*, *64*(1), 89–112. doi:10.1016/S0022-1996(03)00081-3

Lechmacher, W., & Padilla-Taylor, V. (2015). Hurdles Ahead Along the "New Silk Road." *Financial Times Blog*. Available at: http://blogs.ft.com/beyondbrics/2015/09/17/hurdles-ahead-along-the-new-silk-road/

Lee, S. T. (2021). Vaccine diplomacy: Nation branding and China's COVID-19 soft power play. *Place Branding and Public Diplomacy*, 1–15. doi:10.105741254-021-00224-4

Levin, A., Lin, C. F., & Chu, C. S. J. (2002). Unit root tests in panel data: Asymptotic and finite-sample properties. *Journal of Econometrics*, *108*(1), 1–24. doi:10.1016/S0304-4076(01)00098-7

Li, F. (2016). A study on China's foreign direct investment policy. *Globalization*, 10.

Liang, C., Shah, S. A., & Bifei, T. (2021). The Role of FDI Inflow in Economic Growth: Evidence from Developing Countries. *Journal of Advanced Research in Economics and Administrative Sciences*, *2*(1), 68–80. doi:10.47631/jareas.v2i1.212

Li, C., & Tanna, S. (2019). The impact of foreign direct investment on productivity: New evidence for developing countries. *Economic Modelling*, *80*, 453–466. doi:10.1016/j.econmod.2018.11.028

Lichtenberg, F. R. (1992). *R&D investment and international productivity differences* (Working Paper No. 4161). Cambridge.

Li, J., Liu, B., & Qian, G. (2019). The Belt and Road Initiative, cultural friction and ethnicity: Their effects on the export performance of SMEs in China. *Journal of World Business*, *54*(4), 350–359. doi:10.1016/j.jwb.2019.04.004

Li, K. X., Jin, M., Qi, G., Shi, W., & Ng, A. K. Y. (2018). Logistics as a driving force for development under the Belt and Road Initiative–the Chinese model for developing countries. *Transport Reviews*, *38*(4), 457–478. doi:10.1080/01441647.2017.1365276

Li, K., & Lin, B. (2017). Economic growth model, structural transformation, and green productivity in China. *Applied Energy*, *187*, 489–500. doi:10.1016/j.apenergy.2016.11.075

Lill, A., & Babula, R. (2009). The link between openness and long-run economic growth. *Journal of International Commerce and Economics*, *2*, 31–50.

Lim, A. C. (2016). China's 'Belt and Road' and Southeast Asia: Challenges and Prospects. *IPP Review*, 22-27.

Lin, H. (2021). *The Map and Project Overview of China-Pakistan Economic Corridor*. Wechat. https://mp.weixin.qq.com/s/LkjYS34hjGDFkgeYt0Zqmw

Lin, Y. (2016). *International production capacity cooperation: Gathering new impetus for global economic growth*. https://business.sohu.com/20160324/n441896100.shtml

Lipsey, R. E. (2002). *Home and host country effects of FDI*. NBER Working Paper No. 9293.

Lisinge, R. T. (2020). The Belt and Road Initiative and Africa's regional infrastructure development: Implications and lessons. *Transnational Corporations Review*, *12*(4), 425–438. doi:10.1080/19186444.2020.1795527

List of screening mechanisms notified by Member States. (n.d.). Available at: https://trade.ec.europa.eu/doclib/docs/2019/june/tradoc_157946.pdf

Liu, H., Li, W., & Chen, H. (2014). How does cultural fusion affect China's bilateral trade with countries along the "Belt and Road": An empirical test based on micro-trade data from 1995 to 2013. *International Trade Issues, 398*(2), 5-15.

Liu, H., Wang, Y., Jiang, J., & Wu, P. (2020). How green is the "Belt and Road Initiative"? Evidence from Chinese OFDI in the energy sector. *Energy Policy, 145*, 145. doi:10.1016/j.enpol.2020.111709

Liu, W., & Dunford, M. (2016). Inclusive globalization: Unpacking China's Belt and Road Initiative. *Area Development and Policy, 1*(3), 323–340. doi:10.1080/23792949.2016.1232598

Li, X. (2016). *Research on the Influencing Factors and Potentials of Bilateral Trade between China and Countries along with the "Belt and Road"*. Liaoning University.

Li, X., Du, T., & Wang, S. (2019). Research on the Influencing Factors and Potentials of Trade between China and Countries along the "One Belt and One Road". *International Economic Cooperation*, (3), 17–29.

Li, Y. (2018). The greater Eurasian partnership and the Belt and Road Initiative: Can the two be linked? *Journal of Eurasian Studies, 9*(2), 94–99. doi:10.1016/j.euras.2018.07.004

Lo, C. (2015). China's Silk Road strategy. *The International Economy*, 29-34.

Louis, R. (2015). The China-Pakistan Economic Corridor. Regional Dynamics and China's Geopolitical Ambitions. The National Bureau of Asian Research.

Lu, H., Rohr, C., Hafner, M., & Knack, A. (2018). *China Belt and Road Initiative: Measuring the impact of improving transport connectivity on international study.Santa Monica, Calif., and Cambridge*. RAND Corporation. doi:10.1007/978-981-13-0101-8

Lu, M. (2018). *Corporate Social Responsibility and Environmental Responsibility. Another Road to China's Sustainable Development.* Brill Nijhoff.

Luostarinen, R. (1979). Internationalization of the firm. Academiae Oeconomicae Helsingiesnsis, Series A: 30 Helsinki School of Economics.

Macaes, B. (2018). *Belt and road: A Chinese world order.* C Hurst US & Co.

Ma, D., Lei, C., Ullah, F., Ullah, R., & Baloch, Q. B. (2019). China's One Belt and One Road Initiative and Outward Chinese Foreign Direct Investment in Europe. *Sustainability, 11*(24), 7055. doi:10.3390u11247055

Mainguy, C. (2004). L'impact des investissements directs étrangers sur les économies en développement. *Région et Développement, 20*, 65–89.

Malik, D. A. (2017). Modi's Perversion of the CPEC. Institute of Strategic Studies, 1-2.

Manoj, K., Rudra, P., & Dinesh, M. (2020). *Impact of COVID -19 pandemic on foreign direct investment in Nepal from south Asian perspectives.* https://www.scribd.com/doc/215509137/Asian-in-the-Global-Economic

Mardell, J. (2020). *China's Economic Footprint in the Western Balkans.* Bertelsmann Stiftung. https://www.bertelsmann-stiftung.de/en/our-projects/germany-and-asia/news/asia-policy-brief-chinas-economic-footprint-in-the-western-balkans

Marjanović, D., & Domazet, I. (2021). Foreign Direct Investments: A Key Factor for Business Globalization. In Handbook of Research on Institutional, Economic, and Social Impacts of Globalization and Liberalization. IGI Global

Marjanović, D., & Domazet, I. (2021). Foreign Direct Investments: A Key Factor for Business Globalization. In Handbook of Research on Institutional, Economic, and Social Impacts of Globalization and Liberalization. IGI Global. doi:10.4018/978-1-7998-4459-4.ch006

Marjanović, D. (2018). Competitiveness of the Serbian Economy through the Prism of Tax Incentives for Foreign Investors. *Economic Analysis*, *51*(3-4), 95–104. doi:10.28934/ea.18.51.34.pp95-104

Marjanović, D., & Domazet, I. (2018). *Unapređenje makro konkurentnosti – fiskalni aspekti [Improving macro competitiveness - fiscal aspects]*. Institute of Economic Sciences.

Marjanović, D., Jovičić, E., & Stojanović, D. (2021). The Global Distribution of Chinese Investments: Importance for the Economy of Serbia. *Ekonomika (Nis)*, *67*(1), 43–55. doi:10.5937/ekonomika2101043M

Markovic Khaze, N., & Wang, X. (2021). Is China's rising influence in the Western Balkans a threat to European integration? *Journal of Contemporary European Studies*, *29*(2), 234–250. doi:10.1080/14782804.2020.1823340

Markusen, J. R., & Venables, A. J. (1998). Multinational firms and the new trade theory. *Journal of International Economics*, *26*(2), 183–204. doi:10.1016/S0022-1996(97)00052-4

Marshall, A. (1920). *Principles of Economics* (8th ed.). Macmillan.

Martinović, N., & Milović, N. (2021). Dužnička kriza ekonomije Crne Gore – uzroci i posljedice. In Makroekonomska stabilnost i unapređenje konkurentnosti zemalja Zapadnog Balkana. Institut ekonomskih nauka.

Matura, T. (2020). Sino–Hungarian Relations in the 21st Century. In China and Central Europe: Success or Failure? (pp. 117–136). Academic Press.

Matura, T. (2021). *Chinese Investment in Central and Eastern Europe: A reality check*. CEECAS. Available at: https://bird.tools/wp-content/uploads/2021/04/72d38a_ 373928ea28c44c7f9c875ead7fc49c44.pdf

McCaleb, A., & Szunomár, Á. (2017). Chinese foreign direct investment in Central and Eastern Europe. In J. Drahokoupil (Ed.), *Chinese investment in Europe: Corporate strategies and labour relations* (pp. 121–140). ETUI Aisbl.

McCartney, M. (2022). *The Dragon from the Mountains: The China-Pakistan Economic Corridor (CPEC) from Kashgar to Gwadar*. Cambridge University Press.

Mehic, E., Silajdzic, S. & Babic-Hodovic, V. (2013). The Impact of FDI on Economic Growth: Some Evidence from Southeast Europe. *Emerging Markets Finance and Trade, 49*(1), 5-20. doi:10.2753/REE1540-496X4901S101

Melendez-Ortiz, R. (2016). *What's ahead for the WTO: Looking around the corner and beyond.* International Centre for Trade and Sustainable Development (ICTSD). https://voxeu.org/users/ricardomel-ndez-ortiz

Mihaela, P., Waqar, A., & Helian, X. (2018). The impact of institutional quality on foreign direct investment inflows: Evidence for developed and developing countries. *Economic Research-Ekonomska Istraživanja*, *31*(1), 626–644. doi:10.1080/1331677X.2018.1438906

Milovic, N., & Jocovic, M. (2017). Impact of foreign direct investment on competitiveness of montenegrin economy. *Transformations in Business & Economics*, *16*(1), 223-23.

Milovic, N., Jocovic, M., & Martinovic, N. (2020). Analysis of the Impact of Macroeconomic Stability on the Level of Global Competitiveness of Western Balkan Countries. *Journal of Central Banking Theory and Practice*, *2*, 23–37.

Ministry of Foreign Affairs & Chamber Economy of Montenegro. (2021). *Montenegro investment and business opportunities*. Author.

Ministry of Foreign Affairs of the PRC. (2016). Available at: https://www.fmprc.gov.cn/web/zyxw/t1413173.shtml

Mirel, P. (2019). *European Union- Western Balkans: for a revised membership negotiation framework.* https://www.recom.link/ european-union-western-balkans-for-a-revisedmembership-negotiation-framework

Mirković, M. (2019). Montenegro economy briefing: Overview of Foreign Direct Investment Trends in Montenegro. China–CEE Institute, 20(2), 1-4.

Mirza, F. M., Fatima, N., & Ullah, K. (2019). Impact of China-Pakistan economic corridor on Pakistan's future energy consumption and energy saving potential: Evidence from sectoral time series analysis. *Energy Strategy Reviews*, *25*, 34–46. doi:10.1016/j.esr.2019.04.015

Mišev, G., Stanojević, P., & Jeftić, Z. (2018). Neki aspekti bezbednosti srpske infrastrukture na "Novom putu svile". In Novi put svile: Evropska perspektiva Bezbednosni izazovi/rizici unutar Inicijative 16+1 (pp. 193–207). Univerzitet u Beogradu – Fakultet bezbednosti.

Moosa, I. A. (2012). *The Determinants of Foreign Direct Investment in Mena Countries: An Extreme Bounds Analysis. Research Report 0421. Department of Economics and Finance, La Trobe University.* University of Chicago Press.

Morisset, J. (2003). *Does a country need a Promotion Agency to attract Foreign Direct Investment? A small analytical model applied to 58 counties.* https://openknowledge.worldbank.org/handle/10986/18230

Mouritz, F. (2020). Implications of the COVID-19 Pandemic on China's Belt and Road Initiative. *Connections: The Quarterly Journal, 19*(2), 115-124.

Mouritz, F. (2022). *Implications of the COVID-19 Pandemic on China's Belt and Road Initiative*. The Quarterly Journal. doi:10.11610/Connections.19.2.09

Mukhtar, A., Zhu, Y., Lee, Y., Bambacas, M., & Cavusgil, S. T. (2022). Challenges confronting the'One Belt One Road' initiative: Social networks and cross-cultural adjustment in CPEC projects. *International Business Review*, *31*(1), 101902. doi:10.1016/j.ibusrev.2021.101902

Munir, K., & Ameer, A. (2020). Nonlinear effect of FDI, economic growth, and industrialization on environmental quality: Evidence from Pakistan. *Management of Environmental Quality*, *31*(1), 223–234. doi:10.1108/MEQ-10-2018-0186

National Strategy for Agriculture and Rural Development for the period 2021-2027. (2021). Ministry of Agriculture, Forestry and Rural Development.

Naudé, W. (2004). The effects of policy, institutions, and geography on economic growth in Africa: An econometric study based on cross-section and Panel Data. *Journal of International Development*, *16*(6), 821–849. doi:10.1002/jid.1129

NBStat, National Bank of the Republic of North Macedonia. (n.d.). http://makstat.stat.gov.mk/PXWeb/pxweb/mk/MakStat/MakStat__NadvoresnaTrgovija__DetalniPod__DetKumSMTK/150_SMTK_ZEMJI_ml.px/table/tableViewLayout2/?rxid=9f41cd3f-fff2-4841-a0f7-1e2345cf5ed5

NDRC. (2015). *Vision and actions on jointly building the Silk Road Economic Belt and 21st-century Maritime Silk Road.* Available at: https://en.ndrc.gov.cn/newsrelease/201503/t20150330_669367.html

Nepal, R., Nirash, P., Bhawna, T., & Harvie, C. (2021). Energy security, economic growth and environmental sustainability in India: Does FDI and trade openness play a role? *Journal of Environmental Management*, *281*, 111886. Advance online publication. doi:10.1016/j.jenvman.2020.111886 PMID:33421939

Neumayer, E., & Spess, L. (2005). Do bilateral investment treaties increase foreign direct investment to developing countries? *World Development*, *33*(10), 1567–1585.

Nguyen, H. V., Phan, T. T., & Lobo, A. (2019). Debunking the Myth of Foreign Direct Investment toward Long-Term Sustainability of a Developing Country: A Transaction Cost Analysis Approach. *Sustainability, 11*(4569), 1–26. doi:10.3390u11174569

North, D. C. (1990). *Institutions, institutional change, and economic performance*. Cambridge University Press. doi:10.1017/CBO9780511808678

Nourzad, F., & Powell, J. J. (2003). Openness, growth, and development: Evidence from a panel of developing countries. *Scientific Journal of Administrative Development, 1*(1), 72–94.

Nowbutsing, A., Ramsohok, S., & Ramsohok, K. (2012). *The impact of openness on economic growth: Case of Indian Ocean rim countries*. ICTI.

Nugent, J. B., & Lu, J. (2021). China's outward foreign direct investment in the belt and road initiative: What are the motives for Chinese firms to invest? *China Economic Review, 68*, 68. doi:10.1016/j.chieco.2021.101628

Nunnenkamp, P., & Spatz, J. (2002). Determinants of FDI in developing countries: has globalization changed the rules of the game? Kiel Institute for World Economics, 1122.

OECD. (2008). *Benchmark Definition of Foreign Direct Investment: Fourth Edition*. https://www.oecd.org/daf/inv/investmentstatisticsandanalysis/40193734.pdf

OECD. (2018). *China's Belt and Road Initiative in the Global Trade, Investment and Finance Landscape*. OECD Publishing.

OECD. (2018). The Belt and Road Initiative in the global trade, investment and finance landscape. In *OECD Business and Finance Outlook 2018*. OECD Publishing. doi:10.1787/bus_fin_out-2018-6-

OECD. (2019). *FDI Qualities Indicators: Measuring the sustainable development impacts of investment*. https://www.oecd.org/

Office des Changes. (2017). *Echanges Maroc-Afrique Subsaharienne*. Département des Statistiques des Echanges Extérieurs.

Okano-Heijmans, M., & Lanting, D. (2015). *Europe's Response to China's Activism: Balancing Hope and Fear in the New Age of Global Economic Governance*. Clingandael Institute.

Papalia, R. B., & Bertarelli, S. (2015). Trade costs in bilateral trade flows: Heterogeneity and zeroes in structural gravity models. *World Economy, 38*(11), 1744–1762. doi:10.1111/twec.12259

Pardo, R. P. (2018). Europe's financial security and Chinese economic statecraft: The case of the Belt and Road Initiative. *Asia Europe Journal, 16*(3), 237–250. doi:10.100710308-018-0511-z

Pavlićević, D. (2019). Structural power and the China-EU-Western Balkans triangular relations. *Asia Europe Journal, 17*(4), 453–468. doi:10.100710308-019-00566-y

Peel, M., & Fleming, S. (2021, May 2). West and allies relaunch push for own version of China's Belt and Road. *Financial Times*.

Pegkas, P. (2015). The impact of FDI on economic growth in Eurozone countries. *Journal of Economic Asymmetries, 12*(2), 124–132. doi:10.1016/j.jeca.2015.05.001

Pelaudeix, C. (2021). *The rise of China and EU vulnerability*. https://halshs.archives-ouvertes.fr/halshs-03323014/document

Pendrakowska, P. (2018). Poland's perspective on the Belt and Road Initiative. *Journal of Contemporary East Asia Studies, 7*(2), 190–206. doi:10.1080/24761028.2018.1552491

Pereire, K. G. (2006). Jihad in China? Rise of the East Turkestan Islamic Movement (ETIM). Institute of Defence and Strategic Studies Commentaries, 12-23.

Pesaran, M. H. (2004). *General diagnostic tests for cross section dependence in panels*. Cambridge Working Papers in Economics 0435, University of Cambridge.

Petkova, M. (2021). The Environmental Impact of Chinese Projects in the Western Balkans. Association for International Affairs (AMO).

Petrović, L., Stojanović, D., Mitrović, S., Barać, D., & Bogdanović, Z. (2022). Designing an extended smart classroom: An approach to game-based learning for IoT. *Computer Applications in Engineering Education*, *30*(1), 117–132.

Pjanić, M., & Mitrašević, M. (2021). Foreign Direct Investments in Serbia. *Culture of Polis-Journal for Nurturing of Democratic Political Culture*, *18*(44), 253-265.

Pogany, S. I. (1992). Economic Development Agreements. *ICSID Review. Foreign Investment Law Journal*, *7*(1), 1–20. doi:10.1093/icsidreview/7.1.1

Poulain, L. (2011). China's New Balkan Strategy. Central Europe Watch, 1(2), 7.

Pradhan, R. P., Norman, N. R., Badir, Y., & Samadhan, B. (2013). Transport infrastructure, foreign direct investment and economic growth interactions in India: The ARDL bounds testing approach. *Procedia: Social and Behavioral Sciences*, *104*, 914–921.

Prague Security Studies Institute. (2019). *Comparative Analysis of the Approach towards China: V4+ and One Belt One Road*. Available at: https://ceias.eu/wp-content/uploads/2019/05/COMPARATIVE_ANALYSIS_full_05.pdf

Radević, I., & Haček, M. (2019). Decentralisation processes in Montenegrin public administration: Challenges of health system. *Lex Localis*, *17*(3), 471–492. doi:10.4335/17.3.471-493(2019)

Rafay, A., Mahdaliza Idrus, S., Mohamad Yusof, K., & Hasunah Mohammad, S. (2021). A survey on advanced transmission technologies for high bandwidth and good signal quality for high-speed railways. *Indonesian Journal of Electrical Engineering and Computer Science*, *23*(1), 293–301. doi:10.11591/ijeecs.v23.i1.pp293-301

Ramasamy, B., & Yeung, M. (2019). C H. China's one belt one road initiative: The impact of trade facilitation versus physical infrastructure on exports. *World Economy*, *42*(6), 1673–1694. doi:10.1111/twec.12808

Ramasamy, B., Yeung, M., & Laforet, S. (2012). China's outward foreign direct investment: Location choice and firm ownership. *Journal of World Business*, *47*, 17–25.

Rapaille, G. C. (2001). *7 secrets of marketing in a multicultural world*. Executive Excellence Pub.

Rauf, A., Liu, X., Amin, W., Rehman, O. U., Li, J., Ahmad, F., & Bekun, F. V. (2020). Does sustainable growth, energy consumption and environment challenges matter for Belt and Road Initiative feat? A novel empirical investigation. *Journal of Cleaner Production*, *262*, 262. doi:10.1016/j.jclepro.2020.121344

Raza, S. A., Shah, N., & Arif, I. (2019). Relationship Between FDI and Economic Growth in the Presence of Good Governance System: Evidence from OECD Countries. *Global Business Review*. Advance online publication. doi:10.1177/0972150919833484

Reenu, J., & Sharma, A. K. (2015). Trends and determinants of foreign direct investment in India: A study of the post-liberalization period. *South Asian Journal of Management*, *22*(3), 96–98.

Rehman, A., Muhammad, I., Hassan, A. M., & Muhammad, A. (2011). The Impact of Infrastructure on Foreign Direct Investment: The Case of Pakistan. *International Journal of Business and Management*, *6*(5), 268–276.

Rehman, O. U., & Ali, Y. (2021). Optimality study of China's crude oil imports through China Pakistan economic corridor using fuzzy TOPSIS and Cost-Benefit analysis. *Transportation Research Part E, Logistics and Transportation Review*, *148*, 148. doi:10.1016/j.tre.2021.102246

Rencz, F. (2019). *The BRI in Europe and the Budapest-Belgrade railway link*. Briefing Paper.

Righetti, F., Vallati, C., Anastasi, G., Masetti, G., & di Giandomenico, F. (2020). Failure management strategies for IoT-based railways systems. *IEEE International Conference on Smart Computing (SMARTCOMP)*. 10.1109/SMARTCOMP50058.2020.00082

Rodrik, D. (1992). The limits of trade policy reforms in developing countries. *The Journal of Economic Perspectives*, *6*(1), 87–105. doi:10.1257/jep.6.1.87

Rogge, N., & Archer, G. (2021). Measuring and analyzing country change in establishing ease of doing business using a revised version of World Bank's ease of doing business index. *European Journal of Operational Research*, *290*(1), 373–385. doi:10.1016/j.ejor.2020.07.065

Rolland, N. (2017). *China's Eurasian Century? Political and Strategic Implications of the Belt and Road Initiative*. National Bureau of Asian Research.

Ross, J. (2016). *China Strengthening Links with Eastern Europe*. Available at: http://www.china.org.cn/opinion/2016-05/17/content_38470993.htm

Rusu, M. (2000). *Investițiile străine directe*. Paideia Publishing House.

Ruta, M., Dappe, M. H., Lall, S., Zhang, C., Constantinescu, C., Lebrand, M., Mulabdic, A., & Churchill, E. (2019). *Belt and Road Economics: Opportunities and risks of transport corridors*. World Bank Publications.

Sabir, S., Rafique, A., & Abbas, K. (2019). Institutions and FDI: Evidence from developed and developing countries. *Financial Innovation*, *5*(8), 1–20. doi:10.118640854-019-0123-7

Saito, H., & Wu, J. (2016). Agglomeration, congestion, and U.S. regional disparities in employment growth. *Journal of Regional Science*, *56*(1), 53–71.

Samarina, M., & Bondarchuk, E. (2021). Ways to optimize process of modernization of trans-Siberian railway using digital economy technologies. *SHS Web of Conferences, 112*. 10.1051hsconf/202111200033

Samimi, A. J., & Alerasoul, S. M. (2009). R&D and economic growth: New evidence from some developing countries. *Australian Journal of Basic and Applied Sciences*, *3*(4), 3464–3469.

Saraç, T. B. (2009). *Aras¸tırma-Gelis¸tirme Harcamalarının Ekonomik Büyüme Üzerindeki Etkisi: Panel Veri Analizi* [The effect of research-development expenditures on economic growth: A panel data]. *EconAnadolu 2009: Anadolu International Conference in Economics*, Eskis¸ehir, Turkey.

Saud, S., Chen, S., & Haseen, A. (2020). The role of financial development and globalization in the environment: Accounting ecological footprint indicators for selected one-belt-one-road initiative countries. *Journal of Cleaner Production*, *250*, 250. doi:10.1016/j.jclepro.2019.119518

Sayari, K. (2019). Institutional efficiency and attraction of FDI to developing countries. *International Journal of Economic Development*, *11*(7), 54–60.

Sayari, N., Sari, R., & Hammoudeh, S. (2018). The impact of value added components of GDP and FDI on economic freedom in Europe. *Economic Systems. Elsevier*, *42*(2), 282–294. doi:10.1016/j.ecosys.2017.03.003

Seetanah, B. (2009). A Sector-Wise Panel Data Study on the Link between Transport Infrastructure and FDI in Mauritius. *9th Global Conference on Business & Economics.*

Sevba, A. (2020). *With weak pandemic management West opens door to China's influence in Balkans.* https://www.aa.com.tr/

Shakur, S. (2018). Impact of trade cost on China-EU agri-food trade. *Journal of Chinese Economic and Business Studies, 16*(3), 259–274. doi:10.1080/14765284.2018.1482089

Shao, X. (2020). Chinese OFDI responses to the B&R initiative: Evidence from a quasi-natural experiment. *China Economic Review, 61*, 61. doi:10.1016/j.chieco.2020.101435

Shi, J., Hu, X., Li, Y., & Feng, T. (2021). Does The Belt And Road Initiative Reshape China's Outward Foreign Direct Investment In ASEAN? Shifting Motives Of State-Owned And Private-Owned Enterprises. *The Singapore Economic Review, 66*(01), 161–183. doi:10.1142/S0217590819500772

Shiyuan, H. (2002). Ethno-Separatism and Terrorism. *Ethonational Studies*, 4-25.

Siddiqui, K. (2019). One Belt and One Road, China's Massive Infrastructure Project to Boost Trade and Economy: An Overview. *International Critical Thought, 9*(2), 214–235. doi:10.1080/21598282.2019.1613921

Silaghi, M., Alexa, D., Jude, C., & Litan, C. (2014). Do business and public sector research and development expenditures contribute to economic growth in Central and Eastern Europe Countries? A dynamic panel estimation. *Economic Modelling, 36*, 108–119. doi:10.1016/j.econmod.2013.08.035

Silverstein, K. (2019, December 5). *As China's 'Belt And Road' Initiative Replaces U.S. On Global Stage, The Implications for Energy And Trade.* https://www.forbes.com/sites/kensilverstein/2019/12/05/as-the-us-becomes-isolationist-china-is-becoming-globalist-the-implications-for-energy-and-trade/?sh=2eb6804719f4

Sing, G. (2016, March 9). *Chinese support to Pakistan.* New Delhi, India: Ministry of External Affairs.

Singh, P. (2015). The China Pakistan Economic Corridor and India. Institute of Defence Studies and Analyses, 3.

Singhania, M., & Gupta, A. (2011). Determinants of foreign direct investment in India. *Journal of International Trade Law & Policy, 10*(1), 64–82. doi:10.1108/14770021111116142

Siobhan, M., Nadia, R., & Michele, R. (2019). How much will the Belt and Road Initiative reduce trade costs? *International Economics,159.*

Smith, D. F., & Florida, R. (1994). Agglomeration and industrial location: An econometric analysis of Japanese-affiliated manufacturing establishments in automotive-related industries. *Journal of Urban Economics, 36*, 23–41.

Sokhanvar, A. (2019). Does foreign direct investment accelerate tourism and economic growth within Europe? *Tourism Management Perspectives, 29*, 86–96. doi:10.1016/j.tmp.2018.10.005

Soyres, F., Mulabdic, A., Murray, S., Rocha, N., & Ruta, M. (2019). How much will the Belt and Road Initiative reduce trade costs? *Inter Economics, 159*, 151–164. doi:10.1016/j.inteco.2019.07.003

Stakić, N., & Zakić, K. (2016). Challenges of business and financial transformation of China in New Normal Economy. *The Review of International Affairs, 67*(1161), 80–100.

Stancheva-Gigov, I. (2016). Foreign direct investment and economic growth: Empirical analysis. *Economic Development, 18*(1-2), 337–350.

Stancheva-Gigov, I. (2018). Transnational companies and their technological power - investments in technology development and technology transfer. *Economic Development, 20*(3), 55–68.

Stephenson, M. (2020). *Digital FDI: Policies, Regulations and Measures to Attract FDI in the Digital Economy*. World Economic Forum White Paper, September 2020. https://www3.weforum.org/docs/WEF_Digital_FDI_2020.pdf

Stoddard, O., & Noy, I. (2015). Fire-sale FDI? The Impact of Financial Crises on Foreign Direct Investment. *Review of Development Economics, 19*(2), 387–399. doi:10.1111/rode.12149

Stojanović, D. (2020). Analiza realizacije učenja na daljinu u Srbiji za vreme pandemije virusa COVID 19. In Black swan in the world economy 2020 (pp. 121–140). Institut ekonomskih nauka.

Stojanović, D., Stanisavljević, N., & Jovičić, E. (2021). Digital marketing techniques for promotion of "Infrastructure of Serbian Railways." *E-Business Technologies*, 44–46.

Stojanović, D., Bogdanović, Z., Petrović, L., Mitrović, S., & Labus, A. (2020). Empowering learning process in secondary education using pervasive technologies. *Interactive Learning Environments*, 1–14. Advance online publication. do i:10.1080/10494820.2020.1806886

Stojanović, D., & Stanisavljević, N. (2011). Internet u funkciji unapređenja odnosa sa javnošću "Železnica Srbije.". *XI Međunarodna Konferencija E-Trgovina, 2011*, 116–121.

Stokić, A., Stojanović, D., Bogdanović, Z., Despotović-Zrakić, M., & Radenković, B. (2019). Enhancing the customer relationship management in public libraries: Findings from three developing countries. *Library Hi Tech, 37*(2), 251–272. doi:10.1108/LHT-07-2017-0138

Straub, S. (2011). Infrastructure and development: A critical appraisal of the macro-level literature. *The Journal of Development Studies, 47*(5), 683–708.

Sun, Q., Tong, W., & Yu, Q. (2002). Determinants of foreign direct investment across China. *Journal of International Money and Finance, 21*, 79–113.

Su, Z., McDonnell, D., Li, X., Bennett, B., Šegalo, S., Abbas, J., Cheshmehzangi, A., & Xiang, Y. T. (2021). COVID-19 Vaccine Donations—Vaccine Empathy or Vaccine Diplomacy? A Narrative Literature Review. *Vaccines, 9*(9), 1024. doi:10.3390/vaccines9091024 PMID:34579261

Sylwester, K. (2001). R&D and economic growth. *Knowledge, Technology & Policy, 13*(4), 71–84. doi:10.1007/BF02693991

Szijjártó, P. (2019). *The Speech of H.E. Péter Szijjártó in the Hungarian Parliament, Assembly day 72, Speech No. 60.* Hungarian National Assembly.

Szunomár, Á. (2019). China' s investments and infrastructural expansion in Central and Eastern Europe. In S. Jian & H. Guenter (Eds.), *Opportunities and challenges: sustainability of China-EU relations in a changing world* (pp. 84–103). China Social Sciences Press.

Tag & Degirmen. (2022). Economic freedom and foreign direct investment: Are they related? *Economic Analysis and Policy, 73*, 737-752. doi:10.1016/j.eap.2021.12.020

Tamás, M., Ágnes, S., Andrijauskas, K., Bērziņa-Cerenkova, U. A., Brînză, A., Filipova, R., Karásková, I., Karindi L., Krstinovska, A., Liperi, O., McCaleb, A., Pejič, N., Raditya-Ležaić, A., Turcsányi, R. & Vladisavljev, S. (2021). *Chinese Investment in Central and Eastern Europe Data Set.* Central and Eastern European Center for Asian Studies.

Tamás, M. (2021). *Chinese Investment in Central and Eastern Europe - A reality check.* Central and Eastern European Center for Asian Studies.

Tang, R. W. (2019). FDI expansion speed of state-owned enterprises and the moderating role of market capitalism: Evidence from China. *International Business Review*, *28*(6), 101596. doi:10.1016/j.ibusrev.2019.101596

Tan, X., & Zhou, M. (2015). The 21st Century “Maritime Silk Road” Trade Potential and Its Influencing Factors-An Empirical Study Based on Stochastic Frontier Gravity Model. *International Trade Issues*, (2), 3–12.

Tariq Ali, J. H. (2022). Bilateral Economic Impacts of China–Pakistan Economic Corridor.”. *Agriculture*, 144.

Teo, H. C., Lechner, A. M., Walton, G. W., Chan, F. K. S., Cheshmehzangi, A., Tan-Mullins, M., Chan, H. K., Sternberg, T., & Campos-Arceiz, A. (2019). Environmental Impacts of Infrastructure Development under the Belt and Road Initiative. *Environments*, *6*(6), 72. doi:10.3390/environments6060072

The Ministry of Foreign Affairs of the PRC. (2012). *China’s Twelve Measures for Promoting Friendly Cooperation with Central and Eastern European Countries*. Available at: http://www.fmprc.gov.cn/mfa_eng/ topics_665678/wjbispg_665714/t928567.shtml

Ting, D. S. W., Carin, L., Dzau, V., & Wong, T. Y. (2020, March 27). Digital technology and COVID-19. *Nature Medicine*, *26*(4), 459–461. doi:10.103841591-020-0824-5 PMID:32284618

Titus, A. O. (2007). Causality between exports, imports, and economic growth: Evidence from transition economies. *Economics Letters*, *94*(3), 389–395. doi:10.1016/j.econlet.2006.08.025

Tomaszewska, P., & Dahl, M. (2020). Implementation of the Belt and Road Initiative in Selected Balkan States. *Understanding Asia: Political, Economic and Socio-Cultural Dimensions*, 69–85. Retrieved from http://kongresazja.pl/images/pdf/understanding_asia.pdf#page=69

Tomić, V., & Stojanović, D. (2018). Trends and innovations in mobile banking. In Digital transformation (pp. 290–310). Academic Press.

Tonchev, P. (2017). *China’s road: Into the western Balkans*. European Union Institute for Security Studies (EUISS).

Trąpczyński, P. (2013). Determinants of Foreign Direct Investment Performance – a Critical Literature Review. *Oeconomia Copernicana*, *4*(2), 117–132. doi:10.12775/OeC.2013.016

Turcsanyi, R. (2014). *Central and Eastern Europe’s courtship with China: Trojan horse within the EU?* European Institute for Asian Studies. https://www.eias.org/wp-content/uploads/2016/02/EUAsia-at-a-glance-Richard-Turcsanyi-China-CEE.pdf

Ullah, S. H. (2022). Empirical nexus between Chinese investment under China–Pakistan Economic Corridor and economic growth: An ARDL approach. *Cogent Business & Management*.

UN Comtrade. (2002). https://comtrade.un.org/Data/

UNCTAD. (2010). *World Investment Report 2020: International Production Beyond the Pandemic*. https://unctad.org/system/files/official-document/wir2020_en.pdf

UNCTAD. (2014). *World Investment Report, Investing in the SDGs (Sustainable Development Goals) – A Plan of Action*. United Nations.

UNCTAD. (2014). *World Investment Report, investment and the digital economy*. https://unctad.org/system/files/official-document/wir2014_en.pdf

UNCTAD. (2020). *Investment Policy Responses to the COVID-19 Pandemic*. Investment Policy Monitor Special Issue No. 4 (May 2020). UNCTAD.

United Nations, Economic and Social Commission for Asia and the Pacific Committee on Trade and Investment. (2021). *Promoting inward and outward foreign direct investment in the post-coronavirus-disease era.* Seventh session Bangkok, 27–29 January 2021 Item 3 of the provisional agenda, ESCAP/CTI/2021/2. https://www.unescap.org/sites/default/d8files/eventdocuments/CTI7_2_item%203%20FDI%20reissued.pdf

Urata, S., & Kawai, H. (2000). The determinants of the location of foreign direct investment by Japanese small and medium sized enterprises. *Small Business Economics*, *15*, 79–103.

Vernon, R. (1966). International investment and international trade in the product cycle. *The Quarterly Journal of Economics*, *80*(2), 190. doi:10.2307/1880689

Vetrovcova, M. (2018). Towards an "Expectations Fulfilment Gap" in 16+1 Relations? China, the EU and the Central and Eastern European Countries. In 16+1 Cooperation and China–EU Relationship. Budapest: China-CEE Institute.

Visvizi, A., Lytras, M. D., & Jin, P. (2019). Belt and Road Initiative (BRI): New forms of international and cross-industry collaboration for sustainable growth and development. *Sustainability*, *12*(1), 193. doi:10.3390u12010193

Vo, D.H., The Vo, A., & Zhang, Z. (2019). *Exchange Rate Volatility and Disaggregated Manufacturing Exports: Evidence from an Emerging Country*. Academic Press.

Voiculescu, D. (2015). *Investițiile Străine Directe- Vector al dezvoltării economice*. Niculescu Publishing House.

Voorpijl, R. (2011). *Foreign Direct Investments in Kenya: The Gains and Losses of Foreign Involvement*. Radboud University.

Waisová, Š. (2020). China's strategy vis-à-vis Taiwan's diplomatic friends: Is Beijing using dollar diplomacy? *Journal of Comparative Politics*, *13*(1).

Wang, N. C. (2021a). *China Belt and Road Initiative (BRI) Investment Report H1 2021*. Green BRI Centre, International Institute of Green Finance (IIGF).

Wang, C., Lim, K. M., Zhang, X., Zhao, L., & Lee, P. T. L. (2020). Railway and road infrastructure in the Belt and Road Initiative countries: Estimating the impact of transport infrastructure on economic growth. *Transportation Research Part A, Policy and Practice*, *134*, 288–307. doi:10.1016/j.tra.2020.02.009

Wang, N. C. (2021b). *China's Investments in the Belt and Road Initiative (BRI) in 2020, Green BRI Centre, International Institute of Green Finance*. IIGF.

Wang, S., Zhao, D., & Chen, H. (2019). Government corruption, resource misallocation, and ecological efficiency. *Energy Economics*, 85.

Wang, X., Xu, Z., Qin, Y., & Skare, M. (2021). *Foreign direct investment and economic growth: a dynamic study of measurement approaches and results*. Economic Research-Ekonomska Istraživanja., doi:10.1080/1331677X.2021.1952090

Wang, Y. (2016). Offensive for defensive: The Belt and Road Initiative and China's new grand strategy. *The Pacific Review*, *29*(3), 455–463. doi:10.1080/09512748.2016.1154690

Wan, Y. (2019). An Empirical Study on the Influencing Factors of Bilateral Trade between China and Countries Along the "One Belt and One Road". *Exploration of Economic Issues*, (11), 134–141.

Wayne, M. I. (2007). *China's War on Terrorism: Counter-Insurgency, Politics and Internal Security*. Routledge. doi:10.4324/9780203936139

Wen, X., Ma, H. L., Choi, T. M., & Sheu, J. B. (2019). Impacts of the Belt and Road Initiative on the China-Europe trading route selections. *Transportation Research Part E: Logistics and Transportation Review, 122*(September), 581–604.

Were, M. (2015). Differential effects of trade on economic growth and investment: A cross-country empirical investigation. *Journal of African Trade*, *2*(1–2), 71–85. doi:10.1016/j.joat.2015.08.002

Wheeler, D., & Mody, A. (1992). International investment location decisions: The case of U.S. firms. *Journal of International Economics*, *33*, 57–76.

White Paper China's Peaceful Development. (2011). *Information Office of the State Council*. http://www.gov.cn/english/official/2011-09/06/content_1941354.htm

Williamson, O. E. (1975). *Markets, and hierarchies: analysis and antitrust implications: a study in the economics of internal organization*. Free Press.

Wolf, S. O. (2021). *China-Pakistan Economic Corridor of the Belt and Road Initiative*. Springer.

Woodward, D. P. (1992). Locational determinants of Japanese manufacturing start-ups in the United States. *Southern Economic Journal*, *58*(3), 690–708.

Wooldridge, J. M. (2009). *Econometrics: Panel Data Methods*. https://www.cemmap.ac.uk/uploads/cemmap/programmes/Background%20reading%20May%202016.pdf

Wooldridge, J. M. (2002). *Econometric analysis of cross section and panel data*. The MIT Press Cambridge.

World Bank. (2018). *Belt and Road Initiative*. https://www.worldbank.org/en/topic/regional-integration/brief/belt-and-road-initiative

World bank. (2019). *Belt and road economics*. International Bank for Reconstruction and Development / The World Bank.

World Bank. (2019). *Belt and Road Economics: Opportunities and Risks of Transport Corridors*. World Bank.

World Bank. (2021). *Data base*. https://data.worldbank.org/

Xinhua. (2019). *Full text of the Dubrovnik Guidelines for Cooperation between China and Central and Eastern European Countries – Xinhua*. Available at: http://www.xinhuanet.com/english/2019-04/13/c_137973910.htm

Yang, Q., & Zhang, C. (2018). Influencing factors of trade flow between China and the countries along the "Belt and Road". *International Economic Cooperation*, (5).

Yeboah, O. A., Naanwaab, C. B., Saleem, S., & Akuffo, A. S. (2012). *Effects of trade openness on economic growth: The case of African countries*. Academic Press.

Yu, P., Chen, Z., & Hu, Y. (2020). The Impact of Belt and Road Initiative on Regional Financial Integration – Empirical Evidence from Bond and Money Markets in Belt and Road Countries. *Chinese Economy*, *54*(4), 286–308. doi:10.1080/10971475.2020.1857061

Yu, S., Qian, X., & Liu, T. (2019). Belt and road initiative and Chinese firms' outward foreign direct investment. *Emerging Markets Review*, *41*(C), 100629.

Yu, S., Qian, X., & Liu, T. (2019). Belt and road initiative and Chinese Firms' outward foreign direct investment. *Emerging Markets Review*, *41*, 41. doi:10.1016/j.ememar.2019.100629

Zakić, K., & Radišić, B. (2019). China's Belt and Road Investment Projects in the Balkan Countries: Six Years After. *The Review of International Affairs*, *70*(1175), 48–68.

Zaman, M., Pinglu, C., Hussain, S. I., Ullah, A., & Qian, N. (2021). Does regional integration matter for sustainable economic growth? Fostering the role of FDI, trade openness, IT exports, and capital formation in BRI countries. *Heliyon*, *7*(12), e08559. Advance online publication. doi:10.1016/j.heliyon.2021.e08559 PMID:34917822

Zeneli, V. (2020). *The Western Balkans: Low Hanging Fruit for China?* https://thediplomat.com/2020/02/the-western-balkans-low-hanging-fruit-for-china/

Zeren, F., & Ari, A. (2013). Trade openness and economic growth: A panel causality test. *International Journal of Business and Social Science*, *4*(9), 317–324.

Zhai, F. (2018). China's belt and road initiative: A preliminary quantitative assessment. *Journal of Asian Economics*, *55*, 84–92. doi:10.1016/j.asieco.2017.12.006

Zhang, H. (n.d.). Research on the trade potential between China and the areas along the "Belt and Road". *International Trade Issues*, (7), 87–97.

Zhang, J., & Zhang, P. (n.d.). Research on the trade efficiency and influencing factors between China and the "Belt and Road" countries. *International Economics and Trade Research*, (8), 5-24.

Zhang, D., Mohsin, M., Rasheed, A. K., Chang, Y., & Taghizadeh-Hesary, F. (2021). Public spending and green economic growth in BRI region: Mediating role of green finance. *Energy Policy*, *153*, 153. doi:10.1016/j.enpol.2021.112256

Zhang, W., Alon, I., & Lattemann, C. (2019). China's belt and road initiative: Changing the rules of globalization. *Journal of International Business Studies*, 358.

Zhang, Y., & Yu, J. (2018). Transportation infrastructure, proximity effects, and bilateral trade: An empirical study based on trade data between China and the "Belt and Road" countries. *Contemporary Finance*, (3), 98–109.

Zhao, S. (2019). China's Belt-Road Initiative as the Signature of President Xi Jinping Diplomacy: Easier Said than Done. *Journal of Contemporary China*, 1–17. doi:10.1080/10670564.2019.1645483

Zhong, G., Xiong, K., Zhong, Z., & Ai, B. (2021). Internet of things for high-speed railways. *Intelligent and Converged Networks*, *2*(2), 115–132. doi:10.23919/ICN.2021.0005

Zhou, W., & Esteban, M. (2018). Beyond Balancing: China's Approach towards the Belt and Road Initiative. *Journal of Contemporary China*, *27*(112), 1–15. doi:10.1080/10670564.2018.1433476

Zhou, Y. (2004). *China's Diplomacy*. China Intercontinental Press.

Zimmerman, T. (2015). The New Silk Roads: China, the US, and the Future of Central Asia. *NYU Center on International Cooperation*, 13-15.

Zuokui, L. (2016). *Europe and the "Belt and Road" Initiative: Responses and Risks*. China Social Sciences Press.

Zuo, X. (2016). Analysis of the trade influence factors and trade potential between China and neighboring countries under the strategic background of the Silk Road Economic Belt-Based on the Research of the Extended Gravity Model. *Financial Development Review*, (7), 130–145.

Zweers, W., Shopov, V., Van der Putten, F., Petkova M., & Lemstra M., (2020). *China and the EU in the Western Balkans, A zero-sum game?* Clingendael Report.

About the Contributors

Miraj Ahmed Bhuiyan is an associate Prof. at the School of Economics, Guangdong University of Finance & Economics. Dr. Bhuiyan is a graduate and undergraduate supervisor for local and international students. Currently, he teaches international marketing, international economics, cross-cultural business communication, Chinese business culture, etc. His research interests are Economic Integration, Environmental Economics, Green Economy, and so on. He has published more than 25 SCI/ SSCI indexed peer-reviewed journal articles. In addition, he has participated few governmental and provincial research projects.

Isidora Beraha is a Research Associate at the Institute of Economic Sciences in Belgrade. Her scientific interest includes business economics, value chain analysis, research and innovation systems, local economic development, entrepreneurship, and small and medium-sized enterprises. She has published a significant number of scientific papers in the mentioned fields. Since 2019 she has been president of the Scientific Council and Head of the Center for Basic Research of the Institute of Economic Sciences. She is a member of the Serbian Scientific Society of Economists, Society of Economists of Belgrade, and Entrepreneurship Research and Education Network of Central European Universities (ERENET).

* * *

Jihad Ait Soussane is a Ph.D. Candidate in economics at the Faculty of Economics and Management - Ibn Tofail University - Morocco. His research interests include international economics, firm internationalization, foreign direct investment, international trade, public economics, industrial organizations, microeconomics.

Duško Bodroža is a Research Associate in economic sciences. Employed at Institute of economic sciences in Belgrade. He is editor of the scientific journal Economic Analysis: Applied Research in Emerging Markets. He has strong experience in the field of finance and international projects, as responsible for several European and international projects. In his research work, he utilizes different research methods, particularly regarding the international economy and finance as his main fields of research. He has more than 40 different publications; he has been the editor of more than 5 internationally recognized editions of books. Managerial and leadership are his main skills.

Ivana Domazet is a Principal Research Fellow at the Institute of Economic Sciences and Associate Professor at the Faculty for Banking, Insurance and Finance, Union University, Belgrade. She teaches courses on Marketing Management, Market Research and Competitiveness Enhancement (postgraduate studies). Her scientific interest refers to: Improving Competitiveness, Marketing Research and Strategy, CRM and Strategic Management. She published a numerous paper related to foregoing topics. She was President of Scientific Council at the Institute of Economic Sciences (2014-2019). She is: Vice-president of Board member of the Institute of Economics Sciences; Board member of the Institute of Social Science; member of Serbian Scientific Association of Economists and Serbian Marketing Association.

Emanuela Hanes is an independent researcher. Her cooperation includes the Vienna University FH BFI Campus Wien, the University of Salzburg and the University of Graz. Her research interests include China-EU business strategies, RegTech, FinTech, Cryptocurrencies, Geopolitics, Chinese Strategic Planning and Development Policies.

Iulia Iuga holds a PhD in Finance (2002) from Babeş-Bolyai University from Cluj Napoca, Romania and B.S. in Marketing (1997) from Bucharest Academy of Economic Studies, Romania. She has been working in the Finance-Accounting Department at "1 Decembrie 118" University of Alba Iulia since 1999 and she is currently Assoc. professor PH.D. She teaches banking and investment disciplines, such as: Financial-banking management; Risk management and measuring bank performance; Banking techniques and operations; Investment evaluation and financing; Entity financing and investment management; Monetary economy and Financial-banking marketing. Her publications are found in the following fields of science: banking, investment and marketing and has written over 14 books and over 150 articles. She is member of editorial boards of specialized publications and ARACIS expert (The Romanian Agency for Quality Assurance in Higher Education) - Finance field.

Elena Jovičić is a Research Associate at the Institute of Economic Sciences in Belgrade (Serbia). She received her bachelor's, master's and doctoral degrees in international trade from the University of Economics in Prague, Czech Republic. Her fields of research interests include international economic relations, international trade, the competitiveness of the national economy, sustainable development, China-CEEC relations. She is the author/co-author of more than 30 scientific publications. She has been involved in a few research and scientific projects financed by the Ministry of Education, Science, and Technological Development of the Republic of Serbia. She is a Management Committee Member of the COST Action CA18215 - "China In Europe Research Network", and a member of the Serbian Scientific Society of Economists. She is a secretary and member of the editorial board of the Journal of Women's Entrepreneurship and Education (JWEE).

Ijaz Khalid is currently serving as Assistant Professor in the Department of Political Science, Abdul Wali Khan University Mardan, KP, Pakistan. His PhD dissertation emphasized the implications of the foreign direct investment under the China-Pakistan Economic Corridor (CPEC) for foreign policy of major powers most notably Russia and the United States of America (USA). His research interests include foreign investment, foreign policy, development, BRI, CPEC, Pakistan, Russia, USA. His work has appeared in journals of international repute.

Miloš Kolavčić is currently a Ph.D. candidate at Belgrade Banking Academy, Union University. He got Master's and Bachelor's degrees at the Faculty of Economics, the University of Belgrade from the area of Finance and Trade. He has more than seven years of experience in financial consulting.

Zahra Mansouri is an accredited professor at the Faculty of Economics and Management - Ibn Tofail University - Morocco. Her research interests include marketing, international trade techniques, supply chain management and the attractiveness of foreign direct investment.

Darko Marjanovic is a Research Associate at the Institute of Economic Sciences, Belgrade Serbia. Department: Macroeconomics. His scientific interest refers to: Foreign direct investment, Competitiveness and Public finance. He is author or co-authored more than 50 papers, one monograph and participated in numerous national and international scientific conferences. He is a member of the Scientific Society of Economists of Serbia and reviewer in a scientific journal Economic analysis. He is editor-in-chief of an international publication SEE-6 Economic Outlook that shows an overview of economic trends and short-term forecasts for the seven countries of Southeast Europe: Bosnia and Herzegovina, Croatia, Montenegro, North Macedonia, Romania, Serbia and Slovenia. He was engaged in several projects that he funded Ministry of Education, Science, and Technological Development of the Republic of Serbia and Provincial Secretariat for Science and Technological Development of the Autonomous Province of Vojvodina.

Nikola Martinović is a Teaching Assistant in Macroeconomics at the University of Montenegro, Faculty of Economics. In November 2020, he enrolled in PhD studies at the Faculty of Economics - University of Belgrade. The subjects of his interest are the areas of Public Finance, National and International Economy, and National Competitiveness. Representing Montenegro, he won the silver medal at the EuroSkills competition (2018) in the Entrepreneurship discipline. He is a co-author of several scientific papers.

Zhu Meng is an independent researcher. Her research interests include FinTech, Chinese economy and business analytics.

Nikola Milović is a full-time professor at the Faculty of Economics, University of Montenegro. His field research includes Economic Analysis and Politics with a special focus on the EU Economy, National Economy, Economic Integration, and Competition Policy of the European Union. Nikola Milović is the author of one textbook and a (co)author of dozens of articles published in international journals, international monographs, and conference proceedings.

Mirela Mitrašević was born on January 3, 1974, in Tuzla (BiH). She is employed at the Faculty of Business Economics, University of East Sarajevo, where she is engaged as an full professor of Financial Mathematics, Insurance and Risk Management in banks and insurance companies in undergraduate studies and Financial Mathematical Analysis and Insurance Analysis in master studies. She is a member of the Association of Actuaries of the Republic of Srpska and the Association of Actuaries of Serbia. She is the author and co-author of several scientific papers. She has participated in a large number of international symposia and in conducting innovative courses in the field of actuarial science. Scientific affiliation: actuarial science, risk management, finance.

Wycliffe Nyaribo is a senior lecturer and currently the Dean School of Graduate Studies at KCA University Nairobi Kenya. Dr. Nyaribo holds a Ph.D. in Business Administration from MDS University Ajmer India. Dr. Nyaribo has been engaged in teaching research at the university level for the last eighteen years. His area of expertise is management with a special focus on human resource management. Dr. Nyaribo has authored many articles published in peer-review journals. He is a member of professional bodies both locally and internationally In addition to his research work, he has mentored and supervised many master's students. He has also attended and presented papers at international conferences globally. He is also a member of the editorial board of academic journals. Dr Nyaribos' professional mission is to work with a professional team in institutions of higher learning that will utilize his knowledge, skills, and abilities to make a difference in the life of students and the community at large while enhancing his personal growth in academic research and consultancy.

Miloš Pjanić, associate professor, was born in Bačka Palanka (Serbia) on November 18, 1982. He completed elementary school in Gajdobra and high school of economics in Bačka Palanka. Dr. Pjanić graduated from the Faculty of Economics in Subotica in 2006 and obtained his master's degree in 2008. He obtained his PhD from the same Faculty in July 2015 with the thesis entitled "Strategy for Managing the Portfolio of Institutional Investors in the Financial Market of Selected Emerging Countries". He has published over thirty scientific papers in domestic and international journals. Scientific affiliation: finance, insurance and institutional investors, stock exchange business.

Klimentina Poposka is a Full-time professor at the Institute of Economics-Skopje, University "Ss Cyril and Methodious" Skopje in Finance. Her research interest is Banking and Finance and she teaches courses on International Finance, Commercial Banking, Corporative Finance, SME Financing (Master program) and Banking and Financial Market and Institutions (Ph.D. program). She has actively participated in many research and applied projects, published numerous papers and 7 books. She performed various study visits and visiting positions such as: CEU, Budapest; St. Petersburg State University, Russia; CEU, Warsaw; Washington university in St. Louis, USA; Bakakademie, Frankfurt; Federal Reserve Bank of St. Louis, USA; Volksbank eG, Boppard, Germany; Frankfurt School of Finance and Management, Germany; University of Applied Science, Department of Business Administration, Koblenz, Germany; School of Economics and Business, University of Ljubljana.

Nenad Stanisavljević is PR manager in "Infrastructure of Serbian Railways.". He has been working in the railway sector since 1991, and has performed various functions within the railway companies. He received his MA Degree from the University of Belgrade – Faculty of Political Sciences. Currently, he is working towards a PhD degree in Laboratory for E-business at the Faculty of Organizational Sciences, University of Belgrade. His current research interests include e-business, financial markets, railway traffic, internet technologies, and marketing.

Danijela Stojanović is a Research Associate at the Institute of Economic Sciences in Belgrade, Serbia. She received her bachelor's and master's degrees in Economics from the University of Belgrade Faculty of Economics and a doctoral degree in the department for e-business at the University of Belgrade Faculty of Organizational Sciences. Her research interests include e-business, e-education, Internet of things and smart environment, digital marketing, and financial markets. She has been involved in a few research and scientific projects financed by the Ministry of Education, Science, and Technological Development of the Republic of Serbia. She is a member of the COST Action CA18215 - "China in Europe Research Network" and a member of the IEEE and the IEEE Computer Society, Serbia and

Montenegro Section. She has been dealing with the topic of Serbian Railways as a part of her research since 2010 and explores China from economic and technological aspects.

Poshan (Sam) Yu is a Lecturer in Accounting and Finance in the International Cooperative Education Program of Soochow University (China). He is also an External Professor of FinTech and Finance at SKEMA Business School (China), a Visiting Professor at Krirk University (Thailand) and a Visiting Researcher at the Australian Studies Centre of Shanghai University (China). Sam leads FasterCapital (Dubai, UAE) as a Regional Partner (China) and serves as a Startup Mentor for AIC RAISE (Coimbatore, India). His research interests include financial technology, regulatory technology, public-private partnerships, mergers and acquisitions, private equity, venture capital, start-ups, intellectual property, art finance, and China's "One Belt One Road" policy.

Index

F

G

I

L

M

www.ingramcontent.com/pod-product-compliance
Lightning Source LLC
LaVergne TN
LVHW080638011026
849160LV00014B/1256